学会基本动词

一口气追上老外

E & C●著　千太阳●译

吉林出版集团有限责任公司

吉林省版权局著作权合同登记 图字：07-2012-3826
图书在版编目(CIP)数据

学会基本动词，一口气追上老外 / 韩国E&C出版集团著；千太阳译. -- 长春：吉林出版集团有限责任公司，2012.11
ISBN 978-7-5534-0038-9

Ⅰ. ①学… Ⅱ. ①韩… ②千… Ⅲ. ①英语－动词－自学参考资料 Ⅳ. ①H314.2

中国版本图书馆CIP数据核字(2012)第232560号

学会基本动词，一口气追上老外

作　者	（韩）E&C
译　者	千太阳
选题策划	含章行文 · 易人英语
责任编辑	王　平　齐　琳
特约编辑	白秋梅
开　本	147mm×210mm　1/32
字　数	446千字
印　张	18
版　次	2013年1月第1版
印　次	2013年1月第1次印刷
出　版	吉林出版集团有限责任公司
电　话	总编办：010-63109269
	发行部：010-63329002
印　刷	北京佳明伟业印务有限公司

ISBN 978-7-5534-0038-9　　**定价：**45.00元

卷首语

“真没有想到，可以用这么简单的动词进行英语会话！”

自从《学会基本动词，一口气追上老外》出版发行之后，很多读者都表示“真没有想到，可以用这么简单的动词进行英语会话！”，“原本就想好好整理简单的动词，这本书正好把那么多的常用短语都总结到了一本书上”等。在获知了有很多人渴望用常用短语进行英语会话的事实后，我们也为自己的努力能给读者带来帮助而感到高兴。与此同时，有不少读者提出了很多建设性的意见和建议，我们表示十分感谢。

“这种情况下应该这么用”，自己掌握短语

正因为如此，我们开始着手修改之前的版本。这次，我们的目标只有一个，就是怎样才能让读者们兴致勃勃地读完这么厚的一本书。因此最终设置了“这种情况下应该这么用”这一部分，以便让读者们在开开心心地阅读本书的过程中，不知不觉地掌握语句的特定用法。先用我们的母语读一遍例文，就可以轻而易举地理解和记住例句中所使用到的常用短语表达的特定用法。比如说，get a refund是意为“退货”的意思，比起干巴巴的死记硬背，不如先阅读标题为“老婆发胖之后，可以对丈母娘说的话”的句子来引发读者的好奇心，之后在“I'd like to get a refund, please”（麻烦您给我退货）的句子让读者明白get a refund短语的意思，就这样，读者会很轻松地记住，需要退货的时候可以说I'd like to get a refund。

本书中使用了1000多个“这种情况下应该这么用”来说明核心短语的用法，让读者产生更大的兴趣，并能更容易地理解语法难点。另外，为了让读者尽量不去在意书本的厚度，本书中还添加了不少插画，让读者的阅读更加轻松，并且为每个短语附加了一段对话，除此之外还录制了老外的原声发音，给读者们带来了立体感、生动感和身临其境的感觉。

轻松记忆常用短语，从容地进行英语会话

可以毫不夸张地说，能够实现我们像老外一样说话的“希望”正是“常用短语”。因为所有的语言都极力追求便利，其实老外们在日常生活中也会用部分常用短语解决所有问题。在实际会话中，从基本动词衍生出的表达远远超出我们的想象。用go over代替examine，用give back 代替return，用get better代替improve等，基本上没有不能用常用短语表达的话。换句话说，常用短语起到了英语会话中轴的作用。

利用本书学习英语会话不仅能够打下良好的英语会话基础，还是一个接近英语会话核心的明智方法。从现在开始，请尽情地掌握基本动词，从容地享受英语会话吧。英语会话不在远方，在附近也能找到答案。希望本书可以为读者们寻找答案带来帮助。虽然本书为全新修订版，但肯定会存在一些不足之处。无论什么时候都欢迎读者留下宝贵的意见和建议。我们的目的不单单是出书，而是创造出能融汇读者们的意见，让读者产生共鸣的好书。请接受我们由衷的感谢。

这本书有什么与众不同之处？

“选取了50个老外在英语会话中经常使用的非常简单的核心基本动词和27个重要基本动词，并以此为基础，收录了最常用的1000多个短语。”

1.肯定会让读者们对实际会话中最常用的基本动词和由这些动词组成的常见短语感叹不已。

2.在每一个短语下方我们用亲切的母语来解释其义，有助于掌握短语的意义和用法。

3.通过“MORE”轻松掌握每个短语的实际应用和活用表达。

4.通过“这种情况下应该这么用”，让读者们轻松了解每个短语表达的具体适用情况。

5.通过例句和对话，将短语完全转化为自己的财富。

这本书是怎样构成的？

1.Section 1：老外最常用的核心基本动词（Basic Verbs）50

一目了然地整理了老外主要使用的50个核心基本动词和以此为基础在实际生活中经常使用的短语。

2.Section 2：老外喜欢使用的重要基本动词（More Basic Verbs）27

除了50个核心基本动词之外，选取了外国人经常使用的动词，及其使用频率较高的短语。

3.More Expressions

每种动词最后附加了一些入门级的词汇，但都对英语会话有着很大用处，让英语会话学习过程变得更丰富。

4.MP3 音频

50个核心基本动词、附加短语，所有例句及对话都配有老外原声录音。明确一点，老外们用到的动词其实也没什么大不了的，所以抱着追上他们口语的信念，勇敢地大声跟读音频吧。

利用本书应该怎样学习?

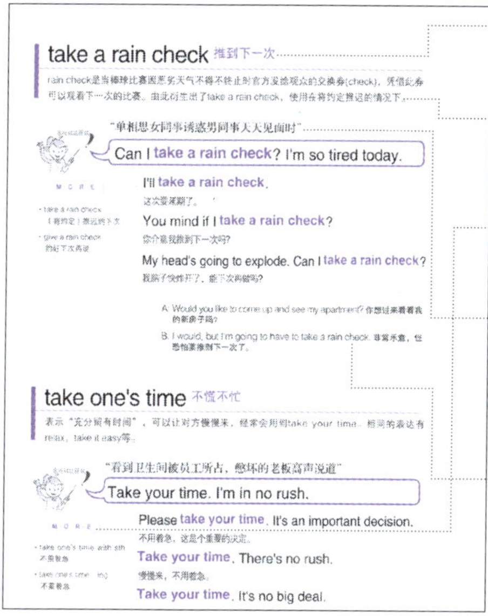

take a rain check 推到下一次

rain check是当棒球比赛因恶劣天气不得不终止时官方发给观众的交换券(check)，凭借此券可以观看下一次的比赛。由此衍生出了take a rain check，使用在将约定推迟的情况下。

"单相思女同事诱惑男同事天天见面时"

Can I take a rain check? I'm so tired today.

MORE

- take a rain check （将约定）推迟到下次
- give a rain check 约定下次再说

I'll take a rain check.
这次要延期了。

You mind if I take a rain check?
你介意我推到下一次吗?

My head's going to explode. Can I take a rain check?
我脑子快炸开了，能下次再做吗?

A: Would you like to come up and see my apartment? 你想过来看看我的新房子吗?
B: I would, but I'm going to have to take a rain check. 非常乐意，但恐怕要推到下一次了。

take one's time 不慌不忙

表示"充分留有时间"，可以让对方慢慢来，经常会用到take your time。相同的表达有relax，take it easy等。

"看到卫生间被员工所占，憋坏的老板高声说道"

Take your time. I'm in no rush.

MORE

- take one's time with sth 不急着急
- take one's time ...ing 不要着急

Please take your time. It's an important decision.
不用着急，这是个重要的决定。

Take your time. There's no rush.
慢慢来，不用着急。

Take your time. It's no big deal.

- **基本动词短语表达**
  由老外最常用的50个核心基本动词衍生出的动词短语。
- **中文解释**
  亲切地解释动词表达的意义与用法。
- **MORE**
  短语表达的实际用法整理。
- **这种情况下应该这么用**
  能够生动形象地再现各种短语的使用状况，有助于高效记忆。
- **例句**
  通过例句和生动的对话说明短语的实际表达的用法，提升对短语的理解程度。

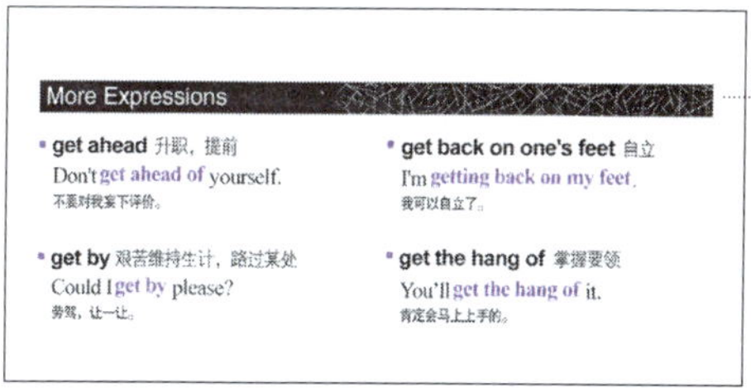

More Expressions

- get ahead 升职，提前
  Don't get ahead of yourself.
  不要对我妄下评价。
- get back on one's feet 自立
  I'm getting back on my feet.
  我可以自立了。
- get by 艰苦维持生计，路过某处
  Could I get by please?
  劳驾，让一让。
- get the hang of 掌握要领
  You'll get the hang of it.
  肯定会马上上手的。

- **MORE Expressions**
  很遗憾没能汇编在条目中，但记住这些表达也会有很大帮助。

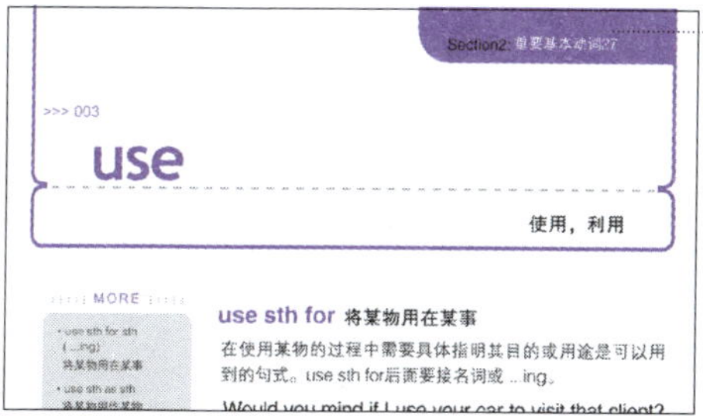

Section2: 重要基本动词27

\>>> 003

use

使用，利用

MORE

- use sth for sth (...ing) 将某物用在某事
- use sth as sth 将某物用作某物

use sth for 将某物用在某事

在使用某物的过程中需要具体指明其目的或用途是可以用到的句式。use sth for后面要接名词或 ...ing。

Would you mind if I use your car to visit that client?

- **More Basic Verbs 27**
  虽然没能进入50个核心基本动词，但同样是老外在日常生活中常用的动词，并整理了多样的短语。

<总共77个!!>

Section 1 Basic Verbs

迫切需要国人记住的老外常用核心基本动词50

- 万能动词 get ·8
- 凡事都要付出的 give ·36
- 拿到手就远走高飞的 take ·50
- 再三挽留也会离去的 go ·71
- 由你到我的 come · 89
- 先做了再说 do ·105
- 存在感十足的 be ·116
- 已经有了却还想要的 have ·134
- 什么都要做 make ·152
- 该知道的都知道了 know ·169
- 喜欢能怎么办 like/prefer ·181
- 得到允许了再做 let ·192
- 持续不变的 keep ·202
- 放在某个地点或状态的 put ·211
- 抓紧了 hold ·221
- 赶紧拿过来 bring ·230
- 只要打个电话就万事俱全 call ·238
- 不看怎么知道 see ·246
- 能听见，没办法 hear/listen ·255
- 渴望时用 want ·263
- 想说什么就说什么 say · 271
- 想告诉你 tell ·283
- 说说看 speak ·294
- 想要和你畅谈 talk ·300
- 不顾挽留离开的 leave ·308
- 跑起来 run ·317
- 不管是人还是机械都要停 break ·326
- 好的开始是成功的一半 start/begin ·333
- 困难时要帮助 help ·341
- 不懂就问 ask ·347
- 要多动脑子想想 think ·356
- 工作不要停 work ·367
- 就是这种感觉 feel ·376
- 转来转去的世界 turn ·385
- 该检查就检查 check ·393
- 我需要你 need ·400
- 那是什么话 mean ·405
- 给我站起来 stand ·412
- 不要摔倒 fall ·421
- 该停手就停手 stop ·428
- 不要离开，留在这里 stay/move ·436
- 相信我 believe ·448

- 让你明确的 set ・454
- 心事重重 mind ・462
- 无论是什么都要找出来 find ・470
- 忘了的东西怎样才能记起来 forget/remember ・477
- 虽然心疼，但该交还得交 pay ・489
- 无论行不行，先试试看 try ・496
- 等到底 wait ・505
- 最后的希望 hope/wish ・511

Section 2 More Basic Verbs

外国人同样常用的重要基本动词27

- send 发送 520
- finish/ end 结束，终止 522
- use 使用，利用 524
- hand 传递，帮助 526
- meet 见面 528
- hang 悬挂，玩 530
- show 展示 532
- play 玩，运动（演奏）534
- save/ spend 节约，储蓄/消费 536
- teach/ learn 教授/学习 538
- drop/ catch 掉落，滴落/抓（住）540
- cut/ hit 砍，切/打，敲击 542
- charge/ cost 罚款/价格为…… 544
- worry/ care 担心/关心，喜欢 546
- eat/ drink/ cook 吃/喝/做料理 548
- pass/ follow 通过，传递/跟随 550
- plan/ prepare 计划/准备 552
- pick/ choose/ decide 挑选/选择/决定 554
- buy/ sell/ deal/ afford/ belong 买/卖/交易/供得起/属于 556
- apologize/ excuse/ thank/ appreciate 道歉/辩解，原谅/感谢/感激 558
- change/ remain 变化/仍然，留下 560
- lend/ borrow/ owe 借给/借来/欠 562
- fill/ file/ fit/ fix 充满/（文件）锉/适合/修正 564
- lie/ lay 躺下，说谎/躺下，放下 566
- pull/ draw 拉，拽/画，拉 568
- ruin/ risk/ hurt 破坏/冒险/伤害 570
- expect 期待，预料 572

Section 1 Basic Verbs

迫切需要国人记住的老外常用

核心基本动词 50

get
give
take
go
come
do
be
have
make
know
like/ prefer
let
keep
put
hold
bring
call
see
hear/ listen
want
say
tell
speak
talk
leave
run
break
start/ begin
help
ask/ answer
think
work
feel
turn
check
need
mean
stand
fall
stop
stay/ move
believe
set
mind
find/ lose
forget/ remember
pay
try
wait
hope/ wish

万能动词

Get

get是个用途非常广泛的万能动词，说得夸张点，单靠一个get就能解决英语会话。根据不同的目的与状况，还能表示“得到”(obtain)，“乘坐”(catch a vehicle)，“到达”(reach)，“理解”(understand)等各种含义，不仅如此还可以像have或make那样表示”使……”的祈使动词，也可以用get+pp形态替代be+pp形态。

基本概念

1 接受(receive)，得到(obtain)，得到（赏罚，学分等），买

I got an e-mail from her yesterday. 我昨天收到了她的邮件。

She got me a cell phone for my birthday. 我生日时，她送给我一部手机。

2 到达，达到，理解

Will you get home okay? 你能自己回家吗?

She did't get the joke. 她没能理解笑话的含义。

3 get (something)+形容词 (pp)变成，使……

He just got married. 他刚刚结婚。

Let's get started. 我们开始吧。

Don't get me wrong. 不要误会。

4 get something+pp (somebody to do)使……

I have to get my car fixed. 我得修车了。

使我的车得到修理

She got me to leave. 是她让我离开的。

<repju'teɪʃən> 名誉(声)；声望(誉)；美名

get a job 就职

get的最基本用法，意为“得到”，“获得”。get a discount表示“得到折扣”，get a reputation表示“出名”，而get a raise表示“得到加薪”。

“媳妇变胖时可以对丈母娘说这句话”

I'd like to get a refund, please.

She **got a new job**.
她找了份新工作。

Guess what? I just **got my license**.
你猜怎么着？我考到驾照了。

I'd like to **get a refund**, please.
我想退货，谢谢。

I've never had an accident or **gotten a ticket** in my life.
我一辈子都没有出过交通事故，也没被开过一张罚单。

A: It's about time we got a raise. 该加薪了。
B: You're telling me. 你说的没错。

<'bɑːgɪn> n ⑴ 买卖合同；成交条件；交易 ⑵ (经讨价还价后)买这的商品；廉价货 v 同上

get something at (from) 从……买到，得到，从……听到

同样表示获得，取得的意思，但通常指在商店花钱买东西或者强调东西的出处，可以说成get sth at (from) ...。

“当朋友炫耀自己在商场打折时淘到好东西时”

I got it at a bargain price at Macy's.

M·O·R·E

- get sth at (from) ...
  从……得到，买到
- Where did you get sth?
  在哪儿买的（弄到的）？

She **got** the necklace **on** sale yesterday.
她在昨天打折时买了这条项链。

I **got** it **at** the flea market. It was just 5 dollars.
在跳骚市场买的，才花了我5美元。

This is for you. I **got** it **from** the gift shop.
给你的，在礼品店买的。

This is not a good chair. Where did you **get** this?
这不是把好椅子，在哪儿买的？

A: Where did you get the information? 你从哪得知的这个消息？
B: I got it from the manager. 从经纪人那里听到的。

get a cold 患上感冒

get会在很多情况下充当have，如果有“get+病名”的形式，就表示“患上……”，“得……”的意思。

“不是一般的感冒(cold)，而是流行性感冒(flu)时”

I've got the flu. Keep away from me.

M·O·R·E

- get a stomachache
  肚子疼
- get a flu
  患上流感
- get a headache
  头疼
- get a sore throat
  嗓子疼

I've **got the runs**.
我拉肚子了。(=I have diarrhea.)

I've really **got a sore throat**. Let's get together later.
嗓子好疼，过两天再聚吧。

I've **got the flu**. Keep away from me.
我患上流感了，不要靠近我。

Don't touch me. I've **got a** really **stiff neck**.
不要碰我，我感到脖子好僵硬。

A: Where does it hurt? 哪里不舒服?
B: I've got a pain in my side since the last weekend. 从上周末开始侧腰部位疼。

get some rest 休息

get后面接休息或睡眠等抽象名词时，如果是get some rest就表示“休息一会儿”，而get any sleep则表示“小睡一会儿”。

“心爱的女朋友突然提出分手，让你彻夜未眠时”

I didn't get any sleep last night.

M·O·R·E

- get some rest
  休息一会儿
- get some sleep
  眯一会儿
- get enough sleep
  睡足

Why don't you **get some rest**?
干嘛不休息一会儿?

I didn't **get any sleep** last night.
我昨天彻夜未眠。

Get some rest and we'll talk more about this tomorrow.
先休息一会儿，这个问题明天再说。

I always **get enough sleep**.
我的睡眠很充足。

A: What do you say we go for a walk? 我们去散步好不好?
B: Sorry, I need to get some rest. 不好意思，我得休息一下。

get somebody 接电话，联系，教训，逮捕

get后面如果接人物的话也有很多意思。像give一样，接电话，联系，教训，逮捕等各种情况下都能表达相应的含义。

"老总对秘书说，要和苏珊通话时"

Please get me Susan.

You can **get me** on the phone.
给我打电话。

Please **get** me **Susan**.
帮我转接苏珊。

Give me **Rick** in sales, please.
请转接销售部的里克。

The police finally **got her**.
警察终于逮捕了她。

A: Sam wants help with his computer. 山姆要找人帮忙看看电脑。
B: Get Helga on the phone. She'll help him. 给赫尔加打电话，她能帮上忙。

get it (me, you) 理解

get用作"理解……"(understand)的意思，I don't get it就是I don't understand it的口语表达方式。可以用you代替it，变成I don't get you。

"对无论提醒过多少次，都会照样迟到的学生"

I don't get it. Why are you late again?

M·O·R·E

- I got it.
  明白了。
- I don't get it (that).
  我不太懂。
- You got it (that) (right).
  没错（就是那样）（知道了）。
- You got it (that)?
  明白（听懂）了？
- Did you get it?
  理解了没？

I need to be with someone who **gets me**.
我需要和理解我的人在一起。

I don't **get it**. Why are you late again?
真搞不懂，你怎么又迟到了？

You **got that right**. It's the best restaurant in town.
你说的没错，这是城里最好的餐厅。

A: Let me know if she likes me, okay? 告诉我她到底喜不喜欢我，好不？
B: You got it. 你知道的。

get the point 理解

同样用get表示“理解”的含义。get the point或get one's point就能表示非常理解对方所说的话。另外，get the picture则表示“理解总体的脉络或状况”。

“考虑到环境问题，原本要说回收利用(recycle)，对方却听成了朗诵(recital)”

Clearly you're not getting the point.

M·O·R·E

- get one's point
  理解某人的意思
- get the picture
  理解，读懂
- get a headache
  你明白了?
- I got the picture.
  明白了，理解了。

I **get the point**. I won't do that.
我明白了，不会再那样了。

All right, I **get your point**.
好了，明白你说的话了。

Now you're **getting the picture**.
你总算理解了。

I **get the picture**, Jill. I know what it means.
我明白了，吉尔。我知道是什么意思了。

A: Do you see what I'm trying to say? 你明白我要说什么吗?
B: I get the picture. 我明白。

get the idea 理解，想出点子

如果单独使用get the idea的话就是“理解”，“明白”的意思，但如果用作get the idea from的话就会变成“从……得到启发”的意思。另外，get the wrong idea则表示“误解”。

Where did you get the idea to do this?

M·O·R·E

- I get the idea.
  明白了。
- get the idea that ...
  想……的主意
- You get the idea.
  你也明白了
  （现在明白了）吧?

I'm beginning to **get the idea**.
我开始懂了。

Where did you **get the idea** to do this?
你是从哪里想出的这种点子?

She seems to **get the idea**.
她好像有主意了。

I just never **got the idea** that they were really happy.
我从没想过他们是不是真的幸福。

A: Did you understand what I said? 明白我说的话了?
B: Oh, sure, I got the idea. 当然明白。

I'll get it 我来

当门铃响时说“我来”或者办公室电话铃响时，旁边的同时嘱咐道“能不能接下电话？”(Will you answer the phone?)时可以用到的短语，表示“我去接”。

“偷偷上传不良信息，不料被警察局打来电话时”

Don't touch the phone! I'll get it.

Don't touch the phone! **I'll get it**.
别碰！我来接。

I'll get it. I guess it's for me.
我来吧，应该是我的电话。

Honey, I'm taking a shower. Would you **get that**?
亲爱的，我正在洗澡。能帮我接个电话吗？

Would you **get that** please? People have been calling to congratulate me all day.
能不能帮忙接个电话？人们一整天都来电话祝贺我。

A: I think I hear the phone ringing. 好像有电话铃在响。
B: I'll get it. You stay here and relax. 我来吧，你在这儿休息。

get one's act together 打起精神

表示将one's act聚集到一块(get together)，换句话说就是“集中”的意思。进一步可以理解为“打起精神”等，与get a grip，get a life，get real表示相同的意思。

“孩子马上要高考了，却以紧张为由沉迷于电脑游戏”

Get your act together.

Get your act together!
给我振作起来！

Let me **get my act together**.
让我回回神。

You have got to **get your act together**.
你必须要打起精神。

A: Come on! Get your act together. 喂！你要打起精神来。
B: But I'm just so tired today. 今天太累了。

get me (you) something 给我（你）拿某物

get为“给某人拿某物”的意思，单纯表示“拿东西”或“给某人买东西”。也可以写成get sth for me (you)。

“当销售员问道需要买什么，或者打算给沉迷于游戏的儿子买点东西时”

What can I **get for** you?

M·O·R·E

- Please get me ...
  请给我……
- I will get you ...
  我给你（买）……

Please **get me some coffee.**
请给我一杯咖啡。

Would you **get that for me**? It's on the table.
能帮我拿那个东西吗？在桌子上。

What did you **get her for** her birthday?
她生日你送什么了？

I will **get you a present** as soon as I get some money.
我赚了钱就马上给你买礼物。

Tomorrow is my birthday. I want you to **get me a present.**
明天是我的生日。我希望你给我买件礼物。

Can you **get me a glass of water**, please?
麻烦您能给我一杯水吗？

Can you **get me a taxi**, please?(= Can you call a cab for me?)
能帮我叫辆出租车吗？

Can I **get you something** to drink? Some coffee or something?
想喝点什么？咖啡或者别的？

Can I **get a steak sandwich and a Coke**?
可以给我一份牛排三明治和一杯可乐吗？

What can I **get for you**?
我能为你做什么？

I('ve) **got something for you.**
我要给你样东西。

A: Would you get me a Diet Coke? 能给我一杯零度可乐吗？
B: Okay. I'll be right back. 好的，您稍等。

A: Oops! I just spilt coffee on my new dress. 哎呀！把咖啡倒在衣服上了。
B: Let me get you a towel. 我给你拿毛巾。

A: I've got a terrible headache. 头疼死了。
B: Can I get you some aspirin? 要不要给你拿点阿司匹林？

get a minute (second) 有时间

get a minute表示有点时间，可以用a second (sec)代替a minute。主要用在让对方稍等片刻时。另外，(for) a minute (second)是“稍等片刻”的意思。

“部长看到员工不务正业，一天到晚只打电话时”

Can I talk to you outside **for a second**?

M·O·R·E

- (You) Got a minute (second)?
  你有时间吗?
- when you get a minute (chance)
  如果有空的话（有闲暇的话）

Hey, Sam, you **got a minute**? I really need to talk to you.
喂，山姆，有时间吗？咱俩说说话。

When you **get a minute** I'd like to talk about the case.
等你有空时聊聊那起事件。

Got a sec? We need to discuss the meeting schedule.
有时间吗？需要商量会议事项。

Can I talk to you outside **for a second**?
能不能在外面跟你谈谈?

A: Can I speak to you privately? 我能私下跟你聊聊吗?
B: I'll be over when I get a minute. 我有时间就找你。

get the feeling 有……的感觉

get the feeling表示“有……感觉”，如果单单用作I get the feeling的话就会变成“有那种感觉”。如果想表达具体的内容，就可以使用get the feeling that主语+动词的形态。

“刚刚与游戏狂结婚的妻子独守空房时”

I **get the feeling** he's more interested in computer games than me.

I'**ve got a feeling** he'll be back.
我感觉他会回来。

I'**ve got a feeling** she will not show up.
我觉得她不会出现。

I **get the feeling** that he's more interested in the computer games than me.
我感觉他喜欢游戏大于我。

I started to **get the feeling** that my secretary is coming on to me.
我突然觉得秘书在诱惑我。

A: I get the feeling she is upset. 她好像受到了打击。
B: Yeah, she's been crying all day. 没错，一整天哭个不停。

get a hold of 抓住，联系，入手

get a hold of 表示“抓住……”或“与……取得联系”，可以简化为a hold或ahold。get a hold of oneself表示抓住自己，意为“冷静”。

“当员工到处寻找以出差为由，却关上手机在桑拿浴享受的老总时”

I can't get a hold of him.

M·O·R·E

- get a hold (ahold) of
  抓住……联系
- get a hold of oneself
  冷静

Let's get her to the hospital. **Get a hold of** her parents.
把她送到医院吧，联系她父母。

I can't **get a hold of** him.
实在找不到他。

Would you **get a hold of** yourself?
能不能消停一会儿?

A: Can you get a hold of an umbrella? 能给我一把雨伞吗?
B: I have one in my briefcase. 我包里有一把。

get to 着手做……

get后面如果加to+动词的话就表示“越来越……”(do sth gradually)，强调随时间的变化过程。最常用的表达有get to know，意为“认识”。

“一点眼力见没有的人问旅行社警卫时”

Do you get to travel a lot?

M·O·R·E

- get to+动词
  着手……
- get to know
  认识

Did you **get to** know the boss at the retreat?
你在培训中认识老总了?

Do you **get to** travel a lot?
你经常旅行吗?

So when do we **get to** meet the guy?
那我们什么时候能见到他?

A: Did you get to know the boss at the retreat? 你是在培训中认识老总的吗?
B: Yes, he is a very nice man. 是啊，他真是一个大好人。

get to somebody 让人不耐烦

作为sth gets to me的形态表示“因某人感到不耐烦”。当然，get to somebody表示“靠近……”，“走近”的含义。

“在和男友分手之后，为了报复，和陌生的男子过了一夜，不料对方不停地来电话”

It's really getting to me.

M·O·R·E

- Sth. gets to me.
  ……让我烦恼
- Sb. gets to me.
  某人在靠近我（走近我）。

I guess the stress **is getting to** me.
好像是因为压力才会这么烦躁。

It'**s** really **getting to** me.
这真烦人。

I'm stuck in traffic, and it is really starting to **get to** me.
遇上堵车了，这让我开始越来越不耐烦。

We've got plenty of time before they **get to** me.
在他们靠近我之前还有很多时间。

A: The noise really gets to me. 噪音很烦人。
B: It's from the construction site. 是从工地传来的。

get to somewhere 到达……

get to+地点名词表示“到达某地”的意思。最常用的短语就是get there (here)，但What have you got there?中，there指对方，表示“你有什么？”

“问朋友、出租车司机或妻子前往目的地的方法时”

What's the best way to get there?

M·O·R·E

- get there
  到那，去那
- get here
  到这

How can I **get there**? Do you know the way?
我怎么去？你知道道路吗？

How long does it take to **get to** the stadium?
需要多久才能到达体育馆？

Can you tell me how to **get to** the nearest subway station?
请问最近的地铁站怎么走？

What have you **got there**? Is that an apple pie?
那是什么？（你拿着什么？）是苹果派吗？

A: I need to get to the Hilton Hotel. 我想去希尔顿大厦。
B: Just go two blocks and turn right. 直走两个街区，然后右转。

get nowhere 毫无效果，没有所得

"get+地点名词"形态的get nowhere表示"哪儿都没有去"的意思。可以比喻为"毫无结果"，主要用作"主语+will get you (us)+nowhere"或I (You) get nowhere (with ...)的形态。

"在升职前夕，为了讨好，给讨厌的部长献上巧克力棒，真令人无语"

That kind of flattery will **get you nowhere.**

M·O·R·E

- Sth. will get you (us) nowhere
  再怎么样，也不会有结果。
- I (You) get nowhere with ...
  ……毫无结果

That kind of flattery will **get you nowhere**.
这种阿谀奉承毫无用处。

This is **getting us nowhere**!
这样下去肯定没有结果！

I'**m getting nowhere** with this report.
编写报告书不太顺利啊。

We **are getting nowhere** with this project.
这个项目毫无进展。

A: I got nowhere asking Jane out. 我邀请简出去过，但毫无用处。
B: She just doesn't want to date you. 她恐怕不想和你约会。

get mad (angry, upset) 生气

这是get用作become的情况。get后面会接形容词，表示"变成……样"，也可以用be代替get。

"看到奥普拉温弗里的身材，誓死决心减肥的大妈"

I'm **getting fat**. I'm going to go on a diet.

M·O·R·E

- get mad at sb.
  生某人的气
- get angry with (at) sb.
  对某人生气
- get upset about (with)
  让某人生气
- get busy 忙碌
- get sick 疼痛
- get fat 长胖
- get serious 变得认真

Don't worry; I'm not going to **get mad**.
不要担心，我不会生气的。

I promise I won't **get angry** anymore.
我发誓，再也不会生气了。

I think you'**re** still **angry with** me.
你是不是还没消气呢。

Why **are** you **upset with** me? What did I do wrong?
你为什么要生我的气？我做错什么了？

A: Don't get mad at your kids. 不要对孩子们生气！
B: They aren't studying hard enough. 谁让他们不好好学习了。

get better 变好

主要用在病情好转或一败涂地的事业开始好转时，最好用作现在进行时的getting better。相反be getting worse 表示越来越糟。

“当对方正处于落榜、失业、失败等痛苦时期时，可以用这句话来安慰对方”

I know it's tough now, but things will get better.

M·O·R·E

- keep getting better 变得越来越好
- keep getting worse 越来越糟

I kept hoping things would **get better**.
我一直希望情况能有所好转。

We think the baby'**s getting better**.
我们觉得孩子越来越健康了。

I was too depressed. It just kept **getting worse and worse**.
我太伤心了，情况越来越糟糕。

I'**m getting better** every day.
我每天都会进步。

A: I will let you know if she's getting better. 她如果有所好转，我就会转告你。

B: I hope she gets better soon. 真希望她早日康复。

get lost 失去方向，消失

“get+p.p.”的形态get lost除了“迷失方向”(lose one's way)以外，还有与get out of here!一样有“走开！”(Go away!)的意思，可以当成“不要烦我了！”(Stop bothering me!)。

“丈夫天天闷在家里，妻子想让他出去活动活动。”

Now get dressed, we're going to the gym.

M·O·R·E

- get hurt 受伤
- get caught in traffic 交通堵塞
- get struck in the elevator 被关在电梯里
- get drunk 醉酒
- get dressed 穿衣服
- get screwed 搞砸
- get tired 疲倦

Why don't you **get lost**?
你怎么不给我消失?

If you **get lost**, just give me a call anytime.
如果迷路了，随时给我打电话。

I have to stop drinking. I **get drunk** easily.
我不能再喝酒了，因为我很容易醉。

I **got screwed**. I lost all the money I had.
我玩完了。所有的钱都砸进去了。

A: Would you please get lost? 你怎么不给我消失?

B: Why are you upset with me? 干嘛对我发脾气?

get caught 被抓，被逮捕，遭遇，被卷进(... up in)

get caught是“被抓”的意思，如果用成get caught up in的话就表示意外遭受的情况。主要用在暴雨天或碰到交通堵塞时。另外，get stuck表示一动不能动的情况。

“公司中迟到的人经常使用到的借口”

I got stuck in traffic this morning.

M·O·R·E

- get caught (for) ...ing 陷入……被抓
- get caught (up) in ... 遭遇……
- get stuck ...ing 被困于……
- get stuck in ... 被困于……
- get stuck with 离不开……

My son **got caught** watching pornos on the internet.
我儿子上网看黄色电影被我发现了。

I **got caught** speeding.
我超速被抓了。

I **got caught** cheating in the class.
我作弊被发现了。

We **got caught in** the storm at the lake.
我们在湖畔遭遇了暴风。

A: How come you're late? 你怎么这么晚?
B: I got caught in traffic. 堵车呗。

get married 结婚

“与某人结婚”时可以用get (be) married to sb，另外get past sth是指“延期”的意思，被用作“通过……或不愿意记住的事情”。

“丈夫搞外遇被发现，老婆正拿着斧头气势汹汹地走过来，丈夫苦苦哀求道”

Can we please get past this?

M·O·R·E

- be (stay) married to 与……结婚

Are you really **getting married**?
你真的结婚了?

I **was married to** Barbara for 30 years.
我与芭芭拉结婚已经有30个年头了。

Jim wants to **stay married to** her because he loves her.
吉姆想和她结婚，因为他非常爱她。

How did you **get past** security?
你是怎么通过安检的?

A: Why don't we get married? 我们结婚怎么样?
B: Never. That's out of the question. 不要，绝对不可以。

get going (started) 开始，着手做

get going (started) 表示“出发”(start) 或“离开”(leave)，“着手做”(start work on)。主要用作Let's get going 或I have to get going的形态，表达时间不够，需要抓紧的情绪。

“明明约好了一起看电影，妻子却化了一个小时的妆”

Come on, honey! Let's **get going**.

M·O·R·E

- get started on (with) sth.
  开始做……
- Let's get started.
  我们开始吧。
- I should get going.
  我要赶紧离开了。
- get sth going
  开始做……(start sth)
- I don't know what you've got going.
  我实在搞不懂我们的计划是什么。

Let's **get started on** the wedding plans!
开始制订结婚计划！

I've got to **get started on** my speech!
现在开始我的演说！

She's really interested in what you **got going on**.
她对你即将着手的事情非常感兴趣。

Whatever you **got going on**, fill me in.
不管你做什么事，都要告诉我。

A: Let's get going. 我们出发吧。
B: Where do you want to go? 我们要去哪儿啊？

get somebody (sth)+介词 让……陷入某种状态

这是彰显万能动词get的威力的短语。如果get sb (sth)后面接副词或介词的话就会变成将sb (sth)“变成某种状态”的意思。具体翻译要根据不同的状况确定。

I promise to **get you out of here** as quickly as possible.

M·O·R·E

- get sb (sth) to+地点
  将某人带到某地
- get sb (sth) in trouble
  让某人陷入困境

We have to **get her to** a hospital.
我们需要把她送到医院。

She **got me in** this room.
她让我进到这个房间的。

She can **get you in** trouble. You'd better stay away from her.
她能给你带来麻烦。你最好离她远点。

The subway will **get you to** the museum.
你坐地铁能到博物馆。

A: Get Tina to a hospital quickly. 尽快把缇娜送到医院去。
B: Did she have an accident? 她出车祸了？

get something straight 矫正，确认

get sth straight表示“矫正……”，“确认……是不是事实”(make sure sth is true)。多用成Let me get sth straight的形态，主要使用在未能理解对方的意思或想要重新确认一下的情形中。

“听说离了好多次婚的朋友又离婚的消息，突然感到非常吃惊和羡慕”

So let me get this straight. You got divorced again?

M·O·R·E

- Let me get this straight.
  说白了就是……

So let me **get this straight**. You got divorced again?

我是说，你又离婚了？

So let me **get this straight**. You didn't know I love you?

换句话说，你不知道我爱你？

Get this straight, okay? I'm not a whore.

弄清楚好不好？我可不是妓女。

Let me **get this straight**, man. You hit your brother?

让我说得清楚点，你打你弟弟了？

A: Let me get this straight. You need money? 就是说，你缺钱？

B: I promise that I'll pay it back. 我发誓一定会还你的。

Don't get me wrong. 不要误会。

当我无意冒犯了对方，伤害对方感情时或可能引起了对方误解时可以用这句话来表达“不要误会”(Don't misunderstand me)。

“一个花花公子深情地吻了一个女孩，一见女孩浑身发抖，立刻解释道”

Don't get me wrong. I just like the kissing.

Don't **get me wrong**, but you look awful.

不要误会，不过你脸色看起来的确不怎么样。

Don't **get me wrong**. I'd love to work with you.

不要误会，我只是喜欢和你一起工作。

A: Do you really hate my shoes? 我的鞋有那么讨厌吗？

B: Don't get me wrong. I think they're OK. 不要误会，我觉得不错。

get it done 结束

这是祈使句的用法。Get+sth+pp表示“使……变成……”的意思。其中最典型的get it done主要是让对方“完成某件事”的意思，多用作Please get it (this) done by的形态。

“老板让员工无论如何在明天之前完成任务，有亲和力的员工会这样回答”

Don't worry. I will **get it done** for you.

M·O·R·E

- Please get it done by ...
  到……为止完成……
- Don't get me started on (about) ...
  不要让我……
  不要提……
- get the car started
  发动车
- get one's hair cut
  理发

Please **get it done** right away.
现在马上做这个。

Please **get it done** by the afternoon.
请在下午之前完成。

We'd like to **get this thing done** today.
我们希望在今天之内完成。

A: Please get it done right away. **请马上做这个。**

B: Don't worry; you can count on me. **不要担心，相信我。**

get somebody to 让某人做某事

同样是祈使句的形态，get sb to do是指“让某人做某事”的意思。与祈使动词have不同，要注意动词前要加to。

“丈夫刚进门就大喊‘I'm home’时，妻子说刚把女儿哄睡”

Shhh! I just **got her to** go to sleep.

You can't **get her to** understand it.
你肯定无法让她理解。

I'm going to **get you to** talk to her.
我会让你和她说话的。

I **got her to** go to sleep.
我让她睡觉了。

A: Can you get her to fix the computer? **能让她修一下电脑吗?**

B: I think she can do it after lunch. **吃完午饭应该可以。**

go get 去取（买）……

go get+是口语中省略中间的and (to)，变成go+V的情况。Let's go 是最典型的用法，可用在"肚子有点饿"或"口渴"的时候。当然，get后面如果接人物的话就会变成"抓住……"。

"看到自己非常信任的男友与自己的闺蜜接吻的场面，瞬间爆发"

I will **go get** a gun and shoot you myself.

M·O·R·E

- go have
  去做……
- go see
  去见……
- go do
  去做……
- go take
  去拿……
- come see
  来看……

Let's **go get** some ice cream.
咱们去吃冰激凌吧。

Do you want to **go get** something to eat?
你要不要出去弄点吃的?

Do you want to **come see** a movie with us?
你想过来和我们一块看电影吗?

A: Let's go get some ice cream. 我们去吃冰淇淋吧。
B: I can't. I have to study. 不行，我得学习。

have got 拥有……

have got在口语中表达的意思与have相同。就像have+名词表示"拥有……"一样，have got+名词也表达"拥有"的含义。只不过除了这种含义之外，就不能用have got代替have。

"看不下去员工们休息的老板向喝着咖啡的员工喊道"

Get back to work! We'**ve got** a lot of work to do!

M·O·R·E

- I've got+名词
  我有……
- You've got+名词
  你有……

I have to run. I'**ve got** so much to do.
我得赶紧走了。有太多事情要做。

I can't stay with you. I'**ve got** other plans tonight.
没办法和你待下去了。我今天晚上有别的安排。

I'**ve got** a date. Wish me luck.
我有个约会。上帝保佑我吧。

Hey, you'**ve got** a boyfriend!
嘿，你有男朋友啊!

A: Why are all the kids so excited? 孩子们怎么那么兴奋?
B: I have got cookies for them. 我给他们拿饼干了。

have got to 应该做……

同理，have got to+动词所表达的含义与have to+动词一样。I've gotta go可以缩略为I gotta go，因此I gotta go的原型是I have got to go。

"妻子只要有空就会出去逛街，无奈的丈夫说道"

You'**ve got to** stop going shopping.

M·O·R·E

- I've got to+动词
  我要做……
- You've got to+动词
  你应该做……

I'**ve got to** run. I'll call you later.
我得赶紧走了。回头给你打电话。

I **have (got) to** go. I have to ring up now.
我要走了。（电话）我得挂了。

You'**ve got to** be kidding!
开什么玩笑!

A: I've got to tell you something. 我有话要对你说。
B: No, no. You don't have to explain yourself to me. 不用了，没必要和我解释。

get together 相见

与meet没有多大区别，但特别指关系好的人聚在一起吃饭喝酒(to have a drink or meal)时就要用get together。名词形式为get-together。

"与不大亲近的大学师弟偶遇之后，睁眼说瞎话"

We should **get together** more often.

M·O·R·E

- get together (with)
  （与某人）见面
- get together on
  ……见面吧
- get-together
  见面

Are we going to **get together** this weekend?
我们这周末聚一聚啊?

I have to **get together with** my mother. It's her birthday.
我得去见妈妈。今天是她的生日。

Let's **get together** (sometime).
我们找个时间坐坐。

A: Let's get together at 3 o'clock in my office. 3点在我办公室见面吧。
B: That'll be fine. See you then. 好的，到时候见。

get in touch with 与某人取得联系

get in touch with表示“与某人取得联系”，或“打电话/发邮件”。这里也会用到keep，此时就表示“与对方保持联系”的持续性，get则将重点放在了“实际举动”上。不过，with+事物的话，就会变成“很了解”的意思。

“遇到好久没见的中学同学，问对方现在有没有联系着的老同学”

You're still in touch with someone from middle school?

M·O·R·E

- get in touch with 与某人联系
- keep in touch with 与某人保持联系
- put sb in touch with 为某人联系某人
- be in touch with 与某人保持联系

Let's **get (keep) in touch**!

我们多联系！

Where can I **get in touch with** her?

我怎样才能联系到她?

Where can I **get in touch with** you tomorrow?

我明天怎么找你?

I tried to **get in touch with** you.

我本来想联系你来着。

A: I heard you talking on the phone. 我听到你打电话了。

B: Your mom was trying to get in touch with you. 你妈正在找你。

get in the way 妨碍

get in the way是挡在某人前行的路上，表示“妨碍”的含义，也可以说成be in the way。想要突出妨碍的事物，就可以说成get in the way of 。

“看到和自己一同进入公司的同事比自己先得到晋升，就会小气地说道”

Your promotion might get in the way of our friendship.

M·O·R·E

- get in the way of+名词 成为……的阻碍
- stand in the way 妨碍
- be in the way 妨碍

I don't want to **get in the way**.

我不想妨碍你。

It won't **get in the way of** anything we're doing here.

那不会妨碍我们做任何事情。

I think they're **getting in the way of** our friendship.

我觉得他们在妨碍我们的友情。

A: There are too many items in this room. 这个房间里有太多东西。

B: Yeah, they always get in the way. 是啊，走路都不方便。

get used to 习惯于……

get used to+名词(...ing)表示适应于(be accustomed to)或习惯于新场所、职业、生活方式等。可以用be 代替get。这种句型也会与过去“常常做某事”的used to 混淆。

“从迈阿密来的交换生在我国凛冽的寒风中瑟瑟发抖”

I just can't **get used to** the cold. I'm from Miami.

M·O·R·E

- get (be)used to+名词 习惯于……
- used to+动词 过去常常做某事
- be used to+动词 被用来做……

Did you **get used to** the weather in Canada?
你习惯加拿大的天气了吗?

I'**m getting used to** it.
我正在慢慢适应。

It happens a lot. You'd better **get used to** it.
经常有的事。你最好习惯。

You need to **get used to** being alone.
你应该习惯独处。

A: Well, the first snowfall is here. 哦，这是初雪啊。
B: We'd better get used to winter. 我们最好习惯冬天。

get along with 与某人和睦相处

get along with表示“与某人维持较好的关系”(have a friendly relationship with)，along后面可以加well，以起到强调作用。

“急匆匆结婚的新婚夫妇各自露出本色之后”

We don't **get along** any more. We fight a lot.

Do you two **get along well**?
你们俩相处得怎么样?

We don't **get along** any more. We fight a lot.
我们没办法相处下去了。我们经常吵架。

I want to **get along with** everyone.
我想和每个人都维持较好的关系。

I don't **get along well with** her.
我和她相处得不是很好。

A: Do you like your little sister? 你喜欢妹妹吗?
B: No, I could never get along with her. 不喜欢，我们的关系不太好。

get around 到处转悠，绕行，躲避，腾出时间做(to)

虽然不太熟悉，但这的确是平时常用的句型。get around表明到处转悠、聚集或回避。另外get around to表明正在着手做原本打算做的事情。

"自己的谎话被拆穿，却辩解道自己本来就打算老实交代"

I was going to **get around to** telling you the truth.

M·O·R·E

- get around sb (sth) 到处转悠，回避(avoid)，说服
- get around to sth (...ing) 腾出时间着手做某事

Word **gets around**.
传闻很可怕。

Is there any way to **get around** it?
有没有办法避开它?

When are you going to **get around to** asking me that?
你打算什么时候来问我?

A: I heard you'll be busy this weekend. 我听说你这周末会很忙。
B: I'm planning to get around to painting the house. 我正打算把房子的漆重新刷一遍。

get away (from) (离……)远去，脱离

表示"摆脱公司的日常生活，休息"(get away from one's work or daily routine)，即"休息"的含义。如果以命令型的语气向对方喊"Get away!"的话，就表示"走开！"，和Get lost!或Beat it!意思相同。

"想要让周围的人免遭女友那致命的'毒屁'时"

Everybody must **get away from** her! She farted again!

I'm glad you were able to **get away** today.
你今天能休息，这真是太好了。

Hey, get back! **Get away from** her!
喂，走开！离她远点！

Why are you trying to **get away from** me?
你为什么要避开我?

A: What's wrong with you? Why're you so angry? 出什么事了？为什么那么生气?
B: Just get away from me! 别管我。

get away with it 成功躲避某事，不受惩罚

get away with尤其指“做完坏事”(do sth wrong)也没有“受到处罚”(without being caught or punished)的情况。with 后面主要跟it。

“原本说要开导自己的女朋友，却索性把她抢了过去，对这种朋友就要说”

You can't let him **get away with that**.

M·O·R·E

- let sb get away with
  轻饶某人

You'll never **get away with it**.
你永远不会逃之夭夭的。

I will not let you **get away with this**.
我不会让你逃之夭夭的。

Trust me; she'll never **get away with it**.
相信我，她肯定不会逍遥法外的。

A: Did they catch the men who robbed the bank? 抓到银行劫匪了吗?
B: No, they got away with stealing a lot of money. 还没有。劫匪们携带巨款而逃。

get somebody (sth) back 拿回，找回

get sb (sth) back表示重新找回某物，是“拿回……”，“找回……”的意思。另外，get back to+后面如果加地点的话就会变成“回到……”。

“虽然女朋友离自己而去，却死心塌地地想要找回她时”

I miss Susan. I'll definitely **get her back**.

M·O·R·E

- get A back（to+地点）
  重新领……回到某地，找回……
- get back（地点）
  回到……
- get back at sb
  报复某人

She wants to **get** her boyfriend **back**.
她想找回前任男友。

I need to **get back to** the office.
我需要回到办公室。

She is using you to **get back at** me!
她在利用你报复我!

A: I lent my cell phone to my brother. 我把手机借给了弟弟。
B: Let's go get it back from him. 我们去要回来吧。

get back to sb (sth) 回头找某人，回到……

打电话时，因为其他重要事情而需要挂机时，可以向对方说“回头再聊”(speak or write to again later)，另外get back to sth表示“回到最开始的话题上”的意思。

“老板在和爱人通话，突然秘书转接了一通重要的电话”

I'm going to **get back to** you on that.

M·O·R·E

- get back to sb first thing in the morning
  明天早上先和某人交谈
- get back to sb on sth
  与某人讨论某事
- get back to sth
  回头再聊某事，回到某事上

I'll **get back to** you when you're not so busy.
等你有空的时候再打给你。

Let me **get back to** you tomorrow on that.
明天我会再找你。

I'll **get back to** you first thing in the morning.
我明天早上就来找你。

You can come here if you want to **get back to** me **on** that.
想要讨论那件事的话，就过来找我。

A: What is going on around him? 他发生什么事了？
B: I'll find out and get back to you. 我问问再告诉你。

get back to work 回到工作上

get to work是开始工作(start working)的意思，这里加入back的get back to work表示休息了一会儿，或者因出门耽搁了一会儿，又重新开始投入工作。老板最常说的话就是“Get back to work”。

“在楼梯与同事聊天消遣，突然被老板发现，急忙解释道”

We were just taking a quick break. We'll **get back to work**.

I'm sorry but I can't talk now. I have to **get back to work**.
不好意思，我不能谈下去了。我得回去工作了。

I'd like to **get back to work** as soon as I can.
我想尽快返回岗位。

I should **get back to work**. See you.
我该回去工作了，回头见。

A: Hey, Frank, have a beer with us. 喂，弗兰克，和我们喝杯酒吧。
B: I'd like to, but I have to get back to work. 我也想，不过现在得马上回去工作。

get down to 开始真挚地做某事

get down to表示“开始认真(serious attention)”的意思，可以在to的后面加business或work等名词。因此get down to business (work)则表示“开始认真地着手做事”。

“明明有很多事情要做，同事们却整天不务正业”

Let's **get down to** business. We have a lot to do today.

M·O·R·E

- get down to business
  着手专注于工作
- get down to work
  开始认真做事
- get down to+地点
  回到某处

We need to **get down to** business.
我们应该干正事了。

Let's **get down to** business.
开始认真做事了。

Well, why don't we **get down to** business?
来，开始好好做事行不行?

A: Let's get down to business. 我们开始做正经事吧。
B: Great, let's start. 好，这就来。

get into 进入，对某事产生兴趣，做某事，争论

get into的基本意义为“进入……”，从这里衍生出的含义有穿衣服，对某事产生兴趣或着手做某事。get into后面如果加学校的话就会变成“进入某某学校”。

“孩子连青蛙都不敢碰，父母却执意让他考医科大学”

I will never **get into** medical school.

M·O·R·E

- get into
  进入……做某事
- get into+学校
  考进某学校，
  进入学校

Can we **get into** this another time? I was sleeping.
我们能换个时间聊吗? 我在睡觉。

I can't **get into** this with you now.
我现在不能和你谈论这些。

What **are** you **getting into**?
你打算干嘛?

Did you guys **get into** a fight?
你们俩打架了?

A: Several workers got into a fight last night. 几个员工昨天晚上打架了。
B: I heard the police arresting them. 我听说警察逮捕了他们。

get off 从某处掉下来，停手，从某处出来

基本意义为“从某处掉下来”，“脱离”，“停手”等。get off (of)表明“从某处掉下”，而get off (of/from) work表示“下班”，“辞职”等。

“心怀鬼胎的男朋友要在午夜下班时来接女朋友”

I get off around midnight. Can I pick you up then?

M·O·R·E

- get off (of)
  从某处掉落，停手
- get off （of (from)）
  下班，辞职
- get sb off the hook
  摆脱责任等
- get sb off (of)
  让某人摆脱某事
- get off one's back
  停止纠缠某人

Would you please **get off** the phone?
那手机你能不能别玩了?

I've just finished work. I just **got off** work.
我刚刚完事，刚下班。

I need a rest. Will you **get off** my back?
我需要休息。你能不能别管我了?

A: This is the subway station where I get off. 我要在这里下车了。
B: I'll see you at the office tomorrow morning. 那明天办公室见。

get on 相处

get on 是相处(get along)的意思，get on sth是指“与某人相处”，而get on with sth表示“继续做某事”。另外，get it on是“开始某事”，get right on则表示“马上开始做某事”。

“深陷失恋的痛苦深渊数年之后，打算回归正常生活”

I'm just impatient to get on with my life.

M·O·R·E

- get on
  与某人相处(get along)
- get on with sb
  与某人相处
- get on with sth
  继续做某事
- get right on sth
  马上开始做某事

How'**re** you **getting on**?
过得怎么样?

You **get on with** it. I quit.
你继续吧，我不干了。

Never mind. Let's **get on with** the game.
不要在意，我们继续玩游戏。

I'll **get right on** it.
我马上就开始。

A: Has Shelia met your cousin Andy? 沙利亚见过你堂兄安迪了?
B: Sure, she gets on with him very well. 是啊，他们俩相处得很好。

get on (off), get in (out) 乘坐，从……上下来

如果像公交或火车这样体积比较大的交通工具则用介词on，如果是小型车辆的话就会用in。当然get in (out)除了车辆以外也表示“进入”，“出来”的含义。

“询问怎么去出版社时”

Take the subway for one stop and get off at Sunae Station.

M·O·R·E

- get on (off)
  乘坐，走下（公交或火车等）
- get in (out)
  乘坐或下（出租车或小轿车等）

Excuse me, is this where we **get on** the train to Chicago?
不好意思，前往芝加哥的火车在这儿上吗？

Could you tell me where to **get off**?
能不能告诉我在哪儿下车？

A: Let's take a ride downtown today. **今天去城里吧。**
B: Do you know where we can get on the bus? **你知道我们应该在哪儿坐车吗？**

get out of 从……出来

“摆脱……”，“离开……”(leave)的意思，如果说Get out of here的话就是表明“你给我消失！”(Go away!)，或者可以对放出无稽之谈的人说这句话来表示“别开玩笑了”。

“恋爱100天纪念日，男朋友却晚了1个多小时才出现在约会地点”

Get out of my face right now!

M·O·R·E

- get out of the way
  让路
- get out of one's face
  在某人面前消失

I'**m getting out of here**.
我得出去了。

I saw them **get out of** the car.
我看见他们下车了。

Get out of the way!
让开！

A: How can I get out of going to that party? **我怎样才能不参加那个派对？**
B: Tell them that you're not feeling well. **就说你身体不好呗。**

get over 战胜或克服（困难，疾病），结束，来

如果后面接人物的话就会表示“忘记某人”， get over (with sth)或get sth over it则表示“结束某事”，“下最终结论”等。另外，get over to+地点是指“来到某处”。

“花花公子最常说的一句话”

I will never get over her.

M·O·R·E

- get over sb (sth)
  克服，战胜，忘记
- get over with sth (get sth over with)
  下结论，结束
- get over（to+地点）
  下结论，结束

I can't **get over** something.
我吓了一大跳。

Let's **get it over** with.
了结它吧。

Get over here! I need to talk to you.
过来！我得和你谈谈。

A: The people got over next to the train. 人们来到了火车旁。
B: They were trying to get onto it. 他们想坐上火车。

get through 战胜，做出

表示“战胜（困难的事情或时期）”，或“结束某件事情”时要用get through (with) sth，与某人做了结时要用get through with sb。另外，get through to sb表示“与某人取得联系”。

“明明轮到自己升职，却被一个无能的手下找关系抢占先机，同事们安慰道”

He's a strong man. He'll get through this.

M·O·R·E

- get through
  战胜
- get through with sth
  结束某事
- get through with sb
  与某人做个了结
- get through to
  与某人取得联系

I don't think I can **get through** the night.
我觉得我没办法平安度过今夜了。

I'm not sure we can **get through** this difficult time.
我不确定我们能不能闯过这次难关。

I'll never **get through** this.
我肯定没办法成功。

I'd like to **get through to** Mr. James.
我想联系詹姆斯先生。

A: I'll never get through this. 我肯定做不出来。
B: You need to try harder. 你应该更努力一些。

More Expressions

- **get ahead** 升职，提前

Don't get ahead of yourself.
不要对我妄下评价。

- **get by** 艰苦维持生计，路过某处

Could I get by please?
劳驾，让一让。

- **get on one's nerves** 刺激某人

It's getting on my nerves. 我看着不顺眼。

- **get up** 起床

I got up at 6:30, like I usually do to feed Mary. 我每天6点半起床喂玛丽。

- **get the sack** 被解雇

Do you think he'll get the sack?
你觉得他会被解雇吗?

- **get wind of** 听到……传闻

I got wind of it. 我听到那传闻了。

- **get a crush on** 一见钟情，相中

I've got a crush on you. 我喜欢你。

- **get (have)a thing for** 喜欢……

He has (got) a thing for her.
他喜欢她。

- **get a move on** 急忙……

I'd better get a move on it.
最好快点。

- **get cold feet** 害怕，紧张

What's the matter? Are we getting cold feet? 怎么了? 紧张了?

- **get back on one's feet** 自立

I'm getting back on my feet.
我可以自立了。

- **get the hang of** 掌握要领

You'll get the hang of it.
肯定会马上上手的。

- **get (take)the hint** 察觉

I get the hint. 我看出眉目了。

- **get+**交通工具 乘坐……

Please get an ambulance. 请叫救护车。
Where can I get a taxi?
我能在哪儿打上出租车?

- **get help** 得到帮助

We got to get help. 我们需要帮助。

- **get one's own way** 为所欲为

What a bitch! She always gets her own way. 贱人! 总是为所欲为。

- **get even with** 报复，返还

Did you get even with him yet?
你报复他了?

The cat got your tongue? 怎么不说话?
I haven't got all day. 我们没时间这样了。
Come and get it. 过来吃吧。
He got worked up. 他生气了（他很了不起）
Get a life! （拜托）打起精神来! 振作起来!
Get real. 给我振作起来!

凡事都要付出的

Give

give与get不同，有“给……”的意思。当然，虽然被get抢走了很多领域，但give sb sth的形态是最常用的表达。尤其当两个宾语交换时需要在中间加一个to，变成give sth to sb。另外，像give a call一样，give后面可以加很多种名词形态来构成多样的短语。

基本概念

1 （向某人）给予，授予

I gave Susan the necklace. 我把项链给了苏珊。

That gives me an idea. 那让我想出了一个好点子。

2 give+动名词 做……

Could you give me a hand? 能不能帮我一下?

I'll give her a chance. 我会给她一次机会的。

3 举行（派对，会议等）

Let's give a party for her. 我们为她举办一次派对吧。

Shouldn't we give a party for him? 我们不应该为他举行一次派对吗?

give somebody something 给某人某样东西

give sb sth是give的最典型表达方式。如果将两个宾语调换位置的话，就要在中间加一个to，变成give sth to sb。

“铁公鸡男朋友好不容易请吃一次高级牛排，但在结账时却说道”

Can you give me a discount for paying cash?

M·O·R·E

- give sb sth
  give sth to sb
  给某人某样东西
- I'll give you a chance.
  I'll give a chance to you.
  我会给你机会的。

Your aunt gave you this shirt.
你姨给了你这件衬衫。

Can you give me $10 worth of gas?
请给我加10美元的汽油。

Can you give me a discount?
能打折吗?

A: Did you get a discount? 打折了吗?
B: Yeah, she gave me 20% off. 嗯，有20%的折扣。

give my love (regards) to 向某人转达问候

这是想要给第三者传达问候时可以用到的表达。give后面要加my regards，my love等，变成give my regards to sb，give my love to sb即可。

“与好友分别，临走前让他给妻子转达问候”

Give my best to your wife.

Give my love to Karen!
帮我给凯伦带个好。

Give my best regards to him when you see him.
如果见到他，就帮我带好。

Make sure you give my love to Cindy.
一定要帮我给辛迪带个好。

Give my best to your folks.
帮我问候你们家人。

A: Give my love to your mom when you see her. 如果看见你妈，帮我转达一下问候。
B: Of course. I'll tell her you said hello. 没问题。我会转告她的。

give (somebody) a call (ring, buzz) (给某人)打电话

give后面如果加上某个行为名词，变成give sb a (an)+名词的形态就表示“做(某事)”。在give sb a call (= call sb)中可以看出，动词的名词形态会变成宾语。

“渴望成为新入学火辣小师妹的导师时”

Don't hesitate to **give me a ring** whenever you need.

M·O·R·E

- give (sb) a ride (lift)
  让某人坐车
- give (sb) a party
  为某人举办派对
- give (sb) a hand
  帮助某人
- give (sb) a call
  给某人打电话
- give (sb) a kiss
  亲吻某人
- give (sb)an answer
  为某人回答
- give (sb) a raise
  为某人加薪

I'll **give you a call** later tonight.
我今晚要给你打电话。

If you have any questions, **give me a call**.
如果你有问题，随时打给我。

Give me a call when you get a chance.
有时间就给我打电话。

I have got your cell phone number. I'll **give you a call**.
我记下你的电话号码了，回头打给你。

Aren't you going to **give me a kiss**?
你不想吻我一下吗?

Have a good day! **Give me a kiss**.
祝你过得愉快！亲我一下。

We need to **give the secretary a raise**.
我们应该给秘书加薪。

Why didn't you **give me an answer** to my question?
你为什么没有回答我的提问?

I will **give you an answer** as soon as I get in.
我会尽快给你答复的。

Could you **give me an answer** by tomorrow?
你明天之前能给我答复吗?

A: I'm going to work on this stuff at home tonight. **我今晚要在家做这件事。**
B: If you have any problems, give me a call. **如果有问题就给我打电话。**

A: Aren't you going to give me a kiss? **你不打算亲我一下?**
B: Okay, I will. 好吧，来。

A: I can't believe they didn't give us a raise. **真不敢相信，他们居然没有给我们加薪。**
B: I guess we'll all be on strike tomorrow. **估计明天我们要大罢工了。**

give (someone) a hand 帮助某人

这是与前文类型相似的表达。a hand表示“帮助”，give sb a hand则表示“伸出援手”。帮助的内容要在give sb a hand后面加 ...ing形式或with+名词。

“妹妹如果完不成作业就会被好好教训一顿，因此开始苦苦哀求姐姐帮忙”

Give me a hand with the homework or I'm dead!

M·O·R·E

- Can you give me a hand（with+名词）?
  能帮我一下吗?
- Give me a hand（with+名词）.
  帮我一下。
- Let me give you a hand（with+动词）.
  我来帮你一把。

Do you think you can **give me a hand** today?
你今天能不能抽空帮我一下?

Give me a hand with this, Tom.
汤姆，帮我一下。

Can you **give me a hand** with this box?
你能帮我搞定这个箱子吗?

A: Could you give me a hand? 能不能帮我一下?
B: What do you need? 你需要我做什么?

give (somebody) a chance 给某人机会

与前几个例句一样的形式，give (sb) a chance表示“给某人机会”，也可以用opportunity代替chance。如果想提到具体的机会内容的话就可以用chance (opportunity) to+动词的形态。

“没能及时交作业，打出的成绩非常不理想时，跑到助教那里求道 ... ”

You have to **give me a chance** to explain.

M·O·R·E

- give (sb) a chance (opportunity)（to+动词）
  给某人机会
- give (sb) one more (another) chance
  再给一次机会

Won't you **give me** just **one more chance**?
你能不能再给我一次机会?

I'll **give you another chance**.
我会再给你一次机会。

I'm going to **give you an opportunity** to do that.
我会给你机会做那件事。

A: Bob did a poor job while working. 鲍勃把工作搞砸了。
B: Give him a chance. He'll improve. 再给他一次机会吧，他肯定能做好。

give (somebody (sth))a try 尝试做某事

就算不能预测成功与否也要试一试，可以用give it a try来表达。此时try表示“尝试”，也可以用shot来取代。

“老板明明不想再见到员工，把他调到了别的部门，这个员工却不解风情地说”

I'm willing to **give it a try**.

I'll **give them a try**.

我会试试的。

Why don't you **give it a try** right now?

你为什么不马上试试?

Give it a try (shot)!

来试试!

Let's **give it a try**.

我们试试吧。

A: My stomach is always hurting these days. 最近总肚子疼。

B: Give this medicine a try. 来试试这个药。

give (somebody) a ride 让某人搭车

give (sb) a ride表明让某人搭车，也可以用a lift代替a ride。另外，如果用get替换give的话就会变成求某人让自己搭车，如果换成offer就会变成提议。

“在饭局中，心怀鬼胎的李部长对女职员们说了一番肉麻的话”

How about I **give you a ride** home?

M·O·R·E

- give (sb) a ride（home/to+地点）将某人送到某地
- get a ride (with sb to+地点) 搭上某人的车
- take sb for a ride 载某人
- go for a ride 出去兜风

I'll **give you a ride** on my way home.

我回家的路上顺道送送你。

Can I **get a ride** with you to the hospital?

我能搭你的车到医院吗?

Need a ride? Get in. I'll drop you off wherever you want.

需要搭顺风车吗? 上来，我载你去。

Do you want to **go for a ride** in my Porsche?

你想坐我的保时捷兜兜风吗?

A: How did they get to the theater? 他们是怎么去的剧场?

B: Rob gave them a ride in his car. 罗波用车送了他们。

give somebody (sth) a break 帮助某人

a break表明在做某件事情的时候暂时中止或休息的意思，因此give sb a break则表示让某人休息一会，或暂时停一下的意思。

“闯红灯被警察抓住时，想要狡辩说自己去赶一个面试，以诱发对方的同情心”

Please **give me a break**! I've got a job interview.

Give me a break. I haven't done this before.
留点情面吧，念在我是初犯。

Oh, **give me a break**. I had only 10 minutes to prepare for this.
关照关照，我必须在10分钟之内准备好这个。

Give it a break (rest)!
给我停手！

You have to **give it a rest**.
你得休息一会儿了。

A: Can I see your license please? 请出示驾驶证。
B: Please give me a break. 拜托，关照关照嘛。

give (somebody) one's word 约定

give sb one's word表明“约定”的意思，主要用作I give you my word（我向你保证）的形态。换句话说，可以理解成I'll promise you，对于被承诺的一方，则是take one's word。

“去女朋友家接女朋友，不料她的哥哥是体育大学的肌肉男”

I **give you my word** I will not touch her.

M·O·R·E

- I will give you my word（that S+V）.
  我向你保证

I will **give you my word** I'll do what I can.
我向你保证，我会尽我所能的。

I will **give you my word** I will not touch her.
我向你保证，绝对不会碰她。

Can you **give me your word** that Jack can be trusted?
你能向我保证，杰克是个值得相信的人吗？

A: Do you think Ralph finished the report? 你觉得拉斐尔写完报告书了？
B: He gave me his word it would be completed. 他向我保证会完成的。

give somebody a hard time 让某人难受，欺负某人

正如字面上的含义，表示“给某人带来艰难的时光”或“让某人难受”。如果宾语变成自己的话give oneself a hard time就表示“自责”的意思。

“公司上司天天都会在下班前留下一大堆业务，愤怒之余可以对他吼一声”

I guess you like to give me a hard time.

M·O·R·E

- give sb a hard time
  让某人难受
- give oneself a hard time
  自责

Please don't **give me a hard time**.
别让我难受。

Why did you **give me such a hard time**?
你为什么要那么欺负我?

Don't **give yourself too hard time**.
不要过于自责。

A: Your clothes are really ugly today. **你今天的衣服真难看啊。**
B: Come on! Don't give me a hard time. **拜托，别欺负我。**

give something some thought 仔细想想……

同样为give A B的表达方式，可以用在对某件事再进一步想想时。最典型的例子就是“我已经想过这个问题了”，此时可以I've been giving (I've given) it some thought。

“学生唐突地问道，是不是一定要毕业，对此老师的反应”

The teacher looked back and gave it some thought.

M·O·R·E

- I've given it some thought and I think ...
  我仔细想过，我觉得……

Maybe you should **give it some thought**.
也许你应该再仔细想想。

You should **give it some thought**.
你应该多仔细考虑考虑。

I'll **give it some thought**.
我会仔细想想的。

I'**ve given it some thought**. I think it would be best for me to leave.
我仔细想过，我觉得离开是最好的选择。

A: I can offer you a job in London. **我可以在伦敦为你提供一份工作。**
B: I must give it some thought before I take it. **在做决定前，我必须仔细考虑考虑。**

give somebody some time 给某人多点时间

表示“给某人多点时间”的意思，在时间处可以用some time，more time，也可以用具体的a few week，a month等。想要说明需要时间的理由的话，就可以在后面加to+动词形态。

“妻子下令，短时间内必须要戒烟，对此向朋友抱怨道”

She didn't give me enough time to quit smoking.

M·O·R·E

- give sb some time+V
  给某人多些时间
- give sb time to+V
  给某人做某事的时间

Give me more time. I'm not a miracle worker.
多给我点时间。我可不是能够创造奇迹的人。

I just need you to **give me some time**.
我需要你再多给我点时间。

You're just going to have to **give me some time** to think about it.
你必须要多给自己留点时间，仔细考虑考虑。

You've got to **give me a few more minutes**.
你必须多给我点时间考虑考虑。

A: I haven't heard from Annie in a few days. 我好几天都没听到安妮的消息了。

B: Give her some time to send you an e-mail. 给她一点时间，她肯定会给你发邮件的。

not give a damn 不干某人的事

俚语中的not give a damn (shit, fuck)表示“对某事毫无兴趣”，但可绝对不能随便用。I don't give a damn (shit, fuck)后面可以加about ... /疑问词S+V的形态，来说明不关心的具体事情。

“不怕被炒鱿鱼的勇敢员工的日常用语”

I don't give a damn what the boss says.

M·O·R·E

- not give a damn (shit) about (what)
  毫不关心某事
  对某事毫无兴趣
- I don't give a damn (shit).
  关我屁事。

You don't **give a damn** about me!
你根本就不在乎我!

I don't **give a shit** what they think.
我才不关心他们在想什么。

A: I quit. I don't give a damn about this company. 我不干了。这公司关我屁事。

B: But you need a job to pay your bills. 不过你需要一份工作来偿还债务啊。

Don't give me that! 不要说那种话！不要装傻！

如果对方拿出毫不讲理的借口或解释，就可以用这句话表示“不要说那种话！”，如果不相信对方的解释或辩解，就可以使用这个句子。另外，Give me that表示“交出来！”

“被狠毒的老板折磨到深夜，却被老婆埋怨为什么这么晚回家”

Don't give me that look. It wasn't my fault.

M·O·R·E

- Don't give me that face (look).
  不要给我看那种脸色（表情）。
- I'll give you that.
  你说的没错。

Don't give me that. I know all the details.
别扯淡。你说过什么自己清楚。

Don't give me that look. It's written all over your face.
别给我摆那张臭脸，你脸上都写着呢。

She's so sexy. I'll **give you that**.
她真性感，你说的没错。

A: Wendy was too full to eat your food. 文迪太饱了，吃不下你做的东西。

B: Don't give me that. She hates my cooking. 别唬我，她不喜欢我的手艺而已。

give it to somebody 单刀直入地说

give it to somebody straight表示“对某人单刀直入地说”。但如果没有straight，单单是give it to sb的话就表示“给某人颜色看看”或“性行为”。但最常用的give it to sb则是前文中提到过的give sth to sb，就是“给某人某样东西”的意思。

“朋友们看到我的名牌手包，羡慕不已，可以自豪地说”

Mike **gave it to** me as a gift.

M·O·R·E

- give it to sb straight
  单刀直入地说
- give it to
  给某人颜色看看，发生性行为
- give it to sb
  给某人某样东西

Give it to me straight.
老实交代。

They really **gave it to** me at the meeting!
他们在会议中好好教训了我一顿！

Give it to someone else. I don't want it.
把它给别人吧，我不想要。

A: How can I break up with my boyfriend? 我怎样才能和男朋友分手呢？

B: Be honest with him. Give it to him straight. 老实交代吧。单刀直入地切入话题。

I'd give anything to (for) ... 为了……什么都可以做，一定要做某事

I'd为I would的简略形式，作为假设方法的表达。to (for)之后的成分为一种条件，表示“如果能够……的话，什么都可以做”。另外，可以用珍贵的my right arm取代anything。

“一心想要和校花简约会的一个男生发自内心的呼唤”

I'd give the world to go out with Jane.

M·O·R·E

- I'd give anything to (for) ...
  我一定要做出……
- I'd give my right arm (the world) to (for) ...
  为了……什么都可以付出。

I'd give anything to have her back.
如果能让她回头，我什么都愿意做。

I'd give anything to be with you again.
如果能重新和你在一起，我什么都愿意做。

I'd give the world to go out with Jane.
不管发生什么事，我都要和简约会。

I'd give my right arm to see my family again.
我要不惜一切代价重新与家人团圆。

A: You look so sad today. 你今天看着很伤心啊。

B: I'd give anything to be with my girlfriend. 如果能和女朋友在一起，我万死不辞。

give birth to 生下……

表示生孩子或引起某种事端，像give birth to sb一样，to后面加上自己生下的孩子即可。

“一口气生下三胞胎的母亲自豪地说道”

I just gave birth to three children.

M·O·R·E

- give birth to
  生孩子，引起事端
- She gave birth to you.
  她生下了你。

You and Jill will **give birth to** a very smart baby.
你和吉尔生下了一个聪明伶俐的孩子。

His wife recently **gave birth to** a beautiful baby daughter.
他老婆最近生下了一个美丽的小女孩。

You think it's easy to **give birth to** seven children?
你觉得生7个孩子容易吗?

A: Gina gave birth to twins last Saturday. 吉娜上个星期六生下了一对双胞胎。

B: Her husband must be so happy! 她老公一定很开心吧!

give away 捐赠，送给，说出秘密

不收取任何报酬，甘愿赠与对方，表示“捐赠”或“错过了机会”等。另外，也会用在说漏秘密（秘诀）时。giveaway作为名词表示白送的商品等。

“妈妈让哥哥把玩具让给弟弟，哥哥非常不满”

This is mine. I don't want to give it away.

M·O·R·E

- give away
  捐赠，送出，说漏秘密
- giveaway
  赠品

I don't want it and I'm going to **give it away**.

我不想留着了，想马上送给别人。

Oh, come to think of it, and maybe we don't have that much to **give away**.

我仔细想了想，好像我们没什么可以送出去的。

Don't **give away** your thoughts so easily.

不要把你的想法随便告诉别人。

A: What will you do with the items in your apartment? 你想怎么处理房间里的东西？

B: I'll give away most of them to my friends. 大部分都送给我朋友。

give back 返还

“返还”(return)给原来的主人，最常用的形态为give me back sth（把某样东西还给我），give you back sth（把某样东西还给你）等。

“在和女朋友分手之后，小心眼男生要对方还所有的礼物”

You've got to give me back my T-shirt.

M·O·R·E

- give me back sth
  把某样东西还给我
- give you back sth
  把某样东西还给你

Give back the money you owe me.

还我钱。

You **give** me **back** my sweater.

把毛衣还给我。

Give me **back** the dress.

把裙子还给我。

I came to **give** you **back** your stuff.

我是来还你东西的。

A: John is going to give back the money he took. 约翰会把钱还回来的。

B: He shouldn't have taken it in the first place. 他一开始就不应该拿。

give in (to) 接受（原本反对的事情），服从……屈服，提交(hand in)

在经过一番劝说之后，接受原本反对的事情。如果是互相争吵的状况，就表示屈服或投降的意思。另外，give in也可以像hand in一样表示“提交某物”。

“在夜店因过度兴奋，遭到了多位女性的谴责时”

I just **gave in to** my basic instincts.

You're going to **give in** eventually.
你最终肯定会接受的。

I am not going to **give in to** this.
我绝对不会屈服的。

We **gave in to** our basic instincts.
我们最终被本能所征服了。

She'll not **give in to** the idea that she will never get married.
她终究不会放弃自己不会结婚的想法。

A: Why are you going on a date with Tim? 你为什么要和提姆约会？

B: He asked me so many times that I had to give in. 他三番五次死缠烂打，我只好投降。

give off something 发出（气味，光，噪声等）

表示发出气味、光、热、声音等。只要是能够发出气味或光的物体，无论人或物都能作为主语。

“对不分昼夜贪图美色的禽兽说一句”

You'**re giving off** the sexual energy all the time.

A woman **gives off** a certain scent when she breathes.
女性在呼吸时会发出奇妙的香气。

The flowers **gave off** a nice smell.
花朵散发出了甜美的花香。

The bathroom **was giving off** a terrible stink.
洗手间发出了刺鼻的恶臭。

Your food **is giving off** a delicious aroma.
你做的食物香气扑鼻。

A: What is that terrible smell? 这可怕的气味到底是什么？

B: That factory is giving off a strong odor. 那家工厂发出来的臭味。

give something over 为某人腾出，传达

give sth over (to sb)表示“给某人传达某物”，与hand over的意义相近，另外，give oneself over表示“专注于或屈服于某事”。

“非常后悔自己的年轻岁月是在赌博中度过的”

He regrets that he **gave himself over** to gambling in his youth.

M·O·R·E

- give sth over to sb
  把某物递给某人(hand over)
- give oneself over sth
  专注于某事
- be given over to sth
  某物被用作特定的目的（hand over）

I'll **give** the money **over to** Charles.

我会把钱转交给查理斯的。

Give it **over to** your mother.

把这个交给你妈妈。

Why don't you **give** this book **over to** Tom?

帮个忙把这本书交给汤姆好吗?

A: Where did your new computer go? 你那台新电脑哪去了?

B: I had to give it over to my brother. 我不得不让给我弟弟了。

give out 发布，发生故障，分发

give out是机械或我们的身体机能“停止正常运作”(stop working)的意思，即“发生故障”(break down)。当然，最常用的形式为表示“分发”(distribute)。

“咖啡社团有一个难缠的家伙，所以想要单独见个面，但咖啡店主拒绝透露个人信息”

We're not supposed to **give out** information on members.

M·O·R·E

- give sth out (to)
  给某人分发某物
- sth gives out
  某物出故障，坏掉

We can **give out** one to everyone who comes into the store.

我们可以给进到店铺里的每位客人发一个。

The hospital won't **give out** any information.

医院不会透露任何个人信息。

The tire **gave out** and completely exploded.

轮胎磨损很严重，最后完全爆开了。

A: There're a lot of ways to celebrate Christmas. 庆祝圣诞节有很多方式。

B: Many people give out Christmas presents. 很多人会分发圣诞节礼物。

give up 放弃

表示放弃或停手，如果单独使用give up，或想要具体说明放弃的事物就可以说成give up sth或give sth up。另外，在指明放弃的行为时，可以说成give up ...ing。

"在大街上看到一对情侣，女方很漂亮，就大胆地对男方说"

I want you to **give up** your girlfriend.

It's not impossible. Don't **give up** yet.
并非不可能，先别放弃。

Don't **give up** too easily.
不要轻易放弃。

I **gave up** smoking for my health.
我为了健康把烟戒掉了。

A: You mean, I should never give up? 你是说，我绝对不能放弃？
B: Exactly! Get out there and try again. 没错！再去试一试。

More Expressions

- **give (...)priority** 把……看成第一位
  I want you to **give this top priority.**
  我希望你把这个看成是当务之急的事。

- **give sth one's OK** 承诺于……
  The boss refuses to **give it his OK.**
  老板拒绝承认。

- **give way to** 谦让
  We will have to **give way to** the new method of production.
  我们必须改变现有的生产方式。

- **give rise to** 产生某种结果，引起
  This decision will **give rise to** a lot of negative publicity.
  这决定会招致很多负面的宣传结果。

- **give somebody pleasure**
  给某人带来快乐
  It **gives me great pleasure** to introduce Mr. Carter. 能介绍卡特先生，是我的荣幸。

- **give oneself a treat** 专注于，享受
  I think I'm going to **give myself a treat**! 我觉得我要开始享受了！

- **give or take**+时间/产量 大概，约
  He's three feet tall, **give or take** an inch. 他个子差不多是三英尺。

Give me five! 拍手！
Don't give an inch! 不要做出半点让步！
I can't give specifics. 我不想详细解释。

拿到手就远走高飞的

Take

表示抓住某物或将某物拿走的意思的take是个与bring正好相反的动词。在表示拿到某物的时候，可以衍生出选择、接受等多种含义，而在表示拿走时，可以加上表示目的地的副词或to+地点名词。另外，像give一样，可以将动作动词的名词形式作为宾语，从而产生出多样的短语。

基本概念

1 抓住，获得，选择，接受

She took my arm. 她抓住了我的胳膊。

I'll take this one. 我选择这个。

2 带走，拿走

I'm just taking my carry-on. 我只带了随身携带的登机行李。

I'll take it to my grave. 我会铭记一辈子的。

3 需要，花费（时间，金钱，努力等）

It took me 5 hours to get here. 来这儿我花了5个小时。

It will take about one week to get the job done. 需要一个星期左右才能完成那件事。

4 take+动名词 做……

Are you going to take a shower right now? 你现在去洗澡吗?

Why don't you take a walk with me? 你要不要和我出去散散步?

take 接受(accept), 选择(choose)

在眼前的几个选项中确定一项的含义。在商店里最终选定一个商品或接受对方建议或忠告时(take sb's advice)，决定工作时(take the job)都可以用take。

“员工要求提升50%的薪水，但只能提升20%时”

I told him he can **take** it or leave it.

I'll **take** it.

我就拿这个了。

Please **take** anything you like from the dessert tray.

请挑选任何喜欢的甜品。

Whichever way you **take**, you will find yourself in front of the station.

不管走哪条路，你都能走到车站。

Take your pick, whatever you want.

无论什么，想拿就拿。

A: What did you say to him? 你对他说什么了?

B: I told him he can take it or leave it. 我跟他说，要么接受，要么放弃。

take one's word for it 相信某人的话

表示接受某人的话(sb's word)，即“相信某人的话”。take it from sb也可以表达相同的含义，另外，have one's word (for it)也是同义句。如果说成give one's word的话就会变成“约定，保证”。

“在介绍他人时，强调他是业内最强人士，让对方相信自己的话”

Take my word for it, he's the best in the business.

M·O·R·E

- take one's word (for it)
  相信某人的话
- take it from sb
  相信某人的话
- have one's word (for it)
  相信某人的话
- give one's word
  保证

We'll have to **take your word for it**.

我们不得不相信你的话。

I'll **take your word for it**.

我相信你。

Take it from me, Mom loves you.

相信我，你妈爱你。

A: Take my word for it. He's a real idiot. 相信我，他真是个白痴。

B: I'll keep that in mind. 我会记住的。

Don't take it personally. 听完不要生气。

take it personally是以个人情绪(personally)接受(take)它(it)，表示以个人的情绪理解对方的话。Don't take it personally.就是在说真心话的时候请对方不要误会或生气的意思。

"绝对无法相信经常说谎的人，郑重地拒绝道"

Don't take it personally, but I won't take your word for that.

M·O·R·E

- take it personally
  想歪，误解，生气
- Don't take it personally, but ...
  听完不要生气

Don't take it personally, but I don't like your new haircut.
听完不要生气，不过我真的不喜欢你的新发型。

He'll **take it personally**.
他听完会不高兴的。

I can't help but **take it personally**.
我忍不住生气。

A: Jerry told me that I'm fat. 杰瑞说我胖了。
B: Don't take it personally. He's unkind. 不要生气，他就是那么讨厌。

I can't take it anymore. 实在无法忍受，忍无可忍。

实在(anymore)没办法接受(can't take)它(it)的意思。表示到了忍无可忍的境界，最常用的形式为I can't take it anymore。

"节食减肥的人实在没办法忍受饥饿，偷偷吃东西时"

I can't take it anymore. I'm so hungry.

M·O·R·E

- get some rest
  休息一会
- get some sleep
  打个盹

Okay, that's it. **I can't take it anymore.**
好吧，我忍不下去了。

I can't take it anymore! I'm putting an end to this!
实在没办法忍下去了！我要做个了结！

I can't take it anymore. I am out of here!
实在是忍无可忍，我不干了！

He couldn'**t take it anymore** so he quit the job.
他实在忍不下去，于是就辞职了。

A: Everyone lies to me. I can't take it anymore. 每个人都对我说谎，我实在忍不下去了。
B: That's not true. I am always honest with you. 其实不然，我总是对你坦诚相待的。

take the blame 接受谴责

同样作为“接受某物”的意义，take将谴责(blame)或责任(responsibility)作为宾语，变成了take the blame或take the responsibility。

“经常狡辩的同事犯下错误之后，在背后说道”

Don't expect her to **take the blame for** that.

M·O·R·E

- take the blame (for ...)
  (对某事)负责
- take (the) responsibility (for (of) ...)
  (对某事)负责

You might **take the blame for** something you didn't do.

你可能在背负莫须有的罪名。

I **take full responsibility for** that.

我对那件事负全责。

We need to **take some of the responsibility** here.

我们需要负点责任。

A: Oh boy, our boss is really angry about the report. 天啊，我们老板听完报告真的有点气愤。

B: Well, I'm not going to take the blame for it. 是啊，我可不要去担责任。

take credit for 付出的努力得到认可，因某事得到认可

这次接受(take)的是对于某次功勋(credit)的认可。虽然有些难以理解，但在日常生活中经常会使用到，也可以用have，get替代take。相反，如果是give credit for的话就是”承认他人的功劳”的意思。

“功劳本不属于自己，但老板却错表扬了自己，出于良心说道”

I can't **take credit for** that. I wasn't part of the project.

M·O·R·E

- take credit for
  因某事得到认可
- give credit for
  承认他人的功劳

I can't **take credit for** this. We both know that this wasn't me.

我可不能独吞功劳。我们俩都知道不应该是我。

You **took credit for** my work, Peter!

彼得！你抢占了我的功劳！

I am sorry I **took credit for** your work.

很抱歉，我抢占了你的功劳。

A: Allison took credit for buying the gift. 埃里森抢占了买礼物的功劳。

B: She should, because she paid for it. 没什么问题啊，本来就是她掏的钱。

take chances (a chance) 冒着危险，碰运气

表示相信命运搏一搏，可以使用take a chance (chances)或take the chance或take one's chances。另外，take a risk (of)也是冒着危险的意思。

"天气预报中说会有暴雨，但执意要出行"

Let's take a chance. We might have some good weather.

M·O·R·E

- take a chance (chances)
  冒着风险，碰运气
- take one's chances
  碰碰运气
- take the chance
  抓住机会，相信命运

I want you to **take a chance** and trust me.
你大可冒险相信我一次。

I'll **take my chances**.
我要碰碰运气。

Sometimes you have to **take chances**.
有时你不得不碰运气。

A: Have you ever gone bungee jumping? 你玩过蹦极跳吗?
B: No, I don't like to take chances. 没有，我不喜欢碰运气。

take the opportunity 抓住机会

与前面的句型有点差异，take the opportunity表示"得到……的机会"，尤其在表达"借机做某事"的时候经常会用到I'll take the opportunity to ...。

"花花公子与漂亮的女生独处，内心强烈呼唤着"

Now I have the perfect opportunity to seduce her.

M·O·R·E

- take the opportunity to do
  得到……机会
- have (get) the opportunity to do
  有……的机会

I'm happy I'm able to **give** you **this opportunity**.
我很高兴能为你提供这次机会。

I'd like to **take this opportunity to** say I'm getting married next month.
我想借此机会跟你说，我下个月要结婚了。

You may not **get an opportunity to** do that research.
你可能没机会做那个研究了。

You can **take this opportunity to** get to know her well.
你可以借此机会多了解了解她。

A: Randy has a chance to start his own business. 兰迪有机会开创他自己的事业。
B: I hope he takes the opportunity. He might get rich. 我希望他能抓住机会，他很有可能会变成富翁的。

take a rain check 推到下一次

rain check是当棒球比赛因恶劣天气不得不终止时官方发给观众的交换券(check)，凭借此券可以观看下一次的比赛。由此衍生出了take a rain check，使用在将约定推迟的情况下。

"单相思女同事诱惑男同事天天见面时"

Can I take a rain check? I'm so tired today.

M·O·R·E

- take a rain check
  （将约定）推迟到下次
- give a rain check
  约好下次再说

I'll **take a rain check**.

这次要延期了。

You mind if I **take a rain check**?

你介意我推到下一次吗?

My head's going to explode. Can I **take a rain check**?

我脑子快炸开了，能下次再做吗?

A: Would you like to come up and see my apartment? 你想过来看看我的新房子吗?

B: I would, but I'm going to have to take a rain check. 非常乐意，但恐怕要推到下一次了。

take one's time 不慌不忙

表示"充分留有时间"，可以让对方慢慢来，经常会用到take your time。相同的表达有relax，take it easy等。

"看到卫生间被员工所占，憋坏的老板高声说道"

Take your time. I'm in no rush.

M·O·R·E

- take one's time with sth
  不用着急
- take one's time ...ing
  不要着急

Please **take your time**. It's an important decision.

不用着急，这是个重要的决定。

Take your time. There's no rush.

慢慢来，不用着急。

Take your time. It's no big deal.

慢慢来，没什么大不了的。

A: I'll be back in ten minutes. 我10分钟后回来。

B: Take your time. It's not that busy. 慢慢来，我不着急。

take medicine 吃药

take后面接medicine或pill，tablet的话就是吃药、服用药物的意思。medication同样可以作为药物的含义与take共同使用。如果是take drugs就会变成“服用非法药物或毒品”。

“儿子患上了严重的流感，却始终不想吃药”

I need you to **take some medicine**.

Are you currently **taking medication**?
你最近在吃什么药吗?

I'**m** not **taking any medicine**.
我没在吃任何药物。

Take one tablet every night before sleeping.
每晚睡觉前吃一片。

I promise I **have** never **taken any drugs**.
我发誓，我绝对没有服用过任何毒品。

A: Our teacher looked terrible this morning. 我们老师今天看起来脸色不好。
B: He should take some medicine for his cold. 他应该吃点感冒药。

take a bus 乘坐巴士

如果take后面接上交通工具(a bus，a taxi)等的话就会变成“乘坐”的意思，如果take后面接道路(road)的话就会变成“去往……的路”。

“醉酒之后想要打车回家时”

I'm going to **take a cab** home.

The easiest way is to **take a taxi**.
最方便的方法就是打车。

Which train should I **take** to Jangnan?
我坐哪列火车可以到江南?

You should **take a bus**.
你应该坐公交。

M·O·R·E

- take a bus (train, taxi, cab)
  乘坐巴士（火车，出租车）
- take the road
  前往……路

A: What is the best way to get to Singapore Department Store?去往新加坡百货商场的最佳路径是什么?
B: Take the bus. You'll be there in twenty minutes. 坐公交吧。二十分钟就到了。

take a lesson 授课

take+科目会变成“听课”，如果是take+考试的话就会变成“考试”。另外，teach sb a lesson表示的不是上课，而是教训一顿，而learn a lesson是得到教训。

“拼命地赚钱就是为了让儿子学钢琴，上英语辅导班”

My son is taking private piano and English lessons.

M·O·R·E

- take a lesson 上课
- give sb a lesson 讲课

I've been **taking** dancing **lessons**.
我一直上着舞蹈课。

I'm **taking** tennis **lessons** three times a week.
我每周上三次网球课。

Why don't you **take** a yoga **class**?
你为什么不上瑜伽课?

A: You can take a lesson in drawing for free.你可以免费上画画课。
B: I'll try it. I like creating art. 我试试吧，我喜欢艺术创作。

take a look (at) 看一眼（某物）

与give的用法一样，take后面如果加动词的名词形式，动名词的话就会变成“做某事”。Look (at)比较常用，但最好选用take+动名词形式的take a look (at)。

“一对恋人请路人给他们照张相”

Can you take a picture of us?

M·O·R·E

- take a shower 洗澡
- take a bath 沐浴
- take a walk 散步
- take a nap 打盹
- take a vacation 休假
- take a rest 休息
- take a seat 坐下
- take a picture 拍照

Would you **take a look at** this paper?
你看看这张报纸呗?

Can I **take a bath**? It won't take long.
我能洗个澡吗? 不会很久的。

Please **take a seat**. Can I get you something to drink?
请坐。喝点什么?

You should **take a rest**. Get some sleep in your room.
你该休息休息了，到你屋里睡一会吧。

A: Take a look at Angela tonight. 今晚看看安吉拉。
B: Wow, I can't believe how beautiful she is. 哦，真不敢相信，她居然这么美。

take a break 休息一会

同样属于take+动名词的一种。break表示暂时停止手上的事情，因此take a break 就表示“休息片刻”，在会话中经常会用到这句。

“在吃完午饭之后聊了一个多小时的天，还厚着脸皮说道”

Well, we're kind of taking a break.

M·O·R·E

- take a break
  休息一会
- be taking a break
  正在休息

I need to **take a break**.
我需要休息一会。

Let's **take a** ten-minute **break**. We've been working hard.
我们休息十分钟吧。工作太累了。

Maybe we should **take a break**.
也许我们该休息一会。

Time to **take a break**. How about some coffee?
休息时间到了，喝杯咖啡怎么样?

A: Shall we take a break now? 现在休息一会怎么样?
B: No, let's keep going. 不了，继续做吧。

take care of 照看，处理

非常熟悉的短语，表示“照顾某人”。另外，如果变成take care of sth的话就可以理解为“处理某事”，如果单独是take care的话就表示“走好”的客套话。

“三伏天热气沸腾时可以为对方着想”

It's important to take care of your health in the summer.

M·O·R·E

- I will (Let me) take care of ...
  我来处理。
- (Please) Take care of ...
  请照看……
- take a good
  好好照顾……，处理

Let me **take care of** it. Don't worry about that.
交给我，不要担心。

Let me **take care of** the bill.
我来买单。

Can you **take care of** my work while I'm away?
我不在的时候你能处理我的工作吗?

A: Could you take care of my dog this week? 你这周能不能帮我照看我的小狗狗?
B: Why? Are you going on vacation? 怎么了? 你要去度假吗?

take time 需要多少时间

take后面如果接时间名词的话就会变成“需要多少时间”的意思，由此衍生出的表达还有it takes+时间+to ...（做某事需要多少时间），how long does it take to ... ?（做某事需要多少时间？）等等。当然，除了时间名词之外还可以接courage等一般名词。

“给亚马逊热带雨林中的土著人买笔记本电脑时”

It takes a while to get used to it.

M·O·R·E

- It takes (sb)+时间+to ...（某人）做某事需要多长时间
- How long does it take to ... 做这件事需要多长时间?
- How long does it take to get to+地点? 去某个地点需要多长时间?

It **takes** around 1 hour **for me to** get there.
去那儿大概需要1个小时。

It **took me a long time to** find you.
找你花了我不少功夫。

It looks like it'll **take a lot of time**.
看起来要费很长时间。

Hold on a moment. It won't **take long**.
稍等片刻，不会很久的。

Be patient. **It takes time to** get what you want.
耐心点。你想得到自己想要的，肯定得花一些功夫。

It will **take a lot of courage to** do that.
需要很大的勇气才能做那件事。

How long does it take to get this done?
完成这个需要多久?

How long does it take to get to the airport?
去机场需要多久?

What **took** you so **long**?
你怎么那么慢?

A: It took David a long time to graduate. 大卫花了好长时间才得以毕业。
B: Yeah, he was in college for seven years. 他在大学待了7年。

A: I haven't cleaned my room this week. 我这个星期没有打扫我的房间。
B: Take time to do that on Sunday. 周日找个时间打扫打扫。

A: How long does it take to cook a turkey? 烹饪一只火鸡需要多久?
B: That depends on how heavy the bird is. 那要看火鸡有多大了。

take somebody to 将某人带到某处

当take被用作移动的意思时，take sb to就表示“将某人带到某处”。to后面大多数情况下会接地点，但也可以变成to+动词，表示“带某人去做某事”。

“约会时从来不结账的女朋友中午突然找过来说道”

Take me to lunch. I'm in the mood for lobster.

M·O·R·E

- I'd like to take you to (out for) ...
  想带你去某处
- Take me to ...
  带我去……

I'd like to **take you to** the restaurant to try some Indian food.

我想带你去尝尝印度美食。

I'd like to **take her out for** dinner on the weekend.

周末我想带你出去吃饭。

Please **take me to** the airport.

请带我去机场。

The train will **take you to** Kimpo airport.

你坐这班火车可以到金浦机场。

A: Where are you going with Elise? 你和爱丽丝去哪儿？

B: I have to take her to a subway station. 我得把她送到地铁站。

take action 采取措施

为了解决某问题，采取必要的行动或措施时可以用take steps。措施的目的可以在action或steps后面加to+动词来表达。

“我们国人频频死于非命时”

We have **to take some steps** to protect the lives of the people.

M·O·R·E

- take steps to
  采取某种措施
- take a legal action
  采取法律措施
- take follow-up measures
  采取后续措施

They decided to **take action**.

他们决定采取措施。

We have to **take steps** to protect ourselves.

我们必须采取措施保护自己。

We are certainly **taking steps** to resolve them.

我们肯定会采取措施解决问题的。

We're **taking some steps** towards stopping this kind of action.

我们正在采取措施阻止这类行为的发生。

A: Sometimes I feel scared when I walk home at night. 有时我一个人回家会非常害怕。

B: You need to take action to protect yourself. 你得想办法保护自己。

take advantage of 利用……

take advantage of sb表明巧妙地利用他人的弱点，以此得到自己想要的利益，take advantage of sth表明肯定意义，即活用某物。

“想把单纯疲劳恢复剂当成万能药卖给老人”

I decided to take advantage of the elderly people.

M·O·R·E

- take advantage of sb 利用某人
- take advantage of sth 活用某物

We're not going to **take advantage of** the situation.
我们不会趁人之危的。

Many people **are taking advantage of** the day off.
很多人利用了休假的时间。

You should feel guilty about **taking advantage of** young people.
你应该为利用年轻人而感到羞耻。

I was hoping to **take advantage of** your expertise.
我希望借用您的专业知识。

A: This is a great price for a new TV. 对于新型电视机来说，这个价格很不错了。
B: You should take advantage of it while it's so low. 你应该好好利用这个机会，趁着它还便宜。

take place 发生，出现

take place为基本短语，表示某种事情发生或出新，可以看成happen的同义词。

“因性交易被抓到警察局的人最不想承认的话”

You admit that prostitution took place there?

Most exchanges **take place** by e-mail, text message, or IM.
很多交易都是通过电子邮件、短信或社交工具实现的。

There's a charity dinner **taking place** downstairs.
楼下有一场慈善晚宴。

The robbery **took place** in a bank downtown.
城镇的一家银行被打劫了。

Our date will **take place** next Saturday.
我们要在下周六约会。

A: What's going to take place in the arena? 竞技场会举行什么活动?
B: There is a pop music concert tonight. 今晚会有一场流行音乐演唱会。

take part in 参与某事

一说到take part in就会想起participate，take part in sth表示参加某事，参与等。

"office politics盛行的公司里，心态正直的人内心呼唤着"

I will not **take part in** such a scheme.

M·O·R·E

- play a part in
  参与某事
- have no part in
  与某事不相关

You're going to **take part in** the camping trip?
你会参加这次野营吗?

My mother **is taking part in** a political protest.
我妈在参加政治游行。

Our friends are going to **take part in** our wedding.
我们的朋友会参加我们的婚礼。

The students like to **take part in** science class.
学生们喜欢上科学课。

A: Did you take part in the festival? 你参加庆典活动了吗?
B: No. I just stayed at home. 没有，我在家待着呢。

take notes 记下，记录，瞩目

take note of表示"关注某事，注意，瞩目"(pay attention)，如果note变成复数的话，take notes就表示做笔记。

"给一个心爱的有夫之妇留下了纸条，不料出现在约会地点的是一个暴力男"

You **left** Jill **a note** to meet her here.

M·O·R·E

- make a note of
  记下笔记
- leave a note
  留言，留下便条

Please **take notes** whatever I tell you to.
记下我跟你说的所有话。

Can you **take some notes** for me?
你能帮我记一下吗?

I was so busy **taking notes**.
我忙着做笔记呢。

A: I won't be able to make it to the presentation. 恐怕我不能出席汇报了。
B: That's okay. I'll take notes for you. 没关系，我会帮你做笔记的。

... will take a second 只需要一会

take a second (minute)表示只需要一会的时间。在嘱咐对方“一会就好”时用成This (it) will just take a minute的形式。当然，如果主语是人的话，就会变成“腾出一点时间去做某事”。

“以健谈闻名的校长在会议上称简单说几句”

It (This) will only take a minute.

M·O·R·E

- It (This) will take a minute (second).
  只需要一会就行。
- sb takes a minute (second) to+动词
  某人腾出一点时间去做某事

It (This) will just take a second.
一会儿就行。

It really is only going to take a minute.
说真的，一会儿就行。

I have to take a minute to check it out.
我只好重新检查一遍。

You want to take a minute to think again?
你愿意再想想吗?

A: Aren't you finished in the bathroom yet? 还有人在洗手间吗?
B: Almost. It will take a second for me to get ready. 快完了，一会儿就好了。

Take it easy. 镇定，慢慢来。

表示向对方说不要慌张时，经常会用到Take it easy形式的祈使句，也可以像I'll take it easy一样，用作一般的陈述句。

“很多女性纠缠的时候，绅士说的话”

Take it easy, ladies. I'm married.

M·O·R·E

- Take it easy.
  镇静，慢慢来。
- take it easy on
  慢慢来，别慌

Just take it easy and try to relax.
冷静一些，放松放松。

Take it easy. We have a lot of time.
别着急，我们还有很多时间呢。

Why don't you take it easy on your girlfriend?
你为什么不好好对待你女朋友呢?

A: I'm looking forward to getting to know you. 我想尽快认识你。
B: Take it easy. We have a lot of time. 慢慢来，我们有很多时间。

take it slow 慢慢来

像之前的句型一样，表示慢慢来的意思。不仅限于某种动作，还可以用于某种关系，表示慎重前行的意思。

"昨天刚刚见面的女生提议要和自己去三天两夜的短途旅行，此时强烈抑制内心的激动，说道"

I'd like that. But I just want to **take it slow**.

He wants to **take it slow**.
他想慢慢来。

I think it's good to **take it slow**.
我觉得最好慢慢来。

Seriously, we'**re taking it slow**.
说真的，我们进度很缓慢。

She wants to **take it slow** in this relationship.
她希望我们的关系慢慢发展。

A: There's a lot of snow on the roads tonight. 今天晚上马路上有很多雪。
B: You'd better take it slow when you drive home. 回家时最好开慢点。

take away 消除，减少

字面意义为拿着(take)走远(away)，表示"抢走某物"，"消除"等意思。另外，take sb's breath away字面意思为"抢走某人的呼吸"，翻译过来就是"让某人大吃一惊"。

"一个疯狂的信用卡使用者被父亲没收了信用卡"

I heard your dad **took away** your credit card.

I still can't believe they **took away** my key.
我真无法相信他们居然拿走了我的钥匙。

Please, Jimmy, don't **take away** my hope.
拜托，吉姆，不要抢走我的希望。

She **took** it **away** and gave it to somebody else.
她把它抢了过去，给了别人。

Surprise me. **Take my breath away**.
吓吓我，最好让我吓破胆。

M·O·R·E

- take away
  抢走；
  让某人吃惊，吓破胆
- take one's breath away
  让某人吃惊，吓破胆

A: What are those men in the truck doing? 那些人在卡车里干嘛呢?
B: They are taking away the school's garbage. 他们在清理学校的垃圾。

take back 拿回(from)，返还，退货(to)，取消说过的话

拿回自己之前给过的东西(take sth back from)，也可以表示返还自己得到的东西(take sth back to)。另外，也可以用在取消自己说过的话时。

"儿子在图书馆借了书，却始终没有还，老妈教训道"

You have to **take** the book **back** to the library.

M·O·R·E

- take back from
  从……拿回
- take back to
  返还给某人

Take back what you said!
收回你说的话!

I just **took back** what was mine.
我只是拿回了原本属于我的东西。

I **took back** my money from her.
我从她那里要回了钱。

A: I heard you had a fight with your girlfriend. 我听说你和你女朋友吵架了。
B: She took back the ring that I gave her. 她把我送她的戒指还给了我。

take down 下降，推到

字面意义为“将某物拉下”，可以表示“放到下面”或“推倒”、“打击士气”等等。另外，有些文章中还会用作“做笔记”。

"工程队的工头想要推倒墙面，做一个凉台"

If the wall is weak, we can **take** it **down** easily.

M·O·R·E

- take down
  拿下某物，推倒，打击士气，做笔记
- take (bring) sb down a notch
  让某人信心受挫，伤害自尊

I'm ready to fight for the little people. **Take down** some bad guys.
我做好了为可怜的人做斗争的准备，我要打倒坏人。

Fine. **Take** her **down** for the next test.
好吧，让她准备下次考试。

Could you **take** it **down** just a notch?
你能不能安静一点?

A: Take down those posters on the wall. 把墙上的海报撕下来。
B: OK, I'll get to work right away. 好的，我马上开始工作。

take from 从某人那里抢夺，掠夺

字面意义为“从某人那里(from)拿走(take)”，也可以表示“接受”。因此take it from me表示“接受我的提议”，即“相信我的话”。

“放在教室书包里的贵重物品遗失时可以说”

Someone in the class took it from my bag.

M·O·R·E

- take from
  从某人那里抢走
- take it from sb
  相信某人的话
- take it from here
  接受，担任
- take it from there
  接受剩下的部分

You can't take my money from me and just go away.
你不能就这么把钱抢走。

Don't take my girl from me.
不要抢走我的女人。

Why don't you guys go home. I can take it from here.
你们回家吧，剩下的我来做。

A: What do you have in your bag? 你包裹里有什么？
B: I took snacks from the kitchen this morning. 我早上从厨房里拿了点零食。

take in 接受，留宿，减少（衣服的尺码），欺骗

字面意义为接受(take)到内部(in)，表示接受为新成员或留宿在家中。另外，如果涉及到服装尺寸，则有改小的意思。

“嫉妒朋友新买的衣服，怂恿她改短衣服的坏心肠女孩”

I think it needs to be taken in.

M·O·R·E

- take sb in
  接受，留宿，欺骗
- take sth in
  改小尺码

They didn't take her in as a new member of the club.
他们没有将她接受为新成员。

I'm sorry but I can't take you in tonight.
很抱歉，我不能留你过夜。

Can you have these pants taken in?
你能改短这些裤子吗？

A: Your mom is the kindest woman I know. 据我了解，你妈妈她是最亲切的人。
B: Yeah, she takes in people who need help. 是啊，她会尽可能地帮助所有人。

take on 担负，对抗

take on有很多含义，最常用的就是表示“担负（极度）困难事情的责任”(accept a job or responsibility)，“雇用”(hire)，“呈现某种形象”。另外，也可以用作“展开斗争”。

“对有求生的欲望敢于面对癌症的人可以说出的话”

I beat cancer. I can take on the world.

M·O·R·E

- take on
  立场，态度

I'm really ready to **take on** more responsibility around here.
我做好了担负任何责任的准备。

Illness can **take on** many forms.
疾病可以呈现很多形态。

You must be a pretty tough guy to take on him.
你居然敢与他对抗，真是一个有魄力的人啊。

So, what's your **take on** this?
那你的立场是什么?

A: That was an exciting fight. 真是一场刺激的打斗。
B: One guy took on two others and won. 是啊，成功一挑二。

take off 脱衣服，飞机（起飞），休息，离开(leave)

off表明从本体逐渐脱离。起飞、脱衣服、申请休假等都可以用take off (to)表示“前往”。

“下午想和女朋友出去玩，找借口请假”

I should take the afternoon off.

M·O·R·E

- take one's eyes off
  停止注视某人

You'll have to wait until the plane **takes off**.
你不得不等到飞机起飞。

Would it be all right if I **took** a week **off** starting tomorrow?
我明天开始请一个星期的假可以吗?

I'd like to **take** the day **off** on Friday.
星期五我想请一天的假。

You're so amazing! I couldn't **take my eyes off** you.
真了不起，我真迷死你了。

A: It seems to me that the room became hot. 好像房间开始变热了。
B: I know. I had to take off my jacket. 是啊，我得脱下外套了。

take out 带出去，取出，取钱，借（书），打包（食物）

具有很多种含义。字面意义为带(take)出(out)，“将某人带出去”，去银行“取钱”，去图书馆“借书”，或去饭店“打包食物”等都可以用这个短语。

“心情天天都很差的姐姐经常会向弟弟撒气”

Just because you got mad, don't take it out on me.

M·O·R·E

- take sb out （for (to) ... ）
  将某人带出去做某事
- take it (anger) out on sb (sth)
  向他人泄愤
- take the words out of sb's mouth
  比某人先张口，打断

Let me take you out to dinner tonight.
今天晚上我请客。

They took me out for some drinks.
他们带我出去喝酒。

Eat here or take it out?
在这吃还是带走?

Don't take it out on me because you feel guilty.
不要因为你惭愧就向我泄愤。

A: Take out these bags and put them in the garage. 把这些包拿出来放到车库里。
B: Are you planning to store them? 你要保管它们吗?

take over 担负任务，占据公司

表示担负任务和工作的短语。如果对象是公司的话，take over就表示占据公司。take over for sb表示”代替某人担负某事”。I'll take over now表示“我来接管剩下的部分”。

“最理想的公司同事。见到他人疲惫就说交给自己”

You're getting tired. Let me take over.

M·O·R·E

- take over
  担负工作或责任，占据公司
- take sth (sb) over to
  把某物带给某人

So then you just took over his business?
所以说你接管了他的生意?

Sam, take over until she gets here.
山姆，帮个忙，直到她回来。

I took it over to the office this afternoon.
我下午把东西带到办公室了。

A: Why're those businessmen in the office? 为什么那些商人在办公室?
B: They plan to take over the company. 他们想并购公司。

take up 开始（工作，业余活动），选择为主题，占据（时间，空间），抢夺时间

表示重新开始某件事情，选择或占据时间和空间。因此，be taken up with表示时间或空间“被占据”，take up a challenge则表示“面对挑战”。

“考取律师或医生的职业资格证需要非常多的精力和时间，说道”

Being a lawyer must **take up** a lot of time.

M·O·R·E

- take sb up on
  接受（招待或提议）
- take up sb's time
  浪费某人的时间

She **has taken up** Taekwondo these days.
他最近在学跆拳道。

Thank you for seeing me. I won't **take up** much of your time.
谢谢你接见我。我不会占用你很多时间的。

I'll **take** you **up on** that.
我会接受你的意见。

A: Have you tried any new hobbies lately? 你最近尝试过任何新的业余活动吗？

B: No, but I plan to take up golf soon. 没，不过我正打算学高尔夫。

More Expressions

- **take checks** 接受支票
  Do you take (accept) credit cards?
  你拿到信用卡了吗？

- **take calls** 接电话
  He won't take my calls.
  他不想接我的电话。

- **take after** 长得像某人
  You must take after your father.
  你长得很像你爸爸。

- **be taken ill** 得病
  He's taken ill. 他生病了。

- **be taken with (by)**被某事吓一跳
  He was taken by surprise. 他吓了一跳。

- **take a message** 接受信息
  leave a message 留下信息
  Could I take a message? 我能转达信息吗？

- **take the place of** 代替某人
  Nothing can take the place of good health. 没有什么可以替代健康。

More Expressions

- **take it for granted** 理所当然地看待某事

  Don't think I take it for granted.

  不要以为我想当然。

- **take a shot** 瞄准，尝试

  Who's going to take the first shot?

  谁先来试试?

- **take A for B** 将A看成B

  Do you take me for an idiot?

  你是把我当成白痴了?

- **what it takes** 成功所需要的资质

  He doesn't have what it takes, does he?

  他不具备应有的素质，不是吗?

- **take a bite** 吃

  She started to take a bite of a sandwich.

  她开始吃三明治。

- **take to sb (sth)**开始喜欢某人**(take a liking to, take a shine to)**

  He seems to have taken to the new secretary. 他好像喜欢上了新秘书。

  They've really taken a liking to me.

  他们开始喜欢我了。

- **take the lead** 提前，站在前沿

  Right after we started getting into it, I took the lead.

  在我们开始之后，我站在了最前沿。

- **take pity (on)** 同情某人

  Does she often take pity on you?

  她经常同情你吗?

- **take A as B** 将A当成B

  I'll take that as a compliment.

  我就当成赞扬了。

What do you take in your coffee?

你在咖啡里放了什么?

It takes money to make money.

用钱赚钱。

I take an interest in you.

我对你感兴趣。

Take it or leave it.

没有选择的余地，爱做不做。

再三挽留也会离去的

Go

不甘心留在原地，不停地移动到其他目的地的动词。语言表达较差的我们，在到某个地方时会说I'll go to，或表示过去式的I went to，还有将来式的I'm going to。除了人之外，在表达某件事情的进行情况时也可以用How's it going? 来表示“最近过的怎么样？”。同样也能表达以动态为特征的机械(car，watch等)的运作。

基本概念

1 去某处，去做某事，（道路）畅通

I have to go now. 我现在要走了。

I went to the post office. 我去了趟邮局。

Does this road go to the station? 这条路通向车站吗?

2 （事情，状况）进行中，变成

How are things going? 过得怎么样?

How did the game go? 游戏结果怎样?

3 go+形容词 变成什么样

She went mad. 她生气了。

4 （机械设备等）运转

The car won't go. 车不动了。

I can't get the watch going. 我的表不走了。

go to 去某地（+名词），去做某事（+动词）

想要表达目的地的话就要用go to+地点，如果想要强调前行的目的就要用go to+动词。另外，go ...ing是指“去做某事”，go to+学校就表示升入某学校，上学等含义。

“高中同学说，我们上了同一所中学”

We went to the same high school.

M·O·R·E

- go to+地点名词
  去某处
- go to+动词
  去做某事
- go ...ing
  去做某事(go shopping, go skiing, go fishing)

I'm going to Florida for a couple of weeks.
我要去佛罗里达待几个星期。

She went to jog in the park.
她去公园散步了。

I'm going shopping today. Want to come along?
我今天要去逛街。你要一起吗?

A: I think it would be better if you went to bed. 我觉得你最好去睡觉。
B: I'm not tired yet. I think I will watch TV. 我还不累，我要看电视。

go (well, fine) （事态或状况）变得……

表示事态或状况向某种形势发展的表达，常用的句型有 ... go well（变得好）、或how ... go? （……怎么样了）。

“朋友刚刚相亲归来，问他感觉怎么样?

How did the date go? Was it good?

M·O·R·E

- go well
  变得很好
- That went well.
  结果不错。
- How did ... go?
  ……怎么样了?
- How's ... going?
  怎么样了?
- That's (just) the way it goes.
  本来就那样

The meeting went well. Good job.
会议很顺利，干得漂亮。

How's your business going?
你生意怎么样了?

How's it going? Did you make any new friends?
怎么样? 交到新朋友没?

How did it go with Caroline last night?
昨天晚上和卡洛琳过得怎么样?

A: How's it going with your new job? 你的新工作怎么样?
B: I have to admit that it's pretty tough. 不得不承认，那是个很棘手的工作。

be going to 将要做某事

be going to 可以理解成助动词“will”的用法。因此be going to+动词中的“going”并不具有“前往”的含义。

“人过中年才得以结婚的老处男的叹息”

Finally, we're going to get married this winter.

M·O·R·E

- be going to+动词 将要去做某事
- be not going to+动词 不会去做某事

Everybody get ready! We **are going to** start now.
大家准备好，我们要开始了。

I'**m not going to** take your word for that.
我不会相信你的话。

I'**m going to** do the laundry.
我要去洗衣服了。

Can you tell me where you'**re going to** stay?
能告诉我你要住哪里吗?

A: Living with you would make me happy. 和你在一起生活，我会很高兴的。
B: That isn't going to be possible! 那是绝对不可能的！

be (get) going 出发，离开(leave)

表示去某个场所，最常用的形态是be going或get going。主要表示不得不去的状况，因此前面会接should, must, had better等词汇。

“想要在聚会中先起身时可以说的话”

I think I should be going.

I guess I'd better **be going**.
恐怕我要先走了。

It's time we should **be going**.
我们该起身了。

I must **be going**. See you in the morning.
我必须先走了。明天早上见。

A: Well, I think I'd better be going now. 好了，我得先走了。
B: Okay, then I'll see you tomorrow at the office. 好吧，那明天公司见。

go wrong 搞错

像get一样，go也会在后面接形容词，表示“变成什么样”的意思。像食品过期(go bad)一样，表示从一个状态转变为另一个状态。go wrong表示“变差”。

“心肝宝贝女儿居然带回了一个老头子要结婚”

I will try to figure out what went wrong.

M·O·R·E

- go bad
  变质
- go grey
  头发变白
- go mad
  疯狂
- go blind
  失明
- What went wrong?
  有没有搞错?
- Something went wrong.
  肯定有问题。

I couldn't take calls. The phone **went dead**.

我不能接电话，电话坏了。

Time flies so fast. My hair'**s going grey**.

岁月如梭，我头发开始变白了。

Where did we **go wrong**?

我们到底错在哪里?

A: Should I buy this new cell phone? 我该不该买这款新手机?

B: It's very cheap. You can't go wrong. 很便宜啊，你肯定不亏。

go get 去做某事

表示“去做某事”的go and (to)+动词形式中，and (to) 被省略。come+动词也可以表示“来做某事”。

“在夜店碰到一些不错的靓妹，正要展现自己无穷的魅力时”

I'll go see if I can get her.

M·O·R·E

- go get+动词
  去做某事
- go have+动词
  去做某事
- go take+动词
  去做某事
- go see+动词
  去见某人

Go get some rest.

去休息一会吧。

You'd better **go see** a doctor as soon as possible.

你最好尽快去看医生。

It's so hot! Let's **go get** some ice cream.

太热了！我们去吃点冰淇淋吧。

I have to **go take** a shower.

我得去洗个澡了。

A: What would you like to do tonight? 你今天晚上想干什么?

B: Let's go see a movie. 我们去看电影吧。

go for a walk 散步

与前面所提到的take a walk具有相同的含义，表示散步。像这样，如果用作go for a+名词形式的话就表示“去做某事”。

“每天都会出去散步的散步狂做出的决定！”

I'm going to **go for a walk** in the pouring rain.

M·O·R·E

- go for a walk (drive, swim)
  去散步（开车兜风，游泳）
- go for a drink (coffee)
  出去喝酒（咖啡）

Do you want to **go for a walk**?
你想出去散步吗?

Want to **go for a ride** on my boat?
想坐我的船出去兜风吗?

Would you two girls like to **go for a drink**?
你们两位女士想喝两杯吗?

A: I'm bored. Shall we go for a walk? 烦死了，我们出去散散步呗?
B: Yes. It will be good exercise. 好吧，就当运动了。

go on a trip 旅行

这次是go on a+名词形式，表示“做某事”。典型的就是go on a trip，表示“去旅行”，go on a ride表示“出去兜风”，还有go on a vacation表示“休假”。

“虽说是个多年单身的老处男，但朋友居然给他介绍了一个未婚孕妇”

I don't want to **go on a date** with a pregnant lady.

M·O·R·E

- go on a trip (cruise)
  （巡游）旅行
- go on a date (diet)
  约会（减肥）

I wanted to **go on a little trip**.
我想去近的地方转转。

I've always wanted to **go on a cruise**.
我一直很想去巡游旅行。

Would you like to **go on a date** sometime?
你想找个时间约会不?

A: Let's go on a date. What do you say? 我们约会吧，你觉得呢?
B: I don't think it would be a good idea. 我不觉得那是个好主意。

go too far 过分

如果某人的行为超过了限度，希望对方停止这种行为的话，就可以说这句话，表示对对方的过分行为表示不满。类似的表达有go overboard。

“辛迪叫同班的一位黑人同学黑鬼(negro)”

Cindy, this time you have gone too far.

You've gone too far. You have to apologize to her.
你太过分了。必须向她道歉。

Her joke went too far. She's so mean.
她的玩笑有点过分了。她太卑鄙了。

I know, I went too far. I won't let it happen again.
我知道我有点过分了。我不会再让它发生了。

He went overboard.
他太过分了。

A: Jim always does dangerous things. 吉姆总喜欢做危险的事情。
B: One day he is going to go too far. 他总有一天会做出过分的举动的。

to go 多余的，打包

(have)+名词+to go的形态表示“还有一些……要做（走）”。如果在饭店表示打包的话，也可以用这个短语来代替take out。

“深怕对自己冷淡的女朋友忘记自己的生日，提醒她道”

Just one week to go until my birthday.

M·O·R·E

- (have)+名词+to go 还有……还要做（走）……
- (I'd like)+食品+to go 打包……
- Will that be to go? 你要带走吗?
- Can I get it to go? 我能带走吗?
- To go (For here), please. 我要打包，谢谢。（在这里吃）

We have to hurry. We have another 10 miles to go.
我们得抓紧点，还有10英里要走。

(I'd like) Two sandwiches and one orange juice to go.
我想打包两个三明治和一杯橙汁。

(Will this be/Is that) For here or to go?
在这里吃，还是带走?

(Do you want to) Eat here or take it out?
在这儿吃还是带走?

A: I'd like two hamburgers and a Coke. 我要两个汉堡和一杯可乐。
B: No problem. Is that for here or to go? 好的，请问在这里吃还是带走?

Here (There) ... go 这（那）有

here和there和go配合能产生很多特殊的表达。有时单纯指某个人走，但也可以用于下列很多特殊的情况。

"性格暴躁的丈夫在公司待了两个月就跑出来了"

There you go again! You're such a jerk.

M·O·R·E

- Here goes.
  我要开始了，准备好。
- Here we go.
  开始了。
- Here we go again.
  又开始了。
- Here you go.
  给你。
- There you go.
  来，接住，我说的没错吧。
- There you go again.
  你又来了。

Oh no! Here we go again!
不！又开始了！

There you go again. Don't be critical of yourself.
你又来了，别再埋怨自己的长相了。

There you go again. Always looking for a girl!
你又开始了！天天找小女孩！

Well, there goes that theory!
天呐，又开始无稽之谈了。

A: Can I borrow five dollars from you? 你能借我5美元吗？
B: Sure you can. There you go. 没问题，给你。

I'm going 我去，我要参加

I'm going表示我马上去(I'm leaving)的意思，或者表示参加或出席某种聚会(I will join)。相反，如果不能出席时，就可以用I'm not going。如果询问别人的话，就可以用You're going?

"为了和恋人约会，原本不打算参加聚会，但被公司同事百般相劝"

All right, I'm going. I'm going.

M·O·R·E

- go on a trip (cruise)
  去（巡游）旅行
- go on a date (diet)
  约会（减肥）

I'm going. I'll see you tomorrow.
我会去的，明天见。

I'm not going. I don't want to see her.
我不去了，不想见到她。

I promise. I'm going. I'll meet you out there.
我发誓我会去，到时候见。

A: I'm going. You'll never see me again. 我走了，你再也见不到我了。
B: Why are you so upset with me? 你为什么那么生我的气？

go easy on 安抚，适当做……

go easy on后面如果接人物的话就是“轻轻安抚”，如果接物体的话就是“不过分地对待”的意思。比如说Go easy on the whisky表示“少喝点威士忌”。

“未婚妻对丈夫的朋友们嘱咐道，单身派对时多照看丈夫，不料”

I told them to go easy on him!

M·O·R·E

- go easy
  安抚，从容，沉着
- go easy on sb
  温柔对待某人，适当做
- easy-going (person)
  从容的，不刻薄的（人）

Go easy, Michael. You don't even know him.
慢慢来，麦克，你甚至还不知道他。

Go easy on me. This is my first time.
照顾照顾我，这是我第一次。

You've got to go easy on butter and cheese.
你得少吃点黄油和奶酪了。

He's an easy-going person.
他是个平易近人的人。

A: Go easy on the hot sauce please. 请少加点辣酱。
B: I forgot that you don't like spicy food. 我忘了你不能吃辣了。

go about 解开，开始，继续自己的事情

go about one's business表示“继续某人的事情”，go about one's lives表示“按照自己原本的方式进行”，同理可以表示按照原本的方式处事或生活。

“每天早上吃完早饭送孩子们上学等一如既往的生活中”

Every day in America, people go about their lives.

I don't even know how I would go about it.
我甚至不知道该怎么着手。

How are you going to go about doing that?
你想怎么开始?

Well maybe you're going about this the wrong way.
你可能做错了。

She watches the students going about their daily business.
她看着孩子们做平时做的事情。

A: So, you're getting a divorce from your husband? 那你要和你丈夫离婚了?
B: Yeah, but I don't go about telling everyone. 是啊，不过我不想告诉所有人。

go against 违抗，违背，不利于……

字面含义为与某事物“相反”(against)，因此表示“违抗某事”，“违背某事”等。即某种状况对……不利或相反。

“撒旦怂恿说，不要违背最原始的本能”

Never go against your basic instincts.

Everything went against her.
她事事不顺。

It goes against everything that I believe to be good.
所有事都与我的期望相背离。

This goes against her Catholic beliefs?
这不是违背了他的天主教信仰吗?

A: Why don't you like that politician? **你为什么不喜欢那个政客?**

B: He goes against everything I believe in. **他所做的一切事情都与我的想法相违背。**

go ahead （督促）让人做，继续，开始（做事）(with)，领先(of)

口语中可以用来表示“允许对方做某事”或“有什么说什么”。原本含义为“领先于……”，或者继续做未完成的工作等等。

“心仪的男生犹豫不决，因此怂恿他申请约会”

Go ahead. Ask me out.

M·O·R·E

- go ahead
  （督促或允许）快点做，继续
- go ahead with
  开始（继续）做某事
- go ahead of
  领先于……

Go ahead, I'm still listening.
继续，我在听。

Go ahead and tell them about that.
快点告诉他们。

I don't think I can go ahead with it because it's wrong.
我觉得我不能再继续下去了，因为它是错的。

You guys go ahead. I'll catch up.
你们继续，我能跟上。

A: Please let me explain why I did that. **请让我解释我的所作所为。**

B: I'm listening. Go ahead, but make it short. **我在听，继续，不过要简短一些。**

go after 尾随某人，追击

go after后面如果接人物名词的话就会表示追上或逮捕某人，如果go after后面接事物的话就表示追求某物。

"明知道对方是有妇之夫，却还是深深迷恋着他"

Why did you go after another woman's husband?

M·O·R·E

- go after sb/sth
  追逐某人，试图获得

I had to go after her to the airport.
我不得不追她到机场。

Do you want to go after her?
你想追求她吗?

I see something, I like it, I go after it.
我只要看到喜欢的，就会毫不犹豫地追。

A: Why did Carl leave the party early? 为什么卡尔走得那么早?

B: He went after his girlfriend. She left early too. 他去追他女朋友了，她也走得很早。

go along (with) 对某事表示赞同（同意），变好，做出

可以联想到"跟着……"(along with)，表示"对某事表示赞同"，如果单独go along的话就表示毫无准备或计划地做下去。

"男生梦想要把女生叫来参加狂欢派对(slumber party)时"

Is she going to go along with this?

M·O·R·E

- go along
  继续，做下去
- go along with
  赞同某人

I'm learning about it as we go along.
我在边做边学。

Although I do not agree with your plan, I'll go along with it anyway.
虽然我不大赞成你的计划，但我还是会遵循你的建议。

I'll go along with that.
我同意。

A: Is it OK if we hold a party on Friday? 我们星期五开派对可以吗?

B: No, I can't go along with that. 不行，我不同意。

go around 到处转悠，（传闻，消息等）传开，路过，不断地……

字面含义为在周边(around)转悠(go)。表示消息或传闻传开或某人“经过某处”。如果是go aroud ...ing形式的话就表示“不停地做某事”。

“一个人只要被骂，就会对骂自己的人上诉”

You can't go around suing people every time they call you names.

M·O·R·E

- (News or rumors) go around （消息或谣言）传开
- go around ...ing 不停地做某事
- be plenty of+名词+to go around 机会均等

Go around town and see what you can pick up.
去城里转转，看看有没有什么可选的。

I don't ordinarily go around kissing guys at parties.
我一般不会在聚会中随便亲别的男生。

There's plenty of fruit and fish to go around.
有足够的水果和鱼供大家分享。

A: Go around and ask for a cigarette. 到处转转，借根香烟。
B: Why? Have you run out of them? 怎么？你都抽完了？

go away 走开，小时，离开（... for+期间）

表示远(away)走的意思，主要以祈使句的形式向对方表示滚开(go away!)。另外，也可以用来表示某种问题或痛苦小，如果是go away for+地点的话则表示“暂时离开”。

“丈夫下班很晚，筋疲力尽，刚洗过澡的妻子却兴致勃勃地冲了过来”

I've had a long day. Go away.

M·O·R·E

- go away for+期间 暂时离开一段时间(leave for a period of time)

Go away! I don't want to see anybody.
走开，我不想见任何人。

Will the pain ever go away? Will I feel better?
痛苦能永远消失吗？我能感觉好点吗？

We should go away for the weekend together.
我们周末应该离开一段时间。

A: I need you to help me with my homework. 我需要你帮我做作业。
B: Go away. I'm too busy to help you. 走开，我太忙了，没空帮你。

go back (to) 回到某处，逆流而上

可以用go back to+地点来表示回到某处，如果要表示暂时停止一会，重新开始时就要用go back to+名词/ ...ing。因此go back out there表示“重新开始跑”。

“去提款机取钱，不料把银行卡留在了ATM里。”

I have to go back to the ATM machine again.

M·O·R·E

- go back to+地点
  回到某处
- go back+时间
  持续了某段时间
- go back to+sth (...ing)
  重新开始做某事

Go back to your seat.
回到你的位置上。

We'll have to **go back to** eating meat.
我们要重新开始吃肉了。

Our relations **go back** at least 20 years.
我们认识有20多年了。

We **go way back**.
我们认识好久了。

A: Can you join us for a few drinks? 你能和我们喝两杯吗?
B: No, I've got to go back to my office. 不行，我得回办公室了。

go by 时间流逝，某人经过，路过，使……流逝

表示“经过某人的身旁”，与as time goes by表示的含义相近。另外，像stop (drop) by一样，有“暂时经过某处”或“以某某之名闻名”的含义。

“回家的路上要去趟杂货店”

Let's go by the grocery for a little while.

M·O·R·E

- go by
  流逝，路经
- go by the name of
  以某人之名
- go by+名字
  被叫做……

Nine months **go by** fast.
九个月过得很快。

I worked ten hours today. I'll **go by** tomorrow.
我今天工作了十个小时，明天会过去一趟。

You used to **go by** the name of “Sam”.
你之前一直被叫做“山姆”。

A: Wow, it seems like summer just started. 哎，貌似夏天才刚刚开始。
B: Now it's autumn. It went by fast. 都到秋天了，时间过得真快。

go for 努力获得某物，想要做某事，喜欢……

for后面的成分就是付出努力所要达到的目的或目标，最典型的用法就是Let's go for it，如果是I would (could) go for ... 的话就表示“期望……”。

“已经结过三次婚的30岁出头男子称要再结一次婚”

I just decided to go for it.

M·O·R·E

- go for
  为了某事付出努力，喜欢……
- I would (could) go for sth
  期望……
- That goes for sth (sb)
  与……相同

Let's **go for** it. I guess we can do it.
我们试试，我觉得能行。

The same **goes for** you.
你也一样。

I never thought you'd **go for** me.
我从没想过你会喜欢我。

A: I want to apply to law school. 我想申请法学院。
B: Go for it. You're smart enough to succeed. 加油，凭你的才华，你肯定能成功。

go into 进入某处，开始（工作，事业），仔细调查（说明）某事。

表示“进入……的内部”，最常用的表达就是进入房间或办公室的内部等。另外，开始某事或某种职业或深陷某事时，可以用来表示“仔细说明或调查”。

“买来丁字裤的丈夫欣喜若狂地让80公斤的妻子试试”

Why don't you go into your room and try this on?

M·O·R·E

- go into details
  仔细检查
- go into labor
  开始工作

I **went into** the store and he got me a soda.
我走进商店，他给我拿了杯苏打饮料。

I have to **go into** intensive therapy right now.
我不得不马上接受集中治疗。

Never **go into** business with somebody you're sleeping with.
千万不要和你同床共枕的人一起经商。

A: I saw a man try to steal some jewelry. 我看到一个男人想要偷珠宝。
B: Go into details. What did he look like? 说得详细点，他长什么样？

go off 去做某事，停止（工作），发射（弹药，警报），响，（机械）不运转

表示分离(off)离开(go)，意味着“向……出发”。另外，也可以用来表示“枪支或闹钟等响起来”。

“随身携带枪支的恐怖分子在通过安检时，警报没有响起，便得意忘形地说”

I'm surprised the detector didn't go off.

M·O·R·E

- (The gun, The alarm, The airbag) go off
  ……发射，响起，爆炸
- go off to
  去做某事
- go off with sb
  与某人同行(go away with)
- go off with sth
  不经允许就拿走某物

I don't want to be 70 when our kids **go off** to college.
我不希望孩子们上大学时我已经70岁了。

I was late again today because the alarm clock didn't **go off**.
我今天又迟到了，因为早上闹钟没响。

She **goes off** to pick fruit.
她去买水果了。

You **went off** with her and you never called.
你和她出去之后就没打过电话。

A: What do you have planned for this weekend? 你这周末打算干嘛？
B: We're going to go off on a camping trip. 我们要去露营。

go on 继续做某事(with)，进行，发生(happen)，（时间）流逝

What's going on? 或As time goes on中常见的go on 的基本含义为“继续”。“on”与“off”不同，表示状态的持续。Go on! 表示激励对方或让对方继续发言。

“这辈子做过最刺激的事就只是做过山车”

He went on about his sexual adventures.

M·O·R·E

- Go on!
  继续！
- go on with (...ing)
  继续做某事
- go on to sth (do) ...
  做下一个事情
- go on (and on) about sth (sb)
  透露关于……的事情

You don't look well. What'**s going on**?
你脸色不好，怎么了？

What'**s going on** with him?
他怎么了？

As time **goes on**, I'm getting weaker.
随着时间的流逝，我变得越来越虚弱。

Shall we **go on to** the next item on the agenda?
我们开始下一个议程项目吧？

A: You look really tired, Karen. 你看起来很疲倦啊，凯伦。
B: I know, but I need to go on with this race. 是啊，不过我得坚持比赛。

go out (with) 与某人约会(go out on a date)

字面意义为“与某人外出”，实际上多表示“男女之间的约会”，“交往”等。类似的表达有前文中提到过的go (out) on a date。另外，向某人申请约会时用ask sb to go out (with)。

“搭过讪的女生太多，没办法一一记清楚，所以事先要确认”

Did I ask you to go out with me?

He's going out with Jane.
他在与简交往。

Jennifer's going to go out with a millionaire.
珍妮弗要与百万富翁交往。

Would you go out with me?
你愿意和我交往吗?

I can't believe Jim went out with my wife!
真不敢相信，吉姆勾搭我老婆!

A: You should go out with us on Friday night. **你这周五晚上应该和我们出去玩。**
B: I'd love to, but I have other plans. **我也想，但我已经有别的计划了。**

go out (to/for) 外出，出去（做某事）

这与字面含义相同，表示外出，至于外出的目的则可以在后面加to或者for来说明。想要出去吃中午饭就是go out for a lunch，出去喝酒就是go out for a drink。

“朋友问道，昨天晚上干嘛了”

We went out for a movie last night.

M·O·R·E

- go out for (...ing)
  出去做某事
- go out to do/go out and do
  出去做某事

Let's go out tonight if you're free.
如果你今晚有空，咱们出去玩吧。

I can't go out tonight. Something's come up.
今天晚上我不能出去了，有点事情要做。

How about going out for a drink tonight?
今晚出去喝一杯怎么样?

A: I'd like to go out for lunch on Friday. **我想星期五出去吃午餐。**
B: Sounds good to me. **我没问题。**

go over 检讨(think over)，检查(examine)

go over的典型含义为“检讨”(think over)或“仔细检查”(examine)。不过go over there或go over to+地点的形式表示“前往某处”。

“女生们一见到偶像就想跑过去强抱一通”

I want to go over there, grab him, and kiss him!

M·O·R·E

- go over to+地点
  前往某处
- go over sth
  检讨某事

I'll go over there and take a look.
我会去看看的。

You want me to go over there now?
你想让我现在过去一趟?

We'll go over your idea during lunch.
我们会在吃午饭的时候好好考虑一下你的建议。

let's go over it again.
我们重新想想吧。

A: I don't know if my report is good or bad. 我不清楚我的报告是好是坏。

B: Let's go over it and see if there are mistakes. 我们来检查一下，看看有没有错误。

go through 经受（困难），经历，通过，查找，做(with)

字面意义为“通过(through)……”，可以指经历，经受，或者为了找某样东西而翻箱倒柜。go through with sth则表示原本的计划和约定不得随意改变。

“让一个少女好运的男生，出于良心发誓道”

I'm not going to let you go through this alone.

M·O·R·E

- go through sth
  经受困难
- go through with sth
  经历某事
- go through the roof
  结束（不大喜欢的事情），激怒(=hit the roof=hit the ceiling)

I'm sorry you had to go through that.
很抱歉让你经受了那种事情。

I don't think I could go through that pain again.
我觉得自己无法再承受那种痛苦了。

In order to get the information, I have to go through all the files.
为了搜集信息，我不得不查找所有档案。

A: Why do I need to empty my pockets? 我为什么要清空口袋?

B: We must go through a metal detector. 我们需要让你通过安检门。

go (well) with 与某人（和睦）相处，选择某项，与某人同行

go with有很多含义。基本上表示“与某人同行”，“相伴”和“与某人和睦相处”，但也可以用I'll go with it（我就要那个）表示“选择某项”。

“花花公子希望和那个女生通宵达旦”

If things **go well**, I'm going to be out with her all night.

Is it all right if I **go with** you?

我和你一起去可以吗?

This skirt and this blouse **go together well**.

这件裙子和上衣很搭。

I'**m going with** it.

我就要这个了。

A: Do you like the dress I am wearing? 你喜欢我穿的衣服吗?

B: Yes, it goes well with your jacket. 恩，很配你的夹克。

M·O·R·E

- go with+sb
  与某人同行
- go well with
  与某人和睦相处
- 事物+go well
  ……顺利
- That went well
  真好
- go with the flow
  顺应……

go without 没有……的日子，在没有……的情况下独自完成

字面含义为“在没有……的情况下继续走”，可以进一步用It goes without saying that来表示“某事无可厚非”。

“老姑娘的独身主义观点”

I don't need sex. I **went without** it the first thirty years.

Just **go without** me.

你自己去吧。

Don't let her **go without** a fight!

不要放过她!

I think it **goes without** saying.

我觉得这很明显。

A: I have no money this week. 我这周没有钱。

B: You'll have to go without beer then. 那你就不能喝啤酒了。

M·O·R·E

- It goes without saying that ...
  ……毋庸置疑
- let sb go without a fight
  给某人放行

More Expressions

- **go for the day** 下班

  He's gone for the day. 他下班了。

- **go to the trouble** 找麻烦

  Please don't go to any trouble for me.
  请不要找我麻烦。

- **go in for** 因为喜欢而做某事，参加……

  My sister went in for a nose job in the past. 我妹妹过去做了鼻梁整容手术。

- **go together** 一起去

  We can all go together.
  我们可以一块儿去。

- **go up** 上升，上去

  What goes up must come down.
  有升必有降。

- **Don't go there** 不要提（那事）

  Look, Michael, can we not go there?
  我说，麦克，咱能不能不提它？

- **go Dutch** AA制

  Let's go Dutch. 我们AA制吧。

- **let somebody go** 让某人走，解雇

  My boss let him go. 我老板开除了他。

- **go nuts** 喜欢某事

  She's going to go nuts for it.
  她会非常喜欢它的。

- **go abroad** 去海外

  I go abroad on business several times a year. 我每年要去国外出差很多次。

- **let go of** 放开某人

  Let go of me. 让我走吧。

- **Way to go!** 好样的！

  Way to go, Peter. I owe you.
  好样的，彼得，我欠你个人情。

- **go all the way** 走到尽头

  They went all the way the other night.
  那天晚上他们走到了尽头。

- **go from bad to worse** 雪上加霜

  The situation went from bad to worse.
  真是雪上加霜啊。

- **go beyond** 超过，超越

  Your fraud goes beyond that.
  你的观点超出了想象。

Have a go at it. 试一试。

Are you going my way?
你和我同路吗？

I'm going in that direction.
我要去那个方向。

Anything goes. 什么都可以。

It's gone. 都结束了。

I couldn't go forward and go back.
我进退两难。

It was touch and go there for a while.
有段时间非常困难。

I'd be the first to go. 我会最先去的。

He really made a go of it! 他真的成功了！

This piano would go for $ 50, 000.
这台钢琴要5万美元。

由你到我的

Come

与go正好相反，表示“来”，不仅限于人或事物的实际空间移动，还包含了某种状况“变成如何”的意思。另外，要注意，I'm coming中的come可以表示向对方走去（在对方的立场来看，是正在来）。因此在打电话请假时，不能说I can't go to work，而应该说I can't come to work。

基本概念

1 来，（向说话的人）走去，来做……

Can I come to see you? 我能去找你吗?

Please come this way. 这边请。

Will you be able to come? 你能来吗?

2 达到，到达，出来

The e-mail hasn't come yet. 电子邮件还没有收到。

The bill comes to $100. 账单高达100美元。

My order hasn't come yet. 我的订单还没到。

3 ……的出身，发生于，出现

Where do you come from? 你从哪里来?

I'm coming. 来了，马上来。

向说话的人或对方移动时使用come，之外移动到第三地点时要用go。因此如果有人叫我，让我移动到对方时不能用I'm going，而应该用I'm coming。

"女儿在楼上看到蟑螂，吓了一大跳"

It's going to be okay. I'm coming.

I'm coming. What is it?
我来了，什么事?

I'm coming. I'm coming. Just hang on.
马上到，马上到，稍等一会。

Hold on! I'm coming.
等等，我来了。

A: If you don't hurry up we'll be late. 你再不快点，我们就迟到了。
B: Okay, okay, I'm coming. Hold your horses! 好了好了，我过去，稍等一会。

come to+动词 着手做某事，来做某事

come to+动词表示"着手做某事"，如果强调come的含义的话，就表示"来做某事"。另外，用到come here的I come here to ... , Did you come here to ... ?等也需要记住。

"去劳教所看望妹妹，却炫耀自己新交往的男朋友，妹妹非常无奈"

Did you come here to tell me about new boyfriend?

M·O·R·E

- come here
  来这
- come here to+动词
  来做某事
- come close to
  靠近……
- come close to ...ing
  差点就……

You'll come to understand me.
你会理解我的。

She came to realize that she was stupid.
她开始意识到自己的愚蠢。

I came to apologize to you.
我是来向你道歉的。

I came here to let you know that I love you.
我是来让你知道，我爱你。

A: I came to see your new car. 我是来看你的新车的。
B: This is it. Do you like it? 就是这辆，怎么样?

How come ... ? 怎么回事?

How come表示对方所处的状况“到底是怎么回事”(How did it happen?)，即“是怎么变成这样的？”，表示询问“理由”。可以像“How come you are late?”一样加入更具体的内容。

“天天抱怨公司怎么怎么不好的朋友依然在上班时”

How come you're still at a job that you hate?

M·O·R·E

- How come?
  怎么了?
- How come S+V?
  怎么会……呢?

How come? Do you have a schedule conflict?
怎么回事? 你的安排冲突了吗?

How come she didn't show up last night?
她昨天晚上怎么会没来?

How come you didn't tell me about that?
你为什么没告诉我?

A: How come you're late? 你怎么会迟到呢?
B: I got caught in traffic. 交通堵塞呗。

Here ... comes ……来这

为了强调“……来到这里”而前置了here。可以写成Here ... comes或Here comes ...。另外，There comes a point (time, moment) when S+V表示“曾几何时……”的意思。

“口口声声说是棒球迷，却躲在最前排看拉拉队表演的禽兽男”

Here come my favorite cheerleaders!

M·O·R·E

- Here it comes.
  来了，又开始了。
- There comes a point (time, moment) when S+V
  曾几何时……

Here he **comes**.
他来了。

Here comes the cocktail waitress.
鸡尾酒服务员来了。

Hey, look! **Here comes** my airplane.
喂，看! 我的飞机来了。

There comes a time when you take that next important step.
你肯定会有翻身的时候的。

A: Here the bus comes. Is your money ready? 公交来了，零钱准备好没?
B: Yeah. Is it still a dollar to ride downtown? 恩，去城镇还是一美元吗?

Come again? 说什么?

在没有听清对方所说的话，或者听到意想不到的话时可以用来反问“说什么?”(What did you say?)，“再说一遍呗?”(Can you say that again?)，当然，也可以用(I'm)sorry? Excuse me?

“在没有听清对方所说的话，要求对方重新说一遍时”

Come again? Say it one more, please.

Good night. Come again.

晚安，再来玩。

Come again? I didn't hear you well.

说什么? 我没听清。

I'm sorry? What did you say?

不好意思? 能再说一遍吗?

A: I plan to quit going to university next week. **我下周打算退学。**

B: Come again? How will you ever get a good job? **说什么? 那你怎么找工作啊?**

come true 实现，成就

come true主要表示愿望，梦想等“变成(come)现实(true)”。这个短语在学校里会经常提到，是个很常用的表达。

“经历过无数次选秀失败的女儿受到父亲的安慰”

But some dreams just don't come true.

Did your wish for a promotion come true?

你希望能够升职吗?

I hope all your wishes come true.

我希望你心想事成。

I'm sure your wish is going to come true.

我相信你的梦想会实现的。

A: Many people want to find true love. **很多人希望找到真爱。**

B: Well, for some people that dream will come true. **是啊，但只有一部分人的愿望才会实现。**

come first 首当其冲

come first字面含义为“第一个到来”，因此表示最重要的东西。如果是工作狂则用Work comes first，如果是医生则用Patients come first。相反，如果是问对方什么是最重要时，就可以用What comes first?

“我们国家什么时候才能享受太平盛世？”

Patients have to come first.

You have a family. Home has to come first for you.
你有个家庭，对你来说家庭就是最重要的。

You always come first with me. Do I still come first with you?
对我来说，你总是最重要的。那我还是你最珍惜的人吗？

I mean, for me, the client comes first.
我是说，对我来说，顾客至上。

M·O·R·E

- My kids come first.
  我的孩子是最重要的。
- You come first.
  你最重要。

A: His children are always successful in school. 他的孩子总能在学校里取得优异的成绩。

B: The children's education comes first. 孩子的教育工作是最重要的。

come and go 来来往往

这个短语看似陌生，但其实很有用处。可以用在自由出入或非永久的擦肩而过等情况下。Have come and gone则是现在完成式的用法。

“有人认为爱情总会变化，但友情是永恒的”

Boyfriends and girlfriends come and go, but our friendship is for life!

This is my home and I want to be able to come and go whenever I want! 出来进去
这是我家，我想什么时候出入就什么时候出入！

I have stomachaches. They come and go in every few minutes.
我肚子疼，每隔几分钟就会疼一次。

There's no chance my mother's already come and gone
我妈妈不可能来过又走了。

A: Has Janet been over to see you today? 加内特今天来看过你吗?

B: No, she comes and goes when she has free time. 没有，她有时间时才会过来。

when it comes to 关于……

该句型在会话中比较常用，when it comes to+名词(...ing)表示“只要是关于……”，用来表示一个人的意见或观点。

“懦弱的小心眼男生无法和女朋友说出分手的话”

I'm not good **when it comes to** breaking up with girls.

Believe it or not, **when it comes to** meeting men, I am shy.

不管你信不信，只要提到男生，我就会害羞。

When it comes to the law, there's absolutely nothing I can do.

只要是关于法律的东西，我就什么都做不了。

I've had some bad luck **when it comes to** relationships.

在维持关系上，我一点运气都没有。

A: Are you sure you can fix my notebook computer? 你确定能修我的电脑吗?

B: Trust me. I'm the best when it comes to computers. 相信我，我在计算机方面算是出类拔萃的。

come to think of it 想想

这是和前面的when it comes to一样常用的句型，come to think of it表示突然产生某种想法。

“出了名的大嘴在阻止自己说出他人的秘密时”

Come to think of it, she doesn't want you to know that.

Come to think of it, you should take a day off.

我想了想，你还是应该休息一天。

Come to think of it, I don't need it anymore.

我仔细想了想，这些我都不再需要了。

Come to think of it, I left my cell phone in the office.

我仔细想了想，发现手机落在了办公室。

A: Damn it! I forgot my glasses today. 糟糕！我今天忘带眼镜了。

B: Come to think of it, I forgot my glasses too. 我仔细想了想，我也忘带了。

come across 偶然遇见(run across, bump into)，偶然看见

在路上或意料之外的场所见到他人时可以用到的典型句式就是come across。当然，偶然碰到的既可以是人，也可以是物品。另外，也可以使用run across, bump into。

"在翻阅邮件时发现了请帖"

Going through her mail, she came across her invitation.

How did you **come across** this information?
你是怎么找到这个信息的?

I **came across** one of his baby pictures last weekend.
我上个周末偶然见到了他的婴儿照。

I **bumped into** him on the stairs.
我在楼道间偶然碰到了他。

A: Let me know if you come across a diamond ring. 如果你看到了一个钻戒，就跟我说一声。
B: Did you lose the ring in my house? 你在我家丢了钻戒吗?

come along 事情进行中，一起去(with somebody)

表示某件事情"进行得很顺利"，"进行中"的含义。如果想表示"与某人同行"可以用come along with sb。Come along! 表示抓紧时间，可以翻译为"快点！"或"快跟来！"等。

"在和朋友们去吃披萨的路上，对偶遇的朋友说道"

Do you want to come along?

M·O·R·E

- be coming along (with)
  ……进行中，进行得很顺利
- come along with sb
  与某人同行

Wow, it's really **coming along**. It looks great.
哇，进行得很顺利啊，看起来不错。

How **are** you **coming along with** your project?
你手上的项目进行得如何?

Can you **come along with** me to the post office?
你能和我一起去趟邮局吗?

Why didn't you just **come along**?
你跟我们一起去呗?

A: My little sister wants to go to the museum. 我妹妹想去博物馆。
B: She can come along if she wants to. 如果她愿意，就把她带上吧。

come around 经过，返回，找回知觉，最终对……表示同意

虽然是个不太熟悉的短语，但come around与come over相同，都表示“经过某地”，或“找回知觉”，也可以用在“最终对……表示同意”上。

“因家庭暴力过于频繁，丈夫离家出走，不安的妻子接受朋友的安慰”

Be patient. Your husband will come around.

M·O·R·E

- come around to+地点
  经过……
- come around
  恢复知觉
- come around
  (to ...ing)
  最终同意……

How did you never **come around** anymore?
你怎么再也不过来了?

She **came around** here before?
她之前来过?

Just give her some time. She'll **come around**.
再给她点时间，肯定会恢复知觉的。

A: I heard Beth likes to visit your mom. 我听说贝斯想拜访你母亲。
B: She doesn't come around here any more. 她再也不会出现了。

come back 回来，回到某人身边，恢复

表示某种状况恢复到以前的状态，但在会话中不仅仅作为单纯回来的含义。come back to+人物(sb)表明“回到某人身边”，come back to+sth表示“回来做某事”。

“同居的爱人离家出走，问他想不想重新回来”

Do you want to come back to my place?

M·O·R·E

- come back
  回来，恢复
- come back to+动词
  回来做某事

Come back and see me.
回来看看我。

I'll **come back** in a couple of hours.
我会在几个小时后回来。

He didn't **come back to** help you.
他没有回来帮你。

You will leave and never **come back**.
你肯定一去不返。

A: I'm really tired of working. 我实在是工作太疲倦了。
B: Okay. It's possible to come back tomorrow. 好吧。可能明天就恢复了。

come down 掉落，下来，患病

come down 具有多种含义，最基本的就是从上方掉落到下方。会话中多用作“教训某人”。另外，come down with则表示“患上”感冒等疾病。

“时间已经很晚了，妻子却不停地擦着粉”

You've got to come down now. We might be late.

M·O·R·E

- come down (to)
  （数值等）下滑，下降，前往……路经
- come down (hard) on sb (sth)
  谴责某人，教训某人
- come down to (with)+病
  减少为，简略为，患上某病

Did you **come down** here to tell me that?
你是专程下来告诉我那件事的?

If you don't **come down**, I'm coming up.
如果你不下来，我就上去。

He's **coming down with** a really bad cold.
他得了严重的流感。

A: I need to go to the third floor of the library. 我得去图书馆三层。
B: We'll go for lunch when you come down. 等你下来，我们再去吃午饭。

come forward 站出来，拿回信息、想法等

字面含义为站(come)出来(forward)，表示为了发言或传递东西而“向前站”。

“明知道学校老大做了坏事，却没有人敢站出来说话”

Everybody knew it, but nobody came forward.

M·O·R·E

- come forward
  站出来
- come forward with sth
  站出来说

Why don't you just **come forward** and tell the police about that?
你怎么不站出来告诉警察?

The boys **came forward** one by one and gave Kate gifts.
男生们一个个站出来给凯特礼物。

Thank you for **coming forward with** this.
谢谢你能指出问题。

A: How did the police find the criminal? 警察们是怎么找到罪犯的?
B: Someone came forward with information about him. 有人站出来举报了他。

come from ……的出身，从……来（出现）

与be from相同，是表示“出身”或“出处”的短语。不过正如以下例句中的那样，实际口语中come from也可以用来表示“事物或想法的出处”。

“出去玩大醉而归的女儿发出阵阵呕吐声时”

The sounds of vomiting **come from** the bathroom.

Where did this cake **come from**?
这蛋糕是从哪儿来的?

This is a great bed. Where did it **come from**?
这床真不错，从哪儿来的?

Where does it **come from**?
你这句话由何而来?

I know where you'**re coming from**.
我知道你是从哪儿来的。

A: I come from a small town in the northern US. 我出生于美国北部的一个小村庄。
B: You must have had cold winters there. 那里的冬天一定很冷吧。

come in 进来，流行

表示进入到内部(in)，用来形容进入到某个空间，或到达或参与某件事情，也可以用来表示流行或新型产品等抽象的概念。另外，come into表示进去，成为……状态等。

“在度假村的走廊看见漂亮的姑娘”

Do you want to **come in** for a beer or something?

Come in and eat with us.
进来和我们一块吃吧。

The shirts **came in** many colors.
这款衬衫有很多配色。

You've recently **come into** a great deal of money.
你最近得到了大笔财产吧。

I didn't **come into** your room.
我没进过你的房间。

A: The new rules will come into effect Monday. 新规定将于星期一生效。
B: Many people are going to be confused. 很多人都会感到非常困惑的。

M·O·R·E

- come in handy
  变得有用
- come in sight
  看见
- come in for
  进来做某事，接受……
- come into effect
  生效

come off 摘掉，掉落，最终变成，成功

如果表示“从某处掉落，出现”的话与get off具有相同的用法。但只有come off表示事情按照原计划顺利进行。会话中经常会见到Come off it!表示向对方怒吼“拉倒吧”。

“本想给出差两年的丈夫一个惊喜，去机场接他，不料”

I saw my husband come off the plane with a young girl.

M·O·R·E

- come off well (badly) 进行得很（不）顺利
- come off as 看着像……(appear to)

I didn't **come off well.**

结果不太理想。

But somehow you **came off as** the bad guy.

不过你看起来有点像个坏人。

I came across the boss when I **got off** the elevator.

我走出电梯时碰到了老板。

A: I really enjoyed talking to your brother. 我真喜欢和你弟弟聊天。

B: He comes off well to the people he meets. 他总会给别人留下很好的印象。

come on 碰到（某事）

“加油！”(cheer up!)，给别人加油的时候，或催促他人说“快点！”，“别磨蹭”(hurry up！)的时候，或者让他人组织过分的行为，表示“好了！”(stop it！)时可以用到这个短语。

“在重症监护室的丈夫处在性命危急的关头，负责的医生却不知廉耻地诱惑她”

How dare you come on to me while my husband is dying!

M·O·R·E

- come on in 进入……
- come on to sb 诱惑某人

Come on! Let's go or we'll be late.

快点，再不走就迟到了。

Why don't you **come on in**?

你为什么不进来?

Are you **coming on to** me?

你是在诱惑我吗?

A: Come on! We'll be late! 快点！我们要迟到了！

B: I'm doing the best I can. 我已经在尽力了。

come out 阐明（实情，结果），出版，出现

某些实情“问世”时(be made public)，就要使用come out。所以电影上映或图书出版时就可以用这个短语。另外，在明确“某人的立场（意见）”时也可以用come out。

“给工作狂同事打电话，让他出来休息休息”

Come out here and get some fresh air.

M·O·R·E

- come out well (badly)
  结果（不）好
- come out wrong
  事情不顺
- come out of
  从……出来，走出困境

When is that movie going to **come out**?
那部电影什么时候上映?

Just **come out** and say it.
老实交代。

There's no way we will **come out of** this.
我们不可能逃出这里。

A: Will you come out to the school's festival? 你会参加学校的庆典活动吗?
B: Of course. I love attending festivals. 当然，我喜欢热闹。

come over 暂时路过（访问）

用作come over+人物（地点）就可以了。Something comes over somebody则表示“某人找到某物”。另外，come by表示“暂时路过某地”或“得到某物”。

“突然来到家门口要进来拜访时”

I'm sorry to **come over** on such short notice.

M·O·R·E

- come over to+地点
  经过某处，拜访
- come over for
  来做某事
- sth come over sb
  某人遇到某事
- come by
  暂时路过（drop by, stop by）,放在手中
- What's come over you?
  你到底怎么回事?

Come over to my place.
来我家吧。

Do you want to **come over** for dinner?
你愿意来吃晚饭吗?

Come by first thing in the morning if you can.
最好明天早上过来。

I'll **come by** for a consult in the morning.
我早上过来商量。

A: Do you want to come over to my place tonight? 你今天晚上想来我家吗?
B: Sure, what time is good for you? 好，几点去合适?

come through 通过，做出，克服（危机，病），符合期待

字面意义为“通过(through)某事进入”，可以表示“承认……”，“成功”，或“克服”某种困难。

“儿子就要做痔疮手术了，妈妈安慰道”

You're going to **come through** this operation just fine.

Our approval didn't **come through**.
还没得到我们的支持。

She will **come through** this.
她会经过考验的。

Excuse me! **Coming through**.
打扰一下！借光。

A: Maybe your dad will lend us some money. 也许你爸爸会借给我们一些钱。
B: He's always come through for me in the past.他以前也经常救我。

come to 来到某处，达到某种状况

come to+地点的愿意为“来到某处”，但come to+名词可以表示“到达某种状态或位置”。特别的，come to an end表示“结束”，come to a close表示“终结”。

“疯狂痴迷派对的朋友不知为何没有参加上次的联欢会”

Why didn't you **come to** the party?

M·O·R·E

- come to that (this)
  达到某种境地
- come to an end
  了结
- come to a close (stop)
  结束
- come to a (the) conclusion (decision)
  获得结论
- If worse (worst) comes to worst
  就算是最差的结果

People **come to** Vegas to get rich.
人们来到拉斯维加斯的目的就是变成富人。

Well, let's hope it doesn't **come to** that.
好吧，只能希望不会变成那样了。

I don't know how it's **come to** this.
我不知道是怎么变成这样的。

The game **is coming to a close**.
游戏快要结束了。

A: The presidential election is almost over. 总统选举快要结束了。
B: It will come to a close on Thursday night. 星期四晚上就结束了。

come up 上来，走过来，发生，出现（某种事态）

当然，最基本的含义为上来，但如果某人想要对我说话而靠近或物体接近时也可以使用这个短语。另外，Something's come up表示某种事情发生，出现。

"觉得辛迪的生日快到了，便问道"

Cindy, don't you have a birthday coming up?

M·O·R·E

- come up
  上来，发生，出现
- Come right up!
  （菜品）出来了！

Can you **come up to** my office for a second?
你能马上来我办公室一趟吗?

She has a birthday **coming up**.
她的生日就要到了。

Something'**s come up**.
出了点事。

A: Are you going back to your hometown? 你要回到家乡吗?
B: I am, but you should come up and visit me. 是啊，不过你要过来找我啊。

come up with 突然想起（追上）

come up with表示突然产生某种想法或计划，(suggest or think of an idea or plan)表示"提出"。"追上"前面的人也叫come up with。

"老板对李部长怒吼，一定要让他想出个新创意"

I promise we'll come up with something.

I've tried and tried, but I can't **come up with** a solution.
我再三尝试过，不过始终找不到合适的解决办法。

So how did you **come up with** this?
你是怎么想到这些的?

You'll **come up with** something else.
你要想出点其他点子。

A: Why haven't you started your report yet? 你怎么还不开始写报告?
B: I need to come up with some ideas for it. 我得先想想。

come with 与某人一起来，与某人一起走

come with somebody 表示“与某人同行”，但如果用在食品或产品上时，Something comes with则表示食物或产品“一同赠出”。

“和爱人提议，一起去纽约旅行”

Please **come with** me on the New York trip.

M·O·R·E

- come with
  与某人一起来，与某人一起走
- What comes with ... ?
  ……还带什么？

I'**m coming with** you.
我要和你去。

What comes with that?
和那个一起的是什么？

Does it **come with** soup or salad and dessert?
汤，沙拉和甜品是一起出吗？

A: Do you want to come with us for drinks? 你要不要和我们一起去喝点？
B: Why not? 好啊。

More Expressions

- **(have) come a long way**
  成功，取得成就
  We'**ve come a long way**.
  我们取得了不小的成就。

- **come to terms with**
  打消念头，接受
  I'**ve come to terms with** it, and you have to too. 我已经接受了，你也要接受。

- **come as a shock** 受到打击
  This might **come as a shock** to you.
  这对你来说可能是一种打击。

- **for years to come** 将来也继续
  It will be okay **for years to come**.
  将来也会如意的。

More Expressions

- **come close** 差点就做某事

  The knife **came close to** touching her cheek. 刀片差点就划到她的脸颊。

- **come loose** 放松，松懈

  The wires **have come loose** in your head! 你脑子短路了！

- **come away** 从 ... 疏远（from），与某人离开，走（with）

  Will you please **come away** from that window? 能不能离窗户远一点？

- **come apart** 破碎，开始走向失败

  The right front tire started to **come apart**. 左前胎开始破裂了。

- **come between** 离间，挤到……中间

  If you try to **come between** me and my husband, I will take you down. 如果你想插足，就让你好看。

- **come for somebody (something)** 来取（领）……

  We had to **come for** you. 我们来带你走。

  We'**ve come for** her things. 我们是来拿她的东西的。

- **be yet to come** ……还没有到

  Just remember that the best **is yet to come**. 记住，最好的日子还没有到来。

I'll come to that. 回头再聊。

I'll come to the point. 我有话直说。

I don't want to wear out my welcome. 我不想大张旗鼓。

You're (very) welcome. 欢迎。

Welcome aboard. 欢迎登机（上船）！

Welcome home. 欢迎回家。

先做了再说

Do

最常用的一个动词，基本含义为“做”。也可以表示过等，另外，do后面接宾语的话可以组成各式各样的短语，如do one's job, do one's best等，还可以接特定的名词(do the dishes, do the laundry, do one's hair)，变成简单的平时生活常用表达。另外，可以用做助词构成否定句和疑问句，也可以像You do? You did what?一样代替前面的动词。

基本概念

1 做，举行，过，生活

What are you doing here? 你在这干嘛呢?

What do you do for a living? 你是干什么的?

I'm doing OK. 我过得很好。

2 分，适当，有用

That will do for me. 对我足够了。

3 do+特定名词：做某事

I hate to do the dishes. 我讨厌洗碗。

Don't forget to do the laundry before you go out. 别忘了出门之前洗衣服。

4 给，带来（损害或利益）

Could you do me a favor? 能帮我个忙吗?

do well 做好

do well表示做好，成功的意思，想要说明成功的内容就可以使用do well with。do fine表示“没关系”，“做得好”，而do okay，do great等表示“过得很好”。

“杰恩去医院拔智齿，害怕得不得了，医生对她说”

You're doing great, Jane. We're almost done.

M·O·R·E

- do well (with)
  做得好，成功
- do fine
  还可以，很好
- do okay
  还可以，过得好
- do great
  过得好

You **did it very well**.
你做得很棒。

I'**m doing great with** Julie.
我和朱莉相处得不错。

You'**re doing great**! Don't you give up!
你做得很好！不要放弃！

A: David, how's it going? 大卫，最近怎么样？
B: I'm doing okay. 我过得很好。

will do 足，有用

在地上捡了个东西，说will do的话就表示……足以，可以接受等。That will do表示“那就够了”，与That'll be fine. That's fine具有相同的含义。在餐厅使用这个句式主要是回答服务员的提问，“That will do?”表示不需要别的了吗？

“在企划会议中没人敢发言时，部长说道”

Don't be shy, any suggestion will do.

M·O·R·E

- That will (won't) do.
  那就够了，决不能那么做。
- Anything will do.
  什么都可以。
- Either will do.
  哪个都行。

Say some words. Any words **will do**.
说说看，什么都行。

Will do. I'll call you on your cell phone.
可以。我会打你手机的。

I don't need much. One of these **will do**.
我不需要太多。一个就够了。

A: Whatever you ask, I will do. 不管你吩咐什么，我都没问题。
B: You are a very loyal friend. 你真是个讲义气的朋友。

do a good job 好样的

在向对方的业绩作出正面评价时可以用到的短语。good也可以替换成nice，great，super,excellent等。但简单的Good job!绝对不能和Good for you!（不错啊！）相混淆。

"刚刚装潢的朋友的房子非常让人满意时"

Your interior designer **did a great job**.

M·O·R·E

- do a good (great) job
  好样的
- Good for you!
  真不赖!

You **did a good job**! I was very impressed.
你干得不错！我很满意。

You **did a good job** here, Michael.
你做得非常棒，迈克尔。

I'm sure you **did a great job**.
我确定你做得很好。

A: I'm baking a cake for Kevin's birthday. **我在为凯文做生日蛋糕。**
B: Do a good job. He deserves something nice. **不错啊。这是他赢得的。**

do one's job 做某人的事

do如果接job或homework的话就表示"做事（作业）"。另外，I'm just doing my job则可以用在有人表扬或妨碍自己的时候，表示"我只是在做分内工作"。

"因社会服务的强行命令，在街道扫大街，却意外地受到他人的表扬"

I'm not an angel. I'm just **doing my job**.

M·O·R·E

- I'm just doing my job.
  分内之事而已。
- Do your job right.
  好好做你的工作。

I **do my job**, and you do yours. All right?
咱们井水不犯河水，好不好?

You can just **do your job**.
你只顾管自己的事情就好。

I **was doing my homework** when you called me.
你给我打电话时我在做作业。

A: He doesn't do his job very well. **他的工作情况不是很顺利。**
B: I know. He's going to be fired soon. **我知道，没多久他就要被炒鱿鱼了。**

do (somebody) a favor 向某人表达好意

有所托付时所用到的话。Could you do me a favor?之后加上嘱咐的内容也可以，但更方便的方法是Could you do me a favor and+动词。表示相同含义的句型有do sb good (harm)。

"丈夫新婚没多久就沉迷于电视或PC游戏中，妻子说道"

Let's go for a walk. Fresh air will do you good.

M·O·R·E

- do (sb) a favor
  向某人表达好意
- do (sb) a favor and+V
  嘱咐某人做某事
- do sb good (harm, damage)
  帮倒忙，受害

Could you **do me a big favor**?
你能帮我个忙吗?

Could you **do me a favor** and bring me a drink?
你能帮我带杯饮料吗?

Do yourself a favor. Get back home today at least by 8 o'clock.
你得多为自己考虑考虑。8点之前回家。

No harm (done).
没什么错。

A: Will you do me a favor? 能帮我个忙吗?
B: Certainly. 没问题。

do something 做某事

虽然不知道要具体做什么，但做是肯定要做的。相反，如果表示什么都不做时可以用do not anything。另外，I'd do anything for you表示为了你，什么都可以做。

"女儿变成了艺人的疯狂粉丝，整天围着他们转，担心的母亲对丈夫说道"

You have to do something about her.

M·O·R·E

- do sth about+名词 (to+动词)
  为某事做……
- do sth+形容词
  做……的事情
- not do anything+adj.
  不做……的事情
- would do anything for
  为某人做任何事

Tom, can you **do something** about this?
汤姆，你能处理这个吗?

You guys! Let's go out. We have to **do something**!
孩子们，我们出去吧，随便做点事情!

Don't get me wrong. I didn't **do anything**.
不要误会我，我没做任何事情。

It's not my fault. I didn't **do anything** wrong.
不是我的错，我没做错任何事。

A: Look, can you do something for me? 瞧，你能为我做点事情吗?
B: Sure, what? 好吧，什么事?

do one's best 使出全力

这是最为常用的表达之一。为了具体说明全力以赴的内容，可以在do one's best之后接to+动词。比如I did my best to do my homework ...

"向女朋友求婚，说自己会赴汤蹈火在所不辞"

I'll **do my best** to make you happy.

I'**m doing my best**! And she is doing her best!

我正在全力以赴，她也是！

I **did my best** under the circumstances.

在这种状况下我全力以赴了。

I will **do my best** to remember your birthday next year.

我会尽量记住你明年的生日的。.

Now you go **do your best**.

现在你要全力以赴了。

A: I want you to study very hard in school. 我想你在学校里努力学习。

B: OK. I'll do my best. 好，我尽量。

do the dishes 洗碗

do是一个杂食性动词，后面可以接多种多样的宾语。当然，都是一些经常使用到的短语，记住它们没什么坏处。

"受到招待的大妈们在吃完晚饭之后要洗碗，主人大妈说道"

Don't worry. My husband is going to **do the dishes**.

M·O·R·E

- do the dishes
  洗碗
- do one's hair
  理发

Why don't you let her **do the dishes**?

你怎么不让她洗碗?

Just go **do the laundry**. I'll take care of your baby.

去洗衣服吧。我会照看孩子的。

Let's **do lunch** sometime.

我们找个时间一起吃午饭吧。

You **did the crime**. You'll be in trouble.

你犯罪了，结果不妙哦。

A: Do you have any plans for tomorrow night? 你明天晚上有安排吗?

B: I really need to do my laundry then. 我得洗衣服。

do this (that, it) 做某事

在说话的过程中，如果提到对话双方都知道的事情，就可以用this，that和it来代替。在这里，具有代表动词性质的do与这些代词相组合，形成了各种表达。

"老大出去约会，最小的出去购物，妈妈让我这个老二看家"

You can't do that. This is so unfair.

M·O·R·E

- do it better
  做得更好
- do it all over again
  重新做
- do this to sb
  为某人做某事
- You did it!
  你成功了！
- I did it!
  我成功了！

I can't **do this**. 我不能下手。

I can **do that** (it, this). 我可以做。

I can **do it better**. 我可以做得更好。

Let's **do it**. 我们开始吧。

Please **do it all over again**. 请重新做一遍。

You can't **do that**! 你不能那么做！

I'll **do that**. 我来做。

You'll **do that**. 就那么办吧。

You **do that**. 请便。

How could you **do this** (that)? 你怎么能这么做?

Let's **do it** again. 重新做一遍。

Why did you **do this** (that)? 你怎么这么做?

You can't **do this to** me. 你不能这么对我。

I **do this** all the time. 我经常会这样。

What **have** you **done to** me? 你对我做了什么?

A: If you have any questions, give me a call. 如果你有疑问，就打给我。
B: I'll do that. 好的。

A: Sorry, I'm seeing a guy. 对不起，我在和别人约会。
B: What! You can't do this to me! 什么！你怎么能这么对我！

A: Let me show you how to do this. 我来教你怎么做。
B: Yeah! That would be great! 啊！那太好了！

be done with 结束

比较常用的表达，表示“结束某事”，比finish用得更多。be done with后面可以接事情，也可以接人物。也可以除去with，单单使用I'm (not) done（没结束），You done?（结束了？）等。

“借了也不会还的朋友再一次要求借钱”

You crossed the line here. I'm done with you.

M·O·R·E

- It's (all) done.
  完了。
- It's done now.
  这么快就结束了。
- (Very) Well done.
  不错。
- All done!
  全部结束！
- What's done is done.
  已经结束了。
- We're done for the day.
  算了吧，停手吧。
- be done ...ing
  结束某事

I'**m done with** that work.
我工作结束了。

I'**m done with** my choices. Now it's your turn.
我选择好了，该你了。

I think I'**m done with** you. Don't call me again.
我觉得和你没什么可说的了，不要再打电话。

Are you **done with** this?
你做完了?

That can't **be done** overnight. You have to look for someone else.
这件事情一整晚都做不完。你得找找别人。

Can it **be done**? If you can't do it, you're fired.
能做完吗? 如果不行，你就会被开除。

She'**s not done with** you. She wants you back.
她和你没完，希望你回到她身边。

Don't worry. I'**m done with** those plans.
不要担心，我已经制订好计划了。

A: Can I take away your plate? 我能收拾碗筷吗?
B: No, I'm not done with my snacks. 不行，我还没吃完呢。

A: Are you done with the Internet? 你上完网没?
B: Yeah, you can shut off the computer. 恩，你可以关电脑了。

A: Are you done with your class today? 你今天的课程结束了?
B: No. I have other classes this afternoon. 没，我下午还有别的课。

... I can do 我能做的事情

do与can相结合而成的表达。 ... (that) I can do可以用来构成多种多样的表达。比如说，表示我已经做完我力所能及的事情，或还没做的事情了。

“到达交通事故现场的119队员在当场死亡的司机面前”

It's too late. There's **not much I can do**.

I did **all I could do**. I'll just wait and see.

我能做的都做了。剩下的就只有等结果了。

That's **all I can do**. Don't expect too much.

我已经尽全力了。期望值不要太高。

I just wanted to give you some gifts. It's **the least I can do**.

我只想给你份礼物。至少是我的诚意。

There's **nothing more I can do**.

我已经尽全力了。

M·O·R·E

- be (do) all sb can do 某人能做的所有事情（做完所有力所能做的事情）
- be the least (best) sb can do 是某人的极限（最小）
- It's the best I can do. 这是我的极限

A: Doctor, is my father going to die? 医生，我爸爸会去世吗?

B: Yes. I did all I could do for him. 恩，我已经尽全力了。

do with （怎样）处理某事，用……弥补，需要……(could do with)

最常用的意思就是“处理……”，“对付……”(deal with)，with之后可以接人物或事物。至于with后面的部分应该怎么理解，要取决于具体的场景大意。

“年迈的部长突然接到了被开除的命令，无奈地说道”

I don't know what I'm going to **do with** myself now.

I don't know what to **do with** that.

我真不知道该怎么办。

I don't know what to **do with** a woman.

我真不知道该怎么对付女人。

What **have** you **done with** Cindy?

你对辛迪怎么样了?

What the hell **are** you **doing with** my client?

你到底对我员工做了什么?

M·O·R·E

- What should I do with ... ? 我该怎么做?
- I don't know what to do with ... 我不知道该怎么办
- What have you done with ... ? What did you do with ... ? 你把……怎么样了? 你在对……做什么?
- What're you doing with ... ? 拿……干嘛呢?

A: What did you do with my history book? 你对我的历史书做了什么?

B: I put it on the shelf above the desk. 我把它放到了桌上的书架里。

do without 过着没有……的生活，……就算不在也无所谓 (can do without)

这次相反，do without 表示"过着没有……的生活（坚持）"。最常用的就是I don't know what I would (am going to) do without形态。另外，can (could) do without句式表示"没有……也无所谓"。

"因加入了人寿保险，可以以低廉的价格接受大手术的病人欣慰地说道"

I don't know what I would **do without** health care.

I don't know what I'd **do without** him.
真不知道没有他该怎么办。

What would I **have done without** you?
如果没有你我会变成什么样?

I mean, what am I going to **do without** you?
我是说，如果你不在，我该怎么办?

What would you **do without** me?
没有我，你该怎么办呢?

A: Smoking is a very unhealthy habit. 抽烟对健康非常不好。
B: I know, but I can't do without cigarettes. 我知道，不过就是无法戒烟。

Neither did I 我也没做

表示我也没有做的neither did I 用来回答对方的问话，这里的did表示对方所提到的行为动词。相反，如果要表示我也一样时要用So do I。

"两个朋友在讨论Tammy有没有说谎"

You think Tammy's lying? **So do I.**

M·O·R·E

- So do I.
  我也是。
- Neither did I.
  我也没有。

Apparently **so do I**. It's OK.
正好我也是，好的。

Honey, **so do I**. I love you too.
宝贝儿，我也爱你。

You don't go to school? **Neither do I.**
你不去学校? 我也是。

A: He never lied to his mother or father. 他从来都不会对他父母说谎。
B: Neither did I. I was a very honest kid. 我也是。我可是个相当诚实的孩子。

Why don't you ... ? ……吧?

Why don't you ... 虽然是疑问句形式，但其实是向对方提议做某事。相当于I want you to ...。另外，Why don't I ... 和Let me ...，Why don't we ... ?和Let's ... 表示相同的含义。

"极度渴望聊天时把朋友叫出来"

Why don't you come over for a cup of coffee?

M·O·R·E

- Why don't you ... ?
  ……怎么样?
- Why don't we ... ?
  ……怎么样?
  我们去……吧。
- Why don't I ... ?
  我来……怎么样?

Why don't you stay here and just hang out with me?

你留在这和我们一起玩吧。

Why don't you ask him to help you?

你问问他帮忙呗?

Why don't we get together on Saturday?

我们星期六见个面呗?

A: I am feeling so tired right now. **我现在好累。**

B: Why don't you go to bed and get some sleep? **你上床休息一会呗?**

You did what? 你说什么?

在没有听清对方的话，或者表示难以置信时所使用到的表达。相反，You did?或You do?表示迎合对方的话，是"是吗?"，"真的?"的意思。

"一辈子没有约过会的朋友昨天居然去见了个女生，难以置信地问道"

You did? What was she like?

M·O·R·E

- You did what?
  你说什么?
- You did?
  是吗?
- You do?
  真的?

You did what? I can't believe it.

你说什么? 真不敢相信。

You did what? How come you always hit your friends?

你说什么? 你怎么能闲着没事就打同学呢?

You did? What was he talking about?

真的? 他说了什么?

You do? That's fantastic!

真的? 很棒啊!

A: I bought a new computer for us to use. **我为我们买了台新电脑。**

B: You did what? I can't afford that. **你说什么? 我可支付不起。**

More Expressions

- **do something over** 重新做一遍 (do again)

  Do it over again. 重新做一遍。

- **do business (with)** 交易

  It's been a pleasure **doing business with** you. 能和你做生意我表示万分荣幸。

- **do the math** 计算，思考

  You **do the math**. 你自己想想。

- **Don't do** 不要做……

  Don't do that anymore. 再也不要那样了。

  Don't ever do that again. 再也不要做那种事情了。

- **the best thing to do** 全力以赴的事情

  What is **the best thing to do** for it?
  最佳方法是什么?

- **do a number on** 欺骗，期满

  You **did a number on** me. 我被你骗了。

  Easy does it. 慢慢来，小心翼翼地，镇定。

Consider it done. 就那么定了。

How do you do that? 你怎么那么做?

That does it. 忍无可忍了，适可而止吧。

Easier said than done. 说着容易做着难。

(It's a) Done deal. 就那么定了。

That is how it's done. 就是这么做。

Please do as you like. 你想干嘛就干嘛。

What do we do now? 现在该怎么办?

What can I do? 我能怎么办?

do's and don'ts 该做的和不该做的

I did it wrong. 是我错了，我错了。

存在感十足的

Be

be不仅像A=B那样表示身份和价值，还可以像be+副词那样表示“在某处”。会话中的用到的be glad to, be sorry, be worried, be angry等be+形容词(pp)形态有着广泛的应用。另外，be+形容词（名词），或否定形态don't be+形容词（名词）形态也需要铭记。

基本概念

1 **在某处**

She isn't at home now. 她现在不在家。

Why is he in such a bad mood? 他心情为什么这么差?

2 **是……**

Will you be my wife? 你愿意嫁给我吗?

Let's just be friends. 我们还是做朋友吧。

3 **be+形容词(pp) ... 是……样**

Why are you so angry with me? 你为什么对我如此生气?

He's really bad at counting numbers. 他在数字方面非常薄弱。

4 **Don't be ... 不要做……**

Don't be such a baby! 不要那么幼稚!

Be a good mother. 当个好妈妈。

be all right (OK) 还好

all right表示还好，不错，因此be all right与be good (fine), be okay表示相同的含义。想要表达某人（某物）不错的话可以用be all right with sb (sth)。另外，be right可以用来肯定对方的话。

"听到楼下有动静，妻子拿着棒球棒悄悄走了下去，丈夫说道"

You're going to **be all right**, honey.

M·O·R·E

- We'll be all right if ...
  如果……的话我们会没事的
- be going to be all right (fine, okay)
  会好的
- be all right with
  与……的关系不错
- be fine by (with)
  ……没关系
- You're right. That's right.你说的没错

Everything's going to **be all right** (fine).
会好的。

It's going to be okay (fine).
会没事的。

If it'**s all right** with you, I'd like to borrow it.
如果你没问题的话，我想明天借一下。

A: I'll go with you to your house. **我陪你回家。**
B: You don't have to walk me home. I'll be okay. **不用了，我自己也没事。**

be there (here) 去，来

去和来虽然有go，come，但会话中经常会用到be there, be here。be there表示"在那里"的意思，可以取代go，而be here表示"在这里"，可以取代come。

"和对方说，大概一个小时之后就能走了"

I can **be there** in about an hour.

M·O·R·E

- I'll (always) be there for you.
  我会帮你的。
- I've been there.
  我知道什么意思了，很理解你的心情，去过。
- We're almost there.
  差不多好了，快完了。

(I'll) **Be right there**.
马上去。

Wait a moment. They are going to **be here**.
稍等一会。他们会来这的。

He really wants you to **be here**.
他真心希望你来这。

A: Make sure that you arrive on time tomorrow. **确认你明天准时到。**
B: Don't worry. I'll be there early. **不要担心，我会早点去的。**

That will be ... 会成为……

表示“会成为……的”。尤其在支付金额时表示“一共消费了……”，可以用到这种句型。That'll be ... 后面接上金额就可以了。另外Will that be ... 的疑问句形态也比较常用。

“饭店服务员拿着账单说，40美元”

Here's your check. That'll be $40.

M·O·R·E

- That'll be ...
  会成为……的
- That'll be all
  那就是全部，终于完了
- Will that be ... ?
  是……吗?

That'll be Here we are, sir. **That'll be** $4.50.
到了，先生，一共是4美元50美分。

Will that be all?
不需要别的了?

Will that be cash or charge?
现金还是刷卡?

A: How much do I owe you? 多少钱?
B: That will be three dollars and twenty-five cents. 应该是3美元25美分。

The point is that ... 重要的是……

在简略地表达重要或核心内容时主要用到的表达，表示“重要的是……”。The thing is that ... 主语+动词也可以。

“职业军人最需要拿手的一项就是“搬家””

The thing is that we're moving again to another city.

M·O·R·E

- The point is that ...
  重点是……
- The point is to+动词
  重点是做……
- The thing is that （...ing/to+动词）...
  重要的是……

The point is that we need to fix the computer.
重点是，我们需要修电脑。

The point is I don't need this right now.
问题是，我现在急需要这个。

The thing is I don't really believe you.
问题是，我不相信你。

A: Could you please get to the point? 你能直接说重点吗?
B: The point is that we are bankrupt. 重点就是我们已经破产了。

There is (are) ... ……有

虽然是最基本的表达方式，但在日常会话中占到的比例很大，可以分为多个类型进行表达。There are (is) ... 表示单单的“……在”，而Here are (is) ... 表示递交物品或意见。

“在军队服役的儿子自愿请求到伊拉克驻军”

There's a chance you could get hurt.

M·O·R·E

- There are (is)+N ...ing
  某人在做某事
- There is no+名词
  某物不存在
- There is no way ...
  绝对不可能……
- Here are (is) ...
  这里有……
- There is a possibility
  有……的可能性

There is a lot of chemistry between you and me.
你和我有太多不和谐。

There is nothing more important than family.
没有什么比家庭更重要。

Here is my card. Call anytime you want.
这是我的名片。随时联系我。

Here are the files you're looking for.
这是你在找的文件。

A: There is a car coming this way. 有辆车向这里开过来。
B: I think that is my brother. 应该是我哥哥。

(Don't) Be ... ……吧，不要……

以be开头的祈使句，可以像Be nice! Be quiet!一样接形容词，也可以像Be a good boy!（听话！），Be a man!（像个男人一样！）一样接名词。另外，Don't be+形容词（名词）用来禁止或拜托对方。

“师弟第一次来到舞厅，前辈拍拍肩说道”

Don't be shy. You'll get used to it soon.

M·O·R·E

- Be+形容词（名词）
  ……吧
- Don't be+形容词（名词）
  不要……
- Don't be a baby.
  别像个孩子一样。

Everyone please **be quiet** for a moment.
大家请稍安勿躁。

Don't be so serious. Let's have fun.
不要当真，玩玩呗。

You're not going to get married? **Don't be** ridiculous.
你不结婚了？别说那种荒谬的话。

Please **don't be** sorry. It's not your fault.
请别自责，这不是你的错。

A: Don't be so hard on yourself. 不要难为自己。
B: You're right. 你说的没错。

have been (gone) to 去过……

have been in (to)+地点表示“到过某处”或“有到访某地的经历”。地点名词可以是暂时到访的车站，也可以是能够久居的纽约New York，还可以是抽象的love，relation等。

“像逛街一样，到处转健身房的人们”

I've been to every gym in my neighborhood.

M·O·R·E

- I have been to (in) ... .
  去过某处。
- Have you (ever) been to ... ?
  你去过某处吗?
- Where have you been?
  你这是从哪里回来?

I**'ve been to** his apartment and he wasn't there.

我去过他家，不过他没在。

Have you **been to** the fifth floor?

你去过五层吗?

You**'ve been in** love before?

你之前谈过恋爱吗?

A: How many times have you been to New York? 你之前去过几次纽约?

B: I've been there twice. 去过两次。

be good at 擅长，对某事有特长

be good (great) at+名词(–ing)表示“擅长（做）某事；而不擅长则用be poor (terrible) at+名词(–ing)。

“经常会装蒜(make up)的人要帮助朋友时”

I'll make something up. I'm good at lying.

M·O·R·E

- be good (great) at+名词(...ing)
  擅长某事
- be poor (terrible) at+名词 (...ing)
  不擅长某事

You can count on me. I **am good at** this.

你可以相信我。我最擅长这个了。

I**'m not great with** figures.

我对数字不感冒。

I don't remember the name of that blond. I**'m terrible at** names.

我不记得那金发女郎的名字了。我对名字不太擅长。

A: I heard you played baseball in high school. 我听说你在高中时打棒球。

B: I'm good at many different sports. 我擅长各种各样的运动。

be happy with (about) ... 满足于…，喜欢

be happy with (about)表示“喜欢或满足某事”。当然，也可以用最常见的be satisfied with。

“如果在公司受到这种夸奖，那肯定是前途无量了”

My boss is so happy with my work.

M·O·R·E

- be happy with (about) sb (sth)
  满足于某事
- I thought you would be happy with (about)
  以为会满足于某事

I'm very happy with my decision.
我很满意我的决定。

I'm not happy about this.
我不大喜欢这个。

What are you so happy about?
什么让你那么高兴?

A: How do you like your new apartment? 你觉得你的新公寓怎么样?
B: I'm happy with it. It's very comfortable. 很满意，很舒服。

be glad to 很开心……

初次见面的人之间常用的客套话Glad to meet you。可以用I'm glad to+动词或I'm glad that主语+动词表示“很荣幸……”。也可以将I'm省略掉。

“主人对宴会中的所有人说道”

I'm glad you're having so much fun here.

M·O·R·E

- I'm glad to+动词 (that S+V)
  很高兴……
- I'm glad to hear that.
  很高兴听到这消息。
- I'm glad you think so.
  我很高兴你能这么想。
- I'm pleased with+名词（to+动词）
  很高兴……

That's great. I'm glad you like it.
不错啊，很高兴你能喜欢。

I'm glad you feel that way.
很高兴你会那样想。

I'm glad you're back. I really need your help.
很高兴你能回来。我真地很需要你。

A: You're always so generous. 你的心肠总是那么好。
B: I'm glad you think so. 很高兴你能那么想。

be angry with 对某人生气

get angry中已经提到过，be angry形态也是非常常用的。要记住，“生气的”形容词和什么样的介词相搭配。

“小心眼老板在身后站着，你却毫不知情地说老板的坏话”

I wonder if the boss is still angry with me.

M·O·R·E

- be angry with (at)
  对……生气
- be mad at (about)
  生……的气
- be upset about (with)
  对……生气

Why **are** you so **angry at** me?
你为什么要生我的气?

Don't **be mad at** him, it's our fault.
不要生他的气，是我们的错。

I'**m not upset about** anything.
我根本没有生气啊。

A: Why are you so angry at me? 你为什么要生我的气?
B: Because you said I was fat and ugly! 因为你说我又胖又丑!

be worried about 担心……

表示“担心……”，可以单独使用I'm worried，也可以使用I'm worried about ... 或I'm worried that主语+动词形态。be concerned about ... 表示“对某事感兴趣”。

“托业考试没有做完，非常担心自己的分数”

I'm just worried about the test results.

M·O·R·E

- I'm worried about sth (sb, ...ing)
  担心某事
- I'm worried (that) S+V
  担心……

I'**m** so **worried about** my wedding ceremony.
我非常担心婚礼。

She'**s** so **worried about** paying the debt.
她非常担心还债的事情。

We **were** all **so worried** we were losing you.
我们非常害怕会失去你。

A: You seem to be worried about something. 你看似有心事啊。
B: I have a job interview this afternoon. 今天下午有个工作面试。

be supposed to ... ……应当做某事

be supposed to+动词表示“应当……”，“将……当成理所当然的事情”。会话中经常会用到的表达。下面整理了be+过去分词 ... 的形态。

“正忙着赚钱的丈夫居然说要放弃事业，转行当歌手”

I'm very disappointed in your decision.

M·O·R·E

- be tied up (...ing)
  忙碌于某事
- be scheduled to
  打算做某事
- be disappointed at (in, to)
  对……感到失望
- be interested in
  对……有兴趣
- be related to
  与……相关（亲戚）
- be surprised to
  对……感到吃惊

Am I **supposed to** meet the client today?
我今天要见顾客吗?

I **am not supposed to** be here.
我不应该在这里。

When **is** he **scheduled to** arrive at the airport?
他预计什么时候到机场?

I'**m not interested in** playing golf.
我对打高尔夫球不感兴趣。

A: When is the show supposed to start? 表演什么时候开始?
B: Just after seven o'clock. 7点准时开始。

be sorry about 对……感到抱歉

简单可以用作I'm sorry about (for)+名词，I'm sorry to+动词，I'm sorry that主语+动词的形态。主要用在道歉或安慰中。另外，在说道歉的具体内容前会说I'm sorry, (but)主语+动词。

“明明说好了会再联系，却忘得一干二净”

I'm sorry I didn't get back to you sooner.

M·O·R·E

- I'm sorry about (for)+名词
  对某事感到抱歉
- I'm sorry (that) S+V
  很抱歉……
- I'm sorry, but S+V
  很抱歉……
- You will be sorry if you don't ...
  如果不……的话，你会后悔的

I'm sorry to hear that.
很抱歉听到那些话。

I'm sorry I'm late again, but I got stuck in traffic.
很抱歉又迟到了。我堵车了。

I am sorry, but I'm going to be a little late.
抱歉，我可能要晚点。

Never do that again. **You'll be sorry** later.
不要再那样了，日后肯定会后悔的。

A: Do you want to break up with me? 你是要和我分手吗?
B: I have to. I'm sorry about that. 没办法。很抱歉。

be able to 能够做

与can表示相同的含义，be able to+动词就是“能够……”的意思。因为不会特别用到will can ... 的形式，因此未来时态的语句中可以用will be able to来代替can。

“连休假都没有，忙得不可开交的职场人士发自内心的呼唤”

I won't **be able to** go on a vacation this summer.

Will you **be able to** attend?
你能出席吗?

We hope you'll **be able to** join us.
我们希望你能加入我们。

How soon will you **be able to** get here?
你要多久才能到那?

Are you sure you'll **be able to** do it?
你确定能做到吗?

A: We hope you'll be able to join us. 我们希望你可以加入我们。
B: I hope so too ... it sounds like fun! 我也是……听起来很不错哦!

be ready 做好了……的准备

就算知道了具体的含义，如果不会实际应用的话就等于不知道。be ready表示“做好了……的准备”，可以写成be ready to (for)的形态。也可以用get代替be，或者将be去掉。

“在犯下了错误之后，不敢负责的胆小鬼”

I'**m not ready to** be a father.

M·O·R·E

- ready to+动词（+名词）
  做好了……的准备
- (I'm) ready to (for)
  我做好了……的准备

Are you **ready to** order your food?
你准备好点菜了吗?

Your room **won't be ready** until one o'clock.
你的房间到1点才可用。

When will it **be ready**? I guess we're going to be late.
什么时候准备好? 我猜我们要迟到了。

A: What would you like to eat? 你想吃什么?
B: We're not ready to order yet. 我们还没想好吃什么呢。

be sure to 一定……

在嘱咐对方一定做某事时所使用到的句式。可以用祈使句的形态Be sure to ... ，也可以说成I'll be sure to ...。

“儿子基本上每次出门都不会锁上房门，妈妈再次叮嘱道”

Be sure to lock the door when you go out.

M·O·R·E

- Be sure to+动词
  一定要做某事
- I'll be sure to+动词
  我肯定会做某事

Be sure to check them all.
一定要检查一遍。

You'll **be sure to** send me flowers first.
你一定要先送我花。

I'll **be sure to** double-check everything from now on.
从现在开始，我一定要检查两遍。

A: I'm going to stay up late tonight. 我今晚打算熬夜。
B: Be sure to brush your teeth before going to bed. 你睡觉前一定要刷牙。

be worth ... 有……的价值

虽然是个众所周知的短语，但实际用起来不太如意。be worth后面可以不加任何介词，直接加名词或动词的 ...ing形式。只不过在名词后面表示“有……的价值”时，要用作worth of。

“稍微有点困难就想着放弃的年轻人经常用到的狡辩”

It's too hard. It'**s not worth** it. I quit.

M·O·R·E

- be worth+名词（...ing)
  有……的价值
- 名词+worth of
  有……的价值

You'd better try. It will **be worth** it.
你最好试试，肯定值得。

Is it **worth** it? Are you sure about that?
这值吗？你确定？

This **is worth** $30,000.
这个值3万美金。

A: That is a very nice sports car. 那是一辆很棒的跑车。
B: It is worth a huge amount of money. 肯定值不少钱。

be better (worse) 更好，更坏

表示比某物更好或更坏时使用到的短语，可以单独使用，也可以加上than 与其他事物做比较。could be better (worse)的含义比较特殊，另外，not ... better则表示最高级。

"but之后的部分如果解释合理的话就会感觉到could be better"

It **could be better**, but it's going to be okay, right?

M·O·R·E

- (Things) Could be better (worse).
  不怎么样，很一般。（马马虎虎）
- (It) Couldn't be better.
  最棒，不能再好了。
- It would be better (for, than, if S+V)
  （对某人，比……如果……的话）更好一些。

That's **better**.
那个更好。

It's **better** than your first plan.
比你的第一个计划好。

It **would be better** if she didn't come tonight.
如果她今晚不来是更好的结果。

A: The coffee here is better than other restaurants. **这里的咖啡比其他餐厅的好。**

B: Is that why you like to come here so much? **所以你经常来这里了？**

It's not that ... 不是……

用来表达否定的句式。It's not that ... 表示"不是那样的"，后面接形容词的话表示"不到那种程度"， It's not that主语+动词就表示"不是那样"，用来否定对方的想法。

"独守空房的妻子抱怨"我们的爱情已经冷淡了！"，丈夫回答道"

It's not that I don't love you.

M·O·R·E

- It's not that (at all)
  （完全）不是那样的
- It's not that+形容词
  并不是那种程度
- It's not that bad
  没那么坏
- It's not (that) S+V
  不是那样的

It's not that we're not having a lot of fun at the party.
我们并没有在聚会中感到无聊。

It's not that we don't care about the employees.
我们并非不关心员工。

It's not that we don't like you.
我们并不是不喜欢你。

A: You really don't like me, do you? **你真的不喜欢我，是吧？**

B: It's not that I don't like you. I just don't know you. **并不是我不喜欢你。只是不太了解你罢了。**

be the one who ... 某人是……的人

属于一种强调的用法，表明“某人才是……的人”。比如说，想要表达“是我做的”时，可以用I'm the one who ... ，“是你做的”时，可以用You're the one who ...。

“在分辨是非时非常有效地表达”

You're the one who should apologize.

M·O·R·E

- I'm (You're) the one who ...
  我（你）才是……的人
- Will sb be the one who ... ?
  某人会是……的人吗?

I'm the one who made him quit smoking.
是我让他戒烟的。

You're the one who ended it, remember?
是你终结的，记得吗?

I guess he's the one who needs a job right now.
我记得他是最近急需找到工作的人。

She's the one who agreed with you!
她就是同意你的人!

A: Pat is going to be fired from our workplace. 帕特要被开除了。
B: I don't want to be the one who tells her. 我可不想告诉她。

be in trouble 处于困境，被教训一顿

be in表示“陷入某种状态”，因此be in trouble表示“陷入困境”。相反，让某人“陷入困境”的话就应该用get sb in trouble，警告某人可能陷入困境时要用will be in trouble if ...。

“虽然已经原谅了无数次，但丈夫再一次到处拈花惹草”

Our marriage is in trouble again.

M·O·R·E

- be in a good (bad) mood
  心情好（坏）
- be in charge of
  对……负责
- be in the way of
  对某人产生妨碍
- be in need of
  需要……
- be in the family way
  怀孕中

You're already in trouble. There's nothing I can do about it.
你已经陷入困境了。我可帮不上你什么。

She's in a good mood tonight.
她今晚心情很好。

I didn't know my wife was in the family way.
我不知道我妻子怀孕的事情。

I'm not in charge of here. Do you want to talk with the manager?
我不是这里的负责人。你想和经理谈谈吗?

A: Give me a hand. I'm in trouble. 帮帮我，我有麻烦了。
B: What kind of help do you need? 我得怎么帮你?

be out of one's mind 丢了魂似的

be out of表明“从……渐渐远去”，因此be out of town表示“出差”，be out of one's mind表示“心不在焉”，而be out of luck表示“运气差”。

“明明是向后倒去，却伤到了鼻梁”

You'**re out of luck**.

M·O·R·E

- be out of town (be out on business) 在出差

I'll **be out of town** all next week.
我下个星期要出差。

He **is out on business**. He will not be in today.
他在出差。今天不会来了。

What are you doing? You'**re out of your mind**!
你在干嘛？失去理智了？

Let's hurry up and do this. We'**re out of time**.
我们抓紧时间做吧，没时间了。

A: I spent all of my money on my stamp collection. 我花了所有钱来收集邮票。
B: Your stamp collection? You must be out of your mind. 收集邮票？你肯定脑子进水了。

be on a first-name basis 关系很好，可以随便叫名字

be on 表示“放在……上面”，“处于某种状态中”。be on the way表示正在路上。be on the phone call表示正在通话，另外，在饭店说be on somebody的话就表示“我来买单”。

“以前一直让人请客，这次要自己掏钱时”

Let me treat you. This one **is on** me.

M·O·R·E

- be on the (one's) way to 正在去往……的路上
- be on sb (the house) 某人来买单
- be on the phone 正在通话
- be on a first-name basis 关系很好

It's going to be okay. I'**m on my way**.
没关系的，我正在路上。

She **is on her way to** the office.
她正在去上班的路上。

We **are on a first-name basis**.
我们关系非常好。

Hold on a moment. The boss **is on the other line**.
稍等一下，老板正在接听别的电话。

A: Have you ever met Mr. Johnson? 你曾经见过约翰逊先生吗?
B: Yes, we're on a first name basis with each other. 是啊，我们关系非常好。

be back 回来

暂时离开位置，再回来的意思。be back可以单独使用，或者附加上详细的内容，接地点或时间的副词。

"与心仪的李经理两人在屋顶独处，去买咖啡"

Don't go anywhere. I'll be back soon.

I'll **be back** (in a minute).
我马上就回来。

He should **be back in** ten minutes. Would you wait here?
他十分钟之内就会回来的。你能在这等吗?

He won't **be back in** the office today.
他今天不会回到办公室的。

M·O·R·E

- be back in a minute
  马上回来
- be back in+地点
  回到某处
- be back to+动词
  回来做某事

A: How soon do you expect him back? 你觉得他能什么时候回来?
B: He should be back in about 15 minutes. 他应该在15分钟之内回来的。

be into 对某事感兴趣

字面含义为"在(be)……的里面(into)"，表示对某种事物或活动感兴趣或专注。be into somebody表示"深深喜欢某人"。

"明知道非常幼稚，却深深陷入了电视节目中"

I'm so into TV shows these days. How about you?

You're not telling me you**'re into** this stuff?
你没告诉我你喜欢这类东西啊?

I can't believe you**'re into** it.
真不敢相信，你居然对这个感兴趣。

You**'re into** porn movies, right? You downloaded a lot?
你非常喜欢成人电影吧? 是不是下了很多?

Since when **are** you **into** jazz music?
你什么时候开始喜欢上爵士音乐的?

M·O·R·E

- I'm not into it.
  我不喜欢。
- She's so into me.
  她对我非常痴迷。

A: Jeffrey seems to be into computer games. 杰弗瑞好像沉迷于电脑游戏。
B: He plays them for hours every evening. 他每天晚上都会玩好几个小时。

be off 离开(Leave)

off包含“分离”和“脱离”的意思，因此be off表示“离开”。想要说明目的地的话就可以使用be off to+名词，想要说明原因的话就可以用be off to+（动词）。另外，be off还具有电器（水龙头）等处于关闭状态的含义。

“团体出游时，肯定会有一两个人早早睡觉，扫大家的兴”

I'm off to bed! You two have fun.

M·O·R·E

- be off（to+地点）
  去往某处
- be off bed
  去睡觉
- be off to+动词
  去做某事

I'm sorry! I must **be off** right now. See you soon.
对不起，我现在得离开了。回头见。

(I'd) Better **be off**. I'll catch you later.
我得走了，回头见。

He'**s off to** see his girlfriend.
他要去见女朋友。

A: Did you turn off the lights before you left? 你离开前关灯了吗?
B: Yeah, the lights are off in the classroom. 恩，教室的灯关着呢。

be over 超越，结束

单纯be over+数字表示“……以上”，也可以与there,here相结合变成be over there (here)，还可以表示某种关系或事情结束。

“明明说好了分手，却不甘心错过如此漂亮的女孩，再三哀求的劣质男”

It's over between us. Forget me.

M·O·R·E

- be over+数字
  ……以上
- be over there (here)
  在那里（这里）
- be over
  （事情，关系等）完全结束

The game (party) **is over**.
游戏（派对）结束了。

The bathroom'**s over there**. Go wash your hands.
洗漱间在那里。去洗洗手吧。

The important thing is it'**s over** and it doesn't matter.
最重要的是已经结束了，而且没有多大意义了。

You have to believe me. It'**s over** now.
你必须相信我，已经结束了。

A: The meeting will be over in two hours.会议再过两个小时就结束了。
B: That's good. I need to get back to work. 很好，我得回去工作了。

be with 与某人在一起，与某人相处

be with表示“与某人在一起”。完成形态have been with somebody表示一直是家人，同事或恋人的关系。另外，如果对方与平时不同，担心对方时可以用What's with ... ?问候。

“深受巨大打击，没心情参加任何活动和酒席的人”

I am not in the mood **to be with** people.

M·O·R·E

- be with
  与某人在一起
- have been with sb
  认识某人
- What's with sb (sth)?
  ……怎么了?

I'll **be right with** you.
我马上过去。

Wait here a moment. The doctor will **be right with** you.
稍等片刻。医生马上就过来。

I **haven't been with** a woman in some time.
我好一段时间没和女士交往了。

She'**s been with** us so long, and she's more like family.
她认识我们很久了，就像家人一般亲切。

I'**ve only been with** one woman my whole life.
我这辈子只交往过一个女士。

You are acting strangely today. **What's with** you?
你今天很诡异啊。怎么了?

What's with you? You're acting like a kid.
你怎么了? 就像个孩子一样。

What's with your clothes? You had a fight?
你衣服怎么了? 你打架了?

A: How can you say that you don't love me? 你怎么可以说你不爱我?
B: It's true. I don't want to be with you anymore.是真的，我不能继续和你交往下去了。

A: How will you be spending the Christmas holiday? 你要怎么度过圣诞假期?
B: I'm going to be with my family at home. 我要在家和家人待在一起。

A: How many women have you been with? 你交往过几个女人?
B: Five. 五个。

be up 结束，心情好，想出点子，准备好做某事

be up表示时间到或心情好，be up for表示“做好了做某事的准备”，而be up to something表示“想出……”。It's up to you里的be up to sb表示“某人来决定”。

“非常想知道分手的女朋友现状如何，对她朋友问道”

Have you heard what she's been up to?

M·O·R·E

- be up
  结束，时间到
- be up for
  准备好
- be up to sb
  某人来决定
- time's up
  时间到

What **have** you **been up** to?
你最近干什么了？

I know what you'**re up to**. You'**re** always **up to** something.
我知道你在想什么。你总会想阴谋诡计。

All this stuff **is up for** auction.
所有这些东西都是用来拍卖的。

A: This project will take me hours to finish. 这个项目要花费我好几个小时。
B: I bet you'll be up all night working on it. 我打赌，你肯定要熬个通宵了。

More Expressions

- **be in touch** 取得联系
  I **will be in touch**. 我会联系你的。
- **be oneself** 平时自己的形象
  Just **be yourself**. 就像你平时一样。
  You'**re not yourself**. 你有点反常啊。
- **be in (out)** 一起做，不做
  You **are in**. 你也一起来吧。
- **be behind** 支持某人，是某人的同伙
  I'**m 100% behind** you.
  我百分之百支持你。
- **be on time** 到时间
  You'**re on time**. 该你了。
- **be on the same page** 有着相同的想法
  We'**re on the same page**.
  我们想的 一样。

More Expressions

- **be off base** 错误，相悖

  You're way off base. 你完全错了。

- **be about to** 想要做某事

  We're about to begin the meeting. 我们正要开会。

- **be in one's** 成为……（年龄）

  She's in her early twenties. 她才20出头。

- **be to blame** 是某人的责任

  You're to blame. 都怪你

  Somebody is always to blame. 不是任何人的责任。

- **It won't be long before …** 不会很久

  It'll not be long before she gets married. 她没多久就会结婚的。

- **be late** 晚

  You're 30 minutes late. 你晚了30分钟。

- **be available to** 有时间做……

  I'm not available to meet you this weekend. 我这周末没空见你。

- **be familiar with** 熟悉于某事

  She's not familiar with the city. 她对这座城市不太熟悉。

- **be allergic to** 对……过敏

  He's allergic to shrimp. 他对虾类过敏。

- **So be it** 随你便，就那么办

  You want to sue me? So be it. 你想告我？请便。

已经有了却还想要的

Have

虽然作用无法与get相比，但从含义的多样性和使用频率上远远比其他动词优越。很多情况下都可以被get替换，大体上表示拥有某物时，无论是人，是物，是食品还是病情。尤其像get一样用作祈使动词，另外，have后面可以接各种各样的动名词，构成多样的短语。

基本概念

1 拥有，具有，有……

Do you have a boyfriend now? 你现在有男朋友吗?

Do you have a room for tonight? 今天晚上有空房吗?

I don't have any brothers. 我没有兄弟姐妹。

2 吃东西，摄取，患（病）

Let's have spaghetti. 我们吃意大利面吧。

I'd like to have a diet Coke. 我想喝减肥可乐。

Do you have a high temperature? 你发烧吗?

3 have+宾语+动词原形(pp) 使……成为……的状态

Have him come downstairs. 让他下楼。

4 have to+动词原形 不得不做某事

I have to make money. 我得挣钱。

You have to go now. 你必须得走了。

have 吃东西，得病

have后面接各种各样的食物的话就表示“吃东西”，与eat相同，因此have a meal就表示“用餐”。另外，have后面如果接疾病名称的话就表示“疼痛”，“患病”。

“因昨夜喝过头了，给老板打电话说今天不上班”

I have a hangover. I have to call in sick.

M·O·R·E

- have a drink
  喝酒
- have dinner (lunch) (with)
  与某人享用晚餐（午餐）
- have the same
  吃一样的
- I'll have the same.
  给我来一样的。

Let's go **have** a drink together, tonight.
我们今晚去喝两杯吧。

What would you like to **have?**
你想吃点什么?

I **have** a high temperature. Get me to the hospital.
我发烧了。带我去医院。

I **have** food poisoning. I can't eat today.
我食物中毒了。今天不能吃东西。

A: Do you have time to have dinner? 你有时间吃晚饭吗?
B: No, not really. I must be going now. 没有，我现在得走了。

have somebody (sth) 使……处于某种状态

have somebody (something) 后面如果接形容词或介词的话会表示“使……处于某种状态”。have one's hand full表示“很忙”，have the phone on vibrate表示“把手机置于振动”。

“故意不接电话，却以手机震动为由”

I had my phone on vibrate. I was a little busy.

M·O·R·E

- have sb (sth)+形容词
  让某人……
- have sb (sth)+介词
  使……处于某种状态

We're going to **have** everything **ready**.
我们得准备好所有东西。

I **have** my hands **full**! Go have fun yourself!
我很忙，你自己好好玩吧!

I **have** a lot **on my plate**.
我得考虑好多事情。

You two really **have** something **going**, don't you?
你们俩相处得很好吧?

A: We have everything ready for the conference. 会议的所有东西都准备好了。
B: Well done. The president will be here soon. 好样的。总裁很快就到。

have somebody+动词 让某人做某事，命令某人

have被用作祈使动词的情况。have+人物+动词则表示让某人做某事。与之前所学的get有相同的含义，但get要在动词前面加to，变成get+人物+to的动词形态。

"好久没见的外甥女要吃甜点"

Take her to lunch and **have her get** dessert.

M·O·R·E

- have sb+动词 让某人做某事
- have sb ...ing 让某人做某事

I'll **have him call** you back.

我会让他给你打电话的。

I will **have my secretary work** on the file.

我会让秘书处理那些文件的。

You **had it coming**! I knew it!

是你自找的！我就知道会这样！

A: We need some help on Saturday night. 我们星期六晚上需要一些帮助。

B: Have Dave work with you until you finish. 让大卫帮你做完吧。

have something+pp 使……成为

让宾语中的"事物"成为"pp"样的意思，即某人让对方做某事。比如说I had my car washed表示我让别人洗我的车，即"使车被洗"。

"方向盘有些不对劲，给朋友打电话询问"

Did you **have it checked** out?

Can I **have these delivered** to this address?

能把这些送到这个地址吗?

Call the police! I **had my bag stolen**!

叫警察！我的包被偷了！

How do I look? I **had my hair cut** yesterday.

我看起来如何? 我昨天理发了。

She **had her teeth pulled** out.

她拔牙了。

A: You look like you are upset. 你看起来不好受。

B: I have to have some of my teeth pulled out. 我得拔几颗牙。

have to+动词 不得不做某事

表示“不得不做某事”，强调动词的“强行”成分。虽然不是助词，但经常会被当成助词来用，过去式为had to，将来时为will have to。

“新婚旅行时看到了妻子的素颜，大吃一惊，从此就喜欢上了值夜班”

I'm sorry I **have to** work tonight.

M·O·R·E

- I have to
  我不得不做……
- I have to admit that S+V
  我不得不承认……
- You have to ...
  你必须……
- You don't have to ...
  你没必要……
- Do I have to ... ?
  不做……也可以?
- What do I have to ... ?
  我必须……吗?
- The first thing we have to do is+动词 ...
  我们的当务之急是……

I'm sorry, but I **have to** cancel my reservation.
对不起，我不得不取消晚上的预约了。

I **have to** go now.
我现在必须得走了。

I **have (got) to** go. I'll call you later.
我必须得走了，回头见。

I **have to** tell you (something). I love being alone.
我得告诉你点事情。我喜欢独处。

Act your age. You **have to** grow up.
能不能成熟点。你得学会长大了。

Do I **have to** make a reservation?
我必须要预约吗?

Do I have to wait here until she gets in?
我必须要在这等她回来吗?

It's totally my fault. **You don't have to** say you're sorry.
都是我的错，你不用说对不起。

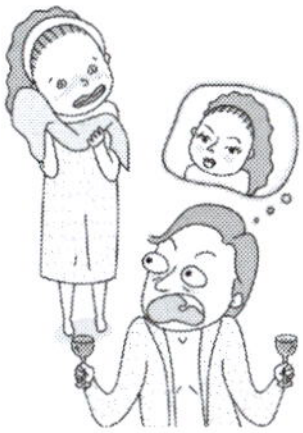

A: You don't have to say you're sorry. 你不必说对不起。
B: Sure I do. It was all my fault. 必须的，都是我的错。

A: I have to leave right away for the meeting. 我得马上去开会了。
B: I'll catch up with you later. 我回头联系你。

A: I'd be pleased if you could join us for dinner. 如果你能和我们共进晚餐就太好了。
B: I'll have to call my wife first. 我得先给老婆打电话。

have+动名词 做某事

与前文中的get或take一样，have也可以将bath, reservation, fight等名词作为宾语，表示做某事。

“人事部的员工上班不太认真，老板找他谈话”

Can we have a talk? It's about your job.

M·O·R·E

- have sb+动词
  让某人做某事
- have sb ...ing
  让某人做某事

I **have a reservation** under the name of James Smith.

我以詹姆斯史密斯的名字预约的。

We're **having a big sale** this week.

我们这周有一场大甩卖。

Did you guys **have a fight**? Who won?

你们俩打架了？谁赢了？

I'**m having a little chat** with her.

我正在和她商量。

A: Ray got drunk and had a fight with his wife. 雷喝醉了，和老婆吵了一架。

B: Did anyone tell him to calm down? 有人劝过他吗？

had better 最好做某事

You'd better+动词是对朋友或晚辈说的话，表示”最好……”的忠告或警告。一般会省略为You'd better, I'd better, we'd better，有时会索性略去had，变成I (We, You), 甚至还会连人称都去掉，变成Better+动词。

“电影快要开始了，爱人却一直待在洗手间里。”

We'd better hurry. The movie starts in ten minutes.

M·O·R·E

- You'd better+动词
  你最好……
- You'd better not+动词
  你最好别做某事

You'**d better** hurry up. We might be late.

你最好抓紧时间。我们可能要迟到了。

You'**d better not** go outside. It's raining.

你最好别出门，外面正在下雨。

You'**d better** do it right now.

你最好现在就做。

A: How can I be successful in the future? 我将来怎样才能成功？

B: You had better find a stable job and make some money. 你最好找一份稳定的工作，挣点小钱。

Rumor has it 听到了……的传闻

喜欢在别人后面说三道四的人们最常用的表达。表示“传闻中说……”，在Rumor has it后面加主语+动词的句式就可以了。它与get wind of具有相同的含义，也可以用word代替rumor。

“职场人士最希望听到的话”

Rumor has it that we're going to get a 10 percent raise.

Rumor has it he's going to quit.
听说他要辞职不干了。

Rumor has it the store's going to shut down.
听说这家店要关门了。

Rumor has it you're going back to New York.
听说你要回纽约了。

A: Brad and Allison were arguing this morning. 拉德和埃里森今天早上吵架了。
B: Rumor has it that they might break up. 听说他们可能要分手了。

May I have ... ? 能给我……吗?

郑重地向对方索取某物时可以用到May I+动词?的形态，而这里的动词就是have。表示“能够给我……吗？”，语气比"Can I have ... ?"更为恭敬。

“海外旅行时经常能在机场听到的话”

May I have your ticket and your passport please?

May I have your email address?
能告诉我你的电子邮件地址吗?

May I have your name again, please?
尊姓大名?

May I have a receipt, please?
能给我开发票吗?

A: Here is your change, sir.找给您的钱，先生。
B: Thank you. May I have a receipt, please? 谢谢，我能索要发票吗?

have somebody (sth) in mind 心里想着某人（某物）

表示“心里(in mind)有着……”，可以用来表达“心里想着什么”，“挂念什么”等。

“提议把患上老年痴呆的母亲独自留在乡下，其他兄弟责备道”

Is this what you have in mind?

Do you **have** any particular restaurant **in mind**?
你想到了特别的饭店吗?

What do you **have in mind**?
你在想什么?

That's not what I **had in mind**.
那和我想的不一样。

A: Do you have any plans tonight? 你今晚有计划吗?
B: Possibly. What do you have in mind? 可能吧。你想说什么?

have something to 有些事情要做

表示“有些事情要做(to do)”的句式。something的位置可以由nothing，anything取代，形成多样的表达。

“该上班了，老婆却连早饭都没做”

Can I have something to eat?

M·O·R·E

- have sth to+动词
  有些事情要做
- have nothing to+动词
  没什么事情要做

I can't go play golf with you. I **have a lot to** do.
我不能和你去打高尔夫了。有很多事情要做。

Do you **have anything to** declare?
你有事情要申诉吗?

It couldn't be better. I **have nothing to** complain about.
好的不能再好了。我没什么可抱怨的。

We **have something to** show you.
我们有些东西要给你看。

A: I can't believe how hot it is today. 真不敢相信今天居然这么热。
B: Let's have a drink to cool down a bit. 我们去喝点饮料降降温吧。

have to do with 与……相关

have to do with表示与某事相关，也可以说成have something to do with。相反，如果没有任何关系的话就可以说成have nothing to do with。

"愚人节那天，在班主任桌上放假蛇的主犯不打自招"

It doesn't have anything to do with me.

M·O·R·E

- have to do with
  与……相关
- have something (nothing) to do with
  与……有（无）关
- not have anything to do with
  与……没有任何关系
- What does it have to do with ... ?
  与……有什么关系?

I think it **has to do with** your kids. Go talk with them.
我觉得这件事和你的孩子们有关。去和他们谈谈。

What does that **have to do with** you?
这和你有什么关系?

Does it **have to do with** your family?
这和你的家庭有关系吗?

I'm sorry about that, but I **had nothing to do with** this.
很抱歉，我和这件事没有任何瓜葛。

A: This weekend's marathon was canceled. 这周末的马拉松取消了。
B: I have nothing to do with that. I'm not a runner. 和我没什么关系。我不是选手。

not have any 一点都没有……

have any+名词一般在否定的句式中表示"……一点都没有"，在疑问句或条件从句表示"有没有……"。

"宅男对仅有的一个朋友说道"

I don't have any close friends except you.

M·O·R·E

- I don't have any+名词
  一点都没有……
- Do you have any+名词
  你有……吗?

What am I supposed to do? I **don't have any** money.
我应该做什么? 我可一毛钱都没有。

Do you have any identification?
你有身份证吗?

What're you doing tonight? **Do you have any** plans?
你今天晚上有事吗? 有没有安排?

Did you get any messages while I was away?
我不在的时候有没有收到留言?

A: Do you have any hobbies? 你有什么爱好?
B: I'm fond of watching movies. 我喜欢看电影。

have a (the) feeling 有……的想法

表示“有某种想法”的主观意愿的语句。可以用表示预感的hunch代替feeling，变成have a hunch。不过，have feelings for则表示“对某人有兴趣”。

“把情人节忘得干干净净的男生变得坐立不安”

I have a feeling she's going to be very angry.

M·O·R·E

- I have a (the) feeling (that) S+V
  有……的想法，好像是……
- I have (strong) feelings for sb
  喜欢某人

I have a feeling that she is not going to show up.
我感觉她可能不会出现了。

I have a hunch he's lying to me. You don't think so?
我感觉他在和我说谎。你不觉得?

I have (strong) feelings for her.
我很喜欢她。

A: I have a feeling it will snow a lot today. 我感觉今天要下很多雪。
B: Me too. The sky looks very dark and stormy. 我也是。天空看起来很阴暗。

have time to (for) 有……的时间

表示有没有时间做某事，have time后面接+动词或for+名词就可以了。另外，time加上the，变成have the time的话，就表示询问时间。

“同学里长得最丑的人天天晚上来电话要和自己约会”

I don't **have time for** this. I have to get up early.

M·O·R·E

- have time to+动词(for)+名
  有时间做某事
- Do I have time to+动词（for+名词）?
  我有……的时间吗?
- Do you have time to+动词（for+名词）?
  你有时间……吗?

I don't **have time for** this right now.
我现在没时间。

Do you **have (some) time**? I need to talk to you.
你有点时间吗? 我得和你谈谈。

Do you **have time to** go there for me?
你有时间替我去趟那吗?

A: Do you have time to talk about the meeting? 你有时间聊聊会议的事吗?
B: Not this morning, but I am free after lunch. 今天早上不行，不过午餐之后可以。

have a question 有疑问

对某人有疑问时可以使用的表达，想要说明提问的对象就可以加for somebody，想要说明提问的内容就可以加about something。

“为了不去服兵役，生生拔下自己的门牙”

I have a question. Why did you do that?

I **have a question**. I need to ask you.
我有个问题，得问问你。

Have you got a minute? I **have a question for** you.
你有时间吗？我有个问题要问 。

I **have a question about** your report.
我想和你聊聊报告书的事情。

A: I have a question. Are we leaving early? 我有个问题，我们早点走吗？
B: Yes, we need to go downtown in a few hours. 恩，我们得尽快到达城镇。

have a problem 有问题，有不满

正如字面含义那样，表示有问题，即不满等情绪，如果没有任何不满或问题的话可以说have on problem with。

“花花公子式的男朋友还会和别的女生见面，断然地和他谈话”

I have a problem with you seeing other girls.

M·O·R·E

- have a (no) problem with sb (sth)
  对某人有（无）不满
- have a problem sb ...ing
  对某人做某事有不满
- Have you had any problems+ ...ing?
  ……方面有问题吗？

I **have no problem with** that.
我没问题。

What's with you? Do you **have a problem with** me?
你怎么了？你对我有不满？

Do you **have a problem with** that?
你对那个不满吗？

A: I have a problem. 我有点问题。
B: Really? What happened? 真的？怎么了？

have a chance 有机会

表示“有……的机会或可能性”，可以用with+名词或to+动词说明机会的具体内容。前文中提到的take a chance表示“抓住机会”，可以理解成冒一次险。

“原本想找个机会道歉，却始终错过机会”

I didn't **have a chance** to apologize to you for what I did.

M·O·R·E

- have a chance with
  有……的可能性
- have a chance to+动词 (of ...ing)
  有……的可能性

I think I **have a chance with** her.

我觉得我和她有可能。

I'm sorry I didn't **have a chance to** call.

很抱歉没能给你打电话。

We might actually **have a chance of** winning this.

我们可能有机会获胜。

A: Shall we go into one of these casinos? **我们找一家赌场进去吧?**

B: No. We don't have a chance of winning any money. **不，我们根本不可能赢钱。**

have a point 有道理，说的没错

have a point表示对主语的话与想法表示赞同，也可以用get取代have，point后面可以加there（在某一方面），变成have a point there。

“没有听明智的妻子的建议，胡乱投资，最终倾家荡产”

She **had a point**. I guess I should have listened to her.

That's true. You **have a point there**.

没错，你说的很对。

I think he might **have a point**.

我觉得他可能说的没错。

Do you **have a point**?

你有重点吗?

A: You're getting fat because you eat too much. **你吃太多了，瞧你胖的。**

B: You have a point. I need to go on a diet. **你说的没错，我得开始减肥了。**

have an appointment 有约

appointment不是朋友之间的约定，而是在医院（美容院）等场所的预约。have an appoinment后面加with somebody就表明约好的对象，也可以用to+动词表示预约的内容。

"之前有牙科的预约，该走了"

I have to go. I **have an appointment with** a dentist.

M·O·R·E

- have an appointment（with ... / to+动词）（与某人/某件事情）有约
- have an appointment 有约
- have a (no) plan 有无计划

I **have an appointment with** Mr. James.
我之前约好了詹姆斯先生。

I **have an appointment to** see Dr. Kim.
我之前约好了金大夫。

I'm afraid I **have another appointment**.
抱歉，我已经有约了。

A: What's the rush? 你怎么这么着急?

B: I have an appointment. And it's very important. 我有个约会。而且非常重要。

have no idea 不知道

have no idea与don't know表示相同的含义，I have no idea表示"我不知道"，如果想说明具体不知道的内容就可以用have no idea疑问词主语+动词或疑问词to do形态。

"整天看着电视购物的妻子看到什么眼睛都瞪得巨大"

Do you have any idea what this means?

M·O·R·E

- I have no idea（疑问词S+V/疑问词to do）不知道（是不是……）
- You have no idea（疑问词S+V/疑问词 to do）你不会知道……
- Do you have any idea（疑问词 S+V/疑问词 to do）? 你知道……吗?

I have no idea what it is.
我不知道这是什么。

I have no idea what you are talking about.
我不知道你在说什么。

I have no idea what to say.
我不知道该说什么。

You have no idea how much I miss her.
你不知道我有多想念她。

A: This room needs to be cleaned right away. 这间房间急需打扫。

B: I have no idea what made it so dirty. 真搞不明白，到底为什么会这么脏。

have enough 充分

表示“……充分”的have enough最基本的用法为+名词，of+名词或to+动词等。另外，I have had表示“足够了”，“已经厌倦了”。

“胖女朋友把5人份的牛排都吃光了，抚摸着鼓鼓的肚皮说道”

I hope you had enough to eat.

M·O·R·E

- have enough（+名词）某物充分
- have enough of+名词 ……足够了
- have enough to+动词 ……足够了
- I've had enough 足够了
- have had it (with) 厌倦了

Where's everybody? I don't **have enough** help.
其他人呢？我可没得到足够的帮助啊。

Get out of my face! I'**ve had enough of** you.
马上消失！受够你了。

That's enough! I'**ve had it**.
够了！已经受够了。

I'**ve had it with** you guys.
我受够你们了。

A: Would you like something from the grocery store? **你让我去商店带点什么吗？**

B: I have enough food right now. **我的食物足够了。**

have no doubt 没错，毋庸置疑

doubt表示疑心，疑惑，have no doubt表示“没有疑心”。可以单独使用I have no doubt，也可以用have no doubt that主语+动词形态。

“儿子在料理方面有着出众的天赋，爸爸鼓励道”

I have no doubt you're going to be a good chef.

M·O·R·E

- I have no doubt 没错
- have no doubt (that) S+V 没错

You're absolutely right. I **have no doubt**.
你说的没错，我深信不疑。

I **have no doubt** you'll do well.
你肯定做得很好。

I **have no doubt** that you're a good doctor.
我知道你是个出色的医生。

A: They have no doubt Sarah will become their manager. **他们确信莎拉会成为他们的经理。**

B: Do they think she is a good person to work for? **他们觉得她适合做这份工作吗？**

have fun 有趣

表示“有趣地，度过愉快的时光”等，在日常生活中使用的频率很高。想要表达“过得非常愉快”时可以用have a lot of fun，分手时想要祝福对方“祝你过得愉快”时可以说Have (a lot of) fun!

“宽容的未婚妻问丈夫，单身派对过得怎么样”

Did you have fun at the bachelor party last night?

M·O·R·E

- have much fun
  很有趣
- have fun with sb
  与某人度过快乐的时光

It **was fun having** you. I enjoyed myself very much.
和你在一起很快乐。我度过了非常美妙的时光。

Did you **have fun with** her?
你和她在一起快乐吗?

I don't want to go. I'**m having fun**.
我不想走，正玩得起兴呢。

A: All of the children had fun at the park. 所有小朋友都在公园度过了快乐的时光。
B: It was a beautiful day to be playing outside. 真是一个适合户外活动的天气啊。

have a good day (time) 祝你过得愉快

一天不如意时可以说I had a bad day，一天很开心时可以说I am having a good time。当然，也可以像have a nice trip一样，接除了day (time)以外的其他名词。

“转学的孩子第一天放学回家，母亲担心地问道”

Did you have a good day at school?

M·O·R·E

- have a good time with sb
  和某人玩得愉快
- I had a big day.
  今天是个非常重要的日子。
- I had a bad day.
  今天真倒霉。

I've got to get some sleep. I **had a rough day**.
我得去睡觉了。今天过得很累。

I'**m having a hard time** these days.
我最近过得不好。

I'm just here with my friends **having a good time**.
我和朋友们在一起玩得很嗨。

Did you guys **have a good time** in Japan?
你们在日本玩得怎么样?

A: I'll be traveling in Europe for three weeks. 我要去欧洲旅行三个星期。
B: Have a good time. I really envy you. 祝你玩得愉快，说实话，羡慕死你了。

have a hard time 在……上碰壁

正如字面含义一样，有了一段非常痛苦的时光(hard time)，表示困难的状况。想要说明具体缘由的话，可以在hard time后面接 ...ing。

"碰到了好久没见的朋友，诉苦说上个月非常辛苦。"

I've been okay, but I **had a hard time** last month.

M·O·R·E

- have a hard time ...ing
  ……很痛苦

You **have a hard time** listening, huh?
你在听力方面花了很大功夫吧?

I **had a hard time** trying to find you.
我花了好大功夫才找到你。

I'**m** still **having a hard time** accepting the decision.
我至今也很难接受那个决定。

I'**m having a hard time** concentrating on what you're saying to me.
我很难听懂你所说的话。

A: Why did he come home early from England? 他为什么提前从英国回来了?
B: He had a hard time adjusting to English food. 他对英国的食物很不适应。

have second thoughts 重新想想

表示"重新想想"的意思。为了修改已经决定的事情而提出建议。如果说not give it a second thought的话就表示"不会重新考虑"，即"不担心某事"。

"马上就要结婚了，可恶的未婚夫却天天大醉而归"

I'**m having second thoughts about** the wedding.

M·O·R·E

- have second thoughts about
  重新考虑
- not give it a second thought
  不担心
- on second thought
  仔细想想

We'**re having second thoughts about** it.
我们正在重新考虑。

Don't **give it a second thought**.
不要担心。

On second thought, I will have another cup of coffee.
重新想了想，我还是再来一杯咖啡吧。

A: Did you decide not to get married to Tim? 你决定不和提姆结婚了?
B: Yes, I had second thoughts about our relationship.恩，我再三考虑了我们俩之间的关系。

have no choice 没有选择的余地

字面含义为没有选择(choice)的余地，表示身不由己的状况，当要表示“不得不做某事”时要使用have no choice but to+动词的形式。

“在抓捕小偷的过程中，小偷反抗到底，警察不得不动用武力”

I had no choice but to use force.

I'm afraid you really **have no choice**.
恐怕你没有选择的余地了。

You **have no choice** in this matter. You just do what you're told.
在这个问题上你没有选择的余地。你就照着我说的做就行。

It's not fair. I'm telling you I **had no choice**.
这不公平，我跟你说过我没有选择的余地。

A: It's too difficult to get a good grade in math class. 在数学课上拿高分太难了。

B: You have no choice. You must get a good grade. 你没有选择。你不得不拿一个高分。

have one's word 相信某人的话

表示“相信某人的话”，可以用promise取代word。另外，give one's word表示“承诺”，have a word (with)表示“与某人交谈”，have words with表示“与某人争论”等。

“这次升职再一次失败的金代理，火冒三丈地去找部长单独谈话”

Can I have a word with you, alone?

M·O·R·E

- have one's word
  相信某人的话
- have a word with
  与某人交谈
- have words with
  与某人争论

I won't do that again. You **have my word**.
我不会再那样了。我向你保证。(= You have my promise.)

I **give you my word**. You will not get a paycut.
我向你保证，你的工资不会减少的。

Do I **have your word** on that?
你对我承诺了吗?

Can I **have a word with** you outside, please?
我能和你去外面谈一谈吗?

A: Do you promise to keep this secret? 你发誓会坚守这个秘密吗?

B: You have my word. I won't tell anyone. 我向你保证，我不会告诉任何人的。

I've had ... 我做过……

I have是现在完成时态，如果说have had的话就表明“从之前开始就一直……”。相反，I've been是I'm ... 的现在完成时态，表示“曾是……”。

“明明天天到处拈花惹草，却不承认”

I've never had a one-night stand in my life.

M·O·R·E

- I've had+名词
  我一直做……
- I've never had+名词
  我没有做过……
- I've been+名词（形容词）
  我之前是……
- It has been+时间+since
  有一段时间……
- How long have you+pp?
  你……多久了?

I've had some personal problems.
我有一些个人问题。

It has been a while since you and I played golf.
我们俩好久没打高尔夫了。

How're you doing? **It has been** a while.
过得怎么样? 好久没见了。

How long **have you been** married?
你结婚有多久了?

A: Is a dog a good animal to keep as a pet? 狗适合当宠物养吗?
B: Sure. I've had dogs since I was a little kid. 嗯，我从很小的时候就开始养狗了。

More Expressions

- **have company** 有人陪同
  I **have company**. 我有人陪同。
- **have money** 有钱
  I **have a lot of money** on me now.
  我现在有很多钱。
- **have no reason to** 没有道理……
  She **has no reason to** hurt me.
  她没道理伤害我。
- **have a heart** 同情
  That was a little girl! Don't you **have a heart**?
  她可是个小女孩，你连一点同情心都没有啊?
- **have the nerve (guts)** 有勇气
  You don't **have the guts**. 你没有勇气。
- **have every right to+动词** 可以做某事
  You **have every right to** be angry with me. 你有足够的理由对我生气。

More Expressions

- **don't have a clue** 完全不知道

  He **doesn't (even) have a clue**.

  他一点都不知道。

- **have everything somebody needs** 得到某人想要的全部

  I **have everything I need**.

  我已经有了我想要的一切。

- **have a baby** 生孩子

  I'm going to **have a baby**.

  我要生孩子。

  What did she **have**? (It's a girl.)

  她生的是男是女？（是个女孩。）

- **have faith in** 相信……

  I **have faith in** you. 我相信你。

- **have an appetite for** 喜欢……

  She **has an appetite for** rap music.

  她喜欢说唱音乐。

- **have a shot** 试一试

  Let me **have a shot** at it. 让我试试吧。

- **have sb over for dinner (to dinner)** 招待某人享用晚餐

  We're going to **have you over for dinner** sometime. 我们会请你吃饭的。

- **have a call** 打电话

  You **have a phone call**. 有你的电话。

  I **have a call** for you. 有人找你。

- **have it in for somebody** 讨厌某人

  I know. She **has it in for** me.

  我知道，她讨厌我。

- **have one's own way** 按照某人的方式做

  I'll **have my own way** on this project.

  我会按照自己的方式做这个项目的。

- **have (got) a thing for** 喜欢某人

  I think he **has got a thing for** her.

  我觉得他喜欢她。

You have the wrong number.
您打错了。

We have a bad connection.
电话信号不太好。

He's a has-been. 他风光不在。

Now there you have me.
现在，你赢了。

Nice place you have here.
很高兴你能来。

I have butterflies in my stomach.
我心跳得砰砰响。

I have a flat tire. 爆胎了。

She has an ax to grind.
她也有别的心思。

She has an eye for it. 她很有眼光。

I had a little fender-bender.
有过小小的摩擦。

You can't have it both ways.
你不能尽善尽美。

What do we have here? 怎么回事？

I have a surprise for you.
我有个惊喜要送给你。

I have no excuse. 我没话说。

You have it right. 你说得没错。

什么都要做

Make

主要表示制作的动词make还有“料理”(cook)，“准备”(prepare)，“成为……”(become)等含义。不过make最明显的特征是作祈使动词“使……”(force)，比前文中的have，get的语气更强。另外，像make a speech，make a call一样，make可以将动名词作为宾语形成多样的短语。

基本概念

1 制作，料理，准备，挣（钱），达成（目标）

Can you make a cup of coffee for me? 能帮我冲一杯咖啡吗?

Can you make the party? 能组织一次聚会吗?

Do you know who makes this product? 你知道这产品是谁做的吗?

2 （经过努力）成为，（自然）成为……

Three and five make eight. 3加5等于8。

Jane will make an excellent model. 简会成为优秀的模特的。

3 使……（make sb (sth)+动词）

Let me make you feel better. 我会让你好受点儿的。

4 使做某事（make sb (sth)+名词（形容词））

You made her upset. 你让她生气了。

Don't make me unhappy. 别让我不开心。

make somebody (sth)+动词 使某人做某事

“make+宾语+动词原形”形态是典型的祈使句型。比具有相同含义的have或get的语气更重，因此make表示一种强制性，无论宾语愿不愿意，都要按照主语的意愿行事。

“儿子的考试成绩一落千丈，被手拿高尔夫球杆的爸爸拖进了书房”

Don't make me go in there!

M·O·R·E

- make it work
  使运转
- make it happen
  使发生

Don't **make me laugh**!
别逗我！

There are ways to **make this work**.
肯定有办法让它动起来的。

You'll **make it happen**. I'm sure about that.
你肯定能成功，我对此坚信不疑。

This sauce is so spicy; it'**s making my mouth burn**.
这酱很辣，我的嘴唇都快爆开了。

A: My television has been broken for a week. 我的电视机坏了一个星期了。
B: Let me look at it. I can make this work. 让我瞧瞧，我能把它修好。

make somebody feel 让某人（的心情）变成……

这是make动词语句中最常用的形态之一。make sb feel+形容词表示“使某人的心情……”，“让某人感觉……”。主语可以是具体人物，也可以是that，it等。

“啤酒肚鼓鼓的中年男友看着像斯巴达勇士”

You're just saying that to make me feel better.

M·O·R·E

- make me feel+形容词
  让我心情……
- make you feel+形容词
  让你心情……
- Don't make me feel ...
  不要让我……

It **makes me feel** great.
因为那事，我心情很好。

You're amazing. You **make me feel** special.
你真不可思议，总让我觉得你是个特别的人。

Don't **make me feel** bad.
不要破坏我的心情。

I'm in a very bad mood. **Make me feel** better.
我心情不好，安慰安慰我吧。

A: Does your boyfriend make you feel happy? 你男朋友让你幸福了吗？
B: Yes. He's my favorite person in the world. 嗯，他是我这世界上最喜欢的人了。

What makes you think ... ? 什么会那么想?

同样是“make+宾语+动词原形”的祈使动词典型语句。字面翻译为“什么让你想……？”，可以理解为“为什么会那么想？”，“怎么那么想？”等询问理由的表达。

“在男朋友钱包里发现了前任女友的照片，开始追问起来，男友称那不是爱情”

Are you trying to **make me think that** you didn't love her?

M·O·R·E

- What makes you think so?
  为什么那么想?
- What makes you think (that) S+V?
  为什么会那么想?
- It (That) makes me think (hat) S+V
  这让我不得不觉得……（我有……的想法）

What makes you think we can live together?
你为什么觉得我们能住在一起?

What makes you think he's seeing someone?
你为什么会觉得他在和别人交往?

What makes you think she did that?
你为什么会觉得是她做的?

Well, **it makes me think that** I could love you.
好，这让我觉得我可以爱你了。

A: It's obvious that he knows something. 很明显，他知道一些事情。
B: What makes you think so? 是什么让你那么想的?

make oneself clear 使明确

make oneself+形容词/分词/副词形态表示“自己陷入某种状态”。make oneself clear是让对方再次确认有没有明白自己的话，可以用understood替代clear。

“明明身患高血压，却天天抽烟的患者”

You have to stop smoking. Do I **make myself clear**?

M·O·R·E

- make oneself clear
  让某人理解某人的话
- make oneself understood
  让某人理解
- make oneself at home (comfortable)
  让某人随意

Do I **make myself clear**?
清楚我说的话了吗?

I didn't **make myself clear**. Let me say that again.
我没说清楚。重新说一遍吧。

Can he **make himself understood** in Japanese?
他能听懂一些日语吗?

Come in and **make yourself at home**.
进来吧，当成自己家就行。

A: No one understood what Jim was saying. 没人听得懂吉姆说的话。
B: He must make himself clear to all of us. 他必须让我们所有人都明白才行。

make somebody (sth)+形容词（名词） 使某人……

这同样是一种祈使动词的用法。“make+宾语”后面接的不是动词而是形容词或名词。表示使宾语……，恋人之间经常会说到You make me happy（有你在很幸福）等等。

“把人请到家里，却旁若无人地打起电话来”

You'**re making me** really **uncomfortable**, so I've got to go.

M·O·R·E

- make sb angry (mad) 让某人生气
- make sb sick 让某人厌恶
- make sb crazy 使某人崩溃

She really **makes me angry**! I have to break up with her.
她真的让我很生气！我必须得和她分手了。

Can you **make it mild**?
你能不能听话?

Don't ever do that again! That **makes me sick**.
再也不要那样了！真让我恶心。

It'll only **make a bad situation worse**.
这只能让事情更糟。

What **makes you so special**?
是什么让你变得如此特别?

What **makes you so sure** I don't have talent?
你凭什么坚信我没有才华?

That'**s making me crazy**! I'm out of here.
这真让我崩溃，我走了。

We ran out of time. Please **make it short**.
我们没时间了，请快点说。

Please **make the slices of bread** really **thick**.
请将面包切成厚片。

A: Please make it neat, short, and to the point. 请简短地表达重点。
B: Okay, how short should I make it? 好吧，我应该说得多简短呢?

A: The cost of school keeps going higher and higher. 学费一直在涨。
B: I know. The increase in cost makes me angry.
就是，正因为学费的问题，我越来越生气。

A: Paul said that he wants to take you out on a date. 保罗说他想和你约会。
B: I'll never go out with him. Paul makes me sick.
我绝对不会和他约会的。一想到保罗我就恶心。

make it right 矫正，好好弄

这是make ...+形容词的用法之一。make it right表示矫正其中的it，可以用来表达对某事物的矫正。

"同学通过作弊不小心得了第一名，赶紧劝他自首"

You'd better make it right if you still have a chance.

You've done a horrible thing, and you have to **make it right**.
是你做出了那么可怕的事情，你应该负责。

I've made a lot of mistakes. I'm going to **make them right**.
我犯下了很多过错，我会一个个纠正的。

That doesn't **make it right**.
那也不能正当化。

A: We argued over the wedding for a long time. 我们在结婚问题上争论了好长一段时间。

B: Make it right with your girlfriend. Buy her some flowers. 好好和你女朋友商量，给她买点鲜花。

make somebody something 为某人做……

为他人做料理时可以在make somebody后面接想要做出的行为或事物等。

"骗子们最常使用的诈骗手法"

I am going to make you a very rich man.

M·O·R·E

- make sb sth
  为某人做（料理）……
- make you sb
  让某人变成……的人，接受某人

If you want I can **make you** some macaroni and cheese for dinner.
如果你想吃的话，我可以给你做点奶酪。

I am going to **make you** some coffee.
我给你冲点咖啡吧。

I'll **make you** something, dad.
我给你做点东西吧，老爸。

A: I want to eat some food right now. 我现在想吃点东西。

B: I'll make you a sandwich and some soup. 我给你弄点三明治和汤吧。

make an effort 努力

在英语会话中，比起动词本身，更愿意用动词的名词形式来表达含义。像前文中的have，take，give一样，make也能造出各种各样的短语。

"在无法释怀的两个男生中间徘徊的女孩"

You have to **make a choice**. You can't have both men.

M·O·R·E

- make an agreement 达成协议(agree)
- make an attempt 试图(attempt)
- make a choice 做出选择(choose)
- make a confession 老实交代(onfess)
- make an excuse 找理由(excuse)
- make an offer 提供(offer)
- make a proposal 提议(propose)
- make a reservation 预约(reserve)
- make an announcement 通告(announce)
- make a mistake 犯下错误(mistake)
- make a speech 做演说(speak)
- make a contribution 做出贡献(contribute)

I have to **make a speech** next week.
我下周得做一次演讲。

It's time for you to **make a choice**.
你该做个抉择了。

Finally, I **have made a choice**. I'm not going.
我终于做出了个决定，我不去了。

We can **make an exception** this one time.
这次我们网开一面。

It's a private party. I can not **make an exception**.
这是个私人宴会，不能有例外。

I have **a confession to make**. You didn't cause the accident.
我有些事情要说。引起这次事故的人不是你。

I've got **a confession to make**. I'm not your mother.
我得老实交代了，我不是你亲生母亲。

Are you here to **make a contribution** to my campaign?
你是来助我选举的吗?

I'm here to **make a big announcement**.
我是来做一个重大报告的。

My father **made me an offer** that I couldn't refuse.
我爸给我提出了一个难以抗拒的提议。

A: We can go to Hawaii or to Tokyo. 我们可以去夏威夷或东京。
B: Why don't you make the choice for us? 你帮我们决定呗。

A: I'm sorry that my homework was turned in late. 很抱歉，作业交晚了。
B: I'll make an exception now, but never again. 这次就算个例外，下不为例了。

A: I think we need to make an offer on the house. 我觉得我们得申请买那座房子。
B: The last thing that we want to do is make the wrong decision. 我最不想做出错误的决定了。

make a reservation 预约

想要预约时间、场所或人员的话，可以用for，at。另外，have a reservation是通过make a reservation而已经预约好的状态，而make an appointment则表示与某人有约。

"结婚纪念日预约了第一次去的高级中国餐馆"

Honey, I made a reservation at China Garden.

M·O·R·E

- I'd like to make a reservation ...
  我想预约……
- make an appointment (with)
  与某人相约

What time can we **make a reservation** for?

我们什么时候能预约?

I'd like to **make a reservation** for eight people at six o'clock tonight.

我想预约，晚上6点，一共8个人。

I already **made a reservation**.

我已经预约好了。

I'm calling to **make an appointment with** Dr. Choo.

我正在打电话和邱医生预约时间。

A: The restaurant looks crowded tonight. 今天晚上饭馆人很多啊。

B: I should have made a reservation for us. 本应该提前预约的。

make a difference 有差别，重要

make a difference表示"有差别"，也可以表示"重要"。另外，否定形式make no difference (not ... any difference)表示没有差别，"无论哪一方都无所谓"，"没关系"等。

"铁公鸡第一次组织派对，却没有人光顾"

A few more people aren't going to make a difference.

M·O·R·E

- make a difference (to sb)
  和某人有关系，重要
- make no difference
  完全无关，没关系
- It's going to make a difference.
  肯定有差异的。
- That makes a difference.
  肯定有不同。

What **difference** does it **make**?

那又能有什么不同?

It's **not** going to **make any difference**.

没有任何关系。

I don't care. It **makes no difference to** me.

我不在乎，这对我来说无所谓。

It's going to **make a big difference**.

肯定会有巨大的差异的。

A: Should I wash the car this afternoon? 我今天下午需要洗车吗?

B: No. It won't make a difference because it's going to rain. 不用了。马上就要下雨了，洗不洗都一样。

make a mistake 失误

想要说明失误的具体内容的话就可以写成make a mistake+... ing的形态。另外，请通过以下例句记住，在说完自己失误(made a mistake)的事情以后，应该怎么把话接下去。

"嫌自己的薪水涨幅不大，去找老板理论"

I think you're making a big mistake.

M·O·R·E

- make a big (huge) mistake
  犯下（巨大的）错误
- make a mistake+... ing
  犯下……的错误

We **made a huge mistake** telling her about that.
我们不该告诉她那些事情。

I **made a mistake**. I admitted it.
我承认我犯错了。

I **made a mistake**. It's my fault.
是我的失误，都是我的错。

I **made a mistake**. I should have told you.
我错了，早应该告诉你的。

A: This math problem looks like it is all wrong. 这道数学题好像完全错了。
B: Maybe I made a mistake when doing it. 我可能做错了。

make a deal 交易，妥协

"与某人交易"是make a deal with sb，Let's make a deal表示"我们就这么办吧"。交易的具体内容要放在接下来的文章中或者使用make a deal to do（决定交易……）形态。

"正想交易，不料对方一语不发"

I can't make a deal if you keep your mouth shut.

M·O·R·E

- make a deal with sb
  与某人交易（妥协）
- make a deal to+动词
  决定交易（妥协）某事

Let's **make a deal** never to fight over it again.
我们以后都不要吵架了。

I'll **make a deal** with you. If you lie to me, I will lie to you.
我跟你说好了，如果你骗我，我就骗你。

I **made a deal** with the boss. He's not going to fire me.
我和老板说好了，他不会炒我鱿鱼的。

A: I am ready to sell my house. 我准备把房子卖了。
B: Let's make a deal. I want to buy it. 我们做个交易吧，我正想买呢。

make a call 打电话

make a call表示打电话，take a call则表示接电话。如果在和对方交谈时突然有重要的电话打进来，就可以说I have to take this call，来请求对方的谅解。

“陪着母亲和女朋友去电影院，突然不见了女朋友”

Your girlfriend went to **make a call**. She'll be back soon.

M·O·R·E

- make a call
  打电话
- take a call
  接电话

I have to go **make a call**. I'll be back.
我得去打个电话了，马上就回来。

She takes out her phone to **make a call**.
她拿出电话拨起号来。

I **made a call to** the life insurance agent yesterday.
我昨天给保险公司打电话了。

A: This party doesn't have many people. 这次聚会来的人不多。
B: Let me make a call. I'll invite some friends. 我打个电话，叫几个朋友过来。

make sense 说得通

make sense一般表示事物主语that或it称为主语，变为“能够理解”，“说得通”。否定形式make no sense或not make any sense则表示“根本说不通”。像“我理解不了”，“你理解不了”一样将人物作为理解的主语时，就可以用make sense to somebody。

“女朋友口口声声说自己能飞上天，对这种无稽之谈的反应”

Your girlfriend can fly? How does that **make any sense**?

That **makes sense**.
说得有道理。

It **doesn't make any sense**.
根本说不通。

Does that **make any sense** to you?
你听懂了吗?

A: Does this e-mail make any sense? 这个邮箱能理解吗?
B: It does sound a little bit strange. 听起来有点奇怪。

make sure 确认，明确某事

make sure表示“确认某事”。主要句型为Let me make sure that ... 用来再次确认对方所说的话,或正相反，可以用Please make sure that ... 的形态向对方表达“请明确……”，“一定要再次确认某事”等等。

“丈母娘担心自己的女儿，跟着小夫妻俩来度蜜月”

I followed you to **make sure** you were okay.

M·O·R·E

- Let me make sure that S+V
  我再确认一下……
- Please make sure (that) ...
  一定要确认……
- I want to make sure ...
  我想确认一下……
- I want you to make sure ...
  我希望你再次确认……

Make sure that you arrive on time tomorrow.
请确认你明天准时离开。

I'll **make sure that** I keep in touch.
我一定会联系你的。

I want to **make sure that** you're okay.
我想确定你过得很好。

A: Make sure that you arrive on time tomorrow. 请确认你明天准时到达。
B: Don't worry. I'll be there early. 不要担心，我会尽快到的。

make money 挣钱

make具有将目标“拿在手上”(gain or reach)的意思。因此make money表示“挣钱”，make a killing (fortune)表示“挣了很多钱”，make a living表示“挣生活费”。

“经常出入赌场的人的口头禅”

I'm here to **make money**.

M·O·R·E

- make money for
  为了……而挣钱
- make a fortune (killing)
  赚了一大笔钱

I **am making (some) money**.
我在挣钱。

They **made a killing** in Las Vegas.
他们在拉斯维加斯大赚了一笔。

I have to **make money** for my education.
我得挣钱交学费。

A: What is the job with the highest salary? 什么工作给的薪水最高?
B: I think doctors make a lot of money. 我觉得应该是医生。

make time 腾出时间

make time是腾出时间做某事的意思。想要表达挤出时间做某事时可以用make time for+名词/...ing或make time to+动词的形态。

"丈夫经常大醉而归，并和妻子大吵，朋友劝道"

Make time to talk to your wife.

M·O·R·E

- make time for+名词(...ing) 腾出时间做某事
- make time to+动词 腾出时间做某事

I make time for her but I don't make time for you.
我虽然能为她腾出时间，但为了你可不行。

I have to make time to write my speech.
我得挤出时间写演讲稿了。

Make time. I'll be expecting you.
挤出点时间，我等你。

A: Always make time to be with your family. 总要挤出点时间陪陪家人。
B: Right. It's important to be close to them. 没错，和他们在一起很重要。

make love (to somebody) 与某人分享爱情

make love是一种委婉的表达，和have sex是同义词。做爱的对象就是make love to somebody。

"面对经常晚归的丈夫，妻子会说"

Our family needs your love.

M·O·R·E

- make love to sb 与某人做爱
- make a move on 追求某人(make a pass at)

He made love to me.
他向我求爱了。

Did he make a pass at you?
他骚扰你了？

They were made for each other.
他们是天生一对。

It's a match made in heaven.
真是天作之合。

A: What is the most romantic thing you've done? 你做过的最浪漫的事情是什么？
B: I made love to my girlfriend on our camping trip. 我和女朋友在野营的时候做过爱。

make it 做到，及时到达

在前文中有所提及，make具有“到达某处”(reach)的含义，最典型的例子就是make it，一般与地点介词to一起用，表示“及时到达”(arrive in time)，也可以用来比喻“成功”(succeed)。

“当最亲近的朋友因出差无法出席婚礼时”

That's too bad! I was really hoping he could **make it**.

M·O·R·E

- make it
  做到，成功
- make it to+名词
  准时到达
- make it on time
  准时到达
- make it on one's own
  独自完成，自立
- I made it!
  我做到了!
- You made it!
  你做到了!

I can't believe I **made it to** the gas station!
真不敢相信，我终于到了加油站!

When can you **make it**?
你什么时候能到?

Can you **make it**?
你能来（约会，聚会等）吗?

We're having a party for Sam. Hope you can **make it.**
我们要为山姆开个派对，希望你能来。

I won't be able to **make it to** the presentation.
我不能参加演出了。

Let's **make it** around four.
我们4点左右见面吧。

I almost didn't **make it to** the party.
我差点没赶上聚会。

I wonder if she **made it** on time.
不知道她能不能准时到。

He **made it big**.
他（事业）成功了。

You'll never **make it** on your own.
你肯定不能自己完成的。

A: Did you hear about the class meeting this weekend? 你听说过周末要开班会吗?
B: It sounds exciting. I hope all the students can make it. 听起来不错，希望所有学生都能到。

A: Ted is having a birthday party tonight. 泰德今晚要开一个生日派对。
B: I can't make it to the party. I'll be working. 我不能参加聚会了，我得不停地工作。

A: I wonder if she made it on time. 不知道她有没有准时到。
B: I'm sure she did. 我敢肯定她到了。

make it through 熬过，挺过（困难的状况）

make it through具有“挺过了痛苦而艰难的状况”的意思，可以单独使用，也可以用作make it through+名词形态。

“3个月内一定要减下20公斤的比赛中”

Some of us will **make it through**, and some won't.

Do you think I can **make it through** today without falling asleep?
你觉得我今天能够坚持不打瞌睡吗?

So don't worry about it. You'll **make it through**.
所以说不用担心，你肯定能挺过去。

The doctor said she wouldn't **make it through** the night.
大夫说，她熬不过今晚了。

He won't **make it through** the surgery unless we do our best.
如果我们没有尽全力的话，他肯定挺不过手术了。

A: Every time I see you, you're studying hard. **我每次看你，你都在认真地学习。**
B: I have to study to make it through medical school. **我一定要努力学习，考上医科大学。**

make a mess of 犯下……

表示“将……搞得一团糟”，在这里make表示“犯下”。相同含义的短语有表示“找麻烦的”make trouble，“捣蛋”的make a scene，“大吵大闹”的make a fuss about等等。

“明明已经签下了离婚协议书，却突然提出要重新开始过”

There's nothing you can do. Just don't **make a scene**.

M·O·R·E

- make a mess of
  将……搞得一团糟
- make trouble
  捣蛋，找麻烦
- make a scene
  捣乱

You **made a mess of** things.
你把事情搞得一团糟。

I'm afraid I'**ve made a mess** here on your desk.
我可能把你的桌子搞乱了。

Don't **make trouble** for me.
别找我麻烦。

Let's not **make a scene**. It's not worth it.
不要捣乱，也没有必要那么做。

A: The storm caused a lot of flooding in the countryside. **暴风雨导致乡下大片洪水泛滥。**
B: Yeah, it made a mess of the city, too. **是啊，在城里也是。**

make fun of 嘲笑

与表示“嘲笑”，“欺骗”的make a fool of具有相近的含义，make fun of后面可以接somebody或something。

“可以对那些总喜欢嘲笑别人身材矮小的人说一句”

Don't make fun of me because of my size!

M·O·R·E

- make fun of
  因某事嘲笑
- make a fool of
  嘲笑……

You're making fun of me?
你在嘲笑我?

Don't make fun of me, okay?
别嘲笑我，行不?

You're making a fool of yourself.
你在自欺欺人。

A: It must be difficult to be a fat person. 做一个胖人肯定很不容易。
B: Many people make fun of fat people. 很多人嘲笑胖子。

make nothing of 无视……

make与much, little, nothing等词结合表示不同的含义。make much of表示“重视某人”，如果用little取代much的话就表示“轻视某人”，如果使用nothing的话就表示“无视某人”。

“与恋人分手之后，在最后一次见面时说道 ... ”

I guess we can make the most of it.

M·O·R·E

- make nothing of
  无视……
- make much of
  重视某人
- make the most of
  最大限度利用……
- make the best of
  (在困境中)付出最大的努力，克服

I can't make anything of it.
我实在无法理解。

Oh, don't make nothing of his question.
不要假装没听见他的问话。

Why does he always make so little of my work?
为什么他总要无视我的工作?

When she stood me up again, I decided to make the best of it.
当她又一次让我大失所望时，我决定不再姑息。

A: The criminal left some clues during the robbery. 罪犯在抢劫过程中留下了一些线索。
B: Yes, but the police made nothing of the clues. 没错，不过警察们却无能为力。

make up one's mind 决心，决定

这是个比较眼熟的句式。make up one's mind用在好坏立场分明的情况，表示“决心做某事”。用一个单词概括就是decide，还可以表示为make a decision。

“朋友总抱怨自己的老板太苛刻，天天喊着要辞职，不过始终做不出决定”

I haven't **made a decision** yet.

I haven't **made up my mind** yet.
我还没做出决定呢。

Hurry up and **make up your mind**.
抓紧时间做决定。

Make up your mind. What time is okay for you?
快点决定，你几点可以？

Did you **make up your mind** about what you're going to do?
你决定要做什么了吗？

A: Are you going to join our team? 你要加入我们队？
B: I haven't made up my mind yet. 我还没决定呢。

M·O·R·E

- make up one's mind
  决定(= decide)
- make a decision
  决定(= decide)

make out 理解，假装，亲热

make out具有很多含义，如“看懂，听懂”(see, hear, or understand with difficulty)，“成功”，“假装是……”等。另外，还能表达“亲热”。

“医生充满了过度的使命感，对待患者过于亲切”

You can't **make out with** your patients.

We can barely **make out** what they're saying.
我们基本上听不懂他们在说什么。

Don't lie to me and **make out** that you don't know what I'm talking about.
不要对我说谎，不要假装没听到我说的话。

I want to **make out with** my girlfriend.
我想和女朋友亲热。

A: How did you make out at the doctor's office? 医生说什么？
B: He told me that I'm in really good health. 他告诉我身体状态很不错。

M·O·R·E

- make out sth (that)
  假装……
- make out with
  做好……
- make sth out
  了解，理解
- make out with sb
  与某人亲热

make up 组成，假装，准备，化妆，和解(with)

make up具有很广泛的含义，在日常生活中经常会用到，表示“编造谎话”，“和解”，“化妆”等。另外，be made up of表示“由……构成”。

“女生们不想让别人看到自己的素颜”

I'm going to go put my make-up on.

M·O·R·E

- make sth up
  假装，准备
- make up
  化妆 (put on one's makeup)
- make up with sb
  与某人和解

I made up a story about that.
那个故事是我编造的。

Is that something you're making up?
你在编瞎话吗?

He didn't recognize me at first without my make-up.
我没化妆时，他第一眼没认出我。

She was trying to make up with you. You should go eat with her.
她想和你和好。你应该和她吃顿饭。

A: I can't tell my parents that we were drinking beer. 我不能告诉父母我喝酒的事情。

B: Make up a story. Tell them you were at the library. 编个瞎话呗。告诉他们你在图书馆。

make up for something 补偿，罚款

用别的东西补偿丢失的东西。make up for后面接上丢掉的东西就可以了。另外，make it up to somebody表示“因自己犯下的错误向对方表示真挚的道歉”。

“人都快打死了，却掏出10美元作为补偿金，说道”

It won't make up for what I did to you, but it's the best I can do.

M·O·R·E

- make up for the lost time
  弥补失去的时间
- make up for the past
  补偿过去
- make it up to sb
  补偿……

That'll give us a chance to make up for lost time.
是补偿逝去时间的时候了。

I'll make up for it tomorrow, okay? I promise.
我明天会补偿的，好不好? 我发誓。

Is there anything I can do to make it up to you?
有什么我可以补偿你的吗?

Let me make it up to you. I'll carry your stuff.
我来补偿你吧，我给你搬东西。

A: Why do I need to work on Sunday? 我为什么要在星期天上班?

B: You have to make up for the days you were absent. 你得弥补你请假的日子。

make do with (without) 用……弥补（不用……弥补）

牙坏了就得补，make do with就表示用某样东西弥补原本需要的东西。

"在网吧玩得昏天暗地，连饭都没顾上吃，回家一看只有一片面包"

I'll make do with what I have here.

M·O·R·E

- make do with 用……弥补
- make do without 不用……弥补

I had to make do with milk in my coffee.
我不得不把牛奶当成伴侣冲咖啡。

You'll have to make do with it.
你必须要弥补它。

I'm afraid you'll have to make do with me.
恐怕你得补偿我了。

A: The economy has been bad all over the world. 全球的经济走势不太好。

B: It's important to make do with what you have. 凭借你的所有支撑下去很重要。

More Expressions

- **be made of (from)** 由……制成

  It's made from eggs! 这是用鸡蛋做的！

- **make friends with** 与某人做朋友

  You have to make friends with him.
  你必须和他做朋友。

- **make ends meet** 收支平衡

  We're barely making money enough to make ends meet.
  我们基本上收支平衡。

- **make off with** 携带……逃跑

  They made off with my MP3 player.
  他们拿着我的MP3逃跑了。

- **make a face** 皱眉

  Don't make a face. 不要皱眉。

- **make a run for it** 逃跑，逃避

  Let's make a run for it.
  我们赶紧逃跑吧。

- **make a day (night) of it** 一天过得愉快

  With your son, you'll make a day of it.
  和你儿子好好玩一天。

That makes two of us.
我也一样（我也那么认为）。

You've got it made.
这次成功都要归功于你。

You've made your point. 你赢了。

Haste makes waste. 欲速则不达。

Make mine the same. 我也要一样的。

该知道的都知道了

Know

这个词是基本上所有人都知道的动词。知道或不知道某事时都会用到 know，这种情况下就只使用了字面上的含义。衍生的短语或句式虽然较少，但 know anything about ... , I know that ... , You don't know that ... 等都是实际生活中经常使用到的表达。好好记住这些，会话就会容易很多。

基本概念

1 知道，认识

Do I know you? 我们认识吗?

Do you know that? 你知道那个吗?

2 对……很了解(of, about)

Do you know about that? 你了解那件事吗?

Do they know about each other? 他们相互了解吗?

3 know that (what) 主语+动词 知道

I know she made a mistake. 我知道她犯下了过错。

My God! I don't know what to say. 天啊！真不知道该说什么。

I know where you live. 我知道你住在哪里。

know it (that) 知道

虽然这个表达不算是短语，但可以将之前提到过的事情取代为it或that，变成know that (it)的形态，实际生活中经常会用到。

“自称是有名人士的经纪人，却被人戳穿”

I knew it. You're not even an agent.

M·O·R·E

- I know that (it).
  我知道。
- I knew that (it).
  我就知道。
- I don't know that.
  我不知道。
- You know that (it).
  你知道的。
- You (already) knew that.
  你（已经）知道了。

I didn't **know that**. But I thought you **knew that**
我不知道，不过我以为你知道呢。

I didn't know you **knew that**.
我不知道你知道。

How do you **know that**?
你是怎么知道的？

A: You're not allowed to have drinks out here. 你不能把饮料带出去。
B: Oh, I didn't know that. 哦，我不知道。

know somebody 认识某人

“认识某人”表示非常熟悉(be familiar with)。know somebody very well表明“与某人非常熟悉”，而know each other表示“互相认识”。

“恋爱中的男女都想找一个外遇，不料在相亲会上见面”

Do you two know each other?

M·O·R·E

- know sb very well
  非常了解某人
- know each other
  互相认识
- know sb as (for)
  知道某人为……
- know sb from
  从……认识到某人，……时的朋友

Do I **know you**? / Don't I **know you**?
我认识你吗？/ 我不认识你吗？

Where do I **know you** from?
我是从哪儿认识你的？

You look familiar. Do I **know you from** somewhere?
你看起来很面熟，我之前在哪儿见过你吗？

I think I **know you from** college.
我觉得在大学时见过你。

A: Is this your first time to meet Cindy? 这是你第一次见辛迪吗？
B: No, but I don't know her very well. 不是，不过我对她不是很了解。

know anything about+名词（否定，疑问句形式）完全不知道……

这是在否定句或疑问句中所使用到的表达方式。在否定句中用来强调否定内容，表示“完全，毫不”等，而在疑问句中表示“对某事了解吗？”。

“在开始赌钱之前，给对方下一颗定心丸”

I **don't know anything about** playing poker.

M·O·R·E

- I don't know anything about ...
  我对……完全不了解。
- I don't know any+名词
  我不知道任何……
- Do you know anything about ... ?
  对……你知道一些吗?
- Do you know any+名词？
  你有知道的……吗?

I **didn't know anything about** this, I swear.
对此我一无所知，真的。

You **don't know anything about** me, do you?
你完全不了解我，是吧?

Do you **know any** good restaurants?
你知道哪儿有不错的餐厅吗?

Do you **know anything about** the virus?
你对病毒了解吗?

A: Do you know anything about chemistry? 你对化学了解吗?
B: Yes, I studied chemistry in college. 嗯，我在大学学过化学。

know (that) 知道……

know后面加上（that 主语+动词），表示“知道……的事实或情况”。与know+名词唯一的不同就是所接的是从句而不是单词。

“妻子快要生了，丈夫却拿着离婚协议书说道”

I **know that** you're busy, but I need to talk to you right now.

Please stop. I **know that** you're lying to me.
算了吧，我知道你在骗我。

My fingers are crossed. I **know** you really want that job.
我替你祈祷，我知道你很需要那份工作。

I don't know that we can afford a Harley.
我不知道能不能买得起那辆哈雷摩托车。

Do you know that there's no liquor in this house?
你知道家里没有酒了吗?

A: Tina was very sick after dinner. 缇娜在用完餐之后非常不舒服。
B: I don't know that the food made her sick. 不知道是不是因为食物的问题。

know when (where) 知道……

这是利用各种疑问词变成I know what/why/how主语+动词的形态，比前文中提到的know that主语+动词的使用频率更高。只不过从句并不是倒序的形态，而是“疑问词+主语+动词”。尤其You don't know+疑问词主要用来抱怨、指责对方。具体例子为You don't know what it's like to+动词（你不知道这是什么）。

“已经有七个男孩了，却还要继续生，口口声声说要组个足球队才罢休”

You don't know what it's like to have a baby.

M·O·R·E

- I know what I'm doing.
  我知道我在干什么。
- I know what I'm saying.
  我知道我在说什么。
- I know what you're saying.
  我知道你在说什么（我也那么想）。
- I know what you're up to.
  我知道你在想什么。
- You know what I mean?
  你知道我在说什么吗?
- I don't know what you are getting at.
  我不知道你到底想要表达什么。
- I don't know what's keeping him.
  我不知道他为什么迟到。
- I know just how you feel.
  我知道你现在的心情。
- You don't know what (how) ...
  你不知道……
- You don't know what it's like to+动词
  你不知道这是什么样的

I **know** exactly **what** you need.
我很清楚你需要什么。

I don't want to be alone. You **know what** I'm saying?
我不想一个人待着。你明白了?

We never **know when** our life is going to change.
我们永远都不知道人生什么时候会改变。

I think I **know where** they came from.
我好像知道他们是从哪儿来的。

I don't even **know how** I feel about her yet.
我都不知道对她是什么感觉。

Do you **know when** the party is?
你知道聚会几点开始吗?

Do you **know where** the train station is located?
你知道火车站在哪儿吗?

You don't know that. You don't know me anymore.
你根本就不知道，你再也不懂我了。

You don't **know how much** I love you.
你不明白我有多么爱你。

A: Do you know when the train arrives? 你知道火车几点到吗?
B: It's scheduled to be here at 7 a.m. 应该是早上7点。

A: Do you know where the bookstore is? 你知道书店在哪儿吗?
B: You can't miss it. It's at the end of this street.
沿着这条路一直走下去，你肯定能看见。

A: I can help find your cat. 我可以帮你找到猫。
B: Thanks. I don't know where she is. 谢谢。我不知道她现在跑到哪里去了。

know when (how, where) to 知道……

这次是疑问词+to+动词成为know的宾语的情况。用作I don't know how(what) to ... 或Do you know how to ... ?就可以了。

"骗女朋友说很擅长滑雪，不料被她拉去滑雪场"

Frankly, I don't know how to ride a skateboard.

M·O·R·E

- don't know how (what) to+动词
  我不知道……
- Do you know how to+动词?
  你知道……吗?

Leave it to me. I know how to handle it.
交给我吧，我知道怎么操作。

I don't know how to say it in English.
我不知道怎么用英语说这个。

I don't know what else to do.
我不知道该怎么用别的方法做。

I don't know what to do.
我不知道该做什么。

I don't know what to get her for her birthday.
想不出她生日应该给她买什么。

You shouldn't have. I don't know how to thank you.
你大可不必，我不知道该怎么谢你。

How stupid I am! I don't know what to say.
我真是笨！竟然不知道该说些什么。

I don't know what to say. I really appreciate it.
真不知道该说点什么，我很感激你。

Do you know how to use it?
你知道怎么使用吗?

Where's Central Park? Do you know how to get there?
中央公园在哪儿? 你知道怎么去那儿吗?

My computer broke. Do you know how to fix it?
我的电脑坏了，你知道怎么修理吗?

A: We're playing cards. Want to join us? 我们在打牌，想一起玩吗?
B: Sure. I know how to play this game. 好的，我知道怎么玩。

A: Here's the present I got for your birthday. 这是我给你的生日礼物。
B: I don't know how to thank you. 真不知道该怎么答谢。

A: I don't know what to do. 我不知道该做什么。
B: You want my advice? 需要建议吗?

let somebody know 告诉某人……

表示对某人告诉接know后面的部分。让我知道可以说let me know，让你知道可以说let you know，也可以单独用一个let me know。

"老鼠的妈妈会对谁说这种话呢，猫还是老鼠？"

I want to let you know how much I care about you.

M·O·R·E

- Let me know if (what) ...
  告诉我……
- I'll let you know ...
  我会告诉你……
- I'd like (I want) to let you know ...
  我想让你知道……

If you need any help, **let me know**.
如果需要帮助，随时告诉我。

Let me know if she likes it, okay?
告诉我她喜不喜欢，好不好？

I just want to **let you know that** we are getting married.
我只想跟你说，我们要结婚了。

A: Let me know if you have any questions. 如果有问题，随时可以提问。
B: I'll keep that in mind. 好的。

know the answer (to) （知道……的答案）

表示知道……的答案，就算不是具体的问题，也可以用来表示"我知道那个"。一般会将前文中提到的问题当成that，用作know the answer to that。

"老板暗示部下升职，把他调到了外地，部下却不解人情地继续工作"

He still doesn't know the whole story.

M·O·R·E

- know the whole story
  很了解…… 掌握……
- He knows what's what.
  他知道真相。

I think I **know the answer to** that.
我好像知道怎么回事。

I think I **know the answer to** this question.
我可能知道这道题的答案。

You **know the answer to** that.
你知道答案的。

You **know your way around** a gun.
你对枪支很了解。

A: When will we go home? 我们什么时候回家？
B: I don't know the answer to that question. 我不能确定。

not know the first thing about 对……一无所知

这是强调“对某事一无所知”的表达。about后面接上要表达的事实就可以了。相似的句型有not know the half of，not know a thing about等。只不过know a thing or two about表示“对某事非常了解”。

“这辈子根本没爬过小山的人竟然谈论起了攀登喜马拉雅山”

You don't know the first thing about climbing.

M·O·R·E

- You don't know the first thing about ...
  你完全不知道……
- I don't know the half of ...
  我不太了解……

I **don't know the first thing about** how to use it.
我完全不知道这个东西的使用方法。

You **don't know the half of** it.
你根本就不知道事态有多么严重。

I **know a thing or two about** playing computer games.
我非常了解电脑游戏。

A: Mary needs help with her computer. 玛丽的电脑坏了，需要帮助。
B: I don't know the first thing about computers. 我对电脑一无所知。

happen to know 偶然知道

happen to+动词表示“偶然……”，I happen to know表示“偶然知道”，Do you happen to know ... ?表示“你知道……吗？”等。

“整天健忘的人肯定要知道”

Do you happen to know where I put my glasses?

M·O·R·E

- I happen to know (about) sth ((that) S+V)
  我偶然知道了……
- Do you happen to koow (about) sth (that) S+V?
  你也许知道……

I **happen to know** you kissed her in the car.
我偶然知道你在车里亲了她。

Do you **happen to know** about Jane?
莫非你了解简?

Do you **happen to know** if there is a good restaurant around here?
你知道这附近哪儿有不错的餐厅吗?

A: Let's eat at an Italian restaurant. 我们去意大利餐馆吧。
B: I happen to know of a great place. 我正巧知道一个不错的地方。

know better than to 知道的比……多

know better than表示“知道的比……多”，“最起码知道……”，换句话说就是“没有那么蠢”。than后面可以接名词或to+动词。

“毫无顾虑地对收养的弟弟说出了真实情况”

You should **know better than to** let him know.

You **know better than** that.

你不至于那么蠢。

I **know better than** that.

该懂的我都懂了。

Of course, she **knew better than to** say this to her husband.

当然，她可没有蠢到把这些告诉她丈夫。

A: Your children are very well behaved. 你的孩子很有教养。

B: They know better than to act badly. 他们已经过了胡闹的年纪了。

as you (probably) know 正如……所知

as you know用来表示“正如你所知”。想要说“正如大家所知”的话就要说成as we know。you know则充当说话前的一种语气词，表示“我说”，“那个”等。另外，as far as somebody knows表示“只要某人知道”。

“虽然有着博士学位，却从来不炫耀，默默做自己的工作”

As far as I know, he hasn't talked about his job.

M·O·R·E

- as you (we) know
  正如你(我们)所知
- you know
  我说，那个，这个
- as far as sb knows
  只要某人知道

As you know, it's my job to interview people.

你也知道，我的工作就是见各种人。

You know, everything is going to be fine.

你知道，一切都会好的。

As far as I know she didn't show up at the party.

据我所知，她没有参加派对。

A: As far as I know they sent it yesterday. 据我所知，他们昨天送过来了。

B: Then it should arrive later today. 那应该在今天晚些时候到。

You know what? 你知道吗？依我看来

引起对方注意的表达You know what? 用在说惊人或有趣的消息之前。表示“你知道吗？”“我说”等等，也可以使用I'll tell you what, Guess what? You know something?

“突然想到了好主意，引起对方注意时”

You know what? I got an idea.

M·O·R·E

- You know something?
  你知道吗？
- I'll tell you what.
  我说。

You know what? Let's not talk.
我说，咱别说话了。

Guess what? I have a date with Cindy.
你猜怎么着？我和辛迪约会了。

I'll tell you what. How about we take a walk tonight?
我说，今天晚上出去走走怎么样？

You know something? I have a date with Gina.
知道不？我和吉娜约会了。

A: You know what? I just got promoted. 你知道吗？我升职了。
B: Good for you! You deserve it. 恭喜啊！是你应得的。

Not that I know of 据我所知可不是……

委婉地表达否定的方式，表示“据我所知不……”。另外，for all I know表示毫不关心，“不知道”，“不管我的事”，而before you know it则表示“在……知道之前”，即“马上”。

“女职员说谎，称自己被上司性骚扰，不过第三方证人说”

Not that I saw. He didn't even touch her.

M·O·R·E

- Not that I know of.
  据我所知可不是。
- Not that I remember.
  我印象里可不是。
- Not that I saw.
  据我看可不是。
- For all I know.
  管我什么事。
- Before you know it
  马上

Not that I know of. Why?
据我所知可不是。怎么了？

For all I know, she's trying to find me.
不知道她有没有在找我。

I'll be back **before you know it**.
我去去就来。

A: Will Sofia be coming over for dinner tonight? 今天晚上聚餐索菲亚能来吗？
B: Not that I know of. 我不太清楚。

God (only) knows! 天知道！

字面含义为只有上帝知道，表示没有人知道的反话。强调不可获知的状况时可以用Nobody knows? Who knows? Heaven (Lord/Christ) knows! 等。

“不懂得珍惜，总是在分手之后说这些有什么用”

God knows I've made a lot of mistakes with her.

M·O·R·E

- God (Lord) knows what S+V!
  ……鬼知道！
- God(Lord) knows that S+V!
  老天作证……

Nobody knows what she's doing.
鬼知道她在做什么。

God only knows what your parents are going to say.
谁知道你父母要说什么。

God knows I owe you so much.
说真的，我欠你太多了。

A: God only knows what my girlfriend will buy. 天知道我女朋友要买什么。
B: Has she gone out shopping again? 她又去逛街了？

know for sure 明确知道

这是在表示很明确地知道某事时用到的表达。可以单独使用为know for sure，也可以使用know for sure if主语+动词的形态。没有自信时，经常会用作否定形式。

“整形医生说，只要修修鼻子，就能变成超级明星”

I don't **know for sure**, but I'm willing to give it a try.

M·O·R·E

- (not) know for sure
  非常肯定（不确定）
- (not) know for sure if S+V
  非常肯定（不确定）某事

All we **know for sure** is that he seems to hate Liz as much as I do.
我们都知道，他像我恨莉斯一样恨她。

I think she might be a lesbian but I don't **know for sure**.
我觉得她是个同性恋，不过不太肯定。

She only suspects something. She doesn't **know for sure**.
她只是在怀疑些什么，不过她也不太确定。

A: I know for sure I'll become a lawyer. 我敢肯定我能成为一个律师。
B: You'll have to study really hard. 你得努力学习了。

know about 对……了解

know about表示“对某事了解”。know all about表示“对某事了如指掌”，而know of表示“听说过……”。

“儿子和一个女孩见面才3天就喊着要结婚”

What else do you know about your girlfriend?

M·O·R·E

- know about
  对某事了解
- know of
  听说某事

I don't know about that.
我不太清楚。

Who is she? What do we know about her?
她是谁？我们对她有多少了解？

Maybe she'll know of something.
她可能听说过一些事情。

A: Do you know of any cool places to hang out? 你知道一些不错的约会地点吗？

B: I know of two or three. 我知道两三处。

be known to (for) 被誉为……

Know被用为被动形态的情况，be known to+动词表示“以……闻名”，be known for+名词则表示“以某物闻名”。

“在背后说老板的坏话，不料被发现，可见前景”

He's been known to fire people for that sort of thing.

M·O·R·E

- be known to+动词
  被誉为……
- be known for+名词
  以某物闻名

The restaurant is well known for its Mexican food.
这家餐厅以美味的墨西哥料理而闻名。

I'm known to be funny.
我可是出了名的幽默大师。

She was known for her cooking.
她的料理水平非常高超。

A: We're going to visit an art museum in Paris. 我们要去逛逛巴黎的美术馆。

B: Paris is known for its artwork. 巴黎是个出了名的艺术圣地。

More Expressions

- **The first thing you need to know is ...** 你得先知道……

The first thing you need to know is that you should go there right now.
你应该知道，最紧要的就是马上去。

- **know the feeling** 知道感觉

I know the feeling. 我知道那种感觉。

- **know A from B** 区分A和B

I know right from wrong.
我能分辨是非。

- **I've never known somebody to ...**

我从没见过某人做某事

I've never known you to pay money.
我从来没见过你花钱。

- **also known as (a.k.a.)**

被誉为……（别名）

He's also know as tom.
人们也称他为汤姆。

- **know-it-all** 万事装懂的人，万事通

I'm smart but I'm not a know-it-all.
我的确聪明，但我可不是万事通。

What do you know (about ...) ?
你了解……吗?
You don't know shit!你知道个屁!
Don't I know it! 你不说我也知道!
Don't you know it!
你说的太对了！真的!
Don't you know?
你不是知道吗？知道我在说什么吧?
What's (there) to know? 不是很明显吗?
You never know. 谁知道呢。
You tell me. (I don't know.)
你告诉我。(我不知道。)
How should I know? 我怎么知道?
I wouldn't know! 我可没理由知道!
That's good to know. 很高兴知道。

喜欢能怎么办

Like/ Prefer

like后面如果接动词时，可以使用to+动词或 ...ing的形式。另外，like与would like的意义不同，like表示一般的喜欢或不喜欢，而would like则表示想要做某事。而且，like像things like that, like I said等词一样可以充当介词，表示“像……”，“正如……”等。

基本概念

1 like+名词 (to+动词 ...ing) 喜欢做某事

I like you best. 我最喜欢你了。
Do you like Korean food? 你喜欢韩国料理吗?
I like listening to pop songs. 我喜欢听流行音乐。

2 would like+名词/to+动词 渴望，想要

Would you like some coffee? 想喝点咖啡吗?
I'd like to speak with Mark. 我想和麦克通话。

3 介词 like 如，像……

You shouldn't say things like that. 你那么说就不对了。
I'm allergic to things like computers. 我特别讨厌电脑之类的东西。

4 prefer 更喜欢，偏好

I prefer to drive during the day. 我更喜欢在白天开车。
Many people prefer warm weather. 很多人更喜欢温暖的天气。
She prefers to listen to classical music. 她更喜欢听古典音乐。

like to+动词 ...ing （一般形式的）喜欢……

如果like后面的宾语是to+动词或 ...ing形式的话，就表示喜欢……不是现在想要做什么，而是“平时喜欢……”。如果要表示眼下渴望得到的东西或想做的事情就要说I'd like ...。

“对万事积极向上的外向人本来就喜欢忙碌的生活”

I'm pretty outgoing, and I like to keep busy.

M·O·R·E

- (don't) like to+动词 (...ing)
  (不)喜欢……
- Do you like to+动词 (...ing)?
  你喜欢……吗?
- like+名词 喜欢某物
  I like it. 我很喜欢。

Is there any special dish that you **like**?

你喜欢什么特别的料理吗?

I hope you **like it**.

我希望你喜欢。

I **like to** play computer games.

我喜欢玩电脑游戏。

Do you **like to** play golf?

你喜欢打高尔夫球吗?

A: Why don't you slow down a bit? **咱慢点走呗?**
B: I like to drive fast. **我喜欢快点开。**

would like to+动词 现在想做某事

would like to+名词表示“眼下想要……”，在饭店点菜时表示“给我来个……”。这是比want+名词形式更恭敬的表达方式。另外，如果would like后面接动词的话则表示“现在想要做某事”，与I'd like to+动词具有相同的含义。

“仅仅加了个Would (d)”，含义就发生变化”

I'd like to play computer games.

M·O·R·E

- would like to+动词
  想做某事
- Would you like to+动词?
  你想做某事吗?
- would like+名词
  想要某物
- would like+名词
  请给我来……
- Would you like+名词?
  你想要某物吗?

I'**d like** two tickets for today's game.

给我两张今天比赛的门票。

Would you like a glass of lemonade?

你要来杯柠檬汁吗?

I'**d like to** propose a toast.

我提议干一杯。

Would you like to come this weekend?

你这周末来吗?

A: I'd like to go shopping for my kids. **我想给孩子们买点东西。**
B: Okay, when would you like to go? **好的，什么时候去?**

I'd like that 我喜欢

I'd like that是I would like that的缩写形式，可以用来对对方的提议表示赞同。表示“那样做我没问题”。相反I like that则表示我喜欢某个状况。

“朋友提议去打猎，我本来就喜欢(like)打猎，因此欣然同意(would like) ... ”

I'd like that very much. I like hunting.

M·O·R·E

- I would like that.
  我没问题。
- I like that.
  我很喜欢。

I'd like that. That sounds sweet.
没问题，听起来很不错。

You're gorgeous. **I like that.**
你真美，我很喜欢。

You want to work for me? **I like that.**
你愿意为我工作？太好了。

A: What do you say we get together for a drink? 我们出去喝两杯怎么样？
B: Oh, I'd like that. 可以啊。

would like somebody to+动词 希望某人做某事

would like somebody to+动词表示希望某人做某事。即拜托对方做某事，多用在介绍朋友时。

“看到一位因交通事故住院的人，向他借手机打电话时”

Is there anyone you'**d like me to** call?

M·O·R·E

- I would like you to+动词
  我希望你做某事
- Would you like me to+动词
  你要我来做某事吗？
- Would you like+名词+pp?
  要做某事吗？

I'**d like you to** stay with me tonight.
我希望你晚上留在这儿。

I'**d like you to** meet my friend, Jim.
我想让你见见我的朋友，吉姆。

Would you like me to close the window?
你要我关上窗户？

Would you like these items delivered?
你要我给你送这些东西？

A: I'd like you to call your parents. 我希望你给你父母打电话。
B: Yeah, I should talk to them soon. 嗯，我马上打。

How do you like ... ? ……怎么样?

How do you like+名词? 表示问对方对某物有什么看法，也可以直接使用一个代词，变成How do you like that?另外，How do you like+动词(...ing)表示询问对方的意向，How would you like ... 是非常急切地询问对方意向。如果would you like与what相结合成为What would you like to+动词或for+名词时，就是问对方眼下渴望什么，想要做什么等。

"拿着名牌香奈儿包去聚会炫耀给朋友们看"

My husband bought this for me. **How do you like** it?

M·O·R·E

- How do you like to+动词(...ing)?
  做某事怎么样?
- How do you like that?
  那个怎么样?
- How would you like+名词?
  你想怎么样? ……怎么样?
- How would you like sth+pp?
  你要把……怎么样吗?
- What would you like for+名词?
  你需要什么? ?
- What would you like to+动词?
  想要做什么?

How do you like the steak?
牛排怎么样?

How do you like the people where you work?
你公司里的人怎么样?

How do you like the new house you moved into?
你的新家怎么样?

How would you like your steak?
您需要怎么烹饪牛排呢?

How would you like your steak cooked?
您需要牛排几分熟呢?

How would you like to pay for this?
您想怎么支付?

How would you like to get together next Monday?
下周一见面怎么样?

What would you like for dinner, beef or fish?
晚上想吃什么? 牛肉还是鱼?

What would you like (to have)?
您想来点什么?

What would you like to have for an appetizer?
想来点儿什么甜点?

What would you like to talk about first?
你想先说什么?

A: How do you like your new job? 你的新工作怎么样?
B: It's stressful. I don't enjoy it. 非常压抑，我不大喜欢。

A: How would you like to pay for this? 你想怎么结算?
B: With my credit card, if it's all right. 如果可以的话，用信用卡吧。

A: Would it be possible to get another drink? 再来一杯可以吗?
B: Sure. What would you like to have? 好的，你想来点什么?

What ... like? ... 怎么样?

What's ... like?与How ... 具有相同的含义。经常会与What does ... look like?作比较，What ... like?表示人物（事物）的性格（性质），而What does ... look like?单纯表示外观（appearance）。

"偶然碰到朋友的妹妹，突然来电"

What's your sister like? Is she a nice person?

M·O·R·E

- What is+名词+like?
  （性格/性质）怎么样?
- What does+名词+look like?
  外观、形象怎么样?

What is your girlfriend like?
你女朋友怎么样?

What is the weather like in New York?
纽约的天气怎么样?

What was the show like last night?
昨晚的演出怎么样?

A: What is the new department store like? 新百货商场怎么样?
B: Awesome! It has a lot of brand-name products. 棒极了！有很多全新的商品。

be like 像……

在这里，like作为一个介词，表示"像……"。I'm like you就表示我和你的想法一样，I'm not like you则表示"我和你不同"。另外，经常会使用It's like形态，可以在后面连接名词（...ing，从句）等。

"聚会上喝过头，回到家中，弟弟莫名其妙地盯着看"

It's not like that. It's not what you think!

M·O·R·E

- It's like+名词（... in/S+V）
  像……相当于……
- know(understand) what it's like to
  我知道……是什么。
- You don't know (You have no idea) what it's like to ...
  你不知道这是什么样的
- It's not like sb to+动词
  不像某人能做出的事情

But you're not like that?
不过你不像那样?

It's like that.
差不多，就是那样。

It's like he hates me. He won't take my calls.
他好像讨厌我，不接我的电话。

I know what it's like to be a teenager.
我知道青少年是什么样的。

A: Dad just put his winter coat on. 老爸刚刚穿上冬大衣。
B: It's like he thinks it will get colder. 他可能觉得要变天了。

things like that 那些事情

things like表示“像那样的事情”。something like that 表示“那种事情”，nothing like that (this)表示“不是那样的”，或者“没有那种东西”，即“最好的”。

“朋友的座右铭就是，好东西一定要分享”

Tom, something like this could ruin your life.

M·O·R·E

- things like that (this)
  那些东西
- something (anything) like that (this)
  那种东西
- nothing like that (this)
  不是那种东西，最好的
- 名词+like that
  那样的，那种

Peter, you can't ask people **things like that**.
彼得，你不能问他人那种问题。

I knew **something like this** was going to happen.
我就知道会发生这种事情。

There is **nothing like that**! It's the best!
没有什么比那好了！那是最好的！

Oh, it's **nothing like that**.
哦，我不是那个意思。

A: I don't want to live with my parents. 我不想和父母住在一起。
B: You shouldn't say things like that. 你可不能说那种话。

like that (this) before 以前，之前

主要用作not see (feel, do) anything like that (this) before 等形态，表示“没见过，没感觉过，没坐过”等表达方式，用于“吃惊”和“强调”。

“看到爸爸的衬衫上有口红的印记，妈妈气得上蹿下跳”

I've never seen her like this before.

Well, I have never seen anything **like this before**.
嗯，我从来没见过这种事情。

I've never felt **like this before**.
我从来没有过这种感觉。

I never did anything **like that before**.
我从来没做过那种事情。

I've seen things **like this before**.
我以前见过这种东西。

A: My stomach really hurts today. 今天胃好疼。
B: Have you ever felt like that before? 你之前疼过吗？

if you like 如果你愿意的话

单独使用if you like的话就表示“如果你愿意”。如果在if you like后面加名词或to+动词，就会变成从句形式，表示“如果……的话”。另外，whatever you like表示“随便你”。

“男女混合旅行的过程中，肌肉男边换衣服，边露出诡异的笑容”

If you like to watch, I'm okay with that.

M·O·R·E

- whatever you like
  随你便
- as long as you like
  你想怎么样就怎么样

If you like, you can go home.
如果你愿意，就回家吧。

If you like it so much, why don't you buy it?
如果你那么喜欢它，为什么不买?

Whether you like her or not, she is a suspect.
不管你喜不喜欢她，她肯定是个嫌疑人。

Take as long as you like.
想拿多少就拿多少。

A: Feel free to stay here as long as you like. 只要喜欢，随便享用。
B: It's very kind of you to say so. 很高兴你能那么说。

Like what? 比如说？怎么？什么样的？

用来问对方某种方式的句式，比如“你是说什么方式？”等。Like this?则表示“这样就可以了？”。

“刚刚退伍的男朋友，成天只会说军旅生活，让女朋友相当不耐烦”

Like what? The soccer game?

M·O·R·E

- Like what?
  比方说?
- Like this?
  这样?

Like what? What do you have to do?
比方说，你必须做些什么?

You need something to do? Like what?
你有事情要做? 比方说?

Are you saying that I've changed a lot? Like what?
你是说我改变了很多吗? 比如?

A: Please bring me some information on the company. 请给我拿些那家公司的相关资料。
B: Like what? 比如呢?

like I said 就像我说的

重复自己之前所说的内容，主要用于再次强调内容。相反，如果表示对方所说的话，就可以用like you said。

"第一次约会，穿得非常艳丽，不料被男朋友拉去看博物馆"

Like I said, I'm going to take you to the museum.

M·O·R·E

- like I said
  就像我说的
- like I said on the phone
  正如我在电话里所说
- like I said before
  正如我之前所说
- like you said
  正如你所说

Like I said, I should go back and get dinner ready.
我再说一遍，我得回家准备晚饭了。

Like I said, it's none of your concern.
我重申一遍，不管你的事。

Like you said, nobody saw anything.
正如你所说，没人看见过什么。

A: Why did you come home so late last night? 昨天晚上怎么回来得那么晚?

B: Mom, like I said, the bus was delayed. 妈，我已经说过了，公交晚点了。

prefer+名词 ...ing 更喜欢……

pefer为比较动词，当文章中含有相互比较的事物或前文中已经提到过比较的事物，就可以用来表示"偏好"，prefer后面的事物是更让主语喜欢的。

"大家来旅行，有人要早早睡觉，有人要去海边玩"

I prefer going to the bar downstairs.

M·O·R·E

- prefer+名词
  更喜欢……
- prefer+ ...ing
  更喜欢做某事
- prefer sb ...ing
  喜欢某人做某事

I **prefer** draft beer.
我更喜欢生啤酒。

Thank you very much, but I **prefer** coffee.
非常感谢，我更喜欢咖啡。

I'm fine being alone. I even **prefer** it.
我自己待着没关系，我更喜欢独处。

I **prefer** you doing the job.
我情愿你来做这份工作。

A: Will he go somewhere warm this winter? 这个冬天他会找个地方避寒吗?

B: No, he prefers mountains and skiing. 不，他更喜欢登山和滑雪。

prefer to do 更喜欢……

这次prefer后面要接to+动词的宾语，表示“更喜欢做某事”，相反prefer not to+动词则表示“宁愿不做某事”。

“用棒球棒拍死大型蚊子之后，自豪地说”

I prefer to be called a "hero".

M·O·R·E

- prefer to+动词 更喜欢做某事
- prefer not to+动词 宁愿不做某事

I prefer to be alone. Please leave.
我更喜欢自己一个人待着，请你离开。

I prefer not to answer that right now.
我宁愿现在不回答。

I prefer not to work on this project.
我情愿不参加这个项目。

A: Shall we take a taxi downtown? **我们打车去城里呗？**
B: We would prefer to walk there. **我们更喜欢走过去。**

prefer A (名词，...ing) to B (名词，...ing) 喜欢A大于B

prefer A to B则表示比起B更喜欢A，A和B可以都是名词或者是动名词 ...ing。需要注意的是，比较对象前面可不是than，而是to。

“结婚之前这样也就罢了，不过结婚之后还这样可就有点”

He prefers playing computer games to watching TV.

M·O·R·E

- prefer A to B 喜欢A大于B
- prefer A ...ing to B ...ing 喜欢做A大于做B

I think I prefer New York to other cities in America.
我觉得在美国，我最喜欢纽约了。

I prefer eating out in a restaurant to sitting around at home.
比起在家待着，我喜欢出去吃。

She prefers text messaging to leaving voice messages.
比起语音留言，她更喜欢发短信。

A: I think I prefer New York to other cities in America. **我觉得在美国，我最喜欢纽约了。**
B: Really? Is there some special reason for that? **真的？有什么特别的理由吗？**

prefer A rather than B 与其做B，不如做A

同样表示比较对象，但用rather than代替了to，表示与其做某事，不如做某事。

"疯牛病时用鸡代替牛，禽流感时用牛取代鸡"

I prefer chicken rather than steak.

Most kids **prefer** to enjoy free time **rather than** study.
很多人在闲暇时间更喜欢娱乐，而不是学习。

She said that she **prefers** traveling **rather than** staying at home.
她说，比起在家待着，她更喜欢出去旅游。

A: I prefer spring rather than summer. 我喜欢春天大于夏天。
B: Me too. Summer is much too hot. 我也是。夏天太热了。

I would prefer+名词(to+动词) 我宁愿做……

像like（主语的喜好）与would like（主语的移向）之间的差异，prefer表示"单纯偏好"，而would prefer表示"希望更……"。I'd perfer后面可以接名词或to+动词的形态。

"考试考砸了，老爸却拿着成绩单想要一科一科算账"

I would prefer not to go into details.

I'd prefer a beer if you have one.
如果你有啤酒，我想喝两杯。

I'd really prefer a mountain bike.
有辆山地车该多好呀。

I think that **I would prefer** the airport limo.
如果是机场大巴就好了。

I'd prefer not to get involved.
我希望不介入其中。

A: Are you ready to eat lunch? 你准备好吃饭了吗?
B: I would prefer to keep working. 我还是再工作一会吧。

I'd prefer it if ... ……就好了

If之后的成分表示与现实不同的希望，或者可以郑重地表示“不要对某人怎么样”。

“对不错的男生告白，不料被他拒绝，感到很惋惜”

I'd prefer it if you weren't gay.

I'd prefer it if you didn't.
如果你不那样就好了。

I'd prefer it if we didn't make an issue out of this at work.
如果我们在工作的时候不把这个当成问题就好了。

I'd prefer it if you didn't call me chicken.
你最好别再叫我胆小鬼了。

I'd prefer it if we could keep it between us.
我希望我们之间的事能成为秘密。

A: I have your glasses at my house. 你的眼镜在我家呢。
B: I'd prefer it if you gave them back. 我希望你还给我。

More Expressions

- **like better** 更喜欢
  What do you **like better**, action or comedy? 动作片和喜剧片，你更喜欢哪种？

- **act like** 就像……一样行动
  Why're you **acting like** a crazy person? 干嘛像个疯子一样？
  Stop **acting like** a child. 别像个小孩一样。

- **eat like a bird** 吃得少
  You **eat like a bird**! 你饭量真小啊。

- **likes and dislikes** 喜欢与不喜欢
  I don't have any strong **likes or dislikes**. 我没有特别喜欢的，也没有特别不喜欢的。

- **like hell** 终究不是，强烈地
  It hurts **like hell**. 疼死我了。

- **I'd like to think ...** 希望是……
  I'd like to think I'm going to dance again. 我希望能重新跳舞。

Do as you like. 随你便。
Just like that! 就是这样！
That's more like it. 那个更好。

得到允许了再做

Let

基本上不会给人带来祈使动词印象的祈使动词。let sb (sth) 形态中，主要记住两种，Let me+动词表示“让我来做某事”，而I will let you+动词则表示“我让你做某事”。另外，Let's+动词表示“我们做某事吧”，与Why don't we ... ?具有相同的含义。原本let us+动词简化成为了let's+动词。

基本概念

1 允许，让做

Let me take care of it. 我来处理吧。

Let me do this for you. 我为你做吧。

2 让我们做某事，不要做某事

Let's go to the coffee shop around the corner. 我们去街角的咖啡馆吧。

3 让某人做某事

Stop the boat. Let me out. 停船，我要出去。

Please let me in. 请让我进去吧。

let me+动词 我来做某事

let me+动词表示“让我来做某事吧”，是在做某事前预告自己的行为的表达。“让我来帮你”是Let me help you，“让我想想”是Let me think about it。

“在蹦极跳顶点瑟瑟发抖的130公斤巨型女”

I believe I can do it. Let me try.

M·O·R·E

- Let me check ...
  让我检查检查……
- Let me know ...
  告诉我……
- Let me think ...
  让我想想……
- Let me try ...
  让我试试……

I think I can fix it. **Let me** take a look.
我好像能修好它。让我瞧瞧。

Would you mind **letting me** check your bag?
你能让我检查一下包裹吗？

Let me think it over again.
让我再考虑考虑。

A: Do you know when the next flight leaves? 你知道下个航班是几点的吗？
B: Just a moment. Let me check. 稍等片刻，让我查查。

let you+动词 让你做某事

这次变成了“让你做某事”的Let you+动词。最常用的形态是I'll let you+动词或I'm going to let you+动词的形态。

“教练不让我这个主力上场，只让我做一些打杂的活”

I just want to let you know that I'm your key player.

M·O·R·E

- I will let you+动词
  我让你做某事
- I'm not going to let you+动词
  我不会让你做某事的
- want to let you know that S+V
  想要告诉你某事

I will not **let you** get away with this.
我不会让你逃脱惩罚的。

We will **let you** know that later.
我们会让你知道的。

I will **let you** know when I find her.
我一找到她就会告诉你。

A: I wanted to let you know I'm getting divorced. 我想让你知道，我要离婚了。
B: But why? You seemed so happy with your husband. 为什么？你和你丈夫看起来那么幸福。

let that (this, it) happen 让那种事发生

let后面用that (this)或it取代事先提到过的事情，let that (this, it) happen表示“让某种事情发生”。主要使用的形态为not let ... happen，表示“不会让那种事情发生”。

“明明说好了要戒烟，却偷偷抽烟，不料被媳妇发现”

I'm not going to **let it happen** again.

M·O·R·E

- not let that (this, it) happen
  不让某事发生

Sorry about that. I won't **let it happen** again.
真抱歉，我不会再让这种事情发生了。

Just don't **let it happen** again, all right?
再也别让这种事情发生了，好不?

We're not going to **let that happen**. I promise you.
我们不会让这种事情发生的，我保证。

He says you **let it happen**.
他说是你招致这种结果的。

A: I'm so sorry. I forgot to call you last night. 很抱歉，我昨晚忘了给你打电话了。
B: Don't let it happen again! I was worried. 再也不要让这种事情发生！我很担心。

Don't let somebody (sth)+动词 不要让某人做某事

let的否定形态，Don't let somebody (something)+动词表示“不要让某人做某事”，也可以表示“不要因为……做某事”，“某人不让做某事”等。

“脾气暴躁的李部长慢慢走过来，负责人小心翼翼地告诫新员工”

Don't let her be with you. She's a real bitch.

M·O·R·E

- Don't let sb+动词
  别让某人做某事
- Don't let sth+动词
  不要因为……做某事

Don't let it bother you.
不要让你自己分心。

Don't let her drink anymore!
别再让她喝了！

Don't let your stupid pride get in the way of you asking for help.
不要让你那没用的自尊心阻碍你求知的道路。

A: Emma really drank a lot of beer tonight. 艾玛今天晚上喝了很多啤酒。
B: I know. Don't let her drive her car home. 我知道，不要让她开车回家。

Let's+动词 做某事

Let's 为Let us 的缩略形式，主要用来表现提议某种行为活动。想要表达“我们去做某事吧”时要用Let's go，表达回头聊时可以用Let's talk later。

“仅仅忘记了一次生日，就大发雷霆，开始翻旧账。”

Let's not talk about the past, please.

M·O·R·E

- Let's+动词 做某事吧
- Let's not+动词 不要做某事了

Let's get together again soon.
我们找个时间见面吧。

Let's do that now and then go for a coffee.
我们马上做完，然后去咖啡馆。

Let's call it a day and get some beer.
我们今天就到这儿，去喝点啤酒吧。

Let's not think about it.
我们别想这个了。

A: What would you like to do tonight? 今天晚上要干什么？
B: Let's go and watch a movie. 我们去看电影吧。

Let's face it 接受、面对现实

需要承认或接受难以面对的事实时用到的表达。Let's face it后面要接需要接受的具体事实。

“只要碰面就会吵架的夫妻俩”

Let's face it. We drive each other crazy.

Let's face it. She's going to leave someday.
我们面对现实吧。她总有一天要离开。

Let's face it. They're not going to help us.
我们面对现实吧。他们不会帮助我们的。

Let's face it. You're not going to find anyone around you.
我们面对现实吧。你周边肯定不会有人。

A: Martha and Adam are always fighting. 玛莎和亚当整天吵架。
B: Let's face it. They don't like each other. 面对现实吧。他们的确不喜欢对方。

Let me see（稍微想想）让我看看，说什么好呢，就是说

按照字面翻译的话就是让我看看，但如果see后面不接任何宾语时就会表示思考或回忆某事。也可以说成Let's see。

"朋友要我还他一年前借的钱"

Let me see. I don't know what you're talking about.

Let me see. How about four o'clock?
让我想想，4点钟怎么样？

What is it? **Let me see.**
是什么？让我看看。

Let me see. I think it was about seven months ago.
让我想想，我觉得应该是7个月以前。

Let me see. Come on. Take a seat and show me.
让我看看，来吧，坐下给我看看。

A: Where should I put this package? 我应该把这些包裹放哪儿？
B: Let me see. Put it on top of the table. 我想想，放在桌上吧。

Let me see something 给我看看某物，看看

这次Let me see后面接上了名词，与之前的情况稍有不同，表示给我看看后面的名词。

"如果有人穿着警察制服要你出示证件的话"

Let me see your badge.

M·O·R·E

- Let me see (Let's see)+名词
  让我看看
- Let me see that.
  让我看看那个。

Let me see it again, if you don't mind.
如果可以的话，我想再看看。

Let me see your license and registration please.
请出示您的许可证和注册证。

That is so funny. **Let me see** that.
真好玩，让我看看。

A: Let me see your new apartment. 让我瞧瞧你的新公寓。
B: OK, but it hasn't been cleaned yet. 好的，不过还没有打扫干净。

Let me see if ... 确认某事，了解某事

Let me see if ... 表示“确认某事”。将不确定或不敢肯定的事情放在If后面就可以了，也可以说成Let's see if ...。另外，可以用what或how等代替if。

“放学时突然下起了瓢泼大雨，给女儿打电话，问她带没带伞”

Let me see if she took an umbrella with her.

M·O·R·E

- Let me (Let's) see if ...
  让我确认某事
- Let me (Let's) see what (how) ...
  让我了解了解某事
- Let me see what can I do.
  让我看看我能做什么。
- Let me see what I got.
  我看看我有什么。

All right, **let me see if** I understand this correctly.
好的，让我看看我能不能搞明白。

Let me just see if I got this straight.
让我看看你有没有明白。

Let's see what happens.
让我看看发生了什么事情。

Let's see how she handles this.
我得确认一下她处理得怎么样。

A: Let me see what you've come up with. 让我看看你提出的方案。
B: It's not much, but it's a start. 还没弄好呢，才刚刚开始。

Let me (just) say 话说

在开始说话前使用的表达。可以单独使用，也可以像Let me say just this（跟你说点事情），Let me say again（换句话说），或和Let me say goodbye一样将具体内容放在Let me say后面。

“弟弟说丢了自己非常珍惜的钢笔，侵入我的房间，开始翻腾起来”

Let me say it again. It's not here.

M·O·R·E

- Let me say this.
  我跟你说。
- Let me say it again.
  我重申一遍。
- Let me say that S+V
  可以说……

Let me say. I am a great lover of soccer.
我跟你说，我是个狂热的球迷。

Let me say this. I am a proud American.
我跟你说，我是个自豪的美国人。

Let me just say again. I love your house.
再说一遍，我非常喜欢你的房子。

A: Have you decided who to vote for? 你决定好要给谁投票了吗?
B: Let me say this. I don't like any candidate. 我想说，哪个候选人我都不喜欢。

Let's (just) say 就当成，假定……

这次为Let me say中的me被us取代的情况，经常会缩略为Let's say，表示“假设……”，用于举例子或作假设。say后面主要接具体从句，但有时也可以接名词。

“婚礼当天，新娘没有出现，也无法联系到”

Let's say she's not going to be here. Then what?

M·O·R·E

- Let's say hello to sb
  给某人打招呼

Let's say I bought a really great pair of shoes.
假设我买了一双非常棒的皮鞋。

Let's say we do.
假设我们做。

Let's say she didn't break the window. Who did?
如果她没打破窗户，那是谁干的?

Let's say we leave him here. What will happen?
假设我们把他留在这里，会发生什么事情?

A: Is Cheryl really going to get divorced? 谢丽尔真要离婚吗?
B: Let's just say she doesn't live with her husband. 假设她不和她丈夫一起住。

let ... go 解雇，忘记

let ... go表示“让……离开”。let sb go则表示“让某人离开”，警察如果说这句则表示“释放某人”，老板则表示“解雇”。另外，let it go还有“忘记”，“放任不管”的意思。

“被自己的心腹手下出卖的朋友”

Let it go. It's all in the past.

M·O·R·E

- let sb go
  让某人离开，解雇
- let it go
  忘记，放任不管
- let go of
  解雇，放开

My boss **let him go** this morning.
我老板今天早上把他解雇了。

Don't **let him go**! I still need him yet.
不要让他走! 我还需要他呢。

(Would you) **Let it go**.
忘掉吧，别管了。

You should **let go of** your anger.
你要学会控制愤怒。

A: You should let your son go on the trip. 你应该让你儿子去旅行。
B: But I'm worried he might have problems. 不过我害怕他会出事。

let alone 不值得一提

可以在否定表达后面接let alone，来说明比前面的内容更差的内容。即not A ... let aloneB中，“B就甭提了，连A也……”。B的成分可以是动词，...ing也可以是名词。

“宅男儿子假期只会在床上滚来滚去”

He wouldn't get out of bed, let alone get out of the house.

M·O·R·E

- let alone+动词 / ...ing/名词 不用提……

We were barely speaking, **let alone** having sex.
甭提做爱了，我们连话都不怎么说。

She's not even going to school, **let alone** not doing homework.
甭提做作业了，她连学校都不怎么去。

She can barely take care of herself, **let alone** a kid.
甭提小孩了，她连自己都照顾不周。

A: Is he going to graduate this year? 他今年能毕业吗？
B: He won't pass his classes, let alone graduate. 甭提毕业了，他就连课程也通过不了。

let somebody in (out) 让某人进去（让某人出去）

let somebody后面接的不是动词而是副词的情况，let somebody in则表示“让某人进入”，let somebody out表示“让某人出去”。let somebody后面也可以接get。

“夜不归宿的丈夫刚回到家，就受到妻子的质问”

Please let me in so I can explain myself to you.

M·O·R·E

- let sb in 让某人进入
- let sb out 让某人出去
- let sb in on 向某人透露秘密

I lost my key. **Let me in**, please.
我把钥匙弄丢了。请让我进去吧。

Who **let you in**?
是谁让你进来的？

Let me get out of here right now. You **let me out**
马上让我出去吧。快点。

I'm going to **let you in on** a little secret.
我要告诉你一个小秘密。

A: Let me in! It's really cold outside. 让我进去！外面非常冷。
B: How long have you been standing outside my door? 你在外面待多久了？

let somebody down 让某人失望

同样是let somebody后面接副词的情况，let somebody down表示“让某人失望”。... let me down, ... let you down等都是常用的形态。

“只拿到99分的孩子被妈妈狠狠教训一顿，现在这个时代啊”

I'm sorry I let you down, mom.

M·O·R·E

- Don't let me down.
  不要让我失望。
- I'll not let you down.
  我不会让你失望的。
- What a letdown!
  真是令人失望啊！

I'll try not to **let you down**.
我不会让你失望的。

You **let me down** this year, Jimmy.
你今年很让我失望啊，吉米。

You didn't **let me down**. You did the right thing.
你没有让我失望，你做的没错。

A: Don't let me down. 不要让我失望。
B: Don't worry. I'll get it done for you. 不要担心，我会帮你做的。

let somebody off 放过某人，照顾某人，让某人出去

具有放开(off)含义，表示“放过某人”。let somebody off the hook也是一样的意思。另外，物理上也可以理解为“释放……”。

“老板对秘书说，会让她坐私人飞机，却总是没有实际行动，只会对她毛手毛脚”

I want you to let me off this yacht.

M·O·R·E

- let sb off
  让某人离开，照看某人
- let sb off the hook
  让某人离开，照看某人，放过某人

I'm not going to give you a ticket. I'm going to **let you off** with a warning.
我不会给你开罚单，这次仅仅是警告。

My boss **let me off** early, so I took the plane.
我老板让我早早离开了，以便让我赶上飞机。

Let her off the plane!
让她下飞机！

A: The bus will let me off near your house. 我坐公交能到你们家附近。
B: Well, come on over and visit me. 好的，过来玩吧。

let something out 放出…… 坦白，大喊

字面意义为把某物释放出去，经常有“将心里的东西释放出来”的意思。另外，也可以理解为“大喊”，“解雇”等。

“借助高端科技成为美女的女孩让朋友们保守秘密”

Don't let it out! Hold it in!

Honey, you can **let it out**.
亲爱的，你可以坦白。

It's all right. **Let it out**.
没关系，直说吧。

Come on, **let it out**.
来，说说心里话。

Do you think we'll feel better if we cry? You know like just **let it out**?
你觉得如果我们哭一场能不能好受点？如果宣泄一下的话。

A: It rained all over my shopping bags. 我的购物袋全被大雨淋湿了。
B: Tilt them over and let the water out. 倾斜一会儿，雨水就会流出来了。

More Expressions

- **let loose** 解开，释放，表露
  She is **let loose** last weekend.
  她上周被释放了出来。

- **let it slip** 无心说出
  Cindy **let it slip** that you're in love with Jane.
  辛迪不小心说出了你和简交往的事情。

- **let somebody in on** 向某人透露秘密
  I'm going to **let you in on** a little secret. 我要告诉你一个小小的秘密。

- **let up** 停止
  We'll go outside after the storm **lets up**.
  我们要等暴风雨停了之后出去。

Don't let the cat out of the bag.
千万要小心别说漏嘴（暴露某种事实或秘密等）。

Live and let live. 宽容对待每个人。

Let it (that) be a lesson to you.
吃一堑长一智。

持续不变的

Keep

最基本的含义为持续某种状态，表示“继续做某事”，要记住比continue常用的keep ...ing。在持续的含义中还包括“保存，保管”，“守约”，“写日记”等。另外，像keep it clean (secret)一样，keep+宾语+形容词的形态也比较常用。

基本概念

1 具有，保有，担负，保管（保存）

Can you keep this book for me? 你能帮我保管这本书吗?

2 继续做某事

Are you going to keep doing that? 你要一直做下去吗?

You keep saying that. 你怎么一直说那话。

3 处于某种状态（keep+形容词），使某物处于某状态（keep+形容词）

You'd better keep it safe. 你最好好好保管。

I kept myself so busy last month. 我上个月一直很忙。

4 留住（人），使停留

What's keeping him? 他为什么会迟到?

I don't know what's keeping him. 我不知道他为什么迟到。

I won't keep you any longer.（打电话时）我不能再耽误你时间了。

keep ...ing 继续做某事

表示“继续做某事”，也可以说成keep on+ ...ing。如果要表达“过去一直做某事”时可以用I kept ...ing。

“女老板非常喜欢可爱的小职员，每次见面都要拍拍他的肩膀”

You just let her **keep doing** that!

M·O·R·E

- Keep ...ing!
  继续做某事！
- kept ...ing
  我过去一直做某事

I **keep** bumping into you.
我们一直碰面。

Keep going straight until you reach the church.
一直走下去，直到你看到教堂。

I **kept** paying for his education.
我一直给他供学费。

A: This report is so hard to finish. 这个报告书很难完成。
B: Keep working. We're almost done. 继续工作，我们快弄完了。

keep going 继续

keep going表示在去往某个地方或做某个事情的时候“继续走”或“继续做”的意思。另外，keep somebody (something) going表示“让某人坚持下来”，“继续做某事”等。

“跟着导航开车，不料差点掉进悬崖”

Keep going! You can't miss it!

M·O·R·E

- keep going (on)
  继续……
- keep sb (sth) going
  继续……

Keep going. I'm listening.
继续，我在听。

Should we go back or **keep going**?
我们要回去还是走下去?

You did your best in this restaurant every day to **keep** it **going**.
你为了维持这个饭店，每天都用尽全力经营。

A: When will we receive our annual budget? 我们什么时候能接到年度预算?
B: Keep going on the sales report. 继续整理你的报告书。

keep one's promise 守约

keep还有遵守的意思，因此keep one's promise表示“遵守约定”。可以用word代替promise。

“一个胆小鬼朋友说如果我敢玩蹦极她就做变性手术，不料我真的完成了”

You don't have to **keep your promise**.

M·O·R·E

- keep one's promise (word)
  遵守约定
- keep a diary
  写日记
- keep a secret
  恪守秘密
- keep early hours
  早早起床
- keep the change
  拿零钱

Here's twenty dollars, and **keep the change**.
这是20美元，不用找了。

Don't worry. Bill always **keeps his word**.
不要担心，比尔总会遵守诺言的。

Could you **keep a secret**?
你能守住秘密吗?

A: Here's thirty dollars, and keep the change. 这是30美元，不用找了。
B: Thanks a lot. Have a nice stay in New York. 非常感谢，祝您在纽约度过愉快的时光。

keep somebody (sth)+形容词 置于某种状态

keep表示持续某种状态，keep+形容词则表示“持续某种状态”。另外，发展为keep somebody (something)+形容词表示“将……置于某种状态”，“使某人做某事”。

“和年轻的女子手挽手一起走，不料被部下发现”

You'll **keep quiet** about that, if you're smart.

M·O·R·E

- keep busy
  保持忙碌
- keep awake
  醒着
- keep quiet (about)
  保持安静（关于某事）
- keep sth private
  保护隐私
- keep oneself busy
  保持自己忙碌

You can count on me. I'll **keep it private**.
你可以相信我，我会保护隐私的。

I **keep myself busy** these days.
我这些天很忙。

It's our responsibility to **keep it secret**.
保守秘密是我们的责任。

A: Why didn't Joe tell us about the money? 乔为什么没有说关于那些钱的事情?
B: I guess he wanted to keep it secret. 我觉得他想把那件事当成秘密。

keep one's fingers crossed 借助幸运

字面意义为双手合十，表示“祈祷幸运的降临”。至于渴望的具体内容要加在on后面，或者可以用that。keep somebody (something)+ing (pp)的句型。

“偶尔这样也就算了，如果凭着自己的美貌天天这样就有点……”

Sorry to have **kept you waiting** so long.

M·O·R·E

- keep one's fingers crossed 祈求幸运
- keep sb waiting 让某人等下去
- keep sb posted (on ...) 给某人传达最新的消息

I'll **keep my fingers crossed** (for you)!
我会为你祈福的！

I'm **keeping my fingers crossed** that he'll pass the exam.
我祈祷他能通过考试。

I've got to go. I'll **keep you posted**, okay?
我得走了。我会告诉你最新的消息，好吗?

Keep me posted on how they are doing.
让我知道有关他们的最新消息。

A: Tomorrow I'm going to ask Amanda to marry me. 明天我要向阿曼达求婚。
B: I'll keep my fingers crossed for you. 我会为你祈福。

keep somebody company 与某人在一起，有某人陪伴

在这里company表示和别人在一起，即“同行”，因此keep somebody company表示“与某人同行”，“不让某人孤单”等。

“刚刚失恋的朋友发短信，说自己很难受”

I'll come and **keep you company**.

M·O·R·E

- keep me company （别人）和我在一起
- keep you company （我）会和你在一起的
- have company 有人同行

Can you **keep me company** this weekend?
你这周末能陪我吗?

Mind if I **keep you company** for a bit?
介意我和你待一会儿吗?

Do you have someone to **keep you company** tonight?
你今晚有人陪吗?

You can drop by right now, but I **have company**.
你可以现在过来一趟，不过我有客人在这儿。

A: I have some free time this afternoon. 今天下午我有时间。
B: Good. You can stay here and keep me company. 太好了，你可以留在这儿陪着我。

keep an eye on 照看，留意，观察

表示“注意观察”(watch carefully)，可以理解为“照看……”或“留意监视”。如果要让别人暂时看着自己的行李，或者拜托别人暂时照看自己的孩子时，可以用这个句型。

“冰箱里的海参不见了，要找到嫌疑人”

You want me to **keep an eye on** her?

M·O·R·E

- keep an eye on sb (sth)
  照看，留意……

I'll **keep an eye on** him.
我会注意他的。

Did they send you over here to **keep an eye on** me?
是他们派你来这里监视我的吗?

Would you **keep an eye on** this for me?
你能帮我注意一下吗?

I need to **keep an eye on** my expenses.
我需要用心理财了。

A: Keep an eye on the cameras, will you? 注意看镜头，好吗?
B: Don't worry about a thing. 不要担心。

keep in touch with 与某人联系

表示互相保持联系，与之前的get in touch有着相近的含义。可以单独使用keep in touch，或者可以加上联系的对象，如keep in touch with somebody。

“关系恶劣的两姐妹会经常保持联系吗”

Do you and your sister **keep in touch**?

M·O·R·E

- keep (get) in touch
  联系，保持联系
- keep (get) in touch with
  与某人联系

Let's **keep in touch**!
我们常联 系!

Do you still **keep in touch with** her?
你现在还和她联系着?

Keep in touch, okay?
保持联系，好吗?

A: Don't forget to drop me a line. 别忘了给我打电话。
B: I'll make sure that I keep in touch. 我保证会联系你的。

keep in mind 铭记于心，记住

前文中提到的have in mind表示“在意某事”，而keep in mind则表示“铭记于心”，“记住某事”等。可以使用keep somebody (something) in mind或keep in mind that主语+动词的形态。

“到别人家做客，离开时主人盛情邀请再次光临”

Thanks. I'll keep that in mind.

M·O·R·E

- Keep in mind (that) S+V
  铭记某事
- Let's keep in mind (that) S+V
  我们好好记住……
- I'll keep that in mind.
  我会好好记住的。

Keep in mind that she will never fall in love with you.
记住，她绝对不会喜欢上你的。

Let's **keep in mind** this is our last chance to do that.
要记住，这是我们最后的机会。

Thanks for coming in. We will definitely **keep you in mind**.
谢谢你能来。我们肯定会记住你的。

A: I want to get a new computer. 我想弄台新电脑。
B: Keep in mind that will cost a lot. 要知道肯定要花不少钱。

keep down 减少，降低（声音），抑制，掩藏

表示维持在以下(down)，可以用在一次性降低或减少某物时。进一步可以表示“抑制……”，“阻碍成功”，“掩藏”。

“楼下投诉说噪声太大，却仍然没有好转”

Keep it down! We got a noise complaint.

M·O·R·E

- keep down
  减少，抑制，掩藏
- keep one's head down
  藏起来
- keep it down
  安静一下 (keep one's voice down)

Would you **keep it down**?
你能安静点吗?

It's not easy to **keep you down** here like this. But I can't let you out.
我知道藏在这里不容易，不过我不能让你出去。

If you're so worried about privacy, just wear a hat, and **keep your head down**.
如果你那么担心隐私，大可以带个帽子，低头走过去。

A: Keep it down in there. I can't sleep. 能不能安静点，我都睡不着了。
B: Sorry, we were being so loud. 不好意思，我们太吵了。

keep ... from+名词 ...ing 阻止某人做某事

这里的keep具有“阻止，抑制”的含义。keep A from+名词(...ing)表示“阻止某人做某事”。需要注意的是，如果少了from，变成keep A+ ...ing的话就表示“让某人做某事”。

“不知道珍惜的老板，一见手下要辞职，极度挽留”

Please don't **keep me from** quitting my job.

M·O·R·E

- keep sb (sth) from+ ...ing/N
  阻止某人做某事
- keep oneself from ...
  控制自己做某事
- keep sb (sth)+ ...ing
  让某人做某事
- keep sth from sb
  不告诉某人某事

They **keep me from** getting work done.
正因为他们，我才没完成工作。

I was just trying to **keep you from** doing something stupid.
我只想阻止你做一些愚蠢的事情。

I moved all our stuff, to **keep it from** them.
我把所有东西都搬过来，以防止他们接近。

A: Terry really misses his ex–girlfriend. 特里非常想念他的前女友。
B: Try to keep him from calling her. 别让他给她打电话。

keep somebody (sth) off 不让某人接近

就像“请不要踏入草坪”(keep off the grass)一样，keep off表示“离……远点”。经常还会用成keep A off (of) B的形态，如果要表示“别碰蛋糕！”，则可以用Keep your hands off the cake。

“电车里挤满了人，一个40多岁的中年男子居然毛手毛脚”

That's my ass. **Keep your hands off** my ass!

M·O·R·E

- keep off
  离……远点
- keep one's hands off
  把某人的手拿开

Hey, **keep off the grass**! Go on and get out of here!
嘿，别进草坪！快点离开！

I think it's a good idea to **keep children off** drugs.
我觉得最好不要让孩子靠近毒品。

Keep your hands off my son!
别碰我儿子！

A: Why is it so quiet in here tonight? 为什么今天晚上这么安静?
B: We decided to keep the TV off. 我们把电视关掉了。

keep up 维持（好状态）

keep up 表示“继续做某事”，“继续维持好状态”，通过up进一步强调了keep的含义，在这里加上with，变成keep up with的话就表示“争取步调一致”。

“给老公做鳗鱼吃的妻子脸上露出了幸福的笑容”

I need you to keep up your strength for tonight.

M·O·R·E

- keep up
  继续做某事，维持
- keep up the good work
  继续努力工作
- keep up with
  追上，不落后，了解

Keep up the good work!
继续好好工作!

Keep it up!
加把劲!

Hey, you got to **keep up** your strength.
喂，你得保持体力。

I've got to **keep up with** him.
我得赶上他。

A: My painting looks really nice. 我的画看起来很不错。
B: Yeah. Keep up the good work. 是啊，继续努力工作。

keep track of 记录某事，不错过某事，知道……的消息

track表示过去的痕迹、踪迹等，keep track of表示注意……在某处或知道某人身上发生了什么事情。相反，lose track of则表示“错过了……而不知道……”等。

“不知道时间的流逝，聊着聊着就晚点了”

I forget to keep track of time. I've got to go.

M·O·R·E

- keep track of
  追踪…… 得到消息，记住
- lose track of
  错过…… 忘记，无法联系

Do you **keep track of** your purchases?
你会记录你买的东西吗?

I always **keep track of** whatever I bring to a party.
我总会记住自己参加聚会时携带了什么东西。

She **lost track of** her son in the accident.
她在一次车祸中与孩子失去了联系。

A: It seems like I never have any money. 好像我总是缺钱。
B: You need to keep track of your spending. 你得记录你的花费。

More Expressions

- **keep away from** 远离……

You can't **keep away from** her.
你无法远离她。

- **keep at** 努力做某事，继续做某事

Please **keep at** it. Don't stop.
继续，不要停。

- **keep somebody out of** 使某人摆脱某事

(Have you) **Been keeping out of trouble**? 没什么问题?

- **keep an open mind** 不要有偏见

I'm trying to **keep an open mind**.
我努力让自己不存偏见。

- **keep your chin up** 加油

Keep your chin up. Things will be getting better for you.
加油！一切都会变好 的。

- **keep something to oneself** 独自珍藏……

There are some things I like to **keep to myself**. 有些东西我想独自珍藏。

- **keep somebody** 使某人迟到

Where **have** you **been keeping yourself?** 你去哪待着了?
What's **keeping him**? 他为什么会迟到?

- **keep a straight face** 呈现严肃的表情

I couldn't **keep a straight face**.
我没办法忍住笑。

- **keep pace with** 与某人保持步调一致，不被甩在后面

It's not easy to **keep pace with** her.
和她保持一致的步调很不容易。

It'll keep. 这是秘密。

Keep your head up. Don't look down.
抬起头，不要看下面。

放在某个地点或状态的

Put

不管是地板上还是桌子上或者脸上，只要涉及到放的动作，就会用到这个动词。比方说put a match to her cigarette表示把烟点着，put the book on the table表示把书放在桌子上，put lotions on her hand表示在脸上涂乳液。当然，如果对象是抽象物体则比喻“使陷入某种状态”。

基本概念

1 放在（地点），放入，放下

I put the papers in the shredder. 把纸张放在粉碎机里。

Don't put all your eggs in one basket. 不要吊死在一棵树上。

2（比喻）提议，赋予，评价，倾注，使处在某种状态

We're putting every effort into it. 我们为此付出了一切努力。

I'll put a smile on your face. 我会让你幸福的。

3 表现

I don't know how to put it. 我不知道该怎么说。

put something in (on) 把某物放在……上，放入

put的最基本含义就是放，在put sth后面接上地点名词就可以了。Where did you put it?表示“你把它放哪儿了？”。

“第一次请男朋友到家里做客，淘气的弟弟把我内衣放在了桌上”

Why did you put my underwear on the desk?

M·O·R·E

- put sth in (on)
  把某物放在…… 放入
- Where did you put ... ?
  你把某物放哪儿了?

I'll just **put** it **in** the kitchen.
我会把它放在厨房里。

You can just **put** it **on** the table.
你可以把它放在桌子上。

Well, should I **put** my coat **in** the bedroom?
那个，我应该把大衣放在卧室里吗?

A: Can I borrow your lawn mower tonight? 今天晚上我能借用一下割草机吗?
B: Sure, I'll put it in your driveway after supper. 好的，我会在吃完晚饭之后把它放在你家门外的车道上。

put ... in danger 使某人陷入危险

这次不是放在某种物理的空间，而是in danger（危险的状态），in a good mood（好心情），at risk（威胁）等抽象的状态。

“女朋友炫耀自己进入了一家保险公司”

She put me in a good mood.

You'**re putting** our lives **in danger**.
你会让我们的生命受到威胁的。

I'**m putting** you **in charge of** my schedule.
我要你负责我的日程安排。

You **put** our relationship **at risk**.
你让我们的关系非常不好。

You **put** your career **on the line**. You might get demoted.
你的事业受到威胁了。你可能会被降职。

A: The storm put the town in danger. 暴风使那座村庄受到了严重的威胁。
B: Yes, many people decided to leave. 是啊，很多人选择离开。

put ... to work 使……启动，使……工作

虽然是相同的脉络，但这次put somebody (something)后面接了to+名词的形态。表示“使……陷入某状态”的put ... to work如果对象是人则表示“使某人工作”，如果是事物，则表示“使……运转”。

“表面上非常宽宏大量，背地里却利用人心的老板”

The boss is so good at **putting** us **to work**.

M·O·R·E

- put ... to death
  使某人受死，处以死刑
- put ... to (good) use
  （好好）利用某物

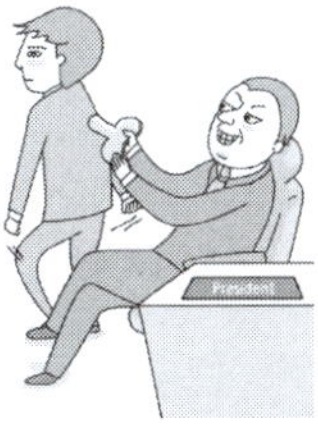

It's time to **put** you **to work**.
得让你开始工作了。

When you're ready, he's going to **put** you **to sleep**.
等你准备好了，他会让你进入梦乡的。

I **put** my computer skills **to good use**.
我很好地利用了我的电脑技能。

I'm just trying to **put** our mistake **to good use**.
我只想好好利用我们的失误。

A: Many people came to help with the festival. 很多人来帮我准备庆典活动。
B: Put them to work setting up things. 让他们开始工作吧。

put A before B 比起B，优先考虑A

put A before B表示重视A大于B，而put something behind somebody则表示忘记某事。

“本来想抗议诈骗电话，不料被对方破口大骂”

How about **putting** it **behind** you? Just let it go.

M·O·R·E

- put A before B
  比起B，优先考虑A
- put sth behind sb
  忘记（不好的事情等）

I **put** my work **before** my family.
我最重视我的家庭了。

I believe a lawyer should **put** his country **before** his client.
我认为，律师应该重视国家大于个人。

You must **put** studying **before** playing.
你必须要先学习，后玩游戏。

A: Jeff is so in love with his girlfriend. 杰夫非常喜欢他的女朋友。
B: He always puts her before himself. 他总把她放在第一位。

put it 表达

How should I put it?（我该怎么表达？）是个比较常用的句型。在这里，put it具有express的含义，表示“表达……”。

“偷偷用同事的信用卡，不小心被发现，却口口声声说是暂时借用一下”

Please don't **put it** like that. I didn't steal your purse.

M·O·R·E

- put it
  表达，表现 (express)
- to put it simply (shortly/briefly)
  简单说来

How should I **put it**?
我应该怎么说呢?

I don't know how to **put this**.
我不知道该怎么说。

Let's **put it** this way.
我这么说吧。

A: Why didn't you go on a date with Steve? 你为什么没和史蒂夫约会?
B: I don't know how to put it, but he seems strange. 我不知道该怎么说，他看起来很奇怪。

put a stop to 结束……

to后面加上a stop（中断），表示“结束某事”。对我们来说，put an end to更为熟悉，不过实际日常生活会话中更多会用到put a stop to。

“知道老教授性骚扰自己女朋友的事情，火冒三丈的男朋友立刻找了过去”

He found out about it and tried to **put a stop to** it.

I'll **put a stop to** that.
我来了结那件事。

Are you saying that we should **put a stop to** this?
你是说我们要中断?

You can **put a stop to** this right now if you want to.
如果你愿意，可以马上结束。

I will talk to him, and we'll **put a stop to** it.
我会和他谈谈的，尽量把这件事了结了。

A: There were three robberies here last week. 上周这里发生了3次抢劫案。
B: The police need to put a stop to that. 警察们应该避免这种事再次发生。

put aside 暂时放在一边，忘记，储蓄(put by)

为了达成其他目的，暂时把眼下的问题、不和谐、差异等放在一边，表示“暂时搁置……”。另外，还有“储蓄”的意思。

“想要玩最新游戏的话，显卡和内存都要升级”

I put some money aside for a new computer.

M·O·R·E

- put aside
  放到一边
- put aside for
  为了……目的而储备
- put by
  储蓄

You need to **put aside** your differences with her.
你应该和她搁置争议。

We have to **put aside** our disagreement and face reality.
我们不得不先放下争议，面对现实。

I had to **put aside** my anger about joining a party.
在加入派对的问题上，我不得不先舒缓我的情绪。

A: We're going to have to put aside our vacation plans. 我们要暂时搁置度假的计划。

B: Why? Don't we have enough money? 为什么？我们的资金不够？

put away 整理，投狱，吃光，击退

表示将某物另行存放，可以用来表达储蓄资金，将犯罪者关进监狱，吃光东西，在游戏或战争中击败敌人等。

“因一次意外的交通事故失去了孩子，而肇事司机却逃之夭夭”

I hope whoever hitting my son gets put away for life.

How many glasses of wine do you **put away** every day?
你每天喝多少红酒?

He is dangerous and I want him **put away**!
他是个危险人物，需要马上关进监狱!

If he's guilty, we're going to **put** him **away**.
如果他有罪，我们肯定会把他打入大牢的。

A: Put away the clothes in your bedroom. 把你房间里的衣服收起来。

B: I'll do that when I have more free time. 等我有时间就去收拾。

put down 放下，记录，教训，谴责，镇压

字面意义为放到下方，表示“记录”，“挂电话”，“（飞机）着陆”，“强行镇定或镇压”，“部分支付”，还有“谴责”等。

“好不容易攒钱买了一款进口车，不料被儿子开出去闯了祸，便拿着高尔夫球杆揍他”

Please forgive me. Just **put down** the club.

M·O·R·E

- put sb down for (as)
  记录
- put sth down to
  将……嫁祸给某人

This is the police! **Put down** your weapon.
警察！放下你的武器！

I'll **put you down** for eight boxes.
你拿走的8箱我都记下了。

I can't believe you **put me down** in front of your friends.
真不敢相信，你居然在众多朋友面前诋毁我！

Tony, stop! **Put me down**! What are you doing?
托尼，停下！放下我！你想干什么？

A: Put down your books and come over here. 放下书本过来。
B: Why? Are you doing something interesting? 为什么？你在弄什么好玩的吗？

put in 设置，腾出时间，交钱，正式邀请

put sth in表示“将……放入……”。在这里主要用到的put in+时间表示“倾注努力和精力”。另外，put in a request (order)表示“邀请（命令）”，put one's faith in表示“相信某人”。

“刚刚升了职，叫部长多多关照”

You know Sue and I both **put in for** a promotion.

M·O·R·E

- put in
  将……放入……内
- put（时间，金钱等）into
  投入……，放入
- put in+时间 (努力)
  付出，倾注
- put in+设施设置
  正式邀请，申请

You've got to **put in** some time.
你得花点时间了。

I can't just walk away! I've **put in** four hours!
我不能放弃！我已经花费了4个小时！

I had **put in** a request to have all my mail forwarded.
我正式申请将我的所有邮件都发出去。

When you **put your faith in** people, they reward you.
如果你相信别人，你肯定会得到回报。

A: Beth is never around anymore. 贝斯再也不会出现在这附近了。
B: She puts in a lot of hours at her new job. 她为了新工作花费了不少精力。

put on 穿衣服，长胖，化妆，假装， 开……

可以用为多种含义的短语之一的put on 最基本表示“放在……上面”。进一步衍生出的含义有“穿衣服”，“化妆”，“打开……”，“播放歌曲”等。

“和女朋友单独在家品尝着红酒，瞬间需要符合氛围的音乐”

I'm going to **put on** some music.

M·O·R·E

- put on+衣服 (体重，化妆品) 穿，长肉，涂抹
- put on+设备 (歌曲) 打开，播放
- put on+音乐会 (话剧) 上演，举行
- put pressure on 给……施压
- put sb on the phone 让某人接听电话

He got up and started to **put on** his jacket.
他起床，然后开始穿外套。

I've **put on** (gained) weight.
我长胖了。

I had to **put on** lotion.
我得沫点乳液了。

Turn off the air conditioner and **put on** the heat.
把空调关了，把暖气打开。

I'm going to **put on** the most romantic song.
我要播放最浪漫的歌曲了。

I want to **put on** a Christmas show tonight. Will you help me?
今晚我想举行圣诞演出，你能帮帮我吗?

You don't have to **put on** a brave face for me.
你不必因为我做出一副勇敢的表情。

I'll **put you on** right away.
马上为您转接（电话）。

I know he is at your place. Just **put him on**.
我知道他在你那里。把话筒给他。

A: You should put on a sweater. It's cold outside. 你得穿上毛衣，外面很冷。
B: I thought it was colder than normal. 我觉得比平时任何时候都冷。

A: I put on too much make-up. I look like a clown. 我化的妆太浓了。看着像个小丑。
B: No, you don't. But I would remove that eyeliner. 没有啊，如果你实在看不惯，我就把眼线去掉。

A: What would you like me to put on your hotdog? 你的热狗要夹点什么?
B: Just some ketchup, please. 番茄酱就够了，谢谢 。

put off 延期，推迟，让他人等待

Don't put off until tomorrow what you can do today（不要把今天的事情推迟到明天）是个家喻户晓的谚语。一般可以用put off形态，也可以用put sth off，如果是动词的话，可以使用put off ...ing。

“懒汉的经典台词，干嘛把明天能做的事情提前到今天”

Why are you doing what you can **put off** till tomorrow?

M·O·R·E

- put (sb (sth)) off
  延期，推迟，
  让他人等待
- put (sb) off ...ing
  推迟……

The meeting has been **put off** until further notice.
会议延期了。

I'll just **put** this **off** till tomorrow.
我就想把这些推到明天做。

I told her it was stupid to **put off** the wedding.
我告诉她，推迟婚礼是不明智的选择。

A: You shouldn't put off that work for much longer. 你不能把工作推迟那么久。
B: I'll try and finish it before I go. 我会在下班前做完的。

put out 关掉（灯，开关），拿出，出版

最基本的含义为将物品放到外边。如果要表达灭火或者关灯的含义时也可以用这个短语。另外，还有“拿出……”，“制作”，“出版”等意思。

“纵火犯想要烧了房子，勇敢的硬汉用尿水浇灭了火”

If you set fire to my house, I'd **put out** the fire by peeing on it.

M·O·R·E

- put out+烟/火
  灭掉
- put out sth
  将某物放到外面，拿出，
  制作，出版
- put out a broadcast
  广播

When I realized I couldn't **put out** the fire, I ran.
当我意识到自己无法灭掉大火时，急忙逃了出来。

Put out the light when you go to sleep.
你睡觉前要记得关灯。

I'm going to **put out** a flyer about the restaurant.
我要发传单，给餐厅做宣传。

A: The fashion magazine will put out a special edition. 时尚杂志会出版特别版。
B: Let's buy a copy and look at the pictures. 我们买来看看照片吧。

put through 电话转接，使某人经历

最具代表性的through短语就是“使某人接电话”，另外，就是“贯通……”，可以由此衍生出“使某人经历”，“经验”等意思。

“搞婚外恋被朋友揭穿，离婚之后在乡下过着艰苦的生活”

Do you have any idea what you put me through?

M·O·R·E

- put sb (sth) through (to) 给某人转接电话
- put sb through+学校 交某人的学费
- put sb through sth 让某人经历某事

I'll **put you through** right away.
马上为您转接。

I never wanted to **put you through** this.
我从来没想过让你经历这些。

Why do you **put me through** this?
你为什么让我经历这些?

A: Your daughter is calling on the other line. **你女儿来电话了。**
B: Put her through to my office. **把电话转接进来。**

put together 收集，构成，整理（综合），合计

字面意义为放(put)在一起(together)，表示收集或整理或综合各种材料。

“在搬家的过程中需要搬运大量的家具，因此让朋友帮忙”

Why don't you help me put together my new furniture?

You **put together** the guest list by tomorrow.
明天把客人的名单整理出来。

Maybe I'll just **put together** another party.
我也许会准备另一个聚会。

How can you quickly **put together** a team?
你怎么能那么迅速地组成一支队伍?

A: Did you put together the photo album? **你整理好相册没?**
B: Yeah, and it looks great. **嗯，这相册看起来很棒。**

put up 竖起，建造，悬挂，启示，高举，抬升，让人留宿

字面意义为将东西高高(up)举起(put)，表示“建造建筑物”，“高挂某物”，“启示”等。另外，还包括“让人留宿”，“用作其他用途”，“提出”等含义。

“电梯里挤满了人，却有人不知廉耻地放臭屁来”

I don't know how you **put up with** it.

M·O·R·E

- put up
  竖起，建造，悬挂，抬升，启示，高举
- put up+钱 付款
- put up
  （因某种目的）拿出，提议
- put sb up
  让某人留宿，过夜
- put up a fight
  宣战，善战
- put up with
  忍受

Why did you **put up** posters for roommates if you don't want them?
既然你不想要室友，干嘛还把招室友的告示贴了出来?

They all **put up** their hands eagerly.
他们都热心地举起了手。

They're already **put up** the money.
他们已经付过账了。

You don't have to **put up with** this.
你不需要忍受这些。

A: How do you put up with him? 你是怎么忍受他的?
B: I just don't take him seriously. 我没把他当回事。

More Expressions

- **put sth on a list** 放入名单内
  You can **put** your name **on a list**.
  你可以将名字记入名单中。

- **put it on one's tab** 某人来付账
  You can just **put it on my tab**.
  把账算在我头上。

- **put forth** 提出(submit)
  I mean the ideas you **put forth** are not that good. 我是说，你提出的点子不太好。

- **put on airs** 自以为是
  You **are** always **putting on airs**.
  你总是自以为是。

- **put somebody in jail** 让某人入狱
  The police **put** me **in jail** for stealing.
  警察以偷窃罪把我关了起来。

- **put somebody out of one's misery** 使……摆脱痛苦
  Just **put** me **out of my misery**.
  不要让我这么悲惨。

- **put something back** 放在原来的位置，放缓，延期
  You just **put** it **back** where you found it.
  把它放在你发现它时的位置。

抓紧了

Hold

最基本的含义为抓在手上。hold something in one's hands (arms)表示手里握着东西。由此衍生的各种含义有握住，拥有，捕捉，忍受等。尤其对事物，有“收容”的意思，像前文中的keep动词那样，可以用hold something+形容词的形态表达“将……维持在某状态”的意思。

基本概念

1 **握在手中，抓住，所有，拥有**

I'm sorry, but could you hold the door? 不好意思，你能帮忙顶下门吗？

2 **召开（会议，聚会），举办，抓住，压制**

The office party will be held tomorrow. 明天会有办公室聚会。

Hold your breath! 憋住气！

3 **维持……的状态**

Hold the window open. 打开窗户。

4 **支撑，容纳（事物主语）**

This meeting room can hold 100 people. 这间会议室可以容纳100人。

This car can hold at least 6 people. 这辆车至少可以容纳6个人。

The bridge won't hold the dump truck. 这座桥可支撑不了一辆大卡车。

hold somebody (sth) in one's hand 将……握在手中

这是hold最基本的含义，使用频率也最高。hold为“将某物握在手中”的意思，可以接各种副词，如in one's hand, in one's arms等。当然，可以用hold+something表示“抓住某物”。

“男朋友考了3次公务员，却都以失败告终，女朋友安慰道”

I'll be here to **hold your hand**.

M·O·R·E

- hold ... in one's hand (arm)
  将……握在手中
- hold ... tight (close)
  抓紧

She is **holding** a shopping bag **in her right hand**.
她右手拎着一个购物袋。

She is **holding** a pillow **in her arms**.
她用胳膊夹着枕头。

Hold her **in your arms**, kiss her, smell the scent of her.
将她搂在怀里，亲吻她，感受一下女人的芳香。

A: Look at the ring my boyfriend gave me. 看看我男朋友送我的情侣戒。
B: Wow, let me hold it in my hand for a minute. 哇，让我试试。

hold a meeting 召开会议

表示召开某种会议或聚会，hold后接的宾语主要有meeting, party, ceremony, funeral, race等。hold比起have更formal一些，日常生活中经常会使用到。

“女儿要组织一次聚会，让朋友在家里留宿”

She plans to **hold a slumber party** this weekend.

We'll **hold our Christmas party** on the 24th.
我们要在24号举行圣诞派对。

The manager will **hold a meeting** for the new staff.
经理会为新员工召开一次会议。

I told my mom not to **hold a birthday party** for me.
我对我妈说，别为我举办生日派对。

A: The company is experiencing many problems. 公司现在遇到了很多问题。
B: We'll hold a meeting to discuss the problems tonight. 我们今晚将召开一次会议来商讨对策。

hold somebody 使某人无法离开

hold somebody表示“抓住某人，不让其离开”，hold somebody hostage表示“抓为人质”，hold somebody prisoner则表示“将某人投入监狱”。

“非常有能力的一位员工突然提出要辞职，着急的老板马上对秘书说”

I need you to **hold** her until I get there.

M·O·R·E

- hold sb hostage 将某人抓为人质
- hold sb prisoner 将某人投入监狱

Hold them right there. I'm on my way.
留住他们，我马上就到。

We captured them. We're **holding** them over at my place.
我们抓住他们了。他们正在我家里关着呢。

I'm not sure **holding** me **hostage** is your best option.
我不知道你们把我当成人质是不是最好的选择。

The girl **was held hostage**.
那个女孩被抓去当人质了。

A: Have the students left the classroom? 学生们离开教室了吗?
B: No, we're holding them until their parents come. 没有，等家长们来了再让他们走。

hold still 静止不动，等待

hold和keep一样，表示维持某种状态，因此hold+形容词表示“某种状态持续”。hold good表示“有效”，hold still则表示“静止不动”，也可以说成keep still。

“insect phobia 丈夫一见到蟑螂就跳到了沙发上”

Calm down. **Hold still**.

M·O·R·E

- hold good 有效
- hold true 事实

Whatever it is, one thing **holds true**.
无论怎样，有一件事是真的。

You're drunk. **Hold still**.
你喝醉了，消停一会儿。

How can I **hold still** when you're touching me?
你碰我的时候，我怎么可能没反应。

A: I don't want you to cut my hair. 别剃我的头发。
B: Hold still and let me get started. 别动，我要开始了。

hold somebody responsible 认为某人会负责

hold somebody responsible (for) 表示“认为某人对某事有责任”，是个比较难的短语。另外，被动时态为be held responsible(accountable) for something。

“校长去卫生间，不料把小便池弄坏了，老师们谴责道”

We're **holding you responsible** for the accident.

M·O·R·E

- hold sb responsible for sth
  认为某人对某事有责任
- be held responsible for sth
  对某事有责任
- hold sth steady
  继续维持……

I'm going to **hold you responsible**.
我觉得你应该负责任。

No, I don't **hold her responsible**.
不，我不觉得她应该负责任。

Hold it steady.
抓着别动。

A: Who broke the window on the house? 谁把那座房子的窗户打碎了?

B: The owners are holding their son responsible. 房子的主人觉得好像是自己儿子弄的。

hold your breath 屏住呼吸，忍住呼吸

这里的hold为“抑制”，“忍受”的意思，因此hold one's breath表示“屏住呼吸”，“紧张”，not hold one's breath表示“不害怕”，“镇定”等，也可以表达不要忍受太久。

“两个愚蠢的人比谁憋气憋得长”

How long can you really **hold your breath** for?

M·O·R·E

- hold one's breath
  屏住呼吸，紧张
- not hold one's breath
  镇定

I can **hold my breath** for 10 minutes.
我可以憋10分钟的气。

Okay, this is going to be tough. **Hold your breath**.
好吧，这可不太容易，紧张起来。

I want you to close your eyes and **hold your breath**.
闭上眼睛，屏住呼吸。

A: I would like to marry a rich guy. 我想找一个富二代嫁了。

B: Sure, but don't hold your breath. 好，不过不要等太久。

hold sth against somebody 怀恨在心

为那些小心眼的人准备的短语。过去对方犯下了某种过错，却始终无法原谅对方，耿耿于怀时可以用到的表达。主要用hold it (that) against somebody的形式。

“踢球的时候，和朋友争头球，不料鼻梁被撞坏，但心胸宽广的我说道”

I'm not going to **hold it against** you. Bad things happen.

I won't **hold it against** you.
我不会埋怨你的。

I don't think you should **hold that against** him.
不要在意他的话。

I said I didn't **hold it against** her.
我说过我对她没有感情。

She won't **hold it against** you. After all, you're her daughter.
她不会埋怨你的，毕竟你是她女儿。

A: I heard that your mom wrecked your car. 听说你妈砸了你的车。
B: She did, but I don't hold it against her. 是啊，不过我不埋怨她。

hold back 阻止，抑制（感情），自制，抽出，隐藏

表示“阻止某种事情的发生”，用于阻止游行群众，抑制感情，或犹豫不决等。另外，还可以用来保守秘密(Keep something secret)。

“已经答应好一起去聚会的男朋友突然和拉拉队队长跑了”

She was staying home **holding back** her tears.

M·O·R·E

- hold sth back
  阻止，抑制感情，掩藏
- hold sb back
  阻止，阻挡，使某人无法做某事
- hold back
  阻止，抑制，隐瞒

She could barely **hold back** the tears.
她无法忍住泪水。

Did he **hold back** information on this issue?
他隐瞒了这个问题的情况？

I didn't **hold back**. I named names.
我没有隐瞒什么，该说的都说了。

Please don't **hold back**.
请不要隐瞒。

A: They asked me to give some money for their trip. 他们要我资助他们旅行。
B: I think you should hold back on paying. 我觉得你得慎重一点。

hold down 阻止，压制，继续维持（职业等）

可以联想将物体压在下方的情形。表示阻止或抓住某人逃跑，抑制物价的上涨等。另外，hold down a job表示“维持原有的职业”。

“借了高利贷去做整容手术，不料因副作用没办法合上双眼”

They **held her down** trying to keep her quiet.

M·O·R·E

- hold sth down
  固定，阻止（价格上升等）
- hold sb down
  阻止，抑制（自由等）
- hold down a job
  维持某人的职业

He couldn'**t hold down** a job. The boss has been so hard on him.

他没能坚持自己的工作。老板对他太坏了。

Hold him down before he runs away.

在他逃跑之前抓住他。

He **held me down** by one arm.

他用一只胳膊抓住了我。

A: The neighbors are always too loud. 邻居总是很吵。

B: Have you asked them to hold down the noise? 你跟他们说过这情况吗?

hold off 延期，推迟

主要用作“推迟”，“延期”等，推迟的对象可以在hold off后面用on sth或(on) ...ing来表示。另外，还具有“阻挡某人”，“使对方无法靠近”，“（雨等）不下”的意思。

“我之所以没邀请她约会，是因为她的头太大”

I **held off** on asking her out because she has a huge head.

M·O·R·E

- hold off on sth
  推迟，延期
- hold off on ...ing
  推迟……

I'll **hold off** until Monday to report to the boss.

我要将汇报的事情推迟到星期一。

Can you just **hold off** for a second?

你能推迟一会吗?

I can't **hold off** on talking to him anymore.

我得马上和他说了。

I **have been holding off on** asking her out.

我一直推迟约她出去。

A: The economy is bad all over the world. 全球的经济情况都不大好。

B: A lot of people are holding off on spending money. 很多人推迟着消费。

hold on 等待

hold on (a minute)为祈使句形态，表示“稍等片刻”或说话的途中“稍等”。另外，hold on或hold on the line表示打电话时让对方不要挂机。

“儿子整天不务正业，沉迷于电脑游戏，老公扛着棒球棒就走进了孩子的房间”

Oh, **hold it**. What are you going to do with that?

M·O·R·E

- Hold on (a minute, a second).
  稍等一会。
- Please hold (= Hold, please).
  请不要挂机。
- hold on (the line).
  请不要挂机。
- hold on to sb (sth)
  继续，固守
- Hold it.
  稍等片刻。

Hold on, let me think it over.
稍等，让我想想。

Could you **hold a second**? I'll check if he's in.
你能等一会吗？我确认一下他在不在。

She had a breakdown and couldn't **hold on to** her job.
她得了神经衰弱，不能再继续上班了。

Betty, **hold it** for ten minutes. We have to get through this.
贝蒂，稍等十分钟。我们马上就结束。

A: Hold on for a minute. I need to talk to you. 稍等片刻，我得和你谈谈。
B: Really? What are we going to talk about? 真的吗？我们要谈些什么？

hold out 伸出（手等），给予（希望等），坚持，抵抗

字面含义为伸出手等，还可以表示“要求到底”或”永不屈服”。

“155cm的前辈与女神一般的女孩分手，便安慰他道”

She's a bitch. **Hold out for** a good girl.

M·O·R·E

- hold out hope of (that)
  产生某种期待
- hold out against
  永不屈服
- hold out for sth
  要求到底
- hold out on sb
  不对某人说重要的话

She **held out** her arms to hug me.
她伸手抱我。

They can't **hold out** much longer.
他们肯定挺不了多久了。

Looks like she's been **holding out on** me.
她好像在隐瞒我什么。

She **is holding out** hope that she'll see her son again.
她重新产生了见儿子的希望。

A: They asked me to work for a small salary. 他们让我以较低的薪水工作。
B: You should hold out for more money. 你应该挺住，要求更高的薪水。

hold to 固守，坚守

hold to 主要用于约定或想法等，表示“信赖”。hold somebody to形式则表示“某人坚守to后面的内容”。

“朋友要给我介绍一个赛车女郎，我突然兴奋起来”

You said you'd do it. I'm holding you to that.

M·O·R·E

- hold to+约定（想法）
  相信某人，信赖，固守
- hold sb to
  使某人遵守……

She didn't **hold to** her promise.
她没有遵守诺言。

I'm going to **hold you to** that.
我会让你遵守承诺的。

I **hold you to** a higher standard. Don't let me down again.
我得满足更高的水平，不要再次让我失望。

A: She promised to give me a book. 她说好了给我一本书。
B: You should hold her to her promise. 你得让她遵守承诺。

hold up 举手，折成，推迟，延期，抢夺

字面含义为将手举起，表示“支撑”，或推迟某事，使某人滞留等。另外，强盗们行凶也可以用hold up。hold up名词为“强盗”，“滞留”等含义。

“早上因交通事故，道路堵得非常严重，便给老板打电话”

I got held up behind a traffic accident.

M·O·R·E

- hold up
  举手，推迟
- hold ... up
  停顿，耽误
- be (get) held up
  被某事束缚
- What held you up?
  为什么迟到?
- What's the hold up?
  为什么这么晚?

Ok, everyone **hold up** your glasses.
好，大家高举手中的酒杯。

I **was held up** by the boss.
因为老板，我才晚的。

Three armed robbers **held up** the casino.
三个带武器的强盗抢劫了赌场。

Hold your hands up!
举起手来!

A: Why isn't the concert starting? 演唱会怎么还不开始?
B: The musicians got held up in a traffic jam. 歌星被堵在路上了。

More Expressions

- **hold your horses!** 减速！镇定！（由骑马时代衍生而来）

  Just **hold your horses**! We have a lot of time. 慢慢来，我们还有很多时间。

- **leave someone holding the bag** 让某人背负罪名

  I **got left holding the bag**. 我背上了黑锅。

- **hold water** 合理

  That'll never **hold water**. 说不通。

- **hold a grudge** 怀恨在心

  Don't **hold a grudge** against me. 不要怨恨我。

- **hold in** 自制

  You'll need that to **hold in** your feelings. 为了控制你的感情，就需要那些。

- **hold your tongue** 住嘴

  You should **hold your tongue** 你给我闭嘴。

赶紧拿过来

Bring

与take表示相反的含义，即带过来。与come的情况相同，take表示将物品拿到第三方地点，相反，bring则表明从对方处拿到本方处。另外，What bring (brought) you to+地点？的句型非常典型，在这种情况下，如果事物充当主语，成为bring somebody to的话就表示“让某人做某事”。

基本概念

1 带来，拿来

You can't bring your pet with you. 你不能把你的宠物带来。

I brought coffee for everyone. 我给大家带来了咖啡。

I forgot to bring a laptop computer for this class. 我上课时忘了带笔记本电脑了。

2 引起，使成为……（事物主语B）

Indigestion may bring about this disease. 消化不良可能引起这种病。

That (Which) brings me to the (main) point. 我想到了重点。

bring somebody something 给某人带来某物

在这里，bring表示“给某人带来某物”。如果先说对象的话，就是bring something for。

“对出差的同事说，回来的路上带邮件”

Please bring me my mail on the way back.

M·O·R·E

- bring me sth
  给我带点……
- Could (Can) you bring me something?
  你能帮我带点东西吗?
- Did you bring me something?
  你给我带了……没?

Could you **bring** me the newspaper?
能帮我带报纸吗?

What did you **bring** me today?
你今天拿什么来的?

We **brought** you some wine.
我们给你拿了几瓶红酒。

A: Thanks, I will return soon. 非常感谢，我会尽快回来的。
B: Bring me a coffee on your way back. 回来的路上帮我带杯咖啡。

bring somebody (sth) to 将某人带到某处，将某物带到某处

之前的句型表示“给我带来某物”，相反，这里是将人物或物品带到别处。因此bring后面要接地点名词或to+名词。

“妻子没带驾照就开车出了门，丈夫急忙把驾照送过去”

She forgot her license so now I have to bring it to her.

M·O·R·E

- bring sb (sth) to+名词（地点副词）
  将……带到某处
- bring sb (sth) with you
  带着，随身携带
- bring ... home
  带到家，拿到家

I never **bring** Jesse **to** the park.
我从来没带杰西去过公园。

Bring her **over here**.
把她带过来。

We'll have to pick her up and **bring** her **to** him.
我们不得不接她，送到他那。

A: The big trip is scheduled for tomorrow. 明天计划有一场大旅行。
B: Remember to bring food to the picnic. 记得带吃的。

What brings (brought) ... ? 怎么回事?

What brings (brought) you ... ?表示询问来到某处的目的（理由），表示“因何事来到这里？”。You后面可以接地点副词或to+名词。一般常用的形态为What brings(brought) you (down) here?

“假装看不见也是一种生存能力，过于老实的经理果然……”

What brings you to the strip bar, boss?

M·O·R·E

- What brings (brought) you here?
  何故大驾光临?
- What brings (brought) you to+地点名词?
  来这干嘛?

So, **what brings you here** at such a late hour?
怎么这么晚了才来这?

So, **what brings you to** New York?
什么风把你吹到纽约来了?

What brings you to the hospital?
你怎么来医院了?

A: What brings you here? I thought you were at home. 是什么风把你吹来的? 我以为你在家呢。

B: I came to pick up some books that I forgot. 我来拿忘在这儿的书。

can't bring oneself to 不忍心……

理解起来比较难的英语短语。直译过来就是“不能做……”，实际上表示“不忍心做某事”。

“非常值得尊敬的初中班主任涉嫌赌博被抓住”

I **can't bring myself to** look at you.

M·O·R·E

- can't bring oneself to+sth
  不忍心……
- can't bring oneself to+动词
  不忍心做某事
- can't bring oneself to tell
  不忍心告诉某人

You **can't bring yourself to** give me one little kiss?
你完全没有亲我的意思吗?

I **couldn't bring myself to** leave her.
我不忍心离开她。

I **can't even bring myself to** say it.
我不忍心说出来。

A: Sam needs to find a better job. 山姆需要找一个更好的工作。

B: He can't bring himself to quit the one he has. 不过他不忍心离开现在的公司。

bring home somebody (sth) 将某人带到家里

bring home a friend（将朋友带到家里）是典型的bring home somebody to+V (for ...)形式。当然，如果宾语是物品的话就表示将某物拿回家里。

“如果丈夫有外遇的话，没准会染传染病”

If he's cheating, he could bring home a disease.

M·O·R·E

- bring home sb
  将某人带回家里
- bring home the bacon (groceries)
  养家糊口

She **brought home** friends to meet her family.
她往家里带了很多朋友见家人。

Bring home a person to help me clean.
带个人回来，帮我打扫卫生。

I **brought home** some people I work with.
我把几个同事带回了家。

He **brought home** Steve for Thanksgiving.
他把史蒂夫带回家过感恩节。

A: I'm going to bring home Bob to meet my parents. 我要把鲍勃带回家见家人。
B: Oh, are you planning to marry him? 哦，你们打算结婚了？

bring about 引起，引发

bring about 表示使about后面的事情发生，可以理解为“带来”，“做出”，“成就”，“招致”，“引起”等含义。另外，最常用的形式为Something+be brought about something。

“在地下坑道或沉没的船只里救出了被困数日的人”

The news brought about a lot of happiness.

That might **bring about** big trouble.
那可能会导致一场大灾难。

The rain **brought about** flooding.
强降雨导致了洪灾。

Her marriage **brought about** two children.
她在结婚之后生了两个孩子。

Our meeting **brought about** a long friendship.
我们的见面使彼此之间的友谊更加长久。

A: The company lost a lot of money last year. 公司去年亏损了不少。
B: I know. It brought about many problems. 就是啊，还带来了不少问题。

bring around 带来，拿来，转移话题，说服，找回意识

字面含义为带(bring)回来(around)，因此bring around表示“带到家里”或“找回意识”。另外，在表达移动某物或分发食物时也可以使用bring around。

“在家里像公主一般成长的女儿不知道在和什么人约会”

Why don't you bring your date around to my office?

M·O·R·E

- bring sb around (to sth)
  将某人带走，
  找回意识
- bring sth around (to sb (sth))
  移动，分发

She is a girl that your friend **brought around**.
她是你朋友带来的。

You can **bring** your coworkers **around** to the party.
你可以把你同事带到聚会来。

Why don't you **bring** the pizza **around** for us?
你为什么不分我们点比萨?

A: Dan doesn't understand my feelings. 丹不知道我的感受。
B: Try to bring him around to the way you feel. 试着让他明白你的心思。

bring back 重新拿回来，让人想起，返还

bring back 正如字面含义，表示将某物拿(bring)回来(back)。可以用来表达“找回回忆”。

“丈夫好久都不关心妻子了，妻子一气之下说道”

Do you know what we need to bring back in this house?

M·O·R·E

- bring sth back for sb
  将某物还给某人
- bring sb back sth
  让某人找回意识
- bring sb back to life
  充满活力

Bring her back here, will you?
把她带回来，可以吗?

They didn't **bring back** any food at all?
他们没有带回任何食物?

It **brings back** bad memories of middle school.
这让我想起了中学时候的不好回忆。

A: Bring back that paper when you're finished with it. 等你弄完了，把那些纸拿回来。
B: Don't worry, I will. 别担心，我会的。

bring down 拉下，使破灭，使崩溃

虽然拿(bring)了回来，但却放在了下方(down)，表示将物品拉下，或降价。在表达“将某物拉下”时，可以理解为“使破灭”，“使崩溃”。

“为了给父亲报仇，刻苦钻研武艺的孩子”

You can bring down the guy who killed your father.

M·O·R·E

- bring down
  拉下，带到某处，降低，打击士气，使破灭
- bring sb (sth) down a notch (peg) (or two)
  打击某人的士气

What'd you **bring me down** here for?
你干嘛把我带到这儿来?

I didn't mean to **bring you down**
我不是诚心让你扫兴。

I've been waiting for the moment when I finally **bring you down.**
我终于等到了击败你的这一天。

A: Hattie got bad news when she went to the hospital. 哈蒂在医院时听到了不好的消息。

B: Oh dear, that will bring down everyone. 天啊，那会让所有人失望的。

bring in 引进，（法）导入，挣钱

具有3种主要含义。首先为某组织或团体“引进外部的人事”，其次为“导入新的法律法规”，最后为“挣钱”。

“非常害怕丈夫的妻子雇人杀害丈夫，不料被他发现”

You bring in a hit man without my approval?

M·O·R·E

- bring in to+动词 (on+名词)
  引入……来做某事
- bring in+钱 挣钱

I have decided to **bring in** an analyst to help us.
我已经决定要引进一名分析师来帮我们。

Did you send a man all the way to Chicago to **bring me in**?
你把一个人派到芝加哥就是为了找我?

My wife **brings in** a lot of money every month.
我老婆每个月都会挣很多钱。

A: I have decided to bring in an analyst to help us. 我已经决定要引进一名分析师来帮我们。

B: Great idea! That is just what we need. 好主意！那正是我们需要的。

bring on 带来，招来

bring on最基本的含义为“拿来某物”，还可以表示招来或引起不好的事情。另外，bring it on一般会在打架时使用，表示“有种就试试”。

“不知道离婚是让人抑郁的最大原因吗”

I'm suffering from stress **brought on** by my recent divorce.

M·O·R·E

- bring on
  带来，招来
- bring it on
  面对（挑战），试试
- bring sth on sb
  让某人经历不幸
- bring sth on (upon) oneself
  自食其果

What **brought this on**?
怎么会这样?

How about I clear the table and **bring on** dessert?
我把桌子收拾一下，端上甜点怎么样?

You want to hit me? **Bring it on**!
你想揍我? 试试啊!

What do you expect me to do? You **brought this on yourself**.
你想要我干什么? 这是你咎由自取。

A: Springtime is a beautiful time of year. 春天是一年四季最好的季节。
B: It brings on the hot weather of summer. 春天会带来炎热的夏天的。

bring out 拿走，带出来，拿出来，表现，发布（产品）

表示将某物带出来(out)，还可以理解为“出示某物”或“公布于众”。

“看到婚礼上恩爱的夫妻就会伤感的中年老处男”

I guess weddings just **bring out** the worst in me.

M·O·R·E

- bring out the best (worst) in sb
  使……处于最好（最差）的状态
- bring sth out in the open
  将……公布于众

I **brought you out** here because I want you to see this girl.
我之所以把你带来，就是为了让你见见这女孩。

We **brought her out of** the streets and gave her a new life.
我们把她从街道中拯救出来，并给了她新生活。

They didn't **bring out** the revised edition yet.
他们还没公布修订版。

A: Bring out the cookies that you made this morning. 把你今天早上亲自做的饼干拿出来。
B: Did you like the way they tasted? 你喜欢他们品尝的方式吗?

bring up 引出（话题），传授，赡养，出现（在电脑画面上）

bring up 相对来说比较纯净。主要有两方面含义，分别是“赡养孩子”和“引出某话题”。另外，也经常会用来表示电脑画面的出现。

“朋友对别人说起我过去的酒后驾驶经历”

Please don't **bring up** the accident again.

M·O·R·E

- bring sb up to+动词 传授某人某事，赡养
- bring sb up as 将某人培育为……

Are you going to **bring up** your children here while you go to school?
你想在上学的过程中把孩子养大?

This isn't the best time to **bring it up**, but you have to get out of here.
现在说这话虽然有点不合适，不过你还是出去吧。

I'm really kind of surprised nobody's ever **brought it up**
很惊讶，居然没有人提到它。

A: Sally gets angry very easily these days. 这几天莎莉非常容易发脾气。
B: I know. I'm afraid to bring up new topics with her. 就是啊，我非常害怕和她说话。

More Expressions

- **bring along** 带走，拿走
  Does he have a single friend that you could **bring along** for me?
  他有没有能够介绍给我的朋友?

- **which brings me to** 正因为如此……
  I got divorced again. **Which brought me to** the strip bar.
  我又离婚了，所以才会来脱衣舞酒吧。

- **bring sth to a close** 结束某事
  Let's **bring this matter to a close**
  我们还是了结了这问题吧。

- **bring ... to one's knees** 使服从，使屈膝
  Use it to **bring any man to his knees**
  用这个让男人们好好听话。

- **bring together** 再回，一起
  We **were brought together** to spend the night together.
  我们聚到一起就是为了过夜。

- **bring a case (charges)** 诉讼
  The district prosecutor refused even to **bring charges**. 地方检察居然拒绝任何诉讼。

It brought me to my senses.
多亏这个，我才可以恢复神智。

只要打个电话就万事俱全

Call

这个世界是离不开电话的。call虽然是众所周知的打电话动词，但原本的含义为“（大声）叫喊”。call somebody chicken就是一个典型的例子。另外，在手机成为人们日常生活的必需品之后，have my phone on vibrate（将手机置于振动），She's on a cellphone（她在用手机通话）等与手机相关的表达就需要好好记住。

基本概念

1 打电话，大声叫喊

Mr. James called you during the meeting. 开会期间詹姆斯先生给你打了电话。

I called but your line was busy. 我打过电话，不过当时占线。

I heard you called this morning. 我听说你今天早上打电话了。

2 召开（会议等）

I'm going to call a meeting tonight. 我今晚要召开一次会议。

3 叫……当成……

What do you call this in English? 这个用英语怎么说?

I'm calling to ... 我打电话是为了……

用在说明给对方打电话的目的。I'm calling to because ... 或I'm calling to+动词都可以。另外，过去式为I called to+动词。

"儿子住校以后，妈妈天天担心，每30分钟就会打一次电话"

I just called to see how you were doing.

M·O·R·E

- I'm calling you because S+V
  我打电话是为了……
- Who's calling please?
  谁的电话?
- I'm calling (called) to+动词
  我打电话是为了……
- This is sb calling.
  我是……

I'm calling you because I saw that you called me.
我看到你给我来了电话，才打给你的。

I'm calling about tomorrow's meeting.
我打电话是为了明天的会议。

I called to apologize.
我打电话是想道歉的。

A: I'm calling to talk to Mr. Kang in the marketing department. 我要打给营销部的姜先生。
B: I'm sorry, but he isn't in the office right now. 不好意思，他现在不在办公室。

call security 叫保安

有时call后面接的不是人，可以是车辆或房子。call+团体/店铺/家等都表示"打电话求帮助"。

"只要喝酒就会疯狂打丈夫的职业摔跤女性"

I realized that I had hurt him, so I **called 911**.

M·O·R·E

- call 911
  打911
- call the police
  叫警察
- call a taxi
  叫出租车
- call sb's house
  给某人家里打电话

Please **call an ambulance**.
请叫救护车。

Could you **call a taxi** for me?
能帮我叫辆计程车吗?

I **called security** to kick him out.
我叫了保安，把他们赶了出去。

A: The baby's not breathing! 孩子不喘气了!
B: Oh, my God! Call 911! 天啊! 快叫911!

give somebody a call 给某人打电话

前面的call表示打电话，这次则变成了名词形式。其中最常用的就是give somebody a call，表示“给某人打电话”，“打电话”等。

“两个人见面才没多久，男孩就提出出去玩一宿，不料被拒绝”

If you change your mind, **give me a call**.

M·O·R·E

- make a call
  打电话
- take a call
  接电话
- expect one's call
  等某人的电话
- return one's call
  回某人的电话
- transfer (direct) a call (one's call)
  转接电话

Give me a call anytime you want.

你随时都可以给我打电话。

I'm available today. **Give me a call** if he needs a drinking buddy.

我今天有空。如果他想喝两杯，就给我打电话。

I'll **give you a call** later tonight.

我今晚会给你打电话的。

I was **expecting your call** all day.

我一整天都在等你的电话。

A: I have to go now. Give me a call sometime. **我得走了。有空就给我打电话。**

B: Oh, but you didn't give me your phone number. **哦，不过你还没告诉我你的电话号码呢。**

a phone call for you 来电话了

表示别人打电话找你，也可以使用you have(got) a call from等。另外，如果对一个正在接听电话的人说有你的电话时可以用There's a call on another line，而当我接电话却有别的电话进来时可以用I have another call。

“女朋友打电话说要拿回之前送过的内衣”

You **got a call from** Cindy. She wants her underwear back.

M·O·R·E

- a phone call for sb
  找某人的电话
- You have a call from sb
  某人给你来电话了

Phone call for you.

找你的电话。 (= You have a phone call)

You **got a call from** the school this morning.

今天早上学校来电话找你。

Excuse me. There's **a phone call for you.**

打扰一下，有电话找你。

A: There's a phone call for you. **找你的电话。**

B: Thank you. I'll take it in my office. **谢谢，我到办公室再接。**

call somebody sth (adj.) 叫某人……

表示叫名字或外号等，be called something表示“被叫做……”，另外，call somebody names表示“骂人”，变成完全不同的含义，因此要注意。

“学校的一个书呆子被蜘蛛咬了一下，居然说‘敢跟学校的老大对抗’”

If you call me chicken again, you're a dead man.

M·O·R·E

- call sb sth
  叫某人……
- call sb names
  骂人
- be called sth
  被叫做……
- call oneself sth
  自称……

What do you **call that** in English?
那个用英语怎么说?

Don't **call me names**!
不要骂我!

You **call yourself** an assistant?
你说你是助理?

You **call yourself** an accountant, but you're terrible at numbers?
你自称会计，却害怕数字?

A: People have been calling Kristie fat. 人们管克里斯蒂叫胖子。
B: She looks like she has been eating too much. 她看起来吃了好多好多。

call it a day 下班

call it a day表示“下班”，也可以成为call it a night或call it quits。同时也要记住两个常用的短语call in sick和call the shots。

“在请了10个星期的病假之后，一般的小病就不好意思请假了”

I can't call in sick after ten weeks of sick leave.

M·O·R·E

- call it a day
  下班，放下手中的事情
  (call it a night, call it quits)
- call in sick
  打电话请病假
- call the shots
  决定

It's coming up on 6:00. What do you say we **call it a day**?
都6点了，我们下班好不好?

What are you doing here? You **called in sick** this morning.
你在这干嘛呢? 今天早上不是打电话请病假了吗?

I'**m calling the shots**.
我来决定。

A: Let's call it a day. 我们下班吧。
B: Sounds good to me. 好主意。

call back 打回电话

接电话不太方便，过一会再打回去的意思(call again)。后面也可以用later或in+时间副词。

“正和女朋友亲热呢，总有人来电话”

I'm making out with my girlfriend. Can you **call back**?

M·O·R·E

· call back in+时间 之后再打电话

Could you **call back** later? I'm tied up right now.

你能过一会再打来吗？我现在有点忙。

I've got to go. I'll **call back** later.

我得挂电话了，回头打给你。

I'll have him **call you back** as soon as he gets home.

我会跟他说，一回到家就给你打电话。

Please **call me back** in ten minutes.

请在10分钟后再打来。

A: Could you tell him to call back after lunch? **你能叫他午餐之后打来吗?**

B: I'll tell him right now. **我现在就跟他说。**

call for 要求，大喊（请求）

for之后的部分就是需要叫喊或打电话的内容。不要固定理解为call for=demand，而是要根据具体的状况理解。因为这还可以表达有人打电话找你(Some guy just called for you)。

“在漆黑的小巷被打劫的人打电话请求帮助”

He was reaching for his cell phone, trying to **call for** help.

Call for an ambulance. She is still alive.

叫救护车，她还有一口气。

She already **called for** a consult.

她已经申请咨询了。

Did anybody **call for** security?

有人报警没?

He **called for** help yesterday.

他昨天请求帮助了。

A: My car is running poorly. **我的车状况不太好。**

B: That calls for a visit to the mechanic. **所以让你去修理师那看看。**

call off 取消，停止

我们比较熟悉的短语，其含义也比较简单。某计划需要终止或取消时可以使用，理解成call off=cancel就可以了。

“虽然出动了搜救队(search party)，却没能找到小狗”

She finally called off the search for her pet.

I want you to end it. I want you to **call off** the wedding.
我希望你能做到取消婚礼。

You can **call off** the roommate search!
别找室友了。

He told me that Leo **called off** his engagement with Jane.
他跟我说，利奥取消了和简的订婚。

The boss had to **call off** the meeting because of the traffic.
因为交通堵塞，老板不得不取消会议。

A: They had a big fight last night. 他们昨晚有过激烈的冲突。
B: I hope they don't call off their wedding. 我希望他们今天不要取消婚礼。

call out 大声呼唤，呼叫，请求帮助

最近因电话的普及，很容易把call当成打电话，但最原始的含义为“叫”。现在也有很多情况用作非打电话的含义。call out就是一个例子，表示“大声呼唤”或“打电话”。

“肯定会有人跨过国境诈骗”

Did you call out everyone's name? Some students are absent.

M·O·R·E

- call out for
  需要……
  打电话订购
- call out to sb (for sth)
  向某人大喊
- call out one's name
  大喊某人的名字，
  叫名字
- be called out to+动词
  呼唤做某事

You're going to **call out** her name and say, “I love you!”
你何不大喊她的名字，说“我爱你！”呢。

She got out of the car and **called out** to Sam.
她从车里出来，大喊着山姆。

From across the street, they heard Michael **call out**
马路对面，传来了麦克的喊声。

A: Winnie got hurt when she was out hiking. 维尼登山的时候受伤了。
B: She had to call out to get someone to help her. 她不得不大喊，让路人帮忙。

call up 打电话

口语中表示“给某人打电话”。一般可以用作call up somebody to+动词或call up somebody+动词的形式。

“就算租车，也要开BMW和女朋友兜风”

He **called up** a car rental agency and reserved a BMW.

M·O·R·E

- call up sb to+动词 打电话做某事
- call up sb and+动词 打电话做某事

Why don't you just **call up** Helen and invite her over?
你怎么不给海伦打电话邀请她?

Call up Tom and tell him we're coming over.
给汤姆打电话，跟他说我们马上到。

I'd like to **call up** Cindy to talk about that.
我想给辛迪打电话聊聊这事。

I want to **call up** someone who'd like to share a conversation.
我想找个人打电话说说这事。

A: Let's call up and order a pizza. 我们打电话叫比萨吧。
B: Great idea. I'm feeling really hungry. 好主意，我现在很饿。

call somebody's cell phone 给某人的手机打电话

如果手机响就会拿出来(take out a cell phone)，用手机打电话(makes a call)交流(talk on my cell phone)。上述的表达为“给某人的手机打电话”，相反call on one's cell phone，(use somebody's cell phone)则表示利用“某人的电话”给“别人打电话”。

“虽然综合业务很重要，不过这也太过分了”

I **was talking on my cell phone**, while making love with her.

M·O·R·E

- call one's cell phone 给某人的手机打电话
- call on one's cell phone 用某人的手机打电话
- talk on one's cell phone 用某人的手机通话

They **called my cell phone** to see where I am.
他们给我的手机打电话，问我在哪里。

Eva made a **call on her cell phone**.
伊娃用自己的手机打了电话。

Dump him immediately. **Use my cell phone**.
马上甩掉他，用我的电话。

A: Why isn't Brad at the party? 为什么布拉德没在派对?
B: Call his cell phone and see where he is. 给他手机打电话，看看他在哪儿。

More Expressions

- **be a close call** 惊险

  That **was a close call**.
  真危险啊，差点。

- **call down** 打电话

  I'll **call down** to see if his car's in the parking lot. 我想打电话确认一下，他的车在不在停车场。

  The boss **called her down** to speak with her. 老板打电话跟她谈谈。

- **call the meeting** 召开会议

  I've **called this meeting** to discuss the stock.
  为了讨论股市的问题，我召开了这次会议。

- **call in** 给某人打电话请求帮助，请求帮助，拜访

  Call in the lawyers. We're getting a divorce. 给律师打电话，我们要离婚了。

- **be one's call** 是某人应该决定的事情

  That'**s your call**.
  那要看你的决定，我会遵循你的意思。

  It's your call. 这是你的事情。

- **be on call** 待机中

  He **was on call** last night, so now he might be asleep.
  他昨晚值班了，现在应该在睡觉。

- **call my own** 我想干嘛就干嘛

  I have no time to **call my own**.
  我可以没有时间做别的事。

- **so-called** 所谓的

  When I was in high school, **so-called** techno music was also very popular.
  我上高中的时候，所谓的高科技舞曲非常流行。

不看怎么知道

See

see表示看眼前的东西，具有“相会”，“交往”和比喻性质的“了解”，“理解”等含义。尤其在分手时经常会用(I'll) See you+时间名词的形式。另外，see与hear同为感觉动词的两大山脉，see somebody/something+动词/ ...ing 的形式表示“见到……做某事”。

基本概念

1 见，凑热闹，相会，交往

I'd like to see a menu, please. 我想看看菜单，谢谢。

Have you seen Bob lately? 你最近见到鲍勃没?

Come and see me next weekend. 下周末来找我。

2 见到某人做某事（see ... +动词（...ing））

I saw you kissing Nina in the park. 我看到你在公园亲妮娜了。

You saw me dancing in the bathroom? 你看到我在洗手间跳舞了?

3 知道，理解，确认

I see. 我明白了。

I don't see that. 我不那么认为。

We'll see. 走着瞧，等等看。

see somebody (sth)+动词(ing) 见到某人做某事

see的最典型句式。see+somebody (something)后面可以加动词原形或 ...ing，而 ...ing可以用来强调动作的进行过程。

"疲劳驾驶的人，应该重重拍他后脑勺"

The boss saw him dozing off behind the wheel.

M·O·R·E

- see sb (sth)+动词 (...ing)
  见到某人做某事
- can't see sb (sth)+ ...ing
  没想到某人会做某事

I **saw her leave** for school this morning.
我今天早上看到她去学校了。

I never **saw her smoke**.
我从来没见过她吸烟。

My wife **saw my secretary hitting** on me.
我老婆看到秘书勾引我。

A: Is Ann still dieting? 安还在减肥吗?
B: No, I saw her eating some cake. 没，我看到她吃蛋糕了。

see somebody 相会，见面

表示与某人见面(meet)，典型的句型有Nice to see you, It's great to see you, It's good to see you等。如果和某人有约，说回头见时可以用I'll see you then，如果见到了很久没见的人，就可以说I haven't see you in years。

"吃完了美味的午餐，回到办公室就被可恶的李部长叫了过去"

He wants to see you in his office.

M·O·R·E

- (It's) Nice (Good) to see you.
  见到你很高兴。
- I'm here to see sb ...
  我是来见……的。

I'm here to **see some** of my relatives.
我是来见见亲戚的。

What a surprise! I didn't expect to **see you** here.
真是个惊喜！我可没想到你会来这。

Haven't I **seen you** somewhere before?
我是不是之前在哪儿见过你?

A: Ms. Norris is here to see you. 诺里斯夫人是来见你的。
B: Okay. Have her come in. 好的，请她进来吧。

(I'll) See you 再见

一般分手时会说I'll see you+时间，表示“……时候再见”。一般I'll会被省略掉，变成See you后面加时间相关的词组，也可以单单说一句See you。

“要加班，没眼色的老婆却要出去吃饭”

I have to get back to the office. **See you** tonight.

M·O·R·E

- See you later.
  回头见。
- See you soon.
  回头见。
- See you tomorrow.
  明天见。
- See you around.
  回头见。

See you in the morning.
明天早上见。

I hope to **see you** again (sometime)
我希望能再次和你相见。

I'll **be seeing you**!
走好，再见！

A: I've got to go. Take care. 我要走了，保重。
B: OK, see you later, nice meeting you. 好，回头见，见到你很高兴。

be seeing somebody 交往

同样为see+人物的形式，如果用作现在进行时则表示“持续见某人”，可以用来表达“男女之间的交往关系”。当然也可以像I'm seeing her again on Thursday 一样，单纯表达见面。

“独身主义的女儿假装自己有男朋友，不料被父母拆穿”

Don't pretend that you'**re seeing somebody**.

M·O·R·E

- be seeing sb
  与某人交往
- see a lot of sb
  与某人相处很长时间

You're late again. Are you **seeing someone**?
你又迟到了，你在谈恋爱吗?

I **am seeing her**. It has been a while.
我在和她交往呢，有一段时间了。

As far as I know, she'**s not seeing anybody**.
据我所知，她还没有男朋友。

Are you still **seeing her**?
你还在和她交往吗?

A: My god, Tracey looks so beautiful. 天啊，特蕾西很漂亮啊。
B: She dresses nicely because she is seeing a rich guy. 她穿的很华丽，因为正在和一个富二代交往。

see a doctor 看医生

表示看医生，在医院“接受治疗”，go to a doctor或visit a doctor也可以。另外，看电影为see a movie。

“看完超人之后，决心长大之后办一个超市”

One day I **saw a movie** that changed my life.

M·O·R·E

- see a doctor 看医生
- see a movie 看电影

I'd like to **see a doctor**.

我要去看医生。

I think we should **see a doctor** soon.

我觉得我们该尽快去看医生。

I **saw that movie** last weekend. It was really good.

我上周末看了那部电影，非常不错啊。

A: Look at this red patch on my arm. 看看我胳膊上的红印。

B: It looks terrible. You should see a doctor. 很吓人啊，你得尽快去医院瞧瞧。

(can) see (that) 明白，原来如此

see在这里表示明白(understand)。I (can) see (that)主语+动词表示“明白”，“清楚”等含义。当然see的原本含义为“见……”。

“在经过数次加班之后，终于要休假了，脸上神采飞扬”

I can see she really needed a vacation.

M·O·R·E

- I (can) see that.
  我知道了。
- I don't see that.
  我可不那么认为。
- Don't you see?
  你不知道吗?
- You'll see.
  你会知道的，等着瞧。

I can see you're not going to be any help.

我觉得你不会有任何作用。

I see that beauty runs in the family.

我看到了那个家庭的和睦。

Did you see that I sent you a text message?

你看到我发给你的短信了吗?

A: Look, there's the Statue of Liberty. 瞧，是自由女神像。

B: Oh, I can see it. 哦，我也看见了。

(can) see what (why, how) 明白……

在这里，see同样表示understand，然而这次后面跟的不是that，而是疑问词。比之前的that情况更为常用。

"办事能力非常差，却因为外表出众继续留在身边的女老板"

I can see why it's hard to fire him.

M·O·R·E

- I (can) see what (why) S+V
  原来是……我知道……了
- I can't see what (why) S+V
  我搞不懂……

I see what you mean.
我知道你的意思了。

I see what this is! You are in love with her!
我知道怎么回事了！你爱上她了！

I can see why he likes you.
我知道他为什么喜欢你了。

I can't see what I'm doing here.
我真不明白我在这干嘛呢。

A: The carpenter worked all day in the house. **木匠整天在家工作。**
B: I can't see what he did here. **真不知道他在这做什么。**

see what somebody (sth) can 看看某人能做什么

在这里see表示"看懂"，"确认"(find out)等含义。表示看看主语在特定问题或状况面前怎么做。

"儿子对工作狂老妈说，请一天假帮自己辅导辅导功课"

I'll talk to my boss and I'll **see what I can** do.

M·O·R·E

- I'll see what ...
  我看看……
- Let me see what ...
  让我看看……

I'll **see what I can** do.
我试试吧。（帮你）

Let's **see what you can** do.
让我看看你的能力。

Here is 100 dollars. **See what you can** do.
这里是100美元，想想要做什么吧。

A: A couple of people came to help us. **几个人来帮助我们。**
B: See what they can do in the kitchen. **看看他们能在厨房干点什么。**

see if 确认……

see if 后面如果接上主语+动词的句子，就表示“确认……是否……”，一般会以I'll see if或Let me see if开始。

“女朋友不接电话，也没有按时赴约”

I just wanted to see if everything was all right.

M·O·R·E

- I'll see if S+V
  确认一下……
- Let me see if S+V
  确认……
- I'll see (Let me see) if I can+动词
  让我看看……能不能做某事
- I want to see if ...
  我想看看……

I'm going to **see if** I can get a room for the night.
我得看看今天晚上能不能弄到房间。

I'll **see if** I can find her.
看看我能不能找到她。

We'll **see if** she wants to come back.
我们看看她是不是想回来。

A: I came here to see if you were finished. 我是来看你有没有做完工作的。
B: No, I still have a lot of work to do. 没有，我还有很多事情要做。

I've never seen ... 头一次见到

如果直译的话就是到目前为止“从未见到过……”，表达惊讶的感情。另外，be the most+形容词+名词(that) I've ever seen的形式表示“在我见到过的所有……当中最……”。

“投了100份简历，无功而返，大醉而归的女儿”

My parents have never seen me drunk!

M·O·R·E

- I've never seen+名词
  第一次见到……
- be the most+形容词+名词+I've ever seen
  是我见到过的……当中最……的

I've never seen anything like it.
我之前从来没见过这种事情。

I've never seen him this happy.
我从没见到过他这么开心。

You're the sexiest woman **I've ever seen**.
你是我见过的最性感的女人。

A: This is my diamond necklace. 这是我的钻石项链。
B: I've never seen diamonds that big. 我从没见过这么大的钻石项链。

the way (as) I see it 在我看来

在这里，see表示“思考（判断）”，因此the way (as) I see it表示“在我看来”。另外，也可以用作be how I see的形式，表示“我对某事的看法为……”，用来表示自己的想法或立场。

“赌场从业人员一看到表演女郎就情不自禁”

As you can see, I have a weakness for showgirls.

M·O·R·E

- the way (as) I see it
  在我看来……
- as you can see
  正如你所知
- how I see
  在我看来……

So **the way I see it**, you've got two choices.
所以说，在我看来你有两种选择。

That's not **the way I see it**.
我可不那么认为。

That's exactly **how I see it**.
我就是那么想的。

That's not **how you see me**, is it?
你不是那样看我的，是吧?

A: Are you going to vote in the election? 你要去参选吗?
B: The way I see it, my vote doesn't matter. 在我看来，我的那一票没什么意义。

wait and see what (if) 观察，留意查看

wait and see 表示“留意观察”，可以用于不急于判断或行动，“慎重地观察情况”。

“经常迟到的人，今天会有什么创意性的辩解呢”

We're going to **wait and see what** she tells us.

M·O·R·E

- wait and see what (if) S+V
  查看，留意

Let's **wait a bit and see how** things develop.
让我们耐心期待事情的进展吧。

We are going to just **wait and see what** happens.
我们耐心等待会发生什么事情吧。

We're going to have to **wait and see if** she remembers anything else.
我们得慢慢观察她能不能记起别的事情。

A: I think he is planning to buy us dinner. 我觉得他要请我们吃饭。
B: Wait and see if he invites us out with him. 耐心等待他邀请我们吧。

see about 处理，检讨

see about表示“对……了解一番”，“确认”等。当对方询问某个问题时，可以用来表达尚不清楚会怎么样，最常用的形式为We'll see about that（我们走着瞧）。

“一个高三学生说不想考大学，只能这么说了”

You're not going to a university? We'll **see about** that.

M·O·R·E

- see about+N/ ...ing
  确认……

Well, we'll **see about** that.
好，我们走着瞧。

Yeah, we'll **see about** that. I am calling her right now.
好，我们走着瞧，我现在就给她打电话。

Could you **see about** getting my notebook back?
你能问问能不能找回我的笔记本吗?

A: Let's go to the theater tonight. 我们今晚去剧院吧。
B: I may be busy. We'll see about the theater. 我可能会有点忙，去剧院以后再说吧。

see through 看破，看穿

表示通过某物观察，“看破……”，另外，将某物观察到底，“坚持到底”或“帮忙帮到底”。see–though就变成了形容词，可以表示“心知肚明的”。

“加班12点才回家，老婆却穿了一件透明的睡衣”

I saw her wearing a **see-through** nightie when I got home.

M·O·R·E

- see through
  看破，看穿，继续做某事
- see sb through (sth)
  帮助某人，帮到底

Can you totally **see through** her shirt?
她的上衣是不是透明的?

The jury would **see through** that.
陪审团会看穿的。

I started doing something charitable and I'm going to **see it through**.
我刚开始参加慈善事业，而且会做到底的。

A: Are you sure John is in his apartment? 你确定约翰在他公寓里吗?
B: Yes. I saw through his window and he's inside. 恩，我通过窗户看到他在里面。

seeing as 因为是…… 正因为(seeing that)

在提及自己所说内容的理由时所使用的表达。主要使用的形式有seeing that 主语+动词或seeing as主语+动词的形式。

"婚礼当天，新娘大喊'我讨厌结婚！'，没有出现在现场"

There isn't going to be wedding today, **seeing as** we have no bride.

There isn't going to be any class today, **seeing as** we have no teacher.
老师今天不在，看来不会上课了。

Seeing that you're the leader, I'd appreciate you saying something.
既然你是我们的领袖，我希望你能说点什么。

Seeing as you've got the most experience, I want you to take this.
既然你最有经验，那你来接管吧。

A: They are too busy to come to the meeting. 他们太忙了，没办法参加会议。
B: Seeing as they can't come, we'll cancel the meeting. 既然他们不能来，那我们就取消会议吧。

More Expressions

- **see off** 送(see you to+地点)

I've been to the airport to **see** my mother **off**. 我去机场送妈妈。
I'll **see you to** the station.
我就送你到车站吧。

- **see eye to eye (with)** 统一

I don't **see eye to eye** with my wife.
我和老婆意见不一。

- **see ... coming** (困难等)临近

I didn't **see it coming**. 我没想到会这样。

- **see ... as ...** 认为……

He'll **see it as** a sign of relief.
他会把它当成释怀的象征。

- **see in somebody** 喜欢某人

What do you **see in** her? 你喜欢她哪一点?
I can't imagine what Tom **sees in** her.
我无法想象汤姆喜欢她。

I (can) see your point. 我知道你的意思了。
I don't see why not. 没问题。
You see that? 看到没? 我说的对吧?
I don't see the need for it.
我觉得没有必要。
You haven't seen anything yet.
这还是小儿科。
I've seen better. 没什么大不了的。
I've seen worse. 还可以。

能听见，没办法

Hear/ Listen

听到声音的意思，与前面的see共同充当重要的感觉动词。像动词see一样，hear somebody (something)+动词形式表示“听到某人做某事”。hear的各种短语中最需要记住的就是表达听到某消息的I('ve) heard that ... 或Have you heard (Did you hear) that ... ?等。

基本概念

1 听见，听到

Excuse me, I didn't hear you well. 不好意思，我没听清你的话。

Did you hear that Cindy got married again? 你听说辛迪又结婚了吗?

I heard you got fired a few weeks ago. 我听说你几个星期前被解雇了。

I heard you and your husband live in Chicago. 我听说你们夫妻俩住在芝加哥。

2 听到某人做某事（hear sb. ... +动词(...ing)）

I heard her singing in the bathroom. 我听到她在卫生间唱歌。

I never heard her talking like that. 我从来没听她那样说过话。

hear it (that) 听到……

主要是在对话的过程中，将听到的消息或声音指代为it或that，用作hear it (that)（听到……）的形式。

“一个人在黑暗里走路，后面突然传来奇怪的声音”

Don't you hear that?

I am glad to **hear that**.
很高兴听到这个消息。

I am sorry to **hear that**. I never expected him to dump you.
很抱歉听到这个消息。我从来没想过他会抛弃你。

What're you talking about? That isn't the way I **heard it**.
你在说什么？这和我听到的完全不同。

M·O·R·E

- Did you hear that?
  你听说了吗？（在听到奇怪的消息之后）
- Did you hear?
  你听过没？
- Do you hear that?
  听到了吧？
- I didn't hear that.
  我没听到。

A: Today has been such a crazy day. 今天真让人发疯。
B: I'm sorry to hear that. What's going on? 很抱歉听到这话，发生什么事了？

hear somebody 听到某人的话

这次hear后面接上了人物，表示“听到某人的话”，“听某人的话”等。想要向对方表达“记住”的话，可以用You heard me。

“一有空就会吵架的楼上夫妇非常令人讨厌”

I can hear you through the ceiling.

I'm sorry I can't **hear you**. Please say it louder.
很抱歉，我听不到。请大声一点。

It's good to **hear your voice**. Where are you now?
听到你的声音真好。你现在在哪？

Did I **hear you** right?
你说的是真的？

I can't (couldn't) **hear you**.
我听不到你的声音。

M·O·R·E

- You heard me.
  小心点。
- I hear you, I hear you.
  我听到了。
- Do you hear me?
  你听到我的话没？

A: I need you to pay attention. Do you hear me? 我需要你集中注意力。听到没？
B: Yes! Calm down. I hear you. 恩！冷静点，我听到了。

hear somebody (sth)+动词 听到某人……

和see一样，hear+sb (sth)+动词表示“听到某人……”。如果使用 ...ing 的话就表示对动作进行过程的强调。

“下班回家，从门外就听到老婆大喊”

What's going on here? I heard you yelling.

We **heard you crying**. Please don't cry.
我听到你在哭泣。别哭了。

I'**ve never heard him make** that sound.
我可从来没听到过他发出那种声音。

I'**ve never heard her talk** like this.
我从来没见过她这么说话。

A: I can hear her talking on the phone. **我能听到她打电话的声音。**
B: Is she talking to her boyfriend? **她是在给男朋友打电话吗?**

hear somebody say (that) 听到某人说某事

属于应用表达范畴hear somebody后面加动词，say that主语+动词的情况。表示“听到某人说某事”的句式有hear me say ... , hear you say ... 等。

“丈夫说，来世也要和你在一起”

I'm very glad to hear you say that.

M·O·R·E

- I heard you say that S+V
  我听到你说那些话了。

I **heard you say that** she was emotionally unstable.
我听你说过她精神不正常。

You **never heard me say that** I love you.
你从来没听我对你说过我爱你。

You **never heard me say** that.
你从来没听我说过那些话。

A: I heard somebody say that it will rain tonight. **我听有人说今天晚上会下雨。**
B: Yeah, we'd better take an umbrella. **恩，我们最好带把雨伞。**

hear (that) 听到

听到的内容过长，用从句表达的情况。I heard that或I've heard that可以用来表达听到的具体内容，用Did you heat that?或Have you heard that? 向对方询问“听说过……吗？”。

“每天上班的老公其实几天前就被解雇了”

I heard you got fired a few weeks ago.

M·O·R·E

- I('ve) heard that S+V
  我听说……
- Have you heard (Did you hear) that ... ?
  你听说过……的消息吗?

I hear you've been promoted.
我听说你晋升了。

I heard you had some fun with her last night.
我听说你昨晚和她玩得很开心。

I heard you were going to get married.
我听说你要结婚了。

Did you hear that she went to China to study?
你听说过她要去中国留学的事情吗?

A: I heard you don't like watching basketball. 我听说你不喜欢看篮球比赛。
B: Right. I prefer to watch baseball games. 恩，我比较喜欢看棒球比赛。

never hear 完全没听过

在没有听到某事时可以说I did't hear或I have never heard ... ,表示“没有听到……”，“没有听过……”。

“明明是自己忘了老婆的生日，还怪老婆情绪不稳定”

I've never heard her talk like that.

M·O·R·E

- I didn't hear ...
  我没听过……
- I have never heard ...
  我从来没听过……

I didn't hear you come in.
我没听到你进来。

I didn't hear you leave the hotel room.
我没听到你走出宾馆房间的声音。

You've never heard that before?
你之前从来没听说过吗?

A: Shawn is going to move to Hawaii. 肖恩要搬到夏威夷去了。
B: I never heard that. Are you sure it's true? 我从来没听说过。你确定这是真的吗?

hear somebody out 听完某人的话

表示听完somebody说的话，中途不打断。主要用来让对方倾听自己的话，常用Please hear me out的形式。

"儿子突然抱来了一个婴儿，说是我孙子"

I'm glad you decided to hear me out.

Please, **hear me out**. This is important.
请听我讲完，这很重要。

Listen, just **hear me out** for a second.
听我把话讲完。

I've been at this for hours. Just **hear me out**.
我已经做四个小时了，听我讲完。

Did she **hear you out**?
她听完你的话了吗?

A: Your idea will never work. 你的主意肯定行不通。
B: Hear me out. It's a good idea. 听我把话说完。它的确是个好主意。

hear about 听有关……的事情

正如字面含义，表示"听有关……的事情"。Hear about后面可以接听话的内容，也可以用hear about somebody ...ing的形式表达"听某人讲的话"。

"因为暴雨侵入屋里，不得不丢掉所有家具的朋友"

We heard about what happened. I'm so sorry.

How did they **hear about** my divorce?
他们是怎么知道我离婚的消息的?

Have you **heard about** her secret boyfriend?
你听说过她的秘密男友吗?

I **heard about** your engagement the other night. Congratulations.
我前几天晚上听说你订婚的事情了，恭喜啊。

I **heard about** you getting married next month.
我听说你下个月结婚。

A: I've heard about the Great Wall of China. 我听说过中国的万里长城。
B: Would you like to go and visit it? 你要去看看吗?

M·O·R·E

- I heard about it.
  我听说过这件事。（但不知道详细的情况。）
- I never heard about any of this.
  我从来没听过这件事。
- I heard about it second hand.
  我听别人说过。
- I've heard all about it.
  我听说了整件事。

hear of 听到……的消息

表示“听到……的消息”，hear of 后面可以加人物，也可以加事物。经常会省略为Never heard of this, Never heard of her等。

“头一次听说人们会给临产前的产妇送去礼物的习俗”

What is a baby shower? Have you heard of that?

I never **heard of** such a thing.
我从来没听说过这种事。

I've never **heard of** you until this morning.
我今天早上才听到你的消息。

I'd never **heard of** that until you told me about it.
在你告诉我之前，我从来没听过那件事。

I'm not kidding. I've never **heard of** this before.
我没开玩笑，我之前绝对没有听说过这件事。

A: Did you ever hear of a ghost living here? **你听说过这里有鬼吗?**
B: No. Who told you there was a ghost here? **没有，谁告诉你这里有鬼的?**

hear from 从某人那里听到

from后面加人物名词的话，hear from就表示“从某人那里听到消息”，“通过某人听到消息”等，主要表达通过第三者了解消息。

“女儿第一次谈恋爱，却没有表露任何事情，着急的妈妈说道”

How was your date? I didn't hear from you all weekend!

M·O·R·E

- I haven't (never) heard from ...
  我从来没听某人说过
- (Have) You heard from somebody?
  你听过某人的消息吗?

I **haven't heard from** him since the divorce.
自从他离婚之后，就再也没有消息了。

Unfortunately, I **never heard from** him.
很不幸，我没听到关于他的消息。

You **heard from** the car sales dealer?
汽车销售商联系你了?

Have you **heard from** Will?
你听说过威尔的消息吗?

A: It's good to hear from you again! **很高兴能再听到你的声音!**
B: I'm glad to be back on the job. **我很高兴能够再回来工作。**

listen (carefully) 注意听，倾听

与hear不同，表示注意倾听。如果没有宾语，单单的be listening 的形式表示“听话”。想要引起对方注意时就要用listen carefully，或轻轻说一声listen，接着把话接下去。

“对方总是重复说过的话，搞得越来越困”

I don't think you're listening.

M·O·R·E

- Listen carefully.
  仔细听我说。
- Listen.
  听我说！

I'm listening.
我在听，快点说。

You're just not listening.
你不听我说话干嘛呢?

Listen carefully. This is very important.
听清楚了，这很重要。

Listen, I'm broke, okay?
听我说，我现在是个穷光蛋，知道了?

A: Look, don't get so upset at me. 喂，不要对我生这么大的气。
B: I'm angry because you're just not listening. 我生气是因为你不好好听我说话。

listen to 听……

listen to后面可以接音乐(music)等可以发出声响的事物，表示主语在“倾听……的声音”，“聚精会神地听”等。

“马上就要出差了，老婆来电话让把孩子接回去，同事看不下去了”

Why are you listening to her? Are you crazy?

M·O·R·E

- listen for
  倾听
- listen up
  倾听，好好听

Are you listening to me?
你在听我说话吗?

He listens to me.
他非常听我的话。

They listened for a response and heard nothing.
他们用心去听了，不过什么都没听到。

All right, everybody, listen up.
很好，大家听我说。

A: What radio station do you listen to? 你一般听哪个广播台?
B: I listen to 88.1(eighty-eight point one) FM radio. 我一般听FM88.1广播。

More Expressions

- (I hear you) Loud and clear
  听得清楚，听明白
  I hear you **loud and clear**. Don't worry about me. 我听得很清楚，不用担心。

- From what I hear(d) 据我所知
  From what I hear, that's going to take a while. 据我所知，那得需要一定的时间。

- So I hear (So I've heard)
  据我所知，据我了解
  You're not a doctor. **So I've heard**.
  据我所知，你不是个医生。

- hear it through the grapevine
  听到传闻
  I **heard it through the grapevine** the other day. 我前几天听到了这个传闻。

- won't (wouldn't) hear of
  不愿意 听……
  My mother **wouldn't hear of** it.
  我妈就是不愿意听那些。

- hear the last of somebody
  某人的抱怨还没有完
  I don't think we'**ve heard the last of** her. 我觉得她的抱怨还没有完。

- never hear the end of it
  会继续说下去
  You will **never hear the end of it**
  你绝对听不完的。

I'm sorry, I'm hard of hearing.
很抱歉，我听力不好。

Now I've heard (seen) everything.
天下之大，无奇不有。

So I've been told/So I hear.
据我了解，是那样的。

You'll never guess what I heard.
你绝对不会猜到我今天听到的事情。

I hear what you're saying.
我知道你说的是什么意思了。

I could hear a pin drop. 真安静啊。

渴望时用

Want

want表示的是想要拥有自己需要的东西(want something)或者是想要做某件事情(want to)的意思，虽然跟前面提到的I'd like意思相似，但是却是用在比较亲近的关系之间的比较直接的一种表达形式。尤其是要表示想要对方做某件事情的时候，用want somebody to来表示就可以了。在生活中经常会遇到想要做什么或者是不想做什么的时候，所以可以把经常用到的表现形式熟记下来，在需要的时候进行活用就可以了。

基本概念

1 想要，需要……(want something)

Do you want a refund? 您想要退款吗?

Do you want some? 想吃一点吗?

2 想做……(want to do)

I want to ask you something. 我想问你一些事情。

I don't want to lose you. 我不想失去你。

Who do you want to speak to? 你想跟谁谈话?

3 想要……给做（want ... to do (形容词，pp)）

I want you to meet my friend. This is Julie. 我想让你见见我的朋友，这是朱丽叶。

I want you to be happy. 我想让你幸福。

I want it fixed. 我想让你帮我修理一下。

want somebody (sth) 想要……

虽然这一表现形式是与表示现在想要的东西的时候使用的I'd like+名词相类似的表现形式，但是要在更加亲近一些的关系之间使用。I want+名词表示的是“需要……”，“想要……”的意思。在want的后面不仅可以加具体名词，而且还可以加类似于advice、privacy这样的抽象名词。

“给那些正在苦恼是辞职不干了呢，还是继续干下去的职场同事们”

Do you want some advice?

M·O·R·E

- I want+名词
  想要…… 需要……
- (Do you) Want+名词 ... ?
  想要……吗?

The boss wants you in his office now.

老板想让你现在就去他的办公室。

Do you want some more?

你还想再要一些吗?

Do you want some help with that?

你需要帮助吗?

A: I want something to drink right now. 我现在想喝点儿东西。

B: Let's go to the bar down the street. 我们去街边的酒吧吧。

want to 想做……

与上面相同，这一表现形式用在比表示“想要做……”意思的I'd like to+动词更亲近一些的关系中间。相反的，当表示不想做……的时候用I don't want to……来表示，当询问对方想不想的时候用Do you want to+动词？来表示。

“当妻子想要生孩子，但是我还没有做好准备的时候”

She wants to start a family, but I'm not ready yet.

M·O·R·E

- I want to+动词
  想做……
- I don't want to+动词
  不想做……
- Do you want to+动词 ?
  想做……吗?

I want to go to a movie tonight.

今天晚上我想去看电影。

I want to talk to you about that right now.

我想现在就跟你谈论一下关于那件事。

I don't want to start trouble.

我不想闹事。

Do you want to get some air?

你想去兜风吗?

A: I am not sure if I want to buy this. 我不知道我需不需要买这件东西。

B: Don't worry. I won't cheat you. 不用担心。我不会欺骗您的。

want somebody to 想让……做……

表示的是跟前边学过的I'd like somebody to相类似的意思，并不是说我要做什么，而是想让somebody做……表示拜托以及邀请的意思。

“跟恋人分手的时候，想让对方舒服一些的公式化的语句”

I just want you to be happy. I mean it.

M·O·R·E

- I want you to+动词 我想让你做……
- Do you want me to+动词？ 你想让我做……吗?
- want sb ...ing 想让某人做……

Don't lie to me. I **want you to** tell me the truth.
不要对我说谎。我想让你对我说实话。

He really **wants you to** be here. I guess he's serious.
他真的希望你能够在这里。我想他是认真的。

Do you **want me to** stay with you? Until when?
你想让我跟你待在一起吗？到什么时候为止?

There are some people I **want you to** meet.
我想让你见一些人。

A: Julie, I want you to meet my friend. This is Peter. 朱丽叶，快打招呼，这是我的朋友彼得。
B: Hi! Nice to meet you. 你好，很高兴认识你。

I want you to know (that) 我想让你知道

这是前面学习过的I want you to+动词的其中的一种表现形式，I want you to know that主语+动词这一表现形式主要用在向对方传达一个非常重要的事实或者是真心的时候。

“向被无心扔过来的石头打死的青蛙说……”

I want you to know how sorry I am.

M·O·R·E

- I want you to know (that) S+V 希望知道……
- I want you to know what (how) 希望知道 ...

I just **want you to know** I love you.
我只是想让你知道我爱你。

I want you to know that I'm going to be there.
我想让你知道我将要去那里了。

I want you to know that nobody thinks you're stupid.
我想让你知道没有人认为你很愚蠢。

We just want you to know how much we care.
我们只想让你知道我们有多么关心这个问题。

A: So, you talked to my boyfriend? 所以说，你跟我男朋友谈过了?
B: I want you to know he still loves you. 我想让你知道他仍然爱着你。

make somebody want to 让某人想做

虽然稍微有些难，但是这是使役动词make与want to相结合组成的表现形式。表示的是“让某人想做”的意思，所以通常用make you want to或者是make me want to来表示。

“当向比自己年轻的男朋友可爱地眨眼或者是撒娇的时候”

It really **makes me want to** have you.

M·O·R·E

- make me want to+动词
  让我想做……
- make you want to+动词
  让你想要做……

He **makes me want to** be a better man.

他让我想要成为一个更好的人。

Thinking of you **makes me want to** puke.

只要想到你就让我想要吐。

Christmas **makes you want to** be with people you love.

圣诞节让你想要跟自己爱的人一起度过。

A: Wow, that food smells delicious. 哇，那份食物闻起来很香。

B: It makes me want to eat it all. 它让我想要把它一口全部吃掉。

want somebody (sth)+形容词 (pp，副词) 想让……变成……形态

在want somebody (something)后面可以加类似于I want you out（出去），I want you out of here（从这里出去）这样的形容词、pp、副词（句）等，表示“想让……变成……形态”的意思。

“如果想让离家出走的妻子回来的话，是不是应该说”

I miss my wife. I **want her back**.

M·O·R·E

- want sb (sth)+形容词(pp)
  想要……变成……形态
- want sb (sth)+副词（句）
  想要……做……
- want ... back
  想把……要回来

I **want you right here**.

我想要你马上到这里来。

I **want it on my desk** first thing in the morning.

我想让你早上早早的把它放在我的桌子上。

When I ask you to do something, I **want it done**!

当我让你做某件事情的时候，就表示我想让你圆满地完成！

A: She gave away all of her designer clothes. 她把自己所有的名牌衣服都捐出去了。

B: Yeah, but she wants them back now. 是的，但是她现在又想全部都要回来。

don't want anything 完全不想

表示的是“什么都不想要”的意思，在anything的后面可以加to+动词，...ing，(that)主语+动词等，表示“什么都不想要”的意思，意译过来就是“绝对不想做”的意思。

“没有眼色，搅和进朋友的结婚纪念日中，还恬不知耻地说”

I don't want anything to spoil your anniversary.

I **don't want anything** from you.
我在你身上什么也不期望。

Now I **don't want anything** going on while I'm gone.
我希望我不在的时候什么都不要做。

I **don't want anything** to upset Betty tonight.
今天晚上我绝对不想让贝蒂伤心。

I **don't want anything** to do with you!
我不想跟你做任何事情，我要跟你分手！

A: Can I get you some coffee or cake? 我能不能给你一些咖啡或者是蛋糕呢？
B: Thanks, but I don't want anything. 非常感谢，但是我什么都不想要。

I just wanted to ... 我只不过想做……而已

这是表示自己的行动以及话语的意图的表现形式。并不是有其他的理由或者目的，“只不过是(just)想做……而已”以此来表达自己真实的想法。I just want to ... 表示“我只不过是想做……而已”的意思。

“努力学习了一会之后想要看一会电视，对无法忍受这些的母亲说”

I just want to watch a little television. What's the big deal?

M·O·R·E

- I just wanted to say ...
  我只不过是想说……而已
- I just wanted to make sure S+V
  我只不过是想确认……而已
- I just wanted to ask you if S+V
  我只不过是想要问一问是否……而已

I just wanted to say thank you.
我只不过是想对你说谢谢。

Well **I just wanted to** say I'm sorry.
我只不过是想对你说对不起。

I just wanted to make sure that you were doing OK.
我只不过是想确认一下你是否顺利。

I just want to tell you that Mr. Brown is fine.
我只不过是想要告诉你布朗先生很好。

A: Where were you this afternoon? 你今天下午去哪里了？
B: I just wanted to go outside for a while. 我只不过是想去外面待一会儿。

All I want is ... 我想要的一切就是……

这是对自己想要的东西进行描述的一个表现形式。表示的是“我想要的一切就是……”的意思，对自己想要的东西进行强调。当想要的是一种行动的时候用All I want to+动词+is ... 来表示就可以了。

“恋爱的时候说的话。让对方听了以后非常不舒服”

The last thing I want to do is to make you feel uncomfortable.

M·O·R·E

- All I want is+名词
  我想要的全部就是……
- All I wanted was (for sb) to+动词
  我想要的是做
- All I want to know is what (when ...) S+V
  我想要知道的是
- The last thing I want to do is+动词
  我最不想做的事情就是

All I wanted was to meet a nice girl like you.
我所希望的就是能够遇到一个跟你一样的好女孩。

All I wanted was for you to like me.
我所希望的就是你喜欢我。

All I want to do is help her.
我想做的就是帮助她。

All I want to know is how fast you run.
我想知道的是你到底能跑多快。

A: I'll give you whatever you would like. 只要是你想要的我全部都给你。
B: All I want is to be loved by you. 我想要的全部就是得到你的爱。

be what I wanted 我想要的就是

what I want表示的是“我想要的东西”，what I wanted表示的是“我曾经想要的东西”，主要是用what I want(ed) (to)的形式来表示“我想要的（曾经想要的）东西是”的意思。Know what I wanted表示的是“知道我想要的东西”。

“由于无法忘记分手的女朋友，要求再见一面之后却不知道该说什么”

I didn't **know what I wanted** to say to her.

M·O·R·E

- This (That) is what I want(ed).
  这（那）就是我想要的。
- This (That) is not what I want(ed).
  这（那）不是我想要的。
- I'll tell you what I want.
  我将告诉你我想要的是什么。
- Here's what I want you to do.
  这就是我想让你做的事情。

That'**s what I wanted** to hear!
那就是我想听到的！

That'**s** actually **what I wanted** to talk to you about.
那就是我想和你说的。

Here'**s what I want to** ask you.
这就是我想要问你的。

Do you **know what I wanted** to do?
你知道我想做什么吗？

A: I'm glad we're going to Hawaii. 我们要去夏威夷了，我真高兴。
B: Me too. This is what I wanted to do. 我也是。因为这就是我所期望的。

What do you want (me) to ... ? 想做什么？你想让我做什么？

这是疑问词what与do you want (me) to结合而成的表现形式。如果去掉(me)的话，表示的就是询问对方想做什么；如果加入me的话，表示的就是询问对方想让我做什么。当然，也可以用where、when来代替what。

“对总是唠叨着让自己嫁人的妈妈发火的时候说的话”

When do you want me to get married?

M·O·R·E

- What do you want (me) to+动词？
  你想做什么？
  你想让我做什么？
- Where do you want (me) to+动词？
  你想在哪里做？
  你想让我在哪里做？
- When do you want (me) to+动词？
  你想什么时候做？
  你想让我什么时候做？

What do you want to eat for lunch today?
你今天午饭想吃什么？

What do you want from me? You're too much.
你到底想从我这里得到什么？你太过分了。

Where do you want to go? Do you want to go home?
你想去哪里啊？想回家吗？

She's gorgeous. **When do you want to** meet her?
她很不错啊。你想什么时候见她啊？

A: I'd like to propose a toast. 让我们干杯。
B: What do you want to drink to? 为了什么呢？

Why do you want (me) to ... ? 你为什么想做？你为什么想让我做？

这一表现形式是why、how、who与do you want to结合而成的。尤其是用who作主语的who wants to+动词？的表现形式一定要记住。

“让妹妹跟那个出了名的花心大萝卜分手的时候”

Why do you want me to stay away from him?

M·O·R·E

- Why do you want (me) to+动词？
  你为什么想做？
  你为什么想让我做？
- How do you want (me) to+动词？
  你想怎么做？
- Who wants to+动词？
  谁想做？

Why do you want me to date other men?
你为什么想让我跟别的男人约会呢？

How do you want to pay me?
你想用什么形式支付给我？

Who wants to go first?
谁想最先离开？

A: Why do you want to break up with me? 你为什么想跟我分手？
B: I'm feeling unhappy with you. 我跟你在一起觉得不快乐。

If you want to ... 如果你想……的话

用if you want (to)来表示条件，在后面可以加命令句或者是“必须要做”、“我将要做”这样的句子。而且还要了解单独使用的if you want (to)或者是if you want me to等表现形式。

“只有采取行动的人才有可能取得胜利。如果想取得成功的话，要像犀牛一样横冲直闯才行”

If you want to date Cindy, you have to ask her out.

M·O·R·E

- If you want to ... , V ...
  如果想……的话就……吧
- If you want to ... , I will ...
  如果你想……的话，那么我将……
- If you want (to)
  如果你想要……的话
- If you want me to do
  如果你想让我做
- If you want to ... , you've got to (you have to) ...
  如果你想……的话，你必须要……

If you want to stay, I'm not going to stop you.
如果你想多待一会儿的话，我不会阻拦你的。

If you want to know about girl stuff, ask Allan.
如果你想问一些与女孩子有关的问题的话，那么去问艾琳吧。

You can come with us, **if you want to**.
如果你想跟我们一起走的话就走吧。

I will keep you company, **if you don't want** me to go.
如果你不希望我走的话，我就留下来陪你。

A: I can meet you there if you want. 如果你希望的话，我就去那里跟你见面。
B: That would be more convenient for me. 那样的话对我来说会更方便一些。

You don't want to ... 最好不要做……

虽然有一定的难度，但是却是经常使用的表现形式。这是当表示最好不要做……的建议以及忠告的时候经常使用的表现形式，也可以写作you wouldn't want to ... 。而且，may (might) want to ... 表示的是“做……还不错”的意思。

“对即使有非常重要的早会，也总是说‘再睡5分钟，5分钟’的丈夫说的话”

You don't want to be late for the meeting.

M·O·R·E

- may (might) want to
  做……应该不错
- wouldn't want to
  做……并不是一个好想法
- You don't want to ...
  你最好不要做……

Well, **you might want to** get used to it.
你最好是熟练掌握。

I wouldn't want to spend tonight with you.
我今天晚上不想跟你在一起。

You wouldn't want to see me lose my job, would you?
你不想看到我失去工作，对不对?

You don't want to know.
你不会想知道的。

A: We're planning to go to a casino. 我们正在计划去赌场。
B: You don't want to waste your money that way. 你应该不想用那样的方式来浪费你的钱。

想说什么就说什么

Say

Say是在表示说话的动词4兄弟say、tell、speak、talk中，最具有概括性，带有最一般性意义的动词。在表示要转达我所说的话的时候(I said that)或者是对对方说过的话再次进行确认的时候(Are you saying that ...？)使用。而且，当手表或者是告示牌作为主语的时候，也带有“写着”、“指”的意思。

基本概念

1 说，讲述

It's time to say good-bye. 现在到了分别的时候了。

You don't have to say you're sorry. 你没有必要说对不起。

2（书、告示板等）写着

Her e-mail says that she will not come over tonight. 她在电子邮件中说她今天晚上不来了。

The clock says 3:15. (three fifteen) 钟表正显示着3点15分。

The label says to take one pill a day. 说明书上说这种药每天吃一片。

3（插入句）比如说，例如

How about getting together next week, say, on Friday? 下周，比如是说周五的时候见面怎么样?

say hi （说你好）打招呼

Hi在见面的时候表示“你好”的意思，所以如果用say hi来表示的话，就是“说你好”或者是向远方的朋友“转达问候”的意思。如果说say good bye的话，就是表示道别的意思，如果说say good night的话，就是表示“晚安”的意思。

“爸爸想让还想看电视的儿子去睡觉的时候”

Time for sleep. Say good night to your mom.

M·O·R·E

- say hi to
  向谁打招呼，说你好，向谁转达问候
- say good-bye
  说再见，跟谁道别
- say good night (to)
  对谁说晚安

I have to go now. I'll have to **say good bye**.
我现在必须要走了。我必须要说再见了。

We just wanted to stop by and **say good night**.
我只不过是想过来对你说晚安。

Say hi to Tony for me.
替我向托尼问好。

A: I'm going to visit Steve and Heather. **我将要去拜访史蒂夫以及赫塞尔。**
B: How nice. Say hi to them for me. **太好了。替我向他们问好。**

say no (to) 反对，拒绝

可以用say no to somebody (something)来表示“反对”、“拒绝”的意思。另外，say so表示的是“那样说”的意思，say more表示的是“再说一些”的意思。

“不管是多么亲密的朋友，想说‘不’的时候就应该说‘不’”

I think I'm going to have to say no to that.

M·O·R·E

- say no (to)
  反对，拒绝
- say so
  那样说
- say more
  多说一些
- Say no more.
  即使不再多说也清楚，即使不用多说也知道是什么意思。

I just can't **say no to** my mother. I'm not like you.
我不能反对我的妈妈。我跟你不同。

Why did you **say yes**? Are you out of your mind?
你为什么同意了？你还正常吗？

It seems weird to you, but everybody **says so**.
虽然你觉得很奇怪，但是大家都是那样说的。

Say no more. I know it's your birthday.
不用再说了。我知道那是你的生日。

A: Robin, are you smoking again? **罗宾，你又开始吸烟了吗？**
B: Yes, I can't say no to cigarettes. **是的，我怎么也戒不了烟。**

say something to 对……说了些什么

Say something表示的是“说了些什么”的意思，在后面可以添加to somebody，about等，而且也可以用anything或者是nothing来代替something。

“把‘f’的音发成‘p’的音的男人，说自己的兴趣爱好是钓鱼（pissing），大家都笑了”

Did I say something funny?

M·O·R·E

- say something to sb
  对某人说一些事情
- say something about
  说一些与某人有关的事情
- say something like that
  说类似于那样的话
- say something+形容词
  说一些……样的话

Can I just **say something to** you as a friend?
我能作为朋友对你说些话吗?

Wait a minute. I'd like to **say something about** Joe.
稍等。我想说一些与乔有关的事情。

Did he really **say nothing about** me?
他真的没有说任何与我有关的事情?

I don't want you to **say anything like that** to her.
我不想让你对她说任何类似于那样的话。

A: Some of my students need to shower more often. 我的学生中有几个需要经常洗澡。

B: I'll say something to them about it. 让我来对他们说吧。

say a word 说，泄露

这个表现形式是因为电影Don't say a word而为大家所熟知的。表示的是“一句话都不要说”的意思，主要以Don't say a word，I won't say a word这样的否定形式使用。

“秘书无意中看到了老板的秘密，对老板说”

I'm not going to say a word to anyone.

M·O·R·E

- Not say a word.
  没有说出口，一句话也没有说。

Here she comes. Don't **say a word**, okay?
她来了。一句话都不要说，知道吗?

I promise I won't **say a word**.
我保证我一句话也不说。

You can count on my help. Just **say the word**.
我可以帮助你。只要你开口。

A: Did you plan a party for Randall? 你是不是为兰德尔准备了一个晚会?

B: It's a surprise. Don't say a word about it. 这是个惊喜。什么也不要告诉他。

have something to say 有话要说

也可以用get来代替have，表示“有话要说”的意思。另外，可以用have something to say to somebody来表示“有话对某人说”，用have something to say about来表示“有一些与……有关的话要说”的意思。

“当要说一些与离职、移民、离婚这样重要的话题的时候说的话”

You guys, I have something to say.

M·O·R·E

- have sth to say to sb
  有话对某人说
- have sth to say about sth
  关于……有话要说
- have nothing to say to (about)
  对某人（关于什么）无话可说

I **have something to say**.
我有话要说。

I **have nothing to say** to you.
我对你无话可说。

If you **have something to say** to me, just say it.
如果你有什么话要对我说，就尽管说吧。

You **have anything to say** about his daughter?
关于他女儿你有什么话要说吗?

A: Before I go any further, Bill has something to say. 在我继续往下说之前，比尔说他有话要说。

B: I handed in my resignation this morning. 我今天早上递交了辞职信。

say much about 说了很多与……有关的话

当要表示说了很多话的时候，可以用say much或者是say a lot来表示。当要表示“对……有很多话要说”的时候，就可以用say much to来表示，同时，当要表示“说很多与……有关的话”的时候，用say much about来表示就可以了。

“当朋友非常内向，喜欢一个人待着，很少说话的时候”

He doesn't say much. He keeps to himself.

M·O·R·E

- say much to sb
  对……说很多话
- say much about
  说很多与……关的话

He doesn't **say much about** it.
他没有说很多与那相关的事情。

She didn't **say much to** me.
她没有跟我说很多话。

We **said a lot of things**.
我们说了很多事情。

A: How does your brother like his job? 你弟弟觉得他的工作怎么样?

B: I don't know. He doesn't say much about it. 我不知道。他不怎么说与工作有关的事情。

say that 说

当say的宾语是主语+动词的时候，需要掌握的最基本的句型就是I said that，You said that，(s) He said that等。

"对那些刚开始同意结婚，后来又反对的父母们说"

You said it was okay! Why did you change your mind?

M·O·R·E

- I said that S+V
  我说过
- I said to sb that S+V
  对……说……
- You said (that) S+V
  你不是说 ... 吗
- I thought you said (that) S+V
  我以为你说的是……
- I'm sorry to say that S+V
  很抱歉对你说……

I said that you had a nice place.
我说过你家的位置很好。

She said she's having a lot of fun with Andy.
她说她跟安迪一起度过了美好的时光。

I thought you said it was okay.
我以为你说没关系呢。

You said it was going to be fun!
你不是说会很有趣吗！

A: Jim said that he'd pick up the tab. 吉姆说了他来结账。
B: In that case I'll have another drink. 那么我就再要点饮料。

You said you wanted ... 你说你想要……吧？

You said you wanted ... 表示的是"你不是说你想要……吗"的意思，对对方刚才说过的话再次进行确认的时候使用。根据情况的不同，有时候还会用在打架的时候。

"如果过于相信一个人的话很有可能会遭到背叛"

You said you wanted to help me, and I believed you.

M·O·R·E

- You said you wanted to+动词
  你说过你想做……吧
- You said you wanted something
  你说过你想要……吧

You said you wanted to get involved.
你说过你也想参与进来。

Come on Tammy! You said you wanted to talk about it.
黛米！你说过你想说这个故事的。

Remember when you said you wanted to be a model?
你还记得你曾经说过你想成为一个模特吗？

You said you wanted to say something.
你说过你想说些事情吧。

A: Why did you buy me tea at Starbucks? 你为什么要给我买茶呢？
B: You said you wanted something to drink. 你不是说你想喝些东西嘛。

I say (that) 我说，我的意思是

使用现在时say的I say (that)形式表示的是“我的意思是”的意思，也就是把自己的意思转达给对方。相反的，you say (that)表示的是“你的意思是”，表示对对方的话进行确认。

“劝说那些总是不停地想要离婚的人们维持现在的婚姻的时候”

I say you have to give your marriage another chance.

M·O·R·E

- I say (that) S+V
  我的意思是让你做
- You say (that) S+V
  你的意思是……吧

I say you show Jill how much you love her.
我的意思是让你向吉尔表示你到底有多么爱她。

You're a man. I say you just do it.
你是一个男人啊。所以我让你勇敢地去做。

I say you leave Sally alone and go get Vicky.
我的意思是让你放开莎莉，去抓住薇琪。

You say you want to meet young girls.
你说你想跟年轻的女孩子见面的。

A: Karen and Harry make such a cute couple. 卡伦与哈里将会成为一对很幸福的情侣。

B: I say they will get married within a year. 我认为他们会在一年之内就结婚。

You're saying ... 你的意思是……吧，你的意思是……吗？

进行时You'r saying ...？表示的是“你现在说的是……的意思吗？”也就是说不信任对方或者是当对方说出了意料之外的话语的时候，表示自己的惊讶或者是生气。相反的，如果是I'm saying ... 的话，表示的是对自己说的话进行整理或者是进行强调的意思。

“对体重达90kg的师母说她非常苗条的时候，有自知之明的师母会说”

You're just saying that to make me feel better.

M·O·R·E

- You're saying S+V
  你的意思是……吗？
  你的意思是……吧
- I'm (just) saying S+V
  我只不过是说……

You're saying you're attracted to your teacher?
你是说你被自己的老师吸引了？

You're saying you don't know anything about this?
你的意思是对于这件事你一无所知？

I'm saying your father was a good man.
我的意思是你爸爸是一个好人。

I'm saying this as a friend. Don't do this to me.
我是作为朋友说这样的话。你不要这样对我。

A: A storm is coming our way. 暴风正向我们这边袭来。

B: You're saying it will snow this afternoon? 你的意思是说今天下午会下雪吧。

Are you saying ... ? 你的意思是……吗?

因为对方的意想不到的话语或者是完全不可理喻的话语而慌张，想要再次进行确认的时候的表现形式。根据文意的不同，既可以表示惊讶，也可以表示厌烦。如果是使用固定的表现形式What are you saying? 的话，那么表示的就是“那是什么意思? ”的意思。

“好不容易把烂醉如泥的乘客送回家的时候，乘客嫌费用过多大声叫嚷的时候”

This is ridiculous. Are you saying this is my fault?

M·O·R·E

- All I'm saying is ...
  我说的意思是……
- What I'm trying to say is (that) ...
  我的意思是……

Are you saying that you're not going to hire me?
你的意思是将不会录用我是吧?

What I'm trying to say is that she's rich.
我想说的是她很富有。

What I'm saying is Allan likes you, not me.
我的意思是艾伦喜欢的人是你，而不是我。

What are you saying? Am I rude?
你说的是什么意思? 我很无礼吗?

A: You'll be sorry if you don't prepare for the test. 如果你不为这次考试做准备的话，你将会后悔的。

B: Are you saying that I should study? 你的意思是我必须要学习吗?

I have to say 我必须要说

在没有办法必须要说些什么的情况下，用这一表现形式表示“必须要说”的意思。也可以用must来代替have to。另外，I want to say表示的是“我想说”的意思。

“对在结婚纪念日，不说带我出去吃饭，甚至是让我给他煮拉面的不懂事的丈夫说的话”

I must say I'm disappointed in you.

M·O·R·E

- I have to (must) say+名词 ((that) S+V)
  我必须要说
- I have to (must) say
  可能
- I want to say+名词 (that, how S+V)
  我想说
  我必须要说

I have to say you are much smarter than me.
我必须要说你比我聪明。

I have to say you really impressed me today.
我必须要说我今天被你感动了。

I want to say thank you.
我想跟你说谢谢你。

I want to say how sorry I am.
我想说我非常抱歉。

A: The economy will get better next year. 经济情况在明年将会有所好转。

B: I have to say I don't believe you. 我必须要说我并不相信你。

I can't say ... 不是……吧，我不能说……

这是当对某件事并不能确定的时候使用的表现形式，跟I'm not sure表示的是相同的意思。另外，I'd say主语+动词中的I'd say是I would (could) say的缩略形式，表示的虽然不能断定，但是“也可以说”。也就是说表示的是“好像是”的意思。

“听说总是在晚上12点之后回家的邻居家的女儿未婚先育”

I can't say that I'm surprised.

M·O·R·E

- I can't (couldn't) say S+V
  不是
- I can't say.
  我不知道
- I'd say (that) S+V
  好像是
- I'd say so.
  好像是那样。

I can't say who did that.
我不知道是谁做的。

I can't say for certain she'll recover completely.
我不能说她已经完全恢复过来了。

I would say that you are around 30 years old.
我觉得你看上去在30岁左右。

I'd say she died when she was about twenty.
她好像是在20岁左右的时候死的。

A: I can't say I've ever been to London. 我从来没有去过伦敦。
B: Would you like to go there with me? 想不想跟我一起去？

Let's say ... 让我们（假定）……试一试，说……怎么样？

进行假定的表现形式。可以用Let's say主语+动词或者是let's just say主语+动词来表示。

“向汽车销售达人询问销售秘诀的时候给出的谦虚的回答”

Let's just say I had a very good month.

Let's just say he's a married man.
让我们假设他是一个已经结了婚的男人。

Let's say that he is going to be there.
让我们假设他要去那里。

Let's say we get out of here. I'll show you around.
让我们离开这里吧。我将带你参观一下周围。

Let's say she came home first.
让我们假设她先回到家。

A: Should we meet on Tuesday or Wednesday? 我们在周二或者是周三见面怎么样？
B: Let's say Wednesday. It's better for me. 周三怎么样？周三对我来说更方便。

What do you say (to) ... ? ……怎么样?

这是向对方提建议的时候使用的表现形式，在what do you say后面可以用主语+动词或者是to+ ...ing (名词)形式来叙述提议的内容。另外，what would you say ... 表示的是"……的话怎么样？"的意思，对对方的反应进行询问。

"在上学的路上对自己喜欢的女学生提议一起散步"

What do you say we go take a walk?

M·O·R·E

- What do you say?
  怎么样?
- What do you say to+名词 (...ing/S+V/if)?
  做……怎么样?
- What would you say?
  要怎么做啊? 你说什么?
- What would you say to+名词/...ing?
  如果……的话，你会怎么说?
- What would you say if S+V?
  如果……的话，怎么样?

What do you say I take you to dinner tonight?
我们今天晚上一起吃饭怎么样?

What do you say we get together for a drink?
我们一起喝一杯怎么样?

Let's go to China in May. **What do you say?**
让我们在5月份的时候去中国吧。怎么样?

What would you say if she stayed with us all night?
让她跟我们一起待一晚上怎么样?

A: What do you say to going for a drink tonight? 今天晚上一起去喝一杯怎么样?

B: Sounds like a good idea! 当然很好了!

How could you say ... ? 你怎么能够说……呢?

因为对方不可理喻的话而发火的时候使用的表现形式。How can (could) you say的后面既可以加名词，也可以加主语+动词的形式。

"因为总让自己加夜班为难自己，所以对老板说'人渣'的时候"

How can you say that to me? I'm your boss!

M·O·R·E

- How could you say+名词 ?
  你怎么能够说……呢?
- How could you say (that) S+V?
  你怎么能说……?
- How can (could) you say that?
  你怎么能够那样说呢?

How can you say that it doesn't matter?
你怎么能说那不重要呢?

How can you say something like that? I'm so hurt.
你怎么能说那样的话呢? 我非常受伤。

How could you say such a thing?
你怎么能够说出那样的话呢?

How could you say yes to that?
你怎么能够同意呢?

A: I have to break up with you. 我要跟你分手。

B: How can you say that? 你怎么能说出这样的话呢?

Who says ... ? 谁说……了?

当对对方的话无法表示同意的时候用Who says主语+动词? 来表示。但是，Who can say主语+动词? 表示的是“谁会说……呢”，也就是说任何人都不知道，也可以用Who's to say主语+动词? 来表示。

“当有传闻说因为公司合并而面临解雇的时候”

Who says I could be the first to get fired?

M·O·R·E

- Who says S+V?
  (反对意见)谁说……的?
- Who's to say S+V?
  有谁能说……呢? (任何人都不知道)
- Who can say ... ?
  谁能说……呢? (任何人都不知道)

What? Who says that?
什么? 谁说的?

Who says I can't handle it?
谁说我不能处理好?

Who says I need someone to take care of me?
谁说我需要有人照顾?

Who's to say it wasn't you?
谁知道那不是你?

A: Who says you need surgery? 是谁说你需要做手术的?

B: My doctor told me it is necessary. 医生跟我说的。

Needless to say 没有说的必要

Needless to say表示的是“没有说的必要”的意思，跟to say nothing of表示的是相同的意思。另外，whatever you say表示的是将会按照对方要求的去做，也可以用Anything you say来表示。

“陷入离婚危机的新婚夫妇，怎么还会给公公婆婆准备饭菜”

Needless to say, I won't be cooking dinner for your parents.

M·O·R·E

- Needless (regardless) to say
  没有说的必要
- to say nothing of
  没有说的必要
- as you say
  按照你说的，就像你说的一样
- Whatever you say
  按照你说的去做
- to say the least
  至少可以说

Needless to say, everyone is shocked, including her.
不用说，包括她在内的所有的人都受到了冲击。

Whatever you say, boss.
只要您吩咐，老板。

As you say, Mr. Smith, this is not a place where you belong.
史密斯先生，就像您说的，这并不是属于您的地方。

Anything you say, honey. What do I have to do now?
完全按照你说的来，亲爱的，接下来该做什么呢?

A: There are a lot of dirty dishes in the sink. 洗碗池里边有很多脏的盘子。

B: Needless to say, you'll have to wash them. 不用多说，你应该去洗碗。

It says here 这里说（写着）

看着某些文件或者是告示板的时候，表示“写着”的意思的表现形式。可以省略掉it，直接用Say here (that)主语+动词来表示。

“看到银行账户上只有5美元时”

It says here that you have 5 dollars in your account.

It says here you're fine.
这里说你已经没事了。

It says here your husband died.
这里说你的丈夫已经死了。

Says here Dr. Smith examined her last week, and everything was fine.
史密斯博士已经给她做过检查了，这里写着一切正常。

A: Look at that big old house. 看看那所又大又老的房子。
B: It says here a president lived in it. 这里说以前在这里住着一位总统。

More Expressions

- **no matter what I say** 不管我说什么
  No matter what I say, don't let me do that again. 不管我说什么，也不要让我再做了。

- **say to oneself** 对自己说
  Before I get up, I say to myself "I'm not a loser." 在我起床之前，我都会对自己说“我不是一个失败者”。

- **They say that ...** 他们说……
  They say time flies. 他们说时光如流水。

- **say ... in English** 用英语说
  I don't know how to say it in English? 我不知道怎样用英语来表述它。

- **have something to say about** 对……发火
  Your father will have something to say about your bad grades. 你爸爸将会因为你的成绩不好而发火。

More Expressions

- **like I was saying** 就像我说过的

  Like I was saying, I'm so sorry.
  就像我说过的，我真的非常抱歉。

- **say something to one's face**
  大胆放心说

  If you want to say something about me, **say it to my face**! 如果你有什么要对我说的，放心大胆地说出来吧！

Say when.（倒酒的时候）可以聊的时候跟我说。

Say cheese.（照相的时候）喊乳酪。

I'll say. 是真的。

You can say that again! 你可以再说一遍！

You said it. 你说的对。

You said that. 你不是那样说了嘛。

What she says, goes.
必须要按照她说的去做。

What can I say?
我无话可说，你还让我说什么？

You don't say!
不会吧！未必吧！真的，不是很明显嘛！

Never say die! 加油！不要示弱！

I know what I'm saying.
我知道我在说什么。

I know what you're saying.
我知道你是什么意思。

I don't know what to say.
我不知道该说什么。

What do you want me to say?
你想让我说什么呀？

What are you trying to say?
你到底想说什么？

Is that what you're saying?
这就是你所说的吗？

What did you say? 你说过什么？你说什么？

Stop saying that! 闭嘴！不要再说了！

What say?/Say what? 什么？再说一遍？

See what I'm saying?
你知道我说的是什么意思吧？

Why do you say that? 你为什么要那么说？

Well said. 是的，就是那样，说的不错。

I wouldn't say that. 我并不同意。

Don't say it!
不想听！我也知道，所以不说也可以。

Easier said than done.
说起来容易做起来难。

I didn't say that. 我没有那样说过。

想告诉你

Tell

比say的语气更强，需要将人物作为宾语(tell me, tell you)。在和对方说话时尤其会产生较强烈的语气，tell somebody to表示“对某人下指示”。想要用在长辈身上就要说ask somebody to。因此在拜托对方告诉我某事时要用Could you tell me what (when, where, how) 的形式。

基本概念

1 讲故事，说话，告诉

I'm here to tell you. 我是来告诉你的。

Please tell me what happened. 请告诉我发生什么事情了。

2 忠告(警告) (tell ... to do)

She told me to save my money. 她让我省钱。

I told you to get out of here. 我跟你说过让你出去了。

3 区分 (tell A from B)

No one is going to be able to tell. 没人会知道的。

tell somebody something 告诉某人某事

Tell A B的形式，具体有tell me something或tell you something还有tell him (her) something等。

"因暴力被抓到警察局的儿子向老师交代实情"

Don't just stand there. Tell me everything!

M·O·R·E

- tell sb the way to
  给某人指路
- tell sb this (that)
  告诉某人这件事

Can you **tell me the way** to the station?
你能告诉我车站怎么走吗?

I'm sorry I didn't **tell you this** before. (sooner)
不好意思，我之前没有告诉你。

Because I am your best friend I can **tell you this**.
因为我是你最好的朋友，才会告诉你的。

A: Tell Sharon that I want to see her. 告诉莎伦，我要见她。
B: Sharon won't be here until this afternoon. 莎伦下午之前不会过来的。

tell somebody about 对某人说起某事

说话的内容并没有确定，而是大致关于某事的，此时就要用tell somebody about 。

"准备第五次结婚的男人在临近结婚时突然想起还没告诉自己的老婆"

Let me tell you about my fourth wife.

M·O·R·E

- Tell me about sth
  告诉我某事
- I didn't tell sb about
  我还没告诉某人某事呢

Tell me about your new girlfriend.
跟我说说你的新女朋友。

I didn't **tell him about** you.
我还没有告诉他你的事呢。

What did Mike **tell you about** her?
麦克是怎么对你说她的?

A: Tell me about you and Jake. 告诉我你和杰克的事情。
B: It's a long story. 说来话长。

tell a lie 说谎

tell后面接不同宾语可以组成多样的短语。典型的就是tell the truth，表示“说出实话”，也可以说成tell me straight。相反则为tell a lie。

“说谎时，总会不由自主地笑起来，被人拆穿”

You always laugh like that when you're telling a lie.

M·O·R·E

- tell the truth
  说出实情
- tell a lie (to+sb)
  对某人说谎
- tell a story
  讲故事，说谎
- tell a joke
  说笑话

You'd better tell him the truth.
你最好跟他说实话。

He was trying to tell us a joke, but we didn't get it.
他本来想给我们说一个笑话，不过我们都没听懂。

He's not good at telling lies.
他不大擅长说谎。

A: My son said he was getting an A in this class. 我儿子说自己能在这次考试中得A。
B: He told a lie. He is doing very poorly. 他说谎了，他的成绩很糟糕。

tell somebody to 让某人做某事

表示“让某人做某事”，与ask sb to不同，可以用在关系无隔膜的人之间，是一种指示性的语气较强烈的表达。绝对不能用在长辈身上。

“已经分手了，前男友还不停地打电话过来”

I told you to stop calling me.

M·O·R·E

- Don't tell me to+动词
  不要叫某人做某事
- I told sb to+动词
  我让某人做某事

Don't tell me to calm down!
不要让我冷静！

I told you to prevent this from happening.
我之前跟你说过，不要让这事情发生。

I told him to drop by for a drink.
我让他路过的时候进来喝杯酒。

He told me to save my money for our honeymoon.
他让我为我们的蜜月旅行攒钱。

A: I need help moving to another apartment. 我要搬到新家了，需要帮助。
B: Tell everyone to come and help you. 让所有人都过来帮你吧。

tell somebody that 对某人说某事

在传达某事实或信息时所使用的表达，tell me (you) 后面要接“that主语+动词”来表示需要传达的具体内容。

“程序突然出了故障，重要的数据都瞬间灰飞烟灭了”

Please **tell me that** you can fix this.

M·O·R·E

- Can you tell me that S+V?
  你能告诉我……吗?
- I will tell him (her) that S+V
  我会告诉他……
- You told me that S+V
  是你告诉我……的

I'll **tell him that** you called.
我会转达他你来过电话了。

Would you **tell him that** James Smith called?
麻烦您转达他詹姆斯史密斯来过电话。

Tell him his brother misses him.
告诉他，他哥哥非常想念他。

Why didn't you believe me? I **told you** he didn't do it.
你为什么不相信我? 我跟你说过不是他做的。

A: You told me that you didn't like Jill. 是你告诉我你不喜欢吉尔的。
B: I didn't mean to say that. 我的本意可不是那个。

tell somebody what 对某人说某事

比前面的tell sb that主语+动词更为常用的表达，首先tell somebody，其次what, when, where等疑问词。

“跟老师打报告，说同学们为什么会打架”

I'll **tell you what** they were fighting over.

M·O·R·E

- Can you tell me what (when, where, who) S+V?
  你能告诉我……吗?
- I will tell him (her) what (when, where, who) S+V
  我会告诉他……的
- Tell me what (when, where, who) S+V
  告诉我……

Can you **tell me what**'s going on there?
你能告诉我那里到底发生了什么事情吗?

Excuse me, can you **tell me what** happened?
不好意思，你能告诉我发生什么事情了吗?

I need you to **tell me who** did it.
你应该告诉我是谁干的。

I'll **tell you what** happened to me yesterday.
我跟你说昨天我碰到过的事情。

A: Will you go grocery shopping for me? 你能去杂货店给我买点东西吗?
B: Can you tell me what you need? 那你需要点什么?

tell somebody how to 告诉某人……的方法

tell someone后面虽然接上了疑问词，但并不是从句的形式。tell someone后面加上what (how) to+动词就可以了。

"一位前辈是出了名的接吻高手，向他请教接吻的秘诀"

I'd like you to **tell me how to** kiss.

M·O·R·E

- Can you tell me how to get to+地点?
  能告诉我去……的方法吗?
- I will tell you how to+动词
  我告诉你这个怎么做

Can you **tell me how to** do it?
你能教我怎么做吗?

Could you **tell me how to** get to Gate 3?
你能告诉我怎么去三号门吗?

Could you **tell me when to** get off?
你能告诉我，应该什么时候下车吗?

You can **tell me how to** go there by e-mail.
你可以用电子邮件告诉我怎么去那儿。

You're going to **tell me how to** do it?
你会告诉我怎么做吗?

I will **tell you how to** make money.
我来告诉你怎么挣钱。

Didn't your mom **tell you how to** treat a lady?
你妈没有教你怎么对待一位女士吗?

You don't tell me what to do! I **tell you what to** do!
不需要你来告诉我这么做！我告诉你怎么做！

This is so complicated. Please **tell me what to** do first.
这太麻烦了，请告诉我应该先做什么。

A: I don't think Ned should take that job. 我不觉得内德应该接那份工作。
B: You can't tell him how to live his life. 你不能干涉他的生活。

A: They are so confused right now. 他们现在非常困惑。
B: You need to tell them what to do next. 你得告诉他们下一步该怎么办。

A: I am going to go jogging for an hour. 我要出去慢跑一个小时。
B: I can tell you when to stop. 我可以告诉你什么时候停。

tell somebody how 告诉某人……方法

这次tell somebody后面接上了how，why，if等，用来表示某种方法或理由或者询问事情的真伪。

"自己一点都不动，只会对别人指指点点"

Tell me why we're going to do this again.

M·O·R·E

- Can you tell me how (why, if) S+V?
  你能告诉我……吗?
- I will tell him (her) how (why, if) S+V
  我会告诉他……的
- Tell me how (why, if)
  告诉我怎么……

Can you **tell me how** this happened?
能告诉我这是怎么发生的吗?

You're not going to the party? Can you **tell me why**?
你不去聚会了? 能告诉我为什么吗?

I'll **tell you how** bad it is.
我跟你说这有多么糟糕。

Tell me if you're still upset about this.
告诉我你是不是还对此耿耿于怀。

A: Could you tell me how I get to the subway? 你能告诉我怎么去地铁站吗?
B: Go straight ahead until you see the sign. 一直走，你会看到标识牌的。

I told you ... 我跟你说过……

用在听不清话或不听话的对象的表达。用I told you to+动词或I told you that主语+动词就可以了。想要表达否定的话就可以说I told you not to+动词，表示"我告诉过你别做某事"。

"怎么可能人人都是蜘蛛侠? 一个朋友说大话，不小心被挂在了屋顶上"

See? **I told you** it was impossible.

M·O·R·E

- I told you to+动词
  我告诉过你……
- I told you (that) S+V
  我跟你说过……

I told you to leave me and never come back again.
我跟你说过离开我，别再回来。

I told you to give him whatever he wants.
我早就跟你说过，他想要什么你就给什么。

I told you that I didn't know exactly where she lived.
我跟你说过，我不大清楚她的住处。

I thought I told you not to come.
我以为我跟你说过别来了。

A: I thought I told you to get out of here. 我好像跟你说过，让你出去。
B: You did, but I don't want to. 你说过，不过我不想。

You told me ... 是你让我……的

You told me to或You told me (that)主语+动词表示“是你让我……的”，用来重复对方以前说过的话。

“嘱咐孩子暂时看管便利店，不料一个强盗闯了进来，儿子就温顺地把收银机交了出去”

You told me to be nice to anyone who comes here.

M·O·R·E

- You told me to+动词
  是你告诉我……的
- You told me (that) S+V
  是你跟我说……的

You told me to call you a cab at 10:00.
是你让我10点叫计程车的。

You told me that you didn't like Jack the other day.
是你曾经告诉我你不喜欢杰克的。

You told me you were going to take me for lunch.
是你跟我说要出去吃饭的。

You're going to throw it away? **You told me** you liked it.
你要把那个扔了？你跟我说过很喜欢它啊。

A: Where is the TV that was here? 原来在这里的电视机呢？
B: You told me to throw it away. 是你让我把它扔了的。

Let me tell you ... 我来告诉你……

用来表达和对方说某事。Let me tell you后面可以直接加名词，也可以about+名词。Let me tell you something为引起对方注意的语句，表示“我有事情要说”。

“姐姐说什么都不愿意嫁人，着急的弟弟想抢先一步结婚”

Let me tell you about my sister.

M·O·R·E

- Let me tell you something (one thing)
  我有话要说 (I have to tell you something)
- Let me tell you what (how) ...
  我来告诉你……

Let me tell you my story.
我跟你说说我的故事吧。

Let me tell you about my plan to open a restaurant.
我来跟你说说开饭店的计划吧。

Let me tell you something. Your girlfriend isn't cute.
我有话要说，你的女朋友长得不好看。

I have to tell you something. It's about your ex-wife.
我得告诉你一些事情。是关于你前妻的。

A: I heard you climbed Mount Everest. 我听说你爬珠穆朗玛峰了。
B: Let me tell you, it was really difficult. 我告诉你，这可相当不容易啊。

Don't tell me ... 不要让我……

作为否定祈使句，Don't tell me后面主要接that从句或疑问句，疑问词句等。Don't tell me! 同样为固定表达，用来对不可理喻的行为表示“真的假的！”，“那是什么话”等。

“被男朋友甩了，被男老板炒了鱿鱼，被男司机调戏了”

Don't tell me men are nice.

M·O·R·E

- Don't tell me that ...
  别跟我说……你不会是……的意思吧
- Don't tell me what ...
  不要跟我说……
- Don't tell me!
  真的假的！

Don't tell me what's in the box.
别告诉我那盒子里有什么。

Don't tell me that it's over between us.
别跟我说，我们俩之间已经没戏了。

Don't tell me that you don't have time to talk.
不要跟我说你没有时间谈话。

Don't tell me that you are seeing another woman.
别告诉我你在和别的女人交往。

A: The car didn't start this morning. 早上汽车发动不起来了。
B: Don't tell me that it's broken again. 不要跟我说，它又坏了。

There's no telling ... 没法知道……

对未来的事情不太确信时可以用到的表达，也可以说成There's no way to tell。There's no telling（没法知道）也可以像There's no way to tell（没办法知道）一样单独使用。

“评价不太好的女老师一拉开抽屉，就蹦出一条蛇来”

There's no way to tell who did that.

M·O·R·E

- There's no telling (knowing) what (how) S+V
  没办法知道……
- There's no way to tell what (who) S+V
  没办法知道……

There's no way to tell who it was.
没办法知道是谁做的。

There's no telling what you think.
没办法知道你在想什么。

There's no telling how long they'll last.
不知道他们会持续多久。

A: Do you think the new business will succeed? 你觉得新生意能成功吗？
B: There's no telling what will happen to it. 没办法知道将来会发生什么事。

You're telling me that ... ? 你对我说……?

表示无法相信对方的话或者吃惊而使用的句型。You are telling me that之后可以接上对方的话。如果单独使用You're telling me!的话则表示强烈的赞同，可以理解为谁说不是呢！，没错！等含义。

"早过了结婚年龄的儿子还深深沉迷于玩具飞机"

You're not telling me you're into this stuff?

M·O·R·E

- You're telling me (that)
  你是说……?
- You're telling me!
  没错，谁说不是呢!
- You're not telling me ... ?
  你不是在跟我说……吧?

You're telling me you didn't try to hit him?
你是说当时你没有想打他?

You're telling me I can't see her?
你是说我没办法见她了?

You're telling me there're a million dollars here?
你是说，这里有一百万美元?

A: I'm going to be busy the night of your party. **你开派对的那天晚上，我应该会很忙。**

B: You're telling me that you won't come? **你是说你不能来了?**

be told 听成……

tell变成被动式，I was told或I have been told表示"听说过……"或"一直听着……"。

"听说前任男友向自己的妹妹表白时"

I was told he was going to ask my sister out.

M·O·R·E

- I was (I've been) told (that) S+V
  我听说……据我所知……
- I was told that
  （某人对我）说过那事情，据我了解
- So I've been told.(So I hear)
  我是那么听到的。

I was told that the doors close at nine.
据我所知，大门会在9点关闭。

I was told you had a question for me.
我听说你对我有个疑问。

I have been told that I'm a very good kisser, all right?
我听说大家认为我是个接吻高手，是吗?

A: How cold is it going to get? **会变得多冷呢?**

B: I was told it will fall below freezing. **我听说要降到冰点以下了。**

I can tell you ... 可以说……也是……

比起对某事实给予断言，不如加上I can('t) tell you that的包装，委婉地传达自己的意向。不过I can('t) tell you what (how)等则表示“我（不）可以告诉你某事”。经常会用到I can('t) tell you that（可以那么说……）的句型。

“在大街上偶然碰到了之前诈骗自己逃之夭夭的朋友”

I can't tell you how great it is to see you.

M·O·R·E

- I can('t) tell you that S+V
  可以那么认为……
- I can('t) tell you what (how) S+V
  我（不）能告诉你……
- I can tell you that.
  可以那么说。
- I can't tell you that.
  我不能对你说。

I can tell you that the prices of cars are a bit high.
我跟你说，汽车的价格有点高。

I can tell you what he's going to find.
我可以告诉你他会找到什么。

I can't tell you how sorry I am.
真不知道怎么表达我的歉意。

A: I really need to make some money fast. 我非常需要一些救济的钱。
B: I can't tell you how to make money. 我可不能告诉你怎么赚钱。

More Expressions

- **tell A from B** 区分A和B
  Can you **tell** Cindy **from** Betty? They're a lot alike. 你能区分辛迪和贝蒂吗？他们长得太像了。

- **tell the difference** 区分差异
  I can **tell the difference** between them. 我能区分他们。

- **tell on** 告状
  I didn't **tell on** you before.
  我之前可没有告过你。

- **all told** 综合
  All told, we earned a lot of money tonight. 今天晚上挣到很多钱。

More Expressions

- **(Do) You mean to tell me ... ?** 你说的是真的?

  Do you mean to tell me I got fired?
  我被炒鱿鱼是真的?

- **tell a soul** 对某人说

  Don't **tell a soul**. 不要说关于这个的话题。

- **kiss and tell** 说漏秘密

  I don't **kiss and tell**.
  我可从来不会说别人的秘密。

- **tell it like it is** 有什么说什么

  Please **tell it like it is**. 请有话就说。

- **I don't know how to tell you this, but** 真不知道该怎么对你说

  I don't know how to tell you this, but your son is in the hospital.
  真不知道怎么开口，你儿子住进医院了。

- **How many times have I told you that ... ?** 我到底说了多少次?

  How many times do I have to tell you? 我跟你说了多少次?

I told you so. 我跟你说过。
See, I told you. 看，我说什么了。
So, tell me. 说说看。
You never can tell. 你绝对不会知道。
Tell me about it. 谁说不是呢。
Tell me another (one). 真搞笑。
Time will tell. 时间会证明一切的。
How can I tell? 我怎么知道?
A little bird told me. 有人告诉我的。
That doesn't tell me much.
那并没有任何意义。

说说看

Speak

speak基本上表示在众人面前说话或演讲。另外，可以表示说某种语言或做汇报等，例如，像speak Chinese并不针对“传达某种信息”，大多情况下强调说话的动作本身。不能像tell那样拥有宾语，想要表达对某人说话时可以用speak to sb。

基本概念

1 说话，讲话

Think before you speak. 说话前多想想。

You should speak to your teacher. 你应该跟你老师谈谈。

2 演讲

I have to speak in public tomorrow morning. 我明天早上有一个演讲。

She is supposed to speak at the meeting. 她要在会议上做汇报。

3 说（某种语言）

Is there someone who can speak Korean? 有人会说韩语吗?

I can't speak English very well. 我的英语说得不是很好。

speak to 对某人说，讲话

表示“与某人交谈”，也可以使用speak with。打电话时表示“请让某人接电话”的Can I speak to “somebody” ?就是个典型的例句。当然，不仅仅用在打电话时。

“我说我是大学的毕业生，分手的女朋友称自己很难相信，而且到处张扬”

Do you mind if I **speak to** her alone for a sec?

M·O·R·E

- Could I speak to ... ?
  我能和某人说话，
  与某人交谈吗?
- I'd like to speak to ... , please
  我想和某人交谈，
  我想和某人说话
- You should speak to ...
  你应该和某人说

Can I **speak to** Mr. Smith?
我能和史密斯先生说话吗?

Can I please **speak to** your manager?
我能和你的经理谈谈吗?

I need to **speak with** you.
我得和你谈谈。

A: Can I speak to John Lange? 请问约翰兰格先生在吗?
B: I'm sorry, he's on another line at the moment. 不好意思，他正在接听别的电话。

speak English 说英语

比较典型的用法，speak后面如果接国家的形容词的话就表示“说某个国家的语言”。主要和can('t)一起使用。另外，not speak a word of表示“一句话也说不了”。如果是外国人之间说“Speak English”的话就表示“说点明白话”。

“明明是韩国人，却不会说我们母语的侨胞们”

Are you sure you don't **speak Korean**?

M·O·R·E

- speak+国家名称的形容词形态名词
  说某种语言
- not speak a word of
  一点都不会说

Does anyone here **speak Korean**?
有人会说韩语吗?

I am sorry but I can't **speak English** very well.
很抱歉，不过我不太会说英语。

But he doesn't **speak a word of English**.
不过他连一句英语都不会说。

A: What language did you use in Europe? 你在欧洲使用什么语言?
B: We spoke English to everyone. 我们对每个人都可以说英语。

speak as 以……的资格说

speak as somebody表示“以……的资格说”，因此speak as a doctor表示作为医生说，speak as a parent表示作为父母说。

“如果‘班主任=爸爸’时，就经常会督促你学习”

I'm speaking as a teacher, not as a father.

May I **speak as** a girlfriend for a second?
我能以女朋友的身份说两句吗?

Are you **speaking as** my husband or as my boss?
你是以我丈夫的身份说话，还是以老板的身份?

Now I'**m speaking as** a doctor.
现在我以一个医生的身份说话。

Can you pick up the phone, **speaking as** me?
你能接电话假装是我吗?

A: What should we do about this problem? 我们应该怎么处理这个问题?
B: I can't speak as your teacher. Ask him. 我不能像老师一样回答，问问他吧。

speak up 大声说，表达意见

表示再大声点(up)说话，在说话或打电话时如果听不清对方的话就可以用这个短语。当然，在表达自己的意见时可以用。另外，speak out还具有大声说话或呐喊的意思。

“房间里只有两个人，却非要偷偷摸摸说秘密”

Speak up. It's hard to hear you when you lower your voice.

M·O·R·E

- speak up
  大声说，说出自己的意见
- speak up for sb
  说出支持某人的话
- speak out
  大声喊出

Could you **speak up**, please?
你能大声点吗?

I can't hear you. You'll have to **speak up**.
我听不清，请大声说话。

If you're going to say something; you're going to have to **speak up**.
如果你想说些什么，就一定大声说出来。

A: Mr. Smith, is this your wallet? 史密斯先生，这是你的钱包吗?
B: Speak up. I can't hear what you said. 大声点，我听不清你的声音。

speak for somebody 表达某人的感情或立场，代言

表示“表达某人的立场，感情和想法等”，如果是speak for yourself的话就表达当对方和我持有不同意见时说出自己的意见，“我不同意你的意见”(I don't agree with you)。

“明知道有罪，却要替对方辩护的律师们的心得”

I think it's our job to speak for her.

M·O·R·E

- speak for sb (when I say ...)
  （在说某事时）为某人辩护
- Speak for yourself.
  那是你的想法。
- Something speaks itself. (themselves)
  不言自明，不言而喻。

I think I can **speak for** both of us when I say I'm sorry.
我觉得当我说抱歉时可以代表我们两个人。

I know I **speak for** Will when I say we've very disappointed.
我知道当我说非常失望时包括了威尔的立场。

I need you to **speak for** someone who can't speak for herself.
你应该为那些不能为自己辩护的人说话。

Speak for yourself. I really hate to jog.
那是你的想法，我非常讨厌慢跑。

A: How can I contact the shop's owner? 我怎么才能联系上商店的主人?
B: I'm his son. I can speak for him. 我是他儿子，有什么话就可以对我说。

Speaking of 说起……

如果是之前已经提到过的话题，就可以用来追加相关的话题。想要具体指明已经提到的对象就可以说Speaking of+名词，想要表达“说到……”，就可以用Speaking of which。

“朋友和他母亲断绝了关系，却不解人情地问道”

Speaking of which, how are things with your mother?

M·O·R·E

- Speaking of+名词
  说到……
- Speaking of which
  话说回来

Speaking of winter, did you go skiing this year?
说到冬天，你今年去滑雪了吗?

Speaking of Brian, I have some big news.
提到布莱恩，我有些特大新闻。

Speaking of which, are you ready to go to lunch?
话说回来，你准备好去吃午饭了吗?

A: These chocolate candies are great. 这些巧克力糖果非常不错。
B: Speaking of chocolate, you should try the cookies. 说到巧克力，你应该尝尝这些饼干。

Roughly speaking 大体上讲

Generally speaking（一般来说）是人们比较熟悉的表达，在这里用roughly替代了generally。另外，还有Frankly speaking（老实说），Strictly speaking（严格来说）等。

“说点什么呢？好像没什么错，但又觉得有点毛病”

Generally speaking, women are smarter than men.

Strictly speaking, you don't deserve this.

严格来说，你没有资格获得这些。

Roughly speaking, the casino is at around 2 miles away.

大体来讲，赌场离这有2英里远。

Frankly speaking, you're not invited to the party.

老实说，你没有被邀请到聚会来。

A: When will we arrive at our destination? 我们什么时候到达目的地？

B: Roughly speaking, it will be in three hours.大概还有三个小时吧。

so to speak 话说回来

从小就须掌握的短语。想要一句话概括或整理自己的想法或状况时可以使用这个短语。用我们的话来说就是“一句话”。

“对新来公司的女员工提醒道，部长有偷窥癖”

He is, **so to speak**, a peeping Tom.

So to speak, she's a maniac.

总之，她就是个疯子。

I'd like to go back to the days when I was young, **so to speak**.

其实，我非常希望回到年轻的时候。

I really want to get out of here, **so to speak**.

说真的，我真想离开这里。

A: What does Sandy do at your house? 珊迪在你们家干嘛呢？

B: She's my housekeeper, so to speak. 其实她是我的女佣人。

speak ill of 谴责某人

喜欢在别人背后说坏话（finding fault with）的人必须要掌握的一个短语。相反，speak well of则表示称赞，高度评价等。

"只要没收了PMP，MP3等物品就从来不会还给学生的小气老师"

All students in the school **speak ill of** that teacher.

M·O·R·E

- speak ill of
  谴责
- speak well of
  称赞
- speak highly of
  高度评价

I'm not good at **speaking well of** others.
我不大擅长称赞别人。

Don't **speak ill of** him.
不要说他的坏话。

Don't **speak ill of** the dead.
不要说死人的坏话。

My father **spoke highly of** President Kennedy.
我爸爸高度评价了肯尼迪总统。

A: They certainly speak well of him there. 他们当然会为他说好话的。
B: That's because he did a great job for them. 那是因为他为他们做了不少工作。

More Expressions

- **no ... to speak of** 基本上没有……
  I have **no** enemies **to speak of**.
  我基本上没有什么敌人。
  I've **never** had a big fight **to speak of**.
  我基本上没有打过像样的架。

- **speak out of turn** 说错话
  I didn't mean it. I **spoke out of turn**.
  我不是故意的，我说错话了。

- **speak one's mind** 老实交代
  She has a lot of nerve to **speak her mind** in front of the boss.
  她有足够的勇气在老板面前说实话。

- **speak of the devil** 说曹操，曹操到
  Well, **speak of the devil**. We were just talking about you.
  说曹操，曹操到。我们正在说你呢。

Actions speak louder than words.
行胜于言。

Don't speak too soon.
不要过早地下结论。

想要和你畅谈

Talk

talk的最大特征就是要和对方分享“意见”。所以谈话的对象要说talk to somebody或talk with somebody，另外，比起单纯的对话，肯定会有某一话题，为了说明话题，就要用talk about something。在一番谈话之后，如果一方被说服，则是talk somebody into，表示“说服某人做某事”。

基本概念

1 对话，说话

(It's been) Nice talking to you. 很高兴和你聊天。

You can't talk to me like that! 你不能那么对我说话！

Can we talk for a minute? 我们能谈几分钟吗？

Sorry, I've got a date. Talk to you later. 不好意思，我有约了，回头再聊。

2 说服 (talk ... into)

You're going to try and talk me into it? 你想说服我做那事？

You're here to talk me out of marrying her. 你是想说服我不和她结婚。

talk to 对某人说

talk to somebody表示“对某人讲话”，体现了talk的最基本含义。以下表达都是比较常用的语句，应好好记住。

“交往的时候，你依我依地，一分手完全变成了两个互不相干的人”

They didn't even **talk to** each other.

M·O·R·E

- It's been good talking to you. 认识你很高兴。
- I want (I'd like) to talk to you. 我想和你谈谈。
- We need to talk. 我们得谈谈。
- Who do you think you're talking to? 你以为你对谁说话呢?

I need to **talk to** Mr. James immediately.
我得马上和詹姆斯先生谈谈。

Can I **talk to** you for a second?
我能和你谈一会吗?

She **is talking to** someone else right now.
她现在和别人说话呢。

A: Is it okay if I phone after lunch? 我吃完午饭打电话行吗?
B: No problem. I'll talk to you then. 没问题，到时候聊。

talk with 与某人交谈

虽然是相同的含义，但这次为talk with somebody，表示“与某人交谈”。也可以把talk当成名词，变为have a talk with。

“老公明明就在旁边，却水火不分地勾搭起来”

Do you mind if I **talk with** your wife?

M·O·R·E

- talk with sb 与某人交谈
- have a talk with sb 与某人交谈
- have a little talk with 与某人说点事
- make small talk with 与某人说会话

We're going to have to **talk with** your daughter.
我们要和你女儿谈谈。

Nice **talking with** you. See you around.
很高兴跟你聊，回头见。

I'm going to **have a talk with** Julie.
我要和朱莉谈谈。

They **are still talking with** a cop at the police station.
他们还在警察局和警察交谈呢。

A: Some students have trouble in classes. 有些学生对课程感到困惑。
B: They should talk with somebody and get help. 他们得和别人谈谈，寻求帮助。

talk about 谈论某事

在指明谈话的对象时要用to，with，但提到内容时要用about。因此“谈论某事”要用talk about。不过偶尔也可以把about去掉。

“见到高三学生不上学，周围的人询问起来”

I don't want to **talk about** what happened to my son.

M·O·R·E

- talk about+名词 (what/how) 谈论某事
- Can we not talk about ... ? 我们能不说某事吗?

I don't want to **talk about** it (this).
我不想谈论这件事。

Wait a minute! **Are** you two **talking about** the same guy?
稍等！你们两个人说的是一个人吗?

Can we not **talk about** that?
我们能不能不说那个?

Can we **talk about** this later? I have to go right now.
我们能回头再说这件事吗? 我现在得走了。

I can't **talk about** it here. It's complicated.
我不能在这说那件事，说来话长。

She's embarrassed. She doesn't want to **talk about** it.
她非常尴尬，并不想谈论这件事。

Do we have to **talk about** this right now?
你现在必须要说这件事吗?

How about we **talk about** this over dinner?
我们吃完晚饭再谈怎么样?

What? What are you **talking about**? That's not possible.
什么? 你在说什么? 那根本不可能。

I don't even know what you**'re talking about**.
我都不知道你们在说什么。

A: Shall we go on vacation together? 我们一起去度假好不?
B: I'm not sure. Let's talk about it. 我不太确定，商量商量吧。

A: I'm going to talk to my boss today.我今天要去和老板谈谈。
B: Are you going to talk about your contract? 你要谈你的合同吗?

A: What do you think about my proposal? 你觉得我的提议怎么样?
B: We need to talk about that. 我们得进一步探讨探讨。

Let's talk 谈论某事

用来向对方提议谈论某话题时用到的Let's talk about表示“我们谈谈某事吧”，Let's talk to somebody表示“我们对某人说说”，Let's not talk表示“我们别提某事”。

“妈妈站在身后，却毫不知觉，乱说话”

Let's not talk to mom about this.

M·O·R·E

- Let's talk (about) ... 我们说说……吧
- Let's talk to sb 我们跟某人说说吧

First of all, **let's talk about** that.
首先，我们说说那件事。

So **let's talk about** what you can do for me.
我们来说说你能为我做什么。

Let's not talk about the past. We'll just let it go.
我们别说过去的事情了，该放的就放手。

A: Let's talk about our plans for tomorrow. **我们说说明天的计划吧。**
B: I really want to go jet skiing. **我很想去玩滑翔机。**

I'm talking 我在说……的事情

这里的talk为现在进行时，经常使用的形态有I'm talking, You're talking和Are you talking ... ?等，其中I'm talking to you 表示听我说说，Are you talking to me?表示是在对我说吗?

“明明说爱得死去活来，离婚之后马上找新欢的男人”

We're talking about our relationship.

M·O·R·E

- I'm (We're) talking ... 我正在说…… 正在与某人说…… 你是在说……
- You're talking ... 正在与某人说…… 你是在说……
- Are you talking ... ? 你指的是……吗? 你是在说……吗?

I'm talking about chicks, not gambling.
我们在说女人，不是赌博。

You're talking to the wrong man.
你找错人了。

Are you **talking about** getting married?
你们在说结婚的事情吗?

A: What are you talking about? **你在说什么?**
B: I'm talking about me having a baby. **我说我已经怀孕了。**

what you're talking about 你说的事情

虽然是比较长的句式，但what you're talking about（你说的事情）或what I'm talking about（我说的事情）都经常会和know等动词相结合，一起使用。

“收养的孩子不知道自己的身世，突然他的亲生母亲出现”

I don't know **what you're talking about**.

I know **what you're talking about**.
我知道你在说什么。

This is exactly **what I'm talking about**.
这就是我想说的。

You know **who I'm talking about**.
你知道我说的是谁。

I have no idea **what you're talking about**.
我搞不清你说的东西。

A: I saw you out with another woman. 我看见你和一个女人出去了。
B: I don't know what you're talking about. 我不知道你在说什么。

talk like that （以那种方式）那么说

like that是“那样”的意思，在这里加上talk，变成talk like that的话就表示“说那种话”。可以用在对方说话很过分或者没礼貌时。

“辛辛苦苦培育的孩子居然不懂得珍惜，说自己的生命制造过程是一场失误”

Don't **talk like that**. You are smart and good-looking.

You don't **talk to me like that**. I am your mother!
你不要那么对我说话，我可是你妈妈！

Jack, you don't **talk like that** to anyone.
杰克，不要对任何人那么说话。

Don't **talk like that**. Everything is going to be fine.
不要说那种话。一切都会好的。

You shouldn't **be talking like that** at all, Sarah.
你不该那么说话的，莎拉。

A: We need to break up soon. 我们得尽快分手了。
B: Don't talk like that. I love you.不要那么说，我很爱你。

talk sb into (out of)+副词 让某人做某事（不做某事）

talk somebody后面接into+名词(...ing)的话就表示“说服某人做某事”，而talk somebody后面接out of+名词(...ing)时可以表示”说服某人不做某事”。

“朋友赌钱输了很多，为了一挽狂澜，想要孤注一掷，急忙劝道”

Don't even bother. You**'re not talking me out of** this.

M·O·R·E

- talk sb into+名词（...ing）
  对某人说……让对方做某事
- talk sb out of+名词 (...ing)
  说服某人不做某事

I **talked him out of** it. You can stop worrying about that.
我让他停手了。你现在不用担心了。

I'm glad you **talked me into** this.
我很高兴你能让我做这个。

How did she **talk me into** doing that?
她怎么可以让我做这种事呢?

I don't know how to thank you. You **talked me into** it.
真不知道该怎么感谢你。是你让我做这些的。

A: I thought Tim wasn't going to bungee jump. 我觉得提姆不会玩蹦极跳的。

B: I talked him into coming along. 是我说服他一起来的。

talk over 商量，讨论

表示“商量”，至于讨论的对象，可以用with somebody表达。相似的句型有talk out，表示为了解决某个问题而进行彻底的讨论。

“非常有能力的员工递交了辞职申请书，老板急忙要给他涨薪水”

Talk it over with your wife. You have 2 days.

I have to **talk it over** with the boss right now.
我现在得马上和老板谈谈了。

We'll **talk it over** at the office tomorrow.
我们明天会在公司商量这件事。

We're going to **talk over** the party plans.
我们要商量商量派对计划。

A: Our plan was a failure. 我们的计划以失败告终。

B: Let's talk over what to do next. 我们商量商量下一步做什么吧。

talk to oneself 自言自语

前面都是与他人说话，这次就是自己对自己说话的情况。换句话说就是“自言自语”，主要用在现在进行时。

“被女朋友甩了，把自己关在房间里，自言自语”

He's standing against the wall, **talking to himself**

I **was talking to myself**!

我在自言自语!

Sam's gone, and she was sitting here **talking to herself** like a crazy person.

山姆走了，她就坐在这里自言自语着，就像个精神异常的人。

Were you just **talking to yourself**?

你是在对自己说话吗?

A: Who was talking in the other room? 谁在房间里说话?

B: Suzy talks to herself sometimes. 苏琪偶尔会自言自语。

More Expressions

- **talk back** 回答，回应

  Don't **talk back** to your teacher.

  不要顶撞你的老师。

- **talk about ... behind one's back**

  在背后说某人的坏话

  She's very good at **talking about me behind my back**.

  她非常喜欢在我背后说我坏话。

- **talk dirty to** 对某人说猥琐的话

  I love when you **talk dirty to** me.

  我非常喜欢你对我说的那些猥琐话。

- **talk one's way out of**

  从困境中摆脱出来

  You're not going to **talk your way out** of this.

  你不可能从这个困境中走出来的。

- **talk some sense into somebody**

  说服某人为人处世重视分寸

  I'd try one more time to **talk some sense into her**.

  我会再试试说服她做事要有分寸。

More Expressions

- **talk sb through sth**
  对某人详细说明，让对方理解
  You want to **talk me through** this?
  你想让我明白这些?

- **talk the same language** 能说得通
  You'**re talking the same language**
  你说的话我都明白。

- **Talk about ...** 在某个领域是最强的
  Talk about selfish!
  没人比你更自私了。

- **small talk** 闲谈，唠嗑
  It was just **small talk**. 只不过是一些闲谈。
  They made **small talk**. 他们唠了一会嗑。

Can we talk? 我们能谈谈吗?
Can we have a talk? 我们能谈谈吗?
I'm sorry I can't talk long.
很抱歉，我待不了多久。
Let's talk. 我们谈谈吧。
Let's talk later. 我们回头再聊。
Look who's talking. 看看谁在说话。
Money talks. 钱是万能的。
Now you're talking! 没错，就是这样!
You're one to talk. 你还说别人。
Keep talking. 继续说。
You're such a big talker.
你真是个健谈的人。
She's a smooth talker. 她的口才非常好。
Let's just talk turkey. 我们该进入正题了。

不顾挽留离开的

Leave

虽然具有多种含义，但最基本的就是不顾挽留离开的行为。无论是离开首尔(leave Seoul)还是前往纽约(leave for New York)都可以使用这个单词。另外，还有在离开时留下了某些东西的意思，如果是有意图的行为则表示托付，如果是失误，就表示忘在那里。还可以像前文中的keep或hold那样，以leave ...+形容词形态表示“将……置于某状态”。

基本概念

1 离开某地，向某地出发，结束某事

He left the office 10 minutes ago. 他10分钟前就离开公司了。

Are you leaving so soon? 你这么快就要走啊?

I am leaving. 我要走了。

She will leave for New York next month. 她下个月要去纽约。

2 留下，托付，（忘记）丢在原地

I left my wallet at home this morning. 我今天早上把钱包丢在家里了。

We're not at home. Please leave a message. 我们不在家，请留言。

3 置于某种状态（leave ... +形容词）

Don't leave the window open. 不要让窗户开着。

leave somewhere 离开某地，出发

最基本的leave表示go away，即从某地出发或离开。可以像he turns to leave（转身离开）那样单独使用，也可以变成leave+地点名词，表示“离开某地”，“起身”等。

“大家为什么把一对孤男寡女留在房间里就出去了呢？”

Everyone has left the room except for Adam and Eve.

M·O·R·E

- leave somewhere for
  离开某地，去往某地
- leave somewhere to+动词
  为了做某事而离开某地

What time does the limo **leave**?
轿车什么时候开?

He got up to **leave** the room.
他起身走出了房间。

Do you want us to **leave** the room?
你要我们走出房间吗?

A: We told Cindy to leave our group. 我们叫辛迪离开我们小组。
B: I want to make sure she stays away. 我想知道，她到底走没走。

Leave for ... 前往某处

很容易和前面的情况相混淆，如果leave+地点名词的话表示“离开某处”，但如果是leave for+地点名词的话则表示“向某处进发”。

“听说要去看大瀑布，兴奋得不得了的孩子们”

We're ready to leave for Niagara Falls.

M·O·R·E

- leave for A
  向某地出发
- leave A for B
  离开A，向B进发

He **left** New York **for** Seoul.
他离开纽约，去了首尔。

He **left for** Boston yesterday.
他昨天前往波士顿。

I **leave for** work at 7 o'clock in the morning.
我早上7点上班。

We have to **leave for** Japan in an hour.
我们得在一个小时之内前往日本。

A: It's time to leave for the party. 该去参加派对了。
B: I'll meet you down in the lobby. 我会在大厅等你。

leave a job 放弃工作

虽然是leave somewhere，但somewhere的位置如果被school, home, country, job或company等名词代替的话就表示“完全退出，离开”。不过，leave work并不是放弃工作，而是“下班”(get off work)的意思。

“为了挣更多的钱，离开令人怀念的公司”

I **left that job** to make more money.

M·O·R·E

- leave a job
  退出工作
- leave work
  下班(get off work)
- leave for work
  上班

I can't **leave this job** at the moment.
我现在不能放弃工作。

We both **left home** when we were 16.
我们都是在16岁的时候离开家的。

He **left work** in the middle of the day to go on a date.
他中午就提前下班回去约会了。

A: I think he's going to leave this company. 我觉得他要退出公司。
B: What makes you think so? 你为什么会那么认为？

leave something 将某物留在某处，留下，忘在某处

这次的leave表示在离开的位置“留下某物”。无论是有意图的还是粗心大意都可以用这个短语来表达。leave something后面主要接地点名词。

“打电话时要找的人不在，只好让对方帮忙记下名字”

You can **leave** your name, and I'll tell him you called.

How much should I **leave** on the table?
我得在桌子上留下多少？

I'd like to **leave** my room key, please.
我想让您保管我房间的钥匙，谢谢。

I think I **left** my keys here when I went out.
我好像走的时候把钥匙落在这了。

Leave it. I'll look at it if I get a chance.
放那吧，有时间我就看。

A: Don't forget to fill out those forms before you go. 别忘了走之前填好那些表格。
B: I'll leave them on your desk before I go. 我走之前会把那些表格放在你的桌子上。

leave somebody 离开某人，分手，托付

leave后面如果接人物的话表达的意思与leave something相似。表示“离开某人”，“与某人分手”或“留下某人”等。另外，还可以理解成较抽象的“使某人做”，“托付”等含义。

“精神状况好好的，妻子却要强行将丈夫监禁在精神病院”

Don’t **leave** me here with these people!

M·O·R·E

- leave sb
  离开，分手，留下
- leave sb sth
  将某物留给某人

I told her I was going to **leave** her.
我告诉过他，我要离开她。

Where does that **leave** me?
那我会怎么样?

You didn't really **leave** me much choice.
你给我留下的选择并不太多。

A: Ted and his wife have separated. 泰德和他老婆分居了。
B: Really? Did she leave him? 真的? 是她离开他的?

leave something+分词/形容词 变成……的状态

与keep具有相近的用法，leave something+形容词(pp)表示“使……处于某种状态”，“因……成为……的状态”。leave the door open是最为常见的表达。

“公司里最后走的人要记得锁门”

It was Nina who **left** the office door **unlocked**.

M·O·R·E

- leave for A
  向某地出发
- leave A for B
  离开A，向B进发

Don't **leave** things **half done**.
做事不要半途而废。

I **left** the door **open** and she must have gotten out.
我没有关门，她肯定出去了。

It's not very good **leaving** candles **unattended**.
点燃的蜡烛如果不注意就不好了。

A: I'm going to bed soon. 我马上要睡觉了。
B: Leave the door to the bedroom open. 把寝室的门给我留着。

Leave somebody alone 不管某人

如果有人对你纠缠不清时就可以喊一句Leave me alone!（别烦我！），leave somebody alone表示“不要管我”。想要强调的话可以说成leave somebody all alone。

“刚刚失恋的女儿最好不要管她”

Leave her alone. She obviously doesn't want to talk.

M·O·R·E

- leave sb alone
  别管某人
- leave sth alone
  不要管……

Could you please just **leave me alone**?
你能不能别管我?

I didn't want to **leave him alone**.
我不想不管他。

I **left her alone** out there.
我把她一个人留在那里。

They're even. So just **leave it alone**.
没什么不公平的，所以不要管了。

A: Tina always wears old clothes. 缇娜总是穿破旧的衣服。
B: Leave Tina alone. She's a nice girl. 别管她，她是个不错的女孩。

leave a message 留下信息

比较常用的电话用语，leave后面接message或note等词时表示“留下信息或笔记”。想要说明传达内容的话可以说message(note) saying that。

“春香给帮子打电话，却没人接听”

You got Ban-ja. **Leave a message.**

M·O·R·E

- leave a message (note)
  留下信息（记下信息）
- leave a message (note) saying that S+V
  留下……的信息

Could I **leave a message**?
我能留个信息吗?

Please, **leave a message** at the tone.
请在提示音后留下信息。

They **left us a message** saying they were getting married.
他们留下信息说，他们要结婚了。

A: Would you like to leave a message? 你能留下信息吗?
B: That's okay. I'll call again later. 好的，我会晚点打过来。

Leave something to somebody 将某事交给某人

表示让somebody负责或决定的意思。稍有变形的Let's leave it at that表示“该做的都做了，别再管了”。

“怀疑丈夫是不是有外遇，想要尾随的朋友们”

Leave it to the pros.

M·O·R·E

- leave sth to sb
  将某事交给某人，让某人负责
- leave it at that
  就留在这个程度吧，已经足够了
- leave it up to
  交给某人
- leave it to sb to+V
  交给某人做某事

Leave it to me to find her.
找她的事情交给我吧。

I'll **leave them to** you when I die.
等我死后会把他们交给你的。

I think we can just **leave it at that.**
我觉得我们可以收手了。

A: Can you introduce me to your boss? **你能把我介绍给你的老板吗？**
B: Leave it to me. I'll schedule an appointment. **交给我吧，我会安排的。**

have something left 留下了……

属于比较特殊的表达方式，have(get) something left表示“留下something”，另外，leftover表示“剩下的东西”。

“已经签好了1年的协议，刚住了两个月，主人就开始催起来”

There are 10 months **left** on my lease.

M·O·R·E

- have sth left
  留下了……
- leftover
  剩下的东西（食物）

We don't **have much time left.**
我们没多少时间了。

I just **have one problem left** that I don't know how to solve.
我还有一道题不知道该怎么做。

It's **leftover** from the wedding.
这是婚礼上剩下的。

We had a lot of liquor **leftover** from the Christmas party.
我们圣诞节派对之后剩下了很多酒水。

A: When can we leave school? **我们什么时候可以离开学校？**
B: In ten minutes. We don't have much time left. **10分钟之后吧，我们剩下的时间不多了。**

leave somebody (sth) behind 不带走，留下

字面含义为留在(leave)后面(behind)，表示“不带走”，“留下”。留下的对象可以是人(somebody)，也可以是事物(something)。

“大义凌然地说敌人交给我，让伤员们先撤离的中卫”

Go ahead. **Leave me behind**.

The four kids ran off, **leaving Parker behind**

四个孩子逃跑了，把帕克留在了后面。

Is that why he **left you behind**?

所以他在把你留了下来?

So how did you manage to **leave her behind** and come here?

你是怎么把她丢在那，自己来到这的?

If you don't get back right now, I'm going to have to **leave you behind**!

如果你现在不马上回来，我就不等你了!

A: Should I bring my suitcase along? **我能带着我的行李吗?**

B: Leave it behind. We'll get it later. **留在这吧，回头再来取。**

leave out 不考虑，除外

leave out表示omit，可以理解为“除外”，“不包括”。在会话中经常会用为be (feel) left out，表示“被忽视”，“不受欢迎”等。

“连个男朋友都没有，却天天想着生孩子”

You'**re leaving out** the most important factor!

M·O·R·E

- leave out (omit)
  除外
- be (feel) left out
  被忽视，不受欢迎

Have much fun! Just **leave me out** of it.

玩得开心点，我就不加入了。

I **have felt so left out** since you left me.

在你离开我之后，我感到非常孤单。

Frankly, I didn't want you to **feel left out**.

老实说，我没想让你感到失落。

A: We just completed the report. **我们刚刚完成报告书。**

B: Don't leave out my data. **不要忘了我的资料。**

leave off 放下手中的事情

off表示远离而去，因此leave off表示“除外”或“放下手中的事情”。经常会用为continue (pick up, talk up) where we left off的形态，表示“从上次停下的部分接着做”。

“正在勾搭女生，突然打进了一通电话，等过一会继续聊”

Shall we pick up where we **left off**?

M·O·R·E

- leave off
  除外，放弃
- continue (pick up, take up) where we left off
  从上次的部分重新开始

Let's pick it up where we **left off**.
我们接着上次继续做吧。

Why don't you just come back down here and we'll pick up where we **left off**?
你最好马上下来，我们接着之前的部分做。

Shall we continue where we **left off** last night?
我们要从昨天晚上停止的部分接着做吗?

A: Did you finish reading the novel? **你读完那篇小说了?**
B: No. I can't remember where I left off. **没有，我不知道读到哪了。**

be on leave 休假中

如果leave作为名词的话就表示“休假”，与vacation具有相近的含义。因此be on leave表示“休假中”，go on leave表示“享受休假”。

“连休假都不去，每天加班的员工需要休息”

You'**re on leave**. You get some personal time.

M·O·R·E

- be on leave
  休假中
- go on leave
  去度假

He **is on leave** now. You can call him later.
他现在在休假，你可以稍后再打过来。

What's going to happen to us when she **goes on leave**?
如果她去度假的话，我们会怎么样?

She'**s going on leave**?
她要去度假了?

Yes. He's in charge of that, but he'**s on leave** now.
恩，他是主要负责人，不过现在正在休假。

A: Does Bill still work in this department? **比尔现在还在这个部门工作吗?**
B: He does, but he's on leave right now. **恩，不过他现在正在休假。**

More Expressions

- **leave a lot (much, something) to be desired** 感到不满足
  Your manner **leaves something to be desired**. 你有点不礼貌啊。

- **leave room for** 给……腾出空间
  Don't get too full. You have to **leave room for** dessert.
  不要吃得太饱，要留着肚子吃甜点。

- **leave somebody out in the cold**
  除外，排外
  We can't **leave her out in the cold**.
  我们不能把她排除。

- **Better left unsaid** 最好别说话，闭嘴
  I think some things are **better left unsaid**. 我觉得有些事情还是不要说为好。

- **Take it or leave it** 爱咋咋地
  I'll give you $30 for your MP3 player. **Take it or leave it**.
  我花30美元买你的MP3播放器。随你便。

跑起来

Run

想象一下在广阔的空间自由地奔跑，就会理解很多含义。约会要迟到了，急忙跑过去，不料中途偶然遇到对方，或者犯了罪会仓皇而逃等一切人类基本的奔跑行为和机械等运转的过程都可以用这个词来表示。将范围扩大到公司或商店等的运营过程也属于这一范畴。名词具有拉肚子(the runs)，或上映等含义。

基本概念

1 奔跑，逃跑

I can run 100 meters in 14 seconds. 我可以在14秒内跑完百米。

I've got to run.我得马上走了。

I run about thirty miles per week. 我每个星期会跑30英里左右。

2 使运作，使做东，上映

The movie runs for more than 3 hours. 这部电影的放映时间长达3个小时。

This computer doesn't run Windows 7 . 这台电脑不能用Windows 7。

3 运营，经营，参加选举(for)

I run a boutique. 我在经营一家美容院。

4 跑步，拉肚子，演出上映，棒球中的得分

I've got the runs. 我拉肚子了。

I have a runny nose. 我流鼻涕了。

run 奔跑，跑动

具有最基本含义的run与to，down，toward等方向介词相结合，表示“向某处跑去”，“跑过去”等。

“下班回家的老婆对全职家庭主夫老公说，想吃饼干”

Run down to the snack bar and get me some cookies.

M·O·R·E

- run (down) to
  向某处跑去，奔去
- run to+动词
  急忙去做某事

I'm going to **run to** the car and get my stuff.
我要马上跑回车里，拿我的东西。

I'm going to **run down to** the emergency room.
我得马上跑到急救室。

You **run to** the DVD store and I'll go get coffee.
你赶紧去趟DVD店，我来买咖啡。

A: How long does it take to finish this race? **完成比赛需要多长时间？**
B: You will have to run for 30 minutes. **你至少得跑30分钟。**

come running 好不容易跑过来，请求帮助(to somebody)

字面含义为跑(running)过来(come)，表示“急忙跑过来”，“跑来”等，另外，还有比喻性质的“好不容易完成”的意思，也可以用flying代替running。

“刚把公司的女上司送到家，出门时突然听到一声尖叫，急忙跑过去一看”

I heard a scream. I **came running back**, and she was naked.

M·O·R·E

- come running (back) to
  跑到某处，跑回某处
- come running out of (from)
  从某处跑来

The kids **came running out of** the house.
孩子们从家里跑了出来。

She didn't **come running back to** you.
她没有回到你身边。

When you hear it, **come running**.
当你听到时，就马上跑过来。

A: Everyone is feeling hungry tonight. **今天晚上每个人都很饿。**
B: They'll come running when I serve dinner. **等我做好晚饭，他们就会跑过来。**

be running late 迟到

run late表示去某处时迟到，经常会用现在进行时be running late的形态。想要表达……迟到，则可以像be late for一样，使用for，变成be running late for。

"公司女上司连番诱惑，却始终不屈不挠，坚决走出来的老徐同志"

I've got to go. I'm running late.

M·O·R·E

- be late for 迟到……
- be running late for 迟到……

He's supposed to be here, but I guess he's **running late**.
他原本应该在这的，我猜他迟到了。

I **was running late for** a meeting.
会议要迟到了。

Let's go right now. We're **running late**.
我们现在就出发，要迟到了。

A: It's after six o'clock right now. 现在已经过了6点。
B: Oh no! I am really running late! 不！我要迟到了！

run errands 跑腿

errand表示受别人的嘱咐，暂时去买点东西或拿点东西，即"跑腿"。去跑腿则可以使用run errands (an errand)，让别人跑腿则可以用send sb on an errand。

"女上司问我必须离开吗，我说是老板有事找我"

I've got an errand. I have to run.

M·O·R·E

- run one's errands 帮某人跑腿
- go on an errand 跑腿
- send sb on an errand 让某人跑腿

I have to **run an errand**.
我得跑个腿了。

I've got millions of **errands to run**.
我要帮别人做很多事情。

Do you mind if I **run a quick errand**?
你介意我去跑个腿吗?

I'm sorry. She shouldn't have you **running errands**.
不好意思，她不应该让你跑腿的。

A: Where is Joseph this morning? 今天早上约瑟夫去哪了?
B: He had to go run errands. 他应该是替人办事去了。

run after 追赶，尾随

字面含义为在后面(after)跑，表示“追赶……”。可以使用在追赶犯人上，也可以单纯表达尾随。

“他夜里突然发现家里有小偷进来，于是”

He took off running after the thief without any clothes on.

M·O·R·E

- come running after 追赶某人
- take off running after 开始追赶某人

Michael ran off and Jane **ran after** him.
麦克一逃跑，杰恩就开始追赶他。

He **ran after** her. They met in the hallway.
他在尾随她，后来在走廊碰到了。

Tom took off jogging again. Susie **ran after** him.
汤姆重新开始了慢跑，苏西也赶了过去。

Hurley took off **running after** Vincent.
何蕾开始追赶文森特。

A: I got to the bus stop as my bus was leaving. 公交马上就要出发了，我急忙跑到车站。

B: Did you still run after it? 你能追上吗?

run around (with) 跑来跑去，忙碌

字面含义为在周边跑来跑去，可以表示因各种事情忙得不可开交的意思。尤其run around with somebody表示“与某人度过不好的时光”。

“想要抓住逃跑的老徐同志，在前院跑来跑去的她”

She is running around the front yard trying to get him.

M·O·R·E

- run around+ ...ing 忙着做某事
- run around with sb 男女间有外遇

Are you **running around** looking for your earring?
你在到处找你的耳环吗?

They **run around** the house with toy airplanes.
他们拿着玩具飞机在房间里跑来跑去。

She'**s running around** telling everyone that she's going to break up with Tom.
她到处张扬，说自己要和汤姆分手。

A: I don't think I can run around the track another time. 我无法再跑一圈了。

B: Hang in there! Just one more lap. 坚持住！只有一圈了。

run away 逃跑，奔跑

字面含义为远远(away)地跑开，表示“逃跑”，“逃离”等。run off还能表示“急忙走掉”，“逃跑”等，因此两者为近义词。

“紧紧追着老徐同志，苦苦哀求道，为什么这么对自己”

Why do you keep running away from me?

M·O·R·E

- run away (from ...)
  (从……)逃跑
- run off (to+名词，to+动词)
  逃跑去做某事，急忙离开做某事
- run away (off) with
  逃跑，逃避爱情

You can't **run away from** that.
你可跑不掉。

I am going to **run away from** you.
我要离你而去了。

Did he **run off to** see his mom?
他急忙离开是为了见他妈妈吗?

A: Some children choose to run away from home. **有些孩子选择离家出走。**
B: They must have difficult lives. **他们肯定活得很不容易吧。**

run something by somebody 与某人商量某事

字面含义为将something拿到somebody处询问意见，或让对方解释，因此run that by me again表示“重新说一遍”。

“老徐同志边跑边说，需要和老婆商量商量”

I'd better run this by my wife.

M·O·R·E

- run sth by sb
  与某人商量某事
- (You'd better) Run it by me.
  和我说说，商量商量

You'd better **run it by** me.
你最好先和我说说。

Just **run it by** Jimmy and tell me what he thinks.
先和吉米商量商量，告诉我他是怎么想的。

Great! You want to **run it by** me?
很好！你要和我说说?

A: This is the plan that I created. **这是我想出的计划。**
B: Run it by my boss and see what he thinks. **跟我老板商量商量，看看他的想法。**

run down 跑下去，被车撞，谴责，出故障，磨损

字面含义为向下方(down)跑去(run)，表示“追击……”或“枯竭”等。另外，还可以表示“被车撞到”或“谴责”。

“老徐，从前院跑了出来，开始向走廊跑去”

He began running down the sidewalk.

M·O·R·E

- run down
  跑下去，追踪，被车撞，谴责
- run (–) down
  疲倦的，破旧的

I'm going to **run down to** the emergency room and check it out.
我得马上去急救室看看。

Could you **run down to** the snack bar and get me some cookies?
你能赶紧去趟快餐店帮我买点饼干吗?

I've been feeling a little **run down** lately.
我最近有点累。

A: Did you go to the gym today? 你今天去体育馆了?
B: Yes, I exercised. Sweat is running down my shirt. 恩，去活动了一会。衣服都湿透了。

run for 参加选举，向……跑去

无论是总统选举还是大学内社团会长的选举，只要是参加选举就可以用这个短语，即以当选为目的出战。但也可以按照字面含义，理解为“向着……跑去”。

“老徐，现在跑出了住宅区，向很多人跑去”

He was running for the street.

M·O·R·E

- make a run for it
  逃跑
- run for one's life
  往死里跑
- run in the election
  参加选举

I don't know who'**s running for** president.
我不知道谁参加总统选举。

He'**s running for** city council.
他参加了市议会的选举。

I guess you don't read the papers. I'**m running for** mayor.
我猜你没有看报纸吧，我要参选市长。

I wasn't planning on **running for** a second term.
我没有参加第二次选举的意向。

A: My uncle says he's going to run for mayor. 我叔叔说他要参选市长。
B: There's no way he will ever win. 他绝对不可能成功的。

run into 向……跑去，碰到困难，偶然遇到某人

字面含义为向内部(into)跑去，可以表示“碰到困难，难关”或“偶然遇到某人”，相近的短语有run (come) across, bump into等。

“在逃跑的过程中碰到了法律大学同学，还不忘恭敬地打个招呼”

He ran into a law school classmate.

If you **run into** any problems, you call me.
如果你碰到任何困难，找我。

I **ran into** her on my way home.
回家的路上偶然碰到了她。

Good (Nice) **running into** you.
见到你很高兴。

A: I ran into Mike this morning. 我今天早上碰到麦克了。
B: How's he doing? 他过得怎么样?

run out(of) 缺乏（某物）(=run short of, run low)

表示某种物品用完，表示“某物不足”，“缺乏某物”等。相似的表达有run short of, run low等。另外，run out on somebody表示“在某人困难时逃跑”。

“老徐正要打车，突然发现身上没钱”

He wanted to catch a taxi, but ran out of money.

M·O·R·E

- run out (of)
  缺乏某物，不足
- run out on sb
  某人困难时逃跑

I **ran out of** gas. Where can we fill up?
没油了，我们去哪可以加油?

I'**m running out of** time.
我没有多少时间了。(I'm running short of time.)

My real dad **ran out on** me before I was born.
亲生父亲在我出生前就离开了。

A: We ran out of paper for the copier. 我们的复印纸用完了。
B: I'll get the secretary to get some more. 我会让秘书去弄点。

run over 向某处跑去，用车撞，上下打量

表示“向……的上方跑去”，可以理解为“被车撞”，“上下打量”等。如果单纯使用run over（+地点）的话就表示“向某处跑去”。

“连钱都没有，正在想应该怎么回家，不小心被车撞了。”

He **got run over** while thinking about how to get home.

M·O·R·E

- run over to
  向……跑去
- run over
  被车撞，上下打量

I'm going to have to **run over** there and beg him to stay with me.
我得马上跑过去，求他留下。

When I **got run over**, I was on my way to propose to you.
当我被车撞到时，正想去向你求婚。

I'd like to **run over** today's schedule.
我想看一看今天的行程安排。

A: How did the car get a flat tire? 那辆车为什么会爆胎?
B: You must have run over some broken glass. 肯定是压到碎玻璃了。

run through 贯通，上下打量，横穿

正如字面含义，表示“横穿(through)”，“某种想法等贯通”。尤其run through one's mind表示“充满某人的脑海”，或“无法令人忘怀”等。

“被车撞倒在地上，却仍然一丝不挂，路人们大饱眼福”

He saw her **running through** the crowd, still naked.

M·O·R·E

- run through
  横穿……，
  贯通，上下打量
- run through one's mind
  使某人无法忘怀

It's **been running through** my mind ever since.
在那次之后，我的脑海中就充满了那件事。

Why are thoughts of that girl **running through** my head?
为什么我久久无法忘怀她的形象?

Okay, let's **run through** it one more time.
好，我们再检查一遍。

A: The students are very excited today. 学生们今天非常兴奋。
B: Tell them not to run through the hallway. 叫他们不要在走廊跑来跑去。

More Expressions

- **run along** 去吧（命令型）

  Now **run along** so your daddy and I can make love.

  去吧，我得和你爸爸亲热亲热了。

- **make a run for it** 逃跑，急忙避开

  Let's **make a run for it**.

  我们赶紧离开吧。

- **be up and running** 运转良好

  Is the office **up and running**?

  办公室情况稳定吗？

- **run in the family** ……是家庭传统

  Good lucks **run in the family**.

  好运是我们家族的传统。

- **run a fever** 发烧

  Jane's still **running a fever**.

  杰恩还在发烧。

- 期间名词**+running** 连续

  Our softball team has lost two years **running**. 我们垒球队连续输了两年。

- **in the long run** 最终

  Well, **in the long run**, it doesn't matter. 最后也没什么关系。

不管是人还是机械都要停

Break

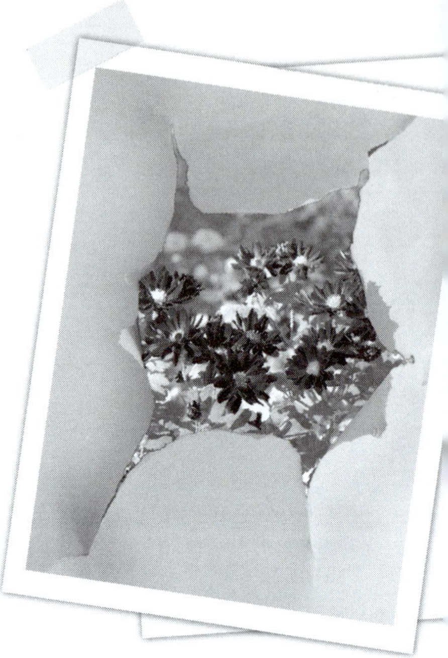

提到break就会想起破坏或断裂等现象，作为动词表示手脚骨折(break one's leg)或电脑等机器出故障。同时可以用来比喻失约等行为(break one's promise)，也可以表示休息一会或者和女朋友分手等。虽然不常用，但将大钱破开也可以说break。

基本概念

1 打破，出故障，ww（法律，记录，约定等）

My son broke the computer. 我儿子把电脑弄坏了。

My display screen is broken! 我的显示器坏了！

She never broke her promise. 她从来不会失约。

2 （为了吃点东西）休息一会

How about we break for a while? 我们休息一会怎么样?

Let's break for coffee. 我们休息一会，喝杯咖啡吧。

3 破钱（大钞换小票）

Would you please break this dollar bill for me? 你能帮我破开这张大票吗?

4 （名词）休息，休假，(TV)广告时间

Would you like to begin after a short break? 你要不要稍微休息一会?

The break is over. 休息时间结束了。

break one's leg 腿部骨折，受伤

break表示“骨折”，经常会使用break one's arm，break one's leg，break one's hip和break one's neck等。

“开车一定要小心，不然就会”

I almost broke my neck kissing in the car.

M·O·R·E

- break one's leg (arm) ...ing 在做某事的时候伤了腿

I have an interview tomorrow and I can't go if I **break my leg**.
我明天有个面试，如果腿骨折了就去不了了。

I didn't know that you **broke your leg**.
我不知道你的腿骨折了。

She **broke my arm**.
她把我的胳膊弄折了。

I **broke my leg** skiing last weekend.
我上周滑雪的时候不小心弄折了大腿。

A: Did you have an accident, Mike? 你出事故了，麦克？
B: I broke my leg while skiing. 我滑雪的时候不小心腿部骨折了。

break one's promise 打破约定

虽然有打破像窗户一样的真实物体的意思，但break也可以将promise, rule, law, habit, record等抽象名词作为宾语，表示“打破……”，“不遵守”，“终结”等。

“立法的人应该以身作则，遵守法律”

No one has the right to break the law.

M·O·R·E

- break one's promise 与某人失约
- break the law (rule, record) 不遵守法律(规则)，打破记录

Well, it looks like they **broke their promise**.
恩，他们好像没有守信。

I will do my best not to **break my promise**.
我会尽量遵守我的承诺的。

Every now and then, we have to **break the rules**.
有些时候，我们不得不违反规则。

You're asking me to **break the law**.
你是在让我违法。

A: Forget about going to the party. 别想着去派对了。
B: I can't break my promise to my friends. 我不能打破和朋友们的约定啊。

break the news to 向某人传达新闻

紧急新闻叫做break news，就像大部分的紧急消息都不是什么好消息一样，break the news to somebody主要表示“将不好的消息传达给某人”。

“员工因公殉职，老板出面要亲自和家人汇报”

I want to **break the news to** her if it's okay with you.

I just accidentally **broke the news** of her infidelity to her husband.
我刚刚不小心把她的绯闻告诉了她丈夫。

I imagine that you were pissed off when she **broke the news**.
在听到她的消息之后，我猜你非常生气。

Let's go **break the news**.
我们去传达消息吧。

A: Jack's mother just died in the hospital. 杰克的母亲刚刚在医院过世了。
B: How can we break the news to him? 我们该怎么跟他说？

break one's heart 让人失望，让人痛心

字面含义为“毁掉一个人的心”，表示“断绝与某人的关系”或“让人气愤或失望”。heartbreaker表示“让人痛心的人”。

“信誓旦旦地保证绝对不会搞外遇，不料老病又犯，伤心地悲痛欲绝”

I trusted you not to cheat on me but you **broke my heart**.

M·O·R·E

- break one's heart
  让某人伤心
- heartbreaker
  让别人伤心的人

You **broke my heart** again.
你再一次伤害了我的感情。

I broke up with a girl who **broke my heart**.
我和伤我心的女朋友分手了。

Don't **break my heart**. Please get out of here.
不要伤我的心。请离开这里。

A: Why did your girlfriend leave you? 你女朋友为什么要离开你？
B: She didn't love me. It broke my heart. 她根本就不爱我。这让我非常伤心。

break for 暂时休息

take a break是众所周知的休息，a break表明暂时放下手中的事情，“休息一会”。在这里如果用作动词的话，break for则表示“为了做某事而暂时休息”。

“孤独的员工召集同事们一起吃午饭”

I'm about to break for lunch. Want to join me?

M·O·R·E

- break for sth
  为了做某事而暂时休息
- take a (short) break
  休息一会
- Give me a break.
  稍微等等，给我机会，停手。
- Give it a break!
  给我住手！

We can talk about that later. I'm about to **break for** lunch.
我们可以回头再聊。我现在要去吃午饭了。

Shall we **break for** a snack? Let's go out.
我们休息一会，吃点快餐呗？出去吧。

Let's **take a ten-minute break**.
我们休息十分钟。

A: OK everyone, let's take a break for lunch. 大家可以去吃午饭了。
B: Thank god. I need to eat some food. 谢天谢地，我得赶紧吃点东西了。

break away 离去，脱离，独立，断绝（关系）

表示断绝而去的意思，物理上的“从某物体脱离”，或抽象的“断绝关系或独立”等都可以用这个短语表达。

“男孩虽然百般挽留，变了心的女孩却渐行渐远”

He grabbed and pulled her, but she broke away.

My son's trying to **break away** from me with a girl he's dating.
我儿子想和他女朋友远走高飞。

He **broke away** from the group and joined us.
他离开了原来的小组，投靠了我们。

I will be there as soon as I can **break away**.
我一出来就会马上赶过去。

A: How do icebergs enter the ocean? 冰山是怎么流向大洋的？
B: They break away from the frozen areas. 是从冰河地区脱离形成的。

break down 击碎，出故障，失败，分解，分离或分类

“机械等破碎”，“出故障”或“失败”等含义。break something down into的形态表示“将某物分类为……”。另外，break down in tears还表示“嚎啕大哭”。

“职场同事的车10年开了30万公里，却又迟到了”

Did your car break down again?

M·O·R·E

- break down
  击碎，出故障
- break sth down into
  将……分类为……
- break(-)down
  故障，挫折

My car **broke down** again.
我的汽车又出毛病了。

Not again! This is the third time you've **broken** my MP3 player!
又来了！这是你第三次弄坏我的MP3播放器了！

Everything can be **broken down** into three categories.
每个东西都可以分为三种类型。

A: Did your car break down again? 你的轿车又出故障了?
B: It did, and that's the third time in two weeks. 是啊，两个星期之内坏了三次了。

break in 侵入，插话，打击

break in(to)的最基本含义为插入或侵入，是小偷的主要工作。break into意味着“开始新的工作”，“突然捧腹大笑”等。

“喜欢尾随的人闯进了别人的家里，差点被抓”

I broke into her house and almost got caught.

M·O·R·E

- break in on (with)
  插话
- break sb (sth) in
  使某人适应
- break into (burst into)
  侵入，开始（新工作），突然爆发（大小，泪水等）

We know who **broke into** your house.
我们知道是谁闯进你的房子了。

Did somebody **break into** my car?
有人撬开了我的车?

I **broke in** my new shoes.
我适应了新鞋。

A: Someone broke into the house and stole things. 有人闯了进来，把东西偷走了。
B: Did anyone call the police about it? 有人叫警察了吗?

break off 打击，折断，脱离，结束（话，关系等），中断

字面含义为“从本体脱离而去(off)”，用来表示对话的结束或关系的中断等。break it off with 多为“与某人分手”(break up with)的意思。

“表面上非常老实，一张嘴就显得非常幼稚的男友非常让人厌烦”

I've got to break it off with Jim.

M·O·R·E

- break off
  折断，打击，脱离，中断
- break it off
  中断关系

Did it **break off** or did someone break it?
是它自己脱落的还是有人弄坏的?

My father **broke off** his affair with Cindy.
我爸爸和辛迪断绝了关系。

If you want, I'll just **break it off with** her.
如果你愿意，我就马上和她断绝来往。

A: The mirror broke off the car door. 镜片从车身掉了出去。
B: It will have to be replaced. 必须要换一个。

break out 出现，发生，突然开始，脱离(... of)

战争，火灾，打斗，病情等突然爆发。另外，“突然开始做某事”也可以用break out of，表示“脱离……”。

“军训的时候有人要逃出去”

Do you ever think about breaking out?

M·O·R·E

- break out
  发生，逃离
- break out into
  突然开始做某事

The fire **broke out** last night.
昨天晚上突然着火了。

I really want to **break out of** here.
我很想从这里逃出去。

She **broke out** into a smile and stood up.
她突然开始大笑，站了起来。

A: What were all of those sirens? 那是什么声音?
B: Three criminals broke out of jail. 3名罪犯越狱了。

break up 生孩子，击垮，分手

最常用的意思是男女之间分手。break up表示“分手”，break up with表示“与某人分手”，we broke up则表示“我们分手了”，I broke up with her表示“我和她分手了”。

“男朋友非常不舍得花钱”

I broke up with him because he's so mean.

M·O·R·E

- break up
  打破，分手
- break up with sb
  与某人分手

I'm going to **break up with** you.
我们还是分手吧。

I **broke up with** Jim because he didn't want to have any children.
我和吉姆分手了，因为他不想要孩子。

Have you seen Mike since you two **broke up**?
在你们俩分手之后，你见过麦克吗?

You'**re breaking up**! Call me again!
你的声音断断续续的！重新打过来！

A: Why did you break up with Anna? 你为什么要和安娜分手?
B: She wants to start a family. I'm not ready. 她想结婚组建一个家庭，不过我还没准备好。

More Expressions

- **be broke** 穷光蛋
  The wedding was expensive. I'**m broke**.
  婚礼费用昂贵，可我一分钱都没有。

- **break through** 闯出，克服难关，成功（breakthrough 新突破口）
  That'll help us **break through** to the trapped miners.
  那个会帮我们找到被困的矿工的。

- **break with** 与某人断绝关系
  I just **broke with** them a week ago.
  我一个星期前就和他们断绝来往了。

- **break wind** 放屁
  Do not **break wind** in the park.
  不要在公园放屁。

- **break even** 收支平衡
  This month, we will barely **break even**. 这个月我们差不多能收支平衡了。

- **break the ice** 打破冷清，开始对话
  Okay, I've got to **break the ice** here.
  好，我先开始说吧。

- **a big break** 好机会
  I don't care! This is **a big break** for me! 我不管！这对我来说是个绝佳的机会！

Tough break! 运气真好！
You sound like a broken record.
你好像在重复同样的话。

好的开始是成功的一半

Start/Begin

start与begin都可以表示“开始”的含义，宾语都可以接名词或to+动词(...ing)。当然，两个词并非没有差异，但最好在各种例句中熟悉两个单词的不同用法。发动汽车要用start a car，而不是begin；起跑线不是beginning line，而是starting line。因此，start多少比begin多一些动态感。

基本概念

1 start：出发，开始做某事，（名词）出发，开始

We'll be starting in a few minutes. 还有几分钟就开始了。

We are going to start now. 我们现在要开始了。

What time does the game start? 比赛几点开始?

2 begin：开始，开始做某事

I think we should begin. 我觉得咱们应该开始了。

It began to rain. 开始下雨了。

Would you like to begin after a short break? 你想休息一会再开始吗?

start to 开始做某事

表示“开始某种行为”，start to+动词或start+ ...ing型都可以。start后面可以接动词不定式或 ...ing。

“是因为耐性不足呢，还是因为刺激呢？”

They started to french kiss in the elevator.

M·O·R·E

- start to+动词
  开始做某事
- start ...ing
  开始做某事

What time do you **start to** board?
你什么时候能登机？

We should **start working** on the report.
我们得开始写报告了。

I just **started driving** this month.
我这个月才开始开车的。

A: How is your cold? 你感冒怎么样了？
B: It's not bad. I'm starting to feel better. 还好，开始康复了。

start something 开始做某事

start表示“开始某事”，后面可以接多种多样的宾语。除了start a company和start a family，还可以像start a fight (fire)一样接其他的名词。

“就算是当了几十年的护士，也不能亲自动手术啊”

Let's start the operation without him.

M·O·R·E

- start a family
  生孩子
- start the car
  发动汽车
- start a company (business)
  开始运营公司（事业）
- start a fight (fire)
  开始战斗（点火）

I can't **start** the car. I don't know what the problem is.
我的车发动不起来了。不知道出了什么问题。

My wife wants to **start** a family this year.
我老婆想在今年怀上孩子。

Did you **start** a fight in the bar yesterday?
你昨天在酒吧打架了？

A: I'm eager to start my vacation. 我很希望赶紧去度假。
B: Where are you going? 你要去哪？

start it 开始

it为之前已经提到过的话题，可以用来明确到底是谁先开始的和各种是是非非。

"专门在论坛说脏话的人组团骂人，不小心被抓"

He started it and got caught in the middle of it.

I **started it** but, now it's scaring me.
是我开始的，不过现在我有点害怕了。

She's the one that **started it**.
是她先开始的。

You **started it**. Everybody knows that!
是你先开始的，大家都知道！

A: Many people were killed in the war. 很多人在战争中丧失了生命。
B: I wonder which country started it. 真想知道是哪个国家先挑起战事的。

starting 先开始做某事

start如果变成starting+时间名词的形态则表示"从……开始"。"从现在开始"为starting now，"从下周开始"为starting next week。

"不喜欢学习的学生们经常会用到的辩解"

I'm going to study hard starting tomorrow.

M·O·R·E

- starting+时间名词
  从……开始做
- starting now (next week)
  从现在（下个星期）开始

I'll be on vacation **starting** next week.
我下周要去度假了。

Would it be all right if I took a week off **starting** tomorrow?
我明天开始请一周的假可以吗?

Starting next month, I'm going to pay you to live here.
从下个月开始，我会给你房租的。

A: I'm going to exercise starting next week. 我要从下个星期开始锻炼。
B: Good. You need to lose weight. 很好，你是得减减肥了。

start off 开始

字面含义为分离开(off)，出发(start)，可以联想到出发的动作。start off后面如果加with的话就表示“以……开始”，如果加to (toward)的话就表示“向某处进发”。

“一个胖子说要通过运动减肥，先从仰卧起坐开始”

I decided to start off with something small like doing sit-ups.

M·O·R·E

- start off sth with (by)
  以……开始
- start sb off with
  帮助某人开始做某事
- start off to (toward)
  向某处进发

I always like to **start off** with a hug.
我总是喜欢先抱一抱。

She **started off** toward the church.
她向教堂进发了。

A: Is it difficult to work in a bank? 在银行里工作很难吗?

B: All employees start off by working long hours. 所有员工一开始都会工作很长时间。

start on 开始某事

像work on一样，on表示某种作业的对象，start on表示“开始某事（作业）”，“使用某物”等。另外，start in on则表示“谴责某人”，“抱怨某人”等。

“交代的事情已经过了好几天，对方却毫无反应”

When can you start on the annual report?

M·O·R·E

- start on
  开始做某事，使用
- start in on
  谴责某人
  (began nagging (yelling))

Sorry I couldn't **start on** your case sooner.
对不起，我不能尽快着手你的案例。

You can **start on** your essay now.
你现在可以开始写论文了。

I told her I was going to leave her and then she **started in on** me.
我跟她说要离开她，她就开始闹我了。

A: The class is waiting to take the exam. 学生们正在准备考试。

B: Have them start on the first part of it. 先让他们做第一部分。

start out 开始，开始从事某职业等

字面含义为向外部(out)开始(start)，表示某种事情或人生，职业等以特定的方式呈现和开始。start out(of)也可以表示“从某处出来”。

“一个有名的作者最开始是从底层做起的”

I started out as a ghost writer.

M·O·R·E

- start out as 以……开始
- start out on (with) 以……开始

He **started out** of the bathroom to the door. She followed him.
他从洗手间走出来，向门口走去，她跟了过去。

It **started out** this way. Nothing caused it to happen.
一开始就这样，没有什么特别的原因。

I actually **started out as** a playwright, and then I went into law.
我其实是以编剧开始的，后来改行学法律。

A: Where will you be traveling this year? 你今年要去哪旅行?
B: I'll start out in Russia and then go to China. 我要从俄罗斯开始，再去中国转转。

start (all) over 重新开始

在这里over表示重复的意思，start over则表示“重新开始”。为了起到强调作用，也可以称为start all over。

“朋友和他老婆离婚了，因此劝他重新开始新生活”

Put your past behind you and start over.

Can we just **start all over**?
我们能重新开始吗?

Maybe we can **start over again**, but things will be different this time.
我们也许可以重新开始，不过已经是物是人非了。

We're going to have to **start all over again**.
我们不得不重新开始了。

A: There are too many mistakes in this report. 这篇报告里有太多错误了。
B: I think we'll need to start over again. 我觉得我们得重新开始了。

start up 开始，建立（公司等），使（发动机等）运转

表示“开始工作或项目”，也可以以start –up作形容词或名词表示“新兴事物”。另外，可以用来表达发动摩托车或汽车等的发动机。

“朋友保证会赚一大笔钱，连预付金都交上去了，却被别人骗了”

I feel like such an idiot! We'd better **start up** again.

M·O·R·E

- start up (sth) with sb 与某人开始做某事
- start up again 重新开始
- start up one's own 开始自己的事业

I **am not starting up with** him again.
我再也不会和他重新开始了。

I can't **start up something with** you.
我没办法和你重新开始。

His heart's too weak to **start up** again.
他根本经受不起重新开始。

The police car **started up** and began to drive away.
警车突然发动，开了出去。

A: Start up the car. We'll be leaving soon. 发动汽车吧，我们马上离开。
B: I'll go get the keys for it. 我要去拿钥匙。

start with 从……开始

虽然也是表示“开始”，但要注明先开始的东西。start with后面可以接人或事物。在饭店可以用来表达“先从……开始”，I'm going to start with cheese salad and then I'll have tuna等。

“卫生局来饭店检查卫生状况”

Maybe we should **start with** the kitchen.

Let's **start with** her and we'll see what we can do.
我们看看我们能做点什么吧，先从她开始。

Which one would you like me to **start with**?
你希望我们先从什么开始?

Let's speak in turn, **starting with** you.
我们轮流说吧，先从你开始。

A: Let's start with a prayer before eating. 吃饭前先祈祷。
B: OK, please go ahead with it. 好的，咱们开始吧。

begin to 开始做某事

就像start可以接to+动词或 ...ing，begin也可以用begin to+动词或begin+... ing的结构。

“没有男子汉气概的男生在气势汹汹的大妈面前说话”

I began to get butterflies in my stomach.

M·O·R·E

- begin to+动词 开始做某事
- begin ...ing 开始做某事

I **began to** like Korean food, such as bulgogi and kimchi.
我开始喜欢上韩国料理了，比如说烤肉和泡菜。

Tom pulled her toward him and they **began to** kiss.
汤姆一把把她拉了过去，两人开始接吻。

I'd like to **begin** repairing it.
我要开始修理它了。

A: Does your son have any hobbies? 你儿子有什么爱好吗?
B: He's begun to collect stamps. 他开始喜欢上集邮了。

begin something 开始做某事

同样与start相近，begin后面可加名词，begin something表示“开始某事”。something可以是各式各样的名词。

“讲述从法学院毕业后，作为律师的种种经历”

She began her career as a lawyer.

M·O·R·E

- begin the trip 开始旅行
- begin the meeting 开始会议
- begin one's career 开始某人的职业生涯
- begin (sth) as 开始做某事

We will **begin the trip** to Cheju Island tomorrow.
我们明天会去济州岛旅行。

Is everyone ready to **begin the meeting**?
大家都准备好开会了吗?

Now you can **begin** the test.
你现在可以开始测试了。

She **began her career** when she got here.
她来到这儿就开始了自己的职业生涯。

A: When can I begin the test? 我什么时候可以开始考试?
B: It will get started in about an hour. 差不多还有一个小时。

begin with (by) 从……开始

用来详细说明开始的对象，可以用begin with或begin by。另外，begin (something) as表示“以……开始”。

“名字叫凯瑟琳，但不知道是以“C”开头的，还是以“K”开头的”

Does her name **begin with** a "C"?

- begin with
  开始某事
- begin by ...ing
  从某事开始

We would like to **begin with** that.
我们先从那个开始吧。

Let me **begin by** saying that a terrible tragedy has occurred here.
我先告诉您，这里发生了一场惨剧。

A: I want to be successful at my job. 我想在事业上大有所成。
B: That begins with a lot of hard work. 那要从努力工作开始了。

More Expressions

- **get started** 开始
  Let's **get started on** the wedding plans! 我们按照婚礼计划开始吧！

- **start from scratch** 从一开始
  I'd like to have lunch again. Let's **start from scratch**.
  我想再吃一顿午餐，我们重新开始吧。

- **from the start** 从一开始
  As I said **from the start**, they don't support us here.
  正如我开始说的，他们并不支持我们。

- **a good start** 好的开始
  That's **a good start**. 那是个好的开始。

- **begin to understand (imagine)**
  开始理解，渐渐理解
  She **began to understand** what the boss was getting at.
  她渐渐明白老板的意图是什么了。

- **in the beginning** 最开始
  That was true, **in the beginning**.
  最开始的确没错。

- **to begin with** 首先，最先要提到的
  I never wanted this baby **to begin with**.
  首先，我从来没想要这个小孩。

困难时要帮助

Help

有困难就要互相帮助。help是帮助别人的意思，最基本的用法为help somebody，还可以用help somebody to+动词，help somebody with something，还有help+动词等3种句式。另外，can't help but to+动词或can't help ...ing表示“不得不……”。

基本概念

1 帮助，提供帮助

Is there anything I can do to help? 有什么我能帮忙的吗?

May I help you? 我能帮你吗?

How can I help you, sir? 需要什么帮助，先生?

I'd be happy to help you. 能帮到你我很开心。

2 帮助某人做某事（+动词（名词））

He sent me to help you with your grief. 他让我来帮你走出悲痛。

Can I help you with anything? 我能帮你什么吗?

3 can't (couldn't) help 不得不……

I can't help but to do that. 我不得不那么做。

I couldn't help feeling sorry for her. 我无法抑制对她的愧疚之情。

help somebody do 帮助某人做某事

help somebody后面一般会省略to，直接加上动词的原形。help后面如果直接接动词的话，就表示“对……形成帮助”。

“死皮赖脸不帮老婆做家务的男人”

If you don't **help me cook**, you're a dead man.

M·O·R·E

- help sb+动词
  帮助某人做某事
- help+动词
  帮助某事

You have got to **help me get** Tammy.
你必须帮我抓住塔米的心。

Well, I think I can **help you get** over him.
我觉得我可以帮助你和他做个了结。

It will **help solve** the traffic problems.
这会有助于交通问题的解决。

A: Come on, help me move this. 过来，帮我搬这些东西吧。
B: I'm sorry! I must be off right now. 不好意思！我现在马上得走。

help somebody with 帮助某人做某事

帮助他人的具体内容如果是名词形态，要加上with，变成help somebody with+名词的形态。

“能力不怎么样，就知道死要面子，只会拒绝朋友们帮助的人”

Why don't you let me **help you with** that?

M·O·R·E

- Can I help you with ... ?
  我能帮你做某事吗?
- Let me help you with ...
  我来帮你做某事吧

Can I **help you with** anything?
我能帮你做点什么吗?

Why don't you let me **help you with** that?
你怎么不让我帮帮你?

I have to **help my son with** his homework.
我得帮儿子做作业。

A: Can I help you with anything? 我有什么可以帮你的吗?
B: No, thank you, I'm just looking around. 不用了，谢谢，我就是随便看看。

help 帮助

help后面也可以不接任何宾语，单独使用。可以将人物作为主语，但也有很多时候主语会变成事物，表示“……有帮助”。

“切肉的时候不小心弄断了菜刀，老公拿着壁纸刀说”

Well, maybe this will help.

(Sometimes) That **helps**.
（有时）那挺有帮助的。

I just wasted my time . That didn't **help**!
我白白浪费了时间，根本没什么帮助！

It might **help**. Just go and try it.
有可能会起到作用。去试试吧。

Leave me alone. You'**re not helping**.
别管我，你不会帮到什么。

A: Did you buy your wife some flowers? 你给你老婆买花了没?
B: That didn't help. She's still mad at me. 根本没用，她还在生我的气。

help yourself (to) 请随便（做某事），您随意

help yourself单独使用，或者help yourself to+食物时则表示对客人说“请您随意”，“您请便”等。to后面如果是不能吃的东西，就表示随便使用。

“来参加聚会的客人找卫生间”

Help yourself to anything in the bathroom.

M·O·R·E

- Help yourself
  请您随意，请便
- Help yourself to ...
  请随意……

Go ahead, **help yourself**. Take whatever you want.
来，不要介意。想吃什么就吃什么。

Help yourself to the cake.
多尝尝蛋糕。

Help yourself to whatever's in the fridge.
冰箱里的东西想拿什么就拿什么。

A: I feel like drinking a cold beer. 我想喝一杯冰的啤酒。
B: There are a few in the fridge. Help yourself. 冰箱里有几瓶，随便拿。

can't help+动词 不得不做某事

用在迫不得已的情况中。可以说成I can't help it，如果想要说明具体的事情，就可以用I can't help but+动词，或I can't help but ...ing的形态。

"在公园碰到了几个流氓调戏自己的女朋友，却拔腿就跑"

I was weak, I couldn't help myself!

M·O·R·E

- I can't help but+动词(...ing)
  我不得不做某事
- (I) Can't help it.
  我也没办法。
- (It) Can't (couldn't) be helped.
  我也迫不得已。
- I cannot help myself.
  我无法抑制自己的感情。

I'm sorry, but **I can't help myself**.
很抱歉，我也没办法。

I can't help but think that he's not a good friend.
我会不由自主地想，他不是个好朋友。

I can't help but pay her the money.
我只能还她钱。

I can't help but think about Lisa.
我没办法忘掉丽萨。

A: I can't help playing computer games every day. **我每天都会情不自禁地玩电脑。**

B: That means you have no time to study. **那就是说你没有时间学习了。**

be a great (big) help (to) （对某人）产生巨大的帮助

在得到巨大帮助之后，用来表达内心感激之情。经常会用现在完成时，You're been a big (great) help（您给予了我巨大帮助）。

"去卫生间，居然没带纸，正好看见地上有别人用过的纸"

That's a big help. You are a life saver.

Thanks. You'**ve been a great help**.
谢谢，你给了我巨大的帮助。

He **was a big help to** us, as always.
他对我们帮助很大，每次都是。

You'**re a big help**. I think I can't live without you.
非常感谢，我不敢想象没了你应该怎么活。

Thank you. You'**ve been very helpful**.
很感谢，你给了我巨大的帮助。

A: I see there is a new secretary in the office. **我看见办公室里来了一位新秘书。**

B: Yes, she is a great help to all of us. **恩，她对我们帮助很大。**

need (some) help 需要（一些）帮助

在这里help变成了名词形式，表示“需要帮助”用need help，表示“得到帮助”用get help。I need your help表示“我需要你的帮助”，Get help!表示“去请人帮忙！”。当然，可以用want替代need。

“完全不会持家的新媳妇，连个鳗鱼料理都做不好”

Help me! I need help! I can't do this!

M·O·R·E

- need (some) help (with)
  需要帮助（做某事）
- need help ...ing
  需要帮忙做某事
- get help
  得到帮助

Can you make time for me? I **need help with** this.
你现在有时间吗？我需要帮助。

We've got to **get help**. Go and call some people!
我们得找人帮忙了。去叫几个人来帮忙！

Do you **want help** or not?
你需不需要帮忙？

A: I need help setting up the computer. 装电脑需要人帮忙。
B: I'll give you a hand after lunch. 我吃完午饭帮你看看。

help somebody out 帮助某人

在somebody陷入困境时可以用来表达“帮助”，即help somebody out with something。

“平时关系非常亲密，不料对方一陷入困境，就袖手旁观”

Are you sure you can't help me out?

M·O·R·E

- help sb out
  帮助某人
- help sb out with
  帮助某人走出困境

Somebody **help me out**!
谁来帮帮我！

Are you sure you can't **help me out**?
你确定你不能帮我？

I'm trying to **help you out** here.
我想帮你离开这里。

Okay, let me **help you out with** this.
好，我来帮你做这个吧。

A: Where are you going right now? 你现在去哪？
B: I'm helping Jen out. She is moving. 我在帮助贞，她正在搬家。

More Expressions

- **with the help of somebody**
  得到某人的帮助，多亏某人的帮助
  I could solve the problem **with the help of** Hellen.
  正因为有了海伦的帮助，我才可以解决这个问题。

- **So, help me (God)** 我保证
  So help me, I will win this lottery.
  我保证，这次可以赢得大奖。

- **Are you being helped?**
  （商店的店员）有人在帮忙吗?
  Yes, thank you. I'**m being helped now**. 很感谢，不过已经有人在帮我了。

不懂就问

Ask/Answer

不懂就要问别人。ask表示询问，要求等，主要使用的结构有ask something或ask somebody something等。另外，和tell不同，ask somebody to+动词表示“拜托某人做某事”，ask for something表示“拜托某事”，“邀请”等。

基本概念

1 询问，质问

Hey, can I ask you something? 喂，我能问你点事情吗?

I have to ask you something. 我得问你点事情。

2 请求（帮助，建言，信息等）

Is that too much to ask? 我要求的是不是太多了?

That's all I ask. 我的要求也就那些。

3 拜托某人做某事 (ask somebody to do)

Did my wife ask you to lie for her? 我老婆让你帮她说谎了?

4 answer 回答

Go ahead and ask. He won't answer. 去问问吧，他不会回答的。

You ask, I'll answer. 你提问，我来回答。

ask somebody something 向某人询问某事

ask me (you) something表示“询问某事”。如果变成anything的话，就变成了“有什么尽管问”。

“当对方好像有什么话要说，却犹豫不决时”

You want to **ask me something**? Don't be shy.

M·O·R·E

- Let me ask you something.
  我来问你点事情。
- Can I ask you something?
  我能问你点事情吗？
- I have to ask you something now.
  我现在得问你点事情。

Is Jill around? I have to **ask her something**.
吉尔在吗？我得问他点事情。

I don't want to lose you. So **ask me anything** you want.
我不想失去你。所以说，有什么尽管问我。

Are you here to **ask me that**?
你是来问那件事的？

A: Can I ask you something? **我能问你点事情吗？**
B: Sure. Go ahead. **好的，说吧。**

ask (somebody) a question（对某人）提问

表示“向某人询问”，是在直入主题之前先铺垫的用语。想要说明具体的内容，就要说question about。

“问女同事老婆的生日应该买点什么”

Can I **ask you a question** about the birthday gifts?

M·O·R·E

- Let me ask you a question.
  我来问个问题。
- Can I ask you a question?
  我能问你个问题吗？

Could I **ask you a question**? It's important.
我能问你个问题吗？非常重要。

Do you mind if we **ask you a few questions**?
你介意我们问你几个问题吗？

May I **ask you a couple of questions**?
我能问你几个问题吗？

A: May I ask you a question? **我能问你个问题吗？**
B: Sure. What would you like to ask me? **好的，你想问我什么？**

ask somebody for a favor 请求某人的帮助

同样为ask A B的形态，前文中出现的do somebody a favor表示“向某人提供帮助”，而ask somebody for a favor表示“请求对方给予帮助”。

“拜托对方一件困难的事情时”

Could you do me a big favor?

I need to **ask you for a favor**. It's urgent.
我得请你帮个忙，非常着急。

I'm calling to **ask you for a favor**.
我打电话是想找你帮个忙。

Can I **ask you for a big favor**?
我能请你帮个大忙吗?

A: Can I ask you for a big favor? **我能请你帮个大忙吗?**
B: Maybe. What do you want me to do? **也许吧，你想让我做点什么?**

ask somebody about 向某人询问某事

用于向他人询问信息的情况。ask somebody about+名词表示“询问某人关于某事的各种信息”。

“朋友们不知道我和男朋友分手了，一直问来问去”

Don't ask me about him again.

M·O·R·E

- I need to ask you about+名词
  有点事情要问你
- Don't ask me about+名词
  不要问我关于……的事情

I need to **ask you about** your brother.
我得向你问问你哥哥的事情。

I have something to **ask you about** the wedding ceremony.
我得向你问问有关婚礼的事情。

Please, don't **ask me about** this again.
请不要再问我这件事了。

I'll **ask her about** this.
我会问她这件事的。

A: The students asked Ed about his trip to Africa. **学生们问艾德有关他去非洲旅行的事情。**
B: What did he say? Was it interesting? **他说什么了? 有趣吗?**

ask somebody to 拜托某人做某事

ask somebody to+动词表示“拜托某人做某事”。用来向对方询问“能请托您帮个忙吗？”。

“和朋友们去济州岛旅行，男朋友突然出现，单膝跪地求婚”

You came down here to ask me to marry you?

M·O·R·E

- I'm going to (have to) ask you to+动词 我得求你帮个忙
- I'm not asking you to+动词 我不是叫你做某事

I'm going to have to **ask you to** leave now.
我现在不得不要求你离开了。

I didn't **ask you to** do it!
我没叫你做那种事情！

I'**m not asking you to** set me up.
我不是来要你给我介绍对象的。

A: Where is the report I asked you to do? 我要你做的报告在哪？
B: I'm still working on it. 我还在做呢。

ask (sb) what (when) 询问某人某事

如果要问的事情有点长，就可以用ask (somebody)+疑问句。以wh ... 开头的疑问词有what, when, where, who, why等。

“女儿把未来的女婿领来了，对他说的第一句话就是”

Can I ask you what school you attended?

M·O·R·E

- Can I ask you wh ... S+V? 我能问问你……吗？
- Can I ask why (not)? 我能问你为什么(不)吗？

Can I **ask you what** happened here?
我能问问你这里发生什么事情了吗？

She will **ask me where** it came from.
她会问我这是从哪来的。

People **ask me why** we're not together.
人们问我为什么我们没在一起。

A: Ask Dad what he wants to do tonight. 问问老爸今天晚上想干嘛？
B: He said he's going to the baseball game. 他说他要去看棒球比赛。

ask (somebody) if (how) （向某人）询问某事

在ask（somebody）后面加if从句或how从句或者how to+动词。最常用的是ask me if。

"在恋爱的初期，大部分人会询问对方的家庭背景，最常用的提问是"

She asked me if I have an interest in movies.

M·O·R·E

- ask sb if S+V
  向某人询问是否……
- ask sb how S+V
  向某人询问怎么……

You never **asked me if** I lived in Germany.
你从来就没问过我有没有在德国住过。

He **asked me how much** I loved my wife.
他问我有多么爱我的妻子。

A: I want to get this report done before I go home. 我想在回家前把这些报告都搞定。

B: Feel free to ask if you have any questions. 如果有问题的话，随时可以找我。

ask oneself 自己问自己，扪心自问

询问的对象不是别人，而是自己，可以在ask oneself后面接if从句或how从句，也可以接how to+动词。

"一个有妇之夫搞外遇被发现，朋友忠告道"

You're going to ask yourself who you want to give up.

M·O·R·E

- ask oneself if (how)
  扪心自问……
- ask oneself how to+名词
  问问自己该怎么做……

Well then **ask yourself** this.
那你问问自己吧。

You should **ask yourself** why you're doing that.
你得问问自己，到底为什么会那么做。

I'd have to **ask myself** what kind of person would do that.
我得好好问问自己，到底什么样的人会做出那种事情。

A: I spent thirty years working in an office. 我在一间办公室待了30多年。

B: Did you ever ask yourself if you enjoyed it? 你有没有扪心自问，自己是不是乐在其中？

ask for 拜托某事

for后面的部分就是需要拜托或期望的事情，for后面如果接人物名词的话就表示“想和某人交谈”。想要指明接受嘱托的人，就可以用ask somebody for。

“两口子离婚了，喜欢找借口的丈夫一直说提出离婚的并不是自己，而是妻子”

She's the one who asked for the divorce.

M·O·R·E

- ask (sb) for
  （向某人）拜托，表达期望
- ask for it (trouble)
  咎由自取
- You asked for it.
  是你咎由自取！
- Couldn't ask for more.
  是你自食其果。

You don't have to ask for my permission.
你不需要得到我的允许。

Why didn't you just ask me for the money?
你为什么没有向我借钱？

She didn't really ask for you, she asked for me.
她找的其实不是你，而是我。

A: I need to ask for some help here. 我得找个人来帮帮忙了。
B: You name it. What can I do for you? 说说看，我能不能帮到你？

ask somebody out 申请约会，招待

最基本的含义为“将某人招待出去吃饭”。进一步可以表示“邀请某人约会”，此时可以用ask somebody out (on a date)。

“一男子将离婚诉讼交给了一名美貌女律师，一见面就要约人家”

Our client asked me out to dinner.

M·O·R·E

- ask sb out for (to)
  将某人邀请出去做某事
- ask sb out (on a date)
  申请约会

I asked Sarah out for dinner tonight.
我今天晚上约沙拉出去吃晚饭了。

He asked me out.
他向我提出了约会。

Are you asking me out on a date?
你是在邀请我出去约会吗？

A: Are you planning to ask Brian out? 你打算约布莱恩出去吗？
B: No, I'm too shy to ask a boy out. 不了，我有点害羞，不好意思约男生出去。

be asked to 被邀请来做某事，听某人的话

be asked to表示“被邀请来做某事，听某人的话”，为ask somebody to do的被动形态，be asked to do就表示对别人说“我接到了……的邀请”。be told to do可以表示相近的含义，只不过指示别人的性质稍微强烈一些。

“接到老板的紧急呼叫命令，急忙跑了过去，没想到对方只是在开玩笑”

I **was told to** get over here right away.

I **was asked to** go there instead of Karl.
我接到了替代卡尔去那里的邀请。

I thought you **were asked to** come home.
我想你应该收到了来我们家的邀请。

I **was asked to** give this to you.
有人让我把这个转交给你。

Two of you will **be asked to** leave.
你们两个要被赶出去了。

A: Why is Alice so excited today? 今天爱丽丝为什么会这么兴奋?
B: Someone asked her out to the dance. 有人约她出去跳舞了。

answer somebody (sth) 向某人回答

只要有人问(ask)，就一定要回答(answer)。answer的后面主要接人物或事物，表示“回答某事，回答某人”，有时可以两个宾语一块用，变成answer sb sth的形态。

“老婆怀孕期间丈夫居然搞外遇，如果问他为什么会这样，他能回答吗”

Go ahead and ask. He won't **answer**.

M·O·R·E

- answer sb (sth)
  回答某人(某事)
- answer sb sth
  回答某人某事
- Don't answer that.
  不要回答这个问题。
- Don't answer now.
  不要现在作答。
- I can't answer that.
  我不能回答那个问题。

Just **answer me this**. Why did we break up?
回答我的问题。我们为什么会分手?

I will expect you to **answer me**.
我非常希望你能答复我。

Don't **answer me**. It's your choice.
不要回答我。这是你的选择。

Why didn't you **answer my e-mail**?
你为什么没有回复我的邮件?

A: Stop wasting time surfing the Internet. 不要浪费时间上网了。
B: I must answer an e-mail before I log off. 我得在退出登录之前回复一封邮件。

answer one's question 回答某人的问题

将具体的问题(question)作为宾语，表示“回答某人的问题”。最常用的结构为answer my (your) question，如果问题有两个以上，则要说成questions。

“对于那些只想着自己感受的人，可以说这么一句”

I'll answer your question if you answer mine.

M·O·R·E

- answer my question
  回答我的问题
- answer your question
  回答你的问题

Don't **answer that question**.
不要回答那个问题。

That didn't **answer my question**.
那并不等于回答了我的问题。

She'll **answer your questions** when she's ready.
她如果准备好了，就会回答你的问题的。

I'm very happy to **answer your questions**.
能回答你的问题，我感到很荣幸。

A: Is your girlfriend dating another guy? 你的女朋友在和别的男人约会吗?
B: I asked her but she wouldn't answer my question. 我问过她，不过她没有回答我的问话。

answer the phone (call, door) 接电话，帮人开门

answer的宾语为the phone, call, door等，表示回应电话，敲门声等。如果自己没办法应付，拜托别人时，可以直接对了解情况的人说“answer it”。

“喝得大醉的老公连手机都不接，很晚才回家”

Why didn't you answer your cell phone?

M·O·R·E

- answer the phone
  接电话
- answer one's cell phone
  接某个人的手机
- answer the door
  去开门

He's not **answering his cell phone**.
他不接手机。

Will you please **answer the phone**?
你能帮我接个电话吗?

Please **answer the door**.
帮忙开下门。

Could you **answer** it for me?
(电话铃响时)你能帮我接一下吗? (门铃响时)你能帮我开个门吗?

A: Did you answer the phone? 你接电话没?
B: I did, but they hung up as soon as I answered. 接了，不过我刚接起来，对方就挂电话了。

give somebody an answer 给某人回复

表示向某人提供解决方法或解答，用give somebody an answer，如果要指出给予解决方案的对象，就可以接介词to。

“辛辛苦苦提升了业绩，要求加薪，老板却装作什么都不知道”

Please **give me an answer** within 3 days.

I thought you could **give me an answer** to my question.
我觉得你能够回答我的问题。

I'd like to **give you an answer** after work.
等我下班了，会给你一个答复的。

I'll **give you a firm answer** by Friday.
我会在星期五之前给你一个准确的回复。

A: Could you give me an answer by tomorrow? 你能在明天之前给我个答复吗？
B: Sure, I'll let you know by tomorrow. 好的，明天就答复你。

More Expressions

- **if you ask me** 如果要我说我的想法

If you ask me, we aren't getting paid enough. 在我看来，我们的薪水还不太充足。
If you ask me, I think it's too good to be true. 在我看来，我觉得这个条件不是很好。
If you ask me, you're making a huge mistake. 要我说啊，你正在犯下一个巨大的失误。

- **Whatever you ask** 随便说什么

I will do **whatever you ask**.
你说什么，我就帮你做什么。

- **All I'm asking is for you to ...** 我对你的期望就只有……

All I'm asking is for you to leave!
能不能拜托你离开啊！

Feel free to ask. 随便问，想问什么就问什么。
Feel free to ask if you have any questions. 如果有问题的话，大可随便问。
May I ask who's calling?
请问您是？（打电话的时候）
It doesn't hurt to ask. 问问又不会损失什么。
Don't ask me. 不要问我。
Don't ask. 别问。
Who asked you? 是谁拜托你的？
Who asked your opinion?
谁问你的想法了？
I shouldn't have asked. 我真不该问。
If there's anything you need, don't hesitate to ask. 如果有什么需要，大可问我。

要多动脑子想想

Think

最需要记住的think典型句式为I think (that) 主语+动词，用来委婉地表达自己的意见，或者用Do you think (that)主语+动词，询问对方的意见。另外，还会经常用I'm thinking of表示“考虑某事”，用来表达自己的打算或意图。此外，表示think最基本含义的think about (of)也需要牢记。

基本概念

1 思考，冥想，检讨

I don't have time to think. 我根本没有时间去想。

Tell me what you're thinking. 告诉我你在想什么。

I think I'm catching a cold. 我好像感冒了。

2 打算做某事，意图……

I'm thinking of ordering a pizza. 我打算订比萨。

Are you really thinking of going? 你真打算去?

3 看待，认为，预想

I thought as much. 我就知道会那样。

think(that) 认为

用来表达自己的想法，I (don't) think则表示说没有自信的话，或者委婉地表达自己的想法，可以理解为“我觉得……”。I guess that也可表示相近的含义。

“因为加班非常劳累，一个员工睁着眼睛睡觉”

I think you need to get some rest.

M·O·R·E

- think (that) S+V
  我觉得……
- don't think (that) S+V
  我觉得……并非……

I **think** you have a problem.
我觉得你有问题。

I **don't think** it's a good idea to leave now.
我觉得现在离开并不是个好主意。

I **don't think** we're met before.
我觉得我们之前没有见过面。

A: I think that my math teacher is an asshole. **我觉得我的数学老师是个混蛋。**
B: What makes you think so? **你为什么会那么想？**

Do you think (that) ... ? 你觉得……吗？

用来询问对方意图或想法。如果用作否定，Don't you think ... ?就可以用来强调自己的想法，或者根据语调的不同，可以表示指责和责备等语气。

“女朋友喝得有点多，意识模糊，男朋友说”

It's 12 o'clock. Don't you think it's time you went home?

M·O·R·E

- Do you think (that) S+V
  你觉得……吗？在你看来是……吗？
- Don't you think S+V ... ?
  你不觉得……吗？

Do you think she'll become a model?
你觉得她能成为一个模特吗？

Do you think we should go there?
你觉得我们应该去那吗？

Do you think there's a chance I could have a date with Susie?
你觉得我能有机会和苏琪约会吗？

Don't you think it's a little too early?
你不觉得有点早？

A: Do you think that it will break again? **你觉得这会重新坏掉吗？**
B: No, I don't think so. I replaced all the damaged parts. **不，我不那么认为。我已经把所有损坏的零件都给换了。**

I thought (that) 我以为…… 我原来在想……

I think的过去式，表示“我以为……”。可以用来表示过去那么认为，也可以用来表示之前是那么想的，但现实却截然相反。

“老婆让我今天早点回家，我满怀期待地回到家，老婆却说自己有约，让我看家”

I thought we had plans for tonight.

M·O·R·E

- I thought I could+动词
  我以为我能……
- I thought we had+名词
  我以为我们……

I thought last night was great.
我觉得昨天晚上很棒。

You let me down. **I thought** I could trust you.
你让我失望了。我以为能相信你呢。

To be honest, **I thought** you lied to all of us again.
老实说，我还以为你又对我们所有人都说谎了。

I thought you were on my side in this fight.
我还以为打架的时候你是站在我这一边呢。

A: I thought you were moving to Chicago. 我以为你要搬到芝加哥去了。
B: I didn't say I was going to move there. 我没有说我要搬过去啊。

I think I will ... 我怕……

I will ... 表示“我要在未来做某事”，如果用I think ... 修饰，就表示“我怕……”，“我还以为”等，可以用来使要表达的内容委婉化。

“喝鸡尾酒的时候，有些人肯定要点这些好东西”

I think I will have a Sex on the Beach.

M·O·R·E

- I think I will+动词
  我怕……
- Well, all right, I think I will.
  知道了，就那么办。

I think I will stay here with her.
我怕我要和她留在这。

I think I'll go say hello to your wife.
我要去和你老婆打个招呼。

That's okay with me. **I think I'll** pass.
我无所谓，就算通过了。

A: Why don't you ask her to join us? 你为什么不邀请她加入我们呢?
B: I think I will. 我正想那么做。

I'm thinking of (about) ...ing 我在考虑……

think of (about)后面如果接动词的 ...ing形式的话就表示“正在考虑……”，用来表达日后的打算等。最常用的句式为I'm thinking of (about) ...ing。

“老公身患高血压、糖尿病、脂肪肝等综合病症，老婆却要给他买比萨”

I'm thinking of ordering a pizza.

M·O·R·E

- I'm thinking of (about) ...ing 我正在考虑……
- I'm thinking of (about)+N 我正在考虑……

I'm thinking of retiring soon.
我正在考虑早点退休呢。

I'm thinking of inviting Anne this weekend.
我正在考虑这周邀请安妮到家里。

I'm thinking about coloring my hair.
我正在考虑染头发。

I'm thinking about moving this chair.
我正在考虑把这个椅子挪掉。

A: What are you going to do with your bonus? 你要怎么处理你的奖金?
B: I'm thinking of going on vacation. 我正在考虑去度假。

think so 那么认为

当赞同对方的观点，表示同意时可以用这个的句式，可以将对方说的话替代为“so”。如果想要进一步强调同意的程度，就可以说“I think so, too（我也那么认为）”。

“不懂得称赞的神奇力量的人只会这么说”

I don't think so. I don't think you can.

M·O·R·E

- I think so 我觉得也是
- I don't think so. 我不那么认为

I'm glad you **think so**.
我很高兴你能那么想。

I **thought so**, too, but she didn't want to see me.
我也那么认为，不过她不愿意见我。

I think we should go. Don't you **think so**?
我觉得我们应该走了，你是不是这样想?

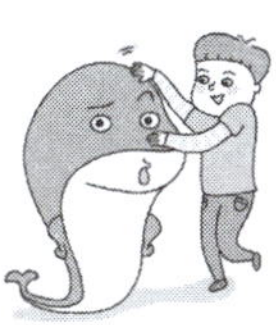

A: Dave might have the key. 大卫可能有钥匙。
B: I don't think so because he wasn't in yesterday. 我不那么认为，因为他昨天没有上班。

think twice 三思，慎重考虑

字面含义为“想两次”，用来表达“慎重考虑”。最常用的结构为think twice before（在做某事前慎重考虑一番）。与短语think over具有相近的含义。

“一个穷光蛋要和一个天仙结婚，简直是不考虑后果”

Why don't you **think twice** before you start a family?

M·O·R·E

- think twice (before)
  （在做某事之前）再三思考
- think hard
  好好考虑考虑
- think positive(ly)
  往正面（肯定）的方向考虑
- think over
  慎重考虑

You should **think twice** before having kids.
你要在生孩子前好好考虑考虑。

I'm going to **think twice** before I try this.
我要在开始前好好考虑考虑。

There's always something bugging you. **Think hard**.
总会有一些事情让你烦恼，好好想想。

Let me have time to **think it over**.
让我找个时间好好想想。

A: Think twice before you choose what to study. 在你决定学什么之前，好好考虑考虑。

B: Yeah, you need to get a good education. 恩，你得接受良好的教育。

... don't you think? 你不觉得？

询问对方的意见，或者加强自己的意愿，可以在说完自己的话之后，加上don't you think?

“丈夫在大街上随意丢烟头，妻子指责道”

It's my civic duty to report it, **don't you think**?

It's about time for some tea, **don't you think**?
到了喝茶的时间了，你觉得呢？

It's a little excessive, **don't you think**?
这有点过分啊，你不这么想吗？

Well, that's a little easy, **don't you think**?
恩，挺容易的，你觉得呢？

It's a little soon for that, **don't you think**?
这有点早了，你不这么认为吗？

A: Angelina is beautiful, don't you think? 安吉丽娜很漂亮，你觉得呢？

B: Sure. Her boyfriend is a lucky guy. 当然，她男朋友很幸运。

... than I thought 比我想的还……

表示真实情况超出自己想象，than的前面通常会接形容词的比较级。

"老公在电话里说是一场小意外，没什么大事，见面一看，原来大腿骨折了"

Oh, my god. It's worse **than I thought**.

The exam was harder **than I thought**.
这次考试要比我想象中的难。

This is going to be harder **than I thought**.
这次要比我想象中的更难了。

You're meaner **than I thought**.
你比我想象中的还吝啬。

You're a lot smarter **than I thought**.
你可比我想象中的聪明得多。

A: A lot of people came to the festival. **很多人都来参加庆典活动了。**
B: I know. The crowd was bigger than I thought. **是啊，人群比我想象中的要拥挤。**

What do you think of ... ? 你觉得……怎么样?

用来询问对方的意见，先说完想要表达的内容，再加上What do you think (of that)?，也可以在What do you think后面接上介词of或about，再加上想要说明的内容，注意要用名词形式或者 ...ing形式。

"40多岁的大妈对做过隆胸手术的朋友们说道"

What do you think of my breasts?

M·O·R·E

- What do you think (of that)? 你觉得（那个）怎么样? 你认为呢? 你自己觉得呢?
- What do you think of (about)+名词（...ing)? 你觉得……怎么样?
- What do you think of (about) sb ...ing? 你觉得某人怎么样?

What do you think of me?
你觉得我怎么样?

What do you think of adding her to our team?
你觉得把她加到我们队里怎么样?

What do you think about me staying the night?
你觉得我留下过夜怎么样?

A: What do you think of this new phone? **你觉得这部新电话怎么样?**
B: It's certainly superior to the one I have. **这肯定要比我那部高级。**

What do you think? 你认为……吗？

Do you think what主语+动词？中的“what”，表示“主语会认为……”。尤其像What do you think I am?（你把我当成什么人了，你以为我是什么样的人？）一样，很有可能成为指责性的语气。

“一帮踢野球的人组成的足球队要和首都专业足球队比赛，开赛前”

What do you think our chances are?

M·O·R·E

- What do you think I am?
  你把我当成什么了？
- What do you think you are?
  你以为你自己是谁啊？
- What do you think you're doing?
  你这是在干什么？

What do you think she's going to do?

你以为她要去干嘛？

What do you think I should order?

你觉得我应该点些什么？

What do you think she wants?

你觉得她想要什么？

A: We have to get a nice gift for Mom. 我们得给妈妈送一个很好的礼物。

B: What do you think she wants for her birthday? 你觉得她生日想要什么？

I think 在我看来

日常生活中不一定要使用正式的I think (that)主语+动词的形态，经常会用简洁的语句表达临时的想法。此时就要用I think，后面接上自己的想法。

“平常看起来很一般，没想到在化妆之后就像变了个人似的”

I think we could be friends.

I think, this is my worst nightmare.

我觉得，这是我做过的最坏的梦。

Since you saw mine, **I think**, you have to show me yours.

既然你看了我的，我觉得你也应该让我看看你的。

I look at you and **I think**, this is what I want.

我凝视着你，感觉这就是我所希望的。

A: Your face looks very pale this morning. 你今天早上气色不太好啊。

B: I think I am going to be sick. 我觉得我要生病了。

... what I think 在我看来

... what somebody thinks表示“某人所想的事情”，后面可以接be, say, do, know等多种宾语，组成各式各样的语句。

“虽然不太准确，但可以猜测辛迪到底发生了什么事”

Let me tell you what I think happened to Cindy.

M·O·R·E

- what I (you) think
  我（你）想的事情
- what I (you) think（主语）+动词
  在我（你）看来……
- You know what I think?
  你知道我是怎么想的吗?
  （在表达自己的想法之前）
- Here's what I think.
  我是这么想的。
- That's what I think.
  那就是我的想法。
- That's (It's) what you think.
  那是你自己的想法。
- Is that what you think?
  这是你所想的吗?

Do you know **what I think**? I think you were right.
你知道我是怎么想的吗? 我觉得你是对的。

That's **what I thought**.
我正好也这么想。

Oh, it's exactly **what you thought**.
哦，这正是你所想的。

Is that **what you think** of me? I'm a mistake?
你是这么看我的? 我的存在本身就是个错误?

We know **what you think**.
我们知道你在想什么。

I was just curious **what you thought** about that.
我就是好奇你是怎么看待那个问题的。

Is that **what I think** it is?
事情是我想的那样吗?

Are they saying **what I think** they're saying?
他们说的事情，我理解对了吗?

You know **what I think** you should do?
你知道我认为你应该做些什么吗?

I don't feel **what you think** I'm feeling.
其实我的感受和你说的不太一样。

A: I saw you today kissing in the hall. 我今天看见你们在走廊里接吻了。
B: That's not what you think. 其实事情不是那样的。

A: I don't like the way you designed this. 我不太喜欢你设计的东西。
B: Bite me. I don't care what you think. 别管我，我才不稀罕你怎么看。

A: Let me know what you think. 让我知道你在想什么。
B: Hmm... I have to think about it for a second. 嗯……我得想一会。

think less of 看扁……

think后面接less或little，nothing等否定词语，再接上of+名词的话就表示“看扁……”，“轻视”，而think much of则表示“看重……”。

“在发生交通事故之后，从小排量车里走出一个黑帮老大型人物，说道”

I really hope you don't think less of me.

M·O·R·E

- think less (little) of
  过低评价，不费心思
- think nothing of
  不介意……无视
- think much of
  (think a lot of)
  重视……

(Please) Think nothing of it. It's no big deal.
不要在意，没什么大不了的。

No, I don't think less of you. Believe me.
不，我很在乎你，相信我。

She's not a big talker so I didn't think much of it.
她可不是大舌头，所以我没有太介意。

A: The teacher drank too much alcohol. 老师喝太多酒了。
B: His students are going to think less of him. 他的学生们要鄙视他了。

think of (about) 想……

think of (about)+名词的话就表示“考虑……”，“想想……”，是个比较常用的短语。也可以用作祈使语句形态的think about (of)，of (about)后面可以接名词或 ...ing的形态。

“儿子天天在家里无所事事的，老爸对他说道”

Why don't you think about looking for a job?

M·O·R·E

- (Just) think of (about)
  想想……
- think about what ...
  想想……

Let me think about it a little more.
让我再考虑考虑。

I haven't thought about marriage yet.
我还没想过结婚的事情。

Let me think about that and I will get back to you.
让我再想想，回头给你答复。

Don't even think about (doing) it. You can't do that.
连想都别想。你可绝对做不了。

A: We may never see each other again. 我们可能再也不用见面了。
B: I don't like to think about that. 我想都不愿意想。

think of ... as ... 认为……是……

利用think of 的表达，think of A as B表示“把A想成B”，“认为”。如果用oneself替掉A的话，think of oneself as则表示“自己认为自己……”。

“老板给手下的待遇很差，员工们异口同声地说”

I always think of him as an asshole.

M·O·R·E

- think of ... as ...
  认为……是……
- think of oneself as
  觉得自己是……

People think of me as a hard worker.
人们觉得我是个工作狂。

Will, I think of you as a friend.
威尔，我把你当成朋友。

I like to think of myself as a freelancer.
我喜欢把自己当成一个自由职业者。

A: You've been friends with Rob a long time. 你和罗波是很久的朋友了。
B: I think of him as my best friend. 我把他当成最好的朋友。

More Expressions

think out loud 大声自言自语

No, I'm just thinking out loud.
没有，我只是在自言自语罢了。

not think straight 不能明确地想到

I don't want to talk about it right now. I can't even think straight.
我现在不想谈这件事。脑子一片混乱。

I think the best thing to do
认为最好的是……

I think the best thing to do is just smile. 我觉得最好的方式就是微笑。

I hate to think ... 我讨厌……想

I hate to think that you have been cheating on me.我不想认为你骗了我。

think it best (for somebody) to
认为这是（对某人）最好的……

I thought it best to work with Tony.
我觉得和托尼一起工作是最好的事情。

I thought it best for us to keep this quiet. 我觉得我们把这个当成秘密是最好的选择。

More Expressions

- **come to think of it** 我想了想

  Come to think of it,why don't you come to the movies with us?

  我想了想，你要不和我们一起去看电影吧?

- **think outside the box**

  创造性地思考和行动

  Is it really impossible for you to think outside the box?

  你能不能想点新鲜的东西?

- **have second thought** 再三考虑

  Don't give it a second thought

  不要担心（差不多得了）。

  I'm having second thought about the wedding.

  我在重新考虑结婚的事情。

- **on second thought** 重新想了一遍

  You know, on second thought, gum wouble be perfect.

  我重新想了想，口香糖应该很不错。

Here's a thought. 我有个好主意。

What are your thoughts here?
你对此有什么想法?

What is he thinking? 他在想什么?

What was he thinking? 他在想什么?

What makes you think so? 你怎么会那么认为?

I thought as much. 我也那么想过。

工作不要停

Work

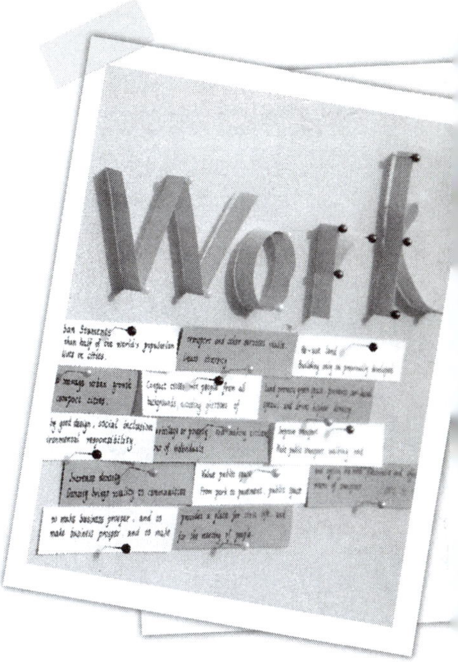

如果单纯理解为“工作”，你就是外行了。当然，在很多情况下会表示“工作”，“上班”等行为。然而，机械等运转正常与否或启动等都可以用这个词来表达，也可以表示某种计划等进行得顺利，老外则更偏好于用work表达后者。而且，表达这种含义的work理解起来不像工作的work那么如意，因此学习过程中要格外注意各种用法。

基本概念

1 工作，上班，研究

I work around 10 hours a day.我每天大概工作10个小时。

Who do you work for?你在哪工作?

Thanks for your hard work. 谢谢你辛勤的工作。

2（机械）等运转正常，启动

It's working fine.这台机器运转正常。

My computer doesn't work.我的电脑不好使了。

My father can't even work an MP3 player. 我老爸连个MP3都不会玩。

3（计划）进行得很顺利，（药）有效果

My plan didn't work well. 我的计划没能顺利进行。

work hard 努力工作

在这里hard为表示努力的副词，因此work hard表示“努力地工作”。Don't work too hard也可以在分别的时候用，表示“不要太累”。

“老板要求员工周末也出来给他工作，此时就得好好说一句”

I work hard all week and I deserve to have fun.

M·O·R·E

- work hard (to+动词)
  为了……而努力工作
- work around the clock
  工作非常认真

It's been a long day. We **worked hard** today.
今天真不容易啊。我们工作得很努力。

We**'re working around the clock**.
我们昼夜不分地工作着。

I**'m working hard** to become a better man.
我要努力变成一个好男人。

A: You have to work hard. Don't let me down. **你得努力工作了。不要让我失望。**
B: I'll do my best, boss. Believe me. **我会尽全力的，老板，请相信我。**

work overtime 加班

同样表达认真努力地工作，work overtime表示“加班”，“工作到很晚”等，与work late具有相同的含义。

“要做的事情太多了，真想用个分身术”

I have to work late again tonight.

M·O·R·E

- work overtime
  加班
- work late
  工作到很晚

I can't meet you for dinner. I have to **work overtime** today.
我今天不能和你一起吃晚饭了，我要工作到很晚。

Are you **working overtime** tonight?
你今天要加班吗?

I don't **work late** tomorrow night. Let's get together then.
我不会工作到很晚，我们到时候见吧。

A: How is your new job? **你的新工作怎么样?**
B: Not so bad. I have to work overtime sometimes, but I like the job.
还不错。有时候我得工作到很晚，不过我喜欢这个工作。

work+时间 工作……时间

work+时间相关名词可以表示工作的时间长度。可以用来回答别人询问工作时间，What are the hours?

“姐姐是个单亲妈妈，而且还要工作到很晚”

My sister is a single mother who **works nights**.

M·O·R·E

- be on a five-day work week
  每周上五天班
- work nights (days)
  上夜班（白班）

You'd **be working a five-day week**, 9 to 5.
你一个星期会上五天班的，早上九点到下午五点。

Are you **on a five-day work week**?
你一个星期要工作五天吗?

I'**m working nights** (days).
我在上夜班（白班）。

A: Why don't I ever see your husband? 我怎么从来就没见过你的老公?
B: He's very tired since he has to work nights. 他每天晚上都要上班，所以很累。

work 正常运转

work主要表达运转有效或运转正常，主语为事物。想要表达使某物正常运转时，就要用make ... work (get ... to work)。

“丈夫昨天夜不归宿，回到家中妻子用尽了各种办法，但他就是一个字都不提”

He didn't say a word. Torturing him didn't **work**.

M·O·R·E

- It works!
  很好使！有效果。
- It doesn't work.
  这不好使，根本不行。

That's not how it **works**.
那样可不行。

It's never going to **work**.
我们绝对不会有结果的。（表示男女之间不会产生火花）

Why didn't it **work**? What was the problem?
为什么不好使呢？出什么问题了?

Never give up! There are ways to make this **work**.
绝对不要放弃！肯定有办法。

A: Is the time on that clock correct? 那个表上的时间准吗?
B: No, it doesn't work. Check the time on your cell phone. 不，那个表不走了。看看你手机上的时间吧。

make it work 使……工作

为前文中提到短语的祈使形态，表示让“it”运转起来。可以用things代替it，make things work也是比较常用的句式。当然，可以像make marriage work一样，接一般名词。

“男朋友从来不相信我，还说要在我的手机上装位置追踪芯片”

You have to trust me to make this relationship work.

M·O·R·E

- make it work
  使……工作起来
- make things work
  使……发挥作用 (get sth to work)
- make a relationship work
  使关系变得可能

We will find a way to **make it work**.
我们会找出让它运转的方法的。

I'm going to need some time to **make it work**.
我需要一些时间来让它运转起来。

The only person that can **make** marriage **work** is you.
我唯一能够结婚的对象就是你。

I thought about what it takes to **make** a relationship **work**.
我想了想什么可以让我们的关系融洽。

A: What do you think about that idea? 你觉得这个想法怎么样?
B: It will be difficult, but we can make it work. 很难，不过我们一定要做出来。

works for somebody 对某人来说……不错，很好

与前面的例句具有相同的含义，事物主语+works for somebody的话就表示“某物对某人很好”，“还不错”等，经常会用在约会时间上。

“在商量约会的时间，问对方7点怎么样”

Does seven o'clock work for you?

M·O·R·E

- 事物主语+work for sb
  对某人来说……可以，还不错

It **works for** me.
我无所谓，我赞成，我没问题。

Does it (that) **work for** you? Tell me what you think.
你觉得怎么样？（你也同意吗？）说说你的想法。

Does this afternoon **work for** you?
今天下午可以吗?

A: Let's see, is Friday all right? 我想想，星期五怎么样?
B: Yes, I guess that works for me. 恩，我应该可以。

work at 努力做某事

work at+地点名词主要表示“在某处工作”(work for)，如果work at后面接事情或者 ...ing形态的话，就表示“为了得到……或者向上，努力尝试”。

“如果这样的话，光合作用就会受阻，面色变得苍白，肚子越来越鼓”

I **worked at** home. I hardly ever go out.

M·O·R·E

- work at+地点
  在某处工作
  认真做某事
  (work for sb)
- work at sth (...ing)
  认真做某事

They think I **work at** Starbucks.
他们以为我在星巴克工作。

How long did you **work at** the store?
你在这家店里工作了多久?

I **worked at** getting the job done.
我用心完成了这项工作。

I tried my best to **work at** this marriage.
这段婚姻我用尽了全力。

A: Learning English can be very difficult. 学英语是非常不容易的。
B: I know, but you have to work at it. 我知道，不过你必须得试试。

work for 在某处工作

work for+名词（公司）表示“为……而工作”，即“在某处工作”，可以用来回答Who do you work for?当然，也可以说成work at (in)。

“老板说自己能保证高速晋升，让我接着工作”

I can't **work for** you anymore. I quit.

M·O·R·E

- Who do you work for?
  你在哪工作?
- I work for (at, in)
  我在……工作

I **work for** a government agency.
我在政府机构工作。

I **work for** an Internet company.
我在一家互联网公司上班。

How long **has** Brian **worked for** you?
布莱恩给你打了多久的工?

She **has worked for** an ad agency since 2003.
她从2003年开始在一家广告公司上班。

A: It's difficult to work for uptight bosses. 和死心眼的老板一起工作是非常不容易的。
B: You can say that again! 谁说不是呢!

work on 做……的工作

work for指工作的地点，而work on则表示工作的对象。work on the report表示编写报告书。只不过work on somebody表示“说服某人”，“给某人带来影响”等。

“公司的周年庆快要到了，正在准备晚会的相关事宜。”

I'm working on what I'm going to say at the ceremony.

M·O·R·E

- work on sth
  做……工作
- work on sb
  说服某人，给某人带来影响
- work on ...ing
  做……工作
- work on what
  从事于……

I **am working on** it.
我正在做。

I'll get to **work on** it right now.
我现在要开始工作了。

I'm going to **work on** this stuff at home tonight.
我今天晚上回到家再开始做。

Let me **work on** this. I'll get it done by tomorrow.
我来负责这个吧，明天就会做完了。

I was **working on** a crossword puzzle when you called this morning.
你今天早上打电话的时候，我正在玩一个十字猜迷游戏。

I'm going to **work on** my music this summer.
这个夏天我要开始准备出专辑了。

It would **work on** me when I was young.
如果我年轻一点的话，没准就能对我有作用了。

What **are** you **working on** now?
你最近干什么呢?

We spent 2 years **working on** our problems.
我们花了两年的时间才解决我们的问题。

A: I'm so stressed out these days. 我最近很不爽。
B: Oh? Do you have to work on a big project? 恩？你得做一个大项目了?

A: I'm going to work on this stuff at home tonight.
我今天晚上回到家再做这个事情。
B: If you have any problems, give me a call. 如果有问题的话，随时联系我。

A: How long have you been working on that project?
你在这个项目上花了多久的时间?
B: I've been working on it all day long. 我一整天都在做这个。

work out 奏效，运动，变成……

虽然是重要的短语，但其含义并不是很明确。首先，用在某种不好的状况时可以表示“变好”，“好转”，而如果接work out+well（badly, all right, OK）等就表示“变得……”。

“有个朋友天生秃顶，直接拿一个未经过检验的脱毛剂让他试试”

Let me know how that works out for you.

M·O·R·E

- sth works out (for/with)
  变好，好转
- sth works out well (badly)
  好转，变差 (turn out)
- sb works out
  某人想出好办法，制订好计划，运动
- work out for the best
  最终会好转

I hope it works out with you and Mike.
我希望你和麦克能够和睦相处。

How did everything work out?
怎么样，事情还顺利吗?

How's that working out for you? Is that good enough?
事情还顺利吗? 够不够?

It never would have worked out. I knew it!
我最开始就知道这肯定行不通。

Let's work it out.
我们好好试试。

Don't worry about a thing. We can work it out.
不要担心，我们能找到解决办法的。

You can count on me. Everything will work out for the best.
你可以相信我。一切都会好转的。

The figures that you gave me don't work out.
你给我的那些数值没有作用。

A: How's that new guy working out? 那个新进公司的员工做得怎么样?
B: Not very well. He's all thumbs. 不太理想，他笨手笨脚的。

A: How did you make out at the lawyer's office?
你到底在那家律师事务所碰到了什么事?
B: In the end everything worked out for the best. 最后一切问题迎刃而解。

A: Keri is in such great shape. 凯利非常健康。
B: That's because she works out every day. 那是因为她每天都坚持运动。

work things out 事情很顺利

利用前面的work out组成的新句型，work things out表示“事情进展得顺利”，“问题得到解决”等。也可以将things放在前面，变成Things don't work out.（事情不太顺利）。

“去见女朋友的父母，对方却嫌弃我不是公务员，无奈之下只好分手”

Things didn't **work out** and he broke up with her.

M·O·R·E

- work things out (with sb)
  与某人进展顺利，问题得到解决。
- Things work out.
  事情很顺利。

I wanted to **work things out** with my husband.
我想和我老公和睦相处。

I'm trying to **work things out** with Eva.
我想和伊娃搞好关系。

Why do I have to **work things out** with a man who used me?
我凭什么要和一个利用我的男人搞好关系?

Things will **work out** all right.
事情会得到解决的。

A: What's going on between you two? **你们两个之间有什么事情?**
B: We're working out our problems. **我们正在试图解决我们之间的问题。**

work up 使……渐渐……

work up 后面接interest, nerve, appetite等词，就表示主语渐渐产生……可以理解为产生兴趣，勇气，食欲等。另外，work ... up表示“让某人生气”，也可以用作get worked up的形态。

“光头老板在街上走，不料从天上掉下鸟屎，从那光亮的脑门上流了下来”

He'**s all worked up**. You'd better keep away from him.

M·O·R·E

- work up+interest (appetite)
  让某人产生兴趣（食欲）
- work sb up
  让某人生气
- work oneself up
  生气
- get worked up (about)
  （对某事）生气

That'll really **work up** your appetite for lunch.
那样的话会提升你的食欲的。

Go **work up** some new ideas and then we'll go over it during lunch.
去想几个好主意来，然后我们吃午饭时好好商量商量。

I just think you'**re getting worked up** over nothing.
我觉得你在为一个莫名其妙的事情发火。

What **are** you so **worked up** about?
你为什么会那么生气?

A: Have you worked up the courage to ask her out? **你敢起勇气约她出去了吗?**
B: I'm still too afraid. **我还是很害怕。**

have a lot of work 有很多事情要做

在拒绝对方的要求或者先离开酒席时可以用到的语句。可以用much代替a lot of，但a lot of work的使用频率更高。另外，还可以用have got代替 have。

“旁边的同事说要下班，不过我还有很多事情要做”

I can't. I have a lot of work today.

M·O·R·E

- have a lot of (much) work to do
  有很多事情要做
- have some work to do
  有一些事情要做

We have a lot of work today.
我们今天有很多事情要做。

Can I go? I've got a lot of work to do today.
我能走了吗？我今天可有很多事情要做啊。

I have so much work to do on the case.
关于那个案例，我有很多事情要做。

I have some work to do in my office.
我办公室里还有些事情要做。

A: What is our plan for tonight? 我们今天晚上有什么计划？
B: We'll be busy. We have a lot of work to do. 我们会很忙的，有很多工作要做。

after work 下班之后

在这里，work变成了名词形式，after work表示“下班之后”，而at work表示“在公司”，因此be at work表示”正在上班”。

“一起吃了午饭，下班之后还要见面的一对情侣”

I'll see you after work, sweetie.

M·O·R·E

- after work
  下班之后
- at work
  在公司（正在上班）

I'll be home right after work.
我下班了就马上回家。

Hey, what are you doing after work?
喂，你今天下班了干什么？

I'm supposed to be at work all night.
我可能得加一整晚的班了。

He likes to play computer games at work.
他喜欢在上班时玩电脑游戏。

A: He needs to be picked up after work tomorrow. 明天下班之后得有个人接他。
B: I'll send a taxi for him. 我会派辆出租车过去的。

就是这种感觉

Feel

可以用来表示心情好与坏的动词。feel后面可以接各式各样的形容词(good，bad，sick)，以表示心情或身体状况。如果很难用一个形容词形容此时此刻的心情的话，可以在I feel like后面接名词或“主语+动词”，用来表达“我现在感觉……”。另外，I feel like ...ing可以理解成为做……的心情，表示“我想要做某事”。

基本概念

1 心情……

I feel much better. 我心情好多了。

How do you feel?你感觉怎么样?

I know just how you feel. 我能理解你现在的感受。

I've never felt like this before. 我从来没有过这种感受。

How are you feeling? 你身体怎么样了?

2 ……的感觉（feel like+名词(主语+动词)）

I feel like an idiot. 我感觉自己像个白痴。

I feel like it's my fault.我感觉这是我的错。

3 想要做某事

I feel like having a drink. 我想喝两杯。

I don't feel like talking to you. 我现在不想和你说话。

feel better (good, great) 心情变好

如果想要表达心情好，就用feel good，如果更好，就用feel great，如果心情变好了就可以说feel better。另外，身体状态或心情好时也可以用feel well。相反，如果心情不好，则可以说feel bad。想要说明心情好或坏的具体原因就可以在后面加about，to，if等。

"到处说女朋友坏话，不小心被发现了"

I didn't mean to make you feel bad.

M·O·R·E

- feel good (bad) (about sth (...ing)) （……事情）心情好（不好）
- feel better (great) (about) （对某事）感觉好点了
- feel well 心情（身体）好
- It (That) feels good (to (if)) （……事情）感觉好
- make sb feel bad 让某人心情变差
- make sb feel better 让某人心情好转

I don't feel well these days.
我这两天身体不太好。

Leave me alone. I'm not feeling well.
别管我。我现在心情不太好。

Don't feel so bad about it.
不要过于伤心了。

I'm not feeling very good today.
我今天心情不是很好。

I feel good about this.
我对这件事感觉不错。

Drink this. It'll make you feel much better.
喝了吧，会让你心情好点的。

I'd feel better if I slept with Diane.
如果能和戴安娜睡觉，感觉一定很好。

It feels good to be taken care of.
有人照看的话，心情就很好了。

A: How are you doing, Jodie? 你最近过得怎么样，周迪？
B: I don't feel good today. I want to go home. 今天感觉不怎么样。我想回家。

A: You feel better now? 你现在感觉好点了吗？
B: Yeah, much. 恩，好多了。

A: You look terrible today. 你今天气色很差啊。
B: I'm not feeling well. I need to lie down. 现在身体不太好，我得去躺一会了。

feel+形容词 （心情，身体）感觉……

除了至今学到的feel better, feel good, feel well之外，还可以加各种形容词，表示主语的心情或身体状况。当然，同理在后面可以加about，that S+V等，来进行附加地说明。

“看到坏心肠老板正在弯腰，冲动之下想要跑过去来一个屁股开花，不过”

I don't really **feel right about** doing this.

M·O·R·E

- feel sick
  身体不舒服
- feel tired
  疲劳
- feel sad
  伤心
- feel weird
  感觉很奇怪
- feel nice
  感觉很好
- feel sure (certain)
  确信
- feel right
  感觉正确
- feel terrible
  感到可怕
- feel stupid
  感觉是个白痴

I **feel really sick** today.
我今天身体不太舒服。

This **feels (very) weird** to me.
感觉很奇怪啊。

I don't know, but it just doesn't **feel right to** me.
我不知道，不过对我来说，这不太靠谱。

You said it. I don't **feel right**, either.
真的，我感觉也不踏实。

I **feel weird about** what happened the other day.
关于上次发生的事情，我感觉有点奇怪。

I **don't really feel right about** doing this.
我觉得做这件事不太好。

Don't make me go there. I **feel at home** here.
不要让我去那，我觉得这里更自在。

You can stop working and go get some rest if you **feel tired**.
如果你累的话，可以停下工作休息一会。

A: I have no energy and feel sick. 我一点力气都没有，感觉不太舒服。
B: This is why you need to exercise. 所以说你得多运动。

A: You have all my sympathy. 我很想同情你。
B: You shouldn't feel sad for me. 你不用为我伤心。

A: I want to go to bed. I feel tired. 我想去睡觉了，很累。
B: That's a good plan. We need rest. 好主意，我们得休息一会了。

feel okay 没关系

用来表达彼此之间的问候。feel okay或feel all right都可以表示"还可以"。

"昨天是和女朋友的第一百天纪念日，不料晚上玩得有点过火"

Are you feeling okay? You look so exhausted.

M·O·R·E

- feel okay about
  认为……没关系

You're feeling okay, David?
你感觉好点没，大卫?

How can you feel okay about this?
你怎么可以说这个还可以?

I actually feel OK! At least about life with my husband.
我其实感觉还可以！至少和我丈夫的关系。

Does that feel OK? Don't hesitate to tell me if it doesn't feel good.
那没关系吗？如果感觉不好，一定要跟我说。

A: Are you feeling okay? 你感觉好点吗?
B: No, actually I'm feeling pretty sick. 不太好，其实今天有点不舒服。

feel like+名词 是……样的感觉

feel后面可以直接加形容词，不过想要加名词的话，就要有一个like，变成feel like+名词的形态。表示"是……样的感觉"。

"连连转战公司的人，突然感觉到自己像一个无业游民"

I'm beginning to feel like a nomad.

M·O·R·E

- feel like+名词
  是……样的感觉
- make sb feel like
  让某人感觉到……

I feel like a new person.
我感觉自己得到了新生。

I can't believe I didn't get a promotion. I feel like such a loser.
真不敢相信我居然没有得到晋升，感觉自己就是个失败者。

How could you say that? You made me feel like an idiot.
你怎么能那么说呢？你让我感觉自己就是个白痴。

A: What should we get to eat? 我们吃点什么呢?
B: I feel like Chinese food tonight. 我今天晚上有点想吃中国饭菜。

feel like (that) 是……样的感觉

与it seems (like), it looks like等相近的表达。含义像I feel like+名词一样，表示“是……样的感觉”。可以理解成用一个句子替代了名词。当然，也可以将like省略掉，变成I feel that+动词。

“做错了事，向女友道歉”

I feel like it's my fault.

M·O·R·E

- feel like S+V
  有……样的感觉
- feel like as if (though) S+V
  就像……疯了似的
- I don't feel like S+V
  我没有感觉到……

I feel like you are not listening to me.
我觉得你没有听我的话。

I still feel like something's not right.
我还是觉得有些不对劲。

I feel like I'm totally lost.
我实在打不起精神。

You probably feel like you don't have a chance.
你可能会觉得你一点机会都没有。

A: I feel like my head is going to explode! 我感觉头都要炸开了。
B: What happened? 出什么事了？

feel like ...ing 想要做某事

feel like后面如果加动词的 ...ing形式的话，就表示“想要做某事”。比如说想要吃什么，想要做什么等等，如果要表示相反的含义，即“不想做某事”时就可以用否定型I don't feel like ...ing。

“谈了三年的恋爱，分手之后非常不适应”

I don't feel like being alone tonight.

M·O·R·E

- feel like+ ...ing
  想要做某事
- I don't feel like+ ...ing
  我不想做某事
- I don't feel like it.
  我不想做这件事。

I feel like having a cup of coffee.
我想喝一杯咖啡。

Leave me alone. I don't feel like doing anything.
别管我，我不想做任何事。

I don't feel like going to play computer games with you.
我不想和你一起玩电脑游戏。

A: Do you want to go out? 你要不要出去？
B: Later. I feel like taking a shower first. 晚点吧，我现在想冲个澡。

feel free to 随心所欲地做某事

让别人不要有负担，想做什么做什么事可以使用的短语。表示“不要犹豫，随便做……”，与Don't hesitate to的含义相近。

“邀请朋友到自己的派对，顺便让他带上女朋友”

Feel free to bring some girlfriends to the party.

M·O·R·E

- feel free to+动词
  随心所欲地做某事
- Don't hesitate to+动词
  毫不犹豫地做某事

Please feel free to have another.
别客气，再来一个。

Feel free to stay here as long as you like.
想待多久就待多久。

Feel free to ask if you have any questions.
如果有问题的话，可以随便问。

A: Feel free to stay here as long as you like. 只要你喜欢，想待到什么时候就待到什么时候。

B: It's very kind of you to say so. 你能那么说，我很高兴。

feel the same way 想的一样，达成共识

虽然是个简单的短语，但在日常生活中的使用频率很高。feel the same way (about somebody) 表示“（对某人）表示赞同”。the same way指代之前提到的对话内容。

“朋友单恋一个人好久了，要想方设法让他面对现实”

I'm sorry but she doesn't feel the same way.

M·O·R·E

- feel the same way about
  对某事持有相同的观点
- have the same feeling
  有一样的感受

I feel the same way.
我也那么认为。

I don't feel the same way about you.
我想的和你有点不一样。

I hope that you feel the same way about me.
我希望你想的能和我一样。

Does he feel the same way?
他也那么想吗?

A: I have a feeling that they are not going to show up. 我有种预感，他们不会出现了。

B: That's funny, and I had the same feeling earlier today. 很有趣啊，今天早些时候也有过相同的预感。

feel for 同情某人

feel for somebody (something) 表示同情处在困境或痛苦中的某人，或由衷地表示痛心，可以理解为“同情某人”，“觉得……惋惜”等。需要注意的是，如果变成have a feel for的形态的话，就表示对……有感觉，喜欢对方等含义。

“刚刚失去了工作，觉得很可怜，不料突然成为了营销成员，瞬间向自己推荐产品”

I don't **feel sorry for** you anymore.

M·O·R·E

- feel for sb
  同情某人的伤痛
- feel for sth
  认为某人很可怜
- feel pity for
  同情某人
- feel sorry for
  觉得某人很可怜

She suffers from depression. We all **feel for** her.
她患上了抑郁症，我们都为她难过。

The boss will like her and **feel for** her situation.
老板会喜欢上她的，并且会同情她的处境。

I **feel for** the loss that they suffered.
我为他们所经受到的痛苦感到难过。

A: I feel for Bette. She looks unhappy. 我觉得贝蒂很可怜，她看起来不大高兴。
B: She's having problems with her parents. 她和她父母之间好像出了点问题。

have a good (bad) feeling about 因某事而心情好（坏）

可以用来表达对事物或人物的感受，心情好坏与否，只要在feeling前面加上自己的感情形容词就可以了。比如说，感到奇怪的话，就是weird feeling。

“初次拜访，却有着似曾相识的感觉，好像在梦里见过”

I **have a weird feeling** I've been here before.

M·O·R·E

- have a good feeling about
  因某事感到心情好
- have a bad (weird) feeling about
  因某事感到心情差（奇怪）

I **had a bad feeling about** this.
我对此事有着不好的感受。

I'**ve got a good feeling about** this.
这件事让我心情很好。

I **have a really good feeling about** her.
我对她的感情很好。

I **have a weird feeling about** this place.
我觉得这个地方有点奇怪。

A: I have a good feeling about this date. 这次的约会我感觉不错。
B: You'll have a good time with Eileen. 你会和艾琳度过愉快的时光的。

have the (a) feeling 有着……的感觉，仿佛是……

可以用为have the (a) feeling (that)主语+动词的形态，that后面的部分the (a) feeling可以解释具体的感受内容。后面如果接of或about的话就表示“对……有感觉”。

“我一直不大同意，单身的母亲就和她的老男朋友分手了”

I **have a feeling** you did it for me.

M·O·R·E

- have the (a) feeling (that) S+V
  感觉是……
- have the (a) feeling about
  有着……的预感

I **have the feeling** you had something to do with it.
我觉得你和那件事有牵连。

I **got the feeling that** your wife was coming on to me.
我觉得你老婆在勾引我。

I **have a feeling** he's going to be very angry.
我预感到他会非常的生气。

I'**ve got a feeling** he'll be back.
我感觉他会回来的。

A: Morton has done a very poor job. 莫尔顿的成果非常差。
B: I have a feeling that he will quit soon. 我有种预感，他马上要辞职了。

have a feeling for 喜欢……

这点a feeling或feelings后面接上了for，因此have a feeling (feelings) for表示“对某人有心”，“喜欢某人”等。

“一般来说，如果女生稍微对男生好点，男生就会有错觉”

I **have feelings for** you. I know you feel something for me.

M·O·R·E

- have a feeling (feelings) for
  喜欢某人

I **have (strong) feelings for** her.
我非常喜欢她。

You'**ve had feelings for** me?
你对我有特殊的感情?

You still **have feelings for** me, don't you?
你还喜欢着我，不是吗?

A: Bob is always calling me. 鲍勃总会给我打电话。
B: You know he has feelings for you. 你知道他对你有感觉吧。

(There's) No hard feelings 没有恶意

There's no hard feelings on my part（不要往坏处想）是比较常见的表达句式。如果说出的话可能会让对方不高兴时，可以说hard feelings for (about)。

“没被老板发现迟到的事情，不料同事口口声声说什么“公平的社会”，给老板打小报告”

No hard feelings. Promise.

M·O·R·E

- No hard feelings about
  不要想歪了
- (There's) No hard feelings on my part.
  听完别不高兴。

There's **no hard feelings** even though I was fired.
虽然我被解雇了，也没什么不高兴的。

No hard feelings about you leaving me behind.
你虽然离我而去，但我并没有什么不高兴。

I know you tired, so **no hard feelings**.
我知道你很累了，所以没有什么不高兴的。

A: I'm sorry I spilled your drink. 很抱歉，我打翻了你的饮料。
B: No hard feelings. I'll get another. 我没生气，再拿一杯就可以了。

More Expressions

- **feel up to+名词 (...ing)**
  有着足以……的力 量
  I don't **feel up to** it. 我觉得没办法做到。

- **feel the need to** 感觉到……的必要性
  You don't **feel the need to** apologize to me.
  你是感觉不到有向我道歉的必要啊。

- **What are your feelings about ... ?**
  你觉得……怎么样?
  What're your feelings about us divorcing?
  你觉得我们俩离婚怎么样?

- **spare one's feelings** 不伤某人的感情
  I was trying to **spare your feelings**.
  我试着不去伤害你的感情。

- **hide one's feelings** 隐藏某人的感情
  Yeah, at least you **hid your feelings** well. 恩，至少你隐藏了自己的感情。

- **hurt one's feelings** 伤害某人的感情
  She's too afraid of **hurting your feelings**. 她非常害怕伤害你的感情。

You got a gut feeling on this?
你对此有着天生的直觉?

I know the feeling. 我知道那种感受。

I have no feelings. (one way or the other) 我没有任何感觉。

转来转去的世界

Turn

turn的最基本含义就像She turned and walked away（她转身离开了）一样表示转变方向，包括身体或脸部方向等。因此，turn left (right) 表示左（右）转，也可以用来表示旋转，比如说旋转开关等等。除此之外，还可以用来替代get或become，变成turn+形容词形态，而且turn+年龄则表示“长到几岁”。

基本概念

1 旋转，翻身，面向（某个方向），转过来，替换

Would you please turn the TV off? 你能把电视机关掉吗?
Go down this street and turn to the left. 沿着这条马路走下去，左拐。

2 变化，改变（turn+名词（形容词））

My mother's hair began to turn grey. 我妈的头发开始变白了。
The weather is starting to turn cold.天气渐渐变冷了。

3 到（年龄，时间）

My wife's just turned 33. 我老婆刚刚33岁。
Our company will turn 100 next month. 我们公司下个月就100周年了。

turn and 转身做某事

turn最基本的含义为转身等转变方向的行为。因此turn and (to)+动词表示“转身做某事”。

“女朋友提出了分手，不甘被甩的男孩甚至追到了女厕所”

He's turning to follow her into the rest room.

M·O·R·E

- turn to
  将身体转向
- turn and (to)+动词
  转身做某事

He **turned to** leave, then turned back suddenly.
他转身离开，随后突然又转过身来。

She **turned to** her side to turned off her cell phone.
她侧身把手机关上了。

They **turned around** and walked back to the office.
他们转身走回了办公室。

A: Where did your friend go? 你朋友去哪了？
B: He just turned to leave the room. 他刚刚转身离开了房间。

turn left (right) 左（右）转

转身可以理解为改变方向。在给别人指路的时候必须要掌握的短语为，turn left表示左转，turn right表示右转。

“如果有人跟你问路了，就可以用这些话回答”

Turn left and go south three blocks and it's on the right.

M·O·R·E

- turn right = turn to the right
  向右侧转去，右转
- turn left = turn to the left
  向左侧转去，左转

Go east for two blocks and then **turn right**.
向东走两个街头，再右转。

Go down this street and **turn to the left**.
沿着这条街一直走到底，左转。

Take this road until it ends and then **turn right**.
沿着这条街一直走到底，右转。

A: Turn left and go straight for 2 blocks. You can't miss it. 左转，再直走两条街，你肯定能找到的。
B: Thank you so much. 非常感谢。

turn one's back on 背对某人，拒绝（帮助），回避

字面含义为将某人的后背(one's back)转过去(turn)（坐下），可以用来表示“回避”，“拒绝某人的帮助”等。拒绝的对象可以用on somebody (something)来表示。

“未婚夫成了下半身残疾，父母强烈要求跟他分手”

How can I turn my back on him?

M·O·R·E

- turn one's back
  暂时离开，背对某人
- turn one's back on sb (sth)
  回避某人，拒绝对方的要求

Why did you **turn your back on** him? I told you to take care of him!
你为什么不管他？我跟你说过要好好照顾他的！

Now I only **turned my back** for a second and she was gone.
我只是暂时离开一会，她就不见了。

Don't **turn your back on** him.
不要避开他。

If you **turn your back on** her, she will try to kill you!
如果你不理她的话，会死得很惨！

A: I am not going to listen to you. 我不会再听你的话了。
B: Don't turn your back while I'm talking! 我说话的时候不要假装没听见。

turn around 改变方向，情况有所好转，使好转

turn around表示将方向旋转180度。可以用来比喻状况的好转或使好转，日常生活中经常会用为“转身做某事”，即turn around to (and)+动词。

“正在兴致勃勃地看恐怖电影，突然有人推门进来，心里一凉”

I turned around to see who was entering the room.

M·O·R·E

- turn around and (to)+动词
  转身做某事
- turn around to look at
  回头看
- turn around
  情况好转

I **turned around to** see where it was coming from.
我转身看他是从哪过来的。

They **turned around** and looked at Tammy.
他们转身看了看塔米。

He **turned around** and said “Again, I'm sorry.”
他转身说道，“再说一遍，我很抱歉”。

A: I think we're lost now. 我感觉我们迷路了。
B: Let's just turn around and go home. 我们沿着原来的方向回家吧。

turn away 转头，回避

turn away具有很多含义，比如说“转头”，“回避”，“拒绝”，“避开”等，也可以用来比喻“赶走”。

“帮儿子输电脑密码，不想让他看到，所以就让儿子暂时回避”

Turn away for a second.

M·O·R·E

- turn away
  转头
- turn away from sb
  避开某人，拒绝

She kept trying to kiss me on the mouth, and I kept **turning away**.
她不断地想要亲吻我，所以我就不停地转头。

Don't you **turn away from** me. Look at me!
不要回避，看着我!

Lord, help us find the strength to **turn away from** evil when it tempts us.
天啊，请赐予我们力量逃出恶魔的诱惑吧。

A: Many people wanted to see the show. 很多人想要看那场演出。
B: They had to turn away people at the door. 他们不得不在入口处把人们驱走。

turn back 转身，回来，使回来

turn back字面含义为转身回来，可以表示“回头看”，“回来”或使别人“回来”等。

“男朋友色迷迷地说找个地方休息一会，不会做别的事情，女孩坚决不同意”

She turned back and decided not to enter.

M·O·R·E

- turn back (to+N)
  转身，回来
- turn back to+V
  转身做某事
- turn sb (sth) back
  使某人回来

Even though she never **turned back**, she knew Tom was behind her.
虽然她没有转身，但却知道汤姆就在她身后。

They both **turned back to** look at the building.
他们同时转身看了看那栋楼。

You have a right to **turn back** if you're scared.
如果你害怕的话，可以回去。

A: A lot of snow is falling. Should we turn back? 正下着鹅毛大雪呢，我们要不要回去?
B: No, let's keep going till we get there. 不，我们得一直走到底。

turn down 拒绝，使变弱，减少

字面含义为转向(turn)下方(down)，可以用来表示“调低电视的声音”，“使变弱”等，另外，还可以比喻“拒绝”等。相反，turn up则表示“放大声音”，“展现……的形象”。

“上层人士的子女要求职，只好把剩下的求职者都拒绝掉”

We turned down over 99% of our applicants.

M·O·R·E

- turn down
  减弱，减少，拒绝
- turn up
  加强，培养，暴露……的面孔

I had to **turn down** a job in Indonesia.
我不得不拒绝印度尼西亚的工作岗位。

Tell the kids to **turn down** the TV.
让孩子们把电视的声音放低。

I don't know what's keeping them, but I'm sure they'll **turn up**.
我不知道他们因为什么事情而迟到，不过我敢肯定，他们迟早会露出真面目的。

A: What are you going to do with the offer? 你要怎么处理那个提案?
B: I'm pretty sure I'm going to turn it down. 我很肯定，我会拒绝的。

turn in 提出，返还，睡觉，告密

turn in 表示“提出……”(hand in)或“进入梦乡”，turn into表示“变成或被换成……”。

“通过一次巨大的工程，女孩变成了绝世整形美女！”

Look at you! You turned into such a beautiful girl!

M·O·R·E

- turn in
  提出，进入梦乡，（向警察）告密
- turn into 变成

Please **turn in** your papers by tomorrow.
请你明天把论文交上来。

You didn't even read it before you **turned it in**?
在你提交之前，连读都没读过?

She went to the police to **turn in** a client.
她为了告发客户，去找了警察。

I had this room **turned into** a nursery.
我把这间房改成了托儿所。

A: Come on everyone. Let's turn in. 大家都过来，我们睡觉啦。
B: But I don't feel sleepy right now. 不过我现在一点都不困啊。

turn on 打开，使某人产生兴趣，使兴奋

turn down (up)为控制音量的大小，而turn on (off)是打开或关闭电源。因此也可以进一步表示让他人产生某种兴趣。

"看到一个身材绝伦的美女，不由自主地说道"

You look great and can always turn me on.

M·O·R·E

- turn on
  打开，使运转，使产生兴趣，使兴奋
- turn off
  关闭，让某人无法产生兴趣，让某人震惊下来
- Whatever turns you on
  随你的便
- You turn me on
  你让我兴奋，我很喜欢你

Do you want me to **turn off** the TV?
你想要我关电视吗?

Turn off the lights before you come to bed.
在上床之前记得关灯。

You have to **turn the gas valve off** before going out.
你出门前必须要把煤气阀门关上。

To be honest with you, I **got very turned on** by you.
老实说，你让我非常兴奋。

A: Who forgot to turn on the alarm? 是谁忘了关掉闹钟?
B: It's my fault. 是我的错。

turn out 结果为……(prove)

有"人们跑出来"，"生产"(produce)，"关闭……"等各种含义，但最常用的是"结果为……"。

"以纯粹的爱情为由，根本没经过测试就结了婚，没想到丈夫脾气非常火爆"

Our relationship turned out to be a disaster.

M·O·R·E

- turn out well (bad)
  变好，变差
- turn out to be+名词
  最终结果为
- It turns out (that)
  结果为
- as it turns out
  正如结果所示

In the end it **turned out** for the best.
最终证明了这个选择是最佳的。

Let's **turn out** all the lights and we'll watch the movie!
我们把所有的灯都关了，看电影吧!

She was engaged to a guy who **turned out to** be gay!
她订婚的那个男的居然是个同性恋!

It **turns out** it was a mistake.
最后才发现大错特错。

A: I'm not sure we can get through this difficult time. 我不太确定，我们能不能走出这个难关。
B: Don't worry. Things always turn out for the best. 不要担心，事情总会变好的。

turn over 翻身，谦让，传递

翻身是最基本的含义，进一步可以表示谦让或传递给别人。在表达谦让时可以用to+somebody (something)。

“在烤牛排的时候，先烤完一面，再对另一面说”

Are you ready to turn over now?

M·O·R·E

- turn over
  翻身
- turn over to
  将……传给……

We **turned over** and faced each other.
我们转身四目对视。

When did you **turn it over**?
你什么时候转手的?

Why didn't you just **turn them over** to me?
你为什么不直接给我呢?

A: I think I hurt the back of my leg. 我感觉大腿后面受伤了。
B: Turn over and let me look at it. 转过身去，让我看看。

turn to 得到帮助，依靠，使身体面向……

turn to+动词正如前文中提到的，表示“转身做某事”；turn to+名词则表示“将身体转向……”，可以用来比喻“处理……”，“依赖……”或“得到……的帮助”等。

“如果陷入困难的话，有人就会依赖自己的信仰”

When people are in trouble, they usually turn to religion.

M·O·R·E

- turn to+名词
  面向……转身做某事
- turn a blind eye to
  回避，假装没看见……
- turn a deaf ear to
  装傻，假装没听见……

Can we **turn to** the case?
我们能集中这个案例吗?

You shouldn't **turn to** drugs to escape from stress.
我们不能依仗毒品来摆脱压力。

I tried to talk to him, but he **turned a deaf ear to** me.
我试着和他说话，不过他总是装作没听见。

A: Everyone seems to love Lisa. 每个人好像都喜欢丽萨。
B: Yes, they turn to her when they need help. 恩，每当他们有困难时，丽萨就会提供帮助。

take turns 依次

在这里turn变成了名词，表示“顺序”，“名次”等多种含义。尤其take turns+... ing表示“按照次序做某事”。

“不小心勾搭上了黑帮老大的女人，悲惨地被每个小弟揍了一遍”

They **took turns** beating me with the sticks.

M·O·R·E

- take turns ...ing
  依次做某事
- be one's turn (to+动词)
  到了某人做某事的时候了
- in turn
  依次
- wait one's turn
  等待某人的顺序

Whose **turn** is it next?
下一个是谁?

Let's speak **in turn** from now on.
我们从现在开始依次说话吧。

They **took turns** looking at each other.
他们互相看着对方。

Maybe **it's my turn to** watch out for you.
也许该我照看你了。

A: I want to use the computer right now. 我现在想用用你的电脑。
B: Not yet. We have to take turns. 现在不行，我们得依次来。

More Expressions

- **turn a profit** 获取收益
  We've barely **turned a profit**.
  我们基本上没有什么收益。

- **turn one's attention to** 对某人有兴趣
  Please **turn your attention to** the big screen. 请注意大屏幕。

- **turn the corner** 渡过难关
  We've finally **turned the corner**.
  我们终于渡过了难关。

- **turn something inside out** 里外颠倒
  It's kind of like **turning a sock inside out**. 这就像把袜子翻过去。

- **turn the tables on** 逆转，报复
  Sam called the police and **turned the table on** the thief.
  他们抓住了小偷，报了警。

- **take a turn for the worse** 恶化
  My grandmother's health **has taken a turn for the worse**.
  我奶奶的病情有些恶化了。

I spoke out of turn. 我说错话了。
I didn't know where to turn.
我不知道该做什么了。

该检查就检查

Check

可以表示阻止，制止，但在日常生活中最常用的含义还是确认或检查。check something可以单纯用来检查某物，也可以用check if来确认某事实。另外，从确认的含义出发，还可以表示宾馆里的登记手续，或者在机场的check-in counter办理托运手续，或在图书馆借书等。

基本概念

1 制止，确认

Do you want me to check again? 你要我重新确认一下吗?

Why don't we check this area again? 我们再检查检查这片区域吧?

Where can I go to check my e-mail? 我到哪里可以查我的邮件?

Honey, I'm just checking. 亲爱的，我只是确认一下。

2 寄（行李），办理登记手续（在宾馆）

How many pieces of luggage are you checking? 你要寄多少行李?

How can I get to the check-in counter? 手续办理台怎么走?

She's checking the coats. 她在寄存大衣。

3 （名词）调查，检查，支票，（饭店）账单

What did the doctor say at your check-up today? 老师今天检查的时候说什么了?

I'll pay by check. 我会给你支票的。

check one's schedule 确认日程安排

check的最常用含义当属“确认”。如果check后面接名词的话就表示“检查某物”，同时代词it，that，this等也可以作为check的宾语。

“十多年没有联系的朋友突然提出要见个面”

I don't know. I'll have to **check my schedule.**

M·O·R·E

- check one's schedule
  检查某人的行程安排
- check one's messages
  确认某人的信息

First of all, let me **check my schedule.**
首先，让我确认一下行程安排。

Do you mind if I **check my messages**?
你介意我确认一下信息吗?

I can **check that** for you.
我可以帮你确认一下。

A: I wonder if we could get together on the 15th. 我在想，我们能不能在15号见面。

B: First of all, let me check my schedule. 首先，我得查查我的日程安排。

Let me check ... 让我来确认……

前文中提到过的let me+动词句式用来检查单纯的对象时可以用作Let me check+名词。经常会简单说一句Let me check（我来确认一下）。

“老公说好像把重要的文件留在了办公室，所以用电话寻求确认”

Hold on. **Let me check.**

M·O·R·E

- Let me check
  我来确认一下
- Let me check+名词
  我来确认一下

Let me check your blood pressure.
我来测测你的血压。

Let me check the computer to see if there are any seats left.
我用电脑查一下，看看有没有剩余的位置。

Just a moment! **Let me check** the other list.
稍等一会！我来查查别的名单。

A: Is that your car alarm going off? 这是你车的警报器在响吗?

B: Let me check outside and see. 让我出去确认一下。

check if (whether) 确认是否……

check后面接从句大多是check if (whether)主语+动词的形式，想要表达“确认某事”的话，就可以用check to see if主语+动词。

“对方只要提到派对就会欣喜若狂，怎么会不来呢”

Please **check if** Paris Hilton is coming to the party.

M·O·R·E

- check to see if (whether) S+V
  确认一下……

I'll check if he's finished working.

我来看看他有没有做完工作。

I'm just checking to see if she's okay.

我就是想看看她有没有事。

A: I need a size ten or eleven. 我要10或11码的。

B: I'll check to see if we have any in stock. 我得查查看我们有没有库存。

double check 再次确认

表示“再次确认”，可以用来表达再次对某事或某物的检查或确认。虽然出门之前确认过了液化气开关已经关闭，但最好再次确认一下，此时就要用double check。

“本来要兴致勃勃地去看话剧，没想到没有买到票，进不去”

I **should have double checked** for our tickets.

Be sure to **double-check** the alarm system.

再次确认一下警报系统。

I need you to **double-check** my meeting this afternoon.

我要你再次确认今天下午的会议。

I'll be sure to **double-check** everything from now on.

我从现在开始会再三确认所有事情的。

Let's **double check**.

我们再检查检查。

A: I think there's something wrong on the account. 我觉得那个账号出了点问题。

B: Let me double check. Just a moment. 我再次确认一下吧，稍等片刻。

check in （在宾馆等）登记，办理出入境手续，寄存（包裹）

表示确认进入(in)或离开(out)时所要经过的手续，因此表示“入住宾馆或住进医院时所需要办理的手续”。也可以说成check into。另外，还能表示“在机场办理出入境手续”，“寄存行李”等。

“到机场时，最先要做的事情就是办理托运手续”

We have to **check in** our bags right now.

M·O·R·E

- check in on sb (sth)
  去确认一下某人
- check in with sb
  通知某人，联系
- Check in, please
  我要办理入住手续
- I'd like to check in
  我要办理登记手续
- check into
  调查某事，（宾馆等）投宿

He **checked in** yesterday and paid with a credit card.
他昨天办理了入住手续，而且是用信用卡支付的。

When's the **check-in** time?
什么时候可以办理入住手续?

Just **check in with** Becky when you're done.
等你做完了，就对贝奇确认一下。

My father just **checked into** the hospital yesterday.
我父亲昨天刚刚住进了医院。

How would you feel about us **checking into** a romantic hotel tomorrow?
你觉得我们明天入住一家浪漫的宾馆怎么样?

Good afternoon. **Checking in**?
下午好，需要住宿吗?

She **checked into** the Hilton for two nights.
她在希尔顿宾馆住了两天。

I need you to **check into** her background.
我需要你查查她的背景。

A: We'll be able to check in at noon. 我们可以在中午办理入住手续。
B: What will we do after we check in? 我们办完手续应该做什么?

A: Security at the airport takes a long time. 机场的安检过程需要很久。
B: I always arrive early to check in. 我经常会提前到那办理手续。

A: Who are you going to call? 你要联系谁?
B: I promised my wife I would check in with her.
我答应过我老婆，会和她联系的。

check out 确认（调查），遥望，办理退宿手续（宾馆），出借（书籍）

是check in的反义词，字面含义为出去(out)的时候确认一下(check)，表示“在宾馆或者医院办理退宿手续”或者“借书”等。不过大多情况下会用作“确认（调查）”，“瞻望某人”等。

“丈夫不到最后一刻从不退房”

He'**s never checked out of** a room a minute before he had to.

M·O·R·E

- check sth out with sb
  与某人确认某事
- I'd like to check out now.
  我想现在办理退房手续。
- Check it (this) out!
  看看这个！确认一下！

I'll **check it out**.

我会确认一下的。

Hey, **check out** that girl! She is really hot!

喂，快点看看那女孩！真性感啊！

Your wife **checked out** two hours ago.

您的夫人在两个小时前办理了退房手续。

I'**m checking out** the restaurant with Tim.

我要和提姆去看看饭店。

A: What time is your check-out? 几点前需要退房？

B: Guests need to check out by 11:00 am. 客人们需要在上午11点办理退房。

check on 确认

check on somebody (something) 可以用来确认某事进行顺利与否，安全与否等。

“朋友不慎住进了医院，给他打电话确认病情”

I'm calling to **check on** the status of a patient.

I called my apartment and **checked on** my grandma.

我给家里打了电话，问奶奶情况怎么样。

Jack ran forward to **check on** what was going on.

杰克急忙跑了过去，确认一下出了什么事。

I **checked on** her but she's a little unstable today.

我今天看了看她，发现她情绪有点不稳定。

Hold on. Let me just **check on** the baby!

稍等，我来看看孩子的情况！

A: Where did Steve and Adrian go? 史蒂夫和阿德里安去哪了？

B: They had to check on their kids. 他们去看孩子有没有事。

check over 仔细检查

check over表示全盘检查一遍，可以理解为“仔细检查”。尤其是医生、技师等专家们经常会用到这个词。

“正走着，一个花盆从天而降，男友急忙检查女友是否受伤”

He'**s checking her over** to make sure she isn't hurt.

M·O·R·E

- check over
  自己检查，（医生等人）进行专业的调查
- have sb checked over
  接受……的检查

It's time you had the doctor **checked over**.

你得找个大夫好好检查检查了。

How long does it take for a mechanic to **check the car over**?

技师检查车辆受损情况需要多久?

The doctor **is checking over** a guy who just got run over by a bus.

医生正在检查刚刚被大巴撞到的男子。

A: You should check over this term paper. **你得好好检查一下期末报告。**

B: Why? Are there mistakes on it? **为什么？难道有什么错?**

check with 询问某人

check with somebody表示“为了确认某事而询问某人”。想要说明具体的询问内容就可以说check with somebody about something。

“丈夫整天待在家里无所事事，总会对加班到深夜的妻子抱怨”

I don't know. I'm going to go **check with** the boss.

M·O·R·E

- check with sb
  询问某人
- check with sb about sth
  询问某人某事

You'd better **check with** the boss.

你最好和老板确认一下。

Did you **check with** security?

你和保安确认过了?

I wanted to **check with** you first.

我想先和你确认一下。

Check with me about stuff like this.

这种事情先和我确认一下。

A: She didn't check with her boss before she began. **她在开始的时候没有和老板确认。**

B: I'll bet she's in trouble with him. **我打赌她肯定有麻烦了。**

check up 调查，确认

check up 表示“调查真伪”，“确认某人的状态”，医生们也会经常用来表示“进行健康诊察”。后面会接on somebody (something)，另外，名词型check (...) up表示“健康诊察”。

“心肝宝贝女儿最近刚刚离婚，独守空房，父母非常担心她的未来”

I just came by to **check up on** you.

M·O·R·E

- check up (on sb (sth))
  确认，调查
- check-up
  （医院）诊察

I'm going to go **check up on** your friend.
我得去看看你的朋友怎么样了。

Your ex-wife came by this morning to **check up on** you.
你的前妻今天早上来过，看了看你的状态。

The doctor can **check up on** him here.
医生可以在这对他进行诊察。

I get a dental **check-up** every six months.
我每六个月就会进行一次牙科检查。

A: Vera doesn't look very healthy these days. 维拉这几天气色不大好。
B: Tell her to schedule a check-up with her doctor. 让她找个时间去看看大夫吧。

check 支票，账单

check 作为名词可以表示“支票”，“账单”等。因此在饭店如果说Check，please的话就表示“请拿账单”。

“如果没什么大事的话，最好take checks（接受支票）。”

I'm sorry, we don't accept **checks** here.

Will you pay for this in cash or **by check**?
您是要付现金还是支票?

I'm going to pay for this **with a check**.
我要用支票支付。

Could I have the **check** please?
我能看看账单吗?

Here's your **check**. That'll be $10.
这里是您的账单，总共10美元。

A: Can I pay for this drink with a check? 我可以用支票支付这瓶饮料吗?
B: No, we only accept cash or credit cards. 不可以，我们只接受现金支付和信用卡支付。

我需要你

Need

Need表示必要，可以用need something或need to+动词的形态表达需要的东西或行为。相反，如果要表达不需要时则可以用I don't need，向对方说没有做某事的必要时可以说You don't need。另外，需要别人做某事时要用need somebody to+动词。

基本概念

1 需要……（need+名词），需要做某事（need to+动词）

If there's anything you need, don't hesitate to ask. 如果你需要什么，尽管跟我说。

I need some rest. 我得休息一会了。

I need to get back to the office.我得回办公室去了。

2 需要某人做某事

I need you to help me with this homework. 我需要你帮我做作业。

Do you need me to go with you?你要我和你一起去吗?

3（名词）必要，要求，义务

I don't see the need to go to school.我不知道为什么要去学校。

I don't see the need for it. 我不觉得有那必要。

need something 需要某物

need后面可以加主语需要或对主语必要的名词。也可以用It (that)替代名词，成为I need it, I don't need it, Do you need that?等。

"同桌借了我一支中性笔，等将近用完了才还回来，我很无奈"

Don't be sorry. I don't **need** it anymore.

M·O·R·E

- I need+名词
  我需要……
- You need+名词
  你需要……
- Do you need+名词?
  你需要……吗?

If you **need** anything, feel free to ask.
如果需要什么，尽管向我要。

I **need** more time to think it over.
我需要多点时间来考虑考虑。

Do you **need** an answer right now?
你现在立马需要答复吗?

A: I need a new bed to sleep on. 我得找个新床睡觉。
B: They sell them at the department store. 百货商场应该有卖的。

need somebody 需要，渴望……

这次need后面接人物。像前面的情况一样，用作I (don't) need, You (don't) need, Do you need ... ?等就可以了。

"只有你自己出人头地，才会有所谓的朋友，一见到你落寞就一个个离你而去"

I don't **need** you or anybody else!

M·O·R·E

- need sb back
  希望某人回来

You can go now. I don't **need** you anymore.
你现在可以走了。我不再需要你了。

We **need you back**. When can you come back?
我需要你回来。你什么时候能回来?

Why do you **need** me anyway?
你到底为什么需要我?

A: Is there a leak in your bathroom? 洗手间漏水吗?
B: Yeah, I need a plumber to fix it. 恩，我得找个水管工修修。

need to 需要做某事，有必要做某事

如果需要的不是某个人物或者事物，而是行为时，可以用need to+动词的形态。另外，need to be+pp形态也比较常用。

“如果老师说了这种话，那你的成绩最多也就是个F了”

I need to talk to you about your mid-term exam.

M·O·R·E

- I need to+动词
  我需要做某事
- need to be+pp
  我需要变成……

I need to stay another day.
我得多待一天。

Hey, stay there! **I need to** talk to you.
喂，站住！我得和你谈谈。

I need to borrow some money.
我得和你借点钱了。

Let's get together. We **need to** talk about something.
我们见个面吧，得和你说点事情。

A: I have to go. I need to get to work. 我现在得走了，要工作了。
B: Don't forget to take your lunch with you. 别忘了把午餐带着。

You need to ... 你应该做某事

虽然同样是need to+动词的形态，但主语如果变成you，即You need to+动词的话就表示“你应该做某事”，而Do you need to+动词？的话就表示“必须做某事吗？”。

“要去旅行了，孩子们兴奋地连安全带都不系，就在车里面乱蹦”

You need to buckle up.

M·O·R·E

- You need+动词
  你需要做某事
- Do you need to+动词?
  你必须做某事吗?

You need to call her right now.
你现在得马上给她打电话。

You need to talk with your teacher.
你得和你的老师谈谈。

Do you need to get up early tomorrow morning?
你早上必须要早起吗?

A: Do you know what I mean? 你知道我说的是什么意思吗?
B: Yeah! You're saying you need to take a day off. 恩！你是说你需要休息一天。

need somebody to 需要某人做某事

不是我要做某事，而是希望somebody做某事的句式。要记住典型句型，I need you to和Do you need me to ... ?

"长得像一匹马，说的话还驴唇不对马嘴，对这种人就要"

I need you to leave right now.

M·O·R·E

- Do you need me+动词?
  你要我做某事吗?

I **need you to** get this done by tomorrow.
我需要你明天之前完成它。

Mom, I **need you to** sign this document. It's for school.
妈，我需要你在这文件上签个名，是学校要的。

You really **don't need me to** live with you.
你真不希望我和你一起住。

Do you need me to go on a vacation with you?
你需要我陪你一起去度假吗?

A: Do you need me to stay longer? 你要我多待一会吗?
B: No, we're all finished. You can go. 不用了，我们完事了。你可以走了。

don't need to 没有……的必要

need to+动词的否定形态don't need to表示"没有做某事的必要"，与don't have to具有相似的含义。表示对方"不必做某事"的I don't need you too也是比较常用的句式。

"经常迟到的学生不知道是诡辩还是狡辩，总会说各种迟到的理由"

You don't need to make an excuse.

M·O·R·E

- You don't need to+动词
  没有做某事的必要
- I don't need you to+动词 (...ing)
  你不必做某事

I **don't need to** know the details.
我不需要知道详情。

I told you that **you don't need to** be here.
我告诉过你，你不需要待在这。

I **don't need you to** help me. I can do it myself.
我不需要你帮我，我可以自己完成。

I **don't need you** fighting for us anymore.
我不需要你为我们打架。

A: I can help you finish your homework. 我可以帮你做作业。
B: You don't need to stay here with me. 你不需要和我一起待在这里。

All I need is ... 我需要的就只有……

强调我最需要的东西时能够用到的表达方法，All I need is ... 为最基本的形式，由此可以衍生出各种变形的用法。is 后面可以接名词或(to)+动词。

“能够从学习的地狱中逃离出来的唯一办法就是电脑游戏，所以”

All I need is a new computer.

M·O·R·E

- All I need is+名词
  我需要的就只有……
  我只需要……
- All I need is to+动词
  我需要做的事情就只有……
- All I need to+do (tell, know) is ...
  我要做（知道，说）的事情就只有……

All I need is five minutes.
我只需要五分钟。

All I need to do is have some more fun.
我只想获得更多的乐趣而已。

All I need to know is who you fell in love with.
我只想知道你到底爱着谁。

A: All I need is a beautiful girlfriend. 我只需要一个漂亮的女朋友。
B: I don't think that you can find one. 我觉得你找不到那么一个人。

(There's) No need to ... 没有……的必要

向对方说“没有……的必要”为There's no need for+名词（to+动词）形态，其中的There's是可以省略的。

“一个考生考试的时候作弊被发现，教授把他叫过来希望他坦白交代”

There's no need to lie to me.

M·O·R·E

- That's all I need to ...
  我需要的就只有……
- be in need of
  需要
- see a need to
  有……的必要性
- meet a need
  满足……的需要

There's no need to be embarrassed.
没有必要感到惶恐。

There's really no need to explain.
真没有必要作解释。

No need to talk about it.
没必要谈论这个话题。

A: You need to clean up this place! 你该打扫这个地方了！
B: I will. There's no need to get angry. 我会的，不过你也没必要生气吧。

那是什么话

Mean

mean具有多种含义，是个比较常用的单词。其中最重要的一个含义就是表示意味，重要的动词和表示吝啬的形容词。尤其为了和人圆滑地交流必须要用到I mean，在确认对方的话时要用you mean ...？，what do you mean ...？而且为了防止对方误解我的话，就要说I don't mean ... 等。

基本概念

1 意味着，意图

Do you mean he might like me? 你是说他有可能喜欢我?

I didn't mean to say that. 我不是故意要和你说那些的。

I didn't mean to hurt you. 我没有想过要伤害你。

2 有着重要性

It means a lot to me. 这对我很重要。

This party meant everything to her. 这个派对对她很重要。

3 （形容词）吝啬的，卑劣的(gross，nasty)

You're so mean. 你太小气了。

That's a mean thing to say! 那是相当卑鄙的事情!

I mean ... 我是说……

如果对方没有听清或听懂我的话，可以用I mean ... 重新解释一遍。可以使用I mean (that)主语+动词的形态，也可以在I mean 后面接从句或想要说的部分。

“一个大公司的财阀老板要用金钱诱惑，不过我还是决然地说并不是因为钱(be into)”

I mean I'm well off but not into money.

M·O·R·E

- I mean ...
  我是说……
- I mean S+V
  我是说……

I mean he's been missing for several days.
我是说他失踪好几天了。

I mean I've been losing weight these days.
我是说这两天瘦了不少。

I mean today, not tomorrow.
我是说今天，不是明天。

A: I don't understand what you're saying. 我不明白你在说什么。
B: I mean I want you to help me. 我是说，我希望你能帮我。

(Do) You mean ... ? 你是说……吧?

这次主语变成了对方，You mean ... 表示无法理解对方的话或者要再次确认对方的话。You mean ... 也经常会出现在口语中。

“儿子正在兴高采烈地玩游戏机，不过并不是我给他买的”

You mean you stole it?

M·O·R·E

- You mean S+V?
  你是说……?
- You mean S+V?
  你是说……?

Do you mean you won't be coming over for dinner?
你是说你晚上不能来吃饭了?

Do you mean he might like me?
你是说他有可能喜欢我?

You mean he got fired?
你是说他被炒鱿鱼了?

So you mean now you're not seeing anyone?
也就是说，你现在没有对象?

A: You mean she acts cruel and spoiled? 你是说她有点没规矩?
B: Not exactly, but she's not a very kind person. 也不完全是那样，我是说她不是什么善良的人。

What do you mean ... ? 你那是什么话?

如果想要再次确认对方所说的话，或者没能理解对方的话时可以用到的短语。实际会话中一般会用what do you mean? 或者在What do you mean后面接主语+动词的形式或者接不大能理解的那段话。

“无论是成绩还是其他方面都出类拔萃的一个学生突然提出要退学”

What do you mean you quit?! You can’t quit!

M·O·R·E

- What do you mean+N?
  你那是什么话?
- What do you mean by+
  你……是什么意思?
- What do you mean by that?
  你那是什么话?
- What do you mean S+V?
  ……是什么意思?

What do you mean you're not so sure?
什么叫你不太确定?

What do you mean you don't remember me?
你说你不认识我? 那是什么话?

What do you mean by that? Am I fat?
你那是什么意思? 是在说我胖吗?

What do you mean you're not coming?
什么叫你来不了?

What do you mean you're going to Paris?
你要去巴黎? 那是什么话?

What do you mean you live here? Since when?
什么叫你住在这? 从什么时候开始?

What do you mean you lost it again?
什么叫你又迷路了?

A: Be a man and take responsibility for your family. **像个男人一样把家庭的责任担负起来。**

B: What do you mean specifically? **你具体指的是什么?**

A: You gained some weight? **你长胖了?**

B: What do you mean by that? Am I fat? **你那是什么话? 我胖吗?**

A: I can't marry you because I don't love you. **我不能和你结婚，因为我根本不爱你。**

B: What do you mean you don't love me? **什么叫你根本不爱我?**

It doesn't mean that ... 这不是……的意思

如果对方可能对我说的话引起误会，则可以用这个表达，以解除对方的误会，纠正自己的话。

"在和一个离过婚的男人拍拖，父母却极力反对"

It doesn't mean he has a problem.

M·O·R·E

- It doesn't mean that S+V
  这不是……的意思
- I guess that means ...
  我猜那是……的意思

It doesn't mean that I don't love you.
这不意味着我不爱你。

It doesn't mean he's great in bed.
这不意味着他的床上功夫了得。

That still doesn't mean you didn't kill him.
那也不能说明你没杀他。

I guess that means we've got something in common.
我猜那是说，我们有很多共同点。

A: The weather today really sucks. 今天的天气真差。

B: It doesn't mean that the weather will be bad tomorrow. 这也不能表明明天的天气就一定差。

mean to 打算做某事

mean to+动词表示"打算做某事"。能和say，tell等动词相搭配使用，另外也会经常使用过去时的meant to+动词形态。

"交往了10多年的女朋友突然提出分手，瞬时举足无措"

You **mean to** tell me you're going to leave me?

M·O·R·E

- I mean(t) to say (tell) ...
  我（本来）想说……
- (Do) You mean to tell me ... ?
  你说的……是真的?

I **mean to say** that we were shocked by the news.
我想说，我们看到那篇报道之后，都吓了一大跳。

I **meant to** leave that stuff at your apartment.
我本来想把那些东西留在你家里的。

I **meant to tell** you, I don't love you anymore.
我本来想告诉你，我不再爱你了。

You **mean to tell** me you can't find a room?
你是想告诉我，你找不到房间了?

A: You didn't pay back the money you owe me. 你欠我的钱还没还呢。

B: I meant to give it to you this morning. 我本来想今天早上给你的。

I didn't mean to ... 我没有打算做某事

为前文中的mean to的应用表达，可以用来防止对方的误解，或者具体说明可能误解的部分。在I didn't mean to后面接上可能误解的部分，或者可以单纯地讲I didn't mean that。

"在学校突然拧开了汽水，不小心溅到了后面的人脸上"

I'm sorry! **I didn't mean to** do that!

M·O·R·E

- I didn't mean that
  我不是故意……的
- I didn't mean to+动词
  我没有打算做某事

Don't be upset. **I didn't mean that.**
不要生气了，我不是故意的。

I didn't mean to offend (insult, upset) you.
我没有想冒犯（侮辱，刺激）你。

I didn't mean to do that. Let me clean it up.
我不是故意要那么做的。让我收拾吧。

I didn't mean to say that.
我不是故意要那么说的。

A: You should have been here an hour ago. 你应该一个小时之前就到了。
B: I didn't mean to be late. 我不是故意要迟到的。

mean it (that) 真心，真的

mean it 或 mean that表示"真心"或"真的"，相似含义的短语有mean business。

"给朋友介绍了一个帅气十足的男生，不料假发被台风卷走"

I mean it. I didn't know about that.

M·O·R·E

- I didn't mean it.
  我不是故意的。
- I mean business.
  我说的是真的，不是开玩笑。

Don't get me wrong. **I don't mean it.**
不要误会我。我不是那个意思。

I mean it. You don't try to call me again.
真的，你别再给我打电话了。

Please, don't laugh anymore. **I mean business.**
别再嘲笑我了，说真的。

You mean it? That would be so much fun!
你是认真的？那会很好玩啊！

A: Are you serious? 你说的是真的？
B: Sure. I mean it. 恩，真心话。

mean a lot 对……有着重大的意义，重要，熟悉

mean 后面接a lot, everything, something, anything等词而组成的短语，可以表达“对某人有重要的意义，没有意义”等，也可以理解为“重要”，“熟悉”等。

“女朋友转身离开，急忙拉住她的袖子，苦苦相求”

You mean everything to me. Please don't go away.

M·O·R·E

- mean a lot to sb (that) （某事）对某人非常重要
- mean everything to sb 对某人有重大的意义
- mean nothing to sb 对某人没有意义
- mean something (anything) to sb 对某人有意义（熟悉）

It **means a lot to** me that you came to my place.
你能来我这儿对我很重要。

I don't know what to say. That **means a lot to** me.
真不知道该说些什么，这对我很重要。

That **means nothing to** me.
这对我没有意义。

It **doesn't mean anything to** me. I don't care.
这对我一点意义都没有，我才不管。

A: Happy birthday sweetheart. I love you. 亲爱的，生日快乐，我爱你。
B: It means a lot to spend the day with you. 生日当天能和你一起过对我很重要。

what somebody mean ……意味着

what I mean（我说的是）与what you mean（你说的是）都会成为know和see的宾语，表示“知不知道我说的话”等，主要用来指交流的内容。

“朋友深陷赌博的深渊，不停地找我借钱”

I know what you mean. You don't have to explain.

M·O·R·E

- what I mean 我说的话……
- what you mean 你说的话……

That's not **what I mean**.
那不是我想表达的。

I'm not sure (I don't know) **what you mean**.
我不太确定你在说什么。

I need to focus on this. You know **what I mean**?
我得专注于这件事，你知道我是什么意思吗？

See **what I mean**?
知道我是什么意思？

A: Do you think he's cruel? 你觉得他很残忍吗？
B: That's not what I meant. I think he's selfish. 我不是那个意思。我觉得他有点自私。

mean no harm 没有恶意

mean no 或 not mean any后面如果接上表示“害处”的harm, offense, disrespect等单词的话就表示“没有恶意”，“没有打算产生负面影响”。

“只要有点钱，女朋友就会花在新款名牌衣服，手提包等上”

I **mean no offense**, but you have to change your lifestyle.

M·O·R·E

- mean no harm (offense)
  没有恶意
- mean no disrespect
  没有想过要使某人不愉快

I really didn't **mean any offense**.
我真的没有任何冒犯之意。

I'm sorry about that. I didn't **mean any harm**.
很抱歉，我并没有恶意。

I **mean no disrespect**, doctor.
医生，我希望您别误会。

A: Jim didn't invite me to his party. 吉姆没有邀请我到他的派对。
B: He probably forgot. I'm sure he meant no harm. 他可能忘了吧，我肯定他并没有恶意。

be meant to 决定做某事

如果mean变成被动形态，即be meant to+动词（for+名词）的话，就表示“本应该做某事”。尤其在表示男女之间有天生缘分的时候就可以用It was meant to be, They were meant to be等。

“被高利贷者抓住，狂打一顿的赌徒，但还是沉迷于赌博”

I feel like I **was meant to** be a gambler.

M·O·R·E

- be mean to+动词（for+名词）
  本应该……
- It was meant to be.
  这是缘分。
- by all means
  当然，肯定，必须
- don't mean maybe
  真的

You know my music **is meant to** inspire.
你知道我的音乐是用来激发灵感的。

I **was meant to** spend the rest of my life with you.
我决定和你度过余下的时光。

I feel like I **was meant to** pick this up.
我觉得我命中注定要选择这个。

I think that **was meant for** you.
我觉得那是你命中注定的。

A: What is all of this money for? 这些钱全都是用来干嘛的?
B: It is meant to buy some furniture. 是用来买些家具的。

给我站起来

Stand

虽然stand只是单纯表示站起来的意思，但也可以用来描述多种情况，如站在路中间(stand in the way)表示“妨碍”，站在旁边(stand by)表示“等待”，“支持”，站在外边(stand out)表示“突出”等。另外，否定形式can't stand somebody (something)表示“无法忍受……”。而且作为名词还可以表示露天卖场或者体育场的看台。

基本概念

1 站起来，站着

Please stand up and follow me. 请站起来跟我走。

She stood up and turned around to face me. 她站了起来，转身面向了我。

I need to get back to the office. 我得回到办公室。

2 忍受，坚持

I just can't stand your friends. 我实在无法忍受你的朋友了。

3（名词）（制成）台，露天，卖场，（体育场）看台

Where's the taxi stand? 出租车停车场在哪里?

stand 站

stand 的最基本含义为站起身来。以此为基础，stand up 表示“站起来”，stand next to表示“站在……的旁边”，而stand ...ing表示“站着做某事”。

“政治家们经常会出绯闻，明知道丈夫出轨而妻子们也会站在旁边保持微笑”

She **is standing next to** him holding his hand.

M·O·R·E

- stand at (in, on)
  站在某处
- stand+(地点) ...ing
  （在某处）站着做某事
- stand next to
  站在……的旁边
- stand in line
  排队

Tom **is standing at** the window waving at her.
汤姆站在窗户旁边向她招手。

Ben **is standing next to** her.
本站在她的旁边。

I **stood there** trying to remember why she left me.
我站在那里，尝试着回想她为什么离开我。

A: Shall we go to a movie tonight? 我们今天晚上要不要去看电影?
B: No, I hate to stand in line to buy tickets. 不了，我不喜欢排队买票。

stand+形容词 处在……的状态

虽然使用频率不是很高，但stand像keep一样，如果接形容词的话则表示“处于……状态”。stand still是最典型的句式，表示“站住”，“静止不动”。

“对妻子过分依赖的丈夫有一天突然发现了一则重大新闻”

I saw my wife **standing close to** a cute guy.

M·O·R·E

- stand still
  坚持，不退缩
- stand firm
  停止，静止不动

It's like time **has stood still** in this room.
在这个房间内，时间仿佛停止了。

They **stood close to** each other.
他们彼此紧贴着站着。

She took a few steps around the desk, to **stand closer**
她向桌子走近了几步，紧靠而立。

A: The children are running around the classrooms. 孩子们正在教室周围跑来跑去。
B: Tell them to stand still or they'll be punished. 让他们站住，要不就罚他们了。

can't stand something (somebody) 不喜欢某事，无法忍受某事

can stand something (somebody)表示“可以接受某事”，平时主要使用它的否定形态can't stand，表示“无法忍受……”，“讨厌某事”等。

“两个儿子为了一个女人大打出手，实在看不下去的老爹说道”

I **can't stand** you two fighting over her.

M·O·R·E

- can stand sth (sb) doing
  接受某人做某事
- can't stand sth (sb) ...ing
  无法接受某人做某事，讨厌
- can't stand to+动词
  无法忍受……
- can't stand the thought of
  无法接受……的想法
- can't stand that S+V
  无法忍受……

I **can't stand this** (you).
我没法忍受这个（你）了。

Oh, God. I **can't stand it** any longer.
哦，天啊，我实在忍不下去了。

I **can't stand the boss**. She sucks!
我实在无法忍受老板了，她真逊！

I **can't stand the smell of** hot dogs. They make me sick.
我实在无法忍受热狗的味道，闻着就恶心。

Why did you invite him? I **can't stand** that guy!
你为什么要邀请他？我实在无法忍受那个家伙！

I **can't stand** you being here.
我无法忍受你在这里。

You **can't stand** me getting closer to her.
你无法忍受我和她靠近。

I **can't stand the thought of** you with another woman!
我实在无法忍受你居然和别的女人在一起！

I **can't stand that** I hurt you.
我无法忍受伤害你的事实。

I **can't stand** to lose. I'm sure I will win.
我无法接受失败，我确定我会胜利的。

A: I can't stand Lindsey Lohan. 我无法忍受琳赛罗涵。
B: Yeah, she is always getting in trouble. 恩，她总是会惹一些麻烦。

A: We're going to have salad before dinner.我们要在晚饭前来点沙拉。
B: Oh no! I can't stand eating salad. 不要啊！我可吃不了沙拉。

A: I can't stand that I didn't get into Harvard.
我真无法接受我没能考进哈佛的事实。
B: It's very difficult to get into that school. 要进入那所大学可不是件容易的事情。

stand in the (someone's) way 妨碍

字面含义为站在(stand)路中间(in the way)，可以理解为“妨碍……”。也可以用be，get等词替换stand，而形成妨碍的对象可以用of来表达。

“虽然非常相爱，但女朋友家境过于好，有点接受不了，对这种朋友就要说”

You shouldn't let anything stand in your way.

M·O·R·E

- stand (be, get) in the way (of)
  妨碍（某事），妨碍
- stand (be, get) in sb's way (of)
  妨碍某人做某事

Ok then. I won't **stand in your way**.
那好吧，我不会妨碍你的。

I'm not going to **stand in your way of** doing it.
我不会妨碍你做那件事的。

Are you going to let that **stand in the way of** us?
你要让那个妨碍我们?

I'm not going to **stand in the way of** that.
我不会形成妨碍的。

A: My girlfriend's parents really don't like me. 我女朋友的父母非常不喜欢我。
B: Are they standing in the way of your marriage? 他们会妨碍你们俩的婚姻吗?

where somebody stands (on) 某人（对……）的立场，想法

字面含义为“某人站着的地方”，可以用来表示“……的立场”，“……的想法”等。比方说where I stand表示“我的立场”，where you stand则表示“你的立场”。

“对方陷入了一起通奸案，询问对方的立场时”

Please let me know where you stand on the law.

M·O·R·E

- know where sb stands (on)
  了解某人（在某个事情上）的立场
- tell A where B stands (on)
  将B（关于某事）的立场告诉A
- from where I stand
  我在的地方，
  在我看来，我觉得
- That is where I stand.
  那就是我的立场。

I'd like to know **where you stand**.
我想知道你的立场。

I was wondering if you could tell me **where I should stand**?
我在想，你能不能告诉我，我应该站在哪个立场?

From where he stood, he looked around the downtown.
他站在那里看了看城镇。

Do you know **where I stand** on the stock market?
你知道我对股市的看法是什么样的吗?

A: Who will Jeff vote for in the election? 杰夫会在选举时支持谁呢?
B: I don't know where he stands on politics. 我不知道他的政治立场。

stand a chance 有机会，有望

字面含义为树立(stand)机会(a chance)，因此stand a chance of表示“有着……的机会”，“有可能性”。相反stand no chance of表示没有机会。

“还没等考试呢，就率先放弃的人比比皆是”

I don't **stand a chance of** passing the exam.

M·O·R·E

- stand a chance (of)
  有（做某事）的机会，有望
- stand no chance (of)
  没有（做某事）机会

I think I don't **stand a chance**.
我觉得我不会有机会的。

Do you think we even **stand a chance**?
你认为我们会有机会吗?

She **stands no chance of** marrying Peter.
她不会有机会和彼得结婚了。

A: Will Australia win a gold medal for skiing? 澳大利亚会获得滑雪金牌吗?
B: No, they don't stand a chance of winning. 不会，他们根本没有胜算。

stand by 等待，支持某人

字面含义为站在(stand)旁边(by)，表示“等待着什么”或者“站在旁边支持”。表示站在后方支持的stand behind也是“支持”的意思。

“结婚刚刚一个星期，丈夫就被公司炒了鱿鱼，妻子说会支持到底”

She promised to **stand by** me.

M·O·R·E

- stand by (sb)
  等待，支持（某人）
- stand behind
  支持

There is a beautiful blonde lady **standing by** the car outside.
外面有个漂亮的金发女郎站在轿车旁边。

I'll **stand by** you.
我会支持你的。

She's the only one who **stood by** me in all this.
她是唯一一个能够支持我所有事情的人。

You're my friend and I will try to **stand by** you through this.
你是我朋友，我会想尽办法帮助你挺过去的。

A: Are you ready for me to help you? 你准备接受我的帮助了吗?
B: Not yet. Just stand by until we start. 还没呢，稍等一会吧，我们马上开始。

stand for 表现，支持

What does FBI stand for?表示“FBI代表什么意思？”。像这样，stand for最主要的含义是用来表示“代表……”，“表现……”。另外，也可以用来表示“支持……”，“为某人说话”等。

“沉迷于微博的朋友问道BBL是什么话”

What does "BBL" stand for?

What exactly does that **stand for**?
那到底是什么意思？

That's what this ring **stands for**.
这就是这个指环的含义。

You said that you **stood for** the poor.
你说你会为穷人说话的。

A: The H on that car stands for Hyundae. **那辆车上面的字母H代表现代。**
B: I've heard they are pretty good cars. **我听说它们都是些不错的车。**

stand out 突出，明显

字面含义单纯表示“站在外面”，而日常生活中常用作“突出”，“显眼”等含义。

“想要突出的话就要努力长高”

I want to be a person who always stands out in a crowd.

M·O·R·E

- stand out
  站在外面，突出
- stand out in a crowd
  鹤立鸡群

She's **standing out** in the rain.
她站在外面淋着雨。

He **stands out** in a crowd because he's so tall.
他站在人群中非常显眼，因为个子太高了。

I can tell. A real lady always **stands out** in a crowd.
我知道。是金子总会发光的。

A: Berry has gotten excellent grades this year. **贝瑞这个学期的成绩非常好。**
B: He stands out from the rest of his classmates. **他是我们班里成绩最突出的。**

stand somebody (sth) up 放鸽子，树立

stand up表示自己起身或者树立其他事物，因此stand somebody up表示使某人站在外面，可以用来表示“放鸽子”，“失约”等。

“一个猥琐男苦苦相求见自己一面，出于恻隐之心来到了约会场所，没想到被放鸽子了”

I can't believe he stood me up the other night.

M·O·R·E

- stand sb up
  放某人的鸽子
- stand sth up
  树立某物
- get (be) stood up
  放鸽子

I don't like being **stood up**!

我不喜欢被放鸽子！

Your sister **stood me up** the other night.

你妹妹那天晚上放我鸽子了。

How could she just **stand me up** on a date?

她怎么能够放我的鸽子呢?

A: Someone knocked the trash can over. 有人打翻了垃圾桶。

B: Stand it up and start putting the trash back inside. 把它扶起来，再把外面的垃圾倒回去。

stand up for 支持，拥护

虽然站了起来(stand up)，但特指为了……而站起来(for somebody (something))，表示“支持……”，“拥护某人”，“替某人说话”等。

“这个世界上有谁没有昧着良心说过话呢”

Many of us are afraid to stand up for what is right.

M·O·R·E

- stand up for sb (sth, what)
  支持……拥护
- stand up for oneself
  不被他人所左右，自立

Could you **stand up for** me, please?

你能帮我说说话吗?

I'm just a guy who **stands up for** what I believe in.

我只是一个相信自己主张的人。

Don't be afraid to **stand up for** what is right.

不要害怕支持正确的观点。

It's time you **stood up for** yourself. Tell him you don't like that.

你是时候自立了。你得告诉他你不喜欢那样。

A: Some students like to study taekwondo. 有些学生喜欢学跆拳道。

B: Well, it helps them stand up for themselves. 恩，对自我防御很有帮助。

stand up to 面对……

字面含义为面向(to)……站起来，因此stand up to表示“对抗……”，“面对”等。另外，stand up to+动词表示“为了做某事而站起来”。

“老板连着两个月让员工加班，对此愤愤不平的朋友”

Why don't you stand up to your boss?

M·O·R·E

- stand up to+动词
  为了做某事而站起来
- stand up to
  对抗……面对……

She **stands up to** follow him to the door.
她站起来跟他走到了门口。

I went there to **stand up to** him.
我是为了勇敢地面对他才去的。

You **stood up to** the boss, nobody does that.
你对抗了老板，没人敢那么做。

A: The teacher treated him very unfairly. 老师对他非常不公平。
B: Did he stand up to the teacher? 他顶撞老师了吗?

stand on one's own (two) feet 双腿而立，自立

stand on+地点表示站在……的上面，即stand on the roof表示站在屋顶上，stand on the table表示站在桌子上。stand on one's own feet表示自己双脚而立，换句话说就是自立，独立等。

“我们在进化的过程中渐渐用双腿行走”

Evolution led man to stand on two feet.

M·O·R·E

- stand on
  站在……的上面
- stand on stage
  站在舞台上
- stand on one's own feet
  双腿而立，自立
- stand on one's head (neck)
  倒立

I can **stand on my own two feet** now.
我现在可以自立了。

I am trying my hardest to **stand on my own two feet**.
我为了自立做出了非常大的努力。

Jim can **stand on** his head for several minutes.
吉姆可以倒立好几分钟。

A: It's time for you to stand on your own two feet. 你已经到了自立的年纪了。
B: But I still need my parents to help me. 不过我仍然需要父母帮我。

More Expressions

- **stand back** 后退

  Just **stand back**. Give me some room.
  后退，给我点空间。

- **stand guard (over sth (sb))**
  监视，小心，警惕

  During my time in the army, I **stood guard** many nights.
  我在服兵役的时候，经常会值夜班。

- **stand trial (for (on))** 站在法庭上

  She's going to **stand trial** for stealing that jewelry. 她会因偷窃罪名站在法庭上的。

- **as it stands (as it is now)**
  按照现在的状态

  As it stands, I won't be getting paid for a while.
  从现在的状态来看，我短期内不会拿到工资的。

I stand corrected. 我承认自己错了。

You don't have a leg to stand on.
你根本就没有任何根据支持你的观点。

You may take the stand.
请站在证人席。

不要摔倒

Fall

fall表示从悬崖上掉下来(fall off a cliff)或倒在床上(fall onto the bed)或在地板或台阶上摔倒(fall down the stairs)等。由此衍生出的还有fall short，表示见底，用光等，另外，fall asleep或fall in love等fall+形容词形式表示陷入某种状态。

基本概念

1 摔倒（在地上），减少，掉落

Did you hurt yourself when you fell? 你摔倒的时候受伤了吗?

She slipped and fell in the shower this morning. 她早上洗澡的时候不小心滑倒了。

2 成为（某种状态）（fall+形容词）

Why did you fall asleep in church? 你怎么在教堂睡觉了?

I'm falling in love with you. 我爱上你了。

fall asleep 睡着

fall用作become含义的典型例句。asleep表示“睡着的”，为形容词形态，两个词共同组成的fall asleep表示“睡着”。尤其fall asleep ...ing表示“做某事的过程中睡着”。

“到底喝了多少酒，直接把头栽进马桶里了”

You fell asleep with your head in the toilet.

M·O·R·E

- fall asleep
  睡着
- fall asleep ...ing
  做某事的过程中睡着

Don't **fall asleep** at the wheel.
不要在开车的时候睡觉。

She **has fallen asleep** waiting for you to call.
她在等你电话的时候睡着了。

A: Have you seen where Tammy is? 你看见塔米在哪里了吗?
B: She fell asleep a few hours ago. 她几个小时前就睡着了。

fall in love 陷入爱河

所有人都喜欢的一句话。在这里fall同样充当了become的作用，想要指相爱的人，就可以用fall in love with somebody。

“俗话说情人眼里出西施，居然指着丑八怪女朋友说”

I fell in love with the most beautiful girl in the world.

M·O·R·E

- fall in love
  坠入爱河
- fall in love with sb
  与某人相爱

She is definitely going to **fall in love with** you again!
她肯定会重新爱上你的!

I've got to stop **falling in love** with strange women.
我不能再和陌生的女人坠入爱河了。

I **fell in love with** my divorce lawyer.
我和我的离婚律师相爱了。

A: They fell in love when they were working together. 他们在一起工作时相爱了。
B: How romantic. Did they get married? 真浪漫。他们结婚了吗?

fall short of 缺乏某物

在这里的fall同样为become的含义，fall short of表示“缺乏某物”，“……不足”等，与be (run) short of有着相同的含义。

“对这次约会非常期待，没想到对方竟是个个头不到150cm的小男人”

He **was falling far short of** her high expectations.

M·O·R·E

- fall short of ...ing
  没有……

Our supply of medicine **fell short**.

我们的药供给不足了。

We help people who **fall short of** cash.

我们帮助那些资金短缺的人。

At least they **fell short of** hitting me.

至少他们没有打我。

A: Did you make enough money to take a trip? 你挣够去旅行的钱了吗?

B: No, I fell short of the amount that I needed. 没有，现有的钱还不够。

fall apart 破碎，搞砸，状态恶化

apart表示“破碎”，因此fall apart表示“完全破碎”。可以用来表示某件事“结果不好”或者“状态恶化”等，经常会用作现在进行时。

“完全没有爱情，纯粹以金钱和权力所促成的婚姻会持续多久呢”

His marriage **fell apart** after a short while.

My entire body **is falling apart**.

我全身都不舒服。

My life **is falling apart**.

我的人生越来越糟糕了。

Things **were falling apart** at home.

家里的事情都乱成一团了。

Everything **fell apart**. We had a big fight and then I got slapped.

所有事情都搞砸了。我们狠狠地吵了一架，我还被抽了一耳光。

A: Are you telling me your car is broken again? 你是说，你的车又坏了?

B: Yeah, it's been falling apart recently. 嗯，最近刚刚坏的。

fall down 倒下，倒塌，失败

最基本的含义为掉在地上，或者从上至下掉落下来，fall down a cliff表示从悬崖上掉下来，fall down the stairs表示在从台阶上摔下来。也可以用来表示“失败”。

“早上起床晚，急急忙忙穿上衣服，就直接上班了”

I fell down the stairs. I'm fine.

M·O·R·E

- sth falls down
  ……倒塌
- fall down the stairs
  从台阶上摔下来

My father **fell down** the stairs the other day.
我爸爸有一天从楼梯上摔了下来。

I **fell down** the stairs and broke my tooth.
我从楼梯上摔了下来，摔掉了牙。

The building **fell down**. Three people were crushed to death.
那座建筑倒塌了，3个人被压死了。

A: There is a lot of ice on the sidewalks today. 今天人行道上结了很厚的冰。
B: Be careful that you don't fall down. 小心点，别摔倒了。

fall for 被（玩笑等）……瞒骗，开始恋爱

是个不常见的短语，具有两种含义。首先可以表示被对方有意图的计谋或谎话“所蒙骗”，其次为fall for somebody的形态，表示“坠入爱河”。

“女朋友说喜欢学校的老大，要提出分手，此时模范生的脑海中”

Why does a girl fall for a bad boy?

M·O·R·E

- Don't fall for it.
  不要被骗。
  (不能坠入爱河。)
- Did you fall for him?
  你喜欢过他?

Don't **fall for it**. He'll only steal your money.
不要被骗。他就是为了骗你的钱。

You **fall for it** every time!
你每次都会被骗!

She's a patient. I can't **fall for** our patients.
她是个患者，我不能喜欢上我的患者。

A: Bonita is the smartest girl in our class. 博妮塔是我们班里最聪明的女孩。
B: I always fall for girls who are intelligent. 我总会喜欢上那些有才华的女生。

fall into 陷入，开始做某事，区分

表示陷入……的内部或摔倒等，可以用来表示倒在床上或在沙发上躺下，也可以表示“开始被……吸引”。

“不能让艺人们的恋爱视频落到坏人的手中”

Don't let this fall into the wrong hands.

M·O·R·E

- fall into place
  说的没错，前后相符
- fall into the hands of
  落到某人的手中

I just **fell into** bed with my clothes on.
我没脱衣服就直接倒在了床上。

She has **fallen into** a black hole of debt.
她深陷债务的巨型黑洞。

Do you want to **fall into** the trap?
你想被骗吗?

It'**s all falling into place**. The happy ending.
所有细节都能对上，真是个完美的结局。

A: How did Patty hurt her leg? 帕蒂的腿是怎么受伤的?
B: She fell into a ditch while she was walking. 她走路的时候不小心掉进了水坑里。

fall off 从……脱离出去，（价格等）下降

字面含义为从本体处脱离(fall)出去(off)。不仅可以用来表示从自行车或屋顶上掉下来，还可以表示衣扣等掉落下来，也可以用来指价格等的下降。

“害怕撞到别人，就和自行车一块儿摔在地上”

I fell off my bike to avoid hitting a person.

M·O·R·E

- fall off
  从……摔下来
- fall off the wagon
  （戒酒的人）重新开始

Nothing big, I **fell off** my bike.
没什么大不了的，我从自行车上摔下来了。

You had an accident. You **fell off** our ladder.
你出事了，从我们的梯子上掉了下来。

Their arms have to be ready to **fall off**.
他们的胳膊差点就脱臼了。

She **has** definitely **fallen off the wagon**.
她重新开始喝酒了。

A: Be careful you don't fall off the cliff. 小心点，别从悬崖上掉下来。
B: This mountain is very difficult to climb. 这座山很难爬啊。

fall on 倒在……上，（生日，纪念日等）是哪一天

表示倒在……上，倒向某人等，可以表示人“倒在……上方”或事物“倒在……上”。也可以用来比喻“纪念日是哪一天”或责任“归咎于某人”等。

“被老婆发现好多次刷卡都是用在酒店上”

He **falls on** his knees in front of her.

M·O·R·E

- (生日，纪念日) fall on+星期
  ……是哪一天
- (工作，义务) fall on sb
  ……是某人的责任，义务
- (邀请) fall on deaf ears
  被无视，被抹杀
- sb falls on hard times
  经历痛苦
- fall on (to) one's knees
  下跪在某人面前
- fall on (to) sb (sth)
  倒下，失去意识
- fall on one's head
  底朝天倒下
- fall on one's back
  后背着地
- fall on the floor
  倒在地上

I can't believe you laughed when I **fell on** the ice.
真不敢相信，我滑倒在冰面时你居然笑我。

I **fell on** the floor this morning.
我今天早上倒在了地上。

My birthday will **fall on** a Sunday this year.
我今年的生日是星期六。

Why does that responsibility always **fall on** us?
为什么那个责任总要归结到我们头上？

He suddenly lost his balance and **fell on** his back.
他突然失去了平衡，向后倒去。

The lunar new year **falls on** a different day each year.
农历春节每年都不会在同一天。

A: What day will you celebrate your birthday? 你哪天庆祝生日？
B: It's going to fall on a Friday this year. 今年应该是星期五。

A: A pile of books fell on me when I was working. 在我工作的时候，一摞书掉了下来，砸到了我。
B: Oh, dear. Did you get hurt by them? 哦，天啊，你受伤没？

A: Did the kids enjoy going skating? 孩子们喜欢滑冰吗？
B: Yeah. They had fun but they fell on their backs a lot. 是的，他们玩得非常开心，不过总会滑倒。

fall out 发生，出现……的结果，斗争

字面含义为向外部(out)掉落(fall)，表示某种事情“发生”，“出现……的结果”等。另外，也可以表示头发或牙齿脱落，而fall out with的形式表示“与某人斗争”。

“印有美女图案的名片从老公上衣口袋里掉了出来”

What is the card that fell out of your jacket?

It wasn't my ring! It **fell out of** his jacket!
这不是我的戒指！是从他的外套里掉下来的！

I **fell out of** your bed this morning.
我今天早上从你的床上掉了下来。

My hair started **falling out**.
我开始脱发了。

We had some kind of big-time **falling out**.
我们大吵了一架。

M·O·R·E

- fall out of bed
  从床上掉下来
- fall out with sb
  与某人斗争

A: So Maggie and Jason have been fighting? 就是说马吉和詹森一直在争吵?

B: Yeah, they fell out over their credit card bills. 嗯，他们因为信用卡账单的事情吵个不停。

More Expressions

- **slip and fall** 摔倒
  She **slipped and fell** and hit her head on the floor. 她滑倒了，头部撞到了地板。

- **fall back on** 依靠，依赖
  She took off her shirt and **fell back on** the couch. 她脱下了衬衫，依靠在沙发上。

- **fall behind sb (sth)** 落后
  I **have just fallen behind on** my homework. 我的作业进度落后了。

- **fall flat on one's face** 向前倒去
  She **fell flat on her face** and broke her nose. 她向前倒了过去，摔坏了鼻子。

- **fall victim (prey) to**
  患病，被……欺骗，被攻击
  We **have fallen victim to** an epidemic.
  我们患上了传染病。
  Laura **fell victim to** her love.
  劳拉被自己的爱所蒙骗了。

- **fall in with** 偶然遇见天作之合，统一
  I was just a kid and I **fell in with** the wrong crowd.
  我当时只是个孩子，碰到一群不良少年。

该停手就停手

Stop

表示停下手中的事情或行为的意思。经常用stop something (somebody)或stop ...ing 的形式表示使某事停下或阻止某人的行动。不过stop to+动词不同于stop+动词，这表示未来做某事而停止，这和try，remember，begin的用法相同。换句话说，stop to fight表示的含义并不是停止战斗，而是停下原来的事情，进入战斗。

基本概念

1 停止，静止，停手

Please stop just before that traffic light. 在红绿灯前停一下。

Stop right where you are. 站在原地别动。

2 中断，使放弃，停下……

Would you stop that? 你能不能停下?

Stop doing that. 不要那样了。

Stop the bus. 把大巴停下。

3 （名词）停止，中止，停车（场）

What's the next stop? 下一个停车场在哪?

Where's the bus stop? 公交站在哪?

stop something (somebody) 让……停止

stop后面接上名词，即stop something表示“使……停止”，“停下”，stop somebody表示“阻止某人的行动”，“使某人停手”。

“和女朋友亲得不可开交，旁边的朋友实在看不下去了，喊道‘你们怎么不去开房间’”

Stop the kissing! Get a room!

M·O·R·E

- Stop it (that)!
  停下（住手）
- stop what sb's doing
  使某人停止做某事

Please **stop** the fighting!
请别吵了！

We couldn't **stop** the bleeding.
我们没办法止住血。

Stop it! I'm serious!
行了，我是认真的！

A: I heard this house has a ghost. 我听说这间房子有鬼。
B: Stop it! You're scaring me. 别说了！我有点害怕。

stop for something 为了做某事而停手，停下来做某事

在前面的句式stop something中间加了一个for，stop for something表示“为了做某事而停手”，for后面的部分就是“停手”，“住手”的原因。

“一家人出去旅行，孩子突然说想吃冰淇淋”

Do you want to stop for ice cream?

M·O·R·E

- stop for sth
  停下来做某事
- stop for a moment
  暂停一下

You can go to the toilet when we **stop for** gas.
我们经过加油站的时候你可以上卫生间。

We **stopped for** a cocktail after work.
我们下班之后经过那里喝了点鸡尾酒。

Can we **stop for** a moment please?
我们能暂停一会吗?

A: Where do you want to stop for breakfast? 你想去哪里吃早餐？
B: Let's go to a pancake restaurant. 我们去pancake餐厅吧。

stop to 停下来做某事，为了做某事而经过

stop to+动词中，to之后的部分为停下来的目的，因此这个句子表示“停下来做某事”，也可以用成stop and+动词，最常用的就是stop to think。

“老婆说今天要加班，却走进了一家酒吧，正巧被下班回家的老公看到”

He stopped to stare at her going into the bar.

M·O·R·E

- stop and+动词
  停下来做某事
- stop to think
  停下来好好想想
- stop to look at (talk)
  停下来看（说）

I just **stopped to** see if I could help.
我就是停下来看看我能不能帮忙。

Okay, then why don't you **stop and go** to bed?
好，要不你停下来去睡觉呗?

Why don't you **stop and ask** for directions?
你为什么不停下来问问路呢?

Don't **stop to think**. Just ... tell me.
不要自己一个人想，和我说说吧。

A: Look at the beautiful scenery. 看看那漂亮的景色。
B: We'll stop to take some pictures of it. 我们得停下来拍几张照片。

stop ...ing 停止做某事

stop something中的something可以被动词的 ...ing替换，成为stop的宾语。该句式表示“停止做某事”，“放下手中的事情”等。

“要学会区分stop to tell a lie和 stop telling me a lie”

Would you please stop telling me lies?

M·O·R·E

- stop for sth
  为了做某事而停下
- stop for a moment
  暂停一下

I always **stop eating** before I feel full.
我每次都吃到饱为止。

I won't stop to smoke. I **stopped smoking**.
我不会停下来抽烟的，我早就戒烟了。

I've had it. **Stop acting** like my mother.
真累啊，别总像我妈似的。

Will you **stop doing** that?
你能住手吗?

A: You have to stop smoking. 你得戒烟了。
B: I know, but it's very difficult. 我知道，不过这很难。

(Please) Stop ...ing! 停下……!

前文中的stop ...ing为祈使句，尤其常用作stop ...ing!的形态。相反，Don't stop ...ing表示“不要停下某事”，即“继续做某事”。

“把女朋友带到了家里，弟弟却不解人情地说出了我和前女友同居的事情”

Stop saying that! Will you say something else?

M·O·R·E

- Please stop bugging me.
  请别烦我了。
- Stop talking.
  别说话了。
- Stop doing that!
  别那么做!
- Stop lying to me!
  别对我说谎了!
- Stop saying that!
  别那么说!

Stop being lazy. You need to study harder.
别那么懒，你得更加勤奋地学习。

Stop looking at me like that.
不要那么看我。

Stop talking to me like you're my boyfriend!
别说得你像我男朋友似的。

Stop saying you're sorry.
别说抱歉的话。

A: Stop jumping on the bed you two! 你们两个，别在床上蹦了!
B: But it's so much fun, Dad. 不过这很好玩啊，老爸。

stop somebody (sth) from ...ing 阻止某人做某事，不让某人做某事

stop somebody from ...ing表示“阻止某人做某事”或“劝别人不做某事”等。

“很久以前就有一个坏习惯，只要看到丈夫的后脑勺就想狠狠地拍一下”

There's nothing to **stop me from** divorcing him.

M·O·R·E

- stop sb from ...ing
  使某人停止做某事

I couldn't **stop you from** doing this.
我不能阻止你做这事。

Why did she **stop me from** dating Adam?
她为什么要阻止我和亚当约会呢?

I came running to **stop her from** leaving.
我跑过来是要阻止她离开的。

A: There are too many items on that table. 桌子上有太多东西了。
B: We need to stop it from falling over. 我们不能让这些掉下来。

stop oneself from ...ing 忍住不做某事

这次控制的不是别人，而是“阻止自己做某事”，可以理解为“自制”，“强忍”等，也可以单纯用作stop oneself。

“老公一天到晚只会洗碗，现在只要看到碗就抑制不住刷碗的冲动”

He tried to **stop himself from** doing the dishes, but couldn't.

M·O·R·E

- stop oneself
  自制，强忍
- stop oneself (from) ...ing
  忍住不做某事

Why did you **stop yourself**?
你为什么忍住了?

I can't **stop myself from** loving you.
我无法阻止自己爱上你。

She **stopped herself from** laughing.
她强忍住了笑容。

A: I'm getting too fat these days. 我这几天长得太胖了。
B: You have to stop yourself from eating too much. 你不能再吃那么多东西了。

can't stop ...ing 不得不做某事

can't为否定，stop从内容上也是否定语。因此否定的否定为强烈的肯定，即can't stop ...ing表示无法停止，换句话说就是“不得不继续做某事”。

“乘坐破旧的船到处游荡，没想到……”

I'm nauseous and I **can't stop** throwing up.

M·O·R·E

- can't stop ...ing
  不得不继续做某事
- can't stop sth (sb)
  无法停止做某事

Ever since you left, I **can't stop** thinking about you.
自从你离开之后，我无法克制思念的心情。

I **can't stop** crying.
我只好一直哭下去。

I'm sure you **can't stop** loving me.
我相信你会一直爱我。

I **couldn't stop** laughing at your story.
听了你的话，我没办法忍住笑。

A: Why are you always so sad? 你为什么总是那么悲伤?
B: I can't stop thinking about my ex-boyfriend. 我一直忘不了前男友。

stop at 停在……

表示停在特定的地点。stop at后面接上要停下的地点名词就可以了。

"在一个陌生的地方，意外地碰见了自己的朋友"

I got lost and had to stop at a store for directions.

Does this train **stop at** Yoksam?
这列火车在yoksam站停吗?

How about we **stop at** the store and get something to eat?
我们在商店停下来去买点吃的怎么样?

Why don't you **stop at** a bar for a couple of drinks?
你为什么不去酒吧喝两杯?

Do you mind if we **stop at** the next motel?
你介意我们停在汽车旅馆旁边吗?

A: Can we stop at someplace to eat? 我们能停下来吃点东西吗?
B: Sure. You must be getting hungry. 好的，你肯定是饿了。

stop by (in) 访问

表示"路过的时候暂时拜访"(make a short visit)，stop by 后面接要停留的地点就可以了，stop in同样表示暂时路过的意思。

"回家的路上得路过干洗店取明天聚会要穿的衣服"

I have to stop by the cleaners on my way home.

Stop by any time after Friday.
星期五之后随时都可以来。

We just wanted to **stop by** and say good night.
我们就是想路过说一声晚安。

I just **stopped by** to see how you're doing.
我就是想经过的时候看看你过得怎么样。

I'll **stop by** the drugstore.
我要去趟药店。

A: Some friends will stop by this afternoon. 今天下午会有一些朋友要来。
B: What time will they be coming? 他们大概几点到?

M·O·R·E

- stop by+地点
  暂时路过某处
- stop by an ATM
  暂时停在自动提款机前面
- stop by and (to) see (how)
  暂时路过见某人
- stop in
  暂时路过

stop off 暂时经过

同样表示脱离原来的方向(off)，暂时停下(stop)。像stop off for a rest一样，stop off for表示“为了做某事而路过”，而stop off at the store中的stop off at表示“路过某处”。

“女朋友在下班的路上路过书店时买了一本自我修养的书”

She stopped off at the bookstore on her way home.

M·O·R·E

- stop off for sth
  暂时路过做某事
- stop off at someplace
  暂时路过某处

I **stopped off at** the Korean deli to get some crackers.
我路过韩国商场时，买了点鞭炮。

I **stopped off** and picked up some dessert for you ladies.
我路过时，给你们几位女士买了些甜点。

Let's **stop off for** a drink.
我们停下来喝点东西吧。

Why don't you **stop off at** my place after work?
你下班后来我家坐坐呗?

A: I need to stop off at the post office. 我得去趟邮局。
B: Me too. I have some letters to mail. 我也是，我有几封信件要邮。

stop over 在旅行地点暂时停下，中途下车

stop over表示“暂时停留”或“短期滞留在旅游地点”。另外，换乘飞机时也可以用来表示暂时停留，其名词形式为stopover。

“飞往芝加哥的路上，需要在洛杉矶换乘”

I stopped over in Los Angeles on our way to Chicago.

M·O·R·E

- stop over for+sth
  为了做某事而暂时路过
- stop over+时间名词
  暂时停留……时间
- stop over in (at)
  旅行过程中暂时停留
- stopover
  短期停留

Why don't you just **stop over** for coffee sometime?
有时间你就过来喝杯咖啡。

Why don't you **stop over** some night for a home-cooked meal?
你有时间的话就过来一块吃顿便饭吧。

We had to **stop over** one night in Los Angeles.
我们得在洛杉矶留宿一晚。

A: The plane is going to stop over in Ireland. 飞机要在爱尔兰停一次。
B: Oh, that sounds like an interesting place. 哦，听起来是个不错的地方。

stop 停车场

stop作为名词时也可以表示前文中的“停止”，“中止”等含义，但在日常生活中最常用的就是公交或地铁等交通工具的“停车场”，如“bus stop”（公交站）。

“看到约会的对象非常讨人喜欢，就想把人带到家里喝杯咖啡的男生”

We’re at my **stop**. Would you like to have coffee?

M·O·R·E

- miss one's stop
  错过车站
- get off at ... station
  在某车站下车

I missed my **stop**.
我过站了。

Take the subway for one **stop** and get off at Paddington Station.
乘坐地铁，过一站在帕丁顿下车。

What's the most convenient **stop** to reach the Chrysler building?
要去克莱斯勒大厦的话应该在哪一站下车？

A: Why are all of those people standing there? 为什么所有人都站在那里？

B: That's a bus stop and they're waiting to go home. 那是一个公交站，他们正等车回家呢。

More Expressions

- **stop short of** 起码不会做（危险的行为）
  She **stopped shot of** hurting herself.
  她至少不会自残。

- **make a stop** 停止
  I need to **make a stop** at the rest area.
  我得在休息区休息一会。

- **stop at nothing** 毫不犹豫地做
  She would **stop at nothing** to impress you.她为了给你留下深刻的印象，什么事情都做得出来。

- **pull out all the stops** 使出全力
  We’**re pulling out all the stops**.
  我们使尽了全力。

- **The buck stops here** 责任我来扛
  Don’t worry. **The buck stops** with me. 不要担心，我会负责的。

不要离开，留在这里

Stay/ Move

stay表示不去别的地方，留在原有的地方。因此stay home，stay here表示留在家里或留在这里，而 stay away from或stay out表示“远离某处”。像前文中的fall，feel，keep，turn一样，如果后面接上形容词，变成stay+形容词形式的话，则表示“处在……的状态”。

基本概念

1 停留，居住，原地不动

Can you tell me where you're going to stay? 你能告诉我你要住在哪里吗?

How long are you planning to stay in the US? 你打算在美国待多久?

2 处在……的状态（stay+形容词）

Please stay calm. 请镇静。

3 （名词）停留，滞留（期间）

Enjoy your stay. 祝你玩得愉快。

We're going to extend our stay in Seoul. 我们打算在首尔多待几天。

4 move 移动，走

Don't move. 不要动。

(It's) Time to move. 该走了。

Let's move it. 我们走吧。

Let's move out. 我们出发吧。

stay and+动词 留下做某事

stop and+动词表示停下来做某事，同理，stay and+动词表示“留下来做某事”。stay像stop一样，可以预示接下来要发生的动作。

“朋友来探病，居然要顺便献个血再走，真是个善良的人”

I think I'm going to stay and donate some blood.

M·O·R·E

- stay and+动词 留下来做某事
- stay to+动词 留下做某事

Would you just **stay and** help me get dressed?
你能留下来帮我穿衣服吗?

I'm going to **stay and** read my book.
我打算留下来看我的书。

I think one of us should **stay and** help her.
我觉得我们之中的一个人应该留下来帮助她。

He **stayed to** see if it was done.
他留下来看看有没有完成。

A: Will you be here this afternoon? 你今天下午会在这吗?
B: Yeah, I'm going to stay and organize my desk. 恩,我打算留下来整理书桌。

let somebody stay 让某人留下来

虽然不能称得上是短语，但在日常生活中经常会使用到。不是我自己做什么，而是让somebody留下来，即挽留的意思。

“来到一对新婚夫妇朋友的家，却不合情理地要求在这里住一个月”

Just let me stay a month.

Will you please **let her stay** with me?
你能让她留下来陪我吗?

We'll just **let her stay** for a month.
我们打算让她待一个月。

If you **let her stay** here, she will stay forever.
如果你让她留在这，她就会一直待下去的。

A: Frank has been living at his uncle's house. 弗兰克一直住在他叔叔家里。
B: His uncle let him stay in the spare bedroom. 他叔叔让他住在一间多出来的卧室里。

stay the same 没有变化，依旧

stay the same表示“完全没有变化，和原来一样”。另外，stay (as)+名词表示“（作为……）留下”。

“自己干了好几年还是个小科员，没想到同时进入公司的同事已经当上部长了”

Do you think we'll **stay friends** after this?

Everything is great! Everything **stayed the same**!
一切都很好！一切都和原来一样！

Promise me that you and I will always **stay the same**.
向我保证，我们永远都不会变。

Is it better if we just **stay friends**?
我们做朋友是不是会好点？

A: Brad Pitt doesn't seem very old. 布拉德·皮特看起来没那么老。
B: He has stayed the same for about 20 years. 他和20年前一样。

stay+形容词 处于……的状态

stay后面如果接形容词或者动词的过去分词的话，就表示“保持……的状态”，“处在……的状态”，是个比较常用的句式。

“给老婆打电话，说要做的事情太多了，不得不加班”

I have to **stay late** because there's a lot of work to do.

M·O·R·E

- stay cool
  沉着
- stay awake
  醒着
- stay late
  留到很晚
- stay loose
  冷静，保持冷静
- stay married
  维持婚姻

What's your secret for **staying healthy**?
你保持健康的秘诀是什么？

Stay cool, Cindy.
冷静点，辛迪。

I'm just trying to **stay awake**.
我就是想清醒一些。

Can we please **stay focused** on my problem here?
我们能集中在我的问题上吗？

A: You have to stay late tonight. 你今天晚上得留到很晚。
B: You can't be serious. I want to go home. 你不是认真的吧。我想回家。

stay home 留在家里

stay后面接副词的情况，在这里home为副词，stay home表示不外出(go out)，留在家里。

"自古以来，独自一个人是很难保证学习效率的"

I tried to **stay home** and study by myself but I can't.

M·O·R·E

- stay home
  留在家里
- stay home from work (school)
  不上班（上学）

Do you mind if we **stay home** tonight?
你介意我们今天晚上待在家里吗?

Do you want to go out or **stay home**?
你想出去，还是想待在家里?

Why don't you **stay home** from work today and just hang out with me?
你今天为什么不请个假和我一起玩呢?

A: Can you afford to go on vacation? **你有时间去度假吗?**
B: No, I will have to stay home this year. **不行，我今年得待在家里。**

stay here 留在这里

stay here (there)表示留在这里（那里），后面经常会接with somebody或表达时间的词组。另外，如果主语变成事物的话，stays here 表示"这是秘密"。

"外婆得了老年痴呆症，妈妈吩咐儿子不要出门，在家照顾她"

Just **stay here**. Keep an eye on your grandma.

M·O·R·E

- sb stays here
  某人留在这里
- sth stays here
  ……是秘密

I'll just **stay here** with you.
我会留在这里陪你的。

I'm going to **stay there** for a while.
我要去那待一会儿。

My mom is waiting for me. I can't **stay here** all night.
我妈正在等我。我不能在这里待一宿。

What is said here, **stays here**.
在这里说的所有话都是秘密。

A: I wish I didn't have to go. **我希望我不去也可以。**
B: Then don't. Stay here. **那就别去了，留在这里吧。**

stay(for) 滞留（一定时间）

如果说stay home (here)是表达停留的地点，那么这个短语就可以用来表示停留的时间，stay后面接时间副词（句子）就可以了。

“朋友提出了非常不靠谱的建议，说要玩电脑玩个通宵”

Let's stay overnight to play computer games.

M·O·R·E

- stay longer
  多留一段时间
- stay another day
  再多待一天
- stay too long
  滞留太久
- stay the night
  留宿(stay overnight)
- stay as long as sb wants
  想留多久就留多久，
  留……时间
- stay for sb (sth)
  因某人留下

I need to **stay** another day.
我得多留一天。

Maybe we should **stay longer** if you want to.
如果你希望的话，我们也许应该多留一段时间。

Are you planning on **staying the night**?
你今天晚上打算熬夜吗?

You can **stay as long as you want**. I don't mind.
你想待多久就待多久，我完全不介意。

Can you **stay for** dinner?
你可以留下来吃晚饭吗?

Can you **stay for** some tea?
你可以留下来喝点茶吗?

A: Would you like to stay longer? **你想多留一会吗?**
B: If you don't mind, I'm ready to leave. **如果你不介意的话，我现在打算走了。**

A: How long are you planning to stay in the US? **你打算在美国待多久?**
B: I'm planning to stay for three weeks. **我打算待3个星期。**

A: Athena, I'm glad you could come by. **雅典娜，很高兴你可以过来。**
B: I can only stay for about ten minutes. **我只能在这里待10分钟。**

stay at 留在某处

想要表达停留的地点就可以用介词at，想表示“留在某人的家中”是可以使用stay at her place，比如说stay at kate's。

“厚颜无耻的人经常会在朋友的家里赖着不走，直到对方把自己赶走”

I'll stay at your place until you kick me out.

M·O·R·E

- stay at+人的名字's
  待在某人的家里
- stay at one's place
  留在某人的家里
- stay at some place
  留在某个地方

I'm staying at the Intercontinental Hotel.
我打算待在洲际酒店。

I stayed at Julie's last night.
我昨天晚上留宿在朱莉的家里了。

Tonight I will stay at my place.
今天晚上我要待在家里。

Can I stay at your apartment again tonight?
今天晚上我能再到你家里住吗?

A: Did you enjoy your stay at our hotel? 你昨天晚上在酒店休息得怎么样?
B: Yes, thank you. It was great. 嗯，挺好的，谢谢。

stay away from 远离，从……脱离

字面含义为从(from)某处脱离开(away)，待在(stay)远处，因此stay away from somebody (something)表示“不靠近……”，“远离某物”等。

“老爸被狐狸精欺骗，丢掉了所有的钱，我急忙劝道”

I'm strongly suggesting that you stay away from her.

M·O·R·E

- Stay away from me!
  闪开!
- Don't stay away so long.
  经常来啊。

Stay away from my daughter or you're a dead man.
离我女儿远点，不然你会死得很惨。

She is so mean. I think you should stay away from her.
她太小气了，我觉得你应该离她远点。

Stay away from the traffic accident.
不要提那次交通事故。

A: What do you think of Brandon? 你觉得布兰顿怎么样?
B: Stay away from him. He's no good. 你最好离他远点，他不是个好东西。

stay back 后退

字面含义为留在(stay)后面(back)，表示不要靠近，或者后退等。可以在后面接上from something来表达需要回避的具体事物。

“和女朋友一起在树林里散步，前方突然出现了一条蛇，急忙对女朋友喊道”

I need you to **stay back** right now!

You have to **stay back**. I have a bad flu.
你不要靠近我，我患上流感了。

Just **stay back**!
离我远点！

Stay back! I'm married.
离我远点！我已经结婚了。

A: Stay back from the side of the mountain. 不要靠近山坡。
B: It looks very dangerous over there. 那里看起来的确很危险。

stay in 留在某处

stay in something表示“留在……的内部”，相反stay out表示“不进入某处，留在外面”。

“朋友不愿意参加派对，只喜欢待在家里自己一个人玩，对这种人说道”

Do you really want to **stay in** your house?

M·O·R·E

- stay in
  留在……的里面
- stay in there
  留在那里，忍受住
- stay out
  留在外面
- stay out there
  留在外面
- stay in touch with
  与某人取得联系

You **stay in** the car. I'll be right back.
你们待在车里。我去去就来。

I can **stay out** as late as I want.
我可以一直待在外面，想几点回去就几点回去。

It's best you **stay in there**.
你能留在这里简直太好了。

Let's **stay outside** for a while.
我们出去待一会儿吧。

A: Look at that rain. I'm going to stay in today. 瞧瞧这雨，我今天要在屋里待着。
B: Me too. I don't want to get wet. 我也是，我可不想变成落汤鸡。

stay out of 不参与某事，不靠近……

字面含义为在某物的外部(out of)，因此stay out of something表示“不靠近……”，也可以用来比喻”不介入某事”。

“住在一起的室友总喜欢对我男朋友说三道四，我的反应是”

You're not his girlfriend. Stay out of it!

M·O·R·E

- stay out of one's way (face)
  从……消失，滚开
- Stay out of trouble.
  祝你万事如意。
- (You) Stay out of this (it)!
  你给我闪开！你不要管。
- (You) Stay out of here!
  （你给我）让开！

If you **stay out of the way** and stay quiet, you stay alive.
如果你不参与，安静地待着，就能捡回一条命。

That's fine, too. Just **stay out of my face**.
那倒无所谓，就是别出现在我面前。

Well, good luck to everyone. **Stay out of trouble**.
好了，祝大家好运，万事如意。

I asked you to **stay out of this**.
我跟你说过不要管闲事。

How many times have I told you to **stay out of** my freezer?
我告诉你多少次了，不要在冰箱附近出现。

Just **stay out of this**. It's not your business.
不用管了，这和你没关系。

Tim, could you just **stay out of** it?
提姆，你能别管了吗？

I told myself to **stay out of** this, but I can't.
我对自己说不要参与这件事，不过我无法做到。

You keep your noses clean. You **stay out of trouble**.
你给我好好待着，不要惹事端。

A: Can I come see what you're doing? 我能看看你在做什么吗？
B: Stay out of here. Can't you see I'm busy? 别凑热闹，没看见我正在忙啊？

A: I hear the police arrested Carlos again. 我听说警察又逮捕了卡洛斯。
B: I know. He can't stay out of trouble. 我知道，他就是不能安分地待着。

A: Why is my ex-girlfriend calling you? 我的前女友为什么要给你打电话？
B: Please stay out of this. 这和你没关系。

stay over 停留，留宿一宿，在外面过夜

stay over特别指晚上不住在家里，在外面过夜，另外，搭乘飞机时中转过程也可以叫做stayover。

“经常对朋友们说在我家疯狂地玩一宿，对方的反应是”

Why don't we have a slumber party? I'll **stay over**.

M·O·R·E

- stay over (for)+时间名词
  待多久
- stay over till S+V
  待到……时候

We'll **stay over** till he shows up.
我们会等到他出现的。

I will **stay over** till your mother comes back.
我会等到你妈回来的。

Do you need me to **stay over** for a couple of days?
你要我再待几天吗?

I've got to get up really early, so you can't **stay over**.
我明天一定要早起，所以你不能住在这儿。

A: Where are your kids tonight? **你的孩子们今晚去哪儿了?**
B: They are staying over with their cousins. **他们要和亲戚们玩一宿。**

stay up 醒着

字面含义为站起来(up)，待着（站起来），表示待到很晚，不睡觉。stay up late表示“熬夜”，stay up all night表示“一整晚不睡觉”。

“如果想说有很多事情要做，没准会通宵达旦”

I have to **stay up** and do a little work tonight.

M·O·R·E

- stay up late
  待到很晚
- stay up until sth
  待到……
- stay up all night (...ing)
  一整晚不睡觉（做某事）

We **stayed up all night** talking.
我们一整晚都在畅谈。

We just **stayed up all night** chatting on the internet.
我们通宵聊天来着。

If you don't mind, I could **stay up late**.
如果你不介意的话，我可以一整夜不睡觉。

A: I feel like I want to go to sleep. **我好想睡觉啊。**
B: You have to try to stay up and study. **你得试试熬夜学习。**

stay with 与某人在一起

stay with sb表示“与某人留下”，stay with后面可以接something，而stay with the company则表示“留下来（继续）上班”。

“丈母娘想女儿了，打算来我们家住几天，看看女儿”

She's coming to stay with me for a couple of days.

M·O·R·E

- stay with
  停留，与某人在一起
- Stay with me!
  听我的话！
  （向即将死去的人）坚持一下！

If you want, you can **stay with** me tonight.
如果你愿意的话，今晚可以留下来陪我。

You can **stay with** me. I can take care of you.
你可以留下来和我在一起，我可以照顾你。

When we get to Chicago, can I **stay with** you?
等我们到芝加哥之后，我能和你在一起吗？

Can you hear me? **Stay with me.**
能听到我的话吗？打起精神。

A: I'd like you to stay with me tonight. **我希望你今晚可以陪我。**
B: I can stay a little longer but I have to go home at twelve. **我可以再多待一会儿，不过12点之前必须得回家。**

move in (out) 搬进来(出去)

move的最基本含义为行动，离开等动态含义，move in表示搬进来，相反move out则表示搬出去。

“交往还没到一个月，男朋友就居然提出无理要求，只好拒绝”

That's really sweet. But I can't move in with you.

M·O·R·E

- move in with
  与某人一起住，同居

I want you to **move in with** me.
我希望你能搬进来和我一起住。

You can't **move in with** me.
你不能和我同居。

I heard that he **moved to** Hollywood.
我听说他搬到好莱坞了。

Why **are** you **moving in with** my son?
你为什么要和我儿子同居？

A: How about I move in with you? **我搬过来和你一起住怎么样？**
B: Well, that would be great. **嗯，那就太好了。**

move on (to) 进行，伴奏，向前推进

move on 中的“on”表示继续进行，因此move on表示持续原来的行为，可以理解为不要停留在这里，继续前行，说下一话题等。

“开会的时候想要进入下一个主题的话，经常会用到这句话”

So let's move on to our next subject.

M·O·R·E

- move on 继续前进
- move on to 前进到……
- move on with 继续进行某事

I failed at this job, so I'm going to **move on**.
这次工作算是失败了，我打算继续前行。

You'll **move on** when you're ready.
等你准备好了就可以进入下一阶段了。

Let's **move on to** number four, shall we?
我们看第四题，好不?

We have to **move on** to Plan B.
我们不得不转入备用计划了。

A: Have we finished this part of the project? 我们完成项目的这个部分了吗?
B: Yes, let's move on to the next part. 嗯，我们进入下一个章节吧。

be moved by 被……打动

move具有打动他人心灵的含义。主要用来表示打动某人的内心，经常会使用被动形态be moved by。另外，还要记住常用的形容词moving（令人感动的=touching）。

“老婆辛辛苦苦收集了十张兑换券，换来了半只烤鸡，激动得不得了，丈夫很感动”

He was moved by his wife's charming story.

She **was so moved by** Jack's story.
她被杰克的故事深深打动。

It was very **touching** speech.
这是一次非常动人的演讲。

Thank you. Your devotion is **touching**.
很感谢，你的奉献精神非常感人。

I **was moved by** the president’s speech.
我被总统的演讲词打动了。

A: We were moved by the people that helped us. 我们被那些帮助过我们的人深深打动了。
B: I think that they were very kind. 我觉得他们都是好人。

get a move on 抓紧时间做某事

表示因为时间已经来不及了，需要抓紧时间的意思，主要会用作祈使句形态的Get a move on!或Let's get a move on!等。另外，如果用make代替get，变成make a move on的话就表示向异性示好。

"爱情上虽然没有国境、年龄的限制，但无论女老师有多么吸引人，至少得等你长大成人"

You must not **make a move on** your teacher.

M·O·R·E

- get a move on
  抓紧时间
- make a move on
  抓紧时间做某事，督促

Get a move on!
快点，没时间了！

I'd better **get a move on** it.
我得抓紧时间了。

If you don't **get a move on**, we're not going to make it.
如果你不抓紧时间，我们就不可能成功了。

He **made a move on** me.
他催促我抓紧时间。

A: Let's get a move on it. I want to leave. 我们抓紧时间吧，我想走了。
B: OK, I'll be ready in ten minutes. 好，我10分钟就准备完了。

More Expressions

- **stay for dinner** 留下来吃晚饭
  I don't think I can **stay for dinner**.
  我觉得没时间吃晚饭了。

- **stay between** 某某之间的秘密
  I have an idea. But it **stays between** us. Agreed? 我有个想法，但是，这是我们俩之间的秘密，你说怎么样?

- **stay clear of** 离……很远，远离
  Stay clear of people who ask for money.
  远离那些和你借钱的人。

- **stay tuned** 固定频道（电视机或收音机）
  Don't go away. **Stay tuned**.
  不要乱换台，就看这个频道。

- **stay put** 静止不动，老实待着
  All right, you two **stay put** right there.
  很好，你们两个站在那里别动。

相信我

Believe

believe经常用believe somebody (something)的形态，表示“相信某人”。不过believe in像believe in luck（相信运气）一样，表示“相信……的存在或依赖”。另外，I believe (that)主语+动词则表示“相信某人会……”，比起委婉的表达自己想法的I think that具有更明确的主张，用来传达自己的信念。

基本概念

1 相信

I don't (can't) believe my eyes. 我真无法相信我的眼睛。

I believe in you. 我相信你。

You don't believe in anything. 你什么都不相信。

2 认为……（believe 主语+动词）

I believe she is the best in her class. 我相信她是班里最优秀的。

I believe he isn't guilty. 我相信他没有罪。

believe it 相信

可以将前面提到过的内容替为it或this (that)，由此而成的believe it (this, that)是实际生活中经常使用到的句式，其含义为相信某事。

"艺人们的X档案，先不管这些到底是不是真的，反正给人带来了新鲜感"

Believe it or not, it sounds exciting.

M·O·R·E

- I believe it.
  我相信。
- I don't believe it (this)!
  我才不相信！
- You won't believe this.
  你无法相信的。
- Can you believe it (this)?
  你能相信这个吗？
- Believe it or not.
  爱信不信。

You'd better **believe it**!
你最好相信这个！

Do you expect me to **believe that**?
你不会是希望我相信那个吧？

I don't **believe this**! You talked to her about that?
我才不相信这些！你跟她说了？

A: The stock market just dropped by 200 points. 股市大跌了200点。
B: Are you sure? I don't believe it. 你确定吗？真是难以置信。

believe somebody 相信某人

这次believe后面接上了人物，表示"相信某人"，"无法相信某人"等。常用的句式有Believe (you) me! I don't believe you!和You don't believe me?等。

"只要开口就会大放厥词；说得天花乱坠，夸张至极，这种人一旦开口，对方就会说"

Of course. I don't believe you.

M·O·R·E

- Believe (you) me!
  肯定是这样的！
  (相信我！)
- I don't believe you!
  我才不相信你呢！
- You don't believe me?
  你不相信我吗？
- I can't believe you!
  我真无法相信你了！

So **believe me**. I know exactly how you feel.
所以说相信我，我很清楚你现在的感受。

I didn't **believe him** because he's always lying to me.
我没有相信他，因为他经常对我说谎。

Nobody's going to **believe her**.
没人会相信她的。

Whatever you say, I **believe you**!
不管你说什么，我都相信！

A: Believe me! I saw a real ghost. 相信我，我真的看到鬼了。
B: I think you are mistaken about that. 我觉得你是看错了。

I believe that ... 相信某事，认为……

如果想要说明的事情有点长，就可以用I (don't) believe that主语+动词的形态。可以用what代替that，其中You are going to believe what ... 可以用在传达非常惊人的事实时。

"有一个朋友称自己在教务处偷到了试题，再高价卖给同学们，听到这话的反应"

You'll never believe what he told me.

M·O·R·E

- I (really) believe (that) S+V
  我（非常）相信某事
- I don't believe (that) S+V
  我不相信某事
- You're not going to believe what ...
  你是无法相信的，
  你肯定会吃一惊的

I still believe that you and Linda are going to get back together.
我仍然相信，你和琳达总有一天会和好的。

I really believe what I did was right.
我非常肯定，我做的事情是正确的。

You're never going to believe what happened to me.
你绝对无法相信发生在我身上的事情。

They are being careful because they believe you are lying.
他们非常谨慎，因为他们坚信你在说谎。

I don't believe what I'm hearing.
我无法相信我所听到的事情。

You are not going to believe what I just did.
你不会相信我刚刚做的事情。

You're not going to believe what just happened.
你绝对无法相信刚刚发生的事情。

You're not going to believe what she said to me this morning.
你绝对不会相信今天早上她对我说的话。

A: What kind of job would you recommend? 你想推荐我做什么样的工作？
B: I believe that you should become a dentist. 我认为你应该当一个牙医。

A: I don't believe that I've met you before. 我觉得我们之前没见过面。
B: My name is Wendy. Nice to meet you. 我叫文迪，见到你很高兴。

A: Martin says his father is very rich. 马丁说他爸爸非常有钱。
B: I don't believe what he told you. 我不相信他跟你说的话。

I can't believe 我无法相信

I can't believe (that)主语+动词并不是否定某事，而是对that后半部分内容的惊讶。当然，可以用what或how等疑问词代替that。

"在体验岁月的无情之前，希望阁下'seize the day'"

I can't believe it was 34 years ago that I married him.

M·O·R·E

- I can't believe that (what, how) ... （吃惊）……无法相信
- I can't believe it. 真的假的！（简直不像话！绝对不可能！）
- I can't believe what I'm hearing here. 我实在无法相信自己在这里听到的事情。
- I can't believe my eyes. 我实在无法相信自己看到的。
- You can't believe how ... 你绝对无法相信……有多么……

I can't believe my team lost the baseball game.
我实在不敢相信我们队居然输掉了棒球比赛。

I can't believe this is happening again.
我真不敢相信，这样的事再次发生了。

I can't believe you did that. You let me down again.
我真不敢相信你居然那样做。你再一次让我失望了。

You can't believe how sorry I am.
你绝对不会知道我有多么难过。

I can't believe they didn't give us a raise.
我真不敢相信他们没有提拔我们。

I can't believe how hot it is today.
实在无法相信，今天简直热死了。

I can't believe it's real.
真不敢相信这是真的。

A: I can't believe that we're breaking up. 真不敢相信，我们就要分手了。
B: I guess all good things must come to an end. 我觉得天下没有不散的筵席。

A: April had ten tickets for the concert. 埃普里尔有10张演唱会的门票。
B: I can't believe she didn't invite us to come with her. 真不敢相信，她居然没有邀请我们一起去。

A: I can't believe what I saw on TV. 真不敢相信在电视上看到的东西。
B: Was it something that interested you? 是和你的兴趣有关的?

Can you believe ... ? 你能相信……吗?

Can you believe (that)主语+动词? 同样表示难以置信的事情，可以理解为“你能相信……吗？”

“虚荣心极强的人就喜欢虚张声势，竟然想尽办法用各种名牌打扮自己”

Can you believe she spent 10 000 dollars while shopping?

M·O·R·E

- Can you believe (that) S+V?
  你能相信……吗?
- Can you believe how ... ?
  你能相信……有多么……吗?

Can you believe he didn't know it?
你相信他不知道这件事吗?

Can you believe she had a date with the teacher?
你能相信她居然和我们的老师约会的事情吗?

Can you believe I found it in your house?
你能相信我居然在你家里找到了这个吗?

Can you believe she got pregnant?
你能相信她怀孕了吗?

A: Can you believe she got pregnant? **你能相信她怀孕的事情吗?**
B: You can't be serious. She's not married yet. **开什么玩笑。她还没结婚呢。**

It is hard (difficult) to believe that ... 实在难以相信某事

可以用来表达非常难以相信的事实，在that后面加主语+动词来表达难以置信的事实就可以了，也可以单单用(It's) Hard to believe!

“就因为多看了几眼，惹得对方极度生气，追逐了好几个小时，最后竟然给杀死了”

It just hard to believe that's what killed him.

M·O·R·E

- It is hard (difficult) to believe that S+V
  实在无法相信某事
- sb find it hard to believe
  实在难以相信

It's hard to believe they didn't come to work.
实在无法相信他们居然没上班。

Why do you **find it so hard to believe**?
为什么你觉得那件事不可信呢?

You may **find this very hard to believe**, but it's true.
你可能觉得难以置信，不过这是事实。

A: It's hard to believe Natalie left. **娜塔莉离开了，真是难以置信。**
B: I wish that she was still here. **她要是能在这儿就好了。**

believe in+人物(事物， ...ing) 相信某人，相信是事实

最基础的句式为believe in somebody (something)，像believe in God一样表示“相信……的存在”，“接受……的事实”等。

“佛教子弟经常会在地铁站等人群繁杂的地方询问陌生人”

Do you believe in past lives?

M·O·R·E

- believe in sb (sth)
  相信……的存在，信赖，相信……的事实
- believe in ...ing
  认为做某事是正确的

I'm still not sure I **believe in** God.
我至今还不太确定自己信不信上帝。

Do you **believe in** heaven?
你相信天堂这回事吗?

I don't **believe in** luck (destiny, miracles).
我不相信运气（命运，奇迹）。

I need you to **believe in** me.
我希望你能相信我。

I **believe in** being nice.
我觉得行善是正确的。

A: Do you believe in UFOs? 你相信不明飞行物的存在吗?
B: It's possible that they exist. 完全有可能存在啊。

More Expressions

- **not believe a word of** 完全不相信某事
  No one is ever going to **believe a word of** that. 没有人会相信这件事的。
- **believe so** 相信如此
  I **believe so**. 我是那么认为的。
  I don’t **believe so**. 我不那么认为。
- **be believed to be** 认为……
  It **is believed** that English is hard **to** learn. 人们通常认为英语学起来很难。
- **believe ... as ...** 认为是……
  Do you **believe** this **as** the truth?
  你相信这是事实吗?

让你明确的

Set

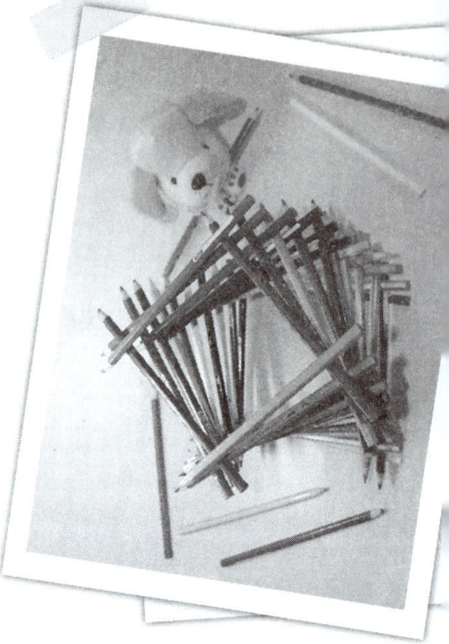

虽然是基本动词，而且虽然因为电脑的问题(set up)已经非常熟悉，但仍然不大容易上口。最常用的含义与put相似，表示“放……”，“放置”，因此可以比喻为“指定模范或标准，例子”等。另外，在设定日期时(set a date)或者在设置机器时也可以使用set。与别的动词不大一样，随着和其他词语的组成不同，其含义也有变化，因此通过例句好好了解一番吧。

基本概念

1 放，放置

She set some flowers on the desk. 她在桌子上放了几束花。

The waiter set our meal in front of us. 服务员把食物放在了我们面前。

2 树立（模范，例子等），展示

Right now, BMWs set the standard for quality cars. 现在宝马成了高质量汽车的标准。

3 定（日期等），设置，调试

We haven't set a date yet. 我们还没定下日子呢。

Would you help me set up the computer? 你能帮我设置电脑吗?

set a date 设定日期（时间）

可以用来表示定结婚的日子，另外，set the clock表示设定时间，set the alarm表示设定闹钟。

"一个老男人终于要娶媳妇了，兴奋地在整个村子里面乱窜"

I'm getting married. We'll set a date soon.

M·O·R·E

- set a date (for)
  定时间（为……）
- set the clock (for)
  设定时间（为……）

Have you set a date? Are you really getting married?
你定下日子了吗？你准备好结婚了吗？

They set the date for May 11th.
他们把日子定在了5月11号。

I set the alarm for a quarter to six.
我把闹钟定在了5点45分。

A: So, you are planning to get married? **就是说，你要打算结婚了？**
B: Yes, but my fiancee and I haven't set a date. **是的，不过我和未婚妻还没有定下日期。**

set a goal 树立目标

表示树立或设定，比方说"设定某种目标"(set a goal)，"创造纪录"(set a record)，"制定规则"(set the rules)，"设定标准"(set the standard)等。另外，"树立榜样"是set an example。

"爸爸经常教导我说，既然已经长大了，就要有个模范的样儿"

You're a grown-up. You have to set an example.

M·O·R·E

- set a goal (record)
  树立目标（创纪录）
- set the rules (standard)
  树立规则（标准）
- set an example
  树立榜样

You'd better set an example for other people.
你最好为别人树立好榜样。

I will set the standard as a teacher.
我作为老师会制订一套标准的。

A: How can I make a million dollars? **我怎样才能挣一百万呢？**
B: You need to set a goal to help you do it. **你得树立正确的目标来给你提供指导。**

set ... free 使……自由，释放

最基本的短语set ... free表示“使……得到自由”，可以用来表示监狱里释放犯人等，“解除某人的约束”。

“虽然说真理会使人得到自由，但人们更喜欢‘虚伪+自由’套装”

The truth shall **set you free**.

How about **setting** your parrot **free**?
把你的鹦鹉放了怎么样?

And you let me go. Just **set me free**.
你让我走吧，放了我吧。

You enjoy him and then **set him free**.
在享受完了之后就放他走吧。

She escaped herself or someone **set her free**.
要么是她自己跑出来的，要么有人放了她。

A: Didn't you have a bird in this cage? 这笼子里不是有一只鹦鹉吗?
B: I did, but I decided to set him free. 是有过，不过我决定把它给放了。

be all set 准备好

be set (for)表示“……定下来”，可以理解为“做好……的准备”。主要用为be all set，与be ready有着相近的含义。

“结婚准备已经做好了，却没有新娘，真是让人无语”

Everything**'s all set for** the wedding except a bride.

M·O·R·E

- (be) all set up for
  为……的准备完成
- (I'm) All set.
  (我)都准备好了。
- Get set (ready)!
  准备好!
- You all set?
  你准备好了?

Are you **all set for** traveling?
你做好旅游的准备了?

Are you **all set to** go? We might be late.
你做好出发的准备了? 我们可能要迟到了。

We**'re all set to** leave. Let's go on a cruise.
我们都做好出发的准备了。让我们踏上巡游之旅吧。

A: I think we're just about ready for the meeting. 我觉得我们刚刚做好了开会的准备。
B: Is everything all set up? 所有的事情都准备好了?

be set to 设定为，为……

set最基本的含义为“设定……”，“确定……”等，其被动形式be set to+动词表示“设定为……”，“确定为……”等。

“父亲据说要在审判中作证”

My father is set to give testimony in the trial.

She's set to receive it when she turns twenty-five.
如果她到了25岁，就可以得到这个了。

I'm sorry, but my phone was set to vibrate.
很抱歉，我的手机设置成振动了。

When are you set to interview Bob?
你什么时候见鲍勃?

A: Is everyone ready to get started? 大家都准备好开始了吗?
B: I think they are set to get to work. 我觉得他们都做好了工作的准备。

set (somebody) to work 开始做事

set to work表示热情而果断地开始工作。反之像set sb to work 一样，如果set后面的宾语为别人时就表示让对方做不情愿做的事情。

“矿山倒塌，救助队员为了抢险，正在努力地工作”

Rescue workers set to work immediately after the mine collapsed.

M·O·R·E

- set to work
  开始工作
- set sb to work
  强制某人做某事

How about we set to work right now?
我们现在开始工作怎么样?

I set the kids to work on their textbooks.
我让孩子们看课本去了。

Let's set them to work painting the house.
让他们给房子刷漆吧。

I'll set you to work organizing the files.
我要让你整理文件。

A: Did you meet the new maid? 你见到新女仆了?
B: Yeah, I set her to work cleaning the bathroom. 嗯，我让她去打扫卫生间了。

set against 使……相反，使产生反感

against具有相反的含义，因此set against表示和睦相处的两个人突然反目成仇或者使对方产生反感。另外，还可以表示反对某事。

"让员工们反目成仇的黑心老板经常使用离间计"

The company tried to set workers against other workers.

M·O·R·E

- set sb against sb
  使互相产生反感
- set sth against sth
  相互比较某物

I'm dead **set against** it.
我绝对不赞成。

The tennis match will **set Andre against** Pete.
网球比赛的双方对手为安德烈和皮特。

Their jealousy **set Tim against** Tom.
提姆和汤姆因强烈的嫉妒心反目成仇。

The football game **set our school against** its rival.
足球比赛在我们学校和死对头之间举行。

A: The tournament will set us against another team. 我们和另外一个队会参加比赛。
B: I'm sure we are going to be the winners. 我相信我们会赢得比赛的。

set aside 单独存放，储备

字面含义为放在(set)旁边(aside)，可以表示"单独存放"或者"储备"。与put aside具有相近的含义。

"活在高消费社会的我们，要活着的日子还长，储备的钱却没多少"

The money we set aside is not enough.

He had money **set aside** for this.
他专门为了这个储备了一些钱。

I **set aside** this weekend to celebrate my wife's birthday.
我安排这个周末给老婆过生日。

I have a lot of time. I **set aside** my whole weekend.
我有很多时间。我把整个周末都腾出来了。

A: Can you set aside your work for now? 你现在能把工作放一边吗？
B: No, this has to be completed today. 不行，手头的工作必须在今天完成。

set off 出发，使工作，使爆炸，让闹钟响起

off表示从本体脱离出去。因此可以表示让机械等运转起来，让炸弹爆炸，或出发做某事。

"到什么地方都能见到这样的孩子……为了好玩按防火警报"

He **set off** the fire alarms at school for fun.

M·O·R·E

- set sth off
  使爆发，使运转
- set off to+动词
  出发做某事

We're going to have to **set it off** manually.
我们得手动启动它了。

They **set off to** get the baby back.
他们接孩子去了。

We **set off to** visit the country.
我们出发去乡下探亲。

We **set off on** a short trip to Tokyo.
我们启程前往东京做短途旅行。

A: Where has your son gone? 你儿子去哪了？
B: He set off to travel around Europe. 他去周游欧洲了。

set on 设定，决定

经常会被用作被动形态，be set on表示"下定……的决心"，set eyes on表示"第一次见到某人"，"相会"，另外，have one's heart set on表示"决定做某事"。

"下定决心离开鸡窝一般的破房子，前往繁华的市中心"

She's got her heart **set on** having a townhouse.

M·O·R·E

- be set on
  设定为……有……的心思
- have one's heart set on
  决心做某事

You'**re still set on** that?
你仍然坚持你的想法吗？

If you'**re set on** divorce, I can help you with that.
如果你决心要离婚，我可以帮你。

I never really **had my heart set on** being a novelist.
我从来就没有决心当一个小说家。

I wanted to marry you the first time I **set eyes on** you.
我在第一眼见到你的时候，就决心一定要娶你。

A: Why doesn't she become a doctor? 她为什么没成为一个医生？
B: Becayse she is set on becoming a lawyer instead. 因为她决心当一个律师。

set out 开始，出发

set out与前文中的set off有着相近的含义，表示“向某处出发”，“出发”，也可以比喻为“开始做某事”。

“开会的时候放屁是对老板大胆的挑战，因此一定要找出凶犯来”

The boss set out to find out who farted in the meeting.

M·O·R·E

- set out
  出发（旅行）
- set out sth (plan, policy)
  说明（书面的计划等）
- set out on sth (to+V)
  开始做某事（为了达到目的）

She **set out to** break some records of her own.
她开始将自己的记录一个个打破。

That evening, she **set out to** break her pattern.
那天晚上，她打破了自己的固有模式。

They **set out to** find out who loved her.
他们开始追查是谁爱上了她。

A: What do you plan to do here? 你打算在这里干嘛?

B: We've set out to find the missing gold coins. 我们决定在这里寻找丢失的金币。

set up 创立(establish)，设定（日程等），欺骗

这是因电脑中的setup而让我们非常熟悉的词组。set up具有多种含义，如树立某事，开始（设定），定下会议的日程安排等。另外，也可以表示“欺骗某人，使某人中计”(make someone be blamed wrongly)等。

“最可疑的放屁者徐博士口口声声说自己发出的声音是出于和椅子的摩擦”

She claimed that someone in the room set her up.

M·O·R·E

- set sb up (for sth)
  欺骗某人（做某事）
- set a meeting up for ...
  将会议定为……

I'd like to **set up an appointment** for Thursday.
我想把约会定在星期四。

Is everything **all set up**?
一切都准备好了吗?

You **set me up**! I will pay you back!
是你陷害我的！（你欺骗我！）我会报仇的！

A: Can I help you, sir? 先生，有什么可以帮忙的吗?

B: I'd like to set up an appointment for next week. 我想把预约定在下个星期。

set somebody up (with sb) 将某人介绍给某人

在提到男女关系时必须要说到的句式，set sb up with表示“将某人介绍给某人”，也可以用fix代替set。

“跟朋友说给我介绍个男生，没想到朋友随便在大街上找了一个猥琐男”

How come you set me up with a stranger?

M·O·R·E

- set (fix) sb up with 将某人介绍给某人
- set sb up on a date 让某人约会，让某人见面

I'm not asking you to **set me up**.
我不是让你给我介绍对象。

You **set me up with** the woman that I've dumped twice.
你给我介绍的女人是我甩过两次的。

Is it okay with you if I **set him up on a date**?
我给他介绍个对象，你不介意吧?

How could you **set me up with** this creep?
你怎么可以给我介绍这么一个怪胎?

A: Phil is the nicest guy I've ever met. 菲尔是我见过的最出色的男生了。
B: Let's set him up with your sister. 给你妹妹介绍介绍吧。

More Expressions

- **set back** 使后退，妨碍
  My plan has been **set back**
  我的计划遭受了挫折。

- **set down** 放下
  Thanks, you can just **set it down** there.
  谢谢，你可以放在那里。

- **set in** 开始
  The shock **set in** 12 hours later.
  12个小时之后冲击开始了。

- **set ... on fire** 放火，使兴奋
  She is the woman who **set my heart on fire**. 她是燃起我心中烈火的女人。

- **set one's mind to** 非常渴望得到……
  I'm sure you could accomplish anything you **set your mind to**.
  我敢肯定，只要你决心做，没有什么是办不成的。

心事重重

Mind

mind可以做为名词，但大多情况下都会使用其动词形式。首先，mind动词最常用的含义为“介意”，“反对”等。因此Do you mind ... ?表示“你介意某事吗？”，而I don't mind ... 表示“我不介意某事”。当然，change one's mind, keep in mind等名词的用法也需要记住。

基本概念

1（否定，疑问句）介意某事，生气

Do you mind if I use your cell phone? 你介意我用下你的电话吗？

Do you mind if I sit here for a second? 你介意我坐在这儿吗？

2 不关心

I don't mind doing what you're going to do. 我才不管你做什么事情呢。

I don't mind if you smoke in the room. 我不会介意你在房间里抽烟的。

3（名词）心，情绪，想法

I'm sorry I lost my mind yesterday. 很抱歉，我昨天失去理智了。

I'll keep that in mind. 我会铭记的。

Do (Would) you mind ...ing? 你介意某事吗?

字面含义为"你介意……吗？"，可以理解为"我能不能做某事？"或者"允许做某事"等，当然如果使用would的话，语气就要比do更正式一些。

"扛着一大堆东西在街上走着，看见旁边走过几个学生，便问道"

Do you mind giving me a hand?

M·O·R·E

- Do (Would) you mind ...ing?
  你介意某事吗?
- Do (Would) you mind sb ...ing?
  你介意某人做某事吗?

Would you mind watching my bag for a moment?
你介意帮我看一下包裹吗?

Do you mind picking me up tomorrow?
你介意明天来接我一下吗?

Do you mind me asking why you didn't go to work?
如果你不介意的话，我想问问你为什么没去上班?

A: Do you mind picking me up tomorrow? 你明天能来接我一下吗?
B: Sure, what time? 好的，几点?

Do (Would) you mind if ... ? 做某事也可以吗?

这次用If从句代替了 ...ing，常用的形态为Would (Do) you mind if主语+动词。在If的后面接上要嘱咐的内容就可以了。

"妈妈正在看肥皂剧，问她介不介意播放音乐"

Do you mind if I turn on the music, mom?

M·O·R·E

- Do (Would) you mind if ... ?
  你介意某事吗?
- Do you mind?
  可以做某事吗？（非常生气要不到此为止？）

Would you mind if I smoke here?
我可以在这里抽烟吗?

Do you mind if I take a look around here?
我在这里四处转转可以吗?

Do you mind if we ask you some questions about her?
我和你问点有关她的事情可以吗?

I'd like to go for a walk. **Do you mind?**
我想出去走走，可以吗?

A: Do you mind if I sit here? 我可以坐在这里吗?
B: No, go right ahead. 没问题，请坐。

I don't mind 我不介意

这次表示“我不介意……”，在I don't mind后面接名词，...ing，或if主语+动词都可以。

“花钱学车，需要找名声最显赫的车先生”

I'd like do speak to Mr. Cha. **I don't mind** waiting.

M·O·R·E

- I don't mind+名词(...ing)
  我不介意某事
- I don't mind that S+V
  我不介意某事
- I don't mind (sb) ...ing
  我不介意某人做某事
- I don't mind if S+V
  我不介意某事

That's all right. **I don't mind** waiting.

没关系，我可以等一会儿。

I don't mind her hanging around with you.

我不介意你和她出去玩。

I don't mind if you ask. Go ahead.

我不介意你向我提问，有话直说。

A: I'd like to smoke a cigarette right now. **我现在想抽烟。**

B: I don't mind if you smoke here. **我不介意你在这里抽烟。**

Never mind 不要在意某事

Never mind!为非常常见的短语，可以用来向对方表示没关系，不要在意等。Never mind后面也可以接名词，...ing，从句等。

“大企业老板对每个小细节都非常在乎，对这种人就要说”

Never mind who's going to handle this.

M·O·R·E

- Never mind (...ing)!
  不要在意（做某事），
  不要在意
- Never mind sb (sth)
  不要在意某人（某事）
- Never mind that (what),
  不要在意……

Never mind that.

不要在意。

Well, **never mind** me. It doesn't matter to me.

好，不用管我了。跟我没什么关系。

Never mind that we don't have it.

我们就算没有也无所谓。

Never mind what I want. What do you want?

不用在乎我想要的东西。你想要什么?

A: How can I make it up to you? **我应该怎么赔偿你呢?**

B: Never mind ... just pay for the damages. **不用在意……交损害赔偿金就可以了。**

I would't mind ... 如果……就好了，想要做某事

可以表示“做某事也没关系”或者“我想做某事”。换句话说，与I would like+名词（to+动词）具有相似的含义。

“大街上有个肌肉男，看完还想多看几遍”

I wouldn't mind seeing more of that guy.

M·O·R·E

- I wouldn't mind sth
  我想做（吃）……
- I wouldn't mind ...ing
  我想做某事

I wouldn't mind a cup of coffee.
我想来一杯咖啡。

I wouldn't mind having some real Chinese food sometime.
我想找个时间品尝一下真正的中餐。

I wouldn't mind sharing a few things with her.
我想和她分享一些东西。

A: Do you have anything planned for tonight? 你今天晚上有安排吗?
B: I wouldn't mind going to a nightclub. 我想去夜店玩玩。

mind one's own business 不干涉别人的事情

Mind your own business!（不要干涉我的事情/做好你的本职工作！）是较常用的表达。相反，mind one's manners, mind one's P's an Q's表示“遵守礼仪”，“注意言行举止”等。

“具有千里眼、顺风耳的同事几乎会干涉别人的所有事情，对于这种朋友就要说”

Look, just mind your own business, okay?

I'**m** just **minding my own business**.
我正在做自己的工作。

Mind your P's and Q's!
注意你的言行举止!

I'll thank you to **mind your own business**.
如果你不干涉别人的事情，我就特别感激了。

Why can't you **mind your own business**? What is your problem?
你为什么要干涉别人的事情？你到底有什么问题?

A: I think I'm going to ask them what they're talking about. 我觉得我应该问问他们在聊些什么。
B: Why don't you mind your own business? 你怎么不管管你自己的事情?

If you don't mind 如果可以的话

是人们比较熟悉的一句话，可以用来请求对方的允许或谅解，有时wouldn't会替代don't，变成if you wouldn't mind的形态。

"女朋友说要一起去看电影，男朋友却想去酒吧"

If you don't mind, I prefer going to a bar.

M·O·R·E

- if you don't (wouldn't) mind
  如果可以的话，如果方便的话
- if you don't mind my saying so
  如果你不介意我说的
- if you don't mind me asking
  如果可以的话我想问

If you don't mind, I'm kind of tired now.
如果你不介意的话，我想说我现在有点累了。

If you don't mind, I'd like to ask you both a few questions.
如果可以的话，我想问你们两位一些问题。

If you don't mind my saying so, you seem a little old to have a baby.
不知道这么说合不合适，你的年龄有点不适合要孩子了。

If you don't mind me asking, why were you so interested in this?
如果不介意的话我想问，你为什么对这个如此感兴趣?

A: If you don't mind, I'm going to leave early. 如果可以的话，我早点过去吧。
B: OK, I think I'll leave early, too. 好的，我正好也想早点出发。

change one's mind 改变主意，变心

mind不仅是动词，作为名词也具有多样的含义。最常用的就是change one's mind，表示"改变主意"，"变心"。

"碰到了自己喜欢的类型，没想到表白被拒，为了以防万一"

If you change your mind, here's my card.

What made you change your mind?
是什么让你改变主意的?

There's nothing you can do to change my mind.
你用什么手段都无法改变我的想法。

You can still change your mind.
你现在还可以改变主意。

Well, call me if you change your mind.
好，如果改变主意的话，给我打电话。

A: Did you want a vanilla ice cream cone? 你想要的是香草味的甜筒?
B: I changed my mind. I want chocolate instead. 我改变主意了，我想要个巧克力的。

take sombody's ming off 使某人忘记

字面含义为“使某人的心远离(off)……”，因此可以表示“让某人忘记……”。可以用keep，get代替take。

“通过购物，可以忘掉日常生活中的诸多烦恼”

I'm just shopping, trying to get my mind off things.

M·O·R·E

- take (get, keep) sb's mind off
  使某人忘记某事

I bought myself a little gift to **take my mind off** my problems.
我给自己买了一个小礼物，让我忘掉所有的烦恼。

Maybe it'll **take your mind off** Betty.
也许这会让你忘掉贝蒂的。

Just try to really **keep Tom's mind off** of it.
试试让汤姆忘掉这件事。

A: Ray drinks too much alcohol these days. 雷这几天喝得太厉害了。
B: It takes his mind off the troubles at his home. 正所谓借酒消愁啊。

put sth (sb) out of one's mind 故意忘记某事

字面含义为“将……放在某人的心之外(out of one's mind)”，因此可以表示“忘记某事”，“不在乎某事”等。相反，have ... on one's mind表示“在意某事”。

“眼看就要被提升了，却因为一些小的问题打不起精神，这种时候就要说”

Whatever it is, put it right out of your mind.

M·O·R·E

- put (get) sth (sb) out of one's mind
  故意不去想某事
- have (get) sth (a lot) on one's mind
  心里有事，在意某事

I just **put that jerk out of my mind**!
我已经把他给忘了。

I just can't get past it. I can't **put her out of my mind**.
我不能就这么忘掉，我无法不去在乎她。

So just **put it out of your mind**.
就让它过去吧。

A: My boss treats me very poorly. 我老板对我非常不好。
B: Put it out of your mind. You can get another job. 别在意了，你可以找一份别的工作嘛。

lose one's mind 失去意识，疯掉

按照字面翻译的话就是“失去意识”(lose)，表示“失去理智”，“疯掉”等。与go (be) out of one's mind具有相似的含义。

“有夫之妇被公司的肌肉男上司勾引出去约会，却搞不清自己为什么会这样”

I'm losing my mind. I can't believe I'm doing this.

M·O·R·E

- lose one's mind
  失去理智
- go (be) out of one's mind
  失去理智，疯掉

I'm losing my mind.

我失去理智了。

You've got to be out of your mind!

你肯定疯了！

What are you doing? Are you out of your mind?

你在干嘛？你疯了？

A: There's too much homework. I'm losing my mind! 作业太多了。我快要疯了。

B: Calm down. Let's take a look at it. 冷静一下。我帮你看看吧。

have half a mind to 考虑到底要不要做某事

表示只有一半的心思（half a mind）。联想一下还未下定决心的状态，犹豫到底要不要做某事时的形象即可。have a good mind表示“非常渴望做某事”。

“看到朋友的老公搞外遇，正在考虑到底要不要和朋友说”

I have half a mind to call her and tell her that.

M·O·R·E

- have (get) half a mind to+动词
  考虑到底要不要做某事
- have (get) a good mind to+动词
  非常渴望做某事

I have half a mind to throw this martini right in your face!

我正在考虑要不要把这杯酒倒在你脸上。

I have half a mind to get out of here right now.

我正在考虑要不要马上离开。

I've got half a mind to contract the company.

我正在考虑到底要不要和这家公司续签合同。

A: Barry just started a fight with Cara. 巴利刚刚和卡拉大吵了一架。

B: I have half a mind to tell him to leave. 我正在考虑要不要让他出去待一会儿。

More Expressions

- have something in (on) mind
  在意某事（注意某事）

  What do you **have in mind**?
  你到底在想什么？

  Do you **have** something else **on your mind**? 你在想别的事情？

- make up one's mind 决心

  I haven't **made up my mind** yet.
  我还没下定决心呢。

- slip one's mind 完全忘记

  It (completely) **slipped my mind**.
  我忘得一干二净。

- cross one's mind 想起某人某事

  The thought never **crossed my mind**.
  我完全想不起来。

  It hasn't even **crossed my mind**.
  我根本就没想到。

- come to mind 突然想到某事

  Nothing **comes to mind**, but I'll check my files.
  什么都想不起来，不过我会去确认一下文件的。

- go (run, flash) through sb's mind
  暂时想

  I wonder what **was going through her mind** when she stood there.
  当她站在那里的时候，我非常好奇她在想什么。

- blow one's mind 使某人惊慌，兴奋

  It **blew my mind**. 我当时非常惊慌。

- set (put) somebody's mind at rest (ease) 专注于某事

  You can **put your mind at rest**
  你可以放心了。

- keep your mind on 专注于某事

  Then stay here and **keep your mind on** your job. You hear me?
  那就留在这儿，专注于你的工作。知道了吗？

Don't mind me. I'm just looking.
不用管我，我只是看看。

I'm trying to keep an open mind.
我试着去掉所有偏见。

Out of sight, out of mind. 眼不见，心不烦。

无论是什么都要找出来

Find/Lose

在find的含义中绝对不能忘记一点，就是像keep，leave一样变成find ... +形容词(v-ing，pp)的话则表示“发现某人……”，即“觉得”。另外，需要区分find和find out。find表示“发现某种实体”，而find out则表示“知道某个事实”。此外，要记住一个常用的短语，find oneself ...。

基本概念

1 寻找，寻求，发现

I lost my passport. I can't find my passport. 我把护照给弄丢了，现在找不到了。

I'm trying to find the National Art Gallery. 我想找国家美术馆。

How did you find such a beautiful girlfriend? 你是怎么找到这么一位如花似玉的女朋友的?

2 知道某人……（形容词）

I find you very attractive. 我觉得你非常有魅力。

I find it hard to believe. 我很难相信它。

3 丢失，失败

I lost my passport. 我把护照弄丢了。

She lost her job last month. 她上个月被炒鱿鱼了。

We're losing the game. 我们要输了。

You're not going to lose him. 你不会失去他的。

We will win, and you will lose. 我们会胜利的，而你就只会是失败者了。

find somebody (something) 寻找……

单纯的find somebody (something)表示“寻找……”，而find somebody something则表示“给某人找某样东西”。

“没有获得学位的儿子为了找工作，每天晚上都会在大街小巷贴传单”

We need to find him a better job.

M·O·R·E

- find sb sth
  给某人找某物
- find sth on the internet
  在网上查找某物
- come to find
  过来找

Where will I **find** you?
我在哪里可以找到你？（你会在哪？）

You know where to **find** me.
你知道应该在哪儿能找到我。

Have you guys seen Jill? I can't **find** her anywhere.
你们见到吉尔了吗？我怎么都找不到她。

I'm trying to **find** Tim before he gets in any more trouble.
我要在蒂姆惹出事端之前找到他。

A: If you find her ring, let her know. 如果你找到了她的戒指就告诉她。
B: Okay, I'll look around for it. 好的，我会找找看。

find somebody (sth)+形容词 (pp, ...ing) 认为某人……

这是find的最常用句式。find A B的结构表示认为A是B。B的位置可以用形容词或过去分词，或者 ...ing。

“上身穿西服，下身穿短裤的新员工真是个性十足啊”

Why do you find it so funny?

M·O·R·E

- find it easy (hard, difficult) to+动词
  认为做某事很容易（很难）

The jury **found her innocent**.
陪审团判定她无罪。

I **find it difficult to** get the job done by tomorrow.
我觉得明天之前完成这项工作有点难度。

I **found that** hard to believe. It came as a shock to me.
我真不敢相信。对我来说这无疑是一个打击。

How did it go? Did you **find it interesting**?
怎么样了？你找到什么有趣的了吗？

A: What happened at Daniel's trial? 丹尼尔的裁决结果出来了吗？
B: They found him guilty of murder. 他们判定他有谋杀罪。

find oneself 具备，寻求……

英语中的find oneself表示“自己发现”，“我怎么样”等。后面如果加地点名词的话，则表示“我在某处”，如果加名词的话就是“给自己找某物”，“寻求”等。

“献血，捐赠，社会无偿服务等善行是每个人都可以做的”

I found myself wanting to do something good.

M·O·R·E

- find oneself+形容词（心情）如何
- find oneself+介词+名词 在某处，处在……的状态中
- find oneself+名词 寻求某物，具备……
- find oneself ...ing 自己在做某事

She **found herself** in Tony's bedroom.
她发现自己在托尼的卧室。

Honey, have you **found yourself** in a family way?
亲爱的，你发现自己怀孕了吗?

You had better **find yourself** another prom date.
你最好找别的对象吧。

One day, you will **find yourself** with gray hair.
有一天，你会发现自己的头发渐渐变白了。

A: I haven't met any guys that I like. 我还没遇到过我喜欢的男生。
B: You're going to find yourself alone. 你不久就会变成剩女的。

find a way 找路，寻找方法

字面含义为“找路”，但多用于比喻义的“寻找方法”。另外，find one's way表示“寻找某人要去的路”，“努力向前进”，“达成”等。

“80多岁的老爷爷太冷了，在网上订购了电暖气，没想到是需要自己组装的”

We've got to find a way to make this work.

M·O·R·E

- find a (better) way to+动词 寻找（更好的）方法
- find one's way 寻找出路，努力前进

She'll get through this. She'll **find a way to** survive.
她一定会挺住的。她会找到生存的方法。

You need to **find a better way to** communicate with your wife.
你得想个办法和你妻子好好交流。

I'm here to help you **find your way** again.
我来是想帮你重新找出路的。

I can not **find my way** out of there.
我找不到出去的路。

A: Tuition for the school has increased again. 学校的学费又涨价了。
B: It's hard to find a way to pay for it. 很难交上学费啊。

find out 知道事实

find是寻找具体的物体，而find out则表示“知道某种事实”。find out后面可以接各种成分，如名词，that从句，if从句等。

“科学的发展（DNA遗传因子）所带来的悲剧”

He found out that Jimmy is not his son.

M·O·R·E

- find out sth
  找出……
- find out if (whether, what, who) ...
  了解……
  知道……的事情
- find out more about ...
  对……多多了解

If you find the document, you'll **find out** the truth.
如果你找到那份文件，你就会知道真相了。

I want you to **find out** if my daughter is using drugs again.
我想知道我女儿是不是又重新开始吸毒了。

We need to **find out** what is going on there.
我们需要知道那里正在发生什么事情。

I **found out** that she didn't love me anymore.
我发现她不再爱我了。

A: I just found out that I got transferred. 我刚刚发现，我被交易了。
B: I'm sorry to hear that. 很抱歉听到这个消息。

find fault with 谴责某人

经常出现的短语find fault with somebody表示“谴责某人”，“怪罪某人”等，与criticize具有相同的含义。

“幼稚的人经常会把所有的过错都推到别人的身上”

Please stop finding fault with people around you.

It doesn't do any good to sit back and **find fault with** your coworkers.
再怎么指责同事的过错也不会有什么好处。

I can't **find fault with** the kitchen.
我对厨房非常满意。

Why do you always pick on me? **Is finding fault with** me is your new job?
你为什么总是喜欢嘲笑我？讽刺我是你的新工作吗？

A: So, you have a difficult relationship with your dad? 就是说，你和你爸爸的关系不太好？
B: He always finds fault with the things I do. 他总喜欢对我做的事情找茬。

lose weight 减肥

该词组可表示通过运动(work out)或节食(go on a diet)使体重减轻，如果要表达增肥，则可以用gain weight 或 put on weight。

“碰到了久违的朋友，没想到对方从圆脸成功转型为瓜子脸”

You look fantastic. Have you lost weight?

M·O·R·E

- lose weight
  减肥
- gain weight (= put on weight)
  增肥

If I eat less, I'll lose weight.
少吃点的话，我可以减掉体重的。

You look like you've lost weight lately.
你最近好像瘦了点了。

She's been weak ever since and she's lost weight.
自从那时候开始她就一病不起，体重也日益减少。

I lost weight. My cholesterol went down.
我减肥了，胆固醇含量也下降了。

A: We both ate a lot of food over the holidays. **我们在假期的时候都吃了不少东西。**

B: We'll need to diet so we can lose weight. **我们得节食减减肥了。**

lose track of 联系中断，错过

track表示“痕迹”，“踪迹”等，of之后的成分就表示错过的具体事情。lose sight of表示“没看见某物”或因为别的事情太忙碌而“忘掉某事”。

“贪图私利的人为了满足自己的“贪欲”，经常不会珍惜家庭的可贵”

Greedy people lose sight of the importance of family.

M·O·R·E

- lose sight of
  没看见，错过
- lose touch (contact) with
  与某人失去联系

I guess I lost track of everybody after high school.
我猜自从高中毕业之后，我基本上失去了和所有人的联系。

I lost track of you, but I always heard about you.
我虽然和你失去了联系，不过经常会听到你的事情。

Yeah. I guess I lost track of time.
恩，我猜我把时间给忘了。

I lost touch with many of my old friends.
我和我的很多老朋友们失去了联系。

A: Where are all of your elementary school friends? **你所有小学同学都在哪?**

B: I've lost track of most of them over the years. **我好几年都没跟他们取得联系了。**

lose one's temper 生气

temper具有情绪，心情等含义，因此lose one's temper表示瞬间失去理性而爆发，生气等。在这种生气的状态中如果和别人“大干了一场”，则可以说lose one's temper with sb。

“恋母癖严重的丈夫至今还得让妈妈帮忙洗澡”

I lost my temper and threw away the wedding ring.

M·O·R·E

- lose one's temper
  突然火冒三丈
- lose one's temper with sb
  与某人大干一场

I am sorry I **lost my temper**, but I was upset.
很抱歉我失去理智了，不过我真的很生气。

I **lost my temper** with the boss.
我对老板发火了。

I **lost my temper** and I was disrespectful to mom.
我失去理智，对妈妈做出了过分的举动。

A: The two taxis had an accident this morning. 今天早上两辆出租车相撞。
B: I'll bet the drivers lost their tempers. 我猜两个司机肯定都气坏了。

be lost 迷路

lost是lose的被动形态，be lost表示迷路。但如果用be lost on sb的话则表示“没能得到某人的理解”，be lost in sth则表示“深陷某事”等。

“公司单方面下令，调派我到地方去工作，我瞬间受到了巨大的打击”

She was quiet and lost in her own thoughts.

M·O·R·E

- be lost (in/on+地点)
  迷路
- be lost in sth
  深陷某事（想法或兴趣）
- be lost on sb
  没能受到某人的关注（理解）
- get lost
  迷路；（祈使句）滚开
- Get lost!
  给我消失！

I think I'**m lost**.
我觉得我迷路了。

If you **get lost** in the maze, don't panic.
就算你迷路了，也不要惊慌。

My boss appears **lost in** thought.
我的老板好像若有所思。

Your joke **is completely lost on** us.
我们完全没有听懂你的笑话。

A: Can you help me? I'm lost. 你能帮我吗？我迷路了。
B: Sure. Where do you want to go? 好的，你想去哪里？

have (get) nothing to lose 没有什么可失去的

have nothing to lose表示“没有什么可失去的”。即，“没什么可损失的”，可以放开了大干一场。

“班里最调皮的学生劝说模范生一起逃课，模范生说道‘你已经没什么可失去的了’”。

You **have nothing to lose**, I have everything to lose.

You've **got nothing to** lose.
你已经没什么可失去的了。

I'**ve got nothing to lose** except you.
除了你，我没什么可以失去的。

We **have absolutely nothing to lose**. Trust me.
我们已经没有退路了，相信我。

Come on, do it. You **got nothing to lose**.
来，试试看。你已经没什么余地了。

A: Are you going to join the Marines? 你要参加海军陆战队?
B: Why not? I have nothing to lose. 为什么不呢? 我已经没什么退路了。

More Expressions

- **lost and found** 失物招领处

  Where is the **lost and found**?
  失物招领处在哪?

  I have got to go and check in the **lost and found**. 我得去失物招领处看看。

- **find one's tongue**
  大吃一惊之后 张口说话

  I couldn't **find my tongue**. 我吓得什么话都说不出。

- **be a real find** 了不起，伟大的发现

  She **is a real find**. 她真的非常了不起。

忘了的东西怎样才能记起来

Forget/Remember

有的时候会忘掉自己的回忆，有些时候会记起忘怀的东西。这次让我们来了解一下“记住和忘记”。最基本的就是表示“忘掉要做的事情”，forget to+动词，和“忘掉已经做过的事情”forget about ...ing。同理，“记住要做的事情”是remember to+动词，而“记住已经做过的事情”就是remember ...ing。

基本概念

1 forget：忘记，记不起来，忘带某物

How could I forget? I forgot to buy her a present. 我怎么给忘了呢？忘了给她买礼物了。

Don't forget to get me a present. 不要忘了给我买礼物。

You forgot? 你忘了？

2 remember：记住

I can't remember which is sister. 我记不清谁是妹妹了。

I know, I remember that! 我知道，我还记得！

forget somebody (something) 忘记某人，忘带某物

forget最重要的含义就是“忘记某人”（记不起来）和“忘带某物”，forget后面可以接人物或事物。

“如果不想忘记，在一起不就行了吗，分手的时候何必说这些话”

One thing you got to know is that I'll never **forget** you.

I think I **forgot** my receipt.
我觉得我忘带收据了。

We had to go back because I **forgot** my jacket.
我们得回去一趟，因为我忘带夹克了。

I hope that we can **forget** the whole thing.
我希望我们能忘掉所有的事情。

Forget her! You don't need her.
忘了她吧！你不需要她。

A: Whoops! I forgot my groceries in the car again. 天啊！我又把食品杂货忘在车里了。

B: Do you want me to go get them for you? 你要我去帮你取来吗？

forget about 忘记，不在意某事，忘记做过的事情

想要表达“忘记抽象的事情或行为”，或者“不在意”时可以在forget something中间加about，变成forget about something (...ing)。当然，forget about后面可以接人。

“公司里的背叛和离间太猖獗了，实在受不了，只好辞职不干”

I try to **forget about** the people around me.

I think it's best that we just **forget about** it.
我觉得我们最好不要去在乎那些。

You should just **forget about** what I said in the office.
我刚刚在办公室说的话，你最好不要在意。

You can **forget about** Tammy, she left us.
你可以忘掉塔米了，是她离开我们的。

A: I'm going to the bank this afternoon. 我今天下午要去银行。

B: Don't forget about the money you need to deposit. 不要忘了你要存的钱。

forget to 忘记要做的事情

表示忘掉要做的事情或者必须做的事情，forget后面接上“to+动词”以表示具体忘记的事情。

“忘了给老婆买生日礼物了，这个丈夫一定会死的很惨”

I forgot to buy her a birthday present.

M·O·R·E

- I forgot to+动词
  忘记要做的事情
- You forgot to+动词
  你忘了要做某事了

I **forgot to** pick up my dry cleaning!
我忘了要去洗衣店拿衣服。

I just **forgot to** return his call.
我忘给他回电话了。

Excuse me? You **forgot to** give me my receipt.
打扰一下，你忘了给我收据了。

A: Why didn't you prepare a report? **你为什么没写报告?**
B: It's my fault. I forgot to do it. **是我的错，我忘了。**

forget that 忘记……

如果忘记的内容有点长，就可以在forget后面加上(that)主语+动词，that后面的部分就是忘记的具体内容。

“明明提出了绝交，男朋友却像个蚂蝗一样，纠缠不清”

Don't call me again. Forget you know my number.

M·O·R·E

- I forget (that) S+V
  忘记……
- Forget (that) S+V
  忘记……

You just **forgot that** I told you this?
你忘了我跟你说的事情了?

You **forgot that** you had that suitcase?
你忘了你有那个箱子?

I can't believe it! I **forgot** you were here.
我简直不敢相信，我忘记了你曾在这儿了。

Forget I said anything.
不用在意我说的话。

A: I'll be going to New York in December. **我会在12月去纽约。**
B: Many people forget that it's cold there in the winter. **很多人都忘了，那时候的纽约非常寒冷。**

forget what 忘记……

forget后面不仅可以接that主语+动词，还可以加what (how) 主语+动词，形成各种句式。

"英国和日本是左侧通行，在那里久居的朋友回国很不适应"

You might **forget which** side of the road to drive on.

M·O·R·E

- I forget what (who) S+V 我忘了……
- I forget how (much, good) 我忘了……有多么……

Don't **forget what** we talked about last night.
不要忘了我们昨天说的事情。

We'**ve forgotten who** he is.
我们忘了他是谁了。

I **forgot how** much I love driving.
我都忘了我有多么喜欢开车了。

I always **forget how** beautiful you are.
我经常会忘了你有多么漂亮。

A: Did you bring the items I wanted? **你把我要的东西带来了吗?**

B: I'm sorry, I forgot what you asked me for. **很抱歉，我忘了你跟我嘱咐的东西了。**

Don't forget to ... 不要忘记……

Don't forget to+动词表示双重否定，"千万不要忘记做某事"，可以用来嘱咐或者让对方注意。

"跟孩子们说，出门的时候千万别忘了锁门"

Hey, kids, **don't forget to** lock the door.

M·O·R·E

- Don't forget to+动词 不要忘了做某事
- Don't forget (that) S+V 不要忘了做某事

See you later. **Don't forget to** e-mail me.
回头见。不要忘了给我发个邮件。

Please **don't forget to** make a backup of those files.
不要忘了帮我弄几分拷贝。

Don't forget that tomorrow is my birthday.
不要忘了明天是我的生日。

A: Take care. And don't forget to e-mail me. **走好，还有别忘了给我发邮件。**

B: I'll do that when I get home! **等我回家就发给你。**

Forget (about) it 忘记，不要在意，行了

固定搭配，在对方表达谢意或歉意时可以用来表示“没关系”，“不要在意”等，也可以用来向对方表示拒绝“No”。

“女朋友是比自己年纪大的职场人士，当对方给我买高档衣服时，至少得表面上推辞一下”

Forget it, it's too expensive.

Let's just **forget it**.
我们不要纠结了。

Forget it. You don't understand.
算了吧，你不明白。

Oh, **forget it**. It's not that important.
哦，算了，不是什么重要的事情。

Forget it. I'm not going to tell you now.
算了吧，我现在不会告诉你的。

A: I didn't buy any candy for you. 我可没给你买什么糖果。
B: Forget about it. I'll buy some later. 算了吧，我回头自己买。

I'll never forget ... 我绝对不会忘记……

表示“永远不会忘记，铭记于心”，说I'll nevet forget something (somebody)就可以了。

“不管什么事情，第一次尝试肯定是令人难忘的”

You will never forget your first time.

M·O·R·E

- I'll never forget ...
  我绝对不会忘记……的
- You'll never forget ...
  你绝对不会忘记……的

You should remember this. **I'll never forget** you.
你要记得，我永远都不会忘了你的。

I will never forget this.
我绝对不会忘记这件事的。

You will never forget me. I'm sure about that.
你绝对无法忘记我的。我非常确信这一点。

I promise you **I will not forget** this.
我答应你，绝对不会忘记这件事。

A: Didn't Elise look great tonight? 今天晚上爱丽丝气色很不错啊？
B: I'll never forget the dress she was wearing. 我绝对忘不了她今晚的着装。

I almost forget 我差点忘了某事

如果在forget前面加副词almost的话就表示“差点忘记某事”，可以用来表示好不容易记起某事。相反，如果加totally (completely)的话就表示“忘得一干二净”。

“突然想起怀孕的事情了，决定要每顿吃两人份的饭”

I totally forgot. I'm pregnant! I have to eat for two!

M·O·R·E

- I almost forgot (about/ to do) ... 我差点忘了某事

Oh, **I almost forgot**. Your file is here.
哦，我差点给忘了，你的文件在这。

I almost forgot about her present.
我差点忘了她的礼物了。

We totally forgot about lunch!
我们把午餐忘得一干二净！

A: I almost forgot to lock the apartment door. 我差点忘记锁门了。
B: You've got to be careful about robbers. 你得小心小偷啊。

remember 记住某事

remember有些时候会单独使用，不加任何宾语。以下是日常生活中较为常用的表达。希望读者们能够熟练地掌握，以便不时之需。

“在同学会上，对方能够记住我，但我却想不起来对方是谁”

You don't have to pretend to **remember**.

M·O·R·E

- I just remembered. 我刚刚想起来。(Now I remember.)
- You remembered! 你还记着呢！
- Just remember. 想想看。
- I don't remember. 我不记得。

Oh! I can't believe he **remembered**!
哦！我真不敢相信，他居然还记得！

Remember back in college? We had a lot of fun.
回想上大学的时候，我们当时很开心。

How can you not **remember** that?
你怎么能想不起来呢？

A: Did you take your vitamins this morning? 你今天早上吃维生素片了吗？
B: I don't remember. I'll take them now. 我不记得了。我现在就吃。

remember somebody (something) 记住……

remember后面可以接somebody或者something，例如：Remember your manners表示“不要乱来，遵守礼仪”等。

“如果记不清楚时，就要老老实实地说自己不记得”

To be honest, I don't remember you.

M·O·R·E

- You remember ... ?
  你记得……吗?
- remember it (that)
  记住……

You **remember** my brother Louis?
你还记得我哥哥路易斯吗?

You **remember** the necklace I gave you last year?
你还记得我去年送你的项链吗?

I **remember** that, it wasn't so bad.
我还记得，还不赖。

A: That Farrell. He went to our high school. 那个人和我们上的是同一所高中。
B: I remember him. He was on the baseball team. 我记得他。他曾经是校棒球队队员。

remember ...ing 记住做过某事

remember后面如果接 ...ing形式的话就表示“记住之前做过的事情”。要和表示“记住将来要做的事情”的remember to+动词区分开。

“到底谈过多少次恋爱啊，怎么连这个都记不住”

I'm sorry, but I don't remember dating you.

M·O·R·E

- remember+... ing
  记住以前做过……
- Do you remember ...ing?
  你还记得做过……吗?

I **remember** reading about this palace.
我记得我读过有关这座宫殿的文章。

Do you **remember** talking to me yesterday?
你还记得昨天晚上和我说过的事情吗?

Do you **remember** having a conversation with this young man?
你还记得和这个年轻人说过话吗?

A: I can't remember going home last night. 我不记得昨天晚上是怎么回家的了。
B: You were half asleep when you left the office. 你离开办公室的时候都快睡着了。

remember somebody (sth) ...ing 记住某人做过某事

和remember ...ing前面的情况一样，都表示记住曾经发生过的事情，但加上somebody后变成了记住别人做过的事情。remember后面接上somebody (something)+ ...ing就可以了。

"年轻的时候曾有个男生求我嫁给他，如今再次碰到了这个男生"

I remember you begging me to marry you.

I don't **remember you doing** the laundry.
我不记得见过你洗衣服。

I **remember people telling** me about it.
我记得别人对我说过这件事。

You **remember me telling** you that joke, right?
你记得我给你讲过这个笑话吧?

How can you not **remember us kissing**?
你怎么能记不得我们接吻呢?

A: I really love to go swimming. 我非常喜欢游泳。
B: I remember you swimming at the beach. 我还记得你在海边游过泳呢。

remember to do 记得要做的事情

与remember+ ...ing不同，remember后面如果接to+动词的话就表示"记住将要做的事情"。

"最近流行着各种病毒，为了不得病，孩子们必须做的事情"

Remember to wash your hands when you get home.

Did you **remember to** buy the toothpaste?
你还记得要买牙膏的事情吗?

Remember to e-mail me.
记得给我发邮件。

Just **remember to** wake us up before you go.
你离开之前记得叫醒我们。

Remember to speak up and don't turn your backs to the audience.
记住要大声说话，不要背对观众。

A: Damn, I forgot a condom. 讨厌，我忘了带安全套了。
B: Just remember to keep it safe. 别忘了小心点。

remember that 记住……

remember后面也可以接从句，经常使用的句式形态有You have to remember ... , I want you to remember ... 等。

"虽然分手了，但我的确真心爱过你"

I want you to remember that I really loved you!

M·O·R·E

- (Do) You remember that ... ?
  你还记得……吗?
- (Do) You remember sth (that) ... ?
  你还记得做过某事吗?
- Remember that (how) ...
  记住……
- You have to remember that ...
  你必须记住……；你要铭记……
- I want you to remember that ...
  我希望你一定记住……

Do you **remember that** you said you were going to get me a present?
你还记得你说过要给我买礼物吗?

She told me to always **remember that** the best was yet to come.
她让我永远都记住，美好的日子终会到来的。

You have to **remember** she's a different person when she drinks.
你必须记住，她一旦喝了酒，就会变成另外一个人。

You have to **remember that** my love for you is real.
你必须记住，我对你的爱是真心的。

I want you to **remember that** I'm a good person.
我希望你记住，我是个好人。

I want you to **remember that** I forgave you.
我希望你记住，我已经原谅你了。

I need you to **remember that** we are all here for you.
我希望你记住，我们来这里都是因为你。

I want you to **remember that** I gave you 500 dollars.
我希望你记住，我给了你500美元。

Remember that you and I aren't friends anymore.
记住，我们已经不再是朋友了。

You **remember that** Christmas we had much fun.
你还记得我们度过的那次美好的圣诞节吗。

A: I'm going to take a nap for a while. 我得小睡一会了。
B: Remember that we're going to a movie tonight. 别忘了我们今天晚上要去看一部电影。

A: How is Tom's mom doing these days? 汤姆的妈妈最近怎么样?
B: Do you remember that she was put in the hospital? 你还记得他妈妈被送进医院的事情吗?

A: I want you to remember that we're having an exam. 我希望你记住，我们要考试了。
B: All of us will need to study for it. 我们所有人都得认真准备考试。

remember what (how) 记住……

remember也可以接以what, why, how等疑问词开头的从句。

"能说出这种话的人，要么是政治家，要么是个精神分裂症患者"

I actually don't remember what I said.

M·O·R·E

- remember what ... 记住……
- remember why ... 记住为什么……
- remember how ... 记住怎样 ...

You **remember what** that is?
你还记得那是什么吗?

Do you **remember why** you dumped the guy?
你还记得你为什么甩了那个家伙吗?

Just **remember how much** we all like you.
请记住，我们有多么喜欢你。

Do you **remember how** your father used to be?
你还记得你父亲以前是什么样的吗?

I can't even **remember what** she looks like.
我甚至都记不清她长什么样。

I can't even **remember why** we were fighting!
我甚至都记不清我们为什么在打架了!

Remember how you hate people talking behind your back?
想想看，你是多么讨厌别人在背地里说你坏话啊。

A: Do you remember what happened during our vacation? 你还记得我们度假的时候发生什么事情了吗?
B: Oh yeah, it rained for five days straight. 当然，那时候连续下了5天的雨。

A: I don't remember why we're being punished. 我不记得我们为什么要受惩罚。
B: It's because we skipped school last month. 是因为上个月逃课的事情。

A: Remember how we planned the party? 还记得我们是怎么计划派对的吗?
B: Sure. I'll make the food and you greet the guests. 当然，我会准备食物，你来接待客人。

remember when 记得什么时候……

人们经常会提到某些事件和地方的回忆。这时候可以用remember when (where)主语+动词或remember+时间名词+when主语+动词的结构。

"记不清上一次见到对方是什么时候的事了"

I'm trying to remember when I saw you last.

M·O·R·E

- remember (the day) when
  记得……的时候
- remember where
  记得在哪里……

Remember when we went to Central Park?
你还记得我们是什么时候去的中央公园吗?

I **remember the day** I got my first pay check.
我还记得我第一天拿到工资的情景。

I **remember when** we first got engaged.
我还记得我们第一次订婚是什么时候。

Do you **remember where** the car was parked?
你还记得车停在哪吗?

A: Remember when we went to the beach? **你还记得我们是什么时候去的海边吗?**
B: I loved walking along the shore when we were there. **在那里的时候，我非常喜欢沿着海岸线走。**

remember the last time when 记住最后一次做某事的时候

经常会出现remember+时间名词+when主语+动词的形态，在这里"时间名词"变成了"the last time (first) time"。表示"记得最后一次(第一次)做某事的时候"。

"如果是个花花公子的话，凡事都要谨慎了，不能随便回答问题"

Remember the first time that you kissed me?

I can't **remember the last time** I stayed up all night.
我不记得上一次通宵达旦是什么时候了。

I can't **remember the last time** I had so much fun.
我不记得上一次这么开心是什么时候了。

I **remember the first time** I asked a girl out.
我还记得我第一次约女生出去的场景。

I **remember the first time** I met you.
我还记得第一次见到你的场景。

A: Let's go to a Mexican restaurant tonight. **我们今天晚上去墨西哥风味餐厅吧。**
B: I don't remember the last time when we ate Mexican food. **我不记得我们上一次吃墨西哥料理是什么时候的事情。**

More Expressions

- **before I forget** 在忘记某事之前

  Before I forget, you got a call from Sam.
  在我忘了之前先跟你说，山姆给你打过电话。

- **Aren't you forgetting ... ?**
  你没有忘记什么吗？

  Look Peter, **aren't you forgetting** anything? 瞧，彼得，你是不是忘了什么？

- **be forgetful** 模糊不清

  I'm afraid I'**m becoming forgetful**.
  我很害怕我变得健忘。

  She'**s very forgetful**. She's older than she looks.
  她非常健忘，她其实比看起来更老。

- **forgive and forget** 忘记和原谅

  Let's **forgive and forget** it.
  我们就让它过去吧。

  Forgive and forget. That's my motto.
  忘掉和原谅，这就是我的箴言。

- **as long as I can remember**
  只要我记得

  I slept more soundly than ever **as long as I can remember**.
  我睡得比之前任何一次都长。

- **be remembered for (as)**
  被记为……

  I'll **be remembered as** the one who saved the company.
  人们会把我记为是拯救公司的人。

- **remember me to somebody**
  替我向某人传达问候

  Remember me to your brother.
  帮我给你哥哥带个好。

- **One thing that we have to remember is that ...** 有件事情我们需要记住

  One thing that we have to remember is that we have to help the poor.
  有件事情我们一定要记住，就是必须要帮助那些贫困的人。

虽然心疼，但该交还得交

Pay

“增加薪水”是我们所有人的心声。表示付钱的表达可以用pay (money) for，另外，“向某人支付”时要用pay somebody money。也可以引申为产生某种好的结果，带来收益，收支平衡等。而pay，作为名词则表示薪水的意思，payraise则表示提高薪水。

基本概念

1 支付（物品，税等）

I can't afford to pay my rent this month. 我这个月没钱交房租了。

We'd like to pay separately. 我们要分开付。

How would you like to pay? 你想怎么支付?

We have to pay first. 我们得先付钱。

2 带来（好结果或利益），收支平衡

Working with you doesn't pay. 跟你一块工作根本没有好处。

You have to keep jogging. It will pay you off in the future. 你得坚持慢跑，肯定会对你的未来有帮助。

3 （名词）支付，付款，薪水

Today's payday.今天要发工资了。

You can spread your payment out over six months. 你可以分六个月进行付款。

pay for 支付……的费用，付出……的代价（被教训一顿）

pay是表示支付的动词。pay for后面需要加支付的事项，表示“需要为……支付”，也可以引申为“付出……的代价”。

“朋友搬进了新家，去他们家拜访的时候问问多少钱买的”

How much did you **pay for** your house?

Let's go eat something. I'll **pay for** dinner.
我们去吃点东西吧。我来请客。

Don't worry. He will **pay for** my lawyer.
不要担心，他会为我支付律师费的。

We would like to **pay for** your airline ticket.
我们想为你支付机票钱。

You get what you **pay for**.
你付出了多少，就会有多少回报。

A: Can I pay for the parking when I leave? 我能不能等离开的时候再支付停车费?
B: I'm sorry, but you have to pay now. 不好意思，您得现在支付。

pay for that 支付……的费用

与pay for用法相似，在日常生活中，如果需要支付的对象已经提到，就可以在后面用pay for it (that, this) 简化。

“在街边买面包，却还要用支票支付”

I'm going to **pay for this** with a check.

You'll **pay for that**!
你会付出代价的！(我们走着瞧！)

How would you like to **pay for this**?
你想怎么支付?

How much did you **pay for that**?
你花了多少钱?

How'd you **pay for them**?
你是怎么买到的?

A: Wow, I ate so much food today. 哇塞，我今天吃得太多了。
B: You'll pay for that. Your stomach is going to hurt. 你肯定会为此付出代价的，胃可能会受损伤。

pay money for (to) 为……进行支付

具体说明支付的费用多少，在pay for的pay和for之间加上金额就可以了。

“老爸说，既然都已经长大成人了，为什么还要为对方支付聚会的费用”

Why should I **pay good money to** go to your party?

M·O·R·E

- pay a lot of (good) money for (to)
  在……上花很多钱
- pay+数字 (money) for (to)
  在……上花了多少钱

I **paid $500 for** this dress.

我花了500美元买了这条裙子。

He **paid a lot of money for** it.

他在这上面花了很多钱。

He **paid good money to** find out how to do that.

他为了寻求解决的方法，花了不少钱。

A: She paid $200 for her new phone. 她花了200美元买新电话。

B: That sounds like a pretty good deal. 听起来真是一桩划算的买卖啊。

pay somebody money 向某人支付

要具体说明支付的对象，用pay somebody for (to)就可以了。somebody后面可以加金额，另外，也可以去掉somebody，表示“花钱做某事”。

“不管是花钱雇人说脏话（post malicious comments）的人，还是自己说脏话的人，都不是好东西”

He **paid me 20 dollars** to post malicious comments.

M·O·R·E

- pay sb+钱+for (to)
  向某人支付多少钱（做某事）
- pay (sb) to+动词 (for)
  （向某人）支付多少钱做某事

She **paid me 50 dollars** not to tell.

她给了我50美元，让我保守秘密。

Her father **pays you for** baby-sitting?

他爸爸花钱雇你看孩子？

You couldn't **pay me to** do it.

你不能花钱让我做这个。

A: You will have to pay me $30,000. 你必须支付3万美元。

B: No way. You must be joking. 没门。你开什么玩笑。

pay in cash 用现金支付

支付的方法大体上有三种，分别是“现金支付”(pay in (with) cash)，“用支票支付”(pay by check)或者“刷卡支付(pay by credit card)”等。

“对于不喜欢刷卡的人来说，或者出于防范犯罪的行为来说，这种制度”

Her hotel bill is always paid in cash.

M·O·R·E

- pay by check = pay for sth with a check 用支票支付
- pay (for sth) in cash 用现金支付（某事）(with cash)
- pay by credit card 刷卡支付(charge sth =buy sth on credit)

Will you be **paying by credit card** or **with cash**?
您是要刷卡呢，还是现金支付?

I'll **pay by check**.
我要用支票支付。

I'm just going to **pay for this with a check**.
我要用支票进行支付。

Can I **pay in** Korean won?
我能用韩元支付吗?

A: How would you like to pay for it? You can use your credit card.
您要怎么支付？可以选择信用卡支付。

B: I'd like to pay in cash. How much is it? 我要用现金支付，一共多少钱?

pay the bill 买单

pay后面也可以不接金额，而是接需要支付的账单(bill)或者税务(tax)，罚款(fine)等。

“在黑道上混的时候难免会遇到说不清的状况，令人非常无奈”

Why should I pay a price? I didn't even do it.

M·O·R·E

- pay the bill 买单
- pay a fine 交罚款
- pay the price 付出代价
- pay rent 交房费
- I'd like to pay the bill, please 我想买单

I'm broke. I don't have money to **pay the bill**.
我穷得叮当响。没有钱买单了。

Just my luck. I have to **pay a fine** for speeding.
我能有什么运气，只好交超速罚款了。

You commit a crime, you **pay the price**.
你犯罪了，就要付出代价。

Can you lend me some money? I've got to **pay rent**!
你能借我点钱吗? 我得交房租了!

A: I forgot to pay the electric bill this month. 我这个月忘了交电费了。

B: Pay the bill as soon as you can. 尽可能快点交。

get paid 得到支付，拿到薪水

get paid表示“以某种代价得到金钱”，可以用来说员工拿到薪水等。如果想表达拿到钱的具体理由，就可以用为get paid for+名词（to+动词）。

“在大街上发传单的人其实很不容易的”

I get paid $10 an hour for this.

M·O·R·E

- get paid (钱)
  拿到多少钱
- get paid for
  因……拿到钱

We're not leaving until we **get paid**!
如果我们拿不到钱，就绝对不会离开！

We work. We **get paid**. You don't owe me anything.
我们工作就有薪水，你没有欠我什么。

Some guys **get paid** a great deal of money for it.
有些人因为这件事得到了一大笔钱。

A: If you ask me, we aren't getting paid enough. 要我说的话，我们拿到的薪水肯定不够。

B: That's true, but we don't have a choice. 没错，不过我们也没有别的选择了。

pay attention 集中注意

pay attention 是我们非常熟悉的短语。表示“集中注意”，用来引起别人的注意力。相反，“不关心”是pay no attention。

“如果对每一个绯闻都非常关心的话，就没有额外的精力管自己的事情了”

I don't pay attention to gossip.

M·O·R·E

- pay (no) attention (to ...)
  （对某事）集中注意力
- pay one's respects
  郑重拜访某人；
  表示尊重

I need you to **pay attention**. Do you hear me?
我需要你专注，听到没?

She ignored me. She didn't **pay any attention to** me.
她无视了我。她根本就不在乎我。

I barely even know her, but I feel like I have to **pay my respects**.
我基本上不怎么了解她，不过我感觉应该尊重她。

A: I need you to pay attention. Do you hear me? 我需要你集中注意力。听到没?

B: Yes! Calm down. I hear you. 好！冷静。我在听。

pay back 还钱

正如pay back的字面含义，表示还钱。即“返还之前借到的钱”，也可以用来表示“报仇”。

“一个值得信任的债务者就要按时偿还所有的债务”

I'm going to **pay you back** every cent.

M·O·R·E

- pay sb back 向某人还钱
- pay back a loan 偿还贷款

I promise I'll **pay you back**.
我发誓，我肯定会还你的。

You can **pay me back** whenever you like.
你想什么时候还，就什么时候还。

I'll **pay you back** all the money you invested.
我会一分不差地把你投资的钱还给你。

You don't have to **pay me back**.
你不需要还我钱。

A: Do you promise to pay me back? **你发誓能还我钱吗?**
B: You have my word. **我保证。**

pay off 产生利益，出现好结果，偿还债务

pay off具有两种含义，一是偿还对方的债务，另一种是像产生利益一样，表示出现了好结果。

“刷卡的时候完全不考虑后果，最后只好卖掉心爱的宝贝以便在规定时间内还款”

I'll sell some jewelry to **pay off** the credit card.

M·O·R·E

- pay off one's debt 偿还债务
- pay off the credit card 刷卡支付

Don't worry about me **paying off your debt**.
不要担心，我肯定会还你钱的。

I've **paid off all my debt**.
我已经还清了所有的债。

Sending that e-mail **has finally paid off**.
发送那封电子邮件带来了好结果。

I'm going to **pay off my credit card**.
我要偿还信用卡借款。

A: What are you going to do with your tax return? **如果得到税金返还，你要做什么?**
B: I'm going to pay off my credit cards. **我要还信用卡的债。**

More Expressions

•pay a visit to 访问

I'll **pay a visit to** the Paul's on my way home. 我要在回家的路上去保罗家看看。

•pay one's dues 负责任；付出代价

I' **ve paid my dues**. 我已经付出了代价。

I **paid my dues** but they would give me hard times.

我已经尽责了，不过他们还是要为难我。

•pay through the nose 背黑锅

You'll **pay through the nose** if you buy a ticket on the day you're leaving.

如果你出发的当天买票的话就会背黑锅的。

•be hell to pay 陷入极度困难的状况

If you change your mind, there's going to **be hell to pay**.

如果你改变想法的话，肯定会陷入巨大的困境。

•pay one's debt to society

（违法的人）付出代价

His dad **paid his debt to society** while he was in prison.

他爸爸在监狱的时候为自己的行为付出了代价。

•pay raise 提升薪水

I got a big **pay raise**! 我的薪水暴涨了！

•check 薪水

I got my first **pay check** yesterday.

我昨天拿到了第一份工资。

无论行不行，先试试看

Try

表示努力，尝试，常用的表达有try hard（努力做），try next time（下次再试试），try again（再试试）等。另外，如果try后面接饮食名词的话就表示尝一尝，而try on表示试试衣服。如果是try to+动词的话，则表示“尝试着做某事”，如果作为名词，例如give a try，就表示试一试。

基本概念

1 试图，努力

If you try, you can do it. 如果你试试的话，肯定能行的。

I'm trying really hard. 我真的非常努力。

Just take it easy and try to relax. 不用担心，试着放松。

2 尝尝（食物），试穿衣服(on)

May I try it on? 我能试穿一下吗?

I'd like to try the steak. 我想尝尝牛排。

3 （名词）试图

Let's give it a try. 我们试试吧。

Give it a try! 试试看!

try something 试试某事

try如果加上something或everything的话就表示试试看。try something后面可以接else, new, different等形容词，try everything后面也可以接to+动词。

"一对情侣边吃饺子，边喝咖啡，说道"

We just wanted to try something a little different.

M·O·R·E

- try sth else (new) 试试别的(新事物)
- try everything (to+动词) (为了某事) 尝试所有的可能性

Let's try something else.
我们试试别的吧。

I've tried everything. I give up.
我已经试过所有的可能性了，我还是放弃吧。

I tried everything to make myself feel better.
我已经尽最大努力让自己心情好点了。

A: I just can't salsa dance as well as other people. 我就是不能像别人那样跳舞。

B: Try something else. You'll find a hobby you like. 试试别的吧。你会找到一个你喜欢的爱好的。

try 尝尝

try后面如果接饮食名词的话就表示"尝尝某食物"。try a steak表示"尝尝牛排"，try some pizza表示"尝尝比萨"。

"一家面包店里的曲奇饼干非常有名，为了尝个鲜，特意来到了这家店"

We came by to try some of your famous cookies

M·O·R·E

- try+饮食名词 尝尝某食物
- try some (of)+饮食名词 尝一点某食物
- I'd like to try+饮食名词 我想吃某食物

I'd like to take you to try some Indian food.
我想带你去尝尝印度料理。

Do you want to try some of my pie?
你想尝尝我亲手做的馅饼吗?

Go ahead. Try a piece.
来，尝一小块。

A: You should try Korean food. It's great. 你得尝尝韩国料理。非常不错的。

B: I've heard that it's quite healthy too. 我还听说那些东西非常健康呢。

try it 试试这个，尝尝这个

可以用代词it，that，this等代替之前已经提到过的东西。想要表示“之前做过吗？”就可以说Have you tried this before，如果想表达“需要试试吗？”，就可以说Should we try it?

“孩子非常贪玩，想要给他做点吃的，他却只顾着玩电脑，任由饭菜慢慢变凉”

You have to **try it** while it's still warm.

Why don't you **try it**?
你怎么不试试看？

We'**ve already tried it** twice.
我们已经试过两次了。

Andy, you must (have got to) **try this**.
安迪，你必须试试这个。

Hey, baby, we **haven't tried it** in the kitchen yet.
嘿，宝贝儿，我们还没在厨房试过这个呢。

A: What do you think about bungee jumping? 你觉得蹦极跳怎么样？
B: It looks fun. I'd like to try it. 看起来很不错。我想试试。

try (it) again 重新试试

try后面可以接副词或副词短语，形成多种表达。表示“重新试试”为try again，表示“努力做”就是try hard，而表示“下次再试试”就是try next time。

“在玩蹦极的时候，经常会有人腿软，不敢跳下去，对此，助教经常会说”

Take a deep breath and **try again**.

M·O·R·E

- try hard
  努力试试
- try next time
  下次再试

Don't give up. Let's **try it again**.
不要放弃，我们再试试吧。

You want to **try it again**?
你想再试试看？

Well, **try harder**. I'm sure you can do it.
好，再努力一些。我敢肯定，你一定能做到的。

You've got to **try harder** next time.
你下次得多努力了。

A: I don't know what I'm going to do. 我不知道我将来要干些什么。
B: Don't worry. You can try again! 不要着急，你可以再试试！

try to 试图做某事，努力

try 后面如果接to+动词的话就表示“试试还没做过的事情”，“尝试”，“努力做某事”等，相反，如果想表达“想尽办法不做某事”时可以用try not to。但try ...ing则表示“试试看……”。

“这种情况下，需要勇气”

She tried to jump cliff.

M·O·R·E

- try to+动词
  尝试做某事，努力做某事
  （try and+动词）
- try+... ing
  抱着试试看的态度做某事
- try hard to+动词
  努力做某事

I **tried to** help her.
我本来想帮助她来着。

I don't get it. What **are** you **trying to** say?
我不太明白，你到底想说什么?

I **tried eating** Korean food. It was delicious.
我尝过韩国料理，挺不错的。

A: If I had his phone number, I would call him. 如果我知道他的号码，我会给他打电话的。

B: Why don't you try to get his number? 那你为什么没试着跟他要电话号码?

I'll try to ... 我会试试看某事

try to+动词是最常用的结构，表示“试试做某事”。而I'm trying to+动词表示“我正在做某事”，用来表达自己所处的状况。

“好不容易才进入到了这家梦寐以求的公司，上班第一天一定要展现出自己最出色的一面”

I'm trying to make a good impression.

M·O·R·E

- I'll try to+动词
  我会试试看做某事
- I'm trying to+动词
  我正在试着做某事，
  我正打算做某事

I'll try to make her feel better.
我会尽量让她感觉好点的。

I'll try to get back as soon as I can.
我会尽可能快点回来的。

I'll try to catch you later.
我回头再试着联系你。

A: I lost my hat at your house yesterday. 我昨天把帽子忘在你们家了。

B: Oh really? I'll try to find it for you. 哦，真的吗？我回去帮你找找看。

Are you trying to ... ? 你是打算做某事吗?

同样为try to+动词的形式，用来询问对方的意图。尤其要记住最常用的表达Are you trying to say (tell me) ... ?，实用性很强。

“一个酒鬼闯了红灯，交警让他出示驾照，不料偏偏这个时候没带”

Are you trying to get me in trouble?

M·O·R·E

- Are you trying to+动词？
  你是要做某事吗?
- Are you trying to say (tell me) that S+V?
  你现在是在说(告诉我)……吗?

Are you trying to threaten me?
你这是要威胁我吗?

What are you doing? **Are you trying to** hurt me?
你在干什么? 你是要伤害我吗?

Are you trying to say that this is wrong?
你是要说这个是错误的吗?

A: Are you trying to cook some food? 你是要做些料理吗?
B: Yeah, I want to make some spaghetti. 恩，我想做点意大利面。

What are you trying to ... ? 你是要做什么?

在Are you trying to+动词前面加上疑问词，可以用What are you trying to ... ?和Why (Where) are you tring to ... ?

“150Kg的老婆在客厅蹦个不停，老公正好回家”

What are you trying to do, my God?

M·O·R·E

- What are you trying to+动词
  你是要做什么?
- What are you trying to do,+动词?
  你到底要干什么，要……?

What are you trying to say?
你到底想要说什么?

What are you trying to do, hit me?
你到底想干什么，打我啊?

Why are you trying to get away from me?
你为什么打算离开我?

A: Excuse me, I seem to have lost my way. 不好意思，我好像迷路了。
B: Where are you trying to go? 您是想去哪里呢?

What I am trying to say is (that) ... 我想说的是……

在表达自己的想法或意图，重新整理一遍思绪时可以用到的句式，与All I'm saying is (that) ... 具有相似的含义。

"每次聚会买单都会消失的人，不知今天怎么了，居然要请大家吃饭"

What I'm trying to say is he's changed.

What I'm trying to say is that she's not rich.
我想说的是，她并不是个有钱人。

What I'm trying to say is I want you to leave.
我想说的是，我希望你离开。

What I'm trying to say is that I didn't mean to hurt you.
我想说的是，我根本就没打算伤害你。

I guess **what I'm trying to say is** I love to drive.
我猜我想说的是，我喜欢开车。

A: I don't understand what you mean. 我搞不懂你是什么意思。
B: What I'm trying to say is I feel lonely. 我想说的是，我感到非常孤独。

Don't try to ... 不要尝试做某事

用try to+动词，可以向对方给予"注意"或"警告"，也可以单独使用Try not to+动词。

"老婆的一些行为惹怒了老公，他说道"

Don't try to make me feel better.

M·O·R·E

- Don't try to+动词
  不要试着做某事
- try not to+动词
  试着不做某事

Don't try to tell me you don't have it.
别告诉我，你身上没有。

Don't try to apologize right now.
现在不要向我道歉。

It's too late. Please **try not to** think about it.
已经晚了。请不要再想这件事了。

A: Teresa and I are going on a first date. 特蕾萨和我今天是第一次约会。
B: Don't try to kiss her when the date finishes. 在约会结束的时候不要想着去亲她。

try for 为了得到某物而努力

try for+名词表示“为了得到某物或者为了达成某种目的而付出努力”。try后面不仅可以接for+名词，还可以接事实。

“暗地里瞒着老板，伪造契约，打算把公司卖出去，不小心被发现”

You'll be tried for the crime you committed.

M·O·R·E

- Let me try sth
  想要占据某物，
  想要得到某物
- be tried for sth
  被判为……

So do you think you will **try for** another adoption?
所以说你在考虑再领养一个?

Do you want to **try for** it again?
你是不是想再挑战一次?

A: My uncle is trying for a job at Samsung. 我叔叔正在为进入三星工作而努力。

B: Great. I've heard it's a good place to work. 很不错啊。我听说这家公司的工作条件很好。

Let me try ... 我来试试……

表示自发的说“我来试试做某事”或者“我会试试做某事，所以再给我点时间”等。可以单独使用Let me try，也可以用作Let me try+名词（to+动词）。

“打电话要找的人不在，只好再打对方手机看看”

Let me try her cell phone.

M·O·R·E

- Let me try sth
  我来试试
- Let me try to+动词
  我来试试做某事

I believe I can do it. **Let me try.**
我相信我能成功的。让我再试试吧。

Let me try that again.
让我重新试试吧。

Does it not taste good? **Let me try** it.
这个味道不好吗？让我尝尝吧。

Let me try to explain it to you in detail.
我来试着给你详细地介绍一下。

A: This math homework is really confusing. 这道数学作业题实在太麻烦了。

B: Let me try to explain it to you. 我来试着给你解释解释吧。

try one's best 使出全力

try后面可以接特定的名词，形成短语。除try one's best之外还有try one's luck，表示“碰碰运气”，try one's patience表示“考验某人的耐心”。

“部分艺人会想尽办法找借口不服兵役，这些人的觉悟”

He **tried his best** to figure out a way to avoid joining the military.

M·O·R·E

- try one's best (luck)
  使出全力（试试运气）
- try one's patience
  考验某人的耐性

I'**m trying my best**. You can trust me.

我正在拼尽全力。你可以相信我。

I will **try my luck**.

我可以碰碰运气。（不管行不行）

She went back to the casino to **try her luck** again.

她回到了赌场，打算再碰碰运气。

You'**re trying my patience**.

你正在挑战我的耐心。

A: My son is not very good at sports. 我儿子不大擅长体育运动。

B: Tell him to try his best when he is on a team. 告诉他，在一个团队里要使出自己的全力。

try on 试试衣服

可以想想从上面套衣服，因此加上了一个on，变成try on。表示为了看衣服合不合身，而试试看。

“陪老婆购物的丈夫积极地给她推荐好东西，真是耐心至极啊”

Just **try something on**. How about this sweater?

Would you like to **try it on**?

你想试试吗?

May I **try on** a pair of shoes?

我能试试这双鞋吗?

Is it okay to **try on** anything I want?

我可以想试哪件就试哪件吗?

A: May I try on a pair of shoes? 我可以试试这双鞋吗?

B: Sure. What size do you need? 好的，您穿多大码?

try out 测试一下（运转正常与否）

表示测试一下某物运转情况怎么样，也可以用在选拔大会或面试中，有时也可以用try out for。

"妻子的料理水平实在不敢恭维，很不幸，她的第一个牺牲者就是可怜的丈夫"

I'd like to **try out** new recipes this time.

M·O·R·E

- try out
  试试看
- try out for
  （运动员等）参加选拔大会(audition for)

She **is trying out** different cookie recipes.
她正在测试各种曲奇饼干的配方。

You'**re trying out** for the cheerleading squad?
你要参加拉拉队员选拔大会?

She **tried out for** the movie.
她参加了电影选秀。

A: I'd like to try out one of your cameras. 我想试试你们的某一台摄像机。
B: Sure, I'll let you borrow whichever one you want. 好的，不论你想要哪一台都可以借你。

More Expressions

- **give it a try** 试试看

I'll **give them a try**.
我会给他们一次机会的。

Maybe I'll **give him a try**.
也许我会给他一次机会。

- **Nice try!**（虽然没能达成目的）好样的!（干得不错!）

It's too bad you lost the contest. **Nice try**. 很遗憾你没能赢得比赛，不过还是好样的!

- **be worth a try** 值得一试

I guess it'**s worth a try**. 我猜，这值得一试。

Just try me. 跟我说说看。给我一次机会。

Keep (on) trying.
继续前进；不要停；继续努力。

Mind if I try? 我试试可以吗?

等到底

Wait

wait表示等待，大多和时间名词等一起使用。wait a minute, wait until或wait an hour等都是常用的结构。另外，wait for表示“等待某人”。can't wait+动词，表示“等不及做某事”，换句话说就是“非常渴望做某事”。而wait on 主要用于饭店等场所的服务，也可以用作：等待。

基本概念

1 等待

Sorry I have kept you waiting so long. 不好意思，让你等了这么久。

I'll wait outside. 我在外面等吧。

I guess we have to wait until he comes back.我猜我们得等到他回来了。

2 服务(wait on)，招待，等待

The staff at the restaurant were busy waiting on customers. 饭店里的服务员们正忙着招待客人呢。

How does he wait on tables dressed like that? 他怎么可以穿着那种衣服给客人们服务呢?

I'm waiting on my girlfriend to call me up. 我正在等我女朋友的电话。

3 （名词）等待，待机

I'm on a wait list. 我的名字在等待名单上。

I've been on the wait list since June. 我自从6月份开始就在等待名单里。

wait until (till) 等到某时候

用来表示等到某个时候，until (till)后面可以接tomorrow, next week等时间名词，或者接主语+动词。

“妈妈抱怨现在的孩子太自私”

You have to **wait until** your father came back to have dinner.

We can't **wait until** Tuesday. We're having a party tonight.

我们不能等到星期二。我们今晚就要举办派对。

We'll just **wait until** Allan gets home.

我们要等到亚伦到家。

Let's just **wait until** I'm on leave.

我们就等到我放假吧。

A: I guess we have to wait until he comes back. **我猜我们得等到他回来了。**

B: When do you think he'll get back? **你觉得他什么时候能回来？**

wait a week 等待一周的时间

表示等待时间的长短，在wait后面接上表示时间的名词就可以了。也可以说成wait for+时间名词。

“父母一直都反对小两口结婚，没办法只能跟他们说已经有孩子了”

We'**ve been waiting a long time** for this.

M·O·R·E

- I can wait+时间
  我可以等多长时间
- I've been waiting+时间
  我已经等了多长时间了

I can **wait a bit longer**.

我可以再等一会。

Just don't **wait too long**. Okay?

不要等太久，好不好？

Why did you **wait two hours** out there?

你干嘛在那里等了两个小时？

I'**ve been waiting four hours** for you to show up.

我一直等你出现，足足等了四个小时。

A: I waited too long to drink my coffee. **我等太久了，咖啡都冷得不能喝了。**

B: Is it cold? Maybe we should order another one. **凉了吗？要不我们再点一杯吧。**

wait outside 在外面等

可以用副词表达等待的地点，比如说wait outside (inside), wait here (there)等。另外，wait out here (there)表示等待的地点为室外。

"本来想逃课出去玩，不料被校长抓了个正着，没办法只好挨训"

You should go back to your class and wait there.

M·O·R·E

- wait outside (inside) 在外面（里面）等。
- wait here (there) 在这里（那里）等。

Would you **wait outside**, please?
你能在外面等等吗?

Wait out here. I'll be right back.
在这里等等。我马上就回来。

Okay, **wait there**, I'll be over in a second.
好的，在那等吧，我马上就完事了。

A: I'm going into the house to talk to Helen. 我要进去和海伦谈谈。
B: OK, I'll wait outside until you're finished. 好的，我会在这等到你出来的。

wait a minute 稍等片刻

表示稍等一会，可以向对方说"wait a minute"，也可以用来暂时中断对方的话，或者在想起什么事情的时候突然说"我突然想到了什么"，可以用second，moment代替minute。

"刚刚做完鼻梁的整容手术，以为没人能看出来，没想到被朋友一眼识破"

Wait a minute, who told you that?

Wait a second, that's not what I meant.
等等，我不是那个意思。

Wait a minute. Hold still.
稍等一会，不要动。

Wait a minute. What are you talking about?
等等，你到底要说什么?

Wait a minute. I forgot something in the car.
稍等片刻，我在车里面落了点东西。

A: I need to buy a new pair of shoes for school. 我得买一双新鞋在学校穿。
B: Wait a minute. Didn't you buy shoes last month? 等等，你不是上个月就买过了吗?

can't wait to 非常想做某事

字面含义为“迫不及待地想做某事”，可以理解为“非常渴望做某事”。can't wait to+动词（for+名词）为常用的结构，与I'm dying to具有相同的含义。

“如果连这个都理解不了，那还不如干脆分手呢”

You're so hot. I can't wait to be a father.

M·O·R·E

- I can't wait to do it
  我想马上就做某事
- I can't wait to tell you this
  我等不及要告诉你这个
- can't wait for sb to+动词
  非常希望某人做某事
- I can't wait until S+V
  我非常渴望做某事

I **can't wait to** see that movie.
我实在等不及看那部电影了。

I **can not wait to** marry you. I am so into you.
我迫不及待地想要和你结婚。我实在太喜欢你了。

I **can not wait to** get to New York.
我非常渴望去纽约。

A: I can't wait for the school holiday. 我巴不得学校的假期快点到来。
B: What will you do with your free time? 那你空闲的时间里打算干些什么？

can (can't) wait 不着急（着急）

虽然can't wait与前面的句式相似，但主语变成了事物，Something can wait表示可以等待，即“不着急”。相反Something can't wait表示等不及，即“很急”。

“半夜四点儿子就起来吵爸爸，让他把电脑打开”

Can't this wait until morning?

M·O·R·E

- This can wait.
  这个不那么着急。
- That can't wait.
  这很急。
- This (That) can('t) wait until ...
  可以等到……（不可以）.

The rest **can wait**.
剩下的部分可以慢慢来。

Can't that wait? Why don't you double check?
不能推迟一些吗？你怎么不再检查检查？

Can't this wait until morning?
不能推迟到明天早上吗？

A: Shall we keep working on the project? 我们要继续做这个项目吗？
B: This can wait. Let's go get some dinner. 这个不着急。我们去吃点饭吧。

wait one's turn 等待某人的顺序

turn作名词，可以表示“顺序”，“次序”等，wait one's turn表示“等待某人的顺序”。

“去买最新款的智能手机4S，看到号码牌上的序号写着100”

She has no choice but to **wait her turn.**

I'm just getting a cookie, so **wait your turn.**
我买来了曲奇饼干，你就再等等吧。

Well, you'll have to **wait your turn.**
恩，你必须等着轮到你。

That's okay, we'll **wait our turn.**
没关系，我们等就是了。

A: Come on, hurry up. I need to use the bathroom. 快点快点，我得马上去洗手间。

B: Wait your turn. You'll be able to use it soon. 等等吧，很快就轮到你了。

keep somebody waiting 让某人等待

没有准时出现在约会地点，而让somebody等待的句型，迟到的人经常会用来表达歉意，即Sorry to have kept you waiting。

“每次都会迟到，还说一些荒唐的理由，这次竟然说地铁站里出现了一头野猪”

I can't stand it. You always **keep me waiting.**

I'm so sorry to **keep you waiting.**
很抱歉让你等我。

Sorry I **kept you waiting** so long.
很抱歉我让你等了那么久。

Come on now, don't **keep me waiting.**
快点，不要让我一直等着。

If you're serious about a guy, **keep him waiting** for at least five dates.
如果你想真心和某个人在一起，就至少让他等五六次约会后再说。

M·O·R·E

- keep sb waiting
  让某人等待
- Sorry to have kept you waiting so long
  很抱歉，让你等了这么久。

A: How was Henry and June's date last night? 昨天晚上亨利和琼的约会怎么样？

B: June kept him waiting for over an hour. 琼让亨利等了一个多小时。

wait for 等待某人

wait for表示“等待某人”，人们最熟悉的短语之一。也可以用wait for somebody to+动词，表示“等待某人做某事”。

“向朋友介绍一个男生，说对方是骑着白马的王子”

I can't **wait for** you to meet him.

M·O·R·E

- wait for sb (sth)
  等待某人（某物）
- wait for sb to+动词
  等待某人做某事
- wait to+动词
  等着做某事

We**'re all still waiting for** someone to come.
我们还在等着有人过来。

I**'ve been waiting for** this a long time.
我已经等了很久了。

I**'m waiting for** my husband. He's bringing the car.
我正在等老公。他去取车了。

A: Could you wait for me in my office? 你能在我办公室里等一会吗?
B: Sure. I'll go and make myself comfortable. 好的，我去随便待着了。

More Expressions

- **wait and see** 观望
  Let's **wait and see** how things go.
  让我们观望事态如何发展。

- wait on 等待……的到达，服务
  We **were waiting on** you to check the desk. 我们正在等你过来检查桌子呢。

- **wait up** 熬夜等待
  Don't **wait up**. 别熬夜等我。

- **wait out** 等到……的结束
  We set up the tents and **waited out** the storm. 我们搭上了帐篷，等待着暴风雨的结束。

What are you waiting for? 你在等什么?
What are we waiting for? 我们在等什么?
Good things come to him (those) who wait. 有志者，事竟成。

最后的希望

Hope/Wish

现在来讲讲希望。先说hope，可以用hope to+动词或hope that。而对于wish来说，wish to 是比较formal的情况，wish somebody something表示“希望某人得到某物”，比方说I wish you a Merry Christmas等。Wish可用为I wish 主语+动词，可以用虚拟语气。

基本概念

1 希望做某事，希望怎么样（hope 主语+动词）

I hope you aren't angry. 我希望你不要生气。

I hope you'll come again. 我希望你再来。

I hope you'll enjoy the party. 我希望你能喜欢这个派对。

2 渴望，希望，如果……就太好了

I wish we were together. 我希望我们能在一起。

I wish you good luck. 祝你好运。

3 （名词Hope）希望，期待，心愿（名词wish）愿望，祝福

My hope is that you won't do that. 我希望你不要做那件事。

I'm sure my wish will come true. 我的愿望肯定能实现。

hope to 希望做某事

可以用来表达自己的希望和期待，在hope后面加to+动词的形式就可以了。在分手时最常用的祝福语为I hope to see you again（回头见）。

“老板非常信任的一个员工出卖了他，手下劝老板，趁早把他给忘了吧”

What do you hope to gain by suing him?

M·O·R·E

- hope to+动词
  希望做某事
- Hope to see you again.
  回头见。

I **hope to** open my own restaurant.
我想开一家我自己的餐馆。

You are the kind of woman I **hope to** marry.
你就是那种我想要娶回家的女人。

You **hope to** do that? Sleep on it.
你想做那件事？睡一觉，好好想想吧。

A: Thank you for inviting me. I really enjoyed it. 非常感谢你能邀请我。我玩得非常开心。

B: Glad to hear that. I hope to see you again. 很高兴你能这么说。希望能再见到你。

hope that 希望……

表达自己希望的用法，在I hope后面接主语+动词就可以了。在送对方礼物时，最常用的话就是I hope you like it。

“心里有一个梦中情人般的艺人，没想到她生活作风有问题”

I hope it's not real.

M·O·R·E

- I hope you enjoyed your meal.
  我希望你用餐愉快。
- I hope I haven't disturbed you.
  我希望我没打扰到你。

I **hope** you two are very happy, I really do.
我希望你们两个幸福，真心的。

I **hope** I can come back again.
我希望我能重新回来。

I **hope that** she gets better soon.
我希望她能早日好转。

A: I hope that we can meet up after school. 我希望我们放学之后能见个面。

B: Yeah, it would be fun to get together then. 恩，到时候应该很有趣。

I'm hoping 如果……的话就好了，想要做某事

不是单纯地希望或期待，而是存在“我想一定做某事”的情绪，常用形式为I'm hoping (that) 主语+动词或I'm hoping to+动词。

“心里有个非常喜欢的男生，生日当天怀着激动的心情邀请他出席”

I'm hoping you'll come to my party.

I'm hoping to sleep with her tonight.
我今晚想和她睡觉。

You're going home? I **was hoping to** get to know you better.
你要回家了？我非常想多了解你一些。

I'm hoping you'll come.
如果你能来就太好了。

I'm hoping that Bob will not show up.
如果鲍勃不出现就好了。

A: I'm hoping that I will become very wealthy. 我希望我变得很富有。
B: You'd better be prepared to work hard. 你最好先做好努力工作的准备。

hope so 希望如此

so为指代之前提到过的内容，因此hope so表示“希望如此”。相反，如果要表达“不希望如此”的话就可以用hope not。

“服用毒品被发现，要上传照片澄清事实”

I **hope so**, but I don't know. People are smarter than you think.

M·O·R·E

- I hope so.
  我希望如此。
- I hope not.
  我希望不会那样。

I hope so, but I can't forget my ex-husband.
我希望如此，不过我实在无法忘掉我的前夫。

Well, you'd better **hope so**.
好，你最好希望如此。

I hope not, but I think so. Who knows?
我不希望如此，不过我觉得很有可能会那样，谁知道呢？

A: I bet you will find a new boyfriend soon. 我敢打赌，你不久就会找到新男朋友的。
B: I hope so, but I can't forget my ex–boyfriend. 我也希望如此，不过我无法忘掉前男友。

Hopefully! 希望，如果幸运的话，恐怕

虽然是单纯的副词，不过可以用来体现希望和期待，在日常生活中经常会出现。在说出自己的希望事项前先提出来就可以了。

"周末出去和朋友们喝酒，开车回家时怀着不被警察发现的侥幸心理"

Hopefully, that isn't going to happen.

If she's my friend, **hopefully** she'll understand.
如果她是我朋友的话，肯定能够理解的。

Hopefully, John's making some progress.
希望约翰能有些进展。

Hopefully, once you taste the dessert, you'll never forget about it.
我觉得，你一旦尝到甜点，就肯定忘不掉。

A: I heard you got sick. How do you feel? 我听说你生病了。你现在感觉怎么样?
B: Terrible. Hopefully I will feel better tomorrow. 糟糕极了，希望我明天能有所好转。

There is hope 有希望

有没有希望可以用There's (no) hope来表示，至于希望的具体内容可以在of后面接上。在条件从句或者否定句中要用There is (not) any of的形式。

"政客们天天都说为国民办事，其实暗地里都忙着装满自己的腰包"

There's is no hope of change our future.

M·O·R·E

- There's hope (of)
  有（……的）希望。
- There's no hope
  没有希望

She's going to continue to think that **there's hope**.
她会继续认为还有一线希望的。

Treatment is difficult and risky, but **there is hope**.
治疗过程非常困难，而且有风险，不过还是有希望的。

Don't say that there is hope when **there is no hope**.
在没有一点希望的时候，千万不要说有希望。

There isn't any hope of you keeping your mouth shut about this.
你肯定没希望保守这个秘密。

A: Did anyone survive the earthquake? 有人在地震中活下来了吗?
B: There is hope that there may be some survivors. 应该有希望找到生还者。

get one's hopes up 产生期待，使产生期待

表示“使某人产生期待”，可以用来使某人的期待高于现实的可能性。主要的例句有Don't get your hopes up（不要过分期待）。

“终于上了一次电视，不过基本上是没人看的频道，却得意洋洋起来”

I just don't want to **get your hopes up** real high.

Don't **get your hopes up**, because probably it's not going to happen.

不要过分期待，因为那种事情基本上不会发生的。

You shouldn't **get her hopes up** like that.

你不能使她产生那样的期待。

Don't **get your hopes up**, honey. You'll just be disappointed.

不要过分期待，亲爱的。你很有可能会失望的。

You'**re not getting your daughter's hopes up**, are you?

你不会让你女儿过分期待，对吧?

A: Rick said he might get a car for his birthday. **里克说他生日可能会得到一辆车。**

B: He shouldn't get his hopes up. A car costs too much. **他不能那么过分期待啊。一辆车太贵了。**

wish to 想做某事

wish to+动词表示“渴望做某事”，虽然乍一看和前面的hope to+动词有着相似的含义，但与hope to 不同，wish to 为更formal一些的表达，经常会用在正式的场合。

“同事的能力虽然不如我，但凭借着高文凭成功晋升，真是令人心寒”

I no longer **wish to** speak with him.

We **wish to** apologize for the late arrival of this train.

我们要为这次火车的晚点表示歉意。

I **wish to** speak to him alone. Can you arrange that?

我想和他单独谈谈。你能安排一下吗?

Do you **wish to** say anything, John?

你有话要说吗，约翰?

A: Many people helped the Thompsons after their house burned. **在托马森的家被烧了之后，很多人都伸出了援手。**

B: They wish to thank everyone who helped them. **他们希望向每个帮助过他们家的人表达真诚的谢意。**

wish somebody something 祝某人某事

与formal的wish to+动词不同，wish somebody something在日常生活中经常会用到，比方说Wish me luck（祝我好运）。

"一辈子没谈过恋爱，就这么走过了25，30岁的老姑娘"

I have no special guy to **wish me** happy birthday.

M·O·R·E

- wish sb a Merry Christmas 希望某人能过一个愉快的圣诞节
- wish sb luck 祝某人好运

I **wish you** a Merry Christmas! Have a lot of fun!
祝你圣诞快乐！开开心心！

I have to go. **Wish me luck**!
我得走了，祝我好运吧！

I just stopped by to **wish you good luck**.
我就是过来祝你好运的。

A: Bobby's team is playing for the championship. 鲍比的队伍要参加冠军联赛了。

B: That's so exciting. Wish them luck for me. 真让人兴奋啊。希望他们能有好运相伴。

I wish ... 我希望

wish的最典型用法，I hope (that)表示希望有足够可能性的事情发生，而I wish (that)则可以用在没有多大可能性的事情上，即与现实背离的愿望。

"一个财阀公司的大老板为了图慈善之名，给孤寡老人分了几包方便面"

I wish I could be more helpful.

M·O·R·E

- I wish I had+名词 我希望我有……
- I wish I could+动词 如果能做某事就太好了

I wish you were here. You would be a big help to me.
我真希望你在这。你肯定会对我产生很大帮助的。

I wish I had a lot of money.
我希望我有很多很多的钱。

I wish I could stay longer, but I have to go now.
我希望我能多留一会，不过我现在就得走了。

A: What do you want to have for dinner? 你晚上想吃点什么？

B: I wish I could have a big juicy steak! 我希望我可以吃一个多汁的牛排！

I wish I had 如果……的话就太好了

这次针对的不是眼下无法实现的愿望，而是过去未能完成的愿望，即可以用来表示忏悔和遗憾。可以使用I wish I had+pp的形式，表示“如果过去……的话该多好啊”。

“为了贪图眼下的安逸，而错过绝佳时机，最终倾家荡产”

I wish I had done things differently.

M·O·R·E

- I wish I had+pp
  真希望当时……
- I wish I hadn't+pp
  如果没有……的话该多好啊Eredees int, publissid ren vivis bon vagil hebatium porum audetis renatus ad finteri convere, C. Ad coenihi caessunum Pat nosti, no.

I wish I had been married to you.
如果和你结婚该多好啊。

I wish I had told you before.
如果之前告诉了你该多好啊。

That's a good point. Now **I wish I hadn't** told Julie.
说的没错。现在我倒希望没和朱莉说起。

I wish he hadn't asked me out on a date.
如果他没约我出去该多好啊。

A: I heard you were drunk and broke a window yesterday. 我听说你昨天喝醉了，还打碎了人家的玻璃。

B: Yeah. I wish I hadn't done that. 恩，真希望那都是假的。

I wish I could, but ... 虽然很希望，但……

郑重地向对方提出拒绝的表达，可以理解为“虽然很不情愿，但……”。but后面要接不得不拒绝的原因。相似的表达有I'm sorry, but ... , I'd love to, but ... 或I'd like to, but ... 等。

“在不想帮助别人的时候，可以故意气对方的话”

I wish I could, but I don't want to.

M·O·R·E

- I wish I could but I can't ...
  虽然我很想，不过……
- I wish I could+动词，but ...
  我很想……，不过……
- I'd like to, but ...
  我很愿意，不过……

I wish I could, but I can't. I have too much work to do.
我也很想，不过不行。我还有很多事情要做。

I wish I could come, but I'm busy on Friday.
我也想去，不过我星期五有点忙。

I'd like to, but I have to go right now.
我也很想，不过我现在得走了。

I'd love to, but I have to go home early tonight.
我也很想，不过我今天晚上得早点回家。

A: Come on over to my house on Sunday afternoon. 星期天下午来我家玩吧。

B: I wish I could, but I have other plans. 我也很想，不过我已经有别的安排了。

I wish somebody would ... 如果某人……就太好了

可以用来表达对somebody的不满情绪，表示如果somebody“怎样的话就太好了”。

“男朋友不管说什么话都会当成玩笑，这次却说要分手”

I wish you would take this seriously.

M·O·R·E

- I wish sb would+动词
  如果……就太好了
- I wish you would
  我希望你能……

I wish you wouldn't talk like that.
我希望你别那么说。

Honey, I wish you would get over her.
亲爱的，如果你能忘掉她该多好啊。

I wish he would just tell me the truth.
我真希望他能把真实情况跟我说说。

A: Do you want me to check again? **你要我重新检查一遍吗?**
B: Well yeah, I wish that you would. **恩，那样就太好了。**

if you wish 如果你愿意的话

在向对方提出某种建议或请求时可以用来表达“如果你愿意的话，如果你喜欢的话”。想要具体表达希望的事项就可以使用if you wish to+动词，另外，as you wish表示回答对方的话，“随你的便”。

“朋友想用一下我那新买的高端智能手机”

You can use my cell phone, if you wish.

M·O·R·E

- if you wish
  如果你愿意的话
- if you wish to+动词
  如果你希望的话
- as you wish
  随便吧，请便

I can help you with your homework, if you wish.
如果你愿意的话，我可以帮你做作业。

You can go now, if you wish.
如果你愿意的话，现在就可以走了。

If you wish to be a writer, you should read a lot of books.
如果你想成为一个作家，就要读很多的书。

A: Can I give you a call tomorrow? **我明天能给你打电话吗?**
B: If you wish. Here is my home phone number. **如果你愿意的话，这是我家里的号码。**

Section 2 More Basic Verbs

外国人同样常用的
重要基本动词

27

- send
- finish/ end
- use
- hand
- meet
- hang
- show
- play
- save/ spend
- teach/ learn
- drop/ catch
- cut/ hit
- charge/ cost
- worry/ care
- eat/ drink/ cook
- pass/ follow
- plan/ prepare
- pick/ choose/ decide
- buy/ sell/ deal/ afford/ belong
- apologize/ excuse/ thank/ appreciate
- change/ remain
- lend/ borrow/ owe
- fill/ file/ fit/ fix
- lie/ lay
- pull/ draw
- ruin/ risk/ hurt
- expect

>>> 001

send

发送

MORE

- send sb sth
  送某人某物
- send sth to sb
  给某人送某物

send somebody something (sth to sb)

向某人送去某物

最基本的send用法，在用send sth时如果要同时说明送去的人和接收的人就要说成send sth to sb或sent sb sth的形式。

I didn't send him an invitation. 我没有给他发请帖。

I should probably send a thank–you letter to her.
我可能要给她送一封感谢信。

- send sb to
  将某人送到某处
- send sb into
  让某人做某事
- be sent to
  被派遣到某处

send somebody to someplace（地点）

把某人送到某处，使某人做某事(into)

这次要送的东西不是事物而是人(person)，send sb to+地点表示"将某人送到某处"，而send sb into表示送往……即"使某人做某事"。

I don't want to send him there. 我不想把他送到那里。

She was sent to the warehouse. 她被派遣到了仓库。

- send (sb) an email
  （向某人）发邮件

send an email (one's apologies) 发邮件（表达歉意）

这种情况下，send的宾语变成了邮件或电脑文件，信息或广播等物体，最常用的就是send an email。

Did you get the e-mail I sent you the other day?
你接到我前几天给你发的邮件了吗?

Please send your mom my apologies, but I won't be attending. 请帮我向您母亲转达歉意，我参加不了了。

- send sth back
  返还，送还
- send sb back
  让某人回去

send somebody (sth) back 返还，还给

将收到的东西返还给他人(return sth to where it came from)，或者让某人回到原来的地方等等(return sb to where he came from)。

Should we send them something back? 我们要把这些送回去吗?

I have to send it back. 我必须得把它送回去。

send away 派某人去拿东西，预定，赶走……

away表示远离，因此send away表示“让某人走开”，“赶走某人”等。不过send away for sth则表示“通过邮政预订某物”。

You really want to send our son away to the prison? 你真打算把我们的儿子关进大牢啊?

I send away for it. You want one of your own? 我预订了那个东西。你也需要一个吗?

MORE

- send (sb) away 赶走，送到……
- send away for 预订

send for 派人去取某物（领某人）

sent for a person表示派人去叫“a person”过来。send for sth像send an ambulance或send the latest catalogue一样，表示“去叫某物”或“发送某物”。

I sent for the offic manager. 我叫人去请经理。

- send for sb 去找人帮忙
- send for a doctor 去叫医生
- send for sth 去找人帮忙

send out 发送，派遣

向发出请帖一样，将同一个东西发给多个人或发送化学物质，广播等。另外，send out后面如果加人物或队伍的话就表示以救助或修理等目的派人。

How about we send out a holiday card this year? 我们今年一起寄贺卡怎么样?

You want a job? You send out a resume! 你想找工作?那就必须得投简历!

- send out sth 发送……
- send out+物质，广播 发送……
- send out+人物 派遣某人
- send out for+饮食 订餐

send in 让人进入

表示让人进入，或者通过邮件发送某物等。

Send her in. 让她进来。

Send in the man who was waiting in the lobby. 让那个在大厅里面等着的男人进来。

- send sb in 让人进来，派遣（警察，军人）
- send sth in 发送（简历，提案等）

send over 派遣，传送，发送……

send over表示让对方来到我这里，或者把东西送到对方处。send over sth表示“派遣……”，而send sb over表示“派遣为……”。

Can you send over some money? 你能给我打点钱吗?

- send over sth 派送某人
- send (sb) over (to) 将某人派遣为……

>>> 002

finish/ end

结束，终止

MORE

- finish sth
  完成某事
- finish ...ing
  完成某事

finish ...ing 结束某事

表示“结束某事”，finish后面经常会接名词，但有时为了表达“结束所做的事情”，可以在finish后面接 ...ing。

Did you finish checking in to your room? 你检查完房间了?

Is it okay if I finish the orange juice? 我把橙汁喝完了也可以吗?

How long does it take to finish it? 完成这些需要多长时间?

- be (have) finished with sth
  完成某事，用完某物
- be (have) finished with sb
  （因生气）与某人了结关系
- finish with sb
  终止交易，
  与某人断绝关系

be finished with 结束某事

be (have) finished with sth表示结束某事或“用完某物，没有利用的价值”等，be (have) finished with sb表示因为生气“与某人停止交谈”，或“终止交易”等。

I'm finished with the work. 我完成了工作。

I'm not finished with you. 我还有话要和你说。

I'm not finished with the report. 我还没有完成报告。

- finish sth off
  终结，吃完东西
- finish off with sth
  结束某事
- finish off sth by ...ing
  通过……结束某事
- finish sb off
  使某人疲惫不堪

finish off 完成，终结

finish off基本上与finish具有相同的含义，表示完成某事，或者吃完东西等。不过finish sb off表示“使某人疲惫不堪”。

Why don't you finish off this pie? 你把这个派吃完了呗?

The guys finished off all of the beer in the fridge. 他们把冰箱里所有的啤酒都喝光了。

finish on time 按时完成某事

在预定的时间内完成某事时可以在finish后面加上on time。

I expect him to finish on time. 我希望他按时完成。

If we don't finish this report on time, I'm going to lose my job. 如果我们不按时完成这个报告，我会丢掉工作的。

finish up 以……结尾，最终变成……

finish up 表示结束的时候到达某个地方或者处于某种状态。另外，finish up后面如果接饮食名词，则表示吃完东西。

Finish up and we'll go out to eat. 赶紧做完手头的事情，我们得出去吃饭。

Did you finish up the work you were doing? 你手头的工作做完了吗?

MORE

- finish up in (with)
  到达（某个地点，状态）
- finish up+饮食
  吃完……
- finish up ...ing
  结束某事

end up with (...ing) 最终以……结尾

end up与finish up具有相同的含义。最常用的形态为end up ...ing。

I ended up getting married and having kids. 我最终结了婚，生了孩子。

You are not going to end up alone. 你肯定不会一个人留下的。

- end up in (with)
  以某状态结束
- end up ...ing
  最终……
- end up as
  以……结束
- end up like
  像……一样结束

bring (put) an end to 结束

这里的end为名词形式。bring (put) an end字面含义为将end（结尾，结束）带到某处，因此可以理解为“结束某事”，“放弃某事”。

I will just put an end to it! 我不干了!

Why don't we put an end to this right now? 你为什么不现在停手呢。

at the end of 在……的结尾

比较熟悉的短语，表示“在……的结尾”。at the end of the day表示最终的意思，也可以用来表达三思之后的判断或结论。

I finally got home at the end of the day! 我终于完成了所有的工作，回到家里!

She is sitting at the end of the table. 她坐在桌子的末端。

- at the end of the month
  在这个月末
- at the end of the day
  最终，最重要的

in the end 最终

同样为非常熟悉的基础短语，可以表示在经过一定时间之后“最终”，“终究”等。

It will work out in the end. 最后肯定会好转的。

In the end, I didn't leave for New York. 最后，我还是没有离开纽约。

>>> 003

use

使用，利用

MORE

- use sth for sth (...ing)
  将某物用在某事
- use sth as sth
  将某物用作某物
- use sth to
  用某物做某事

- be used to+动词
  使用于某事
- be (get) used to+名词
  习惯于某事
- used to+动词
  过去常常做某事

use sth for 将某物用在某事

在使用某物的过程中需要具体指明其目的或用途是可以用到的句式。use sth for后面要接名词或 ...ing。

Would you mind if I use your car to visit that client?
我得去找客户，能不能用一下你的车？

be used to+动词 将某物用在某事

将上面表达中的use sth to变成了被动形态。可以将be used to记为“用某物做某事”。只不过要和下面的be (get) used to+名词及used to+动词相区分开。

A lawn mower is used to cut grass. 割草机是用来割草的。

We used to play together all the time. 我们经常会在一起打球。

You have to get used to it. 你得学会适应。

use one's head (brain) 用脑子，想想看

虽然比较伤别人自尊，不过可以用来谴责或忠告别人，或者让对方避免失误，多想想。

Use your head! How come you fell for it twice? 多动动脑子！怎么能摔两次呢？

I expect you to use your brain this time. 我希望这次你能动动脑子。

get (be) used to 熟悉于某事

很有可能与前面的be used to+动词相混淆。最大的特点是to后面的成分，接动词和接名词(或 ...ing)有着很大差异。

I'm getting used to driving at night. 我在适应夜间开车。

I have to get used to it. 我得学会适应。

You'll get used to it. 你肯定会习惯的。

used to 过去经常做某事

又是一个容易混淆的句式。used to+动词基本上被当做一个介词来用，表示过去的行为或状态，但现在已经不是原来的情况了。

We used to work together. 我们曾经在一起工作过。

I used to be just like you. 我以前也像你一样。

can (could) use 需要……

有点难以理解的句式，一般会用为could use，也可以用作can use。想一想里面的could (can)一词的话就可以知道，use后面的成分还没有得到利用。换句话说，该句式表示希望利用use后面的东西，表示would like to have。

I can use a Coke. 我想喝一杯可乐。

I could use a little help here. 我希望有人能帮一下。

make (good or bad) use of 利用某物

在这里use为名词形式，make use of sth表示“利用某物”，“高效活用”等。当然，如果想要表示利用情况顺利与否，就可以在use前面加上good，bad等形容词。

They made a good use of extra money. 他们很有效地利用了多余的钱。

The children made good use of the toys they got. 孩子们充分使用了收到的玩具礼物。

- make use of
  利用某物
- make good use of
  好好利用某物
- make bad use of
  利用不佳

put ... to (good) use 利用

同样表示利用的句式，不过宾语经常是知识(knowledge)或技术(skill)等，表示利用某物搭乘某种目的或愿望。use前面经常会加good。

I think it'd be better if we put it all to good use. 如果我们能够好好地利用一番就太好了。

It's no use ...ing 再怎么……也没用

向对方忠告时经常使用的表达，表示use后面的部分怎么努力也没用，也可以单独使用一句It's no use!。

It's no use! 没什么用！

Come on, it's no use fighting. 算了，再怎么吵也没用。

- It's no use!
  没用!
- What's the use?
  有什么用?
- What's the use of ...ing?
  ……有什么用呢?
- There's no use (in) ...ing.
  再怎么样也没用。

>>> 004

hand

传递，帮助

MORE

have (got) to hand it to somebody 叹服某人

在口语表达中如果要感叹sb的成功或者作出了某件伟大的事情时，可以用到这个短语。

I've got to hand it to you! 你真了不起啊！

I've got to hand it to you. You are a strong man. 你真了不起，是个男子汉。

hand down 拿下，传递，留给

- hand down (to) 传给某人

给子孙留下贵重的物品或者知识，技术等，或者给比自己年幼的孩子留下不穿的衣服和过期的玩具等。

Grandma handed down some of her jewelry to me.
奶奶给我留下了一些宝石。

hand in 递交(submit)

表示递交某物，但并不是单纯的交给，而是在学校，宾馆，公司等场所上交。term paper（期末报告）上交给学校，或者在办理退房checkout的手续时将房卡还回去都可以使用这个短语。

Did you hand in the report you were working on?
你最近弄的报告交上去了吗？

hand out （给人们）分发，分配(give out)

- hand out leaflet 发传单
- hand out drinks 分发饮料
- handout 传单，广告

虽然同样表示将某物交给某人，但此时具有分发的意思，与give out和distribute具有相似的含义。或者可以用在提出建议(advice)或者信息(information)等。

I stood in the doorway handing out pamphlets.
我站在门口分发着传单。

hand over 谦让（权力等），传递

- have sth over to sb 将某物递给某人
- hand sth/sb over to sb 把某物让给某人

具体表示将汽车钥匙或者书本等交给对方，或者将自己肩上的责任与权限让给对方。

Hand over some money to pay the bill.
给我点钱，我要买单。

give (somebody) a hand 帮助（某人）

hand作为名词虽然有手的意思，但我们也会将它理解为“帮手”的手，因此表示“帮助”(help)的意思。

Can you give me a hand? 你能帮帮我吗?

It's my turn to lend a hand. 这次该我帮助你了。

MORE

- give (lend) sb a hand (to)
  帮助某人（做某事）
- need (want) a hand (...ing)
  需要帮助（做某事）

have one's hand full 非常忙碌

表示两个手从来就没有闲过，因某件困难的事情而“非常忙碌”(to be extremely busy with a difficult job)。想要说明忙碌的原因，就可以用have one's hands full with sth (sb)。

I have my hands full! 我现在忙得很!

She must have had her hands full. 她肯定忙得不可开交。

- have one's hands full with sth (sb)
  因某事而非常忙碌

put something in the hands of 将某物交给某人

hands表示握在手中，put sth in the hands of表示“将某物交给某人”，而give one's hand on sth表示“将某物紧紧握在手中”，“得到”等。

Don't put your fate in the hands of others. 不要把你的命运交给他人。

have (get) somebody (something) on one's hands 某物在手中

表示“某物掌握在手中”，有时单纯指有时间等，而大多数情况下表示需要处理很多棘手的问题。

I've got a little time on my hands. 我现在没有多少空。

You have a lot of time on your hands. 你现在有很多时间啊。

I don't have anything on my hand! 我两手空空!

- have time on one's hand
  有点时间
- have sb (sth) on one's hands
  掌握在手中
- have a hand in
  有关，有联系

get one's hands off 把手拿开

字面含义为将手(one's hands)拿开(off)，可以使用动词take，get或keep等，相反，A be off one's hands则表示“从手心中逃出来”，即不负责A。

Stop it! Get your hands off me! 停下！把你的手拿开！

Would you just take your hands off me? 你能不能把手拿开?

- keep one's hand off
  把手拿开
- A be off on's hands
  不再负责A
- take A off sb's hands
  不再管A

>>> 005

meet

见面

MORE

I'd like you to meet 我来介绍一下

在介绍朋友的时候使用的典型例句。也可以说成I want you to meet sb，如果很忙，或者在熟悉的朋友之间，单叫名字就可以了。

I'd like you to meet my boyfriend. 我来介绍一下我的男朋友。
Everybody, there's someone I'd like you to meet.
我得给你们介绍一个人。

- meed the needs of
满足……的需要
- meet the deadline (goal)
满足最后（目标）
- meet a goal
达成目标

meet the need (satisfaction) 满足需要

meet的宾语如果是need, satisfaction, demand, standard等名词时，meet就表示“满足需要或标准”。相似的句式有meet the deadline, meet a goal等。

The hotel didn't meet our satisfaction.
那家宾馆不是很令人满意。

The loan met Jim's needs while he was a student.
那份贷款满足了吉姆学生时期的需要。

You'll need to hurry to meet the deadline.
你得抓紧时间赶上期限。

make ends meet 收支平衡

ends表示“使能够核对上的东西”。在这里ends表示支出和收入，因此满足两项就表示既没有亏损，也没有盈利，即收支平衡。

We're barely making enough money to make ends meet. 我们挣的钱只够维持收支平衡的。
We need to save money to make ends meet.
我们得攒钱维持收支平衡了。

- meet with sb
与某人见面
- meet with sth
碰到，经历（反对，失败，成功）
- meet up with
偶然见到

meet with 会务，相见，经历，经验，偶然相见

虽然与meet具有相似的含义，不过这里是更加formal的表达，包含了“相见”的含义。另外，meet with后面如果接success, failure, opposition等的话就表示“经历某状况”，”碰到”等。

I'd like to meet with you this afternoon. 我今天下午想见你一下。

I'm here to meet with someone from human resources.
我来这里是要见人事部的人。

have (attend) a meeting 有会议，参加会议

meeting表示会议，因此have a meeting表示参加会议。attend a meeting表示出席会议，hold a meeting表示举办会议等。

Are you going to attend the meeting? 你要出席会议吗?

Did you have a meeting with her yesterday? 你昨天和她开会了?

He's in a meeting right now. 他现在正在开会。

- have a meeting
  开会
- attend a meeting
  出席会议
- hold a meeting
  召开会议
- be in (at) a meeting
  开会

call a meeting 召开会议，召集

表示号召开一次meeting，可以用来表达开会或者“召集会议”。想要说明具体会议内容的话就要说sales meeting，emergency meeting等。

Harris wants to call a meeting to discuss the new proposals. 哈里斯想召开一次会议，讨论讨论新方案。

UN Security Council called an emergency session.
联合国安理会召开了紧急会议。

- call a sales meeting
  召开销售会议
- call an emergency meeting
  召开紧急会议

>>> 006

hang

悬挂，玩

MORE

hang in there 忍受（困难的状况）

被悬挂在悬崖边上，或者砍刀架在脖子上等困难的状况时可以用这个短语来让对方挺住。

I'll be right back. Hang in there. 我马上就回来，在那里忍一会儿。

You're going to be all right. Just hang in there. 你肯定会没事的，稍微忍耐一下。

- hang around
  打发时间，等待
- hang around with
  与某人打发时间
- hang around with+地点
  在某处打发时间，等待
- hang with
  与某人交往，相处

hang around （与某人）相处，到处转悠

虽然表示与特定人物在特定场所，不过没有特别要做的事情，打发时间，或者等待，也可以用成hang with。

He's just really great to hang around with. 他是个非常容易相处的人。

We're just hanging around here. 我们就是在这里玩玩。

It's my last chance to hang with my girlfriend. 这是我和女朋友相处的最后一次机会了。

I'm going to let you hang with Cindy. 我要让你和辛迪相处相处。

- Hang on!
  稍等！(hold on)
- hang on (to)
  紧紧抓住（某物）
- hang on sth
  依靠，继续做某事
- hang on sb's words
  倾听某人的话
- hang onto sth
  继续做某事

hang on 暂时等待（不停顿），紧紧抓住某物

on具有持续的概念，因此hang on表示稍等一会，与hold on 具有相同的含义，另外，hang on to 表示“紧紧抓住某物”，而hang on sth表示“依赖某物”，“继续做某事”。

We're going to take care of you. Just hang on. 我们会照顾你的，稍等一会儿。

Hang on. Don't do this. 等等，千万别这样。

Will you hang on a second? I've got another call. 你能稍等一会儿吗？我有别的电话打进来了。

- hang out (with)
  （与某人）打发时间
- hangout
  经常见面的地方
- hang sth out
  把衣服等挂在外面

hang out (with) 与某人和睦相处

与hang around具有相似的含义，表示没有特别的事情，只是和朋友们打发时间。像这样经常聚会的地点称为hangout。

Just hang out with me. 就和我玩玩吧。
Do you know of any cool places to hang out? 你知道有什么地方可以打发时间吗?

MORE

hang over （担心，烦恼等）不离开脑海

字面含义为悬挂在上方，一般主语为威胁、欠债等负面意义的事情，这些烦恼久久在脑海中徘徊，引起担心和挂念的意思。

The problem is still hanging over my head. 我还在想那道题。
I have a hangover. 好像酒还没醒。
She woke up with the worst hangover of her life. 她醒来的时候，感觉到这次是至今为止最糟糕的一次宿醉了。

- hang over sb's head 久久不能忘怀
- hang over sb (sth) 担心等心情不消失
- hang over 宿醉，后遗症

hang together 一致，对头

根据主语会有含义上的不同，如果某故事或计划等hang together表示“对头”，如果人物变成了主语的话，hang together就表示“互相帮助”。

The speech doesn't really hang together. 这次演说前后不搭。
We must hang together. 我们得相互团结。

- (story, plan) hang together 故事等前后匹配
- (people) hang together 相互帮助

hang up 挂电话

以前的电话都挂在墙上，因此在会用挂电话来表示中断通话。hang up on sb一般表示“单方面挂掉电话”。

Please hang up the phone. 请挂掉电话吧。
Don't hang up. Just listen. 不要挂电话，听我说。

- hang up 挂电话
- hang up on sb 通话过程中挂掉某人的电话
- hang up sth 挂衣服等

get the hang of 掌握处理……的方法，掌握要领

这里的hang 为名词形式，可以用have或get，have (get) the hang of表示“掌握处理……的要领”。

Don't worry. You'll get the hang of it. 不要担心，你肯定会越来越熟悉的。

Are you getting the hang of it? 你现在熟悉了吗?

>>> 007

show

展示

MORE

- show sth by (as) sth
  通过……向某人展示某物
- be shown by (as)
  通过……展示

show somebody the way 给某人指路，告诉某人方法

这里的show表示告诉对方信息或方法，show somebody the way to+动词表示“给某人指路或者告诉某人方法”。

Let me show you another way. 我来给你指别的路吧。

Please show me the way. 请给我带路。

I'll show the way. 我会给你带路的。

- show sb how to
  教某人……的方法
- show sb how S+V
  告诉某人……的方法

show somebody how to 告诉某人……的方法

与前面的表达相似，为show sb how的形态，表示告诉某人……的方法，可以在how后面接how to+动词或How S+V的形态。

Can you show me how to go there? 你能告诉我怎么到那吗?

Please show me how to play the game. 请告诉我怎么玩这个游戏。

Show me how it works. 告诉我这个的工作原理。

- show (sth) that S+V
  证明为……
- be shown to do
  被证明为……
- show sth (sb) to be
  这证明了……
- It goes to show that ...
  正如……
- as shown by (in)
  被……证明

The study shows that ... 根据研究结果……

在阅读理解中经常见到的语句，表示“证明……”(prove)，“表明”，“显示”等，主语经常是事物。

It goes to show just how attractive you are. 这就表明你有多么吸引人。

- show one's emotions
  表露感情
- show an interest in
  对某物表示兴趣

show an interest in 向某人表达好感

这次show的宾语主要为兴趣(interest)，感情(emotions)，感激之情(appreciation)等个人的关心事宜或感情。

Sandy showed her true colors when she got angry. 桑迪在生气的时候，把真面目展现了出来。

show somebody around 让某人观赏，带某人观光

around后面主要会接房子，办公室，室内观光地，购物商场等场所，如果对方表现出了兴趣，则可以带对方转转。

I'm going to show him around town. 我打算带他转转城镇。

Let me show you around. 让我带你转转吧。

show off 炫耀(boast)

如果没有任何目的，单独用一个show off则表示“自夸”，具有否定的感情色彩。另外，show off sth或show sth off表示“出于自豪感而炫耀某物”，如果主语变成了事物，则表示“使某物突出”。

He wanted to show off his new girlfriend, Alma. 他想给大家炫耀炫耀新女朋友，阿尔玛。

show up （在会议或聚会等）出现

表示出现在人们等待的场所，即到达或者来到。不要试着用我们的母语去理解，单单看成来到就可以了。另外，在口语中经常会把up去掉，单独留一个show。

What time do you think you will show up? 你觉得你几点能来?

She never showed up again. 她再也不会出现了。

MORE

- show sb around+地点名词
  待某人转……

- show off
  炫耀
- show sth off
  炫耀某物
- 事物主语+show sth off
  使突出

- show up for
  来到，出现在……
- no show
  没有出现（在约会地点）

>>> 008

play

玩，运动（演奏）

MORE

- play soccer
踢足球
- play computer games
玩电脑游戏
- play games on one's cell phone
用手机玩游戏

paly+运动名词 做……运动

play后面如果接运动竞技名称(basketball, baseball, hockey)或者游戏名称(computer games, cards)的情况，要注意中间不需要加冠词。

I sprained my ankle while playing basketball. 我在打篮球的时候扭伤了脚踝。

- play the piano
弹钢琴
- play MP3 (files)
播放MP3音乐

play the+乐器名 演奏……乐器

play后面如果接乐器时，就需要在乐器前面加冠词，这一点与前面的play+运动不同。另外，play还具有播放CD，MP3文件和播放音乐等含义。

She is good at playing the violin. 她很擅长演奏手提琴。
You used to like playing the piano. 你过去喜欢弹钢琴。

- play a large part in ...ing
在……上起到了重要作用

play a part (role) in 扮演……的角色

如果在话剧，电影等方面的话，就表示在电影中“扮演……角色”，如果在日常生活中就表示“起到……的作用”。

Fred's illness played a part in his decision to retire. 弗雷德的病在一定程度上促使他做出退休的决定。

- play it safe
安全行动(avoid risks)
- play it cool
沉着行动(take it easy)

play it safe 使安全，慎重行事

比较常用的短语为play it safe，play it cool，在这里play具有behave的含义，因此play it safe表示“慎重”(avoid risks)，play it cool表示“沉着行事”等。

If life is short, it's dumb to play it safe. 如果说生命很短暂，那么安于现状就是愚蠢的行为。

You can play it safe if it works for you. 如果合适的话，你就要慎重一些。

- play God
像神一样
- play dead
装死
- play dumb
像傻子一样

play dumb 装傻

电影或话剧中的play表示扮演……的角色，因此play后面如果加dumb, dead, the fool等名词的话就表示“假装”(pretend)的含义。

Don't play dumb! 不要装傻！

Don't play dumb with me! 不要把我当成傻瓜！

play game 玩游戏，耍手段

play games表示为了达成自己的目的而掩藏自己真实的感情，有负面的含义。玩负面意义上的游戏，即“耍手段”等。不过，如果使用单数形式play the game的话就表示堂堂正正玩游戏，即公平竞争。

Don't play games with me! 不要想着耍我！

I don't play games. 我没有在耍心眼。

MORE

- play games with sb
  和某人开玩笑，耍手段
- play the game
  堂堂正正地游戏

play hooky 无端缺席(play truant)

不想上学的孩子经常会做出的行为。并非因故请假，而是无端缺席，这一范畴都可以用该短语表达，也可以使用play truant。truant 指无端缺席的学生，hooky指不上学或不上班的行为。

I don't feel like going to school so I'll play hooky. 我不想上学，所以就逃课了。

- play hooky form (work, school)
  无端缺席（公司/学校）
- play truant
  无端缺席

play hard to get 假装拿不到，假装不关心

play具有“表演”的含义，因此可以理解为“实际行动与内心相背离”。play hard to get为其中的一种表达，主要用在男女之间假装对对方没有感觉，但其实动了心的情况。

Don't start playing hard to get again, John. 约翰，不要假装不关心。

- play hard to get
  假装不在乎

play by oneself 一个人玩

又是上班，又是上学，在很多情况下都会自己一个人玩。在现在这个世道，只有独处地习惯(be very good at playing by himself)才可以适应社会。不过如果对女朋友说I played with myself last night，就有点不合适了……

If you don't want to play by yourself, you should make friends. 如果你不想一个人待着，就得交朋友。

- play by oneself
  自己一个人玩
- play with oneself
  自慰

play a trick on sb 戏耍，开玩笑

愚人节的时候最重要的就是play a trick (tricks) on sb，表示“戏耍某人”。另外，“开玩笑”可以用play a joke on sb来表达。

I thought you were playing a trick on me. 我以为你在耍我。

- play a trick (tricks) on sb
  戏耍某人
- play a joke on sb
  和某人开玩笑，戏耍

>>> 009

save/ spend

节约，储蓄/消费

MORE

- save sb from sth
从……救出某人
- save (one's) face
给面子
- You saved my life
（对方在艰难的时刻帮助了我）多亏了你

save one's life 救某人的命

正如字面含义，表示在对方陷入危险或者处在困难的状况时伸出援手。不一定要救性命，还可以为人挽回颜面，save (one's) face。

Thank you so much, Kate. You saved my life. 非常感谢你，凯特，你救了我的命。
You want me to save your life? 你要我救你的命？
There was no way to save face after I made the mistake. 在我失误后没办法挽回颜面了。

- save to+动词
为了做某事而储蓄
- save enough to ...
攒足了钱做某事
- save up (for)
为了买某物而存钱

save(about)+钱 储蓄……（动词）

表示回头为了买好车或者电脑而存钱的行为，如果想要说明存钱的目的就要在save后面加to+动词或在save (up)后面加for+名词。

I'm saving for a notebook computer. 我正为了买笔记本电脑而存钱。
She wants to save enough to buy a car. 她想存钱买车。

- save sb sth
给某人留下某物
- save sth for sth
为了某人而留下某物
- save (sb) time
节约（某人的）时间

save somebody something (something for something) 为了做某事而储备，留下

同样表示日后为了做某事而储备，这次不仅是钱，还可以指能量，食物以及时间等多种名词。

Hey, save us some pizza. 喂，给我们留点比萨。
I'll save you a parking spot. 我会给你留一个停车位的。
I'll save you a seat. 我会给你占个座的。
Yeah, save it for the cab, okay? 嗯，到计程车里再谈，好不？
I'm going to save you some time. 我不会占你多少时间的。
I will save you a lot of time and energy. 我会让你节约很多时间和精力的。

save somebody …ing 使某人不做某事，减轻某人的……

save表示救助或节省，因此可以用来表示减轻对方的困难或不便。经常会用为save somebody the trouble (bother) ...ing的形态，表示“减轻某人做某事的麻烦”。

Honey, let me save you the trouble. 亲爱的，我来帮帮你吧。

I'm just trying to save you from wasting your time. 我正想帮你节省点时间。

MORE

- save sb ...ing
  使某人不做某事
- save (sb) the trouble of ...ing
  帮助某人减少麻烦
- save oneself
  爱惜某人，减轻麻烦

spend money 花钱

spend的最基本含义为使用consumer的钱。把钱作为宾语，想要表达用钱的目的就可以用for (on)+名词或 ...ing 形态。

You shouldn't spend so much money. 你不应该花那么多钱。

How did you spend so much money? 你怎么花了那么多钱?

Stop spending my money! 别再花钱了!

I can't believe you're going to spend 250 dollars on the lottery! 真不敢相信，你居然花了250美元买彩票!

- spend money on (for) sb (sth)
  为……花钱
- spend money ...ing
  花钱做某事

spend+时间名词+ …ing 在……上花时间

spend的宾语不是金钱而变成了life或time等时间名词，主要表示“在做某事上花时间”。

I will spend the rest of my life trying to make you feel better. 我会用余下的时间让你好受。

I want to spend my life with you. 我想和你共度一生。

I want to spend more time with my family. 我想多和家人在一起。

- spend+时间名词 ...ing
  在做某事上花时间
- spend time on sth
  花时间做某事
- spend (much) time with (together)
  与某人一起度过时光
- spend one's life with (together)
  与某人共度一生

spend the day (night) with (together) 与某人共度今宵

与前面的情况相似，不过这次spend的宾语变成了day，night或Christmas Day, New Year's Day等特定名词。

I want to spend the night with Becky. 我想和贝奇一起过夜。

Why don't you spend Christmas with me?
你为什么不和我过圣诞节?

I would love to spend New Year's day with you.
我想和你一起过新年。

I had to spend all day clearing out stuff.
我不得不花上一整天的时间整理东西。

- spend Christmas with (together)
  与某人一起过圣诞节
- spend the night with sb
  与某人过夜，睡觉

>>> 010

teach/ learn

教授，学习

||||| MORE |||||

- teach+科目at+学校
  在学校教……课
- teach school (college)
  讲课
- teach sb sth
  教授某人某事
- teach sth to sb
  教授某人某事
- teach sb about
  教某人某事

- teach sb to+动词
  教某人做某事
- teach sb how to
  教某人做某事的方法
- teach sb that S+V
  教某人……

- The experience taught sb sth (to do)
  经验之谈
- It taught me that S+V
  这件事教会我……

teach somebody something 教某人某事

teach一般都是老师的工作。在学校讲课或者"教某人某事"等都是比较典型的句式。尤其在指"在学校讲课"时可以不用介词，变成teach school (college)。

Let me teach you a new game. 我来教你一款新游戏吧。

Did your teacher teach you that in your class? 你们老师在学校教过你们？

It's my job to teach you about responsibility. 让你知道什么叫责任，是我的工作。

teach somebody how to 向某人传授……（的方法）

这次变成了"向某人传授……的方法"，内容可以为to+动词，how to+动词或that S+V从句的形态。

I'm just going to teach him how to make pizza. 我要教他怎么做比萨。

I'm trying to teach her how to drive. 我正在教她开车。

That'll teach somebody ... 让某人体会到某事

teach的主语不一定是人。刻骨铭心的经验也可以教会人一些事情，此时主语名词为experience或that (it)等代词。

That'll teach her (him)! 那肯定会让她学到什么的！

I got a speeding ticket. That'll teach me not to drive fast. 我超速被开了罚单。以后肯定会多注意的。

I was taught that 我学到了……

这里teach用成了被动形态，即be taught that S+V的形态，表示主语学会了that之后的内容。

I was taught that it's important to be polite. 我体会到，礼貌是非常重要的。

teach somebody a lesson 教训某人

表示“教训某人”，“教某人一手”，要教训教训(punish)做错事的对象。

I'll teach him a lesson. 我会教训他一顿的。

I'm going to go down there and teach that guy a lesson. 我会下去好好教训他一顿。

MORE

- teach sb a lesson 教训某人
- need to be taught a lesson 某人需要被教训一顿

learn about 学到……的事情

既然有了teach的人，就要有learn的人。learn与teach正好相反，表示“学会”，“学到”，“领悟”等。

You have a lot to learn about men. 关于男人，你还有很多事情要了解。

I'm here to learn about cooking. 我是来学厨艺的。

- learn sth 学到某事
- learn about sth 学到……的事情
- learn (sth) from sb 从……学到某事
- learn from sth 通过某事学到
- learn that S+V 领悟，知道……

learn about 学会……的方法

用to+动词或how to+动词表达学习的内容，即“学会做某事”，“学到……的方法”等。

It'll take you three of four months to learn how to ride a bike. 你学骑自行车得需要三到四个月的时间。

Learn how to hide your feeling! 学会掩藏你的感情!

- learn to+动词 学会做
- learn how to+动词 学会如何……

learn a (one's) lesson 得到教训

正如lesson与teach会经常出现一样，learn a lesson表示得到教训。

Haven't you learned your lesson yet? 你还没有得到教训吗?

I've learned my lesson. 我得到了教训。

- lesson learned 得到的教训

>>> 011

drop/ catch

掉落，滴落/抓（住）

MORE

- drop sb a line when
  留下几行信息
- drop (sb) a line (note) to+动词
  为做某事而留下几行信息

drop a line (note) 写简单的信息

从line或note的字眼中可以知道其含义，用drop代替了send，表示写的并不是正式的信件，而是短短几行话。

Drop me a line. 给我留下信息。

I'll drop you a line. 我会给你写信的。

- drop by for sth
  暂时路过
- drop by for
  暂时路过做某事
- drop in (on sb)
  暂时路过

drop by 访问（突然想见某人），路过

drop by 表示事先不打招呼的访问。同样使用了轻微的drop，表示暂时路过(make a short visit)。

Drop by for a drink (sometime). 有时间就过来玩吧。

Drop in sometime. 有空就过来。

- drop sb (sth) off
  用车接送
- drop sb off on one's way home
  送某人回家
- drop sb at (in)
  让某人在某处下车

drop off 使下车

drop off表示开车的途中使某人下车，或者传递东西。

I'll drop you off at your house tonight. 我今天晚上送你回家吧。

Why don't you just drop me off, and you can come back. 你送我过去再回来呗。

- drop out of college
  大学退学
- dropout
  退学

drop out 淘汰，放弃（学业）

表示在学校或公司等团体生活中退出，尤其指上学的学生半路退学。

The best thing for me to do is to drop out of college and get a job. 对我来说，最好的方法就是退学找工作。

- catch malaria
  患上瘴气
- catch+病名 from
  患病

catch a cold 感冒

与表示下降的drop具有正相反的含义，基本含义为人被某种事物纠缠。最常用的表达为在catch后面接病名，表示患病。

I think I'm catching a cold. Achoo! 我好像要感冒了，啊切！

catch somebody ...ing 抓住某人做某事

表示在对方未能察觉到的情况下发现对方做某事。尤其catch sb in the act指发现某人做坏事。

You caught me. 被你发现了。
You caught me doing it with Tammy. 你发现我和塔米做那件事了。

What's the big deal? 那有什么大不了的?

MORE

- catch sb ...ing
  偷偷看到某人做某事
- catch sb in the act (of ...ing)
  看到某人做某事

be (get) caught in 相见某人，被某人抓住

这次为被动形态，be (get) caught in表示被in后面的状态困住(get stuck)。单单是get caught的话表示罪犯被抓。

I got caught in a shower on my way home. 我回家的路上碰到了瓢泼大雨。
We were caught in a traffic jam. 我们在路上堵车了。

- sb be (get) caught in
  陷入……
- be (get) caught in a shower
  突然遭到暴风雨
- be (get) caught in a traffic jam
  堵车
- get caught
  被抓

catch on 突然理解，流行，贴上……

字面含义为继续(on)追赶，表示吸引人气或者赶时髦，可以想象有一家广播公司的名字就叫Catch On。另外，还表达“非常理解……”。

Wow, you catch on quick. 哇，你的理解能力真强。

Excellent idea! You're catching on. 很不错的想法！你的脑子很好使啊。

My house caught on fire. 我们家着火了。

- catch on (with)
  流行
- catch on (to)
  理解，领悟

catch up with 追上某人

表示赶上(up)某人，可以理解为追赶领先的人或车，或者“赶进度，之前推迟的事情等”。根据不同状况，还可以理解为“回头再说”，还有“逮捕”的含义。

I'll catch up with you in the gym. 回头我们体育馆见。

Catch up with you later! 回头见！

- catch up with
  追赶（之前推迟的事情，领先的人），回头再聊
- catch up with sb
  逮捕，产生影响

>>> 012

cut/ hit

砍，切/打，敲击

MORE

- cut corners to+动词
  为了做某事而节约
- cut cost
  减少开销

cut corners 节约（时间，经费等）

本义为不走弯路，走近路，因此可以表示节约时间，经费，努力等可以缩减的部分，以提高效率。

I had to cut corners to save money. 我得减少开支，存钱了。

This was a real buy. 这东西真实惠。

- cut a deal ...ing
  形成……的条约

cut a deal 达成一致

表示生意谈成(make a business deal)，在口语中想要表达具体的条约内容就可以说cut a deal ...ing。

I cut Sally a deal when she came to my shop. 在莎莉来我店铺的时候，我们就签订了合同。

be cut out for 有……的潜质，适合做某事

虽然看起来比较麻烦，用在某些的确“在某事上有潜质”的人或者适合做某事的人。For后面可以接工作或业务。在这里，cut out表示切除某物制作新东西。

She's cut out for this job. 她非常适合这份工作。

You're not cut out to be a physician. 你不是当医生的料。

- cut back (sth)
  减少（某物）
- cut back on
  减少……

cut back on 减少，缩减

cut back, cut back sth或cut back on sth等句式主要表示“减少支出的经费”，是公司老板非常喜欢的一句话。另外也可以用为“为了健康而调节饮食”上。

We're going to cut back on shopping too. 我们也会减少购物量的。

- cut down (sth)
  减少……的量
- cut down (on)
  减少，缩减，为了健康控制饮食

cut down on 减少，缩减

虽然cut back on具有相近的含义，不过主要用在为了健康减少饮食，烟酒等方面。

She's trying to get me to cut down on sugar. 她想方设法要减少我的糖份摄取量。

cut it out 斩除

表示斩除某物，可以用来表达使某人放弃某事，或者为了健康戒掉不良的饮食或习惯。在口语中Cut it out!会经常出现，表示“算了吧！”，用来回答对方的无稽之谈。

Don't do that! Cut it out! 不要那样！算了吧！
This is useless. We're going to have to cut it out.
这一点用都没有。我们得除掉。

cut off 斩除，中断

表示斩除(off)，可以表达电或天然气等供给的“中断”，“与朋友断交”等。

I was cut off. 电话被挂掉了。

I don't mean to cut you off. 我没有想打断你的话。

- cut sth off
  切除某物
- get cut off
  挂掉电话
- be cut off
  （场所或人）被孤立
- cut sb off
  断绝关系，插嘴，（车辆）危险地闯入

hit the road 出发

在口语中表示开始旅行，出发等踏上道路的举动，另外，hit+地点名词的形态表示“到达某地”。

I am going to hit the road. 我要出发了。

I'd better hit the road. 我最好得出发了。

- hit the road
  出发
- hit+地点名词
  到达某地
- hit the book
  学习

hit the ceiling 激怒

ceiling表示天花板，通过字面含义可以了解，一个人被激怒地顶穿了天花板，也可以用roof代替ceiling。

My wife hit the ceiling when she saw the bill.老婆看到账单时，简直气炸了。

- hit the ceiling (roof)
  激怒
- hit the sack (hay)
  睡觉
- hit the spot
  正是想要的东西

hit it off (with) （与某人）马上熟悉起来

用在那些一见钟情的天作之合上，想要说明对象，就可以用hit it off with。

They really hit it off. 他们就是天生的一对。

- hit it off (with sb)
  （与某人）很快熟悉

hit on 突然想到某事(come up with)，诱惑

在偶然想到妙计时可以用到的表达。不过，用在男女之间的话，就表示“诱惑”。

Are you hitting on me? 你在诱惑我吗？
I hit on a new idea while watching TV. 我在看电视的时候突然想出了新点子。

- hit on (upon) sth
  突然想到点子
- It hit me that ...
  突然产生了……的想法
- hit on sb
  诱惑某人

>>> 013

charge/ cost

罚款/价格为……

MORE

- charge (sb) money (for)
  某人为了某事支付多少
- charge for
  为某事支付多少
- charge rent (an entrance fee)
  支付房租（入场费）

charge somebody money 让某人支付

表示让某人支付某商品或服务的费用。具体的物品或服务内容要接在for后面。

How much did you charge? 一共多少钱?

I charge seven hundred dollars an hour. 每小时700美元。

He charged me twenty bucks. 他要了我20美元。

- charge sth to sb's room
  将费用计在某人头上
- charge sth on sb's account
  将费用计在某人的账户上
- charge sth on
  用信用卡支付
- (Will that be) Cash or charge?
  现金还是信用卡?

charge sth on sb's account 记在某人的账户上

charge除了索要费用的意思之外还具有信用卡支付的含义。就是说不用现金支付，而是用银行账户，信用卡等方式结算。因此在买单时对方一般会说到cash or charge?，此时charge表示信用卡支付。

Would you like to pay by cash or charge? 您是要现金支付，还是信用卡?

I'll charge it, please. 我要刷卡，谢谢。

- charge sb with sth
  因某事起诉（谴责）某人
- be charged with
  被起诉，受到谴责

be charged with 因某事被起诉

charge不仅仅用在结算时，具有多种含义，其中之一就是谴责或者起诉。

I was charged with stealing a cell phone. 我因偷了一部手机而受到了起诉。

You'll be charged with murder. 你会被控告谋杀罪的。

- be in charge of
  负责某事
- put somebody in charge of
  让某人负责某事
- take charge (of)
  负责（某事）

be in charge of 负责某事

charge不仅仅是个动词，作为名词形式最常用的含义就是责任。“负责某事”，“担任某事”都可以用be in charge of来表示。

I'm not in charge of the lab. 我不是这个实验室的负责人。

The boss put me in charge of that. 老板让我负责那件事。

The way you're taking charge is very impressive. 你负责的方式非常独特。

free of charge 免费

charge表示买物品或服务时需要支付的费用，因此free of charge表示不用花钱得到物品或服务。与with no charge具有相同的含义。

Take whatever you want. Free of charge. 想拿什么就拿什么，都是免费的。

MORE

- free of charge
  免费
- with no charge
  免费
- at no extra charge
  没有附加费用

cost somebody money 使某人花费多少钱

cost为动词，cost sb+钱表示某人因买物品或服务而花费了多少钱。

Your mistake cost me a lot money. 你的失误让我蒙受了大笔损失。

That's going to cost you $5000. 你会花5000美元的。

- cost sb+money
  使某人花费多少
- not cost sb a penny
  没有花一分钱

cost a fortune 非常昂贵

在这里没有指明具体的金额，而是在cost后面用到了表示财产的fortune或身体上重要部位an arm and a leg，以表示花费了巨大的金额。

It's so pretty. This must have cost him a fortune.
这个真漂亮，肯定花了他不少钱吧。

- cost a fortune
  非常昂贵
- cost (sb) an arm and a leg
  费用很贵

cost somebody something 使某人失去某物

这次用到的不是金额，而是一般名词。与用钱支付的方式相同，用名词支付就表示“失去某物”，后面的名词主要有job, life, marriage等。

It will cost you your job. 这会让你失去工作的。

It might cost you your life. 这会让你丢掉性命的。

cover the cost (of) 交……的费用

cost作为名词表示价格（费用）或努力（牺牲）。这里cost表示价格，因此cover the cost of表示“交……的费用”。

Who's going to cover the cost of repairs? 谁要交修理费?

I'll pay the cost of a new computer. 买新电脑的钱我来出吧。

- cover the cost of
  交……的费用
- pay the cost of
  支付……的费用
- at the cost of
  以……的费用

>>> 014

worry/ care

担心/关心，喜欢

MORE

· worry about sth (sb)
担心某事
· worry that S+V
担心……

worry about 担心某事

表示担心某事，在worry about后面加上担心的事情就可以了。当然，也可以用worry that从句的方式表达内容。

You worry about me too much. 你过于担心我了。

She worries about everything. 她担心所有的事情。

You don't have to worry about a thing. 你不用担心任何事情。

· be worried about sth (sb)
担心某事
· be worried that S+V
担心某事

be worried about (that) 担心某事

前文中的worry为动词，这次表达使对方担心。被动语态be worried about表示主语“担心某事”。

You're so worried about me. 你太担心我了。

We're worried about getting sued. 我们担心被起诉。

I'm so worried that I might fail the exam. 我非常担心考试没通过。

· Don't worry about sth (sb)
不要担心某事
· Don't worry if S+V
不用担心……
· Not to worry
不用担心……

Don't worry (about) 不要担心（某事）

与前面的worry about虽然是相同的表达，但Don't worry在口语中是个常用的语句，因此单独拿出来整理了一下。

Don't worry. You can count on me. 不要担心，你可以相信我。

Don't worry about a thing. 不用担心任何事情。

Don't worry. It's our treat. 不用担心，我们会做出来的。

Not to worry. She's fine. 不要担心，她没事。

· care about sth
重视某事
· care about sb
关心某人
· care what (how)
关心……

care about 关心某事，担心

care表示因为对方重要或喜欢对方而关心对方，经常用作care about, care what等形态。

I can see how much you care about Becky. 我能看出你对贝奇有多么关心。

You still care about me. 你还在关心我。

care for （肯定）关照，（否定/疑问）喜欢，渴望

care for的用法比较复杂，care for sb (sth) 除了“照看”之外，无论care for sb是肯定还是否定还是疑问，都表示“喜欢”，“渴望”。

(Would you) Care for some coffee? 你想来点咖啡吗?

I don't care for his style. 我不在乎款式。

Would you care to join us? 你希望加入我们吗?

MORE

- care for sb (sth)
  照看，喜欢
- not care for sb (sth)
  不喜欢……
- not care to+动词
  你喜欢……吗?
- Would you care for ... ?
  您想要做某事吗?
- Would you care to ... ?
  你想要……吗?

I don't care about ... 我不在乎……

利用care about组成的多种用法，I don't care about ... /I don't care if (what)或疑问句形态Would you care if ... ?等都比较常用。

I don't care about any of that! 我不在乎任何事情!

I don't care if she's fat or thin. 我才不在乎她是胖还是瘦。

I don't care who he sleeps with. 我才不在乎他和谁睡了。

Do you care if I join you? 我加入你介意吗?

- I don't care about ...
  我不在乎某事
- I don't care what (if)
  我不在乎……
- Would (Do) you care if ... 你介意……吗?

could't care less (if) （对）完全没有兴趣

字面含义表达得很清楚。表示关心(care)少(less)的不能(couldn't)再少，换句话说就是毫不在乎。想要说明不在乎的事情，就可以在about或what (if)后面叙述。

I couldn't care less. 我才不管。

I couldn't care less if she comes or not. 我才不在乎她来还是不来。

- couldn't care less about
  毫不在乎某事
- couldn't care less what (if)
  完全不在乎某事

Who cares about (what)? 有谁在乎……吗?

反问形式句式，虽然没有否定的词汇，但内容表示没有人在乎任何事情。

Who cares what they think? 至于他们想什么，有谁会关心?

Who cares! 没人在乎!

- for all I care (know)
  不在乎某事
- Who cares!
  谁会在乎!

take care of 照看，处理……

care此时变成了名词，take care of后面如果接人就表示“照看”，如果接e-mail等词就表示“处理”。

Let me take care of it. 交给我吧。

Let me take care of the bill. 我来买单。

I'll take care of your son while you're out. 你出门的时候我会照看你的儿子。

- take care
  小心，（问候）保重
- take care of
  照看，处理，买单（费用）

>>> 015

eat/ drink/ cook

吃/喝/做料理

MORE

- be drunk
  喝醉
- DUI(driving under the influence)
  酒驾
- drunken driving
  酒驾
- drink and drive
  酒后驾车

- drink water
  喝水
- drink coffee (tea)
  喝咖啡（茶）

eat lunch (dinner) 吃午餐（晚餐）

这次eat后面接了lunch, dinner, breakfast等名词，最大的特点就是中间不加任何冠词。

What do you want to eat for lunch today? 今天中午吃什么？

get something to eat 吃点东西

something to eat表示吃的东西，即food。因此get (have) something to eat与get (have) food相同，表示吃东西。

Do you want to get something to eat? 你想吃点东西吗？

Let's have something to eat. 我们吃点东西吧。

got drunk 喝醉

酒喝多了难免会醉。最常用的表达就是get drunk。主要使用drunken等pp形态和drunk的形容词形态。

I got drunk easily. 我很容易喝醉。

He's drunk as a skunk (lord). 他醉得一塌糊涂。

drink and drive 酒后驾驶

比喝醉更恶劣的行为就是酒后驾车。不仅是自己，甚至还会威胁到他人的生命。一般会说drink and drive或者用简称DUI。

Don't drink and drive. 不要酒后驾驶。

You're drunk right now. 你已经醉了。

drink coffee (tea, wine) 喝咖啡（茶，红酒）

drink表示喝某种饮料，不一定要用在喝酒上。喝水是drink water，喝咖啡是drink coffee等。

I am not supposed to drink coffee. 我不能喝咖啡。

Do you like to drink juice? 你喜欢喝果汁吗？

get (want) something to drink 拿点喝的东西

something to drink表示喝的东西，因此get (have) something to drink表示拿点喝的东西。

Would you like something to drink? 你要喝点什么吗?

Can I get you something to drink? 我给你拿点喝的好不?

have (get) a drink 喝两杯

喝酒或者饮料的时候要在a drink前面加have，get或take。当然，喝数杯的时候要用drinks或者some drinks。

She's having drinks with her date. 她正在和约会对象喝酒。

He's taking a drink of his soda. 他正在喝苏打水。

- have (get) a drink 喝酒
- have drinks with 与某人喝酒
- have (get) some drinks 喝点酒
- have another drink 再喝一杯
- take a drink (of) 再喝一杯（饮料）

go out for a drink 出去喝酒

have a drink 表示喝酒或喝饮料，如果想要在口语中明确表明“出去喝酒”for a drink的目的的话就要加出门(go out)，见面(meet，join)或经过(drop by)等词组。

How about going out for a drink tonight? 今天晚上喝一杯怎么样?

Drop by for a drink (sometime). 回头喝酒去吧。

- take sb for a drink 带某人出去喝两杯
- get together for a drink 聚在一起喝两杯
- join sb for a drink 见面喝两杯

get (buy) somebody a drink 给某人拿点喝的

喝酒这个事情就应该互相请客。请人喝酒的时候要用get或buy，变成get (buy) somebody a drink。

Why don't you buy her a drink? 请她喝两杯吧。

I'll buy you a drink and explain. 我一边喝酒一边给你解释。

- get sb a drink 带某人出去喝酒
- buy sb a drink 请某人喝酒

cook sth for sb 为某人做料理

cook表示通过食材加热(heat)而制成料理的过程。

Mom is cooking fish for us. 老妈正在给我们烧鱼。

cook somebody a meal (dinner, breakfast) 为某人做料理

想要单单表示“为某人做料理”，而不突出做的东西，就可以用这个短语。

I'll cook you dinner. 我来给你准备晚餐。

My wife loves to cook for our children. 我老婆非常喜欢给孩子们做饭。

- cook (sb) a meal 做料理
- cook (sb) dinner 做晚餐
- cook (sb) breakfast 准备早餐

>>> 016

pass/ follow

通过，传递/跟随

MORE

- pass sb sth
  给某人传递东西
- pass sth to sb
  把某东西递给某人

pass somebody something 传递某人某物

pass表示将某物交给某人，比方说“pass me the salt”。如果把人放在后面就要变成to sb。

Could you pass me that please? 你能帮我拿一下吗？

- pass the exam
  通过考试
- pass the driving test
  通过驾照考试
- pass a law
  通过法案

pass the exam 通过考试

pass后面接各种考试或者法案，表示“通过考试”或“通过法案”等。最常用的短语就是pass the exam。

Do you think she'll pass the exam? 你认为她会通过考试吗？

You'll pass the exam if you study. 如果你学习的话，肯定会通过考试的。

pass away 去世，过世

表示死亡时会常用die，不过用在长辈身上时就要用pass away代替die。

I'm very sorry to tell you your mother has passed away. 很抱歉告诉您，您母亲刚刚去世了。

- pass by sth (sb)
  经过某人的身旁
- pass sb by
  与某人擦身而过

pass by 经过某人的身旁

最原始的含义“经过”，pass by表示“经过某人的身旁”，by后面既可以接人物也可以接事物。不过pass sb by表示没有对sb产生任何帮助，擦身而过。

You just passed by me without saying hi? 你连招呼都不打一声就过去了？

Tom saw a woman pass by with a baby. 汤姆看见一个妇女抱着孩子经过。

- sb pass out
  失去意识
- pass sth out
  失去意识

pass out 失去知觉

表示失去意识(unconscious)，尤其在驾车的时候(behind (at) the wheel)的话，就非常危险了！

He passed out behind the wheel. 他在方向盘上失去了意识。

pass through 通过，经过，经历

虽然是经过但要“通过某个事物”，比方说通过隧道为pass through a tunnel，另外，在旅行过程中路过某地也可以用这个表达。同时也可以用来比喻“经历某事”。

The last train passed through here an hour ago.
最后一班列车一个小时前经过了这里。

pass up 拒绝、错过（机会）

pass up后面接上chance，opportunity或者offer等与机会相关的单词，表示没能抓住机会，错过机会等。

Don't pass up your chance. 不要错过这次机会。

- pass up a chance (opportunity) to
  错过……的机会

follow suit 按照惯例

表示跟着前面的人的惯例行事。尤其在家族里跟随祖先的步伐，可以用follow in one's footsteps。

I'll follow suit. 我也那么做吧。
She went back to eating and her guests followed suit. 她回去重新开始吃了起来，客人们也照做。

- follow suit
  按照惯例
- follow in one's footsteps
  跟随某人的脚步

follow the rules (example) 遵守规则（先例）

与前文中的表达类似，follow后面要加rules，example或lead等名词，表示“跟随……”。

We expect you to follow Jeff's example. 我们希望你按照杰夫的例子。

- follow the rules
  遵守规则
- follow the example of
  按照……的管理
- follow the lead of
  跟随……

follow up 采取后续措施

表示继续尾随收集信息或者采取后续的措施。需要采取后续措施的对象要加在on后面，而方法要加在with后面。比方说，通过邮件对某时间采取后续措施为"follow up on the case with an email"。

She needed to follow up after her proposal was accepted. 她的提议被接受了之后，需要采取后续的措施。

Did the doctor follow up after your operation? 在手术之后，医生采取了后续措施吗？

- follow up (on)
  采取后续措施（做某事）

as follows 如下

想要说明重要的内容或者进入主题之前要说这句话，表示“……如下”。
The main idea is as follows. 主要观点如下。

>>> 017

plan/ prepare

计划，准备

MORE

- plan to+动词
  打算做某事
- plan on ...ing
  计划做某事
- plan out
  周密地计划

plan to do 打算做某事

plan表示树立计划，但在日常生活中经常使用plan to+动词/on ...ing的形态，单纯表示打算做某事。此时可以理解为will或be going to 的代替品。

I plan to stay for a week. 我打算待一个星期。

I thought you had this all planned out. 我以为你已经计划好了。

- as planned
  按照计划
- go as planned
  按照计划进行

as planned 正如计划

如果世界上的所有事情都这样该多好啊。as planned 表示按照原计划，如果使用go的过去式，变成went as planned的话，就表示“按照计划完成了”。

If all goes as planned, I will not be here anymore. 如果所有事情顺利的话，我就不会在这里了。

- make a plan (plans) for
  制订计划（准备）
- work out a plan for
  树立计划

make a plan 树立计划

正如字面含义，make a plan表示“树立做某事的计划”，“做好……的准备”等。

I've already made other plans. 我已经有别的计划了。

I wish I could, but I've made plans to walk around. 我也很想，不过我打算出去走走。

- have a plan for
  有计划
- not have any plan for
  没有任何计划

have a plan 有计划

如果制订了计划，就已经有计划了。have (got) a plan表示“树立……的计划或安排”，否定形式为not have a plan，想要强调的话可以用not have any plans。

Do you have any plans? 你有什么计划吗?

Do you have any plans for summer vacation? 你这个暑假有计划吗?

I've got plans. 我有计划。

No, you were right. I don't have a plan. 不，你说得对，我没有任何计划。

be against (for) the plan 反对（赞成）计划

表示赞成时使用for，反对时使用against。可以将这些用在计划上，即赞成计划是be for the plan，反对计划是be against the plan。

I'm against the plan. 我反对这个计划。

MORE

- be for the plan 赞成计划
- be against the plan 反对计划

... plan is to ... ……的计划是……

想要具体表达计划内容时可以用到的词组，常用Our (My) plan is to+动词的形态。

Our plan is to leave in ten minutes. 我们的计划是十分钟内离开。

Her plan is to hook up with her sister. 她的计划是让你和她妹妹接触接触。

prepare (somebody) for （为某人）准备某事

表示计划将来的事情，准备日程安排等，prepare for sth或prepare to+动词为常用的形态。

I've been preparing for that my entire life! 我用了一辈子计划了这件事情！

I want you to prepare to go to the party. 我希望你做好去派对的准备。

- prepare (sb) for sth 准备某事
- prepare to 准备做某事

prepare something (for) 准备某物

为了做某事而准备something的表达，其用途可以在for后面予以说明，此时可以加人物或事物。

I tried my best to prepare this meal for you. 我已经尽全力为你准备这顿饭了。

- prepare sth for 为了某事而准备某物

have something prepared 准备某物

为被动形态，be prepared to+动词/for+名词表示“做好了……的准备”。

How would you like your steak prepared? 您想要几分熟的牛排？

Did he have a speech prepared? 他准备好演说稿了吗？

be prepared to (for) 准备好做某事

使用了祈使动词have变成了have sth pp的形态。这种表达方式的原因是prepare的主题并不是主语，而是第三者。

I am prepared to let that go. 我已经做好了遗忘的准备。

It's fine. I'm prepared for this. 很好，我做好了准备。

>>> 018

pick/ choose/ decide

挑选/选择/决定

MORE

- pick on sb
  找某人麻烦
- pick on sb (sth)
  选择某人

- pick sb (sth) out
  挑出，识别

- pick sb (sth) up
  抬起某物，扶起某人
- pick oneself up
  起身
- pick sth up
  彻底地清楚，得到，在店铺买东西，得病
- pick sth up
  自行处理，学习，感知（声音等），接电话
- pick sb up
  用车接送
- pick up speed
  提速
- sth pick up
  （状况，经济）好转，向上

- choose from
  从……选择
- choose sb (sth) to do
  选择某人做某事
- choose sb (sth) for
  选择某人为……
- be chosen as (for)
  被选择为……

pick on 找麻烦

正如pick on sb一样，pick on后面如果接人物的话就表示"谴责某人，或者持续找某人的麻烦"(treat sb badly or unfairly)。

Why are you picking on me? 你为什么那么折磨我？

Stop picking on me. 别再折磨我了。

pick out 挑选，选择

表示用手拽出某物，可以用来表达多种含义，其中最常用的就是挑选(select)或"找出……"，"了解"(recognize)等。

Can you help me pick out an engagement ring? 你能帮我挑订婚戒指吗？

pick up 抬起，买，用车接送，向上，加速

可以联想用手抬起某物的动作，发挥想象力理解多种含义。

I picked it up at a flea market for $5. 我在跳骚市场花了5美元买了这个。

Who's going to pick it up? 谁会买单？

I think things are picking up. 我觉得事情会变好的。

choose between (from) 在……中挑选

表示在多个东西或多个人中选择的含义，可以用choose组成多样的短语。

Jill was chosen as the president of our class.吉尔被当选为我们班的班长。

choose to 选择做某事

choose后面选择的如果不是sb (sth)而是某种行为时，则要使用to+动词的形态，表示"选择做某事"。

He chose to live alone. 他决定一个人住。

have a choice 有选择权

choose的名词型是choice，与各种东西相结合所呈现的含义比choose更常用。have a choice表示有选择的机会，而make a choice则是“决定”，“做出选择”的意思。

I don't think you have a choice. 我觉得你没有选择权。

You're right. He made his choice. 你说的没错。他是自己决定的。

have no choice but to 没有其他选择，只能做某事

同样是利用choice组成的表达。从很小的时候就经常听大人说have no choice but to+动词，表示“不得不做某件事”。

I had no choice but to get divorced. 我只好选择离婚。

I had no choice but to use force. 我只好动用武力了。

be somebody's choice 某人的选择

为了突出某人应该决定某问题而在choice前面加上了具体的人物one's。

I mean it was your choice. 我是说，那是你的选择。

decide to do 决定做某事

decide后面必须要接to+动词的形态。在表达“决定了”之前，所决定的内容是一直考虑着的，因此经常会用decided或have decided的现在完成时形态。

I've decided to go to Chicago without you. 我决定不和你一块儿去芝加哥了。

dicide that 决定……

如果决定的内容过长，则可以使用这种句式。经常使用decide that S+V或decide what (who) S+V的形态。

I decided I wanted to come to your party. 我决定参加你的派对。

I decided I'm going to go with her. 我决定和她一起去。

make a decision 做出决定

与decide具有相同的含义，不过英语世界里，经常会用相应的词组代替单个单词，最典型的例子就是make a decision。

She's trying to make a decision about something. 她好像要决定某事。

MORE

- have a (the) choice of
  有……的选择
- have a choice between
  在……之间有选择
- make a choice
  做出选择
- leave sb with no choice
  让某人没得可选

- have no choice but to+动词
  不得不做某事
- have little choice but to+动词
  只好做某事

- be one's choice
  是某人的选择
- It's one's choice to+动词
  做某事是某人的选择

- decide that S+V
  决定……
- decide what (who, whether, when)
  决定……
- decide what (who, how) to
  决定……

>>> 019

buy/ sell/ deal/ afford/ belong

买/卖/交易/供得起/属于

MORE

- buy sb sth
  给某人买某物
- buy sth for sb (sth)
  给某人买某物
- buy (sth) from sb
  从……买到某物
- buy sth for+价格
  以……的价格买到某物

buy somebody something 给某人买某物

表示花钱购买，如果要说“从……买到某物”是要用buy something from，想要表达具体花费的金额，则要用buy something for+金额的形态。

Let me buy you a drink. 我来请你喝两杯吧。

I'll buy you something at the duty free shop, if you want. 如果你愿意的话，我会在免税店里给你买点东西。

buy something on credit 提前购买

如果眼下没有现金，可以承诺日后会支付，先使用商品，这种购物方式就是buy something on credit。字面含义为通过信用(credit)买东西，因此属于一种提前购买行为。

I'd like to buy it on credit. 我想用信用卡购买。

No one bought this on credit. 没有人会延期付款。

- sell sb sth
  向某人卖某物
- sell sth to sb
  向某人卖某物
- sell sth for+价格
  以……的价格卖某物

sell somebody sth (sth to sb) 向某人卖某物

buy的反义词sell表示贩卖物品或服务。不过不仅仅限于购买物品，还可以用在说服对方接纳某种计划或方案时。

I'm going to sell him a coat. 我要向他卖大衣。

She sells candy to kids. 她把糖果卖给了孩子们。

He's not going to sell his car for one thousand dollars. 他不会以一千美元卖掉自己的车。

sell sth on (over) the internet 在网上卖某物

随着通讯技术的发达，网上购物或手机购物已经是种普遍的现象了。

It's good idea to sell ice over the interent. 在网上卖冰块是个不错的想法。

be sold out (of) （某东西）卖完

利用了sell的被动形态，be sold out表示“卖完”，“售罄”等。

We're sold out for the first time. 我们头一次卖完东西了。

Were they sold out of winter coats? 他们卖完了冬季大衣?

MORE

- be sold out fast
  很快售完
- sb be sold out of sth
  某人卖完了某物

deal with 处理……

deal作为动词时需要记住一个最重要的短语deal with。with后面会接sb (sth)，表示“处理”，“解题”，“相处”，“驾驭”等。

He's a difficult man to deal with. 他是个非常不好相处的人。

Deal with it. 打起精神来。

- deal with sb (sth)
  处理，相处，驾驭
- deal with a problem
  处理问题

make a deal 交易，妥协

make a deal表示“与某人交易”，可以用do, strike, cut等动词替换make。不过close a deal的含义并不是结束交易，而是“成功完成交易”。

I'll make a deal with you. 我要和你交易。

Let's make a deal. 我们这样吧。

- make (do) a deal (with) 交易
- strike (cut) a deal
  交易
- close a deal
  成功完成交易

be no big deal 没什么大不了的

big deal表示大交易，自然比喻为“大事”。因此其否定形态be no big deal表示没什么大不了的，不用在意等。

That's no big deal. 没什么大不了的。

What's the big deal? 有什么大不了的?

Don't worry! It's no big deal. 不要担心！没什么大不了的。

can('t) afford+名词（动词） 有（没）空做某事

可以表示经济上能不能够供得起“名词”。一定会和can或be able to相结合使用，名词的位置不仅可以加能够用钱买到的东西，还可以加时间等名词，或者to+动词的形态。

We just can't afford it right now. 我们现在顾不上。

I can't afford to buy you a house. 我们现在可无法给你买座房子。

belong to 属于……

一提到belong就会想到belong to。to后面可以接sb (sth)，其含义为“属于……”，“是某人的”。

You belong to me. You're mine. 你属于我，你是我的。

- belong to sb
  属于某人
- belong to sth
  ……所属

>>> 020

apologize/ excuse/ thank/ appreciate

道歉/辩解，原谅/感谢/感激

MORE

- apologize for sth (...ing)
  因某事道歉
- apologize to sb
  向某人道歉
- apologize to sb for
  因某事向某人道歉

apologize to somebody

向某人（因某事）道歉

apologize表示“对错误的道歉”，如果要说道歉的对象则要用to sb，如果要指明具体的事情，则要用for sth或for ... ing。根据不同的状况，可以单独使用apologize，也可以加上to sb或者to sb for 。

I came to apologize to you. 我是来向你道歉的。

I apologize for that. 我为此道歉。

I just want to apologize for that. 我就是想和你道歉。

- accept one's apologies
  接受某人的歉意
- accept one's sincere apologies
  接受某人诚挚的歉意

accept apologies 接受道歉

对方一旦向你apologize了，那通常都要接受对方的歉意。此时可以使用apology的复数名词形式apologies，变成accept one's apologies。

Please accept my apologies. 请接受我的歉意。

Will you accept my apologies? 你会接受我的歉意吗?

- excuse sb
  原谅某人
- excuse sb for sth (...ing)
  原谅某人某事

excuse sb for 原谅某人做某事

excuse和forgive相似，有原谅的含义，可以用在无礼，不小心等非严重过失上。

Please excuse me for being late. 很抱歉，我迟到了。

Excuse me for being so selfish. 请原谅我那自私的举动。

- excuse sb
  谅解……
- excuse sb from sth (...ing)
  避免某人面临某事
- be excused from ...ing
  暂时离开，不做某事
- sb be excused
  某人可以离开
- if you'll excuse me
  如果您能原谅我

excuse somebody 原谅某人

虽然比较面生，不过在日常生活中经常会用来表示暂时离开，请对方原谅。

May I be excused for a moment? 我可以离开一会吗?

Could you excuse us for a second? 很抱歉，能让一让吗?

You're excused now. 现在可以走了。

If you'll excuse me, I'm going to go back to the office. 如果您不介意，我就回办公室了。

make an (one's) excuse for 为某事找借口

make an excuse (excuses)表示“为某事找借口”。for后面用sth或 ...ing指明具体的事情。

Jamie made an excuse for being late. 杰米找了个借口解释自己为什么迟到。

have no excuse 对某事毫无借口

表示根本找不到借口，have no excuse of表示“对某事毫无借口”，另外，There's no excuse for ... 表示所做的事情太过分了，根本找不到合适的借口让他人理解。

I just ran out of excuses. 我已经没什么借口了。

I have no excuse for not coming home yesterday. 关于昨天没有回家，我没有任何借口。

say thank you (to somebody) （向某人）表达谢意

将"thank you"名词化，say thank you表示表达谢意，如果在后面加to sb则表示“向某人表达谢意”，not know how to thank you表示都不知道该怎么感谢对方了。

I just wanted to say thank you. 我就是想谢谢你。

I just stopped by to say thank you. 我就是过来说声谢谢的。

appreciate it (this, that) 感激某事

比thank更加恭敬和谦逊的话，可以在appreciate后面接具体的名词(support, help)，如果想要表达感激的对象而非事情时，就要用appreciate sb ...ing的形态。

I really appreciate this. 对此我很感激。

This is great. I really appreciate it. 真了不起。非常感激。

I appreciate you giving me a hand. 非常感谢你能帮我一把。

I'd appreciate it if you ... 如果……的话就感激不尽了

经常在信件或者邮件中看到的假设语句。使用了I would，因此在if后面的东西需要变成would (could)+动词或过去式的形态。比起感激，更像是拜托某事。

I would really appreciate it if you didn't tell Dad about this. 如果你不告诉老爸，就太感谢了。

MORE

- make an excuse for sth (...ing)
  为某事找借口
- have an excuse for sth (...ing)
  为某事找借口
- find (look for) an excuse for sth (...ing)
  为某事找借口

- have no excuse for
  关于某事找不到借口
- run out of excuses
  找不到借口
- There is no excuse for ...
  对于某事没有任何借口

- say thank you to
  向某人致谢
- not know how to thank you
  不知道该怎么感谢了

- I appreciate it (this, that)
  非常感激
- I appreciate this, but
  很感激，不过……

>>> 021

change/ remain

变化/仍然，留下

||||| MORE |||||

- change to
  变成……
- change into
  变成，变化

chang something 改变某物

能够改变的所有东西都可以变成宾语，表示改变现有的东西。不过change the baby可不是换什么孩子，而是给孩子换尿布。

I'd like to change my flight. 我想改签航班。

I recently changed jobs. 我最近换了份工作。

Could we change the subject, please? 我们能换个主题吗?

Would you change the oil, please? 请换机油，谢谢!

- change A (in) to B
  将A改为B，使变化
- change sth from A to B
  使某物从A变成B

change A (to B) 将A改成B

表示改变现有的东西。根据不同的状况要选择to或into。如果表示将某物从A改成B，就要用change sth from A to B。

I have to change my ticket from economy to business class. 我得把机票的经济舱改成商务舱了。

- change one's mind about
  改变某人对某事的想法
- have a change of heart
  改变想法（态度）

change one's mind (about)

改变（关于某事）想法

表示改变已经决定的事情或计划等。想要表达改变的对象则要在change one's mind后面加about sth。

I guess she's changed her mind. 我猜她改变主意了。

Why did you change your mind? 你为什么要改变主意?

I've had a change of heart. I don't want to see you anymore. 我改变主意了。我再也不想见到你。

Why the sudden change of heart? 为什么突然改变主意?

- get changed
  换衣服
- get dressed
  穿衣服
- get undressed
  脱衣服

get changed 换衣服

get基本上什么事情都要掺和。get changed可以理解为换衣服(change clothes)。

I'm going to get changed. 我要换衣服了。

Go get changed! 去换衣服!

make a change 变更，变化

将change当成名词，此时和名词change相结合的有make a change。表示向好的方向改变现有的状况。

We need to make a change. 我们得尝试改变。

Starting tomorrow, you have to make a change.
从明天开始，你要做出改变了。

MORE

- make a change to sth
  变更为……

make change 换成零钱

change的第二个名词含义就是零钱。make change表示换成零钱，make change for后面可以接人或者钱。不能和make a change相混淆。

Do you have enough money to make change for a 100 dollar bill? 你能换开一张100的吗？

Here is your change and receipt. 这是找您的钱和收据。

- make change for+钱
  换成零钱
- make change for+人
  给某人找钱
- get change for a dollar
  换成1美元的纸币

remain+形容词 留作……

remain主要用为remain+形容词的形式，就像remain silent一样，其含义与前面的change相反，表示继续留为形容词的状态。

Please remain calm. 请保持安静。
Remain where you are. 站在原地。
The donor asked to remain anonymous. 捐赠者要求匿名。

- remain+形容词
  留为……
- remain+名词
  留为……

The question remains 有问题残留

如果事物变成了主语，以remain结束，或者变成to be+pp的形态则表示虽然处理了各种问题，但“还有……残留”，或者还有“一些事情要做”。

The question remains. Is she going to get married?
问题是，她要结婚吗？

- sth remains
  仍然留下
- sth remains to be+pp
  仍然……

remain at (by, behind) 留在……

remain后面如果接上具体的地点（介词+名词）的话就表示“留在某地”，如remain at home, remain in Korea等。

Bob has chosen to remain at home. 鲍勃决定留在家里。

My wife decided to remain by my side. 我老婆决定留在我身边。

- remain+地点
  留在某地
- remain in bed
  留在床上
- remain at home
  留在家里

>>> 022

lend/borrow/owe

借给/借来/欠

MORE

- lend sb sth
  借某人某物
- lend sth to sb
  把某物借给某人

lend somebody something 把某物借给某人

表示个人或机构“借某物”，与borrow正好相反。需要注意的是，借出去的不仅是钱，还可以是书，椅子等。

If you want, I can lend you some money. 如果你愿意的话，我能借给你一些钱。

Lending friends money is always a mistake. 借给朋友钱不是件好事。

Could you lend me forty bucks? 你能借我40美元吗？

- lend a hand with
  帮助某人做某事
- lend (one's) support to
  帮助某人

lend a hand 帮助

lend表示借，因此可以用来表示向对方“提供”帮助等，不仅有lend a hand，还有lend one's support。

Can you lend me a hand? 你能帮我一下吗？

She asked me if I could lend a hand. 她问我能不能帮个忙。

- borrow sth from sb
  向某人借某物
- borrow sth from
  从……借某物

borrow sth from somebody 向某人借某物

与lend正好相反的动词，表示从他人那里“借某物”，可以借的包括钱和其他多样的名词。另外，与lend不同，borrow并不存在borrow sb sth 的形态。

I need to borrow some money. 我得借点钱了。

I'll never borrow a dress from you again. 我绝对不会再跟你借裙子的。

- owe sb money
  欠某人钱
- owe sb for sth
  欠某人某物
- owe sth to sb
  欠某人……

owe somebody+(money) 欠某人……

表示在得到某件物品或服务之后需要支付相应的费用，或者“欠某人多少钱”等。

How much do I owe you? 我得给你多少钱？

Now, you owe me fifteen bucks. 现在你欠我15美元。

owe somebody sth 欠某人……

虽然没有具体买物品或者借钱，但需要偿还对方所提供的好意时可以用这句话，用sth表达亏欠对方的事情。

You didn' owe me anything. 你根本没有欠我什么。

MORE

- owe sb sth
  欠某人人情

I owe you one 我欠你人情

属于前面的owe sb sth形态，使用频率很高。I owe you one是固定搭配。

It was a great idea. I really owe you one. 这主意很不错，我欠你个人情。

Thanks for coming over. I owe you one. 很感谢你能来，我欠你一份人情。

You guys owe me big time. 你们欠我太多了。

She says you owe her big time. 她说你欠她一个大人情。

- owe somebody big time
  欠某人一个大人情
- owe sb a lot
  欠某人很大人情
- owe sb a great deal
  欠某人很大人情

owe somebody an apology 需要向某人道歉

同样为owe sb sth的句式，不过这次sth的位置变成了特定名词，即apology，explanation，truth等，表示需要道歉，解释或说出真相。

You owe me an apology. 你得和我道歉。

I owe you an apology. 我得和你道歉。

Do I owe her an apology? 我得和她道歉吗?

owe it to somebody 多亏某人，做某事是……的义务

“多亏了他的勇气，我才活下来”可以用owe my life to his bravery，“她是我的救命恩人”要用owe my life to her，同理“欠某人人情”要用owe it to的形态。

I owe it to my colleagues. 多亏了同事们。

I felt like I owed it to him. 我觉得这都要归功于他。

- owe sth to sb (sth)
  多亏了……
- owe it all to sb
  多亏了某人
- owe everything to
  一切都要归功于……
- owe it to sb to+动词
  ……是……的功劳
- owe it to oneself to+动词
  具有……的义务

>>> 023

fill/ file/ fit/ fix

充满/（文件）锉/适合/修正

MORE

- fill sth
  填满某物
- fill sth with
  用某物填满
- be filled with
  装满

fill something 填满某物

fill表示“装满”，经常使用fill A with B的形态，也可以用被动形态be filled with。

The music filled the room. 音乐充满了房间。

The house is filled with guests. 家里挤满了客人。

- fill in sth
  记入某物
- fill sb in (on)
  （向远方的人）传达最近的消息
- fill in for sb
  代替某人做某事

fill in 记入到文件里，装满，通知，代理

同样表示装满，但并不指某空间，而是在文件中“记录必要的事项”。fill in还具有其他含义，fill sb in on表示让远方的人“获知最近的消息”。

You can fill in all the information on the form.
表格里的所有内容都可以填写。

Whatever you've got going on, fill me in. 如果有什么事情，就告诉我。

- fill out sth
  记入（正式书面）
- sb (sb's body) fill out
  长胖

fill out 记入

fill out同样表示在registration（注册申请书），customs declaration（顾客上诉表）等正式“表格中记入信息”。

I've got some paperwork for you to fill out. 有几份文件需要你填写一下。

- fill (the car) up (with)
  加油
- fill up (with)
  装满
- fill (oneself) up (with/on)
  暴饮暴食

fill up 加油

fill大多用在给汽车“加油”上，常用形式为fill it up。另外，除了汽车以外，fill up还表示填满，包括填饱肚子的“暴饮暴食”(eat one's fill; fill one's stomach)。

I ran out of gas. Where can we fill up? 我没油了。去哪儿能加油？

- fit sb well
  （衣服尺寸）合适
- clothes fit
  衣服合适
- be fitted for+衣服
  匹配……的大小（加工）

fit (somebody)+(well, perfectly) （衣服等）合适

fit作为动词表示衣服大小“合适”。作为不及物动词可以用sth fit，作及物动词可以用fit sb well等。

It fits me perfectly. 这非常适合我。

I bought some clothes that actually. 我买了几件很合身的衣服。

fit for (to) 适合……的

fit表示“健康的”或“合适的”等，作为形容词可以使用(be) fit for (to do)的形态。

This house is fit for a sale. 这座房子很适合销售。

I don't think he's fit for being a soldier. 我觉得他不适合当一个军人。

MORE

- fit for sth (...ing)
  适合……的，合适的
- fit to do sth
  健康的，适合的

get fixed 修理（get something fixed 修理某物）

不可能自己一个人修理所有东西，因此需要让别人帮忙，所以会有get sth fixed的说法。

That's how it got fixed! 就是这么修好的！

I never did get my shoes fixed. 我可从来没有修过鞋子。

- get fixed
  修理
- get sth fixed
  修理某物

fix one's hair (make-up) 整理头发（装束）

fix后面如果接头发或者化妆(make up)的话就表示整理头发或者装束。

Sally is fixing her hair in her room. 莎莉正在自己的房间弄头发呢。

My sister is just fixing her makeup. 我妹妹正在补妆。

- fix one's hair for
  弄头发
- fix one's make up
  补妆
- fix one's face
  化妆

fix 准备料理或用餐

fix的另一个重要用法就是在fix后面接lunch，dinner等名词或drink等饮食名词，表示“准备吃的”(prepare)。

She is fixing lunch in the kitchen. 她正在厨房准备吃的。

I'm going to fix you a drink. 我来给你弄杯喝的吧。

- fix+饮食名称
  准备料理
- fix sb sth
  为某人准备某事
- fix oneself sth
  吃……

fix up 确定会议日期等，装修或修缮房间或建筑物

fix up 表示会议或行程“安排确定”，或者“修理”房间等。

The landlord's trying to fix up the place for the new tenant. 房主为了新搬进来的人修理房子。

- fix sb (sth) up
  准备会议等，修理
- fix for sb to+动词
  使某人做某事

fix up with 介绍，提供

基本的含义为准备某物，但如果with后面接事物的话则表示“为某人提供某物”，如果with后面接人的话则表示“向某人介绍某人”。

Yesterday he asked me to fix him up with somebody. 昨天他让我给他介绍对象。

- fix sb (sth) up with sth
  提供……
- fix sb (sth) up with sb
  给某人介绍某人

>>> 024

lie/ lay

躺下，说谎/躺下，放下

MORE

- lie on (in)
  躺在……
- lie down
  躺下，屈服，减少
- lie back
  躺平，向后靠

lie on (in) 躺在……上（过去式为lay）

lie为不及物动词，表示“躺下”，根据躺下的方式，后面会接不同的介词或副词。动词的变化形态为lie–lay–lain。

Tony is lying on the couch watching TV. 托尼正躺在沙发上看电视。

She lay back with her eyes closed. 她闭着双眼躺着。

- sth lie with sb
  （责任/失误等）在某人身上
- sth lie with (in) sth
  （问题/解答等）在……上

lie in 在……

这次不是某人躺着，而是某种问题或责任等在某人身上，主要有blame, responsibility等。

My happiness lies in being with my family. 我的幸福是建立在家庭和睦之上的。

- lie to sb
  对某人说谎
- lie about sth
  关于某事说谎

lie to (about) 向某人（关于某事）说谎

虽然形态和发音相同，但这次的动词变化(lie–lied–lied)却有些差异，可以记住基本的用法，lie to sb, lie about sth等。

You lied to me!你骗了我！

I'm sorry that I lied to you before. 很抱歉，之前骗了你。

Everybody lies on their resume. 每个人都会在简历上说谎。

- tell a lie to sb
  对某人说谎
- tell a lie about sth
  关于某事说谎

tell a lie (to) （向某人）说谎

表示说谎的单词lie不仅具有动词的形式，还可以充当名词，最常用的形态就是tell a lie，后面可以用to接人物，也可以用about sth说明事情。

You shouldn't tell a lie to a client. 你不应该向客户撒谎。

lay something on 将……放在……上

lay为他动词，表示“放下某物”，动词变化形式为lay–laid–laid。而lay cable表示设置电缆，lay carpet表示安装窗帘。

Ron laid his head on table. 罗恩把头靠在了桌子上。

lay the groundwork 打基础

表示的不是单纯的放下，而是为了实现目的而“打基础”，“打地基”，lay后面可以接groundwork或foundation，可以用for后面的部分表示需要成就的事情。

This report will lay the groundwork for the new rules. 这个报告会为新规则的建立提供基础依据。

MORE

- lay the groundwork for 为……打基础
- lay the foundation for 为……打基础

lay emphasis (stress) on 强调某事

lay后面的宾语如果是抽象名词emphasis或stress，变成lay emphsasis (stress)的话就表示“强调”。将想要强调的具体内容放在on后面即可。

My boss lays a lot of stress on completing projects. 我老板格外强调要完成项目。

- lay emphasis on sth (...ing) 强调某事
- lay stress on sth (...ing) 强调某事

lay down 放下，放平，规定，建立

可以表示单纯放下物品，也可以用rules或standards等名词表示“规定”。虽然从语法的角度来讲有一定的问题，但在日常会话中经常会用lay down的含义。

I just want to lay down a couple of ground rules. 我想建立几个基本的原则。

- lay sth down 放下某物
- lay down 躺下
- lay down (rules, standards) 建立规定或标准

lay off 使放弃，停止

最基本的含义为因经济状况等外部原因，公司不得不“裁员”，另外也可以表示“中断”手头的事情。

We're going to be laying off people in every department. 我们要在每个部门削减人员。

Could you lay off, please? 你能停一下吗?

- lay off sb 减员
- lay off (sb) 停止折磨某人
- lay off (...ing) 停手，中断

lay out 展开，舒展

lay out字面含义为铺展到外面，因此可以理解为“展开”，除此之外还可以表达花钱太厉害，仔细说明等各种含义。

I have laid out clean towels on the floor of the bathroom. 我在卫生间的地板上铺了干净的毛巾。

>>> 025

pull/ draw

拉，拽/画，拉

||||| MORE |||||

- pull oneself together
  打击精神
- pull together
  齐心协力
- pull together sth
  统一

pull oneself together 打起精神，振作

pull 表示拉拽。因此pull oneself together表示将一个人受到的打击和愤怒的感情等都拉到一起，表示“打起精神”。

Let's pull together. 我们齐心协力地干吧。

Pull yourself together! 打起精神！

Have some pride.It’s going to work! Pull yourself together. 有点自豪感。肯定会好转的！振作起来。

pull someone’s leg 戏耍

想一想字面含义的话就很好理解了。拉拽别人的大腿，可以理解为和对方开玩笑(for a joke)。

You're pulling my leg. 你在耍我吧？

I thought he was pulling my leg. 我觉得他在耍我。

- pull over
  把车横在路中央
- pull up
  停车，拉（椅子），向上拉

pull over 把车停在路边

在让某人下车或按照警车的指示将车停在路边时要用pull over，而pull up可以理解为向马车一样“停车”。

We're here. Pull over. 我们到了，停车吧。

Pull over right here, driver! 在这停一下，司机师傅！

Pull over to the side of the road. 把车停在路边。

Tim pulled up in front of Jane's house. 提姆把车停在了简的家门口。

- pull sth off
  做出困难的事情
- pull it off
  成功
- pull off (the road)
  把车停在路边

pull off 成功

pull off的最常用含义为“成功完成了困难的事情”，有时还会用成pull it off的形态。除此之外“把车停在路边”，或“快速脱下衣服”等也可以用这个短语。

The thieves pulled off a bank robbery. 小偷们成功抢劫了银行。

I don't think you will be able to pull it off. 我觉得你不可能成功。

pull out 拉拽

最基本的含义为从现有的状态中摆脱出来，或者拉拽，可以用在公司运营状况不良或者公司破产之前离开公司或者开车时超越前面的车辆。

We're pulling out all the stops. 我们正在全力以赴。

Have you had your wisdom teeth pulled out? 你把你的智齿给拔了?

MORE

- pull out
  拉出，脱离，逃离
- pull out
  超车，走出逆境
- pull out all the stops
  用尽全力

draw (somebody) a picture of 画……

draw最基本的含义为用铅笔或毛笔画画。可以将画画的对象用作宾语，也可以使用draw a picture of。另外，draw sb a map表示“给某人画略图”。

She drew a picture of you! 她画了你!

Could you draw me a map? 你能给我画个示意图吗?

- draw sb (sth)
  画……
- draw a picture of
  画……
- draw somebody a map
  给某人画示意图

draw (somebody's) attention to 吸引（某人的）注意力

draw也可以表示拉和拽，由此衍生出的draw sb's attention表示“吸引某人的注意”，而draw a conclusion 表示“下结论”。另外，有时draw还有attract的意思。

The guide drew our attention to the famous painting. 导游让大家把注意力放在一幅名画上。

- draw sb' s attention to
  吸引某人的注意
- draw a conclusion
  下结论
- be drawn to
  被某人吸引

draw near (closer) 走近

draw原本为拉进的意思，因此draw near (closer)表示时间上或空间上的靠近。

She was shy at first, but she drew near later on. 她一开始非常害羞，不过后来就走近了。

draw back 后退

draw back表示因恐惧或惊吓后退的行为，也可以比喻为决定不做某事。

The group drew back from the volcano. 人们逃出了火山区。

- draw back
  后退
- draw back from sth (...ing)
  因不安而决定不做某事
- drawback
  缺点

draw out 引出，在银行提款

draw out表示向外拉拽，引出某物的行为，可以用作银行提款(withdraw)等。

She will draw out money to pay you back. 她会取钱还你的。

- draw sb (sth) out
  引出…… 激励对方多说几句
- draw out+钱
  提款

>>> 026

ruin/ risk/ hurt

破坏/冒险/伤害

MORE

- ruin something
  毁坏某事
- ruin one's weekend
  破坏某人的周末时光
- ruin one's life
  毁掉某人的一生
- ruin one's party
  破坏某人的派对
- ruin it
  破坏

ruin something 破坏某物

ruin表示破坏，经常用在有点可怕的状况，不过在日常生活中常用在破坏美好的时光、周末等。在口语中可以单单说一句ruin it。

You've ruined it! 是你破坏的！

You ruined everything. 你毁了一切！

I hate you! You ruined my life! 我恨你！你毁了我的人生！

You ruined my weekend with Julie. 你破坏了我和朱莉的美好周末。

be (get) ruined 遭到破坏

ruin用为被动式的情况。主语为被破坏的事物，后面可以加be ruined或get ruined。

So nothing got ruined? 所以说没有什么被破坏？

Everything's ruined. 一切都毁了。

- risk sth
  使某物遭受风险
- risk sth ...ing (to+动词)
  冒着危险做某事
- risk sb ...ing
  使某人遭受风险

risk something 使……陷入危机

risk是大家非常熟悉的单词，risk something表示“使……遭受风险”，另外，risk sb ...ing表示“让某人陷入危险”等。

I can't believe I'm risking this again. 真不敢相信，我又陷入了这种危机。

What's the big deal? Let's risk it. 有什么大不了的？我们冒个险吧。

- risk ...ing
  陷入……的危险，敢于……

risk ...ing 敢于做某事

risk也可以表示冒着风险，因此risk ...ing表示“陷入……的危险”或者明明知道会有不好的事情发生却“敢于做某事”。

Did you risk slapping his face? 你打了他一巴掌？

I don't want to risk running into dad. 我不想冒险碰到老爸。

take (run) risk 冒险

这里的risk为名词形式。可以与多种动词相结合，组成各种短语，take或run a risk表示明知道有风险还要尝试。

She wouldn't be afraid of taking a little risk. 她不害怕冒一点险的。

MORE

- turn (run) a risk 冒着风险
- take (run) the risk of ...ing 冒着……的风险
- be worth the risk 值得冒险
- reduce the risk of 减少风险

(somebody) hurt+身体部位 （某人）伤了某处

hurt表示自己或别人受伤，或使受伤，如果要表示某个特定的身体部位受伤，则是人物主语“受了伤”，或者事物“伤害了身体”，也可以将身体部位当成主语。

My leg still hurts. 我的腿还是很疼。

You got hurt when playing golf with my dad? 你在和我爸打高尔夫球的时候受伤了？

- sb hurt+身体部位 ……受伤
- sth hurt+身体部位 因……受伤
- 身体部位+hurt ……疼
- get hurt 受伤(hurt oneself)
- hurt like hell 非常疼

(somebody) hurt somebody （某人）伤害某人

这次指的并不是身体部位，而是精神层面，表示“伤害某人的心”，不仅会产生物理疼痛，而且也会产生精神损伤，其最大特征为主语和hurt的宾语都是人物。

You're hurting me. 你在伤害我。

He's not going to hurt you! 他不会伤害你的！

Did I hurt you in some way? 我伤害你了吗？

Listen, I don't want to hurt her. 听，我不想伤害她。

Somebody is hurt 某人受伤

sb is hurt中的hurt变成了被动语态，表示主语受了伤，sb is hurting中的hurt为自动词，也表示主语经受了不幸的事情，心灵受到了伤害。

I know you're hurt. 我知道你受伤了。

You're angry. You're hurting. 你很生气，肯定很伤心吧。

I'm not sure she's hurting. 我不大确定她是否受伤了。

- sb is (get) hurt 疼，受伤，心情不好，受到迫害
- sb is hurting 某人很伤心，心疼

It (This, That) hurt ……疼

这是个有点特殊的形态，主语为it (this，that)等代词，可以不加任何宾语，也可以用为hurt sb的形态，表示“使某人疼痛”。

It hurts (like hell). 太疼了。

That had to hurt! 肯定很疼吧！

Does it still hurt? 现在还疼吗？

It hurt her so much when he left. 他离开的时候，她非常伤心。

- It (This, That) hurt ……疼
- It (This, That) hurt sb 使某人疼痛

>>> 027

expect

期待，预料

MORE

- expect to+动词
  希望做某事
- expect that
  期待……

expect to do 期待做某事

expect表示某种预料或者计划实现，希望的具体内容要用to+动词或that S+V来表达。

I didn't expect to see you here. 我没想到在这儿会见到你。

Clair is not the one who I expected to fall in love with. 我没想到会和克莱尔陷入爱河。

I expect that she will make a recovery. 我希望她能够恢复。

I never expected they weren't going to show up. 我从来就没想过他们会不出现。

- expect sb (sth) to+动词
  期待某人做某事

expect somebody to 希望某人做某事

这次不是主语希望自己做某事，而是希望他人做某事。

Do you expect me to believe that? 你要我相信那件事?

You're kidding me! You expect her to dump me?开什么玩笑！你想让她甩了我?

- expect sth from sb
  向某人要求某物
- expect sb to+动词
  希望某人做某事
- expect a lot of (much) of sb
  要求某人很多

expect company 等待某人的到来

在这里company不是公司的意思，而是同行者，因此expect company表示“有人会来”。因此have company表示“有同行者”，“有客人”。

I'm expecting somebody. 我正在等人。

I'm expecting company. 我正在等人。

I've been expecting you. 我一直在等你。

expect (a child) 怀孕

这是只有女性才能期待的事情，进行时为being expecting (a baby或 a child)，表示“怀孕”，即快要生孩子了(have a baby)。

I heard Eva is expecting. 我听说伊娃怀孕了。

Are you expecting (a child)? 你怀孕了?

expect somebody back 预料某人回来

当你想找的人不在，询问对方何时回来时必须用到短语expect sb back，尤其在打电话时如果对方不在时也可以用到。

When do you expect him back? 他什么时候能回来?

I didn't expect her back for at least two more days. 我预料她两天之内回不来。

be expected to do 预料……

这是expect作为被动式的情况，be expected to+动词表示预料主语会to+动词。

She was expected to attend the meeting. 希望她能参加会议。

His parents expected him to do well at college. 他的父母希望他在大学表现得很出色。

What do you expect to ... ? 你希望什么?

应用expect的句式，What do you expect to ... ?表示向对方询问期待着什么，What do you expect sb to ... ?表示“希望谁做某事? ”。

What do you expect to see there? 你想去那儿看什么?

What do you expect me do? 你想让我做什么?

- What do you expect to+动词 你希望……?
- What do you expect sb to+动词 你希望某人做什么?

... than I expected 比我预料的还……

如果实际情况比预料的还……，则可以用 ... than I expected，想要表达正如预料，则可以用as expected。

He's taller than I expected. 他比我预料的还高。

She's cuter than I expected. 她比我想象中的可爱多了。